THIRD EDITION

TOP NOTCH 2

TEACHER'S EDITION and LESSON PLANNER

JOAN SASLOW
ALLEN ASCHER

with Daria Ruzicka

Top Notch: English for Today's World   2, Third Edition
Teacher's Edition and Lesson Planner

Pearson Education, 10 Bank Street, White Plains, NY 10606 USA

Staff credits: The people who made up the *Top Notch* team are Peter Benson, Kimberly Casey, Tracey Munz Cataldo, Rosa Chapinal, Aerin Csigay, Dave Dickey, Gina DiLillo, Nancy Flaggman, Irene Frankel, Shelley Gazes, Christopher Leonowicz, Julie Molnar, Laurie Neaman, Sherri Pemberton, Pamela Pia, Jennifer Raspiller, Charlene Straub, and Kenneth Volcjak.

Cover photo credit: Sprint/Corbis
Text composition: TSI Graphics

Printed in the United States of America

ISBN-10: 0-13-381046-1
ISBN-13: 978-0-13-381046-2
4   17

pearsonelt.com/topnotch3e

Photo credits: Original photography by Sharon Hoogstraten, David Mager and Libby Ballengee/TSI Graphics. Page 2 (tl) Image Source/Getty Images, (tl) Gogo Images Corporation/Alamy, (tr) WaveBreakMedia/Shutterstock, (tr) Comstock Images/Stockbyte/Getty Images, (bl) DAJ/Getty Images, (bm) WaveBreakMedia/Shutterstock, (br) Jack Hollingsworth/Photodisc/Getty Images; p. 5 (tl) Daniel Grill/Getty Images, p. 6 (The Forbidden Palace) Rabbit75_fot/Fotolia, (Beijing Duck) Zhangsan/Fotolia, (Two men shake hands) Asia Images Group/Getty Images; p. 7 (Taj Mahal) Saiko3p/Fotolia, (Temple) Searagen/Fotolia, (Ceviche) Ildi.Food/Alamy, (Pyramid of Sun) F9photos/Fotolia, Dabldy/Fotolia; p. 8 (tr) Olly/Fotolia, (tr) Aeroking/Fotolia, (mr) Andrey Arkusha/Shutterstock; p. 10 (snail) Michael Spring/Fotolia, (1) Michael Spring/Fotolia, (2) Syda Productions/Fotolia, (3)Blend Images/Shutterstock; p. 11 (br) Diego Cervo/Shutterstock; p. 12 (1) Luiz Rocha/Shutterstock, (2) Worakit Sirijinda/Fotolia, (3) Aania/Fotolia, (4) Sam Edwards/Caia Image/Glow Images; p. 13 (The Prado Museum) Anibal Trejo/Fotolia, (Tapas) Paul Brighton/Fotolia, (The Millineum Wheel) QQ7/Shutterstock, (Carnaby Street) Image Source/Getty Images, (Eiffel Tower) Wajan/Fotolia, (Tour Boat) Elenathewise/Fotolia, (Ballet) Ria Novosti/Alamy, (Borscht) Cook_inspire/Fotolia, (Colosseum) Pablo Debat/Fotolia, (Gelato) Eldorado/Fotolia, p. 14 (tl) AF archive/Alamy, (tm) AF archive/Alamy, (tr) Pictorial Press Ltd/Alamy; p. 16 (mr) Allstar Picture Library/Alamy; p. 18 (An action film) AF archive/Alamy, (A horror film) BortN66/Fotolia, (A science-fiction film) Innovari/Fotolia, (An animated film) Natalia Maroz/Shutterstock, (A comedy) KPA Honorar & Belege/United Archives GmbH/Alamy, (A musical) Bettina Strenske/Alamy; p. 19 Monkey Business/Fotolia; p. 21 (tl) Gary Conner/Photodisc/Getty Images, (tm) Adam Gregor/Shutterstock, (ml) Eugenia Petrenko/Shutterstock, (mr) Ktsdesign/Fotolia; p. 22 Rich Yasick/E+/Getty Images; p. 23 Nyul/Fotolia; p. 26 (tl) Bjdlzx/E+/Getty Images, (tm) Bjdlzx/E+/Getty Images, (tr) Bjdlzx/E+/Getty Images, (bl) Pejo/Fotolia, (bml) Tom Wang/Shutterstock, (bmr) Zoonar RF/Thinkstock/Getty Images; p. 28 (tl) EpicStockMedia/Fotolia, (br) Racorn/Shutterstock; p. 32 (tl) Cornelia Pithart/Fotolia, (tl) Ludmilafoto/Fotolia, (tm) Razihusin/Fotolia, (tr) Anterovium/Fotolia, (tr) Nyasha/Fotolia, (bl) Mark Peterson/Corbis News/Corbis, (bl) Comstock/Stockbyte/Thinkstock/Getty Images, (bm) (Woman) Chris Ryan/Ojo Images Ltd/Alamy, (Newspaper) Jocic/Shutterstock, (br) Glow Images/Superstock; p. 33 Degree/eStock Photo/Alamy; p. 34 (The Plaza Hotel) Sandra Baker/Alamy, (Rockefeller center) Marcorubino/Fotolia, (Manhattan Skyline) Rudi1976/Fotolia, (Times Square) Richard Berenholtz/Alamy, (Grand Central Station) Forcdan/Fotolia; p. 37 (1) Image Source/Getty Images, (2) Quavando/Vetta/Getty Images; p. 39 (tl bg) Amy Walters/Shutterstock, (tm bg) Horid85/Fotolia, (tr bg) Horid85/Fotolia; p. 44 (1) Supertrooper/Fotolia, (2) Deusexlupus/Fotolia, (3) Algre/Fotolia, (4) National Motor Museum/Motoring Picture Library/Alamy, (5) Yuri Bizgaimer/Fotolia, (6) Rob Wilson/Shutterstock, (7) Supertrooper/Fotolia, (8) Buzz Pictures/Alamy; p. 45 (1) Tracy Whiteside/Fotolia, (2) Arek Malang/Shutterstock, (3) BikeRiderLondon/Shutterstock, (4) R. Gino Santa Maria/Shutterstock, (5) Andresr/Shutterstock; p. 46 Tomml/E+/Getty Images; p. 47 Carlos_bcn/Fotolia; p. 50 (Haircuts) Lester120/Fotolia, (Facials) Valua Vitaly/Fotolia, (Shaves) Yalcin Sonat/Shutterstock, (Manicures) Vladimir Sazonov/Fotolia, (Pedicures) Tomek Pa/Shutterstock, (Massage) Valua Vitaly/Fotolia, (Yoga) Furmananna/Fotolia, (Kickboxing) Erik Isakson/Getty Images, (Pilates) Andres Rodriguez/Fotolia, (Spinning) Wavebreak media LTD/Alloy/Corbis, (Exercise equipment) Hero Images/Getty Images, (Personal trainers) Visionsi/Fotolia; p. 52 (t) (1) Lan 2010/Fotolia, (2) Akova/Fotolia, (3) Ilya Akinshin/Fotolia, (4) Lan 2010/Fotolia, (5) Darak77/Fotolia, (6) Glovatskiy/Fotolia, (b) (1) Picsfive/Fotolia, (2) Coprid/Fotolia, (3) Mile Atanasov/Fotolia, (4) Igor/Fotolia, (5)Isreal Mckee/Shutterstock, (6) Vadim Ponomarenko/Shutterstock,(bg) Madgooch/Fotolia, (7) Toskov/Fotolia, (8) Stephen Coburn/Shutterstock, (9) Monkey Business/Fotolia, (10) Vipman/Shutterstock, (12) Olya6105/Fotolia, (13) Gresei/Fotolia, (14) Hugh O'Neill/Fotolia, (15) Africa Studio/Fotolia, (16) Urfin/Shutterstock; p. 54 (tr) Hola Images/Alamy, (Female speaking on phone) Minerva Studio/Fotolia; p. 56 (tr) Juanmonino/E+/Getty Images, (bl) Racorn/Shutterstock; p. 57 Igor Gratzer/Shutterstock; p. 58 (l) Fotoluminate LLC/Fotolia, (r) Diego Cervo/Shutterstock; p. 59 (1) Holbox/Shutterstock, (2) Tom Cockrem/Stockbyte/Getty Images, (3) Hannamariah/Shutterstock, (4) Eric Lafforgue/Alamy; p. 62 (tl bg) Ilya Zaytsev/Fotolia, (tl) D. Hurst/Alamy, (tr bg) Ilya Zaytsev/Fotolia, (tl) D. Hurst/Alamy, (butter) Coleman Yuen/Pearson Education Asia Ltd, (Fork) Vo/Fotolia, (m bg) Ilya Zaytsev/Fotolia, (Fruit) Koszivu/Fotolia, (Bread,grains,pasta) Nikolay Petkov/Shutterstock, (Vegetables) Ana Blazic Pavlovic/Shutterstock, (Meat,fish,beans) D. Hurst/Alamy, (green napkin) Karandaev/Fotolia, (blue placemat) Aleksandr Ugorenkov /Fotolia; p. 63 (Mushroom diet) Viktor/Fotolia, (Vegan diet) Studio Gi/Fotolia, (Atkins diet) Vladimir Melnik/Fotolia, (Juice Fast) Larisa Lofitskaya/Shutterstock; p. 64 (Sushi) Motorlka/Fotolia, (Mangoes) Volff/Fotolia, (Pasta) Vagabondo/Fotolia, (Ice cream) Unpict/Fotolia, (Asparagus) Africa Studio/Fotolia; p. 67 (Octopus) Denio109/Fotolia, (Shellfish) Maceo/Fotolia, (Tofu) Lilyana Vynogradova/Fotolia, (Steak) Joe Gough/Fotolia, (Broccoli) Ping Han/Fotolia, (Beets) Mitev/Fotolia, (Chocolate) Taigi/Fotolia; p. 68 (tr) Fotandy/Shutterstock, (br) Saje/Fotolia; p. 69 Apollofoto/Shutterstock; p. 70 (a) Shakzu/Fotolia, (Grasshopper) Valeriy Kirsanov/Fotolia, (b) Paul Brighton/Fotolia, (c) Nattawut Thammasak/Fotolia, (d) Africa Studio/Fotolia, (e) Vankad/Fotolia, (f) Uckyo/Fotolia, (Cabbage) Nomad Soul/Fotolia; p. 71 (1,2,3,4) Mariusz Blach/Fotolia, (br) Mourad/Tarek/ Bon Appetit/Alamy; p. 73 (Pad Thai) Narith_2527/iStock/Thinkstock/Getty Images, (Bi Bim Bop) Ain Bagwell/Photodisc/Getty Images, (Chicken Mole) Uckyo/Fotolia, (Potato Soup) Juanmonino/E+/Getty Images, (Tabouleh Salad) M.studio/Fotolia, (Pot Stickers) Chiyacat/Fotolia, (br) Yuris/Shutterstock; p. 74 Lightboxx/Shutterstock; p. 78 Imagesource/Glow Images; p. 79 LightWaveMedia/Shutterstock; p. 80 Pavel L Photo and Video/Shutterstock; p. 81 (tr) Zsschreiner/Shutterstock, (bl) Taka/Fotolia, (br) Eurobanks/Fotolia; p. 82 Monkey Business Images/Shutterstock; p. 83 (t) Rob/Fotolia, (b) Tanya Constantine/Blend/Corbis; p. 85 (1) WaveBreakMedia/Shutterstock, (2) Jeremy Woodhouse/Blend Images/Getty Images, (3) Corey Rich/Aurora/Getty Images; p. 86 (Jewelry) Harshmunjal/Fotolia, (Fashion) Terex/Fotolia, (Pottery) Africa Studio/Fotolia, (Painting) Boyan Dimitrov/Shutterstock, (Photography) Philippova Anastasia/Shutterstock; p. 87 (m) Boyan Dimitrov/Fotolia, (m) Gurgen Bakhshetsyan/Shutterstock, (mr) Rozaliya/Fotolia, (mr) Nils Volkmer/Shutterstock; p. 89 (Monalisa) Dennis Hallinan/Alamy, (Gold Museum) *Cacique Guatavita, known as El Dorado's raft in gold and emeralds, Colombia, Chibcha civilization (or Muisca)*/De Agostini Picture Library/G. Dagli Orti/Bridgeman Images, (National Palace Museum) *Chinese cabbage, Korean, 19th century (jade) / National Palace Museum, Taipei, Taiwan/*Bridgeman Images, (Museum of Modern Art) GL Archive/Alamy; p. 90 (Wood) Pavel K/Shutterstock, (Glass) Sagir/Shutterstock, (Silver) Nolte Lourens/Fotolia, (Gold ring)Lynnette/Shutterstock, (Cloth) NH7/Fotolia, (Ceramic) Deborah McCague/Shutterstock, (Stone) Winnond/Shutterstock; p. 91 (Vase) Nikonbhoy/Fotolia, (Plate) Piero Gentili/Fotolia, (Dolls) Ketsur/Fotolia, (Figure) Kanvag/Fotolia, (Cups) Mrpuiii/Shutterstock; p. 92 Audrey Benson; p. 93 Africa Studio/Fotolia; p. 94 (Stella) AFP/Newscom, (Vincent) De Agostini Picture Library/Getty Images, (Charles) Picture-alliance/Newscom, (Valentino) Splash News/Newscom, (Frida) Bettmann/Corbis, (Henri) Charles Platiau/Reuters/Newscom, (Ang Lee) Fox 2000 Pictures/Album/Newscom; p. 95 (l) Nicholas Piccillo/Fotolia, (m) Michael Jung/Shutterstock, (r) Arek Malang/Shutterstock; p. 96 (a) Pytralona/Shutterstock, (b) Swisshippo/Fotolia, (c) Nerthuz/Fotolia, (d) www.TouchofArt.eu/Fotolia, (e) Yezep/Fotolia; p. 97 (Accademia Gallery) Akg-Images/Cameraphoto/Newscom, (David) Ndphoto/Shutterstock, (Musee d'Orsay) Brian Jannsen/Alamy, (Apples and Oranges) *Apples and Oranges, 1895-1900 (oil on canvas), Cezanne, Paul (1839-1906)/*Musee d'Orsay, Paris, France/Giraudon/Bridgeman Images, (Peru) Eduardo Rivero/Shutterstock, (India) Сергей Чирков/Fotolia, (China) Stockphoto Mania/Shutterstock, (Sweden) Tobyphotos/Shutterstock; p. 98 (Frank) Yulia Mayorova/Shutterstock, (Kathy) Phototalk/E+/Getty Images, (Nardo) Warren Goldswain/Fotolia; p. 100 (tr) Blue Images/Ivy/Corbis, (Monitor,screen) Antiksu/Fotolia, (Mouse) Violetkaipa/Shutterstock, (Touchpad) Tagore75/Fotolia; p. 102 Nikkytok/Fotolia; p. 103 (Joystick) Geargodz/Fotolia, StockLite/Shutterstock; p. 104 (4) Hero Images/Getty Images; p. 106 Chanpipat/Fotolia; p. 107 (l) Glow Images/Fotolia, (r) Kitty/Fotolia; p. 109 (ml) Olix Wirtinger/Fancy/Corbis; p. 115 (Book) Irina Burakova/Fotolia, (Smartphone) Bloomua/Fotolia, (Wallet) Grigoriy Lukyanov/Fotolia, (Coat) Ludmilafoto/Fotolia, (Headphones) Alexander Demyanenko/Fotolia, (Gloves) Spe/Fotolia, (Bag) Nikolai Sorokin/Fotolia; p. 116 (l) Jaroslav Kviz/Profimedia.CZ a.s./Alamy; (m) Tristan Savatier/Moment/Getty Images, (r) AnnaDe/Shutterstock; p. 117 Underwood Photo Archives/Superstock; p. 118 Bikeworldtravel/Fotolia.

Illustration credits: Steve Attoe, pp. 6, 64; Sue Carlson, p. 35; John Ceballos, pp. 25, 37, 49, 121; Mark Collins, pp. 27, 42 (left); Brian Hughes, pp. 24 (bottom), 41; Adam Larkum, p. 61; Pat Lewis, p. 10; Andy Myer, pp. 16 (left, center), 66; Dusan Petricic, pp. 33, 41, 70, 78, 79, 113; Jake Rickwood, p. 24 (top); Geoffrey P. Smith, p. 38; Neil Stewart, p. 119 (center, bottom); Gary Torrisi, p. 46; Anne Veltfort, pp. 16 (right), 31, 42 (right), 66 (top-right), 119 (top).

Text credits: Page 46: *Six Tips for Defensive Driving*, © The Nemours Foundation/KidsHealth. Reprinted with permission; Page 74: *Psychology of Color* from infoplease.com. Reprinted with permission.

Contents

LEARNING OBJECTIVES

	COMMUNICATION GOALS	VOCABULARY	GRAMMAR

UNIT 1
Getting Acquainted
PAGE 2
	• Get reacquainted with someone
	• Greet a visitor to your country
	• Discuss gestures and customs
	• Describe an interesting experience
		• Tourist activities
		• The hand
		• Participial adjectives
			• The present perfect
			  ○ Statements and <u>yes</u> / <u>no</u> questions
			  ○ Form and usage
			  ○ Past participles of irregular verbs
			  ○ With <u>already</u>, <u>yet</u>, <u>ever</u>, <u>before</u>, and <u>never</u>
			GRAMMAR BOOSTER
			• The present perfect
			  ○ Information questions
			  ○ <u>Yet</u> and <u>already</u>: expansion, common errors
			  ○ <u>Ever</u>, <u>never</u>, and <u>before</u>: use and placement

UNIT 2
Going to the Movies
PAGE 14
	• Apologize for being late
	• Discuss preferences for movie genres
	• Describe and recommend movies
	• Discuss effects of movie violence on viewers
		• Explanations for being late
		• Movie genres
		• Adjectives to describe movies
			• The present perfect
			  ○ With <u>for</u> and <u>since</u>
			  ○ Other uses
			• Wants and preferences: <u>would like</u> and <u>would rather</u>
			  ○ Form and usage
			  ○ Statements, questions, and answers
			GRAMMAR BOOSTER
			• The present perfect continuous
			• The present participle: spelling
			• Expressing preferences: review, expansion, and common errors

UNIT 3
Staying in Hotels
PAGE 26
	• Leave and take a message
	• Check into a hotel
	• Request housekeeping services
	• Choose a hotel
		• Hotel room types and kinds of beds
		• Hotel room amenities and services
			• The future with <u>will</u>
			  ○ Form and usage
			  ○ Statements and questions
			  ○ Contractions
			• The real conditional
			  ○ Form and usage
			  ○ Statements and questions
			GRAMMAR BOOSTER
			• <u>Will</u>: expansion
			• <u>Can</u>, <u>should</u>, and <u>have to</u>: future meaning
			• The real conditinal: factual and future; usage and common errors

UNIT 4
Cars and Driving
PAGE 38
	• Discuss a car accident
	• Describe a car problem
	• Rent a car
	• Discuss good and bad driving
		• Bad driving habits
		• Car parts
		• Ways to respond (with concern / relief)
		• Phrasal verbs for talking about cars
		• Car types
		• Driving behavior
			• The past continuous
			  ○ Form and usage
			  ○ Vs. the simple past tense
			• Direct objects with phrasal verbs
			GRAMMAR BOOSTER
			• The past continuous: other uses
			• Nouns and pronouns: review

UNIT 5
Personal Care and Appearance
PAGE 50
	• Ask for something in a store
	• Make an appointment at a salon or spa
	• Discuss ways to improve appearance
	• Define the meaning of beauty
		• Salon services
		• Personal care products
		• Discussing beauty
			• Indefinite quantities and amounts
			  ○ <u>Some</u> and <u>any</u>
			  ○ <u>A lot of</u> / <u>lots of</u>, <u>many</u>, and <u>much</u>
			• Indefinite pronouns: <u>someone</u> / <u>no one</u> / <u>anyone</u>
			GRAMMAR BOOSTER
			• <u>Some</u> and <u>any</u>: indefiniteness
			• <u>Too many</u>, <u>too much</u>, and <u>enough</u>
			• Comparative quantifiers <u>fewer</u> and <u>less</u>
			• Indefinite pronouns: <u>something</u>, <u>anything</u>, and <u>nothing</u>

CONVERSATION STRATEGIES	LISTENING / PRONUNCIATION	READING	WRITING
• Use "I don't think so." to soften a negative answer • Say "I know!" to exclaim that you've discovered an answer • Use "Welcome to ___." to greet someone in a new place • Say "That's great." to acknowledge someone's positive experience	**Listening Skills** • Listen to classify • Listen for details **Pronunciation** • Sound reduction in the present perfect	**Texts** • A poster about world customs • A magazine article about non-verbal communication • A travel poster • A photo story **Skills/strategies** • Identify supporting details • Relate to personal experience	**Task** • Write a description of an interesting experience **WRITING BOOSTER** • Avoiding run-on sentences
• Apologize and provide a reason when late • Say "That's fine." to reassure • Offer to repay someone with "How much do I owe?" • Use "What would you rather do . . . ? to ask about preference • Soften a negative response with "To tell you the truth, . . ."	**Listening Skills** • Listen for main ideas • Listen to infer • Dictation **Pronunciation** • Reduction of h	**Texts** • A movie website • Movie reviews • A textbook excerpt about violence in movies • A photo story **Skills/strategies** • Understand from context • Confirm content • Evaluate ideas	**Task** • Write an essay about violence in movies and on TV **WRITING BOOSTER** • Paragraphs • Topic sentences
• Say "Would you like to leave a message?" if someone isn't available • Say "Let's see." to indicate you're checking information • Make a formal, polite request with "May I ___?" • Say "Here you go." when handing someone something • Use "By the way, . . ." to introduce new information	**Listening Skills** • Listen to take phone messages • Listen for main ideas • Listen for details **Pronunciation** • Contractions with will	**Texts** • Phone message slips • A hotel website • A city map • A photo story **Skills/strategies** • Draw conclusions • Identify supporting details • Interpret a map	**Task** • Write a paragraph explaining the reasons for choosing a hotel **WRITING BOOSTER** • Avoiding sentence fragments with because or since
• Express concern about another's condition after an accident • Express relief when hearing all is OK • Use "only" to minimize the seriousness of a situation • Use "actually" to soften negative information • Empathize with "I'm sorry to hear that."	**Listening Skills** • Listen for details • Listen to summarize **Pronunciation** • Stress of particles in phrasal verbs	**Texts** • A questionnaire about bad driving habits • Rental car customer profiles • A feature article about defensive driving • A driving behavior survey • A photo story **Skills/strategies** • Understand from context • Critical thinking	**Task** • Write a paragraph comparing good and bad drivers **WRITING BOOSTER** • Connecting words and sentences: and, in addition, furthermore, and therefore
• Use "Excuse me." to initiate a conversation with a salesperson • Confirm information by repeating it with rising intonation • Use "No problem." to show you don't mind an inconvenience • Use "Let me check" to ask someone to wait while you confirm information	**Listening Skills** • Listen to recognize someone's point of view • Listen to take notes **Pronunciation** • Pronunciation of unstressed vowels	**Texts** • A spa and fitness center advertisement • A health advice column • A photo story **Skills/strategies** • Paraphrase • Understand from context • Confirm content • Apply information	**Task** • Write a letter on how to improve appearance **WRITING BOOSTER** • Writing a formal letter

	COMMUNICATION GOALS	VOCABULARY	GRAMMAR
UNIT 6 Eating Well PAGE 62	• Talk about food passions • Make an excuse to decline food • Discuss lifestyle changes • Describe local dishes	• Nutrition terminology • Food passions • Excuses for not eating something • Food descriptions	• Use to / used to • Negative yes / no questions **GRAMMAR BOOSTER** • Use to / used to: use and form, common errors • Be used to vs. get used to • Repeated actions in the past: would + base form, common errors • Negative yes / no questions: short answers
UNIT 7 About Personality PAGE 74	• Get to know a new friend • Cheer someone up • Discuss personality and its origin • Examine the impact of birth order on personality	• Positive and negative adjectives • Terms to discuss psychology and personality	• Gerunds and infinitives • Gerunds as objects of prepositions **GRAMMAR BOOSTER** • Gerunds and infinitives: other uses • Negative gerunds

UNIT 8
 	
The Arts
PAGE 86
	• Recommend a museum
	• Ask about and describe objects
	• Talk about artistic talent
	• Discuss your favorite artists
		• Kinds of art
		• Adjectives to describe art
		• Objects, handicrafts, and materials
		• Passive participial phrases
			• The passive voice
			  ◦ Form, meaning, and usage
			  ◦ Statements and questions
			
			GRAMMAR BOOSTER
			• Transitive and intransitive verbs
			• The passive voice: other tenses
			• Yes / no questions in the passive voice: other tenses

UNIT 9
 	
Living in
Cyberspace
PAGE 98
	• Troubleshoot a problem
	• Compare product features
	• Describe how you use the Internet
	• Discuss the impact of the Internet
		• Ways to reassure someone
		• The computer screen, components, and commands
		• Internet activities
			• The infinitive of purpose
			• Comparisons with as . . . as
			  ◦ Meaning and usage
			  ◦ Just, almost, not quite, not nearly
			
			GRAMMAR BOOSTER
			• Expressing purpose with in order to and for
			• As . . . as to compare adverbs
			• Comparatives / superlatives: review
			• Comparison with adverbs

UNIT 10
 	
Ethics and
Values
PAGE 110
	• Discuss ethical choices
	• Return someone else's property
	• Express personal values
	• Discuss acts of kindness and honesty
		• Idioms
		• Situations that require an ethical choice
		• Acknowledging thanks
		• Personal values
			• The unreal conditional
			  ◦ Form, usage, common errors
			• Possessive pronouns / Whose
			  ◦ Form, usage, common errors
			
			GRAMMAR BOOSTER
			• should, ought to, had better
			• have to, must, be supposed to
			• Possessive nouns: review and expansion
			• Pronouns: summary

CONVERSATION STRATEGIES	LISTENING / PRONUNCIATION	READING	WRITING
• Provide an emphatic affirmative response with "Definitely." • Offer food with "Please help yourself." • Acknowledge someone's efforts by saying something positive • Soften the rejection of an offer with "I'll pass on the ___." • Use a negative question to express surprise • Use "It's not a problem." to downplay inconvenience	**Listening Skills** • Listen for details • Listen to personalize **Pronunciation** • Sound reduction: <u>used to</u>	**Texts** • A food guide • Descriptions of types of diets • A magazine article about eating habits • A lifestyle survey • Menu ingredients • A photo story **Skills/strategies** • Understand from context • Summarize • Compare and contrast	**Task** • Write a persuasive paragraph about the differences in present-day and past diets **WRITING BOOSTER** • Connecting ideas: subordinating conjunctions
• Clarify an earlier question with "Well, for example, . . ." • Buy time to think with "Let's see." • Use auxiliary <u>do</u> to emphasize a verb • Thank someone for showing interest. • Offer empathy with "I know what you mean."	**Listening Skills** • Listen for main ideas • Listen for specific information • Classify information • Infer information **Pronunciation** • Reduction of <u>to</u> in infinitives	**Texts** • A pop psychology website • A textbook excerpt about the nature / nurture controversy • Personality surveys • A photo story **Skills/strategies** • Understand vocabulary from context • Make personal comparisons	**Task** • Write an essay describing someone's personality **WRITING BOOSTER** • Parallel structure
• Say "Be sure not to miss ___." to emphasize the importance of an action • Introduce the first aspect of an opinion with "For one thing, . . ." • Express enthusiasm for what someone has said with "No kidding!" • Invite someone's opinion with "What do you think of ___?"	**Listening Skills** • Understand from context • Listen to take notes • Infer point of view **Pronunciation** • Emphatic stress	**Texts** • Museum descriptions • A book excerpt about the origin of artistic talent • An artistic survey • A photo story **Skills/strategies** • Recognize the main idea • Identify supporting details • Paraphrase	**Task** • Write a detailed description of a decorative object **WRITING BOOSTER** • Providing supporting details
• Ask for assistance with "Could you take a look at ___?" • Introduce an explanation with "Well, . . ." • Make a suggestion with "Why don't you try ___ing?" • Express interest informally with "Oh, yeah?" • Use "Everyone says . . ." to introduce a popular opinion • Say "Well, I've heard ___." to support a point of view	**Listening Skills** • Listen for the main idea • Listen for details **Pronunciation** • Stress in <u>as</u> . . . <u>as</u> phrases	**Texts** • A social network website • An internet user survey • Newspaper clippings about the Internet • A photo story **Skills/strategies** • Understand from context • Relate to personal experience	**Task** • Write an essay evaluating the benefits and problems of the Internet **WRITING BOOSTER** • Organizing ideas
• Say "You think so?" to reconfirm someone's opinion • Provide an emphatic affirmative response with "Absolutely." • Acknowledge thanks with "Don't mention it."	**Listening Skills** • Listen to infer information • Listen for main ideas • Understand vocabulary from context • Support ideas with details **Pronunciation** • Blending of <u>d</u> + <u>y</u> in <u>would you</u>	**Texts** • A personal values self-test • Print and online news stories about kindness and honesty • A photo story **Skills/strategies** • Summarize • Interpret information • Relate to personal experience	**Task** • Write an essay about someone's personal choice **WRITING BOOSTER** • Introducing conflicting ideas: <u>On the one hand</u>; <u>On the other hand</u>

TO THE TEACHER

What is *Top Notch?* *Top Notch* is a six-level* communicative course that prepares adults and young adults to interact successfully and confidently with both native and non-native speakers of English.

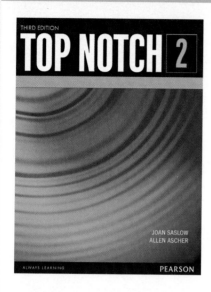

The goal of *Top Notch* is to make English unforgettable through:
- Multiple exposures to new language
- Numerous opportunities to practice it
- Deliberate and intensive recycling

The *Top Notch* course has two beginning levels—*Top Notch Fundamentals* for true beginners and *Top Notch 1* for false beginners. *Top Notch* is benchmarked to the Global Scale of English and is tightly correlated to the Can-do Statements of the Common European Framework of Reference.

Each full level of *Top Notch* contains material for 60–90 hours of classroom instruction. In addition, the entire course can be tailored to blended learning with an integrated online component, *MyEnglishLab*.

NEW This third edition of *Top Notch* includes these new features: Extra Grammar Exercises, digital full-color Vocabulary Flash Cards, Conversation Activator videos, and Pronunciation Coach videos.

* Summit 1 and *Summit 2* are the titles of the 5th and 6th levels of the *Top Notch* course.

Award-Winning Instructional Design*

Daily confirmation of progress

Each easy-to-follow two-page lesson begins with a clearly stated practical communication goal closely aligned to the Common European Framework's Can-do Statements. All activities are integrated with the goal, giving vocabulary and grammar meaning and purpose. *Now You Can* activities ensure that students achieve each goal and confirm their progress in every class session.

Explicit vocabulary and grammar

Clear captioned picture-dictionary illustrations with accompanying audio take the guesswork out of meaning and pronunciation. Grammar presentations containing both rules and examples clarify form, meaning, and use. The unique *Recycle this Language* feature continually puts known words and grammar in front of students' eyes as they communicate, to make sure language remains active.

High-frequency social language

Twenty memorable conversation models provide appealing natural social language that students can carry "in their pockets" for use in real life. Rigorous controlled and free discussion activities systematically stimulate recycling of social language, ensuring that it's not forgotten.

Linguistic and cultural fluency

Top Notch equips students to interact with people from different language backgrounds by including authentic accents on the audio. Conversation Models, Photo Stories, and cultural fluency activities prepare students for social interactions in English with people from unfamiliar cultures.

Active listening syllabus

All Vocabulary presentations, Pronunciation presentations, Conversation Models, Photo Stories, Listening Comprehension exercises, and Readings are recorded on the audio to help students develop good pronunciation, intonation, and auditory memory. In addition, approximately fifty carefully developed listening tasks at each level of *Top Notch* develop crucial listening comprehension skills such as listen for details, listen for main ideas, listen to activate vocabulary, listen to activate grammar, and listen to confirm information.

*We wish you and your students enjoyment and success with **Top Notch 2**. We wrote it for you.*

Joan Saslow and Allen Ascher

* *Top Notch* is the recipient of the Association of Educational Publishers' *Distinguished Achievement Award*.

ActiveTeach

Maximize the impact of your **Top Notch** lessons. This digital tool provides an interactive classroom experience that can be used with or without an interactive whiteboard (IWB). It includes a full array of digital and printable features.

For class presentation . . .

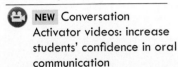 **NEW** Conversation Activator videos: increase students' confidence in oral communication

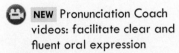 **NEW** Pronunciation Coach videos: facilitate clear and fluent oral expression

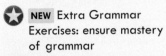 **NEW** Extra Grammar Exercises: ensure mastery of grammar

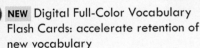 **NEW** Digital Full-Color Vocabulary Flash Cards: accelerate retention of new vocabulary

PLUS

- ▶ Clickable Audio: instant access to the complete classroom audio program
- *Top Notch TV* Video Program: a hilarious sitcom and authentic on-the-street interviews
- *Top Notch Pop* Songs and Karaoke: original songs for additional language practice

For planning . . .

- A *Methods Handbook* for a communicative classroom
- Detailed timed lesson plans for each two-page lesson
- *Top Notch TV* teaching notes
- Complete answer keys, audio scripts, and video scripts

For extra support . . .

- Hundreds of extra printable activities, with teaching notes
- *Top Notch Pop* language exercises
- *Top Notch TV* activity worksheets

For assessment . . .

- Ready-made unit and review achievement tests with options to edit, add, or delete items.

MyEnglishLab

An optional online learning tool

- **NEW** Grammar Coach videos, plus the Pronunciation Coach videos, and Digital Vocabulary Flash Cards
- **NEW** Immediate and meaningful feedback on wrong answers
- **NEW** Remedial grammar exercises
- Interactive practice of all material presented in the course
- Grade reports that display performance and time on task
- Auto-graded achievement tests

Workbook

Lesson-by-lesson written exercises to accompany the Student's Book

Full-Course Placement Tests

Choose printable or online version

Classroom Audio Program

- A set of Audio CDs, as an alternative to the clickable audio in the ActiveTeach
- Contains a variety of authentic regional and non-native accents to build comprehension of diverse English speakers
- **NEW** The entire audio program is available for students at www.english.com/topnotch3e. The mobile app *Top Notch Go* allows access anytime, anywhere and lets students practice at their own pace.

Teacher's Edition and Lesson Planner

- Detailed interleaved lesson plans, language and culture notes, answer keys, and more
- Also accessible in digital form in the ActiveTeach

ABOUT THE AUTHORS

Joan Saslow

Joan Saslow has taught in a variety of programs in South America and the United States. She is author or coauthor of a number of widely used courses, some of which are *Ready to Go*, *Workplace Plus*, *Literacy Plus*, and *Summit*. She is also author of *English in Context*, a series for reading science and technology. Ms. Saslow was the series director of *True Colors* and *True Voices*. She has participated in the English Language Specialist Program in the U.S. Department of State's Bureau of Educational and Cultural Affairs.

Allen Ascher

Allen Ascher has been a teacher and teacher trainer in China and the United States, as well as academic director of the intensive English program at Hunter College. Mr. Ascher has also been an ELT publisher and was responsible for publication and expansion of numerous well-known courses including *True Colors*, *NorthStar*, the *Longman TOEFL Preparation Series*, and the *Longman Academic Writing Series*. He is coauthor of *Summit*, and he wrote the "Teaching Speaking" module of *Teacher Development Interactive*, an online multimedia teacher-training program.

Ms. Saslow and Mr. Ascher are frequent presenters at professional conferences and have been coauthoring courses for teens, adults, and young adults since 2002.

AUTHORS' ACKNOWLEDGMENTS

The authors are indebted to these reviewers, who provided extensive and detailed feedback and suggestions for *Top Notch*, as well as the hundreds of teachers who completed surveys and participated in focus groups.

Manuel Wilson Alvarado Miles, Quito, Ecuador • **Shirley Ando,** Otemae University, Hyogo, Japan • **Vanessa de Andrade,** CCBEU Inter Americano, Curitiba, Brazil • **Miguel Arrazola,** CBA, Santa Cruz, Bolivia • **Mark Barta,** Proficiency School of English, São Paulo, Brazil • **Edwin Bello,** PROULEX, Guadalajara, Mexico • **Mary Blum,** CBA, Cochabamba, Bolivia • **María Elizabeth Boccia,** Proficiency School of English, São Paulo, Brazil • **Pamela Cristina Borja Baltán,** Quito, Ecuador • **Eliana Anabel L. Buccia,** AMICANA, Mendoza, Argentina • **José Humberto Calderón Díaz,** CALUSAC, Guatemala City, Guatemala • **María Teresa Calienes Csirke,** Idiomas Católica, Lima, Peru • **Esther María Carbo Morales,** Quito, Ecuador • **Jorge Washington Cárdenas Castillo,** Quito, Ecuador • **Eréndira Yadira Carrera García,** UVM Chapultepec, Mexico City, Mexico • **Viviane de Cássia Santos Carlini,** Spectrum Line, Pouso Alegre, Brazil • **Centro Colombo Americano,** Bogota, Colombia • **Guven Ciftci,** Fatih University, Istanbul, Turkey • **Diego Cisneros,** CBA, Tarija, Bolivia • **Paul Crook,** Meisei University, Tokyo, Japan • **Alejandra Díaz Loo,** El Cultural, Arequipa, Peru • **Jesús G. Díaz Osío,** Florida National College, Miami, USA • **María Eid Ceneviva,** CBA, Bolivia • **Amalia Elvira Rodríguez Espinoza De Los Monteros,** Guayaquil, Ecuador • **María Argelia Estrada Vásquez,** CALUSAC, Guatemala City, Guatemala • **John Fieldeldy,** College of Engineering, Nihon University, Aizuwakamatsu-shi, Japan • **Marleni Humbelina Flores Urízar,** CALUSAC, Guatemala City, Guatemala • **Gonzalo Fortune,** CBA, Sucre, Bolivia • **Andrea Fredricks,** Embassy CES, San Francisco, USA • **Irma Gallegos Peláez,** UVM Tlalpan, Mexico City, Mexico • **Alberto Gamarra,** CBA, Santa Cruz, Bolivia • **María Amparo García Peña,** ICPNA Cusco, Peru • **Amanda Gillis-Furutaka,** Kyoto Sangyo University, Kyoto, Japan • **Martha Angelina González**

Párraga, Guayaquil, Ecuador • **Octavio Gorduño Ruiz,** Business Training Consultant, Mexico City, Mexico • **Ralph Grayson,** Idiomas Católica, Lima, Peru • **Murat Gultekin,** Fatih University, Istanbul, Turkey • **Oswaldo Gutiérrez,** PROULEX, Guadalajara, Mexico • **Ayaka Hashinishi,** Otemae University, Hyogo, Japan • **Alma Lorena Hernández de Armas,** CALUSAC, Guatemala City, Guatemala • **Kent Hill,** Seigakuin University, Saitama-ken, Japan • **Kayoko Hirao,** Nichii Gakkan Company, COCO Juku, Japan • **Jesse Huang,** National Central University, Taoyuan, Taiwan • **Eric Charles Jones,** Seoul University of Technology, Seoul, South Korea • **Jun-Chen Kuo,** Tajen University, Pingtung, Taiwan • **Susan Krieger,** Embassy CES, San Francisco, USA • **Ana María de la Torre Ugarte,** ICPNA Chiclayo, Peru • **Erin Lemaistre,** Chung-Ang University, Seoul, South Korea • **Eleanor S. Leu,** Soochow University, Taipei, Taiwan • **Yihui Li (Stella Li),** Fooyin University, Kaohsiung, Taiwan • **Chin-Fan Lin,** Shih Hsin University, Taipei, Taiwan • **Linda Lin,** Tatung Institute of Technology, Taiwan • **Kristen Lindblom,** Embassy CES, San Francisco, USA • **Patricio David López Logacho,** Quito, Ecuador • **Diego López Tasara,** Idiomas Católica, Lima, Peru • **Neil Macleod,** Kansai Gaidai University, Osaka, Japan • **Adriana Marcés,** Idiomas Católica, Lima, Peru • **Robyn McMurray,** Pusan National University, Busan, South Korea • **Paula Medina,** London Language Institute, London, Canada • **Juan Carlos Muñoz,** American School Way, Bogota, Colombia • **Noriko Mori,** Otemae University, Hyogo, Japan • **Adrián Esteban Narváez Pacheco,** Cuenca, Ecuador • **Tim Newfields,** Tokyo University Faculty of Economics, Tokyo, Japan • **Ana Cristina Ochoa,** CCBEU Inter Americano, Curitiba, Brazil • **Tania Elizabeth Ortega Santacruz,** Cuenca, Ecuador • **Martha Patricia Páez,** Quito, Ecuador • **María de Lourdes Pérez Valdespino,** Universidad del Valle

de México, Mexico • **Wahrena Elizabeth Pfeister,** University of Suwon, Gyeonggi-Do, South Korea • **Wayne Allen Pfeister,** University of Suwon, Gyeonggi-Do, South Korea • **Andrea Rebonato,** CCBEU Inter Americano, Curitiba, Brazil • **Thomas Robb,** Kyoto Sangyo University, Kyoto, Japan • **Mehran Sabet,** Seigakuin University, Saitama-ken, Japan • **Majid Safadaran Mosazadeh,** ICPNA Chiclayo, Peru • **Timothy Samuelson,** BridgeEnglish, Denver, USA • **Héctor Sánchez,** PROULEX, Guadalajara, Mexico • **Mónica Alexandra Sánchez Escalante,** Quito, Ecuador • **Jorge Mauricio Sánchez Montalván,** Quito, Universidad Politécnica Salesiana (UPS), Ecuador • **Letícia Santos,** ICBEU Ibiá, Brazil • **Elena Sapp,** INTO Oregon State University, Corvallis, USA • **Robert Sheridan,** Otemae University, Hyogo, Japan • **John Eric Sherman,** Hong Ik University, Seoul, South Korea • **Brooks Slaybaugh,** Asia University, Tokyo, Japan • **João Vitor Soares,** NACC, São Paulo, Brazil • **Silvia Solares,** CBA, Sucre, Bolivia • **Chayawan Sonchaeng,** Delaware County Community College, Media, PA • **María Julia Suárez,** CBA, Cochabamba, Bolivia • **Elena Sudakova,** English Language Center, Kiev, Ukraine • **Richard Swingle,** Kansai Gaidai College, Osaka, Japan • **Blanca Luz Terrazas Zamora,** ICPNA Cusco, Peru • **Sandrine Ting,** St. John's University, New Taipei City, Taiwan • **Christian Juan Torres Medina,** Guayaquil, Ecuador • **Raquel Torrico,** CBA, Sucre, Bolivia • **Jessica Ueno,** Otemae University, Hyogo, Japan • **Ximena Vacaflor C.,** CBA, Tarija, Bolivia • **René Valdivia Pereira,** CBA, Santa Cruz, Bolivia • **Solange Lopes Vinagre Costa,** SENAC, São Paulo, Brazil • **Magno Alejandro Vivar Hurtado,** Cuenca, Ecuador • **Dr. Wen-hsien Yang,** National Kaohsiung Hospitality College, Kaohsiung, Taiwan • **Juan Zárate,** El Cultural, Arequipa, Peru

USING YOUR *TOP NOTCH* TEACHER'S EDITION AND LESSON PLANNER

The **Teacher's Edition and Lesson Planner** provides detailed notes for planning and presenting your lessons, plus ideas for extending them. You will find additional support in *ActiveTeach*, a digital tool that goes hand in hand with the Teacher's Edition. *ActiveTeach* provides an interactive classroom experience with or without an interactive whiteboard (IWB).

The instructions here will guide you as you use the teaching suggestions in the Lesson Plans, and explain the printable and digital resources in *ActiveTeach*.

In addition, the authors recommend you consult the **Methods Handbook** for support in developing effective techniques for teaching in a communicative classroom and for teaching tips for achieving the best results with the *Top Notch* course. You can find the **Methods Handbook** in the folder labeled "Methodology" within "Teacher Resources" on *ActiveTeach*. Within "Methodology", you will also find the article "**Great Ideas for Teaching with *ActiveTeach***," which explains numerous ways in which you can use *ActiveTeach* to enhance your in-class lessons.

Overview

Starting with Unit 1, each two-page lesson is designed for a period of 45 to 60 minutes. To plan a class of approximately 45 minutes, use the shorter estimated teaching times as a guide when a range is shown. To plan a class of at least 60 minutes, use the longer estimated times. Your actual teaching time may vary according to your students' needs, your program schedule, and your teaching style. Write your actual teaching time in the space provided for future reference.

Activities labeled *Option* include suggested teaching times that should be added to the lesson.

In addition, these optional digital activities referenced throughout this Teacher's Edition are available in *ActiveTeach* to enrich your lesson.

Vocabulary Flash Card Player

By clicking on the icon, you will have instant access to digital full-color vocabulary flash cards for dynamic presentation, practice, or review.

More Exercises

Additional exercises are provided for each grammar presentation and each reading. The Extra Grammar Exercises can be presented as interactive digital activities, or they can be printed out and distributed as handouts from the "Printable Extension Activities" menu in "Teacher Resources." The Extra Reading Comprehension Exercises can also be presented in the classroom, to be done in class as an oral activity, or they can be printed out from the menu as handouts for written responses.

Conversation Activator Video

This extra speaking support is provided to encourage students to change, personalize, and extend the Conversation Models. This exciting video tool accompanies the Conversation Activator activities in each unit.

The Conversation Activator has two scenes. In Scene 1, actors demonstrate how to change and personalize the Conversation Model. In Scene 2, the actors extend their conversation, saying as much as they can. If you wish, you can print out the video script from the "Teacher Resources" menu in *ActiveTeach*. You can also show a transcript from the video player on *ActiveTeach*.

Pronunciation Coach Video

This extra pronunciation support features a coach who models and expands the pronunciation topic. The video provides animated examples to further clarify the topic and offers further spoken practice.

Top Notch Pop Song Video and Karaoke Video

Designed to provide targeted practice of unit language and improve students' pronunciation, the *Top Notch Pop* songs are accessible in two video formats: first, with a vocalist, and then karaoke-style, without the vocalist. Both videos feature the song lyrics with a "bouncing ball," enabling students to sing or "rap" the songs. Both formats are also available in audio only by clicking the audio icons on the *Top Notch Pop* Lyrics page at the end of the Student's Book. *Top Notch Pop* song activities are available for each unit's song. The activities provide practice of the unit grammar and vocabulary in the songs as well as comprehension exercises of the lyrics. Access the activities from the "*Top Notch Pop* Songs" menu in *ActiveTeach*.

Digital Games

Choose from two games available for additional review and practice of unit language. They can be opened by clicking the icon on the digital Student's Book page in *ActiveTeach*, or they can be accessed in "Teacher Resources" within *ActiveTeach*.

Open Printable extension activities and other resources in *ActiveTeach*

A multitude of additional activities and resources can be viewed and printed from the "Printable Extension Activities" menu in "Teacher Resources" within *ActiveTeach*. Throughout the Lesson Plan notes, the following printable extension activities and resources are referenced with the print icon 🖨 at the suggested point of use in the lesson: Conversation Activator Pair Work Cards, Conversation Activator Video Script, Speaking Activities, "Find Someone Who" Activities, Graphic Organizers, Inductive Grammar Charts, Learning Strategies, Pronunciation Activities, Writing Process Worksheets, Extra Grammar Exercises, Extra Reading Comprehension Exercises. Other available resources, listed at the end of each unit, include Unit Study Guides, Supplementary Pronunciation Lessons, "Just for Fun" Activities, and Oral Progress Assessment Charts.

GRAMMAR BOOSTER **WRITING BOOSTER**

Clicking on ↻ next to the Grammar Booster and Writing Booster boxes on the digital Student's Book page in *ActiveTeach* opens the associated Booster page from the back of the Student's Book. Clicking on the ↺ icon returns you to the lesson you were viewing.

Other Supplements

In addition to the digital and printable extras listed, *Top Notch 2* offers even more supplements. The **EXTRAS** icon throughout the Lesson Plan pages lists additional supplementary components and materials available to support the lesson or individual units.

Supplementary components include:

Workbook Lesson-by-lesson written exercises.

MyEnglishLab An online learning tool with a multitude of features to support students and teachers, including: Grammar Coach videos, immediate and meaningful feedback on wrong answers, remedial grammar exercises, interactive practice of all material presented in the course, grade reports that display performance and time on tasks, and auto-graded achievement tests. The Pronunciation Coach videos and digital vocabulary flash cards used in *ActiveTeach* for presentation and practice are also part of MyEnglishLab, giving students an opportunity to review this content on their own time and at their own pace.

Top Notch TV A highly popular video program which includes a hilarious situation comedy and authentic On-the-Street Interviews. *Top Notch TV* Activity Worksheets provide additional listening and language review and practice. Access the full video program and the worksheets from the "*Top Notch TV*" menu in *ActiveTeach*.

Assessment Ready-made unit and review achievement tests, with options to edit, add, or delete items.

Online Teacher Resources Additional teacher resources are available at **pearsonelt.com/topnotch3e**.

Full Course Placement Tests Accurately place your students into *Top Notch*. Available on CD or online. Includes detailed instructions for administering the test, and guidelines for scoring and placement.

Student's Book icons and *ActiveTeach* icons

The icons used in the Student's Book and *ActiveTeach* are different. Here are the corresponding icons:

	Student's Book icon	ActiveTeach icon
Vocabulary Flash Card Player	DIGITAL FLASH CARDS	V
Extra Grammar Exercises	DIGITAL MORE EXERCISES	★ 🖨
Extra Reading Comprehension Exercises	DIGITAL MORE EXERCISES	★ 🖨
Conversation Activator Video	DIGITAL VIDEO	📹
Pronunciation Coach Video	DIGITAL VIDEO COACH	📹
***Top Notch Pop* Song Video and Karaoke Video**	DIGITAL SONG DIGITAL KARAOKE	🎵 🎤
Games	DIGITAL GAMES	🎮

Grammar Readiness
SELF-CHECK

The Grammar Readiness Self-Check is optional. Complete the exercises to confirm that you know this grammar previously taught in *Top Notch*.

THE SIMPLE PRESENT TENSE AND THE PRESENT CONTINUOUS

A **PRACTICE** Choose the correct verb or verb phrase.

1 We (take /(are taking)) a trip to California this weekend.

2 The flight (arrives /(is arriving)) now. That's great because the flights in this airport usually ((arrive) / are arriving) late.

3 Please drive slower! You (go /(are going)) too fast!

4 ((Does it rain) / Is it raining) often in March?

5 Brandon (goes /(is going)) skiing on his next vacation.

6 We ((like)/ are liking) milk in both coffee and tea.

B **USE THE GRAMMAR** Complete each statement with the simple present tense or the present continuous.

1 In my family, we usually .... *Answers will vary.*

2 Next weekend, I ....

BE GOING TO + BASE FORM FOR THE FUTURE

A **PRACTICE** Complete the conversations with <u>be going to</u>. Use contractions.

1 **A:** What ......are they going to do....... (they / do) after English class?
   B: They 're going to go.................... (go) out to eat.

2 **A:** I 'm going to need.............. (need) a rental car in Chicago.
   B: Are you going to make......... (you / make) a reservation online?

3 **A:** Who ......are you going to call...... (you / call) when your plane lands?
   B: My wife. She 's going to wait.................. (wait) for my call in the airport café.

4 **A:** What ......are you going to do...... (you / do) when you get to New York?
   B: The first thing ....we're going to do........ (we / do) is eat!

5 **A:** Who 's going to be.................... (be) at the meeting?
   B: My colleagues from the office. And my boss ....is going to come....... (come), too.

B **USE THE GRAMMAR** Write your own question and answer, using <u>be going to</u> + a base form.

Q: .... *Answers will vary.*

....

A: ....

....

CAN, HAVE TO, COULD, AND SHOULD: MEANING AND FORM

A **PRACTICE** Choose the correct phrases.

1 We .... a reservation if we want a good room.
  a couldn't make   (**b** should make)   **c** should making

2 Susan doesn't have to wear formal clothes to the office. She .... jeans.
  a can't wear   **b** can wearing   (**c** can wear)

3 Dan can't go shopping this afternoon. He .... drive his children to school.
  a have to   (**b** has to)   **c** doesn't have to

4 They just missed the 3:12 express bus, but they .... the 3:14 local because it arrives too late. They should take a taxi.
  a could take   **b** shouldn't to take   (**c** shouldn't take)

5 The class has to end on time so the students .... the bus to the party.
  (**a** can take)   **b** can to take   **c** can't take

6 I can sleep late tomorrow. I .... go to the office.
  a have to   (**b** don't have to)   **c** doesn't have to

B **USE THE GRAMMAR** Write one statement with both <u>can</u> and <u>have to</u>. Write one statement with either <u>should</u> or <u>could</u>.   Answers will vary.

1 ....

2 ....

OBJECT PRONOUNS

A **PRACTICE** Rewrite each sentence, correcting the error.

1 Please call about it us. Please call us about it.

2 She's buying for you it. She's buying it for you.

3 The brown shoes? She doesn't like on him them. She doesn't like them on him.

4 He wrote for her it. He wrote it for her.

5 They're giving to them it. They're giving it to them.

B **USE THE GRAMMAR** Rewrite each sentence, changing the two nouns to object pronouns.

1 I gave my sister the present yesterday. I gave her it yesterday.

2 The clerk gift-wrapped the sweaters for John. The clerk gift-wrapped them for him.

COMPARATIVE ADJECTIVES

A **PRACTICE** Complete each sentence with the comparative form of the adjective.

1 I think very cold weather is ....worse.......... (bad) than very hot weather.

2 A tablet is ..more convenient. (convenient) than a laptop.

3 A T-shirt is _more comfortable_ (comfortable) than a sweatshirt in hot weather.

4 The clothes in a department store are usually _more affordable_ (affordable) than ones in a small neighborhood store.

5 Orange juice is _better_ (good) for your health than orange soda.

6 Rio is pretty hot in the summer, but Salvador is _hotter_ (hot).

7 If you're getting dressed for the office, you should wear a _longer_ (long) skirt.

B USE THE GRAMMAR Write your own two sentences, using one of these adjectives in comparative form in each sentence: <u>cheap</u>, <u>popular</u>, <u>near</u>, <u>fast</u>. Answers will vary. (cheaper, more popular, nearer, faster)

1 ....

2 ....

SUPERLATIVE ADJECTIVES

A PRACTICE Write statements with the superlative form of each adjective. Answers will vary. The superlative form is shown in parentheses.

1 old _The oldest person in the world is 124 years old._

2 good _(best)_

3 funny _(funniest)_

4 appropriate _(most appropriate)_

5 unusual _(most unusual)_

6 large _(largest)_

7 beautiful _(most beautiful)_

8 short _(shortest)_

9 interesting _(most interesting)_

10 crazy _(craziest)_

B USE THE GRAMMAR Write one statement about yourself, using a superlative adjective. Answers will vary.

....

THE SIMPLE PAST TENSE: STATEMENTS

A PRACTICE Complete the paragraph with the simple past tense.

Chris _went_ (1 go) to New York at the end of the school year. His flight _got in_ (2 get in) late, so he _took_ (3 take) a taxi directly to his hotel and _ate_ (4 eat) something fast at the hotel café. Chris _had_ (5 have) tickets to a Broadway show, and he _didn't have_ (6 not have) time to eat at a regular restaurant. Just before the show, he _met_ (7 meet) his friends in front of the theater. He really _loved_ (8 love) the show. After the show, he _bought_ (9 buy) a book about it. His friends _said_ (10 say) good night, and Chris _walked_ (11 walk) back to the hotel, _drank_ (12 drink) a big glass of cold juice, _went_ (13 go) to bed, and _slept_ (14 sleep) for 10 hours.

B USE THE GRAMMAR Write four statements about what you did yesterday. Use one of these verbs in each statement: <u>go</u>, <u>get dressed</u>, <u>eat</u>, <u>come home</u>   Answers will vary. (went, got dressed, ate, came home)

1 ....

2 ....

3 ....

4 ....

THE SIMPLE PAST TENSE: <u>YES</u> / <u>NO</u> QUESTIONS

A PRACTICE Change each statement to a <u>yes</u> / <u>no</u> question.

1 Phil lost his luggage on the flight. Did Phil lose his luggage on the flight?

2 They drove too fast. Did they drive too fast?

3 She wrote a letter to her uncle. Did she write a letter to her uncle?

4 They found a wallet on the street. Did they find a wallet on the street?

5 Claire's husband spent a lot of money at the mall. Did Claire's husband spend a lot of money at the mall?

6 Ms. Carter taught her children to play the piano. Did Ms. Carter teach her children to play the piano?

B USE THE GRAMMAR Write three <u>yes</u> / <u>no</u> questions. Use each of these verbs: <u>bring</u>, <u>speak</u>, <u>break</u>.

1 ....   Answers will vary.

2 ....

3 ....

THE SIMPLE PAST TENSE: INFORMATION QUESTIONS

A PRACTICE Complete each conversation with an information question in the simple past tense.

1 **A:** Where did you study Chinese?
  B: I studied in Shanghai.

2 **A:** When did you meet your husband?
  B: I met him two years ago.

3 **A:** Who did you call about the problem?
  B: I called my daughter. She always knows what to do.

4 **A:** Who bought your car?
  B: My brother-in-law bought it. He needed a new car.

5 **A:** How long did your parents live in Mexico?
  B: My parents lived there for more than ten years.

B USE THE GRAMMAR Write two information questions in the simple past tense, one with <u>How</u> and one with <u>What</u>.

1 ....   Answers will vary.

2 ....

PREVIEW

CUSTOMS AROUND THE WORLD

Greetings *People greet each other differently around the world.*

Some people bow.

Some people kiss once. Some kiss twice.

Some shake hands.

And some hug.

Exchanging Business Cards

People have different customs for exchanging business cards around the world.

Some customs are very formal. People always use two hands and look at the card carefully.

Other customs are informal. People accept a card with one hand and quickly put it in a pocket.

Getting Acquainted

What about small talk—the topics people talk about when they don't know each other well?

In some places, it's not polite to ask people about how much money they make or how old they are. But in other places, people think those topics are appropriate.

A **PAIR WORK** In your opinion, is there a right way and a wrong way to greet people? Explain.

B **DISCUSSION** In your country, are there any topics people should avoid during small talk? What about the topics below?

- the weather
- someone's job
- someone's religion
- someone's family
- someone's home
- (other) ___

UNIT 1 Getting Acquainted

PREVIEW

Before Exercise A , give students a few minutes to silently read and examine the photos and information about customs.

- Ask a volunteer to read the heading *Customs Around the World.*
- Call on students to read the section headings and the photo descriptions.
- To focus on *Greetings,* ask students for additional ways to greet people and write them on the board. (Possible responses: Pat on the back, nod, smile.)
- Focus on *Getting Acquainted.* Explain that *small talk* is conversation about minor topics. Ask students to name additional topics that can be used for small talk. (Possible responses: the weather, hobbies, work.)

Language and culture*

- Customs vary from culture to culture. In Japan, business cards are always presented to another person with two hands to show respect. In English-speaking countries, hugging or kissing is reserved for friends or close associates. In some cultures, asking about a person's age or salary is acceptable; in English-speaking countries, asking about age or salary can be rude.

*Language and culture notes are provided to offer students enrichment or more information about language and / or culture. Their use is optional.

A Pair work

Suggested teaching time:	3 minutes	Your actual teaching time:	

- For a warm-up, ask *How do you usually greet people?*
- On the board, write What behaviors would be unusual or strange in your country? Why?
- Have pairs discuss the questions; then call on students to share their opinions with the class.

B Discussion

Suggested teaching time:	7–12 minutes	Your actual teaching time:	

- Model the activity by discussing the questions with a more confident student. Review the question and topics in the box with the class. Encourage students to fill in the blank with another conversation topic.
- Divide the class into groups of three and have students read and discuss the questions. Move around the room and help students as needed.
- Review answers with the class. Ask *Which topics would you feel uncomfortable talking about? Most comfortable? What other topics did you think of?*

C ▶1:02 Photo story

Suggested teaching time:	10–15 minutes	Your actual teaching time:

- To prepare students for the activity, have them look at the photos. Ask:
  Do you think the two men know each other well? (No.)
  How do they greet each other in the second photo? (By shaking hands.)
  How do they exchange business cards? (Taka uses two hands to hold the card.)

- Have students read and listen to the conversation once or twice.

- To check comprehension, ask:
  What countries are Leon and Taka from? (Mexico, Japan.)
  Where did they meet last week? (At an IT business conference.)
  Where is the conference going to be next year? (Acapulco.)

- Listen again and review answers with the class.

Language and culture

- *IT* refers to *information technology*.
- *What have you been up to?* means *What have you been doing?* and is commonly used in spoken English. The expression can be used in different tenses; for example, *What are you up to these days? What were you up to?*

Option: *(+5 minutes)* To extend the activity, have pairs role-play the Photo Story. Tell them to replace the names in the book with their own names.

Option: *(+10 minutes)* To challenge students, have them create and role-play their own conversations using the underlined expressions from the exercise. Tell them to imagine they met some time in the past and that now they meet again. For example,
A: *You look familiar. I'm ___.*
B: *Oh, yes, I think we met at ___ last week. I'm ___. . . .*
Volunteers can present their role play to the class.

ENGLISH FOR TODAY'S WORLD The box at the top of this page, titled "English for Today's World," indicates that one or both of the speakers in the Photo Story is not a "native speaker" of English. Remind students that in today's world, they must learn to understand both a variety of standard and regional spoken native accents as well as non-native accents because most English speakers in the world are not native speakers of the language. Language backgrounds are shown in the box so you can point them out to students.

FYI: The subtitle of the Top Notch series is English for Today's World. This is in recognition of the fact that English is a language for communication between people from a variety of language backgrounds.

D Focus on language

Suggested teaching time:	5 minutes	Your actual teaching time:

- To prepare students, point out the underlined expressions in the Photo Story. Ask volunteers to read them aloud.
- Model the activity by doing the first item.
- After students do the matching, have them compare answers in pairs.
- Move around the room and help students as needed.

E Think and explain

Suggested teaching time:	5 minutes	Your actual teaching time:

- Tell students to make notes as they think about and answer the questions. Encourage them to use the underlined expressions from the Photo Story in their answers.
- Point out that the quote to the right shows a sample answer for item 1.
- Review answers with the class.

Answers to Exercise E
1. He thinks he recognizes him.
2. No. He hasn't been doing much.
3. So that they can keep in touch.
4. To show Taka around in Acapulco.

SPEAKING
Pair work

Suggested teaching time:	10–15 minutes	Your actual teaching time:

- Ask students to read the sample advice in the quotes aloud. Explain vocabulary as needed. Ask *Who agrees with each statement?*
- Have students work in pairs. As pairs write their advice, move around the room to provide help with vocabulary and expressions. Tell students to use the same language to give their advice; for example, *Please don't . . . ; Never . . .*
- Invite students to share their advice with the class and explain why it is important.
- Ask the class *Did you find anyone's answers surprising? Whose?*

Workbook

C ▶1:02 **PHOTO STORY** Read and listen to two people meeting in a hotel lobby.

Leon: You look familiar. Haven't we met somewhere before?

Taka: I don't think so. I'm not from around here.

Leon: I know! Aren't you from Japan? I'm sure we met at the IT conference last week.

Taka: Of course! You're from Mexico, right?

Leon: That's right. I'm sorry. I've forgotten your name.

Taka: Kamura Takashi. But you can call me Taka.

Leon: Hi, Taka. Leon Prieto. Please call me Leon. So, what have you been up to since the conference?

Taka: Not much. Actually, I'm on my way to the airport now. I'm flying back home.

Leon: Hey, we should keep in touch. Here's my card. The conference is in Acapulco next year and I could show you around.

Taka: That would be great. I hear Acapulco's beautiful.

Leon: It was nice to see you again, Taka.

Taka: You, too.

D **FOCUS ON LANGUAGE** Find the underlined expression in the Photo Story that matches each explanation.

1 You say this when you want to offer to introduce someone to a new place.   I could show you around.

2 You say this to suggest that someone call or e-mail you in the future.   We should keep in touch.

3 You say this when you're not sure if you know someone, but you think you might.   You look familiar.

4 You say this when you want to ask about someone's recent activities.   What have you been up to?

E **THINK AND EXPLAIN** Answer the questions, according to the Photo Story. Explain your answers. See page T3

1 Why does Leon begin speaking with Taka?

2 Has Taka been busy since the conference?

3 Why does Leon give Taka his business card?

4 What does Leon offer to do at the next conference?

> ❝ Because he thinks he knows Taka. He says, 'You look familiar.' ❞

SPEAKING

PAIR WORK With a partner, discuss and write advice for visitors about how to behave in your country. Then share your advice with the class.

Your advice
1
2
3

> ❝ Questions like *How old are you?* and *How much money do you make?* aren't polite. You shouldn't ask them. ❞

> ❝ Don't exchange business cards with one hand! Always use two hands. ❞

GOAL Get reacquainted with someone

GRAMMAR *The present perfect*

Use the present perfect to talk about an indefinite time in the past.
Form the present perfect with <u>have</u> or <u>has</u> and a past participle.

For regular verbs, the past participle form is the same as the simple past form.
open → open**ed**
study → stud**ied**

Affirmative and negative statements

| We | 've / haven't | met them. | | She | 's / hasn't | called him. |

Yes / no questions

A: **Have** you **met** them?
B: Yes, we **have**. / No, we **haven't**.

A: **Has** she **called** him?
B: Yes, she **has**. / No, she **hasn't**.

Remember: Use the simple past tense to talk about a definite or specific time.

present perfect: indefinite time
I've **met** Bill twice.

simple past tense: definite time
We **met** in 1999 and again in 2004.

Irregular verbs

base form	simple past	past participle
be	was / were	**been**
come	came	**come**
do	did	**done**
eat	ate	**eaten**
fall	fell	**fallen**
go	went	**gone**
have	had	**had**
make	made	**made**
meet	met	**met**
see	saw	**seen**
speak	spoke	**spoken**
take	took	**taken**
write	wrote	**written**

For more irregular verb forms, see page 123.

Contractions
've met = have met
haven't met = have not met
's met = has met
hasn't met = has not met

GRAMMAR BOOSTER p. 126
• The present perfect: information questions

A Choose the correct form to complete each sentence.

1 We've .... the 2:00 express train many times.
   a take   **b** took   (**c**) taken

2 I had breakfast at 9:00, but I haven't .... lunch.
   a have   (**b**) had   **c** having

3 Alison has .... to the mall.
   a went   (**b**) gone   **c** go

4 My younger brother has .... home from work.
   (**a**) come   **b** came   **c** comes

5 They posted some messages yesterday, but they haven't .... anything about their trip.
   (**a**) written   **b** write   **c** wrote

B **PAIR WORK** Complete the conversations with the present perfect or the simple past tense. Then practice the conversations with a partner.

1 A: ......Has Jake met...... our new teacher?
      Jake / meet
   B: Yes, ...he has.... . He ....met.......... her in the office this morning.
                                        meet

2 A: ......Have they been...... to this class before?
      they / be
   B: No, they haven't . They're new at this school.

3 A: ......Have you eaten...... in the new school restaurant?
      you / eat
   B: No, ...I haven't... . Is it good?

4 A: Have your classmates spoken with the school director?
      your classmates / speak
   B: Yes, ...they have.. . They ....spoke.......... with her yesterday.
                                      speak

5 A: ......Has Beth seen...... the new language lab?
      Beth / see
   B: No, ...she hasn't... . But she ....has seen.......... the library.
                                                see

GRAMMAR

Suggested teaching time:	10–15 minutes	Your actual teaching time:

- To introduce the structure, write on the board 1 *They've met* before. 2 *She met him yesterday.*
- Ask:
  Which sentence mentions specific time in the past? (Number 2, *yesterday.*)
  What is the verb in sentence 2? (Met.)
  What tense is the verb? (Simple past tense.)
  Write *simple past tense* above the sentence.
- Read the underlined verb in the first sentence. Then write *present perfect* above it. Explain that this sentence uses the present perfect because it does not mention a specific time in the past. We don't know exactly <u>when</u> she met him.
- To help students identify the difference between specific and non-specific times, explain that a specific time tells them when something happened. Practice this concept by presenting pairs of sentences and asking if the time is specific. For example, *I've read that book. Is this specific?* (Non-specific—at some time in the past.) *I read that book last week.* (Specific—*last week.*)
- Go over the information about statements and *yes / no* questions in the Grammar box. Ask volunteers to read the example sentences. Ask *Which verb is regular?* (Called.) *What is the base form of this verb?* (Call.) *Which verb is irregular?* (Met.) *What is the base form of this verb?* (Meet.)
- Ask a student to read the Remember note in the Grammar box. Point out the specific time references in the simple past tense (1999, 2004). Make sure students understand the meaning of *indefinite* (non-specific) and *definite* (specific). Explain that the example in the present perfect does not have a definite time reference. We don't know when this person has met Bill.
- Ask a student to read the Remember note in the Grammar box. Point out the specific time references in the simple past tense (1999, 2004). Make sure students understand the meaning of *indefinite* (non-specific) and *definite* (specific). Explain that the example in the present perfect does not have a definite time reference. We don't know when this person has met Bill.
- Review the formation of the simple past; remind students that regular verbs form the simple past tense by adding *-ed* to the base form. The past participle form is the same. Explain that irregular verbs do not form the simple past tense by adding *-ed*. The past participle form may be the same as the simple past form or different.
- Direct students' attention to the information in the Contractions box. Point out the contractions in all the example sentences and ask students to give the full form for each (*have–have not; has–has not*). Be sure to explain that short answers in the present perfect only contract the negative form.

Option: GRAMMAR BOOSTER *(Teaching notes p. T126)*

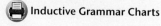 Inductive Grammar Charts

A Choose the correct form . . .

Suggested teaching time:	5–10 minutes	Your actual teaching time:

- Remind students that with the present perfect, the past participle form follows *have* or *has*.
- Review answers as a class.

B Pair work

Suggested teaching time:	5–10 minutes	Your actual teaching time:

- To prepare students for the activity, tell them to circle the definite past time references to help them identify the sentences that use the simple past tense (1B *this morning;* 4B *yesterday*).
- Point out the list of simple past forms and past participles for irregular verbs in the Grammar box. Remind students not to include the past participle in the short answers.
- After pairs have compared answers, have volunteers read the conversations aloud to the class.

Language and culture

- In British English, the past forms of some words can be regular or irregular. For example, you can say *burned* or *burnt, learned* or *learnt, spelled* or *spelt*. The regular past forms of these words are always used in American English.
- The past participle of *get* is *got* in British English; in American English, the past participle of *get* is *gotten*.

Option: (+10 minutes) To challenge your students, have them work in pairs to prepare two short conversations. Tell students to use the present perfect in the question and the simple past tense or the present perfect in the response. Move around the room to provide help and answer questions. After finishing, have pairs role-play their conversations for the class. Ask the class to listen for the verb form and any definite time references in the response. After all the pairs have finished, review the verbs with the class.

C Grammar practice

Suggested teaching time:	5 minutes	Your actual teaching time:

- To help students identify which sentences require the simple past tense, tell them to circle the definite past time references. (1. This morning; 3. In 2013; 7. Last September)
- Have students compare answers in pairs.
- Review answers with the class. Refer to the Grammar box on page 4 if needed.

  Extra Grammar Exercises

CONVERSATION MODEL

A ▶1:03 Read and listen . . .

Suggested teaching time:	2 minutes	Your actual teaching time:

These conversation strategies are implicit in the model:
- Use "I don't think so" to soften a negative answer.
- Say "I know!" to exclaim that you've discovered an answer.

- To prepare students for the activity, ask *What's happening in the picture?* (A man is introducing two women.) *Is this a business or a social situation?* (Social.)
- After students read and listen to the conversation, make sure they understand the conversation strategies by asking comprehension questions; for example, *Does Audrey recognize Hanah right away?* (No.) *Does Hanah recognize Audrey?* (Yes.)

B ▶1:04 Rhythm and intonation

Suggested teaching time:	3 minutes	Your actual teaching time:

- Have students repeat each line chorally. Make sure they:
  - use rising intonation for . . . *have you met Hanah?*
  - use falling intonation for . . . *I'd like you to meet Audrey* and *How have you been?*

PRONUNCIATION

A ▶1:05 Listen to how the sound . . .

Suggested teaching time:	3 minutes	Your actual teaching time:

Pronunciation Coach Video

- After students have listened to and read the sentences, tell them to listen again, paying attention to the disappearing /t/ sound of the negative contraction.
- Have students listen a third time and repeat in the pauses.

B Now practice saying . . .

Suggested teaching time:	2 minutes	Your actual teaching time:

- For more practice, have pairs say the sentences to each other. Listen for correct sound reduction. Provide help as needed.

 Pronunciation Activities

NOW YOU CAN Get reacquainted with someone

Conversation activator

Suggested teaching time:	13–18 minutes	Your actual teaching time:

Conversation Activator Video

- *Note:* You can print the script or you can show a running transcript on video player on the ActiveTeach. The script also appears on page 181 of this Teacher's Edition.
- To review getting reacquainted with someone, refer students to the Conversation Model.
- Ask a volunteer to read the Ideas list. Ask *Which of these places do you go to often? Why? At which places do you usually meet new people?*
- Have students fill in their own idea and share answers with the class.

DON'T STOP! Extend the conversation. Encourage students to continue the conversation by using topics in the box.

- For more support, play the Conversation Activator Video before students do this activity themselves. In Scene 1, the actors use different words in the gaps from the ones in the Conversation Model. In Scene 2, the actors extend the conversation. After each scene, ask students how the model has been changed by the actors.
- Be sure to reinforce the use of conversation strategies. On the board, write *Body language*. Demonstrate the use of appropriate gestures and facial expressions; for example, looking puzzled when responding "I don't think so . . ." to the question *Have we met before?*
- Model the activity by role-playing with a more confident student. Take the role of Student A and use student names; for example, *Peter, have you met Mary?* Then extend the conversation by using a situation from the Ideas and Don't stop! boxes.
- Divide the class into groups of three. Tell students to fill in the blanks and continue the conversation. Encourage students to refer to the Ideas list for places where they might have met.
- Move around the room and help students as needed. Remind them that *small talk* is conversation about minor topics.
- Make sure students change roles and start a new conversation at least once.

Option: (+10 minutes) To expand the activity, ask groups to perform their introductions. Have other groups write down the body language they observe. To demonstrate, write *Student A stood very close to Student B. Student B moved his hands around a lot. Student A smiled and looked friendly.* After each introduction, ask *Was the person introduced using a first or last name? How did the people greet one another?*

 Conversation Activator Video Script; Conversation Activator Pair Work Cards

EXTRAS

Workbook or MyEnglishLab

Speaking Activities: Unit 1, Activity 1

C **GRAMMAR PRACTICE** Complete the message with the present perfect or the simple past tense.

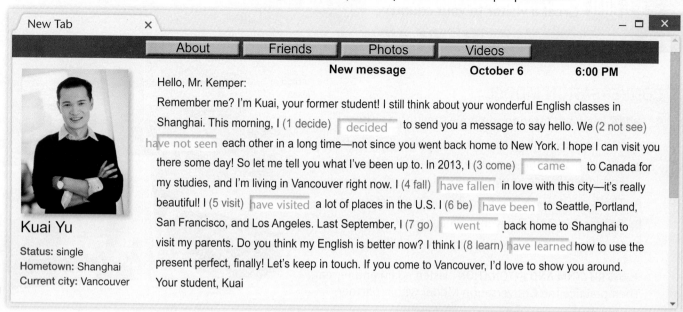

New Tab   ✕   — ☐ ✕

| About | Friends | Photos | Videos |

New message   October 6   6:00 PM

Hello, Mr. Kemper:

Remember me? I'm Kuai, your former student! I still think about your wonderful English classes in Shanghai. This morning, I (1 decide) ___decided___ to send you a message to say hello. We (2 not see) ___have not seen___ each other in a long time—not since you went back home to New York. I hope I can visit you there some day! So let me tell you what I've been up to. In 2013, I (3 come) ___came___ to Canada for my studies, and I'm living in Vancouver right now. I (4 fall) ___have fallen___ in love with this city—it's really beautiful! I (5 visit) ___have visited___ a lot of places in the U.S. I (6 be) ___have been___ to Seattle, Portland, San Francisco, and Los Angeles. Last September, I (7 go) ___went___ back home to Shanghai to visit my parents. Do you think my English is better now? I think I (8 learn) ___have learned___ how to use the present perfect, finally! Let's keep in touch. If you come to Vancouver, I'd love to show you around.

Your student, Kuai

Kuai Yu

Status: single
Hometown: Shanghai
Current city: Vancouver

CONVERSATION MODEL

A ▶1:03 Read and listen to people getting reacquainted.

A: Audrey, have you met Hanah?

B: No, I haven't.

A: Hanah, I'd like you to meet Audrey.

C: Hi, Audrey. You look familiar. Have we met before?

B: I don't think so.

C: I know! Last month. You were at my sister Nicole's party.

B: Oh, that's right! How have you been?

B ▶1:04 **RHYTHM AND INTONATION** Listen again and repeat. Then practice the Conversation Model with a partner.

PRONUNCIATION *Sound reduction in the present perfect*

A ▶1:05 Listen to how the sound /t/ of the negative contraction "disappears" in natural speech. Then listen again and repeat.

1 I haven't been to that class.

2 He hasn't met his new teacher.

3 They haven't taken the test.

4 She hasn't heard the news.

B Now practice saying the sentences on your own.

NOW YOU CAN   Get reacquainted with someone

CONVERSATION ACTIVATOR With two other students, practice making introductions and getting reacquainted. Use your own names and the present perfect. Then change roles.

A: .... , have you met .... ?

B: No, I haven't.

A: .... , I'd like you to meet ....

C: .... You look familiar. Have we met before?

B: ....

DON'T STOP!
• Say how you have been.
• Say more about the time you met.
• Introduce other classmates.

Ideas
You met ...
• at a party
• at a meeting
• at a friend's house
• in another class
• (your own idea) ___

GOAL Greet a visitor to your country

The Forbidden Palace

CONVERSATION MODEL

A ▶1:06 Read and listen to someone greeting a visitor.

A: Welcome to Beijing. Have you ever been here before?

B: No, it's my first time. But yesterday I went to the Forbidden Palace. It was fantastic!

A: That's great. Have you tried Beijing duck yet?

B: Beijing duck? No, I haven't. What's that?

A: It's a famous Chinese dish. I think you'll like it.

B ▶1:07 **RHYTHM AND INTONATION** Listen again and repeat. Then practice the Conversation Model with a partner.

Beijing duck

DIGITAL FLASH CARDS

VOCABULARY *Tourist activities around the world*

A ▶1:08 Read and listen. Then listen again and repeat.

climb Mt. Fuji

go sightseeing in New York

go to the top of the Eiffel Tower

try Korean food

take a tour of the Tower of London

take pictures of the Great Wall

B **PAIR WORK** Use the Vocabulary to say what you have and haven't done.

❝ I've climbed two famous mountains. ❞

❝ I haven't tried Indian food. ❞

GRAMMAR *The present perfect: already, yet, ever, before, and never*

Use ever or before in yes / no questions about *life experiences*.

Have you **ever** eaten Indian food?   Has he been to Paris **before**?

Use yet or already in yes / no questions about *recent experiences*.

Have you toured Quito **yet**?   Has she **already** been to the top of the Eiffel Tower?

In affirmative and negative statements

We've **already** seen the Great Wall.   We haven't tried Beijing duck **yet**.
They have **never** visited Mexico.   They haven't **ever** visited Mexico.
He's been to New York **before**.   He hasn't been to Boston **before**.

Always place **before** and **yet** at the end of statements and questions.

Be careful!
I **have never** (OR **haven't ever**) been there.
NOT I ~~haven't never~~ been there.

GRAMMAR BOOSTER p. 126
• Yet and already: expansion, common errors
• Ever, never, and before: use and placement

CONVERSATION MODEL

A ▶1:06 Read and listen . . .

Suggested teaching time:	2 minutes	Your actual teaching time:

These conversation strategies are implicit in the model:
• Use "Welcome to ___" to greet someone to a new place.
• Say "That's great" to acknowledge someone's positive experience.

• Have students look at the pictures on the right. Ask *What city is this?* (Beijing.) *What are the two people doing?* (Shaking hands and introducing themselves.)

• After students listen and read, ask comprehension questions: *Has the man been to Beijing before?* (No.) *Where did he go yesterday?* (To the Forbidden Palace.)

• Point out that Beijing duck is a famous Chinese dish.

• Point out that the expression *been to a place* only occurs in the present perfect. It is a very common way of saying *have visited a place*.

B ▶1:07 Rhythm and intonation

Suggested teaching time:	3 minutes	Your actual teaching time:

• Have students repeat each line chorally. Make sure they:
  ◦ use rising intonation for *Have you ever been here before?* and *Have you tried Beijing duck yet?*
  ◦ use falling intonation for *What's that?*

VOCABULARY

A ▶1:08 Read and listen . . .

Suggested teaching time:	2 minutes	Your actual teaching time:

 Vocabulary Flash Card Player

• Invite volunteers to give the location of the places pictured, or tell students where they are. (*Mt. Fuji*—Japan; *Statue of Liberty*—New York; *Eiffel Tower*—Paris; *Tower of London*—England; *the Great Wall*—China)

• Ask *What are the tourists pointing to in the second picture?* (The Statue of Liberty.)

> **Language and culture**
> • **From the Longman Corpus:** A common mistake by English learners of all language backgrounds is to say *do sightseeing* instead of *go sightseeing*. However, *do some sightseeing* is a common expression in spoken English.

 Learning Strategies

B Pair work

Suggested teaching time:	5 minutes	Your actual teaching time:

• Write on the board *What tourist activities have you done?* and *Which haven't you done?* Read each question aloud. Model the activity by providing one or two of your own answers. Have students work in pairs to answer the questions using the vocabulary and their own information. Remind them to use the present perfect.

• As pairs are discussing their answers, move around the room and help students as needed.

• To review answers, have individuals report to the class a tourist activity that their partner has done; for example, *Ken has gone to the top of the Eiffel Tower.*

Option: (+5 minutes) Have students use the bold words in the Vocabulary to talk about other tourist activities they have done; for example, *I have gone sightseeing in Madrid. I have taken pictures of the Brooklyn Bridge.*

GRAMMAR

Suggested teaching time:	7 minutes	Your actual teaching time:

• Write on the board the examples under the first rule. Explain that *before* means before now and refers to an indefinite time in the past. Point out that *ever* is placed before the past participle, and *before* is placed at the end of the sentence. Point out that *ever* and *before* can be used in the same sentence: *Have you ever been to London before?* Then have students read the Be careful! note.

• To introduce the use of *yet* and *already,* write the second line of examples from the Grammar box on the board. Underline *yet* and circle *already* in the questions. Ask a student to read aloud the rule and examples while you point out the placement of *yet* at the end of the sentence and *already* before the past participle. Stress that each question is about activities a person has or hasn't done a short time ago.

• Ask volunteers for additional questions with *yet.* Have students answer in the affirmative or negative using *yet* or *already*; for example, *Have you seen this movie yet?* (Yes, I have already seen it. No, I haven't seen it yet.).

• Explain that *yet, already,* and *ever* are optional. They emphasize the lack of a specific time reference.

• Have students underline the affirmative statements. (We've already seen the Great Wall; He's been to New York before.) Point out that *They have never* and *They haven't ever* have the same meaning. Direct students' attention to the Be careful! box. Remind them that *never* always follows an affirmative verb.

> **Language and culture**
> • In British English, the present perfect is used with a past action that has a result in the present; for example, *David has lost his keys.* In American English, the present perfect and the simple past are both used, but the simple past is more common; for example, *David lost his keys.*

Option:  **GRAMMAR BOOSTER** *(Teaching notes p. T126)*

 Inductive Grammar Charts

A Grammar practice

Suggested teaching time:	3 minutes	Your actual teaching time:

- Model the activity by doing the first item with the class and writing it on the board. Then ask several students the question. Remind them to use the present perfect in their answer.
- As students write the statements and questions, move around the room.
- Review the statements and questions with the class.

B ▶1:09 Listen to activate grammar

Suggested teaching time:	8–10 minutes	Your actual teaching time:

- To prepare students for the activity, tell them to look at the pictures and read the captions. If students don't know, explain that *ceviche* is raw fish marinated in lemon juice, oil, and spices.

AUDIOSCRIPT

CONVERSATION 1 [M = Indian]
M: Welcome to India! Is this your first time here?
F: Yes, it is.
M: Really! Have you been to Agra yet?
F: Oh, that's where the Taj Mahal is, right? No, I haven't.
M: You should definitely take a tour. It's amazing.
F: Actually, I'm going there on Friday. I will!

CONVERSATION 2 [F = Japanese]
M: This is my second time in Japan.
F: Well, welcome to Kyoto. Where else have you been?
M: So far, I've been to Tokyo and Osaka. Tomorrow I'm going sightseeing here.
F: Kyoto is fantastic. You're going to enjoy it!

CONVERSATION 3 [M = Peruvian]
F: This is my first time in Peru. I've heard the food is great here.
M: Yes, it is. We're really proud of our food. Have you tried ceviche?
F: No, I haven't. Is it good?
M: Excellent.

CONVERSATION 4 [F = Spanish]
F: Welcome to Mexico City! Is it your first time?
M: Yes.
F: When did you arrive?
M: Last week. I've done so much, but for me the best was climbing the Pyramid of the Sun.
F: When did you do that?
M: Yesterday. It was incredible.

CONVERSATION 5 [M = Brazilian]
M: Welcome to Rio de Janeiro! Have you been here before?
F: Well, I've been to São Paulo before, but this is my first time to Rio.
M: Really! Have you seen Sugarloaf yet?
F: No, I haven't. But I plan to.
M: Oh, you should. It's amazing. Take lots of pictures!

C Write five questions . . .

Suggested teaching time:	5–8 minutes	Your actual teaching time:

- To review, write *yet, already, ever,* and *before* on the board. Ask students where these words appear in a present perfect statement or question. Provide or have students provide examples, such as before the past participle or at the end of a question.

- Have students work in pairs to ask each other their questions. Remind students to use the present perfect in their answer.

 Extra Grammar Exercises

 Learning Strategies

NOW YOU CAN Greet a visitor to your country

A Notepadding

Suggested teaching time:	5–10 minutes	Your actual teaching time:

- Ask students for examples of tourist activities and popular dishes and drinks in their country. Make a list on the board of the most popular items.

B Conversation activator

Suggested teaching time:	5–10 minutes	Your actual teaching time:

 Conversation Activator Video

- *Note:* You can print the script or you can view a running transcript on the video player on the ActiveTeach. The script also appears on page 181 of this Teacher's Edition.

DON'T STOP! Extend the conversation. Encourage students to continue the conversation by asking each other for information about other places and tourist activities listed on their notepads.

- For more support, play the Conversation Activator Video before students do this activity themselves. In Scene 1, the actors use different words in the gaps from the ones in the Conversation Model. In Scene 2, the actors extend the conversation. After each scene, ask students how the model has been changed by the actors.
- Be sure to reinforce the use of the conversation strategies; for example, to sound excited when saying "That's great!"
- Model changing and extending the conversation by role-playing with a more confident student. Play the role of Student A.
- To maximize their speaking practice, make sure that students change roles and start a new conversation at least once.

 Conversation Activator Video Script; Conversation Activator Pair Work Cards

C Change partners

Suggested teaching time:	5–10 minutes	Your actual teaching time:

- Have students form new pairs by counting off 1, 2, 3, 4. Tell students 1 and 3 to form pairs and students 2 and 4 to form pairs.

EXTRAS

Workbook or MyEnglishLab

Speaking Activities: Unit 1, Activity 2

A **GRAMMAR PRACTICE** Use the words to write statements or questions in the present perfect.

1 (you / go sightseeing / in London / before)
Have you gone sightseeing in London before?
2 (she / already / try / Guatemalan food)
She has already tried Guatemalan food.

3 (they / ever / be / to Buenos Aires)
Have they ever been to Buenos Aires?
4 (we / not take a tour of / Prague / yet)
We haven't taken a tour of Prague yet.

B ▶1:09 **LISTEN TO ACTIVATE GRAMMAR** Listen and complete the questions, using the Vocabulary. Then listen again and complete the short answers.

Questions

1 Has she ....taken a tour........ of the Taj Mahal yet?
2 Has he ....gone sightseeing........... in Kyoto yet?
3 Has she ever ....tried.................... ceviche?
4 Has he already ....climbed..... the Pyramid of the Sun?
5 Has she ever ....been............ to Rio de Janeiro before?
6 Has she ....taken a tour........... of Sugarloaf yet?

Short Answers

....No...., she ..hasn't.... .
....No...., he ..hasn't.... .
....No...., she ..hasn't.... .
....Yes...., he ....has.... .
....No...., she ..hasn't.... .
....No...., she ..hasn't.... .

The Taj Mahal • India

A temple • Kyoto, Japan

Ceviche • Peru

The Pyramid of the Sun • Mexico City

Sugarloaf • Rio de Janeiro, Brazil

C Write five questions about tourist activities in your city or country. Use <u>yet</u>, <u>already</u>, <u>ever</u>, and <u>before</u>.

Have you ever tried our seafood dishes?

1 ....
2 ....
3 ....
4 ....
5 ....

DIGITAL
MORE
ERCISES

NOW YOU CAN Greet a visitor to your country

A **NOTEPADDING** On the notepad, write at least five activities for a tourist in your city or country.

B **CONVERSATION ACTIVATOR** With a partner, change the Conversation Model to greet a visitor to <u>your</u> country. Use the present perfect. Suggest tourist activities in your city. Use your notepad. Then change roles.

DIGITAL
VIDEO

A: Welcome to .... Have you ever been here before?
B: No, it's my first time. But yesterday I ....
A: .... Have you .... yet?
B: .... **DON'T STOP!**

- Ask about other places and tourist activities.

Activity	Description
try Beijing duck	It's a famous Chinese dish.

Activity	Description

C **CHANGE PARTNERS** Practice the conversation again, asking about other tourist activities on your notepad.

GOAL Discuss gestures and customs

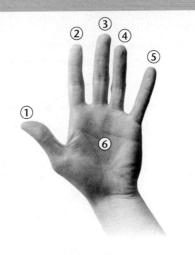

BEFORE YOU READ

DIGITAL
FLASH
CARDS

▶1:10 **VOCABULARY • *The hand*** Read and listen.
Then listen again and repeat.

1 thumb
2 index finger
3 middle finger
4 ring finger
5 pinkie
6 palm
7 fist

READING ▶1:11

We talked to June Galloway about her book,
Get off on the Right Foot: Don't Let the Wrong Gesture Ruin Your Day.

English is the world's international language. But in your book, you've focused on non-verbal communication. Why is that so important?
Well, gestures and other body language can have different meanings in different places. Something that you think is friendly or polite could come across as very rude in another culture. I've described many of these customs and cultural differences so my readers don't get off on the wrong foot when they meet people from places where the culture differs from their own.

Can greeting someone in the wrong way really lead to misunderstanding?
In some cases, yes. The firm handshake a North American expects may seem quite aggressive in other places. And a light handshake—which is normal in some countries—may seem unfriendly to a North American.

In what ways can hand gestures lead to misunderstanding?
Well, as an example, we assume all people indicate the numbers one to ten with their fingers the same way. But in fact, they don't. While North Americans usually use an index finger for

"one," most Europeans use a thumb. North Americans extend all ten fingers for "ten." However, Chinese indicate the numbers one to ten all on one hand. For example, an extended thumb and pinkie means "six," and a fist means "ten." Imagine how confusing this can be when you're trying to communicate quantities and prices with your hands!

What other gestures can cause confusion?
Take the gesture for "come here," for example. In North America, people gesture with the palm up. Well, in southern Europe, that gesture means "good-bye"! And in many Asian countries, the palm-up gesture is considered rude. Instead, people there gesture with the palm down.

I've heard that, in Japan, pointing with the index finger is not polite. Is that right?
Yes. Japanese prefer to point with the palm open and facing up.

Surely there must be some gestures used everywhere, right? What about the thumbs-up sign for "great"?
Sorry. That's extremely rude in Australia and the Middle East. This is why it's so important to be aware of these cultural differences.

What gesture do you use . . .

. . . for the number six?

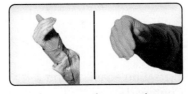

. . . for "Come here": palm up or down?

. . . for pointing? Do you use your index finger or an open palm?

BEFORE YOU READ

▶ 1:10 **Vocabulary**

Suggested teaching time:	5 minutes	Your actual teaching time:	

V **Vocabulary Flash Card Player**

- Have students listen and repeat the hand vocabulary. To make sure they understand the vocabulary, hold up your hand. Point to your thumb and say, *What is this?* (Thumb.) Continue with the other parts of the hand.
- Tell students that there are two other names for the index finger: forefinger and pointer.

▶ 1:11 **READING**

Suggested teaching time:	12–17 minutes	Your actual teaching time:	

- To introduce the topic, call on students to look at the photos in the article. Ask *Which of these gestures do people use in this (your) country? Are any of these gestures considered rude? What other gestures do people use in these situations?*
- Ask students to imitate the gestures they are comfortable with and to demonstrate additional gestures people use in their country and say what they mean. (Possible responses: shrugging shoulders: I don't know; raising eyebrows: I don't believe you; waving: hello or good-bye)

Language and culture

- In many European countries, *Come with me* is gestured palm up, but in many cultures this is considered rude and it is done palm down. In some Asian cultures, an open palm is preferred for indicating a third person. In Chinese culture, there are gestures for the numbers 6 through 10 using one hand.

- Before students read, write on the board *body language* and ask students what they think it means. (Gestures and other non-verbal communication.)
- Have students read the article. Then have students read the article again and underline the different gestures mentioned (indicating numbers, "Come here" hand gesture, pointing, "great" hand gesture).
- Ask *How are gestures different from speech? Do you think gestures can be more powerful than words? Give examples.* (Possible responses: Gestures express meaning without words. Some gestures can be understood between people who speak different languages. Some gestures can make people feel friendlier, angrier, or more interested.) Have students form small groups to share their opinions.

A Identify supporting details

Suggested teaching time:	3–5 minutes	Your actual teaching time:	

- Review the answers with the class. Have a student read a statement, say if it is true, and explain why by giving an example from the text.
- Write *get off on the wrong foot* on the board. Ask *Can anyone explain what this means?* Tell students to scan the article for this expression and underline it (last sentence of the first response in the interview). Have pairs focus on the context to figure out the meaning of the expression. Then have students share ideas with the class. Explain that *to get off on the wrong foot* means to make a bad start.
- Model the use of this expression by saying *We got off on the wrong foot when I arrived late for the job interview.* Then tell students to think of different situations in which this expression can be used.

Option: (+10 minutes) To challenge students, ask pairs to create three additional true / false statements using the information in the text. Tell students not to include the answers. Combine pairs into groups of four and have them exchange statements. Have students support their answers by giving an example from the text.

B Relate to personal experience

Suggested teaching time:	5–8 minutes	Your actual teaching time:	

- Divide the class into groups of three to discuss the questions.
- If appropriate for your students, have students describe or demonstrate to the class the gestures that surprised them and share their experiences.

Option: (+10 minutes) To challenge students, ask pairs to create a list of do's and don'ts for gestures in their culture. Tell them to use ideas from the article and class discussion. Have students share their lists with the class.

⭐🖨 **Extra Reading Comprehension Exercises**

 **Discuss gestures and customs**

A Pair work

Suggested teaching time:	5 minutes	Your actual teaching time:	

- Ask *When you travel, should you follow the customs of the place you are visiting? Why or why not?*
- Before students read the tips, tell them to read the country names in parentheses at the bottom of the tip. Ask *Has anyone visited these countries?*
- After pairs have read and discussed the tips, as a class talk about which tips also apply in the students' culture.

Language and culture

- In North America, a common excuse for lateness is *I'm stuck in traffic* or *I'm working late*. A more general excuse is *I'm running late* (I'm behind schedule), and it is an acceptable way to inform someone that you won't be on time.
- Clauses that start with *If* present a particular condition or situation in the future. *You should* is used to offer advice.

Option: (+10 minutes) To extend the activity, do a short role play. Call on a student to read the tip on the bottom left. Ask two volunteers to role-play getting a server's attention by making eye contact and using hand gestures.

B Notepadding

Suggested teaching time:	5–10 minutes	Your actual teaching time:	

- To prepare students, read the list of Topics and explain any new vocabulary as needed. Encourage students to write their own topic in the blank.
- Model the activity by writing on the board:
  Topic: Showing respect to older people.
  Customs: [Write customs.] Then say a bit more about them.
- As pairs do the activity, walk around the room, encouraging them to analyze the topic further by answering the questions. Help students as needed.

Option: (+5 minutes) To extend the activity, tell groups to write rules for another topic.

Language and culture

- In English-speaking countries, when children greet adults they don't know, they look them in the eye and say *hello*. They may also shake hands. Depending on the formality of the relationship, children call adults by their title and last name (Mr. Anderson) or just by their first name (John).

C Discussion

Suggested teaching time:	5–10 minutes	Your actual teaching time:	

Text-mining: Review the instructions with the class, then have students skim the article and underline appropriate language. For example, *get off on the wrong foot; lead to a misunderstanding; take [the gesture for "come here"], for example; [Japanese] prefer;* etc. Write students' findings on the board for them to refer to during the discussion.

- In pairs, students discuss the customs. Then call on pairs to share their list of customs with the class.

Option: (+10 minutes) For additional practice, brainstorm or suggest additional topics; for example, how to act in a workplace, how to behave in a classroom. Have small groups write rules for them.

Option: (+3 minutes) To extend the activity, ask *What are the consequences of not following customs in your culture?* (Possible responses: People don't respect you, they don't want to talk to you or invite you to their homes.)

EXTRAS

Workbook or MyEnglishLab

 Speaking Activities: Unit 1, Activity 3

A **IDENTIFY SUPPORTING DETAILS**   Check the statements that are true, according to the article. Write **✗** next to the statements that are not true. Explain your answers.

☑ 1 In most of Europe, a thumb and an index finger mean "two."

☒ 2 In North America, a thumb and a pinkie mean "two."

☑ 3 Japanese point at pictures with an open palm facing up.

☒ 4 To be friendly, North Americans greet others with a light handshake.

☒ 5 Everyone uses the thumbs-up sign for "that's good."

> *True. Galloway says most Europeans begin with the thumb. So the index finger is the next finger after that.*

B **RELATE TO PERSONAL EXPERIENCE**   Discuss the questions.

Have you ever been surprised by someone's gestures or body language on TV, in the movies, or in real life? What did you see? What do you think the action meant? Why were you surprised?

NOW YOU CAN Discuss gestures and customs

A **PAIR WORK**   Read the travel tips about gestures and customs around the world. Compare your own gestures and customs with those described. Do any of them seem strange or rude?

Travel Tips ✈

If someone gives you a gift, thank the person and open it right away. (Ecuador)	When a visitor is leaving your home, you should walk with that person out the door. (Korea)	If you are going to be more than 15 minutes late for a party, lunch, or dinner, you should call to explain. (United States)	To gesture that something is good, hold your hand up, palm facing out, and slowly bring all your fingers to the thumb. (Turkey)
If you want to get a server's attention, it's more polite to use eye contact rather than hand gestures. (Kenya)	When greeting people, older people should always be greeted first. (Mongolia)	Before you enter someone's home, you should take off your shoes. (Ukraine)	

B **NOTEPADDING**   With a partner, choose a topic and discuss your country's customs. Then write notes about your country on the notepad.

Topic: *showing respect for older people.*
Customs: *It's not polite to disagree with an older person.*

Topic:

Customs:

Are the rules the same for both men and women? How about for young people or older people? Explain.

Topics
- showing respect to older people
- do's and don'ts for gestures
- topics for polite small talk
- invitations
- visiting someone's home
- giving gifts
- offering or refusing food
- touching or not touching
- (your own topic) ___

Text-mining (optional)
Find and underline three words or phrases in the Reading that were new to you. Use them in your Discussion.
    For example: "body language."

C **DISCUSSION**   Tell your classmates about the customs you described on your notepad. Does everyone agree?

GOAL Describe an interesting experience

BEFORE YOU LISTEN

A ▶1:12 **VOCABULARY** • *Participial adjectives* Read and listen. Then listen again and repeat.

The safari was **fascinating**. (They were **fascinated**.)

The ski trip was **thrilling**. (They were **thrilled**.)

The sky-dive was **frightening**. (They were **frightened**.)

The food was **disgusting**. (They were **disgusted**.)

B Write lists of things you think are fascinating, thrilling, frightening, or disgusting.

C **PAIR WORK** Compare your lists.

❝ I've never eaten snails. I think they're disgusting! ❞

❝ Really? I've tried them, and I wasn't disgusted at all. They're good! ❞

LISTENING COMPREHENSION

A ▶1:13 **LISTEN TO CLASSIFY** Listen to the three interviews. Then listen again and write the number of the speaker described by each statement.

...3... **a** travels to have thrilling experiences

...1... **b** describes differences in body language

...2... **c** was disgusted by something

...1... **d** is fascinated by other cultures

...2... **e** tries to be polite

...3... **f** does things that other people think are frightening

Andrew Barlow

Nancy Sullivan

Mieko Nakamura

BEFORE YOU LISTEN

A ▶1:12 Vocabulary

Suggested teaching time:	3 minutes	Your actual teaching time:

 **Vocabulary Flash Card Player**

- Explain that many past participles ending in *-ed* and present participles ending in *-ing* are used as adjectives.
- Point out that the participial adjectives ending in *-ing* describe something (the safari, the ski trip, the sky-dive, the food). (*Fascinating* means extremely interesting. *Thrilling* means causing a person to suddenly have a strong feeling of excitement. If something is *frightening*, it makes a person afraid or scared. *Disgusting* means very unpleasant, causing a person to feel sick.)
- The participial adjectives ending in *-ed* describe how the people feel (in each example *They*). Have students read and listen.

🖨 **Learning Strategies**

B Write lists . . .

Suggested teaching time:	5 minutes	Your actual teaching time:

- On the board, draw the chart below or print out the graphic organizer and have students fill it in with the activities from Exercise A.

Fascinating	Thrilling	Frightening	Disgusting

- Tell students to create their own charts and provide examples for each participial adjective.

🖨 **Graphic Organizers**

C Pair work

Suggested teaching time:	5–7 minutes	Your actual teaching time:

- Point out the picture of a snail. Model the language by asking two students to read the samples in quotes. In pairs, have students compare their lists from Exercise B and respond by giving their opinions. Move around the room and listen for correct use of participial adjectives.

🖨 **Learning Strategies**

LISTENING COMPREHENSION

A ▶1:13 Listen to classify

Suggested teaching time:	5 minutes	Your actual teaching time:

- To prepare students, call on a volunteer to read the numbers and names under the pictures. Review the example to make sure students understand the task. Then play the interviews and have students listen.

- Tell students to read the statements. Let them listen again and match the statements to the speakers.
- Review answers with the class. Allow students to listen again, if necessary.

Language and culture

- Note that these expressions are used in spoken English and in informal situations:
  ○ *Oh, boy!* is an exclamation used to express surprise. It is similar to *Wow!*
  ○ *Thanks, but no thanks* is an abbreviated, informal way of saying *Thank you for offering me [something], but I don't want it, thank you.*
  ○ *For real?* is a less formal way of saying *Really?*

AUDIOSCRIPT

INTERVIEW 1 [F = U.S. regional]
- **M:** This is Nick Krakauer, and you're listening to *World Reflections*. We're talking today with Nancy Sullivan from Minneapolis in the United States. Hi, Nancy.
- **F:** Hi, Nick.
- **M:** So, Nancy, I understand you're a real traveler—that you've visited over twenty-five countries around the world.
- **F:** That's right.
- **M:** Tell us some of the places you've been to.
- **F:** Well, I've been to countries all over . . . North and South America, Europe, Asia . . .
- **M:** What have been the most fascinating places for you to visit?
- **F:** Hmmm . . . Well, I like visiting countries where the culture is really different from my own. That's what I find most interesting. Different body language, different foods . . . you know.
- **M:** You told me earlier you've been to India. What was that like?
- **F:** Oh, India is fantastic.
- **M:** And what was so different about it?
- **F:** Well for one thing, when people say "yes," they shake their heads from side to side instead of up and down, like I do.

INTERVIEW 2 [M2 = Australian English]
- **M1:** Nick Krakauer here, hosting *World Reflections*. Today's guest is Andrew Barlow from Perth, Australia. G'day, mate!
- **M2:** G'day to you.
- **M1:** So, Andrew, I understand you've been a teacher overseas, is that correct?
- **M2:** I <u>have</u> been, yes.
- **M1:** And I understand you have an interesting story about something you ate once in one of those countries.
- **M2:** That's right.
- **M1:** Tell us about it.
- **M2:** Well, this happened when I got my first teaching job in a very small village. The people in the village wanted to thank me for coming, so they prepared a meal with a lot of really delicious dishes.
- **M1:** That must have been nice.
- **M2:** It was. But there was one thing that I thought was kind of, well, disgusting. They had these tiny little fish that were still alive . . . they were moving on the plate.
- **M1:** Whoa!
- **M2:** Yeah. You're supposed to put one in your mouth and swallow it whole.
- **M1:** Oh, boy!
- **M2:** Look, I was their guest and I didn't want to be impolite, so I tried one. But I could feel it moving as it went down into my stomach. I tried a few, to be nice. But I just didn't know how to say "thanks, but no thanks" without being rude.

AUDIOSCRIPT continues on page T11.

B ▶1:14 Listen for details

Suggested teaching time:	7–10 minutes	Your actual teaching time:

- Have students skim the questions. Ask *Can you answer any of these questions without hearing the audio again?* Students do the exercise and try to answer. Let them listen again and take notes. If necessary, allow students to listen once more before checking answers.

- Have students work in pairs to compare answers. If students are still missing information, play the interviews again.

Option: (+5–10 minutes) For a challenge, role-play the interviews in pairs. Assign roles (interviewer and Nancy, Andrew, or Mieko). Encourage students to try to remember as many details from the interviews and use them in their role plays. Move around the room and help students as needed. Invite students to present their role plays to the class.

 Learning Strategies

NOW YOU CAN Describe an interesting experience

A Notepadding

Suggested teaching time:	5–10 minutes	Your actual teaching time:

- Model the activity by relating some of your own experiences. Write the chart below on the board, filling in your own information. Note that the answers in this chart are merely possible responses.

	Fascinating	Strange or disgusting	Thrilling or frightening
Place	Mexico	Mongolia	Tanzania
Activity	Visited pyramids, went sailing, took cooking classes	Tried camel meat	Took pictures of lions

- Read the questions and review vocabulary as needed. Then ask students to skim the language in the Recycle box. Encourage students to refer to it as they answer the questions.

- Move around the room and help students as needed.

 Graphic Organizers

B Pair work

Suggested teaching time:	10–15 minutes	Your actual teaching time:

- Model the activity with a more confident student by talking about something you wrote on the board and using language from the Recycle box.

- Be sure to include conversation strategies from previous lessons, such as "That's great!"

DON'T STOP! Extend the conversation. Encourage students to continue the conversation by using the ideas in the box.

- Move around the room and listen for the correct use of present perfect and simple past.

Option: (+5 minutes) For additional practice, have students follow up by asking classmates when they had each experience. Ask *When did you take a tour of the Great Wall of China?* Remind students to use the simple past tense when referring to a definite time in the past.

C Group work

Suggested teaching time:	5 minutes	Your actual teaching time:

- To preview the picture, ask a volunteer to read the caption. Ask *Has anyone ever gone hang gliding or done anything dangerous? How did you feel? Were you frightened?* Ask *Was the experience thrilling? Were you thrilled?*

- To model the activity, call on a volunteer to read the sample in quotes. Then have students share their partner's experience with the class. Encourage them to use the participial adjectives from the Vocabulary on page 10.

Option: (+5 minutes) To challenge students, have them describe an experience without using participial adjectives. Have the class guess if they are describing something *disgusting, thrilling, frightening,* or *fascinating.*

EXTRAS

Workbook or MyEnglishLab

 Speaking Activities: Unit 1, Activity 4; "Find Someone Who . . ." Activity

AUDIOSCRIPT Continued, for page T10 (Listening Comprehension)

INTERVIEW 3 [F = Japanese]
- **M:** We're back on *World Reflections*. My next guest is Mieko Nakamura from Sendai, Japan. Welcome, Mieko.
- **F:** Hi, Nick.
- **M:** Mieko, I've been told that you've traveled a lot and you've done some unusual things.
- **F:** I have.
- **M:** That you especially like to do, well, things that would be kind of frightening for most people.
- **F:** I guess that's true. But not scary to me. Just very exciting.
- **M:** So tell us about what you've done.
- **F:** Well, for one thing, I've gone swimming with sharks. Twice!
- **M:** What?!
- **F:** Swimming with sharks.
- **M:** For real? And you didn't find that scary?
- **F:** Well, I didn't do it alone. I was with a group. But swimming so close to the sharks was really thrilling.
- **M:** And what else?
- **F:** Last year I climbed Mount Everest.
- **M:** The world's highest mountain?
- **F:** Yes.
- **M:** I'll bet it was really cold.
- **F:** It was. But I was really thrilled to be standing on the top of the world.

B ▶1:14 **LISTEN FOR DETAILS** Listen again and answer the questions in complete sentences.

1 Nancy Sullivan
  a How many countries has she visited? She visited over 25 countries.
  b What did she notice about gestures in India? When they say yes, they shake their heads from side to side.

2 Andrew Barlow
  c What did the people in the village do to thank him? They prepared a meal with a lot of delicious dishes.
  d Why did he eat something he didn't want to? He didn't want to seem rude.

3 Mieko Nakamura
  e What has she done twice? She has gone swimming with sharks.
  f How did she get to "the top of the world"? She climbed Mount Everest.

NOW YOU CAN Describe an interesting experience

A **NOTEPADDING** Answer the questions. Explain what happened. Write as many details as you can.

Have you ever been someplace that was really fascinating?
Have you ever eaten something that was really strange or disgusting?
Have you ever done something that was really thrilling or frightening?

B **PAIR WORK** Ask your partner about the experiences on his or her notepad.

DON'T STOP!
 • Ask more questions.
 • Ask about other experiences: "Have you ever . . ."

🔄 **RECYCLE THIS LANGUAGE.**
climb [a mountain]
go sightseeing in [Italy]
go to the top of [the Eiffel Tower]
try [snails]
take a tour of [New York]
take pictures of [the Taj Mahal]

C **GROUP WORK** Choose one of the experiences your partner told you about. Tell your classmates about your partner's experience.

❝ My partner went hang gliding last year. She was frightened, but it was really thrilling. ❞

hang gliding

REVIEW

A ▶1:15 Listen to the conversation with a tourist in Vancouver and check <u>Yes</u> or <u>No</u>. Then listen again and write the answers to the questions, using <u>yet</u> or <u>already</u>. See page T12 for answers.

Has she. . .		Yes	No	
1	been to the Vancouver Aquarium?	☑	☐	*Yes. She's already been to the aquarium.*
2	visited Gastown?	☑	☐	....
3	been to the top of Grouse Mountain?	☐	☑	....
4	seen the Capilano Suspension Bridge?	☐	☑	....
5	tried dim sum?	☐	☑	....
6	gone to the top of the Harbour Centre Tower?	☑	☐	....

B Use the photos to write questions using the present perfect with <u>ever</u> or <u>before</u>. Don't use the same verb more than once.

1 Brazilian barbecue

2 Mount Fuji, Japan

3 Oriental Pearl Tower, Shanghai, China

4 Venice, Italy

Answers will vary, but may include the following:

1 Have you ever eaten Brazilian barbecue?

2 Have you climbed Mount Fuji before?

3 Have you ever gone to the top of the Oriental Pearl Tower in Shanghai, China?

4 Have you been to Venice, Italy, before?

C Write sentences about the topics. Use the present perfect.

1 I've been to the top of the Taipei 101 Building.

1 tall buildings you've been to the top of

2 cities or countries you've visited

3 foods you've tried

4 mountains or high places you've climbed

WRITING

Write about one of the interesting experiences you talked about in Lesson 4. Describe what happened, where you were, who you were with, and how you felt.

I've had a few frightening experiences in my life.

Last year, I was on vacation in . . .

WRITING BOOSTER p. 143
- Avoiding run-on sentences
- Guidance for this writing exercise

For additional language practice . . .

♫ **TOP NOTCH** POP • Lyrics p. 153
"Greetings and Small Talk"

DIGITAL SONG | DIGITAL KARAOKE

REVIEW

A ▶1:15 Listen to the conversation . . .

Suggested teaching time:	5–7 minutes	Your actual teaching time:

- After students have listened to the conversation, ask them to read the questions aloud, starting each one with *Has she . . .* Model the activity by doing the first item: *Has she been to the Vancouver Aquarium yet?*
- Let students listen again and check the boxes. Have students write the full answers with *yet* or *already* on the right. Remind students that *yet* appears at the end of a statement or question. *Already* appears between *have* and the past participle.
- Ask students to compare answers in pairs and then listen again to confirm answers.

AUDIOSCRIPT

[M = Canadian English; F = Spanish]
M: Welcome to Vancouver! When did you get here?
F: Just yesterday, thanks.
M: Oh, that's great. Have you done any sightseeing yet?
F: Yes, I have. I've already been to the Vancouver Aquarium.
M: I love the Aquarium.
F: And I took a tour of Gastown.
M: Cool! Have you been to the top of Grouse Mountain yet?
F: Not yet. Is it nice?
M: Oh, yeah! The sky ride up is great. You shouldn't miss it. And you should definitely visit the Capilano Suspension Bridge. It's a great place to take pictures.
F: Oh, that sounds great. You know, everyone tells me I should try dim sum while I'm here.
M: Definitely. It's really delicious. And they bring the food right to your table and you choose what you want.
F: Sounds like fun. Oh, did I mention that I went to the top of the Harbour Centre Tower this morning?
M: No. Actually, I've never done that myself.
F: You should. It's a beautiful view. Vancouver's a great city.
M: Well, I hope you enjoy your stay.
F: Thanks.

Answers to Exercise A
2. Yes. She's already visited Gastown.
3. No. She hasn't been to the top of Grouse Mountain yet.
4. No. She hasn't seen the Capilano Suspension Bridge yet.
5. No. She hasn't tried dim sum yet.
6. Yes. She's already gone to the top of the Harbour Centre Tower.

B Use the photos to write . . .

Suggested teaching time:	5 minutes	Your actual teaching time:

- Preview the activity by calling on students to read the captions on the photos.
- Review the use of *ever* and *before* by asking *Where do we place* ever *in a sentence?* (Before the past participle.) *Where do we place* before *in a sentence?* (At the end.).
- Have students write questions about the photos using the past perfect. Remind them to use a verb only once. (Possible verbs: try, taste, have, be, climb, ride, take, see.)
- Move around the room and help students as needed.
- Have students compare questions in pairs and then ask each other the questions. Review answers with the class.

C Write sentences about the topics . . .

Suggested teaching time:	5 minutes	Your actual teaching time:

- Ask a student to read the topics. Then have a volunteer read the sample answer. Ask students to share buildings they have been to the top of. Listen for the correct use of the present perfect.
- Have students complete the rest of the exercise individually and then compare answers in pairs or small groups.
- Review answers with the class. Write student answers on the board. Ask the class who else has done the different things.

Option: (+5 minutes) For additional practice, ask students to write down when they did the different things. Review using the present perfect and simple past to contrast definite and indefinite times.

WRITING

Suggested teaching time:	10–15 minutes	Your actual teaching time:

- To prepare students, ask them to look at the notes they made on page 11. Tell students to choose one experience to write about. Encourage them to make some additional notes about the topic.
- Tell students to write a paragraph about their experience. Remind them to use the present perfect to refer to an indefinite time in the past and the simple past tense to refer to a definite time in the past.
- Have students read their paragraphs to the class. After each student has read, invite students to comment using *I've done . . . , too.* OR *I've never . . .*

Option: 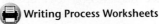 *(Teaching notes p. T143)*

 Writing Process Worksheets

Option: *Top Notch* Project

Idea: Have students prepare a tourist information pamphlet with sightseeing recommendations and culture tips.

- Have students brainstorm tips for tourists. Divide the class into two groups, one to think of ways to behave and one to think of ways not to behave. Have groups write one to two sentences for each tip.
- Collect the paragraphs on places to see, things to do, and the tips. Put them together and make enough copies for each member of the class.

🎵 🎤 *Top Notch Pop* Song Video and Karaoke Video

 Digital Games

ORAL REVIEW

Before the first activity, give students a few minutes of silent time to look at the photos and travel brochure.

Pair work 1

Suggested teaching time:	6–8 minutes	Your actual teaching time:	

- To introduce the activity, tell students to look at the travel brochure. Ask volunteers to read aloud the names of a country's city, tourist attractions, and foods, and then to identify the country. Ask *Has anyone ever been to any of these cities?* OR *Do you know anyone who has ever been to any of them?*

- With a student, model a conversation between the people in the picture. Start by reading the example sentence (*Welcome to Paris . . .*).

- Have pairs choose a city and role-play a conversation there. Refer students to the Conversation Model on page 6 to review expressions and language they should recycle. Remind students to use the simple past tense when referring to a definite time in the past and the present perfect for indefinite time references.

> **Possible responses . . .**
> **A:** Welcome to Moscow. Have you been here before? **B:** No, I haven't. **A:** Have you been to the Bolshoi Theater yet? **B:** Yes, it was very interesting! **A:** Have you eaten borscht yet? **B:** Yes, I have.

> **Language and culture**
> - *Tapas* are Spanish appetizers, *gelato* is Italian ice cream, and *borscht* is a Russian stew made from beets.

Option: (+10 minutes) To practice fluency, conduct a class poll to find out how many students have been to Europe or some other region closer to their country. Invite students to share where they have been and what they've seen, eaten, and experienced.

Pair work 2

Suggested teaching time:	7–10 minutes	Your actual teaching time:	

- Working in pairs, have students create a conversation for the three people in photo 2. Tell students to imagine they've met before and are getting reacquainted during a tour of Europe. Refer students to the Conversation Model on page 5. Tell students to be creative using the information in the travel brochure.

- Invite students to role-play their conversations. Listen for the correct use of the simple past and present perfect.

> **Possible responses . . .**
> **A:** [Rita], have you met [Adrian]? **B:** No, I haven't. **A:** [Adrian], I'd like you to meet [Rita.] **C:** Hi, [Rita]. You look familiar. Have we met before? **B:** I don't think so. **C:** I know! Last week. You were on the tour of the Colosseum in Rome. **B:** Oh, that's right! It was beautiful, wasn't it?

Pair work 3

Suggested teaching time:	7–10 minutes	Your actual teaching time:	

- Have students work in pairs and imagine they are touring Europe. Tell them to ask each other questions using the present perfect and the information in the travel brochure. Ask a student to read the sample question.

- Move around the room and listen for the correct use of the present prefect. Help students as needed.

Option: (+10–15 minutes) For a challenge, have students write postcards that describe what they have done, eaten, and seen, but the postcards cannot reveal the location. Then have students read their postcards aloud while the class guesses the locations.

> **Option: Oral Progress Assessment**
>
> - Use the images on page 13 for an oral test. Encourage students to use the language practiced in this unit.
>
> - Invite a student to role-play a conversation with you.
>
> - Point to the two people. Say *We see each other near the Eiffel Tower, we introduce ourselves, and then get reacquainted.*
>
> - Then say *Greet me in one of the cities in the travel brochure and ask me about things I've seen and tried.*
>
> - Evaluate the student on intelligibility, fluency, correct use of grammar, and appropriate use of vocabulary.

 Oral Progress Assessment Charts

EXTRAS

On the Internet:
- Online Teacher Resources: pearsonelt.com/topnotch3e/

Additional printable resources on the ActiveTeach:
- Assessment
- Just for Fun
- *Top Notch Pop* Song Activities
- *Top Notch TV* Video Program and Activity Worksheets
- Supplementary Pronunciation Lessons
- Conversation Activator Video Scripts
- Audioscripts and Answer Keys
- Unit Study Guides

ORAL REVIEW

PAIR WORK

1 Create a conversation for the man and woman in photo 1. Imagine the man is welcoming the woman to his city. Choose one of the cities in the travel brochure.

Welcome to Paris. Have you been here before?

2 Create a conversation for the three people in photo 2. Imagine they get reacquainted during a tour of Europe.

A: Have you met __?
B: Actually, you look familiar. Have we met before?
C: Yes, I think we have. We were at the . . .

3 Look at the brochure and imagine that you are on one of these tours. Ask and answer questions, using the present perfect.

Have you tried tapas yet?

Tour **Europe**

SPAIN	FRANCE	ITALY	THE U.K.	RUSSIA

Madrid, Spain
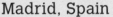

The Prado Museum — Tapas

Paris, France
The Eiffel Tower — Tour boat on the Seine River

Rome, Italy

The Colosseum — Gelato

London, the U.K.

The Millennium Wheel — Carnaby Street

Moscow, Russia
Ballet at the Bolshoi Theater — Borscht

✔ **NOW I CAN**
- [ ] Get reacquainted with someone.
- [ ] Greet a visitor to my country.
- [ ] Discuss gestures and customs.
- [ ] Describe an interesting experience.

COMMUNICATION GOALS

1 Apologize for being late.
2 Discuss preferences for movie genres.
3 Describe and recommend movies.
4 Discuss effects of violence on viewers.

UNIT 2 Going to the Movies

PREVIEW

WebFlicks Stream to watch instantly or add disc to your wish list

Log In | Your account | Help

Leonardo DiCaprio

Click on to preview movies.

Titanic 3D   1997 (3D 2012)
194 minutes
This 1997 blockbuster disaster movie (11 Oscars!) is the true story of the ill-fated ocean liner *Titanic*. But it's also a 194-minute love story. Rose (Kate Winslet), an unhappy young woman, falls in love with Jack (DiCaprio), a poor artist who gives her life meaning. The scenes of the sinking of the magnificent *Titanic* are truly frightening. An epic classic romance!
Genre: Romantic drama, disaster

Blood Diamond   2006
143 minutes
DiCaprio stars as an ex-criminal involved in the violent diamond trade during the 1999 civil war in Sierra Leone. He joins up with a fisherman (Djimon Hounsou) to try to find a pink diamond that they think can change both of their lives. This thrilling action movie will keep you sitting on the edge of your seat.
Genre: Action, drama

The Great Gatsby   2013
143 minutes
This beautiful adaptation of F. Scott Fitzgerald's fascinating 1925 novel of the same name tells the story of neighbors from the fictional town of West Egg on New York's Long Island in the summer of 1922. The main character, a mysterious millionaire, Jay Gatsby (DiCaprio), falls in love with the beautiful Daisy Buchanan (Carey Mulligan), but the story ends in tragedy.
Genre: Romantic drama

Stream

Stream

Stream

Add disc to your wish list

Add disc to your wish list

Add disc to your wish list

More DiCaprio movies

BY GENRE

comedy   crime
drama   romance
action   disaster

BY TITLE

The Man in the Iron Mask (1998)   The Aviator (2004)   Shutter Island (2010)
The Beach (2000)   The Departed (2006)   Inception (2010)
Gangs of New York (2002)   Body of Lies (2008)   The Wolf of Wall Street (2013)
Catch Me If You Can (2002)

A PAIR WORK Did you see any of these DiCaprio movies when they were in the theater? If so, tell your partner about them. If not, is there one you would like to see now? Explain why.

B DISCUSSION Where do you like to see movies: at home or in a movie theater? Explain your reasons.

Going to the Movies

PREVIEW

Before Exercise A, give students a few minutes of silent time to examine the website.

Suggested teaching time:	7–12 minutes	Your actual teaching time:

- For a warm-up, ask the class general information questions about movies. For example:

    How do you decide which movie to buy or rent? Where do you buy or rent movies?

    Do you ever look at movie websites?

- Ask:

    Do you like to preview movies before buying or renting them? If yes, how do you do this? (Possible responses: Online, on TV during commercials, at the movies in the coming attractions.)

    What are other ways of finding information about movies? (Possible responses: Online, in newspapers, from friends.)

    Do you ever rent or buy movies online? If not, where do you buy or rent movies? (Possible responses: Buy in store, rent from video store, record on a DVR.)

- Write WebFlicks on the board. Point out that it is the name of the website and explain that *Web* is an abbreviation for *World Wide Web* (Internet) and a *flick* is a slang word for *movie.*

- Tell students to skim the website. Then ask *Which actor does this website focus on?* (Leonardo DiCaprio.)

> **Language and culture**
> - To *stream* a movie is to watch it online without downloading any files.
> - An *adaptation* is a play or movie that is based on a book.
> - *Ill-fated* means destined to have an unhappy ending.

A Pair work

Suggested teaching time:	3–5 minutes	Your actual teaching time:

- Tell pairs to talk about the movies they've seen and which ones they'd like to see.

- Survey the class to see who has seen which movies. Ask *Which movies seem more interesting to you? Why?*

Option: *(+10 minutes)* To extend the activity, write the following questions on the board and have pairs scan the article for the underlined words. Point out that these words will lead them to the answers. To make this more interesting, turn this into a team competition. The first team that finds all the correct answers wins.

Which movie stars DiCaprio with <u>Kate Winslet</u>? (*Titanic.*)

Which movie is <u>194</u> minutes long? (*Titanic.*)

What happened in <u>1999</u> in <u>Sierra Leone</u>? (There was a civil war.)

Who plays Daisy Buchanan in <u>The Great Gatsby</u>? (Carey Mulligan.)

Option: *(+10 minutes)* To challenge students, assign each pair one film description to read and summarize for the class. After students have presented their summaries, check comprehension by asking the class these questions:

Which movie is a love story about the characters Rose and Jack? (*Titanic.*)

Which movie is set in Sierra Leone? (*Blood Diamond.*)

Which movie happens in the summer of 1922? (*The Great Gatsby.*)

B Discussion

Suggested teaching time:	10 minutes	Your actual teaching time:

- Divide the class into groups of three for discussion.

- To help discussion, draw the graphic organizer below on the board or print it out and distribute it to students. Tell students to fill in their reasons.

	Watch at home	Watch in the theater
Pros ✓		
Cons −		

- After students have completed the activity, ask students to share their preferences.

Option: *(+5 minutes)* As an alternative approach, use the two categories to take a class survey. Tell students to raise their hand for their preference. Write the numbers on the board next to the category. Survey the class again, dividing students by gender or favorite colors. Ask students to make sentences using *would rather* with the results.

 Graphic Organizers

C ▶1:18 Photo story

Suggested teaching time:	10–15 minutes	Your actual teaching time:

- Preview the photos and ask these questions:
  Where are the people? (In a movie theater.)
  What titles of movies can you see in the background? (*Ice Age, Gangs of NY,* and a section of a title *Casabl . . .*)
  Ask students if they can guess the full title of the last movie. If they can't, inform them that it's *Casablanca,* a movie classic from 1942. See the culture note for more information on the movie.
  Have you seen any of these movies? If yes, what were they about? If not, what do you think they are about?

- After students read and listen to the conversation, check comprehension. Ask:
  Does Anna like violent movies? (No, she can't take all the fighting.)
  Does Peter like animated movies? (No, he can't stand them.)
  What movie do Peter and Anna agree on? (*Casablanca.*)

- Tell students that Peter is a native speaker of English from Jamaica.

- As students read and listen to the conversation a second time, have them underline any vocabulary they need help with. Explain as needed.

Language and culture

- *Classic* or *a classic* is often used for a movie, book, song, or other work that is well known and has been considered for a long time to be of very high quality. For example, *Casablanca* is a classic film from 1942. The movie won numerous awards and is one of the most popular films of all time.
- The expression *A big [DiCaprio] fan* can also be stated *A big fan of [DiCaprio].* The word *fan* is used to talk about celebrities, sports, or other hobbies.
- It is very common in spoken English to say you are *(not) in the mood for [something]* or *(not) in the mood to [do something].*
- The pronoun *they* can be used to refer to people in general rather than a specific group of people. This usage is common in spoken English when someone is giving a popular opinion about something.
- Make sure that students understand these terms:
  Nope is a very informal way of saying "no."
  I just can't take [something] means I can't handle it or I can't cope with it.
  I can't stand [something] means I don't really like it.
  Now you're talking is an informal expression meaning I agree with you.
  When someone offers to pay for something such as food or drinks, he or she will often say *It's my treat* or *It's on me.*
  It's a deal means we've come to an agreement [on what to do].

D Focus on language

Suggested teaching time:	5 minutes	Your actual teaching time:

- Model the activity by doing the first item with the class.
- Tell students to look at the underlined text to find the answers to the rest of the clues. Walk around the room and help students as needed.

- For weaker students, write the underlined words and phrases on the board (not in the order of the answers). Have students look for these words and phrases in the Photo Story to help them answer the questions.

a bunch of	can't stand	Frankly
it's my treat	I've heard	I missed

E Infer meaning

Suggested teaching time:	2 minutes	Your actual teaching time:

- If necessary, quickly review these parts of speech: a *noun* is a word that names a person, place, or thing; an *adjective* is a word that describes a noun.
- Read the directions aloud and explain that, unlike Exercise D, the answers have no hints. Have students work in pairs to find the answers.
- As pairs work together, walk around the room and help students as needed.

F Think and explain

Suggested teaching time:	3 minutes	Your actual teaching time:

- To prepare students, tell them to skim the questions. Point out that *How do you know?* follows each question. Explain that they need to give a reason for each item.
- Model the first item for the class. Read the first two questions and ask a student to say the answer to the first question (Leonardo DiCaprio). Then ask *Is anyone here a big DiCaprio fan?*
- As pairs complete the exercise, walk around the room and help students as needed.
- Review answers with the class.

SPEAKING

Pair work

Suggested teaching time:	5–10 minutes	Your actual teaching time:

- For a warm-up, ask *What movies have you seen recently? Did you see these at the movie theater? If not, where?*
- In pairs, have students brainstorm lists of movies in town and answer the questions. If students don't know what movies are playing in their town, tell them to make a list of some of their favorite movies and talk about them.
- Ask individuals to share their answers with the class.
- As an alternative approach, tell students to look up movie listings for homework and bring them to class. Alternatively, bring a newspaper to class so students can look up movie listings.

 EXTRAS

Workbook

C ▶1:18 **PHOTO STORY** Read and listen to a conversation at a movie theater.

Anna: So, what are you in the mood for? They've got a bunch of great classic movies tonight.

Peter: They sure do. Hey, you're a big DiCaprio fan. I missed *Gangs of New York* when it was playing. Have you ever seen it?

Anna: Nope, I haven't. I've heard it's pretty violent. Frankly, I just can't take all that fighting.

Peter: Yeah. It *is* supposed to be pretty bloody. . . . What else?

Anna: Well, there's *Ice Age*. They say it's spectacular. What do you think?

Peter: Hmm. To tell you the truth, I can't stand animated films. Sorry. I've just never liked them. I think I'd rather see something . . .

Peter: Hey! What about *Casablanca*?

Anna: *Casablanca*? Now you're talking! And by the way, it's my treat. You paid last time. What do you say?

Peter: It's a deal! I'll get the popcorn.

D **FOCUS ON LANGUAGE** Find underlined words or phrases in the Photo Story that have almost the same meaning as the ones below.

1 "I'll pay." It's my treat   3 "To tell you the truth, . . ." Frankly   5 "I didn't see . . ." I missed

2 "really don't like" I can't stand /4 "a lot of" a bunch of   6 "They say . . ." I've heard
can't take

E **INFER MEANING** With a partner, discuss, find, and underline . . .

1 a noun that has the same meaning as "movie." film

2 two different adjectives that are related to "fighting" or "killing." violent, bloody

3 an adjective that means "really great." spectacular

F **THINK AND EXPLAIN** First answer each question. Then explain your answer with a quotation from the Photo Story.

1 What actor does Anna like? Leonardo DiCaprio   3 What movie does Anna suggest? Ice Age.
  How do you know?   How do you know?
  Peter says, "Hey, you're a big DiCaprio fan."   She says, "Well, there's Ice Age."

2 Did Anna see *Gangs of New York*? No   4 Who is going to pay for the popcorn? Peter
  How do you know?   How do you know?
  She says, "Nope, I haven't."   He says, "I'll get the popcorn."

SPEAKING

PAIR WORK Make a list of movies playing in your town. Which movies would you like to see? Which movies would you not like to see? Give reasons for your answers.

GOAL Apologize for being late

GRAMMAR *The present perfect: for and since; Other uses of the present perfect*

Use **for** and **since** to describe periods of time that began in the past. Use **for** to describe a length of time. Use **since** with a specific time or date in the past.

How long have you been here?	I've been here **for ten minutes**. (a length of time)
	I've been here **for many years**. (a length of time)
	I've been here **since eight o'clock**. (a specific time in the past)

Be careful!
They've lived here since **2013**.
NOT They've lived here ~~since five years~~.

Other uses:

• with **always**: I've **always** wanted to see *Car Planet*.

• with **ordinals and superlatives**: This is **the third time** I've seen *Ping Pong*. It's **the best** movie I've ever seen.

• with **lately, recently**, or **just**: Have you seen a good movie **recently (or lately)**? I've **just** seen *The Beach*—what a great movie!

• with **still** or **so far**: You **still** haven't seen *Tomato Babies*? I've seen it three times **so far**!

GRAMMAR BOOSTER p. 127
• The present perfect continuous: unfinished actions
• Spelling rules for the present participle: review, common errors

A **GRAMMAR PRACTICE** Choose the correct words to complete the paragraph.

I've been a big fan of Penélope Cruz (1 **for** / since) more than twenty years. I've followed her career (2 **since** / so far) I was in high school. That means I've watched every movie she's made (3 for / **since**) 1993, except for *Vicky Cristina Barcelona*. I (4 yet / **still**) haven't seen that one, but I plan to see it soon. I've (5 still / **always**) loved Penélope's work. I've (6 since / **always**) been the first person in line at the theater when her movies open. Of the movies Penélope has made (7 **lately** / always), the most interesting ones to me are *To Rome with Love* and *I'm So Excited*. I think they're the (8 **best** / just) movies she's made (9 **so far** / still). I've (10 always / **already**) seen them twice!

B **PAIR WORK** Take turns asking and answering the questions. Use the present perfect in all your answers.

1 Is there a movie you've always wanted to see?

2 Have you seen any good movies recently?

3 What's the best movie you've ever seen?

4 What's the worst movie you've ever seen?

5 How many movies have you seen so far this month?

6 Is there a classic movie that you still haven't seen?

VOCABULARY *Explanations for being late*

A ▶1:19 Read and listen. Then listen again and repeat.

I overslept.

I missed the bus.

I couldn't get a taxi.

I couldn't find a parking space.

I got stuck in traffic.

B **PAIR WORK** Think of two other explanations for being late.

GRAMMAR

Suggested teaching time:	5–10 minutes	Your actual teaching time:

- Have a student write the examples on the board. Circle *since eight o'clock* and *for ten minutes*. Point out that we use *since* + present perfect to talk about a specific start time or date in the past, and we use *for* + present perfect to describe a period of time that started in the past.

- Model the use of *since* and *for* by having a student ask you *How long have you been here?* Respond *I've been here since 3:00.* OR *I've been here for six hours.*

- Write on the board *since 3:00, since this morning, since I was a child, for six hours, for two days, for five months, for a long time.* Ask students to create additional sentences using these phrases. Make sure students use the present perfect + *since* or *for* and that they note the information in the Be careful! box.

- Read "Other uses" and example sentences. Ask students for examples of ordinal numbers (first, second, eighteenth) and the superlative (the nicest, the oldest, the strangest) and write these on the board.

- Point out the placement of the underlined words:
  - *always, just* come between *have* + past participle.
  - *lately, recently* come at the end of a sentence in the present perfect.
  - *still* comes at the beginning of a sentence before *have* + past participle.
  - *so far* comes at the beginning of a sentence before *have* + past participle OR at the end of a sentence in the present perfect.

- Review the placement of *already* and *yet*:
  - *already* comes between *have* + past participle or at the end of a sentence in the present perfect.
  - *yet* comes at the end of a sentence in the present perfect.

- To explain usage, ask questions and have students respond with the present perfect. For example: *Have you always wanted to see* Car Planet? *Have you seen* Ping Pong *before? Have you seen a good movie lately?* Encourage students to use the example answers or their own answers.

> ### Language and culture
> - When *still* is used in negative sentences, it shows surprise that a situation has continued; for example, *You still haven't seen* Avatar? means *I'm very surprised that you haven't seen* Avatar *yet.*
> - **From the Longman Corpus:** It is common for English learners across all language backgrounds to confuse *since* and *for*. For example, *I have stayed here since one week.*

Option: **GRAMMAR BOOSTER** *(Teaching notes p. T127)*

 Inductive Grammar Charts

A Grammar practice

Suggested teaching time:	3 minutes	Your actual teaching time:

- To prepare students, tell them to circle all the dates or times in the past (2. I was in high school; 3. 1993) and underline the period of time (1. More than twenty years.)

- Point out the placement of *for, since, still, always, lately, so far,* and *already* in the sentences.

- Have students compare answers in pairs. Then review answers with the class.

B Pair work

Suggested teaching time:	3 minutes	Your actual teaching time:

- To prepare students for the activity, have them find and circle the words in the questions that indicate the present perfect is needed. (1. always; 2. recently; 3. the best / ever; 4. the worst / ever; 5. so far; 6. still.)

- Model the use of the present perfect by reading aloud item 1. (Is there a movie you've always wanted to see?)

- While students ask and answer the questions, walk around the room and make sure their answers include the present perfect. Point out that they can answer item 2 with either *recently* or *just.*

 Extra Grammar Exercises

VOCABULARY

A ▶1:19 Read and listen . . .

Suggested teaching time:	3 minutes	Your actual teaching time:

V Vocabulary Flash Card Player

- Use the pictures and captions to preview the vocabulary. Explain the meaning of *get stuck in traffic* (not be able to move) and *miss the bus* (have it leave without you).

- After students listen and practice, ask *Have you ever used these explanations for being late? What were you late for? Are you usually late? If yes, why?*

- Have students listen and practice again.

 Learning Strategies

B Pair work

Suggested teaching time:	2 minutes	Your actual teaching time:

- On the board, write *I'm sorry I'm late.* Invite a volunteer to explain why. For example, *My car had a problem.* Write the explanation on the board.

- Have students write two other explanations for being late and share them with the class. (Possible responses: I was lost. There was an important meeting. I got an important phone call.)

- Ask *Have you ever made up (invented) an explanation for being late? If yes, what did you say? What was the real reason?*

C ▶1:20 Listen to activate vocabulary

Suggested teaching time:	5–7 minutes	Your actual teaching time:

- If necessary, review the explanations for being late under Vocabulary on page 16.
- Point out that each conversation does not give an explicit excuse. Students must infer the excuse.

AUDIOSCRIPT

CONVERSATION 1
F: Ted, where were you?
M: I'm so sorry. I went to bed after two last night and I didn't hear the alarm clock ring. What time is it?
F: It's 8:30! The meeting starts in fifteen minutes! Thank goodness you're here now!

CONVERSATION 2
M1: Where's Maude?
M2: I don't know. She called me from her car ten minutes ago. She said she was here but she was trying to park her car near the building. I wonder what happened.
M1: Me, too.

CONVERSATION 3
F1: Look at all these cars! Where did they come from?
F2: I have no clue. And today's a holiday! Usually there aren't any cars on the road at this hour.
F1: We're definitely going to be late.

CONVERSATION 4
M: Oh, no! There goes the number 5 bus.
F: Uh-oh. We're going to be late. The next bus doesn't come for another half hour.
M: Let's see if we can find a taxi.
F: In the rain? No way. Everyone wants a taxi when it rains.

PRONUNCIATION

▶1:21 **Notice how the sound /h/ . . .**

Suggested teaching time:	2 minutes	Your actual teaching time:

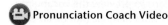 **Pronunciation Coach Video**

- Have students pay attention to the disappearing /h/ sound as they listen.

 **Pronunciation Activities**

CONVERSATION MODEL

A ▶1:22 **Read and listen . . .**

Suggested teaching time:	2 minutes	Your actual teaching time:

These conversation strategies are implicit in the model:
- Apologize and provide a reason when late.
- Say "That's fine." to reassure.
- Offer to repay someone with "How much do I owe?"

- Have students use the photo to predict the conversation. Have them cover the sentences in the conversation and try to guess what each person is saying. Have students read and listen to check their predictions.

- Have students listen again. Then ask *Why is Speaker A late?* (She got stuck in traffic.) *What movie did they want to see?* (*The Love Boat.*) *Will they see that movie?* (No.) *Why not?* (Because it's sold out.)

B ▶1:23 **Rhythm and intonation**

Suggested teaching time:	3 minutes	Your actual teaching time:

- Have students repeat chorally. Make sure they:
  - use rising intonation for *Have you been here long?*
  - use falling intonation for *How much do I owe?*
  - stress *my* in *Next time it's my treat.*

NOW YOU CAN Apologize for being late

A **Add four more movies . . .**

Suggested teaching time:	3–5 minutes	Your actual teaching time:

- Have students fill in the blank slots on the sign with movies of their choice.

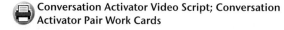 **Learning Strategies**

B **Conversation activator**

Suggested teaching time:	7–10 minutes	Your actual teaching time:

Conversation Activator Video

- *Note*: You can print the script or you can show a running transcript on the video player on the ActiveTeach. The script also appears on page 182 of this Teacher's Edition.

DON'T STOP! Extend the conversation using the ideas in the box. Give students a few minutes to skim the Recycle box.

- For more support, play the Conversation Activator Video before students do this activity themselves. In Scene 1, the actors use different words in the gaps from the ones in the Conversation Model. In Scene 2, the actors extend the conversation. After each scene, ask students how the model has been changed by the actors.

- Working with a more confident student, model how to change and extend the conversation in a role play.

Conversation Activator Video Script; Conversation Activator Pair Work Cards

C **Change partners**

Suggested teaching time:	7–10 minutes	Your actual teaching time:

- Invite pairs to present their role plays to the class.

EXTRAS

Workbook or MyEnglishLab

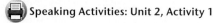 **Speaking Activities: Unit 2, Activity 1**

C ▶1:20 **LISTEN TO ACTIVATE VOCABULARY** Listen to the conversations. Complete the sentences, inferring the information and using the Vocabulary.

1 Ted's late because he .... overslept ....

3 They're going to be late because they .....are stuck in traffic.....

2 Maude probably .....couldn't find a parking space..... .

4 First they .....missed the bus..... . Then they probably .....couldn't get a taxi.....

PRONUNCIATION *Reduction of* h

▶1:21 Notice how the sound /h/ often disappears in natural speech. Read and listen. Then listen again and repeat.

1 How long have you waited?

2 Where have you been?

3 What has he read about the film?

4 When did he buy the tickets?

5 What's her favorite movie?

6 Who's his favorite star?

CONVERSATION MODEL

A ▶1:22 Read and listen to someone apologize for being late.

A: Have you been here long?

B: For about ten minutes.

A: Sorry I'm late. I got stuck in traffic. Did you get tickets?

B: Yes. But the 8:00 show for *The Love Boat* is sold out. I got tickets for *Paradise Island.* I hope that's OK.

A: That's fine. How much do I owe?

B: Nothing. It's on me.

A: Well, thanks! Next time it's my treat.

B ▶1:23 **RHYTHM AND INTONATION** Listen again and repeat. Then practice the Conversation Model with a partner.

NOW YOU CAN Apologize for being late

A Add four more movies to the showtimes.

B **CONVERSATION ACTIVATOR** With a partner, personalize the Conversation Model with your movies and explanations. Then change roles.

A: Have you been here long?

B: For ....

A: Sorry I'm late. I .... Did you get tickets?

B: Yes. But .... I hope that's OK.

A: ....

Stuck in Traffic	7:00	9:00	11:00
	7:30	9:35	[7:30 sold out]
	7:45	10:20	midnight
	8:00	11:00	[8:00 sold out]
	7:50	10:10	

DON'T STOP!

- Say more about the movie.
- Offer to pay.
- Discuss what to do after the show.

RECYCLE THIS LANGUAGE.

[Titanic 3] is sold out.
We missed __.
It started __ minutes ago.
I've already seen __.
That's past my bedtime!
I'm not a [Naomi Watts] fan.

I've heard [it's spectacular].
They say [it's pretty violent].
How much do I owe?
It's on me.
It's my treat.

C **CHANGE PARTNERS** Practice the conversation again, making other changes.

DIGITAL FLASH CARDS **VOCABULARY** *Movie genres*

A ▶1:24 Read and listen. Then listen again and repeat.

an action film

a horror film

a science-fiction film

an animated film

a comedy

a drama

a documentary

a musical

B **PAIR WORK** Compare your favorite movies for each genre.

> 66 My favorite animated film is *Frozen*. 99

C ▶1:25 **LISTEN TO INFER** Listen and write the genre for each movie in the chart. Then circle the movie if the people decided to see it.

D **DISCUSSION** Which movies sound good to you? Listen again if necessary. Explain your choices.

Movie	Genre
1 (The Bottom of the Sea)	documentary
2 Tango in Tap Shoes	musical
3 The Ant Who Wouldn't Die	horror film
4 (Chickens Never Wear Shoes)	comedy
5 (Goldilocks Grows Up)	animated film
6 The Equalizer	action film
7 Twelve Angry Women	drama
8 (City Under the Sea)	science fiction

GRAMMAR *Ways to express wants and preferences*

<u>Would like</u>

Use <u>would like</u> + an infinitive (<u>to</u> + a base form) to politely express or ask about wants.

I'd like to go to the movies.
Would she like to see *The Dancer*?
What would your friends like to do?

| I / She / We / They | 'd like | to see a comedy. |

Be careful!

Would you rather see *Titanic*? Yes, **I would**.
  NOT Yes, I ~~would rather~~.
Would they like to go out tonight? Yes, **they would**.
  NOT Yes, they ~~would like~~.
Would your parents like to go to the early show?
  Yes, **they would**. NOT Yes, ~~they'd~~.

<u>Would rather</u>

Use <u>would rather</u> + a base form to express or ask about a preference between two or more activities.

Would your children rather see an animated film or an action film?
What would you rather do: go to a movie or a play?
She'd rather see a less violent film than *Gangs of New York*.

| I / He / We / They | 'd rather | see a drama. |

Use <u>would rather not</u> + a base form to express a negative preference.

We'd rather not watch TV tonight.

Yes / no questions

Would you like to see a documentary?
Would they rather stay home?

short answers

Yes, I would. / No, I wouldn't.
Yes, they would. / No, they wouldn't.
  OR No, they'd rather not.

GRAMMAR BOOSTER p. 128
• Expressing preferences: review, expansion, and common errors.

VOCABULARY

A ▶1:24 Read and listen . . .

Suggested teaching time:	2 minutes	Your actual teaching time:

 Vocabulary Flash Card Player

- After students listen and practice, ask them *Which is your favorite genre?*

 Learning Strategies

B Pair work

Suggested teaching time:	3–6 minutes	Your actual teaching time:

- Have students write down their favorite movie for each genre. If students don't have a favorite movie, have them list any movie they know of in that genre. Have them share opinions.

> **Language and culture**
> - The words *movie* and *film* are generally used interchangeably, but *movie* is more common in American English.
> - In British English, people often say they are *keen on* something to express a strong liking for it.

C ▶1:25 Listen to infer

Suggested teaching time:	10 minutes	Your actual teaching time:

- Have students read the movie titles and guess their genres.
- As they listen, have students fill in the genres in the chart and compare their guesses. Allow students sufficient time to write.
- Have students listen again. Instruct them to circle each movie the speakers decided to see.
- Have students work in pairs to compare answers.

> **Language and culture**
> - The idiom *I'm game* means *I'm interested in doing something that someone else suggests*.
> - *I'll be up all night* is an expression that, in this context, suggests the person will be too scared to sleep.
> - *Let's give it a try* is another way of saying *let's try doing something*.
> - *Count me out* is an expression meaning *don't include me in your plan*.

AUDIOSCRIPT

CONVERSATION 1
F: I saw this great movie on TV last night.
M: Really? What was it?
F: *The Bottom of the Sea.*
M: What was it about?
F: It explored underwater life in the South Atlantic and Indian Oceans. I learned so much. It's on again tonight. I don't mind seeing it again. Want to watch it with me?
M: Absolutely!

CONVERSATION 2
M: Let's download a movie to watch. It's too cold to go out. What do you think?
F: I'm game. What are you in the mood for?
M: My mom said *Tango in Tap Shoes* was great.
F: Well, I guess if you like to watch a lot of music and dancing.
M: I do. Don't you?
F: To tell you the truth, not really. Let's get something else.
M: OK.

AUDIOSCRIPT continues on page T22.

D Discussion

Suggested teaching time:	3–6 minutes	Your actual teaching time:

- Have students listen again to track 25. Ask them to choose one movie they would like to see. Ask them to explain what in the description of the movie made it sound good; for example: *I think* The Bottom of the Sea *sounds great. I love documentaries, and I love things about the sea.*
- As a culminating activity, ask *What genres does this class like most?* Make a list of the top movies on the board. Tell students to vote on their favorite genres.

GRAMMAR

Suggested teaching time:	7–12 minutes	Your actual teaching time:

- Go over the first rule and examples. Make sure students understand that *would like* is followed by *to* + a base form. Point out that *would* is often contracted to *'d* and that its form remains the same with different subjects.
- For the *Would rather* rules and examples, explain that *I'd rather (not)* + a base form is used to choose between two or more things. Model possible responses to the example questions: *They'd rather see an action film. I'd rather go to a play.*
- Go over the yes / no questions and answers and the information in the Be careful! Box. To check understanding, ask *Would you like to watch TV tonight? Would you rather play video games?* Make sure students' short answers include the full form of *would* or *wouldn't* but do not include *rather* or *like*.

Option: GRAMMAR BOOSTER *(Teaching notes p. T128)*

 Inductive Grammar Charts

A Grammar practice

Suggested teaching time:	5 minutes	Your actual teaching time:

- Remind students that short answers to *yes / no* questions with *would* use only the full form of *would* or *wouldn't*.
- After students complete the conversations, review the responses with the class.

B Pair work

Suggested teaching time:	3 minutes	Your actual teaching time:

- Model a conversation with a stronger student. Ask, *Would you like to see [name of movie]? (Yes, I would OR No, I wouldn't.)* Ask, *What would you rather see: a horror movie or a science fiction movie? (I'd rather see [a horror movie].)*
- Have students ask and answer questions in pairs. Ask a few students to role-play their conversations for the class.

 Extra Grammar Exercises

CONVERSATION MODEL

A ▶1:26 Read and listen . . .

Suggested teaching time:	2 minutes	Your actual teaching time:

These conversation strategies are implicit in the model:
- Use "What would you rather do?" to ask about preference.
- Soften a negative response with "To tell you the truth, . . ."

- Introduce the conversation by having students look at the picture. Ask *Where are the people?* (At home.) *What do you think they are talking about?* (What they want to do.)
- After students read and listen, ask them comprehension questions. For example:
  Does the woman want to stream a movie or go to the theater? (Go to the theater.)
  Does the woman like horror movies? (No, she can't stand them.)
  What do the people agree to do? (See a documentary.)

B ▶1:27 Rhythm and intonation

Suggested teaching time:	3 minutes	Your actual teaching time:

- Have students repeat each line chorally. Make sure they:
  ◦ pause after *see*
  ◦ use rising intonation with *Horror City* and fall with *Love in Paris*
- Point out that *What would you . . . ?*, and *How about a . . . ?* are language chunks. The words are spoken together quickly without pausing between them: *whatwouldyou . . .*

▶1:28 Ways to agree on a plan

- Have students listen and repeat the expressions in the box. Encourage them to replace *that works for me* with the other two expressions when they practice the conversation.

NOW YOU CAN   Discuss preferences for movie genres

A Conversation activator

Suggested teaching time:	5–8 minutes	Your actual teaching time:

 Conversation Activator Video

- *Note:* You can print the script or you can show a running transcript on the video player on the ActiveTeach. The script also appears on page 182 of this Teacher's Edition.

DON'T STOP! Extend the conversation. Encourage students to ask each other additional questions about the movies and to express more movie preferences. Write some possible questions on the board:
What's that movie about? Who is in the movie? What other movie genres do you like?

- For more support, play the Conversation Activator Video before students do this activity themselves. In Scene 1, the actors use different words in the gaps from the ones in the Conversation Model. In Scene 2, the actors extend the conversation. After each scene, ask students how the model has been changed by the actors.
- Review the language in the Recycle box. Remind students to use the language from the Recycle box and to cross out phrases as they use them.
- Be sure to reinforce the conversation strategies. For example, make sure that students use appropriate facial expressions and body language when giving a negative response with "To tell you the truth."
- Model extending the conversation as you role-play with a more confident student. Play the role of Student A.
- Have students list four to five movies and movie stars. Then have them role-play the conversation.
- Invite volunteers to perform their role plays for the class. After each role play, ask *What movie did they decide to see?*

Conversation Activator Video Script; Conversation Activator Pair Work Cards

B Change partners

Suggested teaching time:	5–8 minutes	Your actual teaching time:

- To form new pairs, have students count off alternating A and B. Then have them find a new partner with the same letter.
- In their new pairs, have them practice the conversations again, this time pretending to be in front of a movie theater.
- Encourage students to try to think of movies currently playing in theaters and to use the recycled language.
- Walk around the room and listen for use of recycled language as well as rhythm and intonation.
- Invite pairs to share their role plays with the class.

EXTRAS

Workbook or MyEnglishLab

 Speaking Activities: Unit 2, Activity 2

A **GRAMMAR PRACTICE** Complete the conversations about wants and preferences.

1. A: (I like /(I'd like)) to see *Star Wars X* again. Would you? It's at the CineMax.

   B: Actually, (I'd rather. /(I'd rather not.)) Let's stay home.

2. A: (Do you like /(Would you like)) to stream something on TV?

   B: Yes, (I'd like. /(I would.))

3. A: What would you rather ((see)/ to see): a science fiction film or a comedy?

   B: Me? ((I'd rather)/ I rather) see a science fiction movie.

4. A: There's a musical and a horror movie on TV. ((Would)/ Does) your husband rather see the horror movie?

   B: Yes, (he would rather. /(he would.))

5. A: My sister ((would like to)/ would like) go to the movies on Friday.

   B: Great. ((I would)/ I would like), too.

B **PAIR WORK** Use <u>would like</u> and <u>would rather</u> to ask your partner about movies he or she would like to see and his or her preferences.

> " Would you like to see *Boomerang*? "

> " What would you rather see: a documentary or a drama? "

CONVERSATION MODEL

A ▶1:26 Read and listen to people discussing their movie preferences.

A: What would you rather do: stay home and stream a movie or go to the theater?

B: I'd rather go out. Is that OK?

A: Sure! . . . Would you rather see *Horror City* or *Love in Paris*?

B: Are you kidding? I can't stand horror movies, and to tell you the truth, I'm not that big on love stories.

A: Well, how about a documentary? *The Great Wall of China* is playing, too. I've heard it's great.

B: That works for me!

▶1:28 **Ways to agree on a plan**
That works for me.
It's a deal!
Great idea!

B ▶1:27 **RHYTHM AND INTONATION** Listen again and repeat. Then practice the Conversation Model with a partner.

NOW YOU CAN Discuss preferences for movie genres

A **CONVERSATION ACTIVATOR** Write the names of some movies. With a partner, change the Conversation Model, using your own movies. Then change roles.

A: What would you rather do: stay home and stream a movie or go to the theater?
B: I'd rather .... Is that OK?
A: .... Would you rather see .... or .... ?
B: Are you kidding? I can't stand .... , and to tell you the truth, I ....
A: Well, how about .... ?

DON'T STOP!

- Say more about the movies and express more movie preferences.

B **CHANGE PARTNERS** Change the conversation again, using different movies.

BEFORE YOU LISTEN

DIGITAL FLASH CARDS

A ▶1:29 **VOCABULARY • *Adjectives to describe movies*** Read and listen. Then listen again and repeat.

funny something that makes you laugh

hilarious very, very funny

silly not serious; almost stupid

boring not interesting

weird very strange or unusual, in a negative way

unforgettable something you are going to remember

romantic about love

thought-provoking something that makes you think

violent bloody; with a lot of fighting and killing

B **PAIR WORK** Write the title of a movie for each adjective. Then tell your partner about your choices.

a funny movie	
a hilarious movie	
a silly movie	
a boring movie	
a weird movie	
an unforgettable movie	
a romantic movie	
a thought-provoking movie	
a violent movie	

LISTENING COMPREHENSION

A ▶1:30 **LISTEN FOR MAIN IDEAS** Listen to the movie reviewer. Write a check next to the movies he recommends, and write an ✗ next to the ones he doesn't.

1 ☒ *Popcorn* 2 ☑ *The Vacation* 3 ☑ *Aquamundo* 4 ☒ *Wolf Babies*

B ▶1:31 **LISTEN TO INFER** Listen carefully to each movie review again. Based on the reviewer's opinion, circle one or more adjectives to describe each movie.

1 *Popcorn* (weird)/ funny /(boring)

2 *The Vacation* (romantic)/(violent)/(unforgettable)

3 *Aquamundo* (boring / violent /(thought-provoking))

4 *Wolf Babies* (violent)/ boring / hilarious)

C ▶1:32 **LISTENING: DICTATION** Listen to the following excerpts from the reviews. Complete each statement, based on what you hear.

POPCORN ★

① First up is *Popcorn*, a new ....comedy... starring David Bodine and Judy Crabbe. ② Unfortunately, *Popcorn* is a complete waste of ....time.... .

THE VACATION ★ ★ ★ ★ ★

③ Our next film, *The Vacation*, is a well-acted and ....serious... ....drama.... . ④ I highly ....recommend this.... wonderful ....film.... .

AQUAMUNDO ★ ★ ★

⑤ *Aquamundo* is no ....science.... ....fiction.... film; it's based on real scientific research. ⑥ A ....beautiful.... film. Don't ....miss.... ....it.... .

WOLF BABIES ★ ★ ★

⑦ Adults will find the story ....stupid...., but children won't forget these ....bloody...., scary scenes for a long time.

BEFORE YOU LISTEN

A ▶1:29 Vocabulary

Suggested teaching time:	3 minutes	Your actual teaching time:

 Vocabulary Flash Card Player

- To check understanding, ask *What word describes a movie with a lot of fighting?* (Violent.) *What word describes a movie about love?* (Romantic.) *What word describes a movie that isn't interesting?* (Boring.)
- If necessary, have students listen and practice again.

🖨 **Learning Strategies**

B Pair work

Suggested teaching time:	5–10 minutes	Your actual teaching time:

- Have students discuss and complete the chart with movies they know.
- As a class, ask students which movie they named for each adjective. After each movie title, ask *Has anyone seen this movie? Do you agree that it is [funny / silly / boring / etc.]?*

Option: (+5 minutes) For additional practice, write the model below on the board. Have students role-play the conversation in pairs, using adjectives from the Vocabulary.

A: What's the last movie you saw?
B: ___.
A: Was it ___?
B: ___.

LISTENING COMPREHENSION

A ▶1:30 Listen for main ideas

Suggested teaching time:	4–6 minutes	Your actual teaching time:

- Read the movie titles aloud and tell students to listen to the movie reviewer while looking at the movie titles. Play the audio once or twice and have students listen and complete the task. If necessary, play the audio again.
- Have students compare answers in pairs. Then have them listen again to confirm answers.
- Explain language as needed.

> ### Language and culture
> - *They won't sleep for a week* suggests that the children will be too scared to sleep all week. It is similar to the expression *I'll be up all night.*
> - The word *unfunny* is not a true word. The prefix *un-* means *not* and is sometimes used emphatically at the beginning of a word to create "new words."
> - When a movie is called *a complete waste of time* it means that it was not good. Seeing it would be wasting your time.

Option: (+5 minutes) For additional practice, have students listen for selected details. Then play the listening as many times as necessary for students to complete the exercise. For example, before playing the audio, ask:
  Who's talking? (Cinema Sid.)
  Which movie is a comedy, Popcorn *or* The Vacation? (*Popcorn.*)
  Is Aquamundo *a science-fiction film?* (No.)
  Is Wolf Babies *an appropriate film for children?* (No.) *Why?* (It's very scary.)

AUDIOSCRIPT See page T21.

B ▶1:31 Listen to infer

Suggested teaching time:	5–8 minutes	Your actual teaching time:

- To prepare students, have them skim the adjectives listed next to each movie title. Tell them to guess the answers based on their previous listening.
- Play the audio again and have students listen and then circle the adjective(s) that best describe(s) each movie.
- Have pairs compare answers. If necessary, allow students to listen again.
- Review answers with the class.

Option: (+5 minutes) Have students work in small groups to discuss which movie they would choose to see. Encourage them to give reasons. For example, *I'd choose to see* Wolf Babies *because I like scary movies.*

C ▶1:32 Listening: dictation

Suggested teaching time:	8–13 minutes	Your actual teaching time:

- To prepare students, have them skim the statements with blanks. Explain that these are excerpts from the reviews and that now they will listen intensively for specific words to complete the blanks.
- Have students listen twice and fill in the blanks with the words they hear.
- To support weaker students, write the words they need to complete this exercise on the board (not in the order of the answers): beautiful, comedy, film, miss it, recommend, science fiction, serious, drama, time, this, stupid, bloody.

> **AUDIOSCRIPT**
> 1. First up is *Popcorn*, a new comedy starring David Bodine and Judy Crabbe.
> 2. Unfortunately, *Popcorn* is a complete waste of time.
> 3. Our next film, *The Vacation*, is a well-acted and serious drama.
> 4. I highly recommend this wonderful film.
> 5. *Aquamundo* is no science fiction film; it's based on real scientific research.
> 6. A beautiful film. Don't miss it.
> 7. Adults will find the story stupid, but children won't forget these bloody, scary scenes for a long time.

NOW YOU CAN Describe and recommend movies

A Pair work

Suggested teaching time:	7 minutes	Your actual teaching time:

- To introduce the activity, call on individual students and ask *Do you often read movie reviews? Do you ever choose a movie based on reviews?*

- After you read the title of the article, have students scan the reviews for the movie titles. Ask *Has anyone seen any of these movies? Are any of these titles anyone's all-time favorite movie?*

- Make sure that students understand the meaning of *out of work* (unemployed).

- After students read the reviews to themselves, check comprehension. Ask:
  Which movie is a drama? (Casablanca.)
  Which movie is a documentary? (Grizzly Man.)
  Which movie is a comedy? (Tootsie.)

- Finally, have pairs discuss which movie they would rather see and why.

> **Language and culture**
> - Exaggeration is often used for emphasis in spoken English. For example, when Rebecca says that she's *just seen Casablanca for the hundredth time,* she is exaggerating a bit. Saying that *Casablanca is the most romantic movie in the world* is another use of exaggeration to stress how much she likes this movie.

B Notepadding

Suggested teaching time:	5 minutes	Your actual teaching time:

- If students haven't seen any movies recently, let them make notes about any movie they have seen. To review, refer students to the movie genres listed on page 18 and to the adjectives listed on page 20. Encourage students to use other adjectives as well.

- Walk around the room and help as needed. Remind students that a movie can be categorized in more than one genre. For example romantic comedy.

C Group work

Suggested teaching time:	8 minutes	Your actual teaching time:

- To review, have students scan the language to be recycled. Ask volunteers for definitions of the different adjectives. Help students as needed.

DON'T STOP! Extend the conversation. Encourage students to ask each other additional questions about the movies on their notepads.

Text-mining: To prepare students for the activity, tell them to skim the article and underline useful language. For example, *[the ending is] unforgettable; [it] always make me cry; one of the most [hilarious romantic comedies] of all time; if you want a good laugh.*
- Write students' findings on the board for them to refer to during the discussion.
- After groups describe and recommend the movies on their notepads, have groups share their answers.

Option: (+5 minutes) As an alternative, have students work in pairs to create clues about the movies described in the reviews. Then have the rest of the class guess the movie. For example, *This movie is one of the most hilarious romantic comedies of all time.*

Option: (+5 minutes) To challenge students, have pairs think of several clues about movies they have seen. Have the rest of the class guess the movie. Encourage pairs to provide more clues if students have difficulty guessing. For example, *This movie stars Leonardo DiCaprio and Kate Winslet. It's an epic classic romance. (Titanic.)*

EXTRAS

Workbook or MyEnglishLab

 Speaking Activities: Unit 2, Activity 3; "Find Someone Who . . ." Activity

> **AUDIOSCRIPT** for page T20 (Listening Comprehension)
>
> Good evening, movie lovers. This is Cinema Sid with quickie reviews and recommendations. Here are some of this week's openings.
> First up is *Popcorn*, a new comedy starring David Bodine and Judy Crabbe. Unfortunately, *Popcorn* is a complete waste of time. The acting is terrible. The story's not at all interesting—as a matter of fact, I can't remember much about it—except that it was very strange. And for a movie that's supposed to be funny, it's not. You'll cry, not laugh, at spending your money on this silly, unfunny comedy but with the usually very funny David Bodine.
> Our next film, *The Vacation*, is a well-acted and serious drama. Gene Wildman and Amy Collins play a couple who meet and fall in love, then travel to Rwanda on an innocent vacation. War breaks out and you don't know 'till the end if they'll manage to get on the last plane to leave. An intelligent and interesting story. I highly recommend this wonderful film. There's some blood, so if you can't stand fighting or killing—it is a war film, after all—dòn't see it. But if you like a good story you won't forget, this one's for you.
> Also reviewed this week is *Aquamundo*. *Aquamundo* is no science fiction film; it's based on real scientific research. Filmmaker Hans Schmerling shows the many medical uses of water around the world. From the underwater births of the Sheldrake Islanders to the water cures in Swiss hospitals, Schmerling illustrates how water can heal the world. While many people may think it's a silly idea, the film argues that it can actually happen. It makes you think about the importance of water. A beautiful film. Don't miss it.
> Finally, our last film this week is *Wolf Babies*. Whatever you do, don't take the kids to see this movie! They won't sleep for a week after they see this terrible story about human children captured by wolves. After they capture the children, the wolves take them into the woods and change them forever. Then, when the children return to their families, they hunt younger children and capture them for the wolves. Adults will find the story stupid, but children won't forget these bloody, scary scenes for a long time.

A **PAIR WORK** Read the short movie reviews and choose the movie you think sounds the most interesting. Then compare movie choices. Explain your reasons.

WHAT'S YOUR ALL-TIME FAVORITE MOVIE?

Phil Ito Toronto, CANADA

I've just seen *Tootsie*. What a great movie—perhaps one of the most hilarious romantic comedies of all time. Before I saw the movie, I thought the plot sounded both weird and silly, but it wasn't. Dustin Hoffman stars as out-of-work actor Michael Dorsey, who dresses as a woman to get a part on a TV drama. But problems begin when he falls in love with his co-star, Jessica Lange, who doesn't know Michael is a man. If you want a good laugh, be sure to see this funny, funny film!

Angela Teixeira Fortaleza, BRAZIL

When someone says that documentaries are boring, I say, "You have to see *Grizzly Man*," one of the most thought-provoking documentaries of all time. This 2005 movie by German director Werner Herzog tells the true story of the life and death of Timothy Treadwell, who lived for 13 years among bears in the Alaska wilderness. Treadwell believed that he could live near bears without danger. In the end, however, Treadwell and his girlfriend are killed by bears. Even if you would rather avoid violence, go to see *Grizzly Man* because there is no actual violence on screen.

Rebecca Lane Miami, USA

I've just seen *Casablanca* for the hundredth time. It's the most romantic movie in the world, and there's no movie I would rather see. Humphrey Bogart and Ingrid Bergman star as former lovers who meet after many years. They're still in love and have to make some difficult choices. The ending is unforgettable and always makes me cry. This movie was made in 1942, but it's always "new." I guess that's what makes it a classic.

B **NOTEPADDING** Write notes about a movie you've seen recently. (It's OK if you don't have all the information.)

Title of film:

Genre:

Stars:

Director or producer:

Adjectives that describe the movie:

What the movie is about:

C **GROUP WORK** Describe and recommend the movies on your notepads. Use adjectives from the Vocabulary and other adjectives you know.

DON'T STOP!
• Ask questions.

RECYCLE THIS LANGUAGE.

Questions	More adjectives	
Was it [funny / silly / scary]?	thrilling	exciting
Who was in it?	fascinating	great
What kind of movie was it?	frightening	interesting
Do you recommend it?	disgusting	bloody
What was it about?	scary	unusual
	popular	terrific
	awful	pretty good

Text-mining (optional)
Look at the reviews in Exercise A. Find and underline three words or phrases that were new to you. Use them in your Group Work.
For example: "falls in love with . . ."

GOAL Discuss effects of violence on viewers

BEFORE YOU READ

WARM-UP At what age do you think it's safe to permit children to see violent movies and TV shows? Explain.

READING ▶ 1:33

Can Violent Movies or TV Programs Harm Children?

Many people say that children have become more aggressive in recent years—that is, they are more likely to fight with their friends, sisters, and brothers. A number of scientific studies have reported that watching violence can, in fact, cause a growth in aggression. According to the research, two kinds of programs and movies encourage aggressive behavior in young children more than others: (1) realistic violent action programs and movies, and (2) violent cartoons.

One disturbing conclusion is that the effects of violent viewing last for many years. One study showed that children who watched violent TV programs when they were 8 years old were more likely to behave aggressively at age 18. Furthermore, as adults they were more likely to be convicted of violent crimes, such as child abuse and murder.

Studies have also demonstrated that watching violent movies and TV shows can affect children's attitudes towards violence in the world around them. Children who watch a lot of fighting and bloodshed tend to find it "normal" and may accept more violence in society. They may even begin to commit violent acts themselves.

Very often, characters in movies and on television who commit violent crimes are not sorry for their actions and don't face consequences or punishment. When children see fictional characters who are criminals like these, they learn that doing bad things is OK. For children, who are growing and developing, this is a bad message. It's important for them to see that our society doesn't tolerate crime.

So what can we do? With young children, we have the power to control the TV programs and movies they watch, so we can protect them from seeing any violence at all. However, with older children it's impossible to completely prevent their exposure to violence. But we can try to limit the number of hours they spend watching it. And when children have seen a violent film or TV show, it's important to discuss it with them, to help them understand that violence is not a normal part of life.

A **UNDERSTAND FROM CONTEXT** Circle the correct word or phrase to complete each statement, according to the information in the article.

1 (A realistic /(An aggressive)) person is someone who is likely to fight with others.

2 Scientific studies have reported that some kinds of movies and TV programs can (limit /(encourage)) aggressive behavior.

3 One kind of violent crime is ((murder)/ bad behavior).

4 A word that means almost the same thing as hurt is (help /(harm)).

5 It's difficult to (permit /(prevent)) older children from seeing any violence on TV and in movies.

6 Research has suggested that ((a consequence)/ an advantage) of watching violent films is aggressive behavior.

BEFORE YOU READ

Warm-up

Suggested teaching time:	3–5 minutes	Your actual teaching time:

- To introduce the topic, take a class poll. Ask *How many of you think that it's safe to allow children to see violent movies and TV shows? How many think it can be dangerous for children to watch them?* Write the numbers on the board.

- Ask the warm-up question. Then tell the class that you will ask these questions again after the reading.

▶1:33 READING

Suggested teaching time:	10–15 minutes	Your actual teaching time:

- Tell students to look at the photo. Ask *What do you see?* (A child watching a cartoon of people fighting.)

- Read aloud the title of the article and ask students to predict what it will be about. Ask *Do you think the article will agree or disagree with the question?*

- Have students read the article. Then have them read it again and underline sentences that answer the question in the title.

- Ask students to share the sentences they underlined in the article. Ask *Do you agree with the statement that children who watch a lot of violence become less sensitive to it in the real world?* Remind students to give examples to support their opinion.

- Indicate the numbers on the board from the poll in the warm-up. Take the poll again to see if students have changed their opinions after reading the article.

A Understand from context

Suggested teaching time:	5–8 minutes	Your actual teaching time:

- If students need help doing this exercise, tell them to try to find the words in the answer choices in the article. If they find a word, suggest that they read the sentences near it (the context) to understand what the word means.

- Have students share their answers with the class.

AUDIOSCRIPT Continued, for page T18 (**C** Listen to Infer)

CONVERSATION 3
- **F:** Let's go to the movies.
- **M:** OK. You've got the newspaper right there. What's playing?
- **F:** Hmmm. Let's see. . . . Hey! What about *The Ant Who Wouldn't Die?*
- **M:** Stop that! You've got to be kidding. You know I hate those scary pictures. I'll be up all night.

CONVERSATION 4
- **F:** I rented some DVDs. Want to see one?
- **M:** That depends. What did you get?
- **F:** Let's see . . . I got *Chickens Never Wear Shoes.*
- **M:** That's a joke, right?
- **F:** I think that's the point. I'm in the mood for a laugh. This one looks really funny.
- **M:** OK. Let's give it a try.

CONVERSATION 5
- **M:** So what should we see?
- **F:** Nothing violent, OK? Something we could take the kids to.
- **M:** Hmmm. This looks safe: *Goldilocks Grows up*. It's based on the children's book.
- **F:** Who's in it?
- **M:** No one's in it! But three famous actors do the voices of the bears. I think the art was drawn by Disney Studios. It won a prize.
- **F:** That sounds perfect.

CONVERSATION 6
- **M1:** Hey! *The Equalizer* is at the Strand.
- **M2:** *The Equalizer*? What's that?
- **M1:** You can't be serious. It's that new Daniel Craig film. Lots of car crashes and people jumping out of airplanes.
- **M2:** Count me out. Those kinds of films drive me crazy.
- **M1:** OK. I'll see what else is playing.

CONVERSATION 7
- **M:** Let's see *Twelve Angry Women.*
- **F:** No way. It sounds too serious. I'd like to see something light tonight. What about a comedy or a musical?
- **M:** Don't you like a good story that keeps you interested until the end?
- **F:** No. When I go to the movies I like to be entertained. When I want a good story, I read a book. What else is there?

CONVERSATION 8
- **F:** *City Under the Sea.* What's that about?
- **M:** It's about these people—well, they're not really people. They're some kind of creatures from Mars or Jupiter—I'm not sure. Anyway, they can live in air or water. They come here and build a city under the sea, near India. And then . . .
- **F:** So?
- **M:** What do you mean so? It sounds terrific to me.
- **A:** OK. But you're buying the popcorn.

B Confirm content

Suggested teaching time:	5–8 minutes	Your actual teaching time:	

- Have students work in pairs and look back at the article to find information to answer the questions. Tell them to underline the relevant information as they find it. (1. Par. 1; 2: Par. 1; 3: Par. 3; 4: Par. 4; 5: Par. 5)
- Ask pairs to share their answers with the class.

C Evaluate ideas

Suggested teaching time:	5–10 minutes	Your actual teaching time:	

- On the board, write *Violence is not a normal part of life.* Ask *Who agrees with this statement? Who doesn't?*
- Give students a few minutes to make notes supporting their ideas on this statement. Then call on individuals to share their opinions with the class.

 Extra Reading Comprehension Exercises

NOW YOU CAN Discuss effects of violence on viewers

A Complete the chart . . .

Suggested teaching time:	7 minutes	Your actual teaching time:	

- To prepare students, have them read the headings on the chart and the explanations for the ratings.
- After students complete the chart, have them compare their charts with a partner. Ask *Do you recognize each other's titles? If yes, do you agree with the ratings?*

B Notepadding

Suggested teaching time:	5 minutes	Your actual teaching time:	

- Have students read the questions. Ask *How are young viewers different from adult viewers?*
- After pairs discuss the movies or shows, have students share their responses with the class. If students have answered *No* to either question, have them explain why. Invite students who also know the movie or television show to say if they agree or disagree.

C Discussion

Suggested teaching time:	10 minutes	Your actual teaching time:	

Text-mining: Focus students' attention on the box. Tell students to skim the article on page 22 and underline new language. For example, *a number of scientific studies have reported . . . , one disturbing conclusion is . . . , studies have also demonstrated . . .*

Then write students' findings on the board for them to refer to during the discussion.

- Ask volunteers to read the sample answers in the quotes. Point out the words in bold type. *I think . . . ; I agree / disagree; I feel that . . .* Encourage students to use these words as they discuss the questions in small groups. Walk around the room and help as needed.

- Invite volunteers to give their answers to the class. Ask students to share any differing opinions.
- Ask *Do you think it is possible to protect children from violence on TV, in movies, and in video games? If yes, how can we do this?*

Option: (+15 minutes) To challenge students, have them prepare a debate on one of the questions from the discussion. Divide the class in half and assign each half the negative or positive answer. Tell each group to prepare arguments to support the assigned answer. Allow students to refer to the article for ideas. Have the groups share their arguments, allowing each side to respond. Write the arguments on the board. Then have students read the arguments to determine which group made a stronger case.

Option: (+15 minutes) Have students write a short essay answering one of the three questions. Encourage students to first write a list of arguments supporting their point of view. Have them develop the arguments and give examples in two or three paragraphs.

EXTRAS

Workbook or MyEnglishLab

 Speaking Activities: Unit 2, Activity 4

B **CONFIRM CONTENT** Discuss the questions, using the information in the article.
Then share your answers with the class.

1 According to the article, what are some ways that viewing violence can affect children?

2 What kinds of programs and movies are most harmful?

3 According to the article, some studies show that viewing violence can have effects that last for many years. What are some of these long-term effects?

4 What bad "message" can come from violent programs and movies?

5 What suggestions does the article make to help parents prevent the bad effects of violent TV programs and movies in very young children? In older children?

C **EVALUATE IDEAS** Do you agree with the article that "violence is not a normal part of life"? Explain your answer.

NOW YOU CAN Discuss effects of violence on viewers

A Complete the chart with three films or television shows you know. Rate the level of violence from 0 to 3, with 3 being the most violent.

Title	Medium	Level of Violence
The Dark Knight Rises	film	2

0 = not violent, 1 = somewhat violent, 2 = violent, 3 = ultra violent

B **NOTEPADDING** Write notes about the most violent film or TV show on your chart.

Should children see it? Why? / Why not?
Is it OK for adults to see it? Why? / Why not?

C **DISCUSSION** Discuss the effects of violence on viewers. Use the information from your notepad to help you express your ideas. Here are some questions to consider in your discussion:

• In your opinion, are there some people who should not see violent movies? If so, who?

• Is the effect of viewing violence the same in children and adults?

• Does violence encourage adults to behave aggressively?

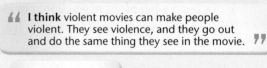

❝ **I think** violent movies can make people violent. They see violence, and they go out and do the same thing they see in the movie. ❞

❝ **I agree . . .** ❞

❝ **I disagree. I feel that . . .** ❞

Text-mining (optional)
Find and underline three words or phrases in the Reading that were new to you. Use them in your Discussion.
For example: "a bad message."

REVIEW

A ▶1:34 Listen to the conversation about movies. Check the correct description of each movie.

1

- ☑ a romantic film
- ☐ a documentary about Brazil
- ☐ a horror movie

2

- ☑ an animated police story
- ☐ a weird love story
- ☐ an unforgettable comedy

3

- ☑ an unforgettable movie
- ☐ a weird police story
- ☐ an animated children's film

4

- ☐ a documentary about cooking ham
- ☑ a musical tragedy
- ☐ a silly comedy

5

- ☐ a documentary
- ☑ a movie only for adults
- ☐ an animated musical

6

- ☑ a comedy
- ☐ an animated film
- ☐ a drama

B Complete the conversations. Choose the correct verbs and adverbial expressions, and write the movie genres.

1 A: (Have you seen) / Did you see) a good ...comedy... (just / lately))?

B: To tell you the truth, no. But last night (we've seen / we saw) a great ..action film...

2 A: How many times (have they seen)/ did they see) *War of the Worlds*?

B: That remake of the old science fiction movie? I think (they saw it /they've seen it) twice (still /so far).

3 A: Sally is such a ...musical... fan. How long (has she waited)/ did she wait) for this film to come out on DVD?

B: She's waited (for)/ since) at least six months.

4 A: I (didn't see /haven't seen) a ...drama... as good as *Twelve Angry Men*.

B: Really? I (lately /still) (didn't see /haven't seen) it.

C Complete each statement or question with <u>for</u> or <u>since</u>.

1 That film has played at the Metroplex ...for... two weeks.

2 *The Talking Parrot* has been available to stream online ..since.. last Tuesday.

3 I've loved animated movies ..since.. I was a child.

4 Have you been here ...for... more than an hour?

5 I've been a fan of science fiction movies ...for... over thirty years.

6 I've been in the ticket line ..since.. 6:30!

For additional language practice . . .

♫ **TOP NOTCH POP** • Lyrics p. 153
"Better Late Than Never"

| DIGITAL SONG | DIGITAL KARAOKE |

WRITING

Write two paragraphs about violence in movies and on TV. Explain why some people think it's harmful and why others think it isn't.

WRITING BOOSTER p. 144
- Paragraphs
- Topic sentences
- Guidance for this writing exercise

REVIEW

A ▶1:34 Listen to the conversation . . .

Suggested teaching time:	10 minutes	Your actual teaching time:

- To prepare for the activity, have students look at the pictures and guess what kind of movie each represents.

- To review vocabulary, write on the board *This movie looks [adjective]*. Refer students to the adjectives from the Vocabulary on page 20.

- Have students listen to the conversation while looking at the possible responses. Ask:
  Who's talking? (A man and a woman.)
  What are they reading? (Movie reviews in a newspaper.)
  Which movie have they already seen? (Fracas in Caracas.)

- Have students compare answers in pairs. Have them listen again to confirm answers, if necessary. Ask *Were any of your guesses at the beginning of the exercise correct?*

AUDIOSCRIPT

M: Here are the movie reviews.
F: What do they say about *Follow Me to Rio*?
M: Hmmm. Follow . . . Me . . . to . . . Rio . . . Oh, here. "Wonderful love story. Very romantic." How about that?
F: Hmmm. I'm not sure. What do they say about *Streets of Saigon*?
M: "This weird movie starts out as a police drama but, incredibly, ends up as an animated children's film." Sounds too weird for me. Let's forget *that* one. Here. This sounds great. *Clouds Over Mount Fuji*. "Unforgettable."
F: I don't know. I saw the trailer. It doesn't sound that interesting to me. What else is there?
M: *Hamlet, the Musical*. Have you heard about that one? It's a musical of the famous Shakespeare tragedy. What do you think of that?
F: Not much, actually. Sounds really silly.
M: Well, what about *Inside the Sahara*? I think that's a documentary—your favorite, right?
F: Isn't that a Matson film? I don't think that's a documentary. His films are always very violent. Yeah—look here at the review. "Only for the brave. Very violent. Children under seventeen not admitted." That's not for me.
M: Well, that leaves only one other film: that comedy *Fracas in Caracas*, which we've already seen. I'd rather not see it again, would you?
F: Actually, no. It was pretty funny, but once is enough. It wasn't the best thing I've ever seen, anyway.
M: Well, it sounds like *Follow Me to Rio* is it. How about you follow me to the movies!
F: Deal!

Language and culture

- A *trailer* is a movie preview that is shown in movie theaters before the full-length film. It's a short advertisement that includes scenes from the movie and is designed to make viewers want to see it.
- A *fracas* is a noisy fight. This term usually appears in writing and is rarely used in spoken English.

Option: (+10 minutes) To extend the activity with speaking practice, have students work in small groups to discuss which movie they would choose to see. Encourage them to give reasons; for example, *I'd choose to see* Streets of Saigon. *I like police dramas and animation, and I really love weird movies.*

B Complete the conversations . . .

Suggested teaching time:	3 minutes	Your actual teaching time:

- Tell students to use the pictures to identify the film genres. Then have them write the genres in the appropriate blanks. To provide extra support, write the words they will need to complete this exercise on the board: *comedy, action, science fiction, musical, drama.*

- Before students do the rest of the exercise, remind them to be aware of the placement of adverbial expressions (*lately, just, still,* etc.) and to look for past time references when deciding between using the simple past and present perfect.

- Review answers with the class.

C Complete each statement or question . . .

Suggested teaching time:	2 minutes	Your actual teaching time:

- Have students underline times or dates in the past (2. last Tuesday; 3. I was a child; 6. 6:30.) and circle periods of time (1. Two weeks; 4. more than an hour; 5. over thirty years.) Point out that in item 3, *I was a child* functions as a time in the past.

- Review the present perfect with *since* + a time or date in the past and *for* + a period of time.

- Have students compare answers in pairs.

WRITING

Suggested teaching time:	15 minutes	Your actual teaching time:

- To help students organize their arguments, draw the chart below on the board. Model possible arguments by inviting individual students to the board to fill in their ideas.

- Have students fill in the chart with their own ideas. Then have them use the chart to help them write their paragraphs. Also refer students to the article on page 22 and the opinions on page 23 for ideas.

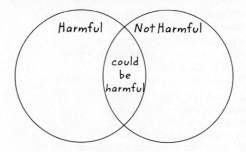

Option: **WRITING BOOSTER** *(Teaching notes p. T144)*

 Graphic Organizers; Writing Process Worksheets

 Top Notch Pop Song Video and Karaoke Video

 **Digital Games**

ORAL REVIEW

Before the first activity, give students a few minutes of silent time to look over the picture.

Pair work 1

Suggested teaching time:	12 minutes	Your actual teaching time:

- To introduce the activity, call on a volunteer to read the movie titles and times at the top of the illustration. Tell pairs they will guess the genres, imagine what the movies are about, and choose actors to star in the movies. Read the model to the students.

- Refer students to the list of movie genres on page 18 and the list of adjectives to describe movies on page 20.

- Walk around the room as pairs work. Provide help as needed.

- As a class, have groups share their ideas about the movies.

> **Possible responses . . .**
>
> *Cult of Blood* is a horror movie. It's about a group of teens on vacation in Texas. People in their group die. It's pretty violent. The movie stars Kristen Stewart, Robert Pattinson, and Jackie Earle Haley.
>
> *Ticket to the Moon* is an animated movie about some dogs that fly to the moon. It's a comedy. We chose Steve Carell and Cameron Diaz to star in this movie.

Pair work 2

Suggested teaching time:	5 minutes	Your actual teaching time:

- Model the activity by role-playing an example conversation with a more confident student.

> **Possible responses . . .**
>
> **A:** I'm sorry I'm late. I couldn't find a parking space.
> **B:** I got tickets for *Ticket to the Moon* at 8:00. I hope that's OK.
> **A:** I love a good science-fiction movie. How much do I owe?
> **B:** Nothing. It's on me.
> **A:** Thanks. Next time it's my treat.
>
> **A:** Do you want to see *Ticket to the Moon*?
> **B:** Actually, I'd rather not. The reviews were terrible.
> **A:** How about *Cult of Blood* at 9:00?
> **B:** OK. I like horror films. They say this one is very good.
>
> **A:** So, what did you think of the movie?
> **B:** Actually, not much. It was too weird.
> **A:** I thought it was great.
> **B:** Yes, but you like sci-fi films. I don't.
> **A:** Well, that's what makes the world go 'round.
>
> **A:** Which would you rather see—*Ticket to the Moon* or *Love in Paradise*? It doesn't matter to me.
> **B:** Well, I've already seen *Ticket to the Moon*.
> **A:** I just hope *Love in Paradise* isn't silly.
> **B:** My friend said it was the best romantic drama she's ever seen.

Option: *(+10 minutes)* To challenge students, have them make up short reviews for each movie in the picture. Make sure they include the genre and use at least two adjectives.

Option: Oral Progress Assessment

- Use the illustration on page 25 for an oral test. Encourage students to use the language in this unit.

- Invite a student to role-play a conversation with you. Play the role of the woman holding the tickets, and have the student play the role of the man.

- Evaluate the student on intelligibility, fluency, correct use of grammar, and appropriate use of vocabulary.

 Oral Progress Assessment Charts

Option: *Top Notch* Project

Have students prepare real movie reviews and then present their reviews to the class.

- Write on the board a list of things students can include in their reviews. For example: *title, genre, movie stars, director, what the movie is about, adjectives to describe the movie.*

Idea: Students research movies in ads or on the Internet and prepare posters with pictures and their own written reviews.

- When the groups have finished their reviews, have a spokesperson from each group read the review(s) to the class.

EXTRAS

On the Internet:
- Online Teacher Resources: pearsonelt.com/topnotch3e/

Additional printable resources on the ActiveTeach:
- Assessment
- Just for Fun
- *Top Notch Pop* Song Activities
- *Top Notch TV* Video Program and Activity Worksheets
- Supplementary Pronunciation Lessons
- Conversation Activator Video Scripts
- Audioscripts and Answer Keys
- Unit Study Guides

ORAL REVIEW

PAIR WORK

1 With a partner, guess the genre of the three movies. Imagine what the movies are about and choose actors to star in the movies. Present your ideas to the class. Use the following as a model.

We think "Love in Paradise" is a romantic movie. It's about a man and a woman who meet and fall in love in Hawaii.

2 Create a conversation for one of the couples. Say as much as you can. For example:

It's 7:30. Did we miss "Love in Paradise"?

SOLD OUT

Cult of Blood
7:20   9:00   Midnight

Love in Paradise
7:15   9:45

Ticket to the Moon
8:00   10:00

✓ NOW I CAN

- ☐ Apologize for being late.
- ☐ Discuss preferences for movie genres.
- ☐ Describe and recommend movies.
- ☐ Discuss effects of violence on viewers.

COMMUNICATION GOALS
1 Leave and take a message.
2 Check into a hotel.
3 Request housekeeping services.
4 Choose a hotel.

UNIT 3 Staying in Hotels

PREVIEW

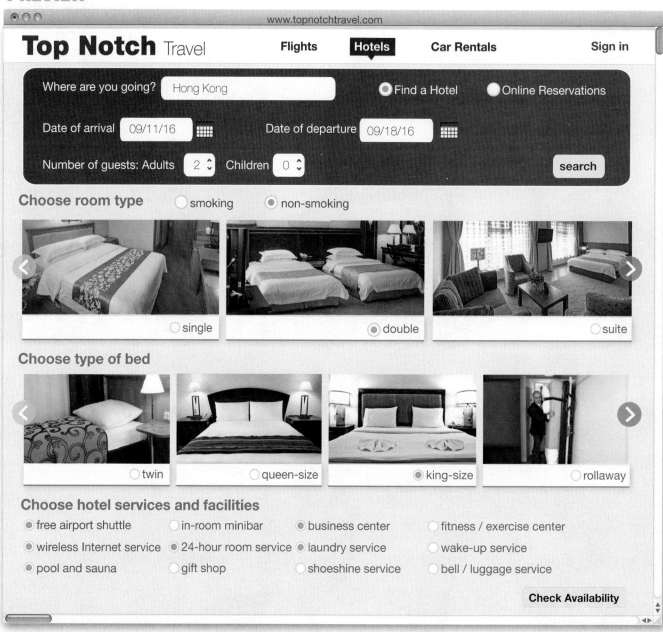

DIGITAL FLASH CARDS

A ▶2:02 **VOCABULARY** • *Hotel room types and kinds of beds* Read and listen. Then listen again and repeat.

1 a single room   4 a smoking room   7 a queen-size bed
2 a double room   5 a non-smoking room   8 a king-size bed
3 a suite   6 a twin bed   9 a rollaway bed

B **PAIR WORK** Have you—or has someone you know—ever stayed at a hotel? Tell your partner about it, using the Vocabulary and the facilities from the website.

UNIT **3** Staying in Hotels

PREVIEW

Before Exercise A, give students a few minutes of silent time to examine the website.

Suggested teaching time:	10–12 minutes	Your actual teaching time:	

- For a warm-up, ask *Do you know names of hotel chains?* (Hilton, Intercontinental, Marriott, etc.)
- Have students skim the list of hotel services. Explain vocabulary as needed. For example, an *airport shuttle* is a small bus that picks up or drops off hotel guests at the airport.
- Ask *What are the benefits of making online hotel reservations?* (Possible responses: You can access hotel information from anywhere at any time; you can see pictures of the rooms; you can get information about hotel services; you can check availability and make reservations without a phone call.)

FYI: The Speaking exercise on page 27 will cover hotel services in more detail.

Language and culture
- A *suite* is a group of rooms that connect together.

A ▶2:02 Vocabulary

Suggested teaching time:	2–5 minutes	Your actual teaching time:	

 **Vocabulary Flash Card Player**

- To prepare students for the activity, have them skim the list of words and phrases. Tell students to scan the website for each term and to look at the pictures to help them understand.
- After students read and listen once, ask:
  How many beds are in a single room? (One.) *In a double room?* (Two.)
  When is a suite a good choice? (Possible responses: When the hotel guest needs a meeting room; when the hotel guest wants to work.)
  What type of room do you prefer in a hotel?
  Which is bigger, a twin or a queen-size bed? (A queen-size bed.)
  Which is smaller, a king-size bed or a rollaway? (A rollaway.)
- Have students listen again and repeat.

Language and culture
- A *single room* can also be called a *single,* and a *double room* can be called a *double.* Beds can also be called *a twin* (the same as a single), *a queen, a king,* and *a rollaway.* A *full-size* or *double bed* is larger than a twin and smaller than a queen. *Smoking* and *non-smoking* are abbreviations for *smoking room* and *non-smoking room.*

Option: (+10 minutes) On the board, write the list of possible hotel guests below. Have students work in pairs to decide the best hotel room features for these guests, using the pictures to help them. Then have students form groups of four and have them share their ideas.

Possible Hotel Guests
1. *a student, non-smoker*
2. *a family of five non-smokers (parents and three small children)*
3. *a husband and wife, smokers*
4. *two friends, non-smokers*
5. *two co-workers, one smoker*

B Pair work

Suggested teaching time:	5 minutes	Your actual teaching time:	

- For a warm-up, poll the class. Ask *Has anyone here ever stayed in a hotel? Who stays at hotels often? How often?*
- After pairs discuss the question in the book, ask students to share their opinions with the class. If students have never stayed in a hotel and don't know anyone who has, tell them to imagine what type of room they would like to stay in. Have them compare ideas with a partner.

C ▶2:03 Photo story

Suggested teaching time:	10–15 minutes	Your actual teaching time:

- To prepare students for the activity, tell them to look at the photos. Ask:

  Where are the people? (In a hotel.)

  Who are the people? (A guest and a hotel clerk.)

  What is the woman doing? (She is either entering or leaving the hotel.)

- Have students read and listen to the conversation. Check comprehension by asking:

  What is the guest at the desk doing? (She's checking out, leaving the hotel.)

  Did she enjoy her stay? (Yes, it was satisfactory; very nice.)

  Does she pay with cash or a credit card? (With a credit card.)

  How is she getting to the airport? (She's taking the shuttle.)

  What does she want to do before she leaves? (Pick up a few things at the gift shop.)

  Who is going to help her with her luggage? (The bellman.)

Language and culture

- *Check out* means to pay one's bill and leave a hotel. It is the opposite of *check in.*

D Focus on language

Suggested teaching time:	3 minutes	Your actual teaching time:

- To prepare students for the activity, point out the underlined words in the Photo Story. Read them or call on a student to read them aloud.

- As pairs match words from the story with the definitions in the exercise, walk around the room and help students as needed.

- Review answers and explanations with the class.

E Think and explain

Suggested teaching time:	5 minutes	Your actual teaching time:

- Model the activity by calling on a student to read the first sentence. Ask *Is this true or false?* (False.) Have students explain why it is false. (The woman is checking out.)

- Have students skim the Photo Story individually to find the answers. Walk around the room and help students as needed.

- Have students compare answers in pairs. If necessary, review answers with the class.

Option: (+10 minutes) To challenge students, have pairs create a series of true and false statements for another pair to answer using the information in the Photo Story. Tell students not to use the four items from the exercise. Help students as needed. Then have pairs exchange statements with another pair and decide which statements are true or false.

SPEAKING

Suggested teaching time:	10–15 minutes	Your actual teaching time:

▶2:04 Hotel services

- Before they do this exercise, have students listen and repeat the hotel services vocabulary in the box.

- To ensure comprehension, ask about services and call on individuals to explain them. For example:

  A: *What is [a wake-up service]?*

  B: *A wake-up service provides a phone call to wake a hotel guest up at a requested time.*

- After pairs complete the matching part of the exercise, ask *Which services are important to you?* Go over the sample answer in quotes. Then have them discuss which services they think are important.

- Review answers with the class. Ask students to share the services they wrote.

Workbook

C ▶2:03 **PHOTO STORY** Read and listen to someone checking out of a hotel.

Guest: Good morning. I'm checking out of Room 604.

Clerk: I'll be happy to help you with that. Was your stay satisfactory?

Guest: Yes. Very nice. Thanks.

Clerk: Did you have anything from the minibar last night?

Guest: Just a bottle of water.

Clerk: OK. Let me add that to your bill.

Clerk: And would you like to put this on your Vista card?

Guest: Yes, I would, please. By the way, I need to go to the airport.

Clerk: Certainly. If you're in a hurry, I'll call you a taxi. But if you'd rather take the free airport shuttle, there's one leaving in twenty minutes.

Guest: Great. I'll take the shuttle. Why pay for a taxi? And that'll give me time to pick up a few things at the gift shop before I leave.

Clerk: No problem. I'll ask the bellman to give you a hand with your luggage. He'll let you know when the shuttle's here.

Guest: Thanks so much.

Clerk: You're welcome. Have a safe trip, and we hope to see you again.

D **FOCUS ON LANGUAGE** Find underlined words and phrases in the Photo Story with the same meaning.

1 pay with
   put this on

2 help
   give you a hand

3 leaving
   checking out of

4 OK
   satisfactory

5 don't have much time
   're in a hurry

E **THINK AND EXPLAIN** Explain why each statement is false, using information from the Photo Story.

1 The guest is staying for a few more days.

2 The guest has complaints about the hotel.
   1. The guest says she's checking out.
   2. The guest says her stay was very nice.

3 The guest pays the bill in cash.

4 The shuttle is arriving in an hour.
   3. The guest says she'd like to put this on her Vista card.
   4. The clerk says the shuttle will be leaving in twenty minutes.

SPEAKING

Match each picture with a hotel service from the list. Which services are important to you? Explain why.

1 wake-up service   2 bell service   3 shoeshine service   4 airport shuttle

5 laundry service   6 minibar   7 room service

▶2:04 **Hotel services**
airport shuttle
bell service
laundry service
minibar
room service
shoeshine service
wake-up service

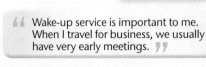

" Wake-up service is important to me. When I travel for business, we usually have very early meetings. "

GOAL Leave and take a message

CONVERSATION MODEL

A ▶2:05 Read and listen to someone leaving a message.

A: Hello? I'd like to speak to Anne Smith. She's a guest.

B: I'll ring that room for you . . . I'm sorry. She's not answering. Would you like to leave a message?

A: Yes. Please tell her Tim Klein called. I'll meet her at the hotel at three this afternoon.

B: Is that all?

A: Yes, thanks.

B ▶2:06 **RHYTHM AND INTONATION** Listen again and repeat. Then practice the Conversation Model with a partner.

GRAMMAR *The future with* will

You can use will or won't + a base form to talk about the future.

Contractions
will = 'll
will not = **won't**

Affirmative statements

He will call back tomorrow.

Negative statements

We won't be at the hotel this afternoon.

Questions

Will she meet us at the restaurant?   Yes, she will. / No, she won't.
Will they take a taxi to the hotel?   Yes, they will. / No, they won't.

When will the shuttle arrive? (In about ten minutes.)
What will you do in New York? (Visit the Empire State Building.)
Where will they go on their next vacation? (Probably Los Angeles.)

Who will Ana call when she arrives? (She'll call the front desk.)
BUT
Who will call the front desk? (Ana will.)

> **Remember:** You can also talk about the future with be going to, the present continuous, or the simple present tense.
> I'm going to call again at 4:00.
> They're meeting at noon at the hotel.
> She arrives on PanAir Flight 24 tonight.

> **GRAMMAR BOOSTER** p. 129
> • Will: expansion
>   Will and be going to
>   other uses of will
> • Can, should, and have to: future meaning

A **FIND THE GRAMMAR** Look at the Conversation Model again. Circle two uses of will.

B **GRAMMAR PRACTICE** Complete the statements and questions in the messages, using will or won't. Use contractions when possible.

1 Message for Ms. Yalmaz: Ms. Calloway called. ......**She'll call**...... back later this evening.
   she / call

2 Message for Mr. Ballinger: ...**your colleagues won't be**... at the Clayton Hotel until after 5:00.
   your colleagues / not / be

3 Message for John Torrence: Your boss called. ......**He'll need**...... a recommendation for a nice restaurant for tonight.
   he / need

4 Message from Mark Smith: ......**Who will take**...... us to the airport after the meeting?
   who / take

5 Message for Ms. Harris: ...**Your brother won't arrive**... at the airport before 6:00.
   your brother / not / arrive

6 Message from Janis Torres: ...**The conference call will start**... at 3:00 tomorrow, London time.
   the conference call / start

7 Message from Mrs. Park: ......**Do I have to**...... come in to the office early tomorrow?
   I / have to

8 Message for Ms. Grady: ...**Where will you meet**... us tomorrow?
   where / you / meet

CONVERSATION MODEL

A ▶2:05 Read and listen . . .

Suggested teaching time:	2 minutes	Your actual teaching time:

This conversation strategy is implicit in the model:
• Say "Would you like to leave a message?" if someone isn't available.

• Have students look at the pictures. Ask *What are the people in the pictures doing?* (Talking to each other on the phone.)
• To check understanding, have students read and listen again and then ask comprehension questions:
  What is the name of the caller? (Tim Klein.)
  Who is he calling? (Anne Smith.)
  Where is he calling her? (At her hotel.)
  What message does he leave for her? (He'll meet her at the hotel at 3:00 this afternoon.)

Language and culture
• Another common way to say *She's not answering* is *There's no answer.*
• *to ring* means to phone or to call someone. In North America, *ring* is usually used by receptionists; *call* is used more frequently in other situations.
• *Is that all?* in this situation means *Is that the entire message?* Be sure to use rising intonation with this question.

B ▶2:06 Rhythm and intonation

Suggested teaching time:	3 minutes	Your actual teaching time:

• Have students repeat each line chorally. Make sure they:
  ◦ use rising intonation for *Hello?* and falling intonation for *I'd like to speak to Anne Smith.*
  ◦ put stress on *Anne Smith* and on *Tim Klein.*
  ◦ use rising intonation for *Would you like to leave a message?* and *Is that all?*
• Explain to students that rising intonation is especially important with the question *Is that all?* If the intonation is flat or goes downward, the question can sound rude.

GRAMMAR

Suggested teaching time:	5–10 minutes	Your actual teaching time:

• As you introduce the first grammar rule, highlight that *will / won't* are used with the base form of a verb.
• Point out to students that the short answer with *will*, as with other modals, appears without the base form and that in affirmative short answers *will* is not contracted, but in negative short answers *will* is contracted. For example:
  A: *Will you be at the party tomorrow?*
  B: *Yes, I will. / No, I won't.*

• As you read the Remember tip and the example sentences, point out the future time (4:00) used with the present continuous and the future time word (tonight) used with the simple present tense.
• Go over the information in the Contractions box.
• Go over the questions with students. Point out the placement of *will* and the base form in each question.

FYI: Although grammar books often provide clear usage distinctions between the forms above with future meaning, these distinctions are rarely observed in practice. In spoken English, the form that is used often depends on the formality of the conversation.

Language and culture
• *Can't* and *won't be able to* are often used to soften refusals that would sound harsh if stated directly. For example, *I can't / won't be able to meet you for lunch.* sounds much more polite than *I won't meet you for lunch* or *I'm not going to meet you for lunch.*

Option: GRAMMAR BOOSTER (*Teaching notes p. T129*)

🖨 **Inductive Grammar Charts**

A Find the grammar

Suggested teaching time:	2 minutes	Your actual teaching time:

• After students complete the activity, review the answers with the class. (I'll ring that room . . .; I'll meet her . . . .)

B Grammar practice

Suggested teaching time:	3 minutes	Your actual teaching time:

• To prepare students, tell them to skim the sentences. *Which two sentences are negative?* (Items 2 and 5.) *How do you form the negative with* will? (Won't.)
• After students complete the exercise, have them compare answers in pairs.
• Review answers with the class and answer any questions.

 Extra Grammar Exercises

C ▶2:07 Listen for details

Suggested teaching time:	5 minutes	Your actual teaching time:

- Have students skim the phrases on the message slips.
- Have students listen and complete as much of each message slip as they can and then listen again, filling in any information they missed.
- Students can compare answers in groups.

AUDIOSCRIPT

CONVERSATION 1
M: Hi. Can I speak with Judy Diller, please?
F: You bet. Who shall I say is calling?
M: Marc Pearl.
F: Oh, I'm sorry, Mr. Pearl. She stepped out. Can I take a message?
M: Sure. Please tell her I called. I'll be at the Savoy Hotel for the next two days. I'd like her to call me back.
F: You got it. Could you spell your last name for me?
M: Of course. P-E-A-R-L.

CONVERSATION 2 [F = Australian English]
F: Hello. I'd like to speak to a guest named Hank Pitt.
M: I'll ring him up for you . . . I'm sorry. There's no answer. Would you like to call back later?
F: Actually, I'd like to leave a message. Please tell him Vicky Denkus called. I'll be at 444-0987 till six o'clock. He can call me at that number.
M: That's D-E-N . . .
F: D-E-N-K-U-S.
M: I'll give him your message, Ms. Denkus.

CONVERSATION 3
F: Hi. This is Carol Braun calling. Is Collin Mack in?
M: No, he isn't, ma'am. He's out of the country till next week.
F: Oh. Well, can you give him a message for me?
M: Of course.
F: Please tell him Carol Braun called. That's B-R-A-U-N. And I'll call him again next week.
M: Very good.

CONVERSATION 4
M: Hello. I'd like to speak with Patricia Carlton in Room 1408.
F: One moment, please . . . Sorry, sir. There's no answer at that extension. Would you like to leave a message?
M: Yes, please. This is Sam Hill calling. H-I-L-L. I'll definitely be at the meeting at 3:00. So I'll see her then.
F: I'll see that she gets your message.

PRONUNCIATION

A ▶2:08 Notice that each contraction . . .

Suggested teaching time:	3 minutes	Your actual teaching time:

 Pronunciation Coach Video

- Have students read the sentences. Make sure they pronounce each contraction as one syllable and then have them listen to the audio to check.
- Have students listen again and repeat in the pauses.

🖨 **Pronunciation Activities**

B Look at the message slips . . .

Suggested teaching time:	2 minutes	Your actual teaching time:

- Have students work in pairs..

NOW YOU CAN Leave and take a message

A Frame your ideas

Suggested teaching time:	5 minutes	Your actual teaching time:

- Write the questions below on the board. Make sure that students answer the questions in each message.
    1. Who are you calling?
    2. What is the phone number?
    3. What do you need to tell this person?
- Walk around the room and help students as needed.

B Conversation activator

Suggested teaching time:	10–15 minutes	Your actual teaching time:

 **Conversation Activator Video**

- *Note:* You can print the script or you can show a running transcript on the video player on the ActiveTeach. The script also appears on page 182 of this Teacher's Edition.
- Make sure students fill out the form completely.

DON'T STOP! Encourage students to use the ideas in the box and the language in the Recycle box to continue their conversations.

- For more support, play the Conversation Activator Video before students do this activity themselves. In Scene 1, the actors use different words in the gaps from the ones in the Conversation Model. In Scene 2, the actors extend the conversation. After each scene, ask students how the model has been changed by the actors.
- Model extending the conversation by role-playing a phone call with a more confident student. Use language such as *Could you repeat that?* and *How do you spell that?*
- Have pairs role-play their phone calls. Tell students to write down each message and to check with their partners to make sure they understood it correctly.

🖨 **Conversation Activator Video Script; Conversation Activator Pair Work Cards; Learning Strategies**

C Change partners

Suggested teaching time:	5–10 minutes	Your actual teaching time:

- Assign students new partners and have them create new conversations, leaving new messages. Walk around the room and listen for the use of recycled language.
- Invite pairs to share their role plays with the class.

EXTRAS

Workbook or MyEnglishLab

 Speaking Activities: Unit 3, Activity 1

C ▶2:07 **LISTEN FOR DETAILS** Listen to the phone messages. Then listen again and complete each message slip, according to the information you hear. Use the future with <u>will</u> in each message.

1

☎ **PHONE MESSAGE**

FOR: *Judy Diller*
FROM: ☑ Mr. ☐ Ms.
 ☐ Mrs. ☐ Miss *Pearl*
☐ Please call ☐ Will call again
☐ Wants to see you ☐ Returned your call

Message: *He'll be . . . at the Savoy Hotel for two days.*

2

☎ **PHONE MESSAGE**

FOR: *Hank Pitt*
FROM: ☐ Mr. ☑ Ms.
 ☐ Mrs. ☐ Miss *(Vicky) Denkus*
☑ Please call ☐ Will call again
☐ Wants to see you ☐ Returned your call

Message: *She'll be at 444-0987 till 6:00.*

3

☎ **PHONE MESSAGE**

FOR: *Collin Mack*
FROM: ☐ Mr. ☐ Ms.
 ☐ Mrs. ☑ Miss *(Carol) Braun*
☐ Please call ☑ Will call again
☐ Wants to see you ☐ Returned your call

Message: *She'll call next week.*

4

☎ **PHONE MESSAGE**

FOR: *Patricia Carlton*
FROM: ☑ Mr. ☐ Ms.
 ☐ Mrs. ☐ Miss *(Sam) Hill*
☐ Please call ☐ Will call again
☐ Wants to see you ☐ Returned your call

Message: *He'll be at the meeting at 3:00. He'll see you then.*

PRONUNCIATION *Contractions with* <u>will</u>

A ▶2:08 Notice that each contraction is one syllable. Read and listen. Then listen again and repeat.

1 I'll call back later.

2 She'll be at the Frank Hotel.

3 He'll bring his laptop to the meeting.

4 We'll need a taxi.

5 You'll have to leave at 6:30.

6 They'll meet you in twenty minutes.

B Look at the message slips you wrote in Exercise C above. Read each message aloud, using the correct pronunciation of the contracted form of <u>will</u>.

NOW YOU CAN Leave and take a message

A **FRAME YOUR IDEAS** On a separate sheet of paper, write four messages you could leave someone.

B **CONVERSATION ACTIVATOR** With a partner, change the Conversation Model. Leave your own messages. Your partner completes the message slip. Then change roles.

A: Hello? I'd like to speak to ....
B: I'll ring that room for you . . . I'm sorry. ....
 Would you like to leave a message?
A: Yes. Please tell ....
B: Is that all?
A: ....

WHILE YOU WERE OUT . . .
FOR: _____

☐ Mr. ☐ Ms. ☐ Mrs. ☐ Miss _____ called.
Phone: _____
☐ Please call back
☐ Will call again

Message: _____

DON'T STOP!

- Leave another message.
- Confirm that you've understood the message correctly.
- Ask for more information.

🔁 **RECYCLE THIS LANGUAGE.**

How do you spell your last name?
Could you please spell that for me?
Could you please repeat that?
What's your ___?

C **CHANGE PARTNERS** Leave other messages.

GOAL Check into a hotel

GRAMMAR *The real conditional*

Conditional sentences express the results of actions or conditions.

if clause (the condition)   result clause (the result)
If the business center is still open,   I'll check my e-mail.

Real conditional sentences express factual or future results. When the result is future, use will in the result clause.
(A factual result: Use present tense in both clauses.)
If a hotel room **has** wireless Internet, guests **don't have to go** to a business center to check e-mail.
(A future result: Use present tense in the if clause and future with will in the result clause.)
If she **checks in** early, she**'ll get** the room she wants.

Questions
If they **don't have** a non-smoking room, **will** you **stay** at a different hotel?
Where **will** you **go** if they **don't have** a room for tonight?
If there **are** no rental cars at the airport, what **will** they **do**?

Be careful!
Never use will in the if clause.
If you hurry, you'll catch the shuttle.   NOT   If you ~~will hurry~~, you'll catch the shuttle.

In conditional sentences, the clauses can be reversed with no change in meaning.
In writing, use a comma when the if clause comes first.
If the fitness center is still open, I'll go swimming.
I'll go swimming if the fitness center is still open.

> **GRAMMAR BOOSTER** p. 130
> • The real conditional: present and future; usage and common errors

---

A   **UNDERSTAND THE GRAMMAR**   Write <u>factual</u> if the conditional sentence expresses a fact.
Write <u>future</u> if it expresses a future result.

<u>factual</u> **1** If you make your reservation in advance, you save a lot of money.

<u>future</u> **2** She'll miss the 11:00 shuttle if she doesn't check out early today.

<u>factual</u> **3** If a guest is in a hurry, a taxi is faster than the shuttle.

<u>future</u> **4** We will call your room this evening if there are any messages.

<u>factual</u> **5** If you request a suite, you usually get free breakfasts.

<u>future</u> **6** You'll have to pay a daily fee if you want wireless service.

B   **GRAMMAR PRACTICE**   Complete the real conditional statements and questions with correct forms of the verbs.

1 .....<u>You won't be able</u>..... to order breakfast at the restaurant if .....<u>you don't hurry</u>..... .
         you / not / be able   you / not / hurry

2 If ....<u>they get</u>.......... a suite on their next cruise, ...<u>they'll be</u>.......... a lot more comfortable.
         they / get   they / be

3 .....<u>Will you reserve</u>..... a room with a king-size bed if ....<u>it is</u>.............. affordable?
         you / reserve   it / be

4 .....<u>Will someone give</u>..... me a hand if ....<u>I need</u>.............. help with my luggage?
         someone / give   I / need

5 Who ....<u>will we call</u>.......... if ....<u>we need</u>.......... laundry service?
         we / call   we / need

6 ....<u>Will I have to</u>.......... pay if ....<u>I use</u>.............. wireless Internet service?
         I / have to   I / use

7 If ....<u>you request</u>.......... a rollaway bed, ...<u>someone will bring</u>.... it to your room.
         you / request   someone / bring

8 Where ....<u>does she go</u>.......... if ....<u>she needs</u>.......... to make copies?
         she / go   she / need

GRAMMAR

Suggested teaching time:	10–15 minutes	Your actual teaching time:

- Go over the first rule and example. Write the example on the board. Explain that the *if* clause gives information about an action or condition: the business center is still open. The result clauses gives information about what will happen as a result of that action or condition: *I'll check my e-mail.*

- Read through the real conditional rules and examples. Make sure that students understand that the present tense is used in both clauses for factual results, but the future tense with *will* is used in the result clause for future results. Write the following examples on the board and ask students to tell you which tense to use in each:

  Factual result: If students have a test, they ___ (study) a lot. (Study.)

  Future result: If I have a test tomorrow, I ___ (study) a lot. (Will study.)

- Go over the examples of questions. Tell students that they are all questions about future results. Point out that word order in the *if* clause does not change for questions, but in the result clause, *will* comes before the subject (*will you stay. . . ?*).

- Direct students' attention to the Be careful! information. To test understanding of the first rule, write the following examples on the board:

  1. *If we will miss the bus, we will take a taxi.*
  2. *If we miss the bus, we will take a taxi.*

  Ask, *Which sentence is correct?* (2.) Cross out *will* (miss) in sentence 1.

- Go over the remaining rules about reversing clauses and adding commas in the Be careful! information.

Option: **GRAMMAR BOOSTER** *(Teaching notes p. T130)*

A Understand the grammar

Suggested teaching time:	5 minutes	Your actual teaching time:

- Remind students that sentences that express future results have *'ll*, *will*, or *won't* in the result clause. Also point out that the result clause can come first in the sentence.

- Review answers with the class.

B Grammar practice

Suggested teaching time:	5–7 minutes	Your actual teaching time:

- Complete the first item with the class. Ask *Which part of the sentence do you add* will *to: the* if *clause or the result clause?* (The result clause.) *Which part of this sentence is the result clause?* (The first part.) Call on volunteers to complete the item and write the answer on the board: *You won't be able to order breakfast at the restaurant if you don't hurry.*

- Have students complete the rest of the exercise in pairs.

- Review answers with the class.

 **Extra Grammar Exercises**

AUDIOSCRIPT Continued, for page T31 (Listen for Details)

M: Let me check. Yes. There's a room available on the eighth floor.
 F: Great. Thanks.
M: Are all those bags yours, ma'am?
 F: Yes, they are.
M: I'll ask the bellman to give you a hand.
 F: Thanks so much.

CONVERSATION 2
M: Hi, I'm checking in. The name's Lewis.
 F: Yes, sir. That's a single—non-smoking—with a twin bed?
M: There must be some mistake. My wife and son are joining me tonight. I'm sure I asked for a king-size bed and a rollaway.
 F: I'm so sorry, sir. Let me check . . . OK. No problem. We have a non-smoking room available with a king-size bed. I'll ask the bellman to bring up that rollaway for you right away.
M: Thanks.

CONVERSATION 3 [M = Japanese]
M: Good morning. I have a reservation under the name Fujimoto. That's F-U-J-I-M-O-T-O.
 F: Fuji . . . moto. OK. That'll be a double for three nights?
M: That's right.
 F: And would you like a queen or a king-size bed?
M: A queen is fine, thanks.
 F: And you reserved a smoking room?
M: Correct. By the way, is it too late to get breakfast?
 F: Actually, the restaurant closes in twenty minutes. Why don't you go ahead and have breakfast now, and I'll finish checking you in when you're finished. I'll ask the bellman to take your bags to your room.
M: Perfect. Thank you.

CONVERSATION 4
F1: Hi, I'm checking in. The reservation's under the name Anderson.
F2: Yes, ma'am. That's a double room—smoking?
F1: A double room? Actually, I reserved a suite. Non-smoking.
F2: I'm so sorry, ma'am. Let me check again.
F1: I have important meetings all week. So I really need that suite.
F2: I'm sorry. . . that was <u>Janet</u> Anderson, right?
F1: Janet? I'm sorry. It's <u>Diane</u>. Diane Anderson.
F2: Diane Anderson. . . I do apologize. I'm showing an executive suite for you, non-smoking with a king-size bed.
F1: Thank you!
F2: I'll get the bellman to help you with your bags.

CONVERSATION MODEL

A Read and listen . . .

Suggested teaching time:	2 minutes	Your actual teaching time:

These conversation strategies are implicit in the model:
- Say "Let's see" to indicate you're checking information.
- Make a formal polite request with "May I ___?"
- Say "Here you go" when handing someone something.
- Use "By the way, . . ." to introduce new information.

- Have students look at the picture. Ask *Who are the people?* (A guest and a hotel clerk.) *What is the woman giving the clerk?* (Her credit card.)

- After students have read and listened to the conversation, write the phrases below on the board. Ask students to explain them or to suggest other ways of saying them.
  The name's Baker (My name is Baker. OR The reservation is under the name Baker.)
  a double (One double bed.)
  non-smoking (You can't smoke in the room.)

Option: (+5 minutes) To extend the activity, have students listen again. Ask:
Is the woman arriving or leaving? (Arriving: "I'm checking in.")
How many nights is Ms. Baker staying at the hotel? (Two nights.)
How is she going to pay for the room? (With a credit card.)
What time do you think it is? (Almost 9:00; the restaurant is going to close soon.)

B Rhythm and intonation

Suggested teaching time:	3 minutes	Your actual teaching time:

- Have students repeat each line. Make sure they:
  ◦ use rising intonation for *Non-smoking?*
  ◦ say *By the way* without pausing between words
  ◦ use rising intonation after *. . . is the restaurant still open?*

Option: (+2 minutes) For additional practice with fluency, have students use the version of the Conversation Model without pauses. Tell them to try to speak in unison with the audio.

C ▶ 2:11 Listen for details

Suggested teaching time:	5–8 minutes	Your actual teaching time:

- Be sure students understand these expressions: *On a high floor* means not near the ground floor; to *give someone a hand* means to help someone do something.

- Have students listen to the conversations and complete the chart.

- To check their answers, have students listen again and then compare their answers in pairs.

- Review answers with the class.

AUDIOSCRIPT

CONVERSATION 1 [M = Indian]
F: I'm checking in. The name is Patel. P-A-T-E-L.
M: Welcome, Ms. Patel. That'll be a king-size bed for two nights, correct?
F: That's right.
M: Smoking or non-smoking?
F: Non-smoking, please. And can I get a room on a high floor?

AUDIOSCRIPT continues on page T30

🖨 Learning Strategies

NOW YOU CAN Check into a hotel

A Conversation activator

Suggested teaching time:	10 minutes	Your actual teaching time:

🎥 Conversation Activator Video

- *Note:* You can print the script or you can show a running transcript on the video player on the ActiveTeach. The script also appears on page 183 of this Teacher's Edition.

- Tell students to look at the hours of operation of the various facilities in the pictures. Ask volunteers to read the captions. Ask *Which of these facilities are important to you in a hotel?*

- Give students a few moments to brainstorm other facilities at hotels they might use.

- Be sure to reinforce the use of the conversation strategies. For example, make sure students pause and check information after saying "Let's see."

- Model the activity by role-playing a conversation with a more confident student.

DON'T STOP! Extend the conversation. Encourage students to ask each other additional questions about services and facilities.

- For more support, play the Conversation Activator Video before students do this activity themselves. In Scene 1, the actors use different words in the gaps from the ones in the Conversation Model. In Scene 2, the actors extend the conversation. After each scene, ask students how the model has been changed by the actors.

🖨 Conversation Activator Video Script; Conversation Activator Pair Work Cards

B Change partners

Suggested teaching time:	5–10 minutes	Your actual teaching time:

- Tell students to form new pairs by working with the person on their left.

- If time permits, have volunteers present their conversations to the class.

EXTRAS

Workbook or MyEnglishLab

🖨 Speaking Activities: Unit 3, Activity 2

CONVERSATION MODEL

A ▶ 2:09 Read and listen to someone checking into a hotel.

A: Hi. I'm checking in. The name's Baker.

B: Let's see. That's a double for two nights. Non-smoking?

A: That's right.

B: May I have your credit card?

A: Here you go. By the way, is the restaurant still open?

B: It closes at 9:00. But if you hurry, you'll make it.

A: Thanks.

B ▶ 2:10 **RHYTHM AND INTONATION** Listen again and repeat. Then practice the Conversation Model with a partner.

C ▶ 2:11 **LISTEN FOR DETAILS** Listen to guests check into a hotel. Complete the information about what each guest needs.

	Type of bed(s)	Non-smoking room?	Bell service?
1	king-size	☑	☑
2	king-size & rollaway	☑	☑
3	queen	☐	☑
4	king-size	☑	☑

NOW YOU CAN Check into a hotel

DIGITAL VIDEO

A **CONVERSATION ACTIVATOR** With a partner, role-play checking into a hotel. Change the room and bed type, and ask about a hotel facility from the pictures. Then change roles.

A: Hi, I'm checking in. The name's ....
B: Let's see. That's a .... for .... night(s). Non-smoking?
A: ....
B: May I have your credit card?
A: Here you go. By the way, is the .... still open?
B: It closes at .... But if you hurry, you'll make it.
A: ....

DON'T STOP!
- Ask about other services and facilities.

Business Center Hours
9 AM to 5 PM

Fitness Center Hours
6 AM to 9 PM

Sauna Hours
11 AM to 8 PM

Pool Hours
6 AM to 10 PM

Gift Shop Hours
8 AM to 9 PM

B **CHANGE PARTNERS** Practice the conversation again. Discuss other room and bed types and hotel facilities.

BEFORE YOU LISTEN

DIGITAL FLASH CARDS

A ▶2:12 **VOCABULARY** • *Hotel room amenities and services* Read and listen. Then listen again and repeat.

We need. . .

extra towels.

extra hangers.

skirt hangers.

an iron.

a hair dryer.

Could someone. . .

make up the room?

turn down the beds?

pick up the laundry?

bring up a newspaper?

take away the dishes?

B **EXPAND THE VOCABULARY** Complete the statements and questions with other items you know. Then compare items with a partner. *Answers will vary.*

1 We need extra ....*glasses and coffee cups*................................... .

2 We also need ....

3 Could someone pick up my .... ?

4 Could someone bring up .... ?

5 Could someone take away the .... ?

Ideas
- dirty towels
- breakfast / lunch / dinner
- bags / luggage
- a coffee maker
- a rollaway bed
- laundry bags
- (your own idea) __

LISTENING COMPREHENSION

A ▶2:13 **LISTEN FOR MAIN IDEAS** Decide if the guests are satisfied or not. Then explain your answers.

Room 586
☑ Satisfied
☐ Not satisfied

Room 587
☐ Satisfied
☑ Not satisfied

B ▶2:14 **LISTEN FOR DETAILS** Listen again and complete each statement.

Room 586
The guest wants someone to take away ......*the dishes*......., bring up ......*extra towels*...... and ......*a hairdryer*......, and pick up *a load of laundry*.

Room 587
The guest wants someone to ....*make up*........ the ....*room*........, bring up ....*skirt hangers*...., and ......*turn down*...... the ....*beds*........ .

BEFORE YOU LISTEN

A ▶2:12 Vocabulary

Suggested teaching time:	3 minutes	Your actual teaching time:

V Vocabulary Flash Card Player

- To prepare students for the activity, tell them to look at the pictures and read the hotel room items and services.
- Have students listen and practice. If it is likely they have stayed in a hotel, ask *Which items do you often need in a hotel? Which services have you requested in a hotel?* If you teach young students, ask them which services their parents might need or have requested.
- Ask students to listen and practice again.

> **Language and culture**
> - Students may also hear the expression *bring over a newspaper. Bring over* is used when the speaker is on the same floor; *bring up* is used when the speaker is on a higher floor. *Bring over* and *bring up* both imply physical movement toward the speaker.

Option: (+5 minutes) As an alternative, have students listen for the stressed words in each phrase and underline them. Review the answers as a class.

B Expand the vocabulary

Suggested teaching time:	7 minutes	Your actual teaching time:

- To prepare students, call on individuals to read the list of Ideas. Make sure that students understand that *a rollaway bed* is a folding bed on wheels that can be rolled into and out of a room to provide an extra bed.
- Tell students to add their own idea to the list and then complete the exercise.
- Have students compare answers in pairs.

LISTENING COMPREHENSION

A ▶2:13 Listen for main ideas

Suggested teaching time:	5 minutes	Your actual teaching time:

- Tell students that they will listen for the main idea: whether the guests are satisfied or not. Have them complete the activity.
- Have students compare answers in pairs. Play the audio again to have students confirm their answers.

Option: (+5 minutes) For additional practice, have students role-play two-line phone calls to the front desk requesting different items and services. On the board, write:

A: We need an iron. Could someone bring extra hangers?

B: ___

Brainstorm possible responses for the hotel staff. (Possible responses: No problem. I'll take care of that right away. Of course. I'm sorry. Yes, sir / ma'am.)

> **AUDIOSCRIPT**
>
> CONVERSATION 1
> **M:** Front desk. How may I help you?
> **F:** Hi. This is Room 586 calling.
> **M:** Hello, Mrs. Williams. Is everything OK?
> **F:** Oh, fine. Thanks. Listen. We just finished breakfast. Could someone come and take the dishes away?
> **M:** Of course, ma'am.
> **F:** Also, I was wondering if someone could bring extra towels. Oh—and we could use a hair dryer, too.
> **M:** No problem, ma'am. I'll take care of that right away. Anything else I can help you with?
> **F:** Oh, I almost forgot! I have a load of laundry. Could someone pick that up?
> **M:** No problem.
>
> CONVERSATION 2
> **M1:** Front desk. How may I help you?
> **M2:** This is Room 587.
> **M1:** Yes, Mr. Rogers. What can I do for you?
> **M2:** Well, this place is a mess. I need someone to make up the room right away.
> **M1:** I'm sorry, sir. I'll take care of that for you.
> **M2:** And my wife needs some of those—what are they called—skirt hangers?
> **M1:** Yes, sir. We can send some up for you.
> **M2:** Wait, hold on. Here she is.
> **F:** Hello? Front desk?
> **M1:** Yes, Mrs. Rogers.
> **F:** Last night nobody turned down the beds. I'd like turn-down service every night, please.
> **M1:** I'm so sorry, ma'am. If you want turn-down service, we'll certainly make sure you get it.
> **F:** I'd certainly appreciate it. I thought this was a <u>nice</u> hotel.
> **M1:** My apologies, ma'am. You'll get turn-down service tonight.
> **F:** Thank you.

B ▶2:14 Listen for details

Suggested teaching time:	10–15 minutes	Your actual teaching time:

- To preview the activity, have students read the statements before they listen. Then have them fill in the missing words as they listen. Tell them to listen again and fill in any missing information.
- Have students check answers in pairs.
- Review answers with the class. If necessary, play the listening again.

Option: (+10 minutes) As an alternative approach, draw the chart below on the board and also distribute copies to the class. Tell students to take notes as they listen. Have students use their notes to complete the chart. Then have them compare answers in pairs.

Room 586	Room 587

 Graphic Organizers

NOW YOU CAN Request housekeeping services

A Pair work

Suggested teaching time:	10–15 minutes	Your actual teaching time:

- Preview the activity by telling students to spend a few minutes studying the pictures.

- When students have finished, review the vocabulary by asking individuals what is happening in some of the pictures. Ask *What do these people need?*

- To support weaker students, refer them to the Vocabulary exercise on page 32 to review what to say to housekeeping.

- Have students work in pairs to tell each other what the guest might be saying and take notes.

- Review answers by asking pairs to share their answers.

Option: (+10–15 minutes) As an alternative approach, turn the exercise into an information-gap activity. Each pair will have a Student A and a Student B. Tell Students A to cover the right half of the page; they should look at the illustrations of the man's conversation. Tell Students B to cover the left side of the page; they should look at the illustrations of the woman's conversation. Write this example on the board:

A: *What's happening in your first picture?*
B: *Well, the woman is ___.*

B Pair work

Suggested teaching time:	10–15 minutes	Your actual teaching time:

- To prepare students for the activity, have students read the language in the Recycle box. Ask volunteers to read each line, filling in any blanks with their own words. For example, *I need wake-up service.* Remind students of other responses they know for the front desk clerk (*No problem; Of course; I'm sorry; Yes, sir / ma'am*). *Point out the rising intonation of Is the ___ still open?* and the falling intonation of the other questions.

DON'T STOP! Extend the activity by using the ideas in the box to continue the conversation.

- Model the role play with a more confident student by playing the role of Student A.

- Walk around the room as students role-play. Encourage them to use all the language in the Recycle box. Help students as needed.

- Remind pairs to exchange roles of clerk and guest and to play the other guest in the illustration.

Possible responses . . .

I'd like to order (some) dinner / a snack / (some) lunch / (some) breakfast.
Could someone bring up an iron? / Can someone iron my shirt?
I've finished my meal. Could someone take away my dirty dishes? / Can I make a reservation for dinner?
Is the sauna still open? / What time does the sauna close?
I don't have a skirt hanger. / Could someone bring a skirt hanger?
Could someone bring up a hair dryer / some extra towels?
I'd like someone to make up my bed.
Is the shop still open? / What time does the shop open /close?
I'd like to leave a message for [Mike Jones] in [Room 543].

EXTRAS

Workbook or MyEnglishLab

 Speaking Activities: Unit 3, Activity 3

A PAIR WORK Look at the pictures. With a partner, discuss what you think each hotel guest is saying.

B PAIR WORK Role-play a telephone conversation between one of the guests and hotel staff. Use your ideas from Exercise A. Then change roles. Start like this:

A: Hello. Room Service. How can I help you?
B: Hi, I'd like to order . . .

DON'T STOP!
- Complain about other problems.
- Ask about the hotel facilities and services.
- Leave a message for another hotel guest.

RECYCLE THIS LANGUAGE.

Hotel staff	Hotel guest
Hello, [Gift Shop].	Is the [sauna] still open?
Is everything OK?	What time does the [business center] close / open?
I'm sorry to hear that.	Could someone __?
Let me check.	The __ isn't / aren't working.
Certainly.	The __ won't turn on.
I'll be happy to help you with that.	I need __.
	I'd like to order [room service].
	I'd like to leave a message for __.

BEFORE YOU READ

EXPLORE YOUR IDEAS What do you think is the best way to get information about a hotel?

☐ by word of mouth
☐ from an online hotel booking service
☐ from a travel guide book
☐ from a travel agency
☐ other ....

READING ▶ 2:15

www.topnotchtravel.com

Top Notch Travel

Flights | **Hotels** | Car Rentals | Sign in

Our best picks for New York City ● $ Budget ● $$ Moderately priced ● $$$ Expensive ● $$$$ Very expensive

The Plaza Hotel $$$$ — Most famous

Located just across from New York's fabulous Central Park, this is as near as it gets to the best shopping along New York's famous Fifth Avenue. This 1907 hotel, with its beautiful fountain, is a famous location in many popular movies and books. Rub shoulders with the rich and famous. Attentive hotel staff available on every floor—service doesn't get much better than this!

Amenities: 4 restaurants • full-service spa and health club • concierge • business center • 24-hour room service • twice-daily housekeeping service   **More Info**

The Plaza Hotel's famous fountain

Broadway at Times Square Hotel $$ — Most convenient

In a great location—next to Times Square and the best Broadway musicals and plays, this convenient hotel is two blocks from the subway, ten minutes from Rockefeller Center, and ten blocks from the Museum of Modern Art.

Amenities: 24-hour business center • 24-hour front desk • fitness center • free Wi-Fi • wake-up service   **More Info**

Rockefeller Center

YOTEL $$$ — Most high-tech

Popular with young travelers, this very cool high-tech hotel, located only two blocks from the Port Authority bus station, offers automatic electronic check-in and robot bell service! A kitchen on every floor offers free hot drinks and a way to prepare your own food. And super-strong Wi-Fi service makes connecting to the Internet fast and headache-free. Enjoy Yotel's Latin-Asian restaurant and entertainment, or hang out at New York's largest roof garden.

Amenities: 24-hour front desk • laundry • currency exchange • tour desk • ATM • concierge service • fitness center • free Wi-Fi   **More Info**

The Manhattan Skyline

Casablanca Hotel $$ — Most unusual

Conveniently located near Times Square and more than fifty restaurants and two major museums, this award-winning hotel has lots of atmosphere—it's decorated in a colorful authentic Moroccan style. Its friendly, helpful staff make your stay an experience you won't forget, and it's also surprisingly affordable!

Amenities: 24-hour front desk • free Wi-Fi • free passes to nearby health club • free breakfast • free coffee, tea, cookies, and fruit all day • Italian restaurant on first floor   **More Info**

Times Square

For the budget minded

Hotel Pennsylvania $
A huge 1,700-room hotel and a great value. Traveling with your cat or dog? Pets are welcome.

The Hotel Newton $
Even though it's far from many of New York's most popular attractions, it features large clean rooms and wonderfully comfortable beds for a good night's sleep. Sorry, no pets.

The Gershwin Hotel $
Around the corner from the Empire State Building, this artistic 1903 historic hotel is just a short walk to Grand Central Station and the United Nations Building. Every room displays a famous artist's painting.   **More Info**

Grand Central Station

BEFORE YOU READ

Explore your ideas

Suggested teaching time:	5 minutes	Your actual teaching time:

- To introduce the reading topic, have students answer the question individually. If you teach young students, ask what they think their parents' opinion would be.

- After students answer the question, ask the class *What is the best way to choose a hotel? Why?* Write student responses on the board and rank them in order of popularity.

- Tell students to skim the Reading. Ask *What is the article about?* (Some of the best expensive and inexpensive hotels in New York City.)

- Ask *Where did the information in this article come from?* Tell students to scan the article for the answer. (topnotchtravel.com, a website.)

Option: (+5 minutes) Brainstorm different factors in choosing a hotel. (Possible responses: Price, location, room size, things people say about the hotel, services, facilities such as restaurants, fitness center, sauna.) Have groups discuss factors that are important to them or their parents when choosing a hotel. Ask students to give reasons.

▶2:15 READING

Suggested teaching time:	15 minutes	Your actual teaching time:

- To prepare students for deciding which hotel they like best, have students think about important factors in choosing a hotel while they read. If necessary, write some examples on the board: *price, location, room size, things people say about the hotel, services, facilities.*

- Point out the key with the dollar sign rating. Ask
  Which type of hotel is the least expensive? (Budget.)
  Which type of hotel costs more, the "Moderately priced" or the "Expensive"? ("Expensive.")

- Have students scan the reading for the dollar sign ratings. Ask:
  Which hotel is rated "Very expensive"? (The Plaza Hotel.)
  Which hotels are rated "Moderately priced"? (The Broadway at Times Square Hotel and the Casablanca Hotel.)
  Which hotel is the most expensive? (The Plaza Hotel.)
  Which hotels are the least expensive? (Hotel Pennsylvania, The Hotel Newton, The Gershwin Hotel.)

- After students read, ask *Which hotel would you rather stay at? Which factor(s) helped you decide?*

Language and culture

- Although students should be able to understand the hotel guide without knowing every word, you may want to explain the following:
  as near as it gets: very close
  rub shoulders with [someone]: meet and spend time with someone
  attentive: listening or watching carefully
  concierge: someone in a hotel whose job it is to help guests with problems
  automatic electronic check-in, robot bell service: the hotel has no human staff to check guests in or carry their luggage; these services are done by computers or robots
  headache-free: with no problems
  atmosphere: the feeling that a place gives you
  affordable: not expensive

Option: (+5–10 minutes) To challenge students, have them work in small groups to discuss their opinions of price ranges for each category. Write on the board the four price categories *very expensive, expensive, moderately priced, budget.* After they have finished their discussion, ask groups to share their answers with the class. Write their answers on the board.

Option: (+5–10 minutes) Have students describe the best hotel and the worst hotel they ever stayed at. Encourage them to refer to the hotel guide for services and facilities the hotels had or didn't have.

 Learning Strategies

A Draw conclusions

Suggested teaching time:	10–15 minutes	Your actual teaching time:

- Introduce a scanning technique. Say *Read the statements about the people. Read for hints to help you find information to complete the advice.*

- Model the technique by doing item 1 with the class. Ask *Where does Carl Ryan like to stay?* (Near the Theater District.) *What can you find in the Theater District?* (Musicals and plays.) *Which part of New York has lots of musicals and plays?* (Broadway/Times Square.) *Which hotels are near Times Square?* (The Broadway at Times Square Hotel or the Casablanca Hotel.)

- Have students read the remaining items to find the key words to scan for in the reading. (Possible responses: 2. great beds; 3. Wi-Fi service; 4. comfortable, lots of services; 5. different/interesting; 6. dog.)

- Tell students to make notes on the reading as they scan. Then have them fill in the blanks.

B Identify supporting details

Suggested teaching time:	5 minutes	Your actual teaching time:

- As students compare answers from Exercise A, explain that they need to provide reasons (supporting details) for their answers. Tell them to refer to their notes on the reading. Walk around the room and help students as needed.

- Review the answers with the class. Make sure to check understanding by asking students to explain their answers.

Option: (+5 minutes) To extend the activity, ask questions. For example:
Which hotel has a large roof garden? (Yotel.)
Which hotel accepts pets? (Hotel Pennsylvania.)
Which hotel is very famous? (The Plaza Hotel.)
Which hotel has a Moroccan theme? (The Casablanca Hotel.)
Which hotel is very convenient? (The Broadway at Times Square Hotel.)

 Extra Reading Comprehension Exercises

NOW YOU CAN Choose a hotel

A Frame your ideas

Suggested teaching time:	5–10 minutes	Your actual teaching time:

- Have a volunteer read the list of factors. To check comprehension, ask *If price is not at all important to you, what number would you rate it?* (1.) *If location is extremely important to you, what number would you rate it?* (5.)

- Have students rate each factor.

- After students complete the activity, take a survey to find out which factors are most important. Discuss the results of the survey.

B Pair work

Suggested teaching time:	5–10 minutes	Your actual teaching time:

- Have students work in pairs to locate the hotels on the map and circle them. Then tell students to read the names of the tourist attractions. Ask:
  Has anyone ever been to New York?
  If yes, what tourist attractions did you visit?
  If no, what tourist attractions would you like to visit?
  Do you think location is important in choosing a hotel?

- Tell students to refer to the ratings they gave the factors in Exercise A (Frame Your Ideas) as they choose their hotel.

Text-mining: Focus students' attention on the Text-mining box. Ask a student to read the text. Have students skim the article and underline helpful language; for example, *as near as it gets.* Review the answers and write students' findings on the board for them to refer to during the discussion. To help discussion, print out the graphic organizer and distribute to students.

- Have pairs discuss the advantages and disadvantages of their choices.

 Graphic Organizers

C Survey and discussion

Suggested teaching time:	5–10 minutes	Your actual teaching time:

- Write a list of all the hotels on the board. Survey how many students chose each hotel and write the number next to the hotel.

- Ask a volunteer to share his or her choices. Then ask if any other students chose the same hotel. If any did, have them add any other reasons.

- Call on a student who chose a different hotel. Follow the same procedure of asking other students who chose the same hotel to add their comments. Repeat until all students have spoken.

Option: (+5 minutes) Say *I would like to stay at a hotel close to the Empire State Building, and I don't want to spend much money. Where should I stay?* (The Hotel Pennsylvania or the Gershwin Hotel.) Have students follow the model to state their preferred location and price and to ask where they should stay. Ask students to share their preferences with the class. Based on each student's preference, have the class give suggestions for an appropriate hotel.

EXTRAS

Workbook or MyEnglishLab

Speaking Activities: Unit 3, Activity 4; "Find Someone Who . . ." Activity

A **DRAW CONCLUSIONS** Complete each statement with the name of a hotel (or hotels) from the Reading. Then compare choices and reasons with a partner.
(Answers will vary but may include the following:)

1 On his vacations, Carl Ryan, 43, likes to stay near the Theater District. If he stays at
........*the Broadway at Times Square Hotel or the Casablanca Hotel*........, he'll be near the Theater District.

2 Stella Korman, 35, doesn't like the beds in most hotels. However, if she stays at
................*the Hotel Newton*................, her room will definitely have a great bed.

3 Mark and Nancy Birdsall (22 and 21) are always online. If they stay at the
................*Yotel*................, the Wi-Fi service is not only free, but it's really fast.

4 Lucy Lee, 36, will pay more for a hotel that is very comfortable and offers a lot of services. If she stays at
................*the Plaza Hotel*................, she'll be very happy.

5 Brenda Rey prefers hotels that are different and interesting. If she stays at
Yotel or Casablanca Hotel or the Gershwin Hotel, she'll find them different from other hotels.

6 James Kay always travels with his dog, Louie. If he stays at ....*the Hotel Newton*................, Louie will have to stay home.

B **IDENTIFY SUPPORTING DETAILS** Compare responses in Exercise A with a partner. If you disagree, explain why you chose a particular hotel.

NOW YOU CAN Choose a hotel

A **FRAME YOUR IDEAS** What's important to you in choosing a hotel? Rate the following factors on a scale of 1 to 5.

	not important			very important
price	1 – 2 – 3 – 4 – 5			
room size	1 – 2 – 3 – 4 – 5			
cleanliness	1 – 2 – 3 – 4 – 5			
location	1 – 2 – 3 – 4 – 5			
service	1 – 2 – 3 – 4 – 5			
amenities	1 – 2 – 3 – 4 – 5			
atmosphere	1 – 2 – 3 – 4 – 5			

B **PAIR WORK** Find each hotel from the Reading on the map. Discuss the advantages and disadvantages of each. Then choose a hotel.

" The Casablanca Hotel sounds like it has a lot of atmosphere. It's affordable, and the location is good. "

Text-mining (optional)
Find three words or phrases in the Reading that were new to you. Use them in your Pair Work.
For example: "conveniently located."

C **SURVEY AND DISCUSSION** Take a survey of how many classmates chose each hotel. Discuss and explain your choices.

" Most of us chose the Hotel Newton because . . . "

REVIEW

A ▶2:16 Listen to the phone conversations in a hotel. Then listen again and complete each statement, using words from the box.

bell	room	dinner	hangers	make up the room
laundry	shoeshine	towels	wake-up	turn down the beds

1 She wants someone to bring up ......_dinner_...... . She also needs ......_wake-up_...... service.

2 He needs ......_laundry_...... service, and he wants someone to bring up extra ......_hangers_...... .

3 She wants someone to _make up the room_ , and she wants someone to bring up extra ......_towels_...... .

4 He needs ......_shoeshine_...... service and ......_room_...... service.

B What hotel room or bed type should each guest ask for?

1 Ms. Gleason is traveling alone. She doesn't need much space. ......_a single room_......

2 Mr. and Mrs. Vanite and their twelve-year-old son Boris are checking into a room with one king-size bed. ......_rollaway bed_......

3 Mike Krause plans to use his room for business meetings with important customers. ......_suite_......

4 George Nack is a big man, and he's very tall. He needs a good night's sleep for an important meeting tomorrow. ......_king-size bed_......

5 Paul Krohn's company wants him to save some money by sharing a room with a colleague. ......_twin beds_......

C Write real conditional statements and questions. Use the correct forms of the verbs and correct punctuation.

1 if / it / rain this morning / Mona / not go / to the beach
   If it rains this morning, Mona won't go to the beach.

2 if / you / walk to the restaurant / you / be there in fifteen minutes
   If you walk to the restaurant, you'll be there in fifteen minutes.

3 Mr. Wang / get a better job / if / he / do well on the English test tomorrow
   Mr. Wang will get a better job, if he does well on his English test tomorrow.

4 what / Karl / do / if / the airline / cancels his flight
   What will Karl do if the airline cancels his flight?

5 if / you / not like / your room / who / you / call
   If you don't like your room, who will you call?

For additional language practice . . .

🎵 TOP NOTCH POP • Lyrics p. 153
"Checking Out"

| DIGITAL SONG | DIGITAL KARAOKE |

WRITING

Write a paragraph about the hotel you chose in Lesson 4. Explain why you would like to stay there. What are its advantages and disadvantages?

I would like to stay at the Hotel Casablanca.

Atmosphere is very important to me and . . .

WRITING BOOSTER p. 145
• Avoiding sentence fragments with
  <u>because</u> or <u>since</u>
• Guidance for this writing exercise

A ▶ 2:16 Listen to the phone . . .

Suggested teaching time:	5 minutes	Your actual teaching time:

- To prepare students for the activity, tell them to silently read the hotel amenities and services in the box. Introduce the context for the listening by saying *Two people are having a conversation. Who do you think they are?* (A hotel guest and a hotel clerk.) Then have students listen to the conversations.

- Have students listen again and complete the activity. Be sure to allow time for them to write the answers. Then have them compare answers with a partner.

- To support weaker students, tell them to read the sentences and complete the exercise before they listen again. Permit them to listen a third time so they can check their answers and make any changes.

AUDIOSCRIPT

CONVERSATION 1
M: Room service. How may I help you?
F: Hi. I want to order something for dinner in my room.
M: What would you like to order?
F: I'll have the grilled chicken.
M: Anything to drink?
F: No, thanks. Oh, and could someone call me at 7:00 tomorrow morning?
M: You can call the front desk for that, ma'am. I'm sure they can help you.

CONVERSATION 2 [F = British English]
F: How may I help you?
M: Hi. I've got a bunch of dirty clothes up here. I wonder if someone could come by and pick them up?
F: I'll take care of that right away, sir. Is there anything else?
M: Oh, right. There aren't enough hangers in the closet.
F: No problem, sir. I'll send someone up with some more.

CONVERSATION 3
M: Can I help you?
F: Hi. I just got back from a meeting and my room is a mess. No one made the bed, and there are towels all over the floor in the bathroom.
M: I'm so sorry, ma'am. I'll send someone up right away.
F: Thanks. And frankly, my husband and I could use more towels. Would that be a problem?
M: Of course not, ma'am.

CONVERSATION 4 [M = Spanish]
F: Front desk. How may I help you?
M: Hi. I just wanted to let you know that I'm leaving my shoes outside my door. Could someone come up and get them?
F: Absolutely, sir.
M: Also, my wife and I are a little hungry. We haven't had dinner yet. Can we still get something?
F: No problem, sir. I'll connect you with someone who can take your order right away.

B What hotel room . . .

Suggested teaching time:	3 minutes	Your actual teaching time:

- Refer students to the Vocabulary on page 26 to review.

- Have students compare and explain their answers in pairs.

C Write real conditional statements . . .

Suggested teaching time:	5–7 minutes	Your actual teaching time:

- Remind students that in real conditional statements and questions, the *if* clause is in the present tense and the result clause is in the future tense (with *will / won't*). In questions, the word order of the *if* clause remains the same, and the word order in the result clause changes.

- Also point out that students need to add a comma when the *if* clause comes first in the sentence.

- Have students compare answers in pairs.

WRITING

Suggested teaching time:	15–20 minutes	Your actual teaching time:

- In groups, have students review the things that are most important to them (or their parents) in a hotel. Draw the chart below on the board and ask students to copy it. As they talk about hotel services and facilities, have them complete the chart with advantages and disadvantages.

HOTEL SERVICES

Advantages	Disadvantages

- Have students follow the model and begin with *I would like to stay at Hotel X . . . .*

- Remind students to separate complete thoughts in very long sentences by using a period and starting another sentence.

- After students complete the writing assignment, tell them to check their papers. Ask *Does every sentence have a subject and verb? Do the subjects and verbs agree?*

- Then have students exchange papers with a partner. Tell them to ask their partner questions if something is not clear.

Option: **WRITING BOOSTER** *(Teaching notes p. T145)*

 **Writing Process Worksheets**

 *Top Notch Pop* **Song Video and Karaoke Video**

 Digital Games

ORAL REVIEW

Before the first activity, give students a few minutes of silent time to look over the pictures.

Pair work 1

Suggested teaching time:	5–9 minutes	Your actual teaching time:

- To introduce the activity, have students look at the photos and illustrations and identify the guests and the hotel employees.
- To prepare students for the conversation, review possible problems guests can have at hotels.
- Model the activity by role-playing an example conversation with a more confident student.

Option: (+5 minutes) For additional practice, have pairs write their conversations in dialogue form and exchange their conversations with another pair for comments.

> **Possible responses . . .**
> **A:** Hello, is this the front desk? **B:** Yes. Can I help you? **A:** This is Room 816. I have a couple of requests. **B:** Yes? **A:** I'd like extra towels and an iron. And could someone turn down the beds every evening? **B:** Yes, no problem. **A:** Thank you very much. That would be great. And could someone please take away my breakfast dishes? **B:** Of course. I'll send someone up right away.

Pair work 2

Suggested teaching time:	5–8 minutes	Your actual teaching time:

- If necessary, quickly review key language for taking messages and write it on the board.
- Tell students to find a new partner. Remind them to use *will* in their conversations.

> **Possible responses . . .**
> **A:** Front desk. Can I help you? **B:** Yes, thanks. I'd like to leave a message for Natalie Bond. **A:** Yes? How do you spell that? **B:** Natalie: N-A-T-A-L-I-E. Bond: B-O-N-D. **A:** That's Natalie; N-A-T-A-L-I-E. Bond: B-O-N-D. **B:** Please tell her Steve Bond called. I'll be at the hotel tomorrow morning at 10:00. **A:** OK. I'll leave her the message. **B:** All right. Thank you.

Option: (+5 minutes) Have students create additional messages to leave a hotel guest. They can begin with *I'll meet her / him . . . , I'll call her / him . . . , I'll arrive / leave at . . .* , etc.

Pair work 3

Suggested teaching time:	5–8 minutes	Your actual teaching time:

- Tell students to use the information in the Directory on the right side of the page in their conversations.
- Model the activity by role-playing an example conversation with a more confident student.

> **Possible responses . . .**
> **A:** Hello, I'm checking in. The name's Anderson. **B:** Hello, Mr. Anderson. That's one double for three nights, correct? **A:** Yes, that's right. Here's my card. **B:** Thank you. **A:** Is the business center still open? I really need to check my e-mail. **B:** Yes. If you hurry, you'll be able to check your e-mail. It closes at 4:00. **A:** OK, thank you.

Option: (+3 minutes) To help motivate students, turn the review stage into a competition. Divide the class into teams. Have teams work together for two minutes to brainstorm hotel services and facilities. The team that provides the most services and facilities is the winner.

Option: Oral Progress Assessment

- Use the images on page 37. Encourage students to use the vocabulary, grammar, rhythm, and intonation practiced in this unit.
- Point to the different people and ask the questions below.
  - *What time is it?*
  - *What is the man asking the front desk?*
  - *What message is the woman leaving?*
  - *What facilities does the hotel have?* (Have students refer to the information on the directory.)
- Invite a student to role-play a telephone conversation with you. Play the role of the front desk clerk and ask the student to play the man talking on the phone.
- Evaluate the student on intelligibility, fluency, correct use of grammar, and appropriate use of vocabulary.

 Oral Progress Assessment Charts

Option: *Top Notch* Project
Have students invent hotels and write a guidebook with hotel reviews.

Idea: Write on the board: *hotel name, location, price, atmosphere, room size, cleanliness, services.* Tell students to include this information in their reviews. Have students write their reviews in small groups. Finally, gather all the reviews into a guidebook.

EXTRAS

On the Internet:
- Online Teacher Resources: pearsonelt.com/topnotch3e/

Additional printable resources on the ActiveTeach:
- Assessment
- Just for Fun
- *Top Notch Pop* Song Activities
- *Top Notch TV* Video Program and Activity Worksheets
- Supplementary Pronunciation Lessons
- Conversation Activator Video Scripts
- Audioscripts and Answer Keys
- Unit Study Guides

ORAL REVIEW

PAIR WORK

1 Create a conversation between the hotel guest in Room 816 and the woman at the front desk. Ask for hotel services or complain about a problem. Start like this:

Hello? Is this the front desk?

2 Create a conversation between the man at the front desk and the caller. Use <u>will</u>. Complete the message slip. Start like this:

A: *Front desk. Can I help you?*
B: *Yes, thanks. I'd like to leave a message for . . .*

3 Create a conversation between the two men at the front desk. Check into or check out of the hotel. Discuss hotel amenities, services, and schedules. Start like this:

Hi. I'm checking in. The name's ....

☎ **PHONE MESSAGE**

FOR: _____
FROM: ☐ Mr.   ☐ Ms.
        ☐ Mrs. ☐ Miss _____
☐ Please call   ☐ Will call again
☐ Wants to see you   ☐ Returned your call

Message: _____
_____
_____

THE BELMAR

DIRECTORY

Business Center	2
9:00 AM – 4:00 PM	
Gift Shop	Lobby
9:00 AM – 9:00 PM	
Fitness Center	3
6:00 AM – 10:00 PM	
Spa	5
10:00 AM – 3:00 PM	
Belmar Café	12
8:00 AM – 11:00 PM	

RECEPTION

THE BELMAR HOTEL

✓ **NOW I CAN**

☐ Leave and take a message.
☐ Check into a hotel.
☐ Request housekeeping services.
☐ Choose a hotel.

UNIT 4 Cars and Driving

COMMUNICATION GOALS

1 Discuss a car accident.
2 Describe a car problem.
3 Rent a car.
4 Discuss good and bad driving.

PREVIEW

Eight Habits of Bad Drivers

How many drivers in your city . . .

❶ speed?

☐ none ☐ some ☐ most ☐ all

❷ tailgate?

☐ none ☐ some ☐ most ☐ all

❸ talk on the phone?

☐ none ☐ some ☐ most ☐ all

❹ text while driving?

☐ none ☐ some ☐ most ☐ all

❺ weave through traffic?

☐ none ☐ some ☐ most ☐ all

❻ don't stop at red lights?

☐ none ☐ some ☐ most ☐ all

❼ don't signal when turning?

☐ none ☐ some ☐ most ☐ all

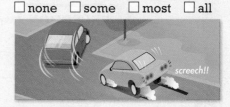

screech!!

❽ pass in a no-passing zone?

☐ none ☐ some ☐ most ☐ all

DIGITAL FLASH CARDS

A ▶2:19 **VOCABULARY • Bad driving habits** Read and listen. Then listen again and repeat.

> speed
> tailgate
> talk on the phone
> text while driving
> weave through traffic
> not stop at red lights
> not signal when turning
> pass in a no-passing zone

B **PAIR WORK** Compare surveys with a partner. Discuss and explain your answers.

❝ Some drivers in my city talk on the phone while they're driving. It's terrible. ❞

❝ Lots of taxi drivers turn without signaling. I don't like that. ❞

PREVIEW

Before beginning Exercise A, give students a few minutes to look over the survey about bad driving habits.

Suggested teaching time:	10 minutes	Your actual teaching time:	

• Check comprehension by asking:
  What is this survey about? (Bad driving habits.)
• Ask students to guess the meaning of each habit based on the pictures.

A ▶2:19 Vocabulary

Suggested teaching time:	3 minutes	Your actual teaching time:	

V Vocabulary Flash Card Player

• Have students read the vocabulary in the box and listen to and repeat the words.
• Tell students to look at the pictures of each bad driving habit in the survey. Make sure students understand all the vocabulary.

B Pair work

Suggested teaching time:	6–8 minutes	Your actual teaching time:	

• Before students complete the survey, ask *Are there a lot of bad drivers in this city? What are some of their habits?*
• Have students complete the survey individually.
• To prepare students for the discussion, go over the sample quotes. Model the activity by making a couple of comments of your own about the survey, explaining your answers. For example: *Some drivers tailgate in our city. I don't like that because it can cause accidents. If the car in front stops suddenly, the second car will hit it.*
• Have students compare their surveys.
• Call on pairs to share their answers with the class.

Option: (+5 minutes) Have a class discussion on the bad driving habits in the surveys. Ask *Which bad driving habits do you think are the worst or most dangerous? Which do you think are not so bad?* Have students give their opinions.

C ▶ 2:20 Photo story

Suggested teaching time:	12–17 minutes	Your actual teaching time:

- To prepare students for the story, tell them to look at the photos. Ask:
  Where are the two men in the first picture? (On a street.)
  What are the men doing in the first picture? (Meeting / Shaking hands.)
  Where are the two men in the second and third pictures? (In a coffee shop.)
  What are the men doing in the second and third pictures? (Talking and drinking coffee.)
- Tell students to close their books and listen to the conversation.
- To check comprehension, ask:
  Who is Brad buying a present for, and why? (Marissa, his wife, for their fifth anniversary.)
  What did Brad just see? (An accident. A taxi hit a bus.)
  What was the taxi driver doing? (Texting while he was driving.)
  What does Mason say about driving in the city? (It's always been bad, but now it's really bad because everyone's texting and talking on the phone instead of paying attention to the road.)
- Have students open their books and read and listen to the conversation.

> **Language and culture**
> - In the third part of the Photo Story, the word *just* means "simply."

D Focus on language

Suggested teaching time:	3–5 minutes	Your actual teaching time:

- If students need help, tell them that the quotations are underlined in the Photo Story. Encourage them to find each quotation and read the sentences around it (the context) to figure out what it means.
- Have students compare answers in pairs.

E Think and explain

Suggested teaching time:	3–5 minutes	Your actual teaching time:

- Tell pairs to find the quotations in the Photo Story to figure out what they mean. (Item 1 is in the first part of the story, and item 2 is at the end of the third part of the story.)
- Call on pairs to share their answers with the class. Write the best answers on the board.

SPEAKING

Discussion

Suggested teaching time:	15 minutes	Your actual teaching time:

- Model the activity for the class by answering the questions yourself. For example: *1. Have you ever seen an accident?* (Yes.) *2. Where was it?* (In a parking lot.) *3. What was the cause of the accident?* (A man was talking on the phone while he was driving. He hit another car.) Explain that students should not answer all the questions. If they have seen an accident, they should answer questions 2 and 3. If they haven't seen an accident, they should answer questions 4, 5, and 6.
- Have students complete the questions individually and then work in groups to tell other students about the accidents they have seen or heard about.
- Call on groups to share their answers with the class.

Option: *[+5 minutes]* Write a few bad driving habits on the board. For example:

talking or texting while driving
speeding
tailgating

Ask *Was this the cause of the accident you saw or heard about?* Read each cause aloud and have students raise their hands if they have seen or heard about accidents that were caused by these bad driving habits.

EXTRAS

Workbook

C ▶2:20 **PHOTO STORY** Read and listen to a conversation between two old friends.

15 minutes later

Mason: Brad! Long time no see.

Brad: Mason! You're right. It *has* been a long time. How've you been?

Mason: I can't complain. What about you? How's the family?

Brad: Great! I was just going in here to pick up a present for Marissa. Tomorrow's our fifth anniversary.

Mason: Congratulations! . . . Hey! Let's have a cup of coffee and catch up on old times. There's a nice coffee place right around the corner.

Brad: You won't believe what I just saw.

Mason: What?

Brad: This taxi was coming around the corner, and he hit a bus! Someone said the guy was texting while he was driving.

Mason: You've got to be kidding! Was anyone hurt?

Brad: I don't think so.

Mason: Thank goodness for that.

Brad: I just can't stop thinking about that accident.

Mason: I know. The driving in this city has always been bad, but now everyone's texting and talking on the phone instead of paying attention to the road.

Brad: You can say that again! You shouldn't multitask while you're driving a car.

D **FOCUS ON LANGUAGE** Match each numbered sentence with one of the quotations from the Photo Story.

1 I've been fine. b

2 I totally agree with you. e

3 I'm so happy for you! a

4 I'm glad nothing terrible happened. d

5 Really? That's unbelievable. f

6 It's great to see you again. c

a "Congratulations!"

b "I can't complain."

c "Long time no see."

d "Thank goodness for that."

e "You can say that again!"

f "You've got to be kidding!"

E **THINK AND EXPLAIN** Discuss with a partner.

1 What did Mason mean when he said, "Let's have a cup of coffee and catch up on old times."?
Let's go somewhere for coffee and talk about the old days and what has happened since we last saw each other.

2 What did Brad mean when he said, "You shouldn't multitask while you're driving a car"?
You shouldn't do other things (like texting or talking on the phone) when you're driving a car.

SPEAKING

DISCUSSION Discuss an accident you know about. Answer the questions.

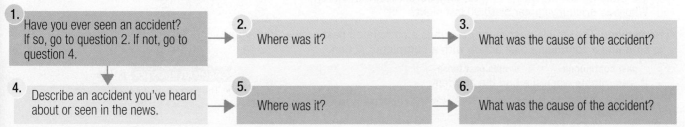

1. Have you ever seen an accident? If so, go to question 2. If not, go to question 4.

2. Where was it?

3. What was the cause of the accident?

4. Describe an accident you've heard about or seen in the news.

5. Where was it?

6. What was the cause of the accident?

GOAL Discuss a car accident

VOCABULARY Car parts

A ▶2:21 Read and listen. Then listen again and repeat.

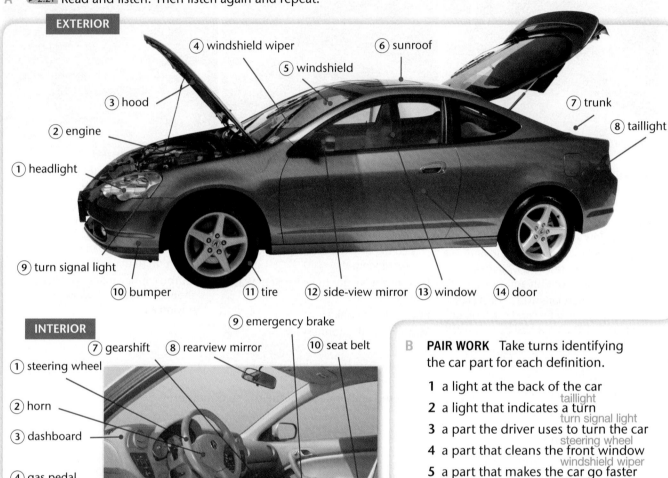

EXTERIOR

④ windshield wiper
⑥ sunroof
⑤ windshield
③ hood
⑦ trunk
② engine
⑧ taillight
① headlight
⑨ turn signal light
⑩ bumper   ⑪ tire   ⑫ side-view mirror   ⑬ window   ⑭ door

INTERIOR

⑨ emergency brake
⑦ gearshift   ⑧ rearview mirror   ⑩ seat belt
① steering wheel
② horn
③ dashboard
④ gas pedal
⑤ brake pedal
⑥ clutch

B **PAIR WORK** Take turns identifying the car part for each definition.

1 a light at the back of the car
   taillight
2 a light that indicates a turn
   turn signal light
3 a part the driver uses to turn the car
   steering wheel
4 a part that cleans the front window
   windshield wiper
5 a part that makes the car go faster
   gas pedal
6 a part that keeps passengers safe
   during an accident   seat belt
7 a light that helps the driver see the road
   headlight
8 a place in the back for carrying things
   trunk

GRAMMAR The past continuous

The past continuous describes an activity that continued during a period of time in the past or at a specific time in the past.

The car **was making** a funny sound while they **were driving**.
Were the headlights **working**? (Yes, they were. / No, they weren't.)
Who **was driving** your car at 10:00 last night?

Remember: The simple past tense describes a <u>completed</u> past action. Use <u>when</u> to combine a continuing past action with a completed action.

        past continuous   simple past tense
        It **was raining** when she **had** the accident.

> Form the past continuous with <u>was</u> or <u>were</u> and a present participle.
> The other driver **was speeding**.

GRAMMAR BOOSTER p. 131
• The past continuous: other uses

VOCABULARY

A  2:21 Read and listen . . .

Suggested teaching time:	10–15 minutes	Your actual teaching time:

V Vocabulary Flash Card Player

- For a warm-up, tell students to close their books. Write on the board:

CAR

EXTERIOR (outside)   INTERIOR (inside)

> **Language and culture**
> - In British English, the car *hood* is called the *bonnet*, the *trunk* is called the *boot*, the *turn signal* is called the *indicator*, the *gas pedal* is called the *accelerator*, and *tire* is spelled *tyre*.

B Pair work

Suggested teaching time:	5 minutes	Your actual teaching time:

- Encourage pairs to do the exercise without looking at the book. Then have them refer to the book to check their answers.
- Move around the room and help students as needed. Review answers with the class.

Option: (+10 minutes) Using the exercise above as a model, assign each student one or two car parts and have them write definitions. Have students form groups and take turns reading their definitions aloud while the other students try to name the car parts.

GRAMMAR

Suggested teaching time:	8–13 minutes	Your actual teaching time:

- To make it clear how to form and use the past continuous, write on the board *The car was making a funny sound while they were driving.* Underline the verb forms, and explain that the past continuous is formed with the simple past of *be* and the present participle of the main verb. Read the rule in the Grammar box and the examples.

- On the board write *She was driving home when she had an accident.* Draw this time line:

Explain that the past continuous (was driving) talks about an action that continued in the past. The simple past (had an accident) talks about an action that happened and then ended in the past. Make it clear that the simple past action interrupted the action in the past continuous; it was not finished. Point out that *when* shows these actions happened at the same time.

Option: GRAMMAR BOOSTER *(Teaching notes p. T131)*

 Inductive Grammar Charts

AUDIOSCRIPT for page T41 (Listen to Activate Grammar)

CONVERSATION 1
M: Oh, no! What happened to your car?
 F: A tree fell on it in the storm.
M: Look at your windshield!
 F: Yeah. I'm going to have to get it replaced.

CONVERSATION 2 [F = Spanish]
 F: Oh, no! What happened to your hood?
M: I had an accident. I hit a parked car.
 F: How did that happen?
M: I fell asleep.

CONVERSATION 3 [M = Korean]
M: I can't drive my car. I had an accident.
 F: I'm sorry. What happened?
M: The brakes failed and I hit a tree.
 F: Oh, no. Was there much damage?
M: Well, I'll have to replace the bumper and the right headlight.

CONVERSATION 4
 F: I had an accident.
M: Oh, no! What happened?
 F: This other car smashed into my trunk.
M: Was anyone hurt?
 F: No. But the car is going to cost an arm and a leg to fix.

A Grammar practice

Suggested teaching time:	4 minutes	Your actual teaching time:	

- To help students understand when to use each tense, write these questions and answers on the board: *Did the action continue during a period of time? (Use past continuous.) Did the action occur and then end? (Use simple past.)*
- Model the activity by doing the first two items with the class. As students complete the exercise in pairs, encourage them to refer to the board and ask themselves the questions as they work.
- When pairs have finished, tell them to compare answers with another pair. Review answers with the class.

 Extra Grammar Exercises

B ▶2:22 Listen to activate vocabulary

Suggested teaching time:	5 minutes	Your actual teaching time:	

- Write these car parts on the board: *windshield, hood, brakes, headlight, trunk.* Point to the item on the cars in the pictures. Refer students to the Vocabulary on page 40.
- After students complete the exercise, have them compare answers in pairs.
- Have students listen again. Point out the typical spoken reduction of *going to* to *gonna* in Conversation 4.
- Ask *What caused the damage in each picture?* (1. A tree fell on the car. 2. The driver fell asleep. 3. The brakes didn't work. 4. Another car hit the car.)
- Review answers with the class.

> **AUDIOSCRIPT** See page T40.

CONVERSATION MODEL

A ▶2:23 Read and listen . . .

Suggested teaching time:	2 minutes	Your actual teaching time:	

> These conversation strategies are implicit in the model:
> - Express concern about another's condition after an accident.
> - Express relief when hearing all is OK.
> - Use "only" to minimize the seriousness of a situation.

- Have students look at the picture. Ask *What do you think the two women are talking about?* (Something serious.) *How do you think the women are feeling?* (Upset, worried.)
- Check comprehension after students read and listen. Ask *What happened to Speaker A?* (She had a car accident.) *Why? What happened?* (The driver behind her was tailgating and hit her car.) *Was there any damage?* (A taillight broke.)

B ▶2:24 Rhythm and intonation

Suggested teaching time:	3 minutes	Your actual teaching time:	

- Have students repeat each line. Make sure they:
  ○ put stress on *sorry.*
  ○ use rising intonation for *Are you OK?* and *Was there much damage?* and use falling intonation for *How did it happen?*

▶2:25 Ways to respond

- Have students listen and repeat the expressions in the box. Make sure they use the correct intonation to show concern and relief.
- Make sure students know that for the conversation the phrases under "With concern" can take the place of "I'm so sorry" and "Oh, no!" The phrases under "With relief" can take the place of "Thank goodness."

NOW YOU CAN Discuss a car accident

A Write what . . .

Suggested teaching time:	5 minutes	Your actual teaching time:	

- Tell students to look at the first picture (The driver wasn't paying attention) as they write their sentences.

B Conversation activator

Suggested teaching time:	8–13 minutes	Your actual teaching time:	

 Conversation Activator Video

- *Note:* You can print the script or you can show a running transcript on the video player on the ActiveTeach. The script also appears on page 183 of this Teacher's Edition.
- To provide more support, tell students to look at the three pictures without captions. Ask *What is happening in these pictures?* Write students' answers on the board. (Possible responses: The driver is speeding. The driver is tailgating. The driver is talking on the phone.)
- Encourage students to use the pictures and the vocabulary in the Ways to Respond box in their conversations. Model a conversation with a more confident student.

> **DON'T STOP!** Encourage students to keep their conversations going by asking more questions. For example: *Where was the accident? Was there more damage? What happened to the other driver?*

- For more support, play the Conversation Activator Video before students do this activity themselves. In Scene 1, the actors use different words in the gaps from the ones in the Conversation Model. In Scene 2, the actors extend the conversation. After each scene, ask students how the model has been changed by the actors.

 Conversation Activator Video Script; Conversation Activator Pair Work Cards; Learning Strategies

C Change partners

Suggested teaching time:	5 minutes	Your actual teaching time:	

- Encourage students to use the accidents they talked about in groups for the Speaking exercise on page 39 when they role-play the conversation again with new information.

EXTRAS

Workbook or MyEnglishLab

Speaking Activities: Unit 4, Activity 1

A GRAMMAR PRACTICE Complete the paragraph with the past continuous and the simple past tense.

I .... *had* .... an accident yesterday. I .... *was driving* .... slowly and I'm
      1 have   2 drive
sure I .... *was paying* .... attention. But I .... *was waiting* .... for a phone call. When
        3 pay   4 wait
the phone .... *rang* .... , I .... *answered* .... it. Suddenly, the car in front of me
        5 ring   6 answer
.... *stopped* .... , and I .... *hit* .... it. I certainly .... *learned* ....
      7 stop   8 hit   9 learn
my lesson! Luckily, I .... *wasn't speeding* .... when I .... *had* .... the accident.
             10 not speed   11 have

B ▶2:22 **LISTEN TO ACTIVATE VOCABULARY** Listen to the conversations about accidents.
Write the number of each conversation in the box under the picture. Then listen again
and write the car part or parts that were damaged in each accident.

| 3 | bumper, right headlight | 2 | hood | 1 | windshield | 4 | trunk |

CONVERSATION MODEL

A ▶2:23 Read and listen to a conversation about a
car accident.

A: I had an accident.

B: I'm so sorry. Are you OK?

A: I'm fine. No one was hurt.

B: Thank goodness. How did it happen?

A: Well, the other driver was tailgating,
and he hit my car.

B: Oh, no! Was there much damage?

A: No. I'll only have to replace a taillight.

> ▶2:25 **Ways to respond**
>
> | With concern | With relief |
> |---|---|
> | I'm so sorry. | Thank goodness. |
> | Oh, no! | What a relief! |
> | How awful! | That's good. |
> | I'm sorry to hear that. | |
> | That's terrible. | |

B ▶2:24 **RHYTHM AND INTONATION** Listen again and repeat.
Then practice the Conversation Model with a partner.

NOW YOU CAN Discuss a car accident

A Write what the driver was doing. Use the past continuous.

B **CONVERSATION ACTIVATOR** With a partner, change the
Conversation Model, using the pictures. Then change roles.

A: I had an accident.
B: .... Are you OK?
A: ....
B: .... How did it happen?
A: Well, ... , and .... hit my car.
B: .... Was there much damage?
A: ....

DON'T STOP!

• Ask more questions
about location, other
damage, the other
driver, etc.

*The driver wasn't
paying attention.*

C **CHANGE PARTNERS** Discuss other accidents.

VOCABULARY *Phrasal verbs for talking about cars*

A ▶2:26 Read and listen. Then listen again and repeat.

| turn on | turn off | pick up | fill up | drop off |

B Complete the sentences with the two parts of each phrasal verb.

1 The car's almost out of gas. Let's go in here so I can ......*fill*...... it ......*up*...... .

2 It's raining, and I can't ......*turn*...... the windshield wipers ......*on*...... . They aren't working.

3 Can I use your car this afternoon? I can ......*pick*...... it ......*up*...... at 3:30 if you don't need it then.

4 We have to return the rental car before 6:00. Let's ......*drop*...... it ......*off*...... early at the airport and get something to eat, OK?

5 I can't ......*turn*...... the air conditioning ......*off*...... . It's freezing in here!

GRAMMAR *Placement of direct objects with phrasal verbs*

Phrasal verbs contain a verb and a particle that together have their own meaning.

main verb   particle
turn   +   on   =   start (a machine)

Many phrasal verbs are separable. This means that a direct object noun can come before or after the particle. <u>Turn on</u>, <u>turn off</u>, <u>pick up</u>, <u>drop off</u>, and <u>fill up</u> are separable.

direct object   direct object
I'll **drop off** the car. OR I'll drop the car off.

Be careful! With a separable phrasal verb, if the direct object is a pronoun, it must come before the particle.

I'll **drop** it **off**. (NOT I'll ~~drop off it~~.)
Did you **fill** them **up**? (NOT Did you ~~fill up them~~?)
Where will they **pick** us **up**? (NOT Where will they ~~pick up us~~?)

GRAMMAR BOOSTER p. 131
• Nouns and pronouns: review

PRONUNCIATION *Stress of particles in phrasal verbs*

A ▶2:27 Stress changes when an object pronoun comes before the particle. Read and listen. Then listen again and repeat.

1 A: I'd like to pick up my car.
  B: OK. What time can you pick it up?

2 A: They need to drop off the keys.
  B: Great. When do they want to drop them off?

VOCABULARY

A ▶2:26 Read and listen . . .

Suggested teaching time:	3 minutes	Your actual teaching time:

V Vocabulary Flash Card Player

- For a warm-up, write these phrasal verbs on the board: *turn on, turn off, pick up, fill up, drop off*. Then mime the action and ask *What am I doing?* For example, you might mime flipping a light switch on and off. If students are uncertain about the difference, when you flip the switch off, mime finding your way around a dark room.

- Have students listen and repeat as they look at the pictures to understand the different terms.

- To check comprehension, ask *What's the opposite of turn on?* (Turn off.) *What's the opposite of drop off?* (Pick up.)

- After students listen and practice, ask:
  What is the person turning on? (The engine.)
  Who is picking up a car—the man or the woman? (The woman.)

- Then have students listen and practice again.

B Complete the sentences . . .

Suggested teaching time:	3 minutes	Your actual teaching time:

- To prepare students, have them read the sentences and underline the context clues before they fill in the blanks. (1. Out of gas; 2. raining, windshield wipers; 3. car; 4. return, airport; 5. air conditioning, freezing.) Encourage students to review the phrasal verbs in the Vocabulary.

- After students complete the exercise, have them compare answers in pairs, referring to the context clues they underlined.

GRAMMAR

Suggested teaching time:	8–12 minutes	Your actual teaching time:

- To introduce the concept of phrasal verbs, write on the board *turn on, turn off, fill up*. Underline the main verbs and circle the particles. Explain that verbs are often combined with prepositions or adverb particles to form phrasal verbs which have their own meaning. Phrasal verbs are very common in spoken English. Write on the board *pick up, drop off*, and call on volunteers to underline the main verbs and circle the particles.

- After students silently read the first two rules and examples in the Grammar box, write on the board *turn on / engine; turn off / engine; pick up / car*. With the class, write a sample sentence on the board. Then have students create sentences by placing the direct object noun before the particle and then after the particle. (Turn the engine on, Turn on the engine; Turn the engine off, Turn off the engine; Pick the car up, Pick up the car.) Ask students to write their sentences on the board.

- Call on a student to read the Be careful! note in the Grammar box. Where possible, model the appropriate placement of the pronouns by rewriting the sentences on the board with direct object pronouns. (Turn it on. Turn it off. Pick it up.)

> **Language and culture**
>
> **From the Longman Corpus**
>
> - *Turn on* and *start* mean the same thing. *Start* is more frequently used with things such as cars and engines, whereas *turn on* is typically used with car lights, radios, and household appliances such as televisions and computers.
> - It is common for English learners across all language backgrounds to mistakenly place the direct object pronoun after the participle of phrasal verbs, especially *pick up*. Make sure students are aware that this is incorrect.
> - Other phrasal verbs are "inseparable," meaning direct objects (nouns and pronouns) cannot come between the verb and the particle. Examples of inseparable phrasal verbs are *call for, get on, get off,* and *care for*. Contrasting the syntax of separable and inseparable phrasal verbs is not recommended for students at this level.

Option: **GRAMMAR BOOSTER** *(Teaching notes p. T131)*

 Inductive Grammar Charts

PRONUNCIATION

A ▶2:27 Stress changes . . .

Suggested teaching time:	3 minutes	Your actual teaching time:

📹 Pronunciation Coach Video

- After students read and listen to the pairs of sentences, tell them to listen again, paying attention to the change in stress, and to repeat during the pauses.

- Tell students to take turns reading the sentences in pairs. Move around the room and listen for correct use of stress.

Option: (+2 minutes) For additional practice, write these sentences on the board:
Take away the dishes. Take them away. Take the dishes away. / Turn on the TV. Turn it on. Turn the TV on. / Look up the information. Look it up. Look the information up.
As students read the sentences, make sure they change stress when the object comes before the particle.

 Pronunciation Activities

B Grammar / Vocabulary practice

Suggested teaching time:	3–5 minutes	Your actual teaching time:

- To make sure that students understand the task, explain that they need to use the cues in parentheses to write a follow-up to the sentence in the book.
- Prepare students by asking them to underline the main verb and the particle of the phrasal verbs. Then have them circle the direct object pronoun. (Phrasal verbs: 1. turn on; 2. drop off; 3. turns off; 4. pick up; 5. fill up; Pronouns: 1. them; 2.–5. it.) Ask *Does the direct object pronoun go before or after the particle?* (Before.)
- Have students compare unscrambled sentences with a partner and then practice reading them. Remind students to pay attention to the change in stress when an object pronoun comes before the particle.

 Extra Grammar Exercises

CONVERSATION MODEL

A ▶2:28 Read and listen . . .

Suggested teaching time:	2 minutes	Your actual teaching time:

> These conversation strategies are implicit in the model:
> - Use "actually" to soften negative information.
> - Empathize with "I'm sorry to hear that."

- Preview the conversation by looking at the picture and asking *Who are the people in the picture?* (A car rental agent and a renter.) *What do you think they're talking about?* (The rental car.) *Does the woman on the left look happy?* (No.)
- Tell students to close their books and listen to the conversation. Then ask:
  Are there any problems with the car? (Yes. The windshield wipers aren't working.)
  Did the renter fill up the car with gas? (Yes.)
- Have students open their books and read and listen as you play the conversation again.

B ▶2:29 Rhythm and intonation

Suggested teaching time:	3 minutes	Your actual teaching time:

- Have students repeat each line chorally. Make sure they:
  - use rising intonation for *Was everything OK? Any other problems? Is the gas tank full?*
  - pause slightly after *actually.*
  - say *I'm sorry to hear that* without pausing.

C Find the grammar

Suggested teaching time:	2 minutes	Your actual teaching time:

- After students find the direct objects, write on the board:
  I'm dropping off <u>my car</u>.   I just filled <u>it</u> up.
  Ask *What is the placement of each direct object?* (*My car* appears after the verb and particle *drop off*; *it* comes after the verb *fill* and before the particle *up*.)

NOW YOU CAN   Describe a car problem

A Notepadding

Suggested teaching time:	3–7 minutes	Your actual teaching time:

- To prepare students for the activity, encourage pairs to brainstorm as much vocabulary as they can on their own. Refer students to page 40 for more vocabulary.
- Move around the room and help students as needed.

B Conversation activator

Suggested teaching time:	5–10 minutes	Your actual teaching time:

 Conversation Activator Video

- *Note:* You can print the script or you can show a running transcript on the video player on the ActiveTeach. The script also appears on page 184 of this Teacher's Edition.
- Be sure to reinforce the use of conversation strategies; for example, using "actually" to deliver unexpected information and using a sympathetic facial expression when saying "I'm sorry to hear that."
- Model extending the conversation with a more confident student by playing the role of Student A.
- Have pairs practice the conversation. Encourage pairs to refer to their notes as they continue the conversation.
- For more support, play the Conversation Activator Video before students do this activity themselves. In Scene 1, the actors use different words in the gaps from the ones in the Conversation Model. In Scene 2, the actors extend the conversation. After each scene, ask students how the model has been changed by the actors.

Conversation Activator Video Script; Conversation Activator Pair Work Cards

C Change partners

Suggested teaching time:	5 minutes	Your actual teaching time:

- Move around the room and help students as needed. Make sure students change roles and change the conversation at least once.

D Option

Suggested teaching time:	10 minutes	Your actual teaching time:

- Give students a few minutes to skim the language in the Recycle box, then review as needed. Encourage students to use all the language in the Recycle box by telling them to check off each question or phrase as they use it.

EXTRAS

Workbook or MyEnglishLab

 **Speaking Activities: Unit 4, Activity 2**

B **GRAMMAR / VOCABULARY PRACTICE** Write statements or questions, placing the direct objects correctly. Then practice reading the sentences aloud with a partner. Use correct stress.

1 The taillights aren't working. (can't / I / on / them / turn) .....I can't turn them on..... .

2 They're expecting the car at 10:00. (off / drop / 10:00 / at / I'll / it) .....I'll drop it off at 10:00..... .

3 It's too cold for air conditioning. (button / which / off / it / turns) .....Which button turns it off..... ?

4 Thanks for fixing the car. (it / pick / what time / I / can / up) .....What time can I pick it up..... ?

5 The car is almost out of gas. (up / please / fill / it) .....Please fill it up..... .

CONVERSATION MODEL

A ▶2:28 Read and listen to someone describing a car problem.

A: I'm dropping off <u>my car</u>.

B: Was everything OK?

A: Well, actually, the windshield wipers aren't working.

B: I'm sorry to hear that. Any other problems?

A: No. That's it.

B: Is the gas tank full?

A: Yes. I just filled <u>it</u> up.

B ▶2:29 **RHYTHM AND INTONATION** Listen again and repeat. Then practice the Conversation Model with a partner.

C **FIND THE GRAMMAR** Find and underline two direct objects in the Conversation Model.

NOW YOU CAN Describe a car problem

A **NOTEPADDING** Write two or more possible car parts for each car problem.

won't open / close:	*the sunroof, the hood . . .*
won't turn on / off:	
(is / are) making a funny sound:	
(isn't / aren't) working:	

B **CONVERSATION ACTIVATOR** With a partner, change the Conversation Model. Report a problem with a car. Use your notepad for ideas. Then change roles and problems.

A: I'm dropping off my car.
B: Was everything OK?
A: Well, actually ....
B: .... Any other problems?
A: ....

C **CHANGE PARTNERS** Describe other car problems.

D **OPTION** Role-play a conversation in which you report an accident when you drop off a rental car. Describe the accident. Say what you were doing when you had the accident, using the past continuous. Then change roles. Start like this:

A: I'm dropping off my car. I had an accident . . .

RECYCLE THIS LANGUAGE.

Oh, no!	Yes, the [taillight]
How did it happen?	is broken.
Is there any damage?	isn't working.
Was anyone hurt?	won't turn on / off.
	is making a funny sound.

BEFORE YOU LISTEN

A ▶2:30 **VOCABULARY • Car types** Read and listen. Then listen again and repeat.

DIGITAL
FLASH
CARDS

❶ a full-size sedan

❷ a compact car

❸ a convertible

❹ a sports car

❺ a station wagon

❻ a minivan / a van

❼ an SUV

❽ a luxury car

B **PAIR WORK** Which car would you like to drive? Which car would you *not* like to drive? Discuss with a partner, using the Vocabulary.

❝ I'd like to drive the luxury car because people will think I have a lot of money. ❞

❝ Really? I'd rather drive the convertible. It's really cool. ❞

LISTENING COMPREHENSION

A ▶2:31 **LISTEN FOR DETAILS** Listen. Write the car type that the speakers discuss in each conversation.

1 ....SUV........ 2 ....minivan........ 3 ....compact........ 4 ....luxury car........

B ▶2:32 **LISTEN TO SUMMARIZE** Listen again. Write a check mark if the caller rented a car. Then listen again. Write the reasons the other callers <u>didn't</u> rent a car.

☑ **1** ....

☐ **2** The company didn't have a minivan available at the right time. ....

☑ **3** ....

☐ **4** The caller was too young. ....

BEFORE YOU LISTEN

A ▶2:30 Vocabulary

Suggested teaching time:	3 minutes	Your actual teaching time:

V Vocabulary Flash Card Player

- After students listen and repeat, personalize the vocabulary by asking:
  Do you have a car? If yes, what type?
  Would you rather have a different type of car? If yes, what type?

> ### Language and culture
> - An *SUV (sports utility vehicle)* is also called a *four-wheel-drive vehicle. Four-wheel drive* means that all four wheels of the car—not just the two rear or front wheels—get power from the engine. Four-wheel drive makes it easier to get out of mud, sand, or snow and to drive on rough roads.

FYI: Depending on its size, a *sedan* can be categorized as a *compact* or *full-size* car. If a *sports car* has a roof that opens, it can also be a *convertible*.

 Learning Strategies

B Pair work

Suggested teaching time:	6–8 minutes	Your actual teaching time:

- To prepare students, review the vocabulary and the sample quotes, explaining vocabulary as needed.
- Model the activity by responding to the questions with your own information.
- Call on pairs to share their car preferences with the class.

Option: *(+10 minutes)* To extend the activity, have students discuss in groups which type of car fits their personality and lifestyle. Tell them to give reasons to support their choices. As an alternative to this activity, have pairs guess which car type fits the other person's personality.

LISTENING COMPREHENSION

A ▶2:31 Listen for details

Suggested teaching time:	5 minutes	Your actual teaching time:

- With books closed, have students listen to the conversations. Ask *Who is Clarence?* (An agent at Wheels Around the World, a rental car agency.) *Who is he talking to?* (Four customers.)
- To provide more support, before you play the audio again, write the four different kinds of cars on the board (out of order). Tell students to listen for these words in the conversations. For example:
  luxury car, minivan, compact, SUV
- After students complete the activity, have them compare answers in pairs.

B ▶2:32 Listen to summarize

Suggested teaching time:	11–12 minutes	Your actual teaching time:

- Read the directions and have students listen again for who rented a car. Then have them listen again to write the reasons people didn't rent cars.
- Ask students to compare answers in pairs. Then review answers with the class.

AUDIOSCRIPT

CONVERSATION 1 [F = Russian]
- **M:** Good morning. Wheels Around the World Rentals. This is Clarence. How may I help you today?
- **F:** Good morning. I need a rental car in La Paz.
- **M:** In Bolivia?
- **F:** That's right. I'm arriving on Tuesday, December 18th.
- **M:** At the La Paz El Alto airport?
- **F:** Yes, at 6:30 A.M.
- **M:** And what kind of car do you need?
- **F:** Something with four-wheel drive. Do you rent SUVs?
- **M:** Yes, we do.
- **F:** Great.

CONVERSATION 2
- **M1:** Good morning. Wheels Around the World Rentals. This is Malcolm. How may I help you today?
- **M2:** Good morning. Do you have a minivan available?
- **M1:** For what date, please?
- **M2:** For today.
- **M1:** And at which location?
- **M2:** Downtown.
- **M1:** Let me check. . . . Well, we have one coming in later today. A customer is returning it at about 4:00.
- **M2:** Four o'clock? No. Unfortunately that's too late. You won't have anything available sooner?
- **M1:** Not a minivan. I'm sorry, sir.
- **M2:** OK. Thanks, anyway. I'll try another company.

CONVERSATION 3 [F = British English]
- **M:** Good morning. Wheels Around the World Rentals. This is Clarence. How may I help you today?
- **F:** Hello? This is Ingrid Katz. Do you rent cars in the U.S.?
- **M:** Yes, Ms. Katz. Where do you need the car?
- **F:** At the Miami airport. On October the 4th, returning the car on October the 7th at the airport again.
- **M:** What kind of car were you looking for?
- **F:** Something small. A compact.
- **M:** Miami. Let me check . . . OK. We have compacts in Miami. Would you like me to reserve one for you?
- **F:** Oh, yes, please.

CONVERSATION 4
- **M1:** Good morning. Wheels Around the World Rentals. This is Malcolm. How may I help you today?
- **M2:** Good morning. I'd like to rent a car on Saturday. A luxury car, preferably white . . .
- **M1:** Yes?
- **M2:** Do you rent by the hour? I only need it for Saturday night.
- **M1:** Well, we do, at $25 an hour for luxury cars, but do you mind my asking you your age?
- **M2:** Excuse me?
- **M1:** How old are you?
- **M2:** I'm eighteen.
- **M1:** I'm sorry, sir. You have to be twenty-five to rent a car.

 **Rent a car**

A Pair work

Suggested teaching time:	8–11 minutes	Your actual teaching time:

- As pairs read each description, have them underline context clues that suggest which car would be best for each person. (1. Doesn't have a lot of luggage, needs a car for local travel; 2. Drive on some rough roads, car with four-wheel drive; 3. Husband and three children, plan to do a lot of shopping; 4. Wife and two children, lots of clothes and presents; 5. Invite three doctors to dinner, likes to drive.)
- After students suggest car types and reasons, tell them to work with another pair to compare their answers.

B Notepadding

Suggested teaching time:	7–10 minutes	Your actual teaching time:

- For a warm-up, ask some general questions:
  Have you or anyone in your family ever rented a car?
  If yes, did you make the reservation in person? On the phone? Online?
  What type of car did you (or your relatives) rent?
  Where did you go?
- Call on students to suggest destinations that would require a rental car.
- Review the headings on the notepad. Then have students work individually and make notes.

C Role play

Suggested teaching time:	15–20 minutes	Your actual teaching time:

- Ask pairs to study the car types on page 44 and decide which one best fits their needs for the trip they planned in Exercise B. If none of the pictured cars are appropriate for them, tell them to suggest another car and explain why they prefer it.

- After students have made their decisions, give them a few minutes to skim the language in the Recycle box, then review vocabulary as needed. Encourage students to use all the language in the Recycle box. Tell them to cross out each question or statement as they use it.
- Model the conversation by role-playing the phone call with a more confident student. Play the role of the caller and sit back-to-back to simulate an authentic phone conversation. Model using repair strategies such as *Sorry, can you repeat that?* or *Sorry, I don't understand. How do you spell that?*
- Have pairs role-play the agent and caller. Encourage pairs to make up a name for the rental agency they are calling.
- Move around the room and make sure students exchange roles and change the conversation at least once.
- Invite volunteers to role-play their calls for the class. As pairs perform, have the other students listen and take notes on which car is rented, and the reason for renting it. Review answers with the class.

Option: (+5–10 minutes) For additional practice, tell students to imagine that they are on a business trip and need to rent a car for five days. Have pairs discuss which of the cars they would pick.

EXTRAS

Workbook or MyEnglishLab

 Speaking Activities: Unit 4, Activity 3

A **PAIR WORK** Read about each customer at Wheels Around the World, an international car rental company. Choose the best type of car for each person. Discuss reasons with your partner.

> " A compact car is good for driving in a big city. It is easier to park in a small parking space. "

①

Background: Ms. Potter is a businesswoman from Boston, in the U.S. She is flying to Dallas to attend a business meeting. She doesn't have a lot of luggage. She only needs a car for local travel around Dallas.

Customer Profile

Car type: ....

Reason: ....

②

Background: Ms. Park is a tourist from Busan, Korea, visiting western Australia with her cousin. They enjoy hiking and fishing, and they're planning a road trip through the Lake District. They plan to drive on some rough roads, so they want a car with four-wheel drive.

Customer Profile

Car type: ....

Reason: ....

③

Background: Ms. Kimura is a tourist from Osaka, Japan, visiting national parks and cities in the western part of the U.S. with her husband and their three children. They plan to do a lot of shopping, too.

Customer Profile

Car type: ....

Reason: ....

④

Background: Mr. Lucena is a banker from Curitiba, Brazil. His son is getting married in Valparaíso, Chile. He wants to drive to Valparaíso from the airport in Santiago, Chile with his wife and their two other children for the wedding. They have a lot of clothes and presents for the wedding.

Customer Profile

Car type: ....

Reason: ....

⑤

Background: Dr. Andrade is from Pereira, Colombia. He's flying to an international medical conference in La Paz, Bolivia. He has invited three doctors to dinner and after-dinner entertainment. He likes to drive.

Customer Profile

Car type: ....

Reason: ....

B **NOTEPADDING** Plan a trip for which <u>you</u> need a rental car.

Destination	Pickup date	Drop off date	Number of companions	Activities

C **ROLE PLAY** With a partner, role-play a phone call to Wheels Around the World to rent a car for the trip you planned on your notepad. Choose one of the car types from the Vocabulary on page 44. Discuss the trip and your needs. Then change roles.

RECYCLE THIS LANGUAGE.

Agent
Hello. Wheels Around the World.
What kind of car [do you need / would you like]?
How many people are you traveling with?
When will you [pick up / drop off] the car?
Where will you drop off the car?
Would you rather rent [a full-sized sedan] or [an SUV]?

Caller
I'd like to make a reservation.
I'd like a [compact car].
I'd rather have a [van].
I'm traveling with [my husband].
It's a [business trip / vacation].
I [have / don't have] a lot of luggage.
Do you accept credit cards?

GOAL Discuss good and bad driving

BEFORE YOU READ

A ▶ 2:33 **VOCABULARY • *Driving behavior*** Read and listen. Then listen again and repeat.

Bad or aggressive drivers . . .

honk their horns

stare at other drivers

gesture at other drivers

flash their lights at other drivers

Good drivers . . .

pay attention

observe the speed limit

maintain a safe following distance

And don't forget . . .
speed
tailgate
talk on the phone
text while driving
weave through traffic
not stop at stoplights
not signal while turning
pass in a no-passing zone

B **WARM-UP** In your opinion, which of the bad and aggressive driving habits are the most dangerous? Why?

READING ▶ 2:34

FEATURE ARTICLE

Six Tips for Defensive Driving

We all know that not everyone drives well. Some people tailgate, gesture, weave through traffic, and honk—classic signs of the aggressive driving that causes one third of all car crashes. But more and more people are now talking on the phone, eating, and even watching TV as they drive—examples of the multitasking and inattentive driving that is a growing cause of accidents. Although we can't control the actions of other drivers, the following defensive driving tips can help us reduce the risks caused by our own driving and the bad driving of others.

1 **Slow down.** Driving too fast for weather or road conditions gives you less time to react to dangers on the road ahead of you. Also, as you increase your speed, your car becomes harder to control and takes longer to come to a stop.

2 **Follow the "3-second rule."** The greatest chance of a collision is in front of you. Maintaining a safe following distance of three seconds behind the car in front of you will give you enough time to react if that car slows or stops suddenly.

3 **Pay attention to your surroundings.** Be aware of where other vehicles are and what is happening on the road. Check your rearview and side-view mirrors frequently. Before changing lanes, always look over your shoulder to check your "blind spots"—areas to the side and rear of your car that aren't visible in your mirrors.

4 **Signal your intentions early.** Use turn signals to let other drivers know what you're going to do before you do it. This helps other drivers understand your plans so they can make their own defensive driving decisions.

5 **Expect the unexpected.** Assume that other drivers will make mistakes. Plan ahead what you will do if another driver breaks a traffic law or cuts you off. For example, don't assume that a vehicle coming to a stop sign or a red light is going to stop. Be prepared to stop your own car if necessary.

6 **Don't take others' aggressive driving personally.** Other people will drive badly. They're not thinking about you. If you permit them to make you angry, it can affect your own driving and lead to an accident. When other drivers show signs of aggressive driving, just slow down or pull over to let them pass.

BEFORE YOU READ

A ▶2:33 Vocabulary

Suggested teaching time:	3–5 minutes	Your actual teaching time:

V Vocabulary Flash Card Player

- Point out the term *Aggressive* in the first subhead. Explain that *aggressive* means angry or threatening.
- Have students read and listen to the vocabulary, and then have them listen and repeat. Answer any questions.
- Direct students' attention to the other bad driving habits in the "And don't forget . . ." box.

B Warm-up

Suggested teaching time:	3–6 minutes	Your actual teaching time:

- To introduce the topic, have students discuss the questions in small groups.
- Review answers as a class.

Option: (*+3 minutes*) To extend the discussion, ask *Which of these aggressive driving behaviors have you experienced? Have you ever done any of these things on the road? What was the result?*

▶2:34 READING

Suggested teaching time:	10–15 minutes	Your actual teaching time:

- Preview the article by reading the title aloud and asking *What is this article about?* (How to drive defensively.) *What do you think* defensive *means here?* (To avoid an accident.)
- Look at the picture and ask *Is he driving defensively? Why not?* (No. He's eating, drinking, and talking on the phone while driving.) *Do you ever do any of these things while driving?*
- Encourage students to activate their knowledge of the topic by closing their books and using the vocabulary to write four defensive driving tips with a negative imperative of their own. For example, *Don't honk your horn.* Then have them read the article.
- As students read the article, move around the room and provide help with any unfamiliar vocabulary as needed.
- After students have finished reading, ask *Did you see any of your tips in the article? Which ones?*
- Review the answers with the class.

> ### Language and culture
> - *To multitask* means to do many things at the same time; the prefix *multi* means *many*.
> - A *collision* is a crash.
> - To *maintain a safe following distance* means to keep driving at a safe distance from another car.
> - To *cut someone off* means to suddenly drive in front of them.
> - *To pull over* means to drive your car out of traffic; for example, onto the shoulder of a highway or the curb of a road.
> - *To take something personally* means to believe that actions or words are directed only at you, not other people.

Option: (*+10 minutes*) For additional practice, have students listen to the audio. Pause at the end of each numbered tip and ask students to summarize each tip.

 Learning Strategies

A Understand from context

Suggested teaching time:	3 minutes	Your actual teaching time:

- Have students scan the choices to complete each statement. Explain any words students don't know, or refer them to the article to find explanations in context.
- Have students complete the exercise individually. Then have them compare answers in pairs. Answer any remaining questions.

Option: (+3 minutes) As an alternative approach, before students circle the correct word or phrase, have them number the paragraphs in the Reading. Tell them to scan the article for the answer to each item in the exercise. Have students write the paragraph number where the answer can be found next to the item and work in pairs to complete the exercise.

Option: (+10 minutes) In pairs, have students look at the tips each of them wrote down before the Reading. Have them choose three tips to add to those in the article. Encourage students to write several sentences for each tip explaining what they mean. Have pairs share their ideas with the class.

B Critical thinking

Suggested teaching time:	5–7 minutes	Your actual teaching time:

- Write the question on the board for students to refer to: *How can defensive driving help drivers avoid accidents?*
- Have students write a list of ideas in pairs. Refer students to page 46 for ideas, if they need help.
- Combine pairs into groups of four to discuss their lists. Move around the room and help students as needed.

Option: (+15 minutes) To challenge students, have a brief debate. On the board, write *Should using cell phones while driving, including hands-free devices, be against the law?* Divide the class in half to form two groups and assign each group either the negative or affirmative answer. Tell each group to prepare arguments to support or oppose the assigned answer. Allow students to refer to the article for ideas and have groups share their arguments, allowing each side to respond. Write the arguments on the board. Then review the arguments and have students vote on which group made a stronger case.

 Extra Reading Comprehension Exercises

NOW YOU CAN Discuss good and bad driving

A Pair work

Suggested teaching time:	5 minutes	Your actual teaching time:

- Refer to the pictures on page 46 to review vocabulary.
- After students complete the survey, have them figure out their score and compare it with their partner's.
- Invite students to share their scores. Ask *Do you think your score accurately reflects your driving behavior? Why?*

Language and culture

- *Cool as a cucumber* is an idiom that means always calm and in control of one's emotions. This idiom may come from the fact that the inside of a cucumber stays cool even in warm weather.

Option: (+5–10 minutes) To extend the activity, write these questions on the board: *Do you think the laws against bad driving are strong enough? Why? How do you think better driving behavior could be encouraged?* Have students discuss the questions in small groups and share their answers with the class.

B Notepadding

Suggested teaching time:	7 minutes	Your actual teaching time:

- Allow students to complete the activity individually. Then place them in pairs to compare lists.
- Ask *Why do you think people do the things on your bad drivers list?* Have groups discuss. (Possible responses: People are in a hurry so they speed, tailgate, cut off other drivers, and weave through traffic. Because people talk and text on their phones while they drive.)

C Discussion

Suggested teaching time:	10–12 minutes	Your actual teaching time:

- For a warm-up, say *Raise your hand if you think you're a good driver. Raise your hand if you think you're a bad driver. An OK driver.* Write the numbers of students in each category on the board. Ask *How many of you know someone who is a bad driver?* Circle the bad driver numbers.

Note: If your students don't drive yet, you can say *Raise your hand if you think you'll be a good driver, a bad driver, or an OK driver.*

Text-mining: Review the instructions with the class, then have students skim the article and underline appropriate language. For example, *. . . is a growing cause of accidents; defensive driving tips can help us reduce . . . ; slow down or pull over . . . ; be prepared to stop your own car if necessary.* Write students' findings on the board for them to refer to during the discussion.

- Have students work in groups to discuss the question in the book. Encourage students to come to an agreement on their conclusion. Assign one student the role of taking notes.
- Review the group conclusions with the class.

EXTRAS

Workbook or MyEnglishLab

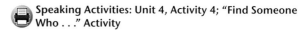 Speaking Activities: Unit 4, Activity 4; "Find Someone Who . . ." Activity

A **UNDERSTAND FROM CONTEXT** Circle the correct word or phrase to complete each statement.

1 A person who is doing more than one activity at the same time is (multitasking / driving defensively).

2 Following the "3-second rule" means maintaining a safe (road condition / following distance).

3 Tailgating, gesturing, and honking are three examples of (inattentive / aggressive) driving.

4 Not paying attention is an example of (inattentive / aggressive) driving.

5 *Collision* and *crash* are two words that mean (danger / accident).

6 A part of the road that you can't see in your mirrors is called a (blind spot / lane).

B **CRITICAL THINKING** How can defensive driving help drivers avoid accidents? Explain your opinion, using the Vocabulary and examples from the Reading or from your own experience.

NOW YOU CAN Discuss good and bad driving

A **PAIR WORK** Complete the survey and then compare surveys with a partner.

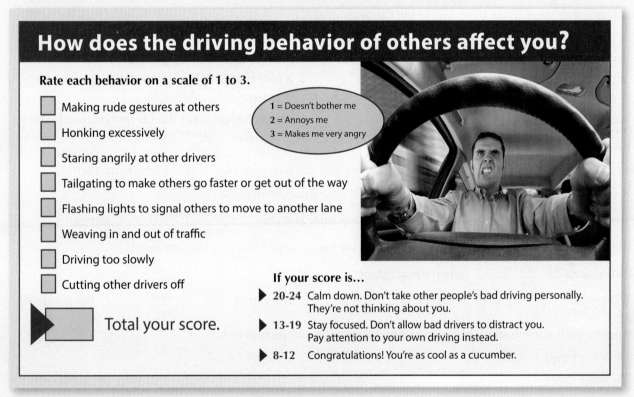

How does the driving behavior of others affect you?

Rate each behavior on a scale of 1 to 3.

☐ Making rude gestures at others

☐ Honking excessively

☐ Staring angrily at other drivers

☐ Tailgating to make others go faster or get out of the way

☐ Flashing lights to signal others to move to another lane

☐ Weaving in and out of traffic

☐ Driving too slowly

☐ Cutting other drivers off

1 = Doesn't bother me
2 = Annoys me
3 = Makes me very angry

Total your score.

If your score is…

▶ 20-24 Calm down. Don't take other people's bad driving personally. They're not thinking about you.

▶ 13-19 Stay focused. Don't allow bad drivers to distract you. Pay attention to your own driving instead.

▶ 8-12 Congratulations! You're as cool as a cucumber.

B **NOTEPADDING** Describe what good and bad drivers do. Use the Vocabulary.

Good drivers . . .	Aggressive drivers . . .
use their turn signals	flash their lights at others

C **DISCUSSION** Discuss good and bad driving. What percentage of drivers do you think are bad or aggressive? Use your notepad for support.

Text-mining (optional)
Find and underline three words or phrases in the Reading that were new to you. Use them in your Discussion.
For example: "slow down."

REVIEW

A ▶2:35 Listen to the conversations. Then complete the statements with words and phrases for bad or aggressive driving.

1 The other driver just .... *cut* .... them .... *off* ....

2 Jim's mother says he's .... *tailgating* ....

3 The driver behind them is .... *honking* .... at them.

4 The driver opened his window and .... *gestured* .... at them.

5 The driver is .... *flashing his lights* .... because he wants to pass.

6 The driver is .... *weaving through traffic* ....

7 The driver is .... *staring* .... at them.

B Read each definition. Write the name of the car part.

1 a window on the top of the car:
.... *sunroof* ....

2 a part that stops the car: .... *brakes* ....

3 a window the driver looks through to see the cars in front: .... *windshield* ....

4 a place where the driver can find information about speed and amount of gas: .... *dashboard* ....

5 a part that people wear to avoid injuries in an accident: .... *seat belt* ....

6 a part that prevents the car from moving when it's parked: .... *emergency brake* ....

C Complete each statement or question about driving. Use the past continuous or the simple past tense.

1 I .... *was not paying attention* .... , and I .... *had* .... an accident.
    not pay attention   *have*

2 The other driver .... *did not stop* .... at the stop sign, and she .... *was not wearing* .... a seat belt.
    not stop   *not wear*

3 He .... *was talking* .... on a cell phone, and his car .... *damaged* .... my trunk.
    talk   *damage*

4 Who .... *was driving* .... when the accident .... *occurred* .... ?
    drive   *occur*

5 Where .... *were* .... they .... *standing* .... when they .... *saw* .... the accident?
    stand   *see*

D Complete each conversation, putting the phrasal verbs and objects in order.

1 A: Won't the car start?

    B: No. I can't .... *turn it on* ....
       it / turn / on

2 A: Do you need gas?

    B: Yes. Please .... *fill it up* ....
       up / fill / it

3 A: Hey, you haven't turned on your headlights.

    B: Oops. Thanks. I can't believe I forgot to .... *turn them on* ....
       turn / on / them

4 A: Can All Star Limo drive us to the airport?

    B: Yes. They'll .... *pick us up* .... at 5:30.
       us / pick / up

For additional language practice . . .

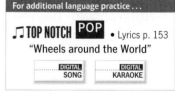

♫ TOP NOTCH **POP** • Lyrics p. 153
"Wheels around the World"

DIGITAL SONG | DIGITAL KARAOKE

WRITING

Write a short paragraph about the differences between good and bad drivers. Include language from pages 38, 44, and 46 in your paragraph.

WRITING BOOSTER p. 146
• Connecting words and sentences: And, In addition, Furthermore, and Therefore
• Guidance for this writing exercise

A ▶ 2:35 Listen to the conversations . . .

Suggested teaching time:	10 minutes	Your actual teaching time:

- For review, refer students to the aggressive driving behaviors in the Vocabulary on page 46. To support weaker students, write these expressions on the board for students to refer to.

- Before students listen, have them read the fill-in statements. Then play the audio once or twice for students to listen and fill in the blanks. If necessary, play the audio one more time.

AUDIOSCRIPT

CONVERSATION 1
  F: Oh, my gosh! Did you see that?
  M: No. What happened?
  F: That guy in the white van just turned in front of us. I almost hit him.
  M: Wow! What's *his* big hurry?

CONVERSATION 2
  F: Jim, don't you think you're driving a little too close to the car in front of us?
  M: No way. I've got great reaction time.
  F: Well, you'd better have good brakes!

CONVERSATION 3
  M: Hey, keep your shirt on, mister.
  F: What is *wrong* with that guy? He does that at every light.
  M: Who knows. Some people can't stand to wait two seconds after the light changes.
  F: Yeah. But the rest of us can't stand all that noise!

CONVERSATION 4
  M1: Did you see what that guy just did?
  M2: No, I didn't.
  M1: He just opened his window and gave me some kind of sign with his hand.
  M2: What's that supposed to mean?
  M1: I don't want to know.

CONVERSATION 5
  F1: Why's that guy behind us doing that with his lights?
  F2: Beats me. Maybe he wants to pass.
  F1: Well, he can be my guest. With all this traffic he won't get very far.

CONVERSATION 6
  F: Look at the way that guy's driving. He just passed us on the left and now he's passing that car on the right.
  M: There he goes again. Now he's in the left lane passing another car.
  F: Unbelievable. He thinks he owns the road!
  M: You know what bugs me? There's never a policeman around when people drive like that.
  F: You can say that again!

CONVERSATION 7
  M: Why is that man looking at us like that? He looks so angry.
  F: You're right. He does.
  M: Yeah. But why's he doing that?
  F: He probably doesn't like the way you drive. Don't even look back at him.

B Read each definition . . .

Suggested teaching time:	3 minutes	Your actual teaching time:

- Encourage students to try to do the exercise without referring to the Vocabulary on page 40. Then have pairs compare answers and refer to the car images.

C Complete each statement or question . . .

Suggested teaching time:	3 minutes	Your actual teaching time:

- Encourage students to check their answers in pairs by asking each other *Did the action continue during a period of time in the past?* Use the past continuous. *Did the action occur and then end?* Use the simple past tense.

- Call on volunteers to name the actions that occurred and ended. (1. had an accident; 2. did not stop; 3. damaged my truck; 4. the accident occurred; 5. they saw.)

D Complete each conversation . . .

Suggested teaching time:	3 minutes	Your actual teaching time:

- If necessary, remind students to place the direct object pronoun before the particle.

- As students compare their responses and practice reading the conversations, tell them to pay attention to the change in stress when an object pronoun comes before the particle.

WRITING

Suggested teaching time:	10 minutes	Your actual teaching time:

- To prepare for writing, refer students to their notepads on page 47. Tell students to find a partner who was not in their discussion group and discuss the ideas from their notepads.

- If students have trouble organizing their ideas, tell them to write about two people they know; for example, one who's a good driver and one who's a bad driver.

- Have students check their papers for errors. Ask *Does every sentence have a subject and verb? Do the subjects and verbs agree?*

- Have students exchange papers with a partner and ask each other questions if something is not clear.

Option:  **WRITING BOOSTER** (*Teaching notes p. T146*)

 Writing Process Worksheets

🎵 🎤 *Top Notch Pop* Song Video and Karaoke Video

 Digital Games

ORAL REVIEW

Before the first activity, give students a few minutes of silent time to become familiar with the pictures.

Group story

Suggested teaching time:	10–15 minutes	Your actual teaching time:	

• To prepare, have students look at the four pictures and say all the words they know. Write them on the board.

Possible responses . . .
> car rental, agent, woman, man, SUV, service station, fill up, speeding, not paying attention, talking on a cell phone, accident, damage, hood, bumper, broken headlights

• Tell students to give the characters names and create a story about them. Remind students to use the simple past tense for finished actions and the past continuous for actions that continued during a period of time in the past.

Possible responses . . .
> John and Melissa Green picked up their rental car in Temuco on January 16. They rented an SUV. First they filled up the car with gas. John was not a good driver. Most of the time he was speeding and not paying attention. Melissa was not paying attention because she was talking on her phone, and John wasn't watching the road. Then he saw a lot of cows in the road. He had an accident. Luckily, no one was hurt. But there was damage to the car. They will have to replace the headlights and fix the hood and the bumper. Melissa called the rental agency and told them about the accident.

Pair work 1

Suggested teaching time:	5–10 minutes	Your actual teaching time:	

• Assign each pair one of the illustrations. Before students create conversations, have them scan the illustration and suggest all possible scenarios. Encourage students to look back at the unit for vocabulary and ideas.

Possible responses . . .
> January 16
> **A:** Hello. My name is Melissa Green. I have a reservation. **B:** Yes, of course. A compact car, right? **A:** No, I requested an SUV. **B:** OK, no problem. We have an SUV available. You'd like the car for two weeks, right? **A:** Yes, that's right. **B:** I'll need your driver's license and a major credit card. **A:** Here you go. **B:** Here are the keys. Enjoy your trip!
>
> January 17
> **A:** Fill it up, please. **B:** Yes, ma'am. Anything else? **A:** Can you check the engine, please? It's making a funny noise. **B:** Can you drop off the car later? **A:** Actually, can you look at it right away? We're traveling. **B:** OK. I have some time now. **A:** Thank you very much.
>
> January 18
> **A:** Look at that mountain! **B:** Yes, it's beautiful. Sally, this is Melissa. We're in Chile! **A:** We can climb to the top tomorrow. **B:** What? Oh, OK. Sally? We're having so much fun. We rented a great red SUV. We're going to climb a mountain tomorrow.

Pair work 2

Suggested teaching time:	5–10 minutes	Your actual teaching time:	

• To prepare students for the activity, tell them to look at the illustration and suggest all possible scenarios. Encourage students to look back at the unit for vocabulary and ideas.

Possible responses . . .
> **A:** Good morning, Multi Car Rentals. This is Pedro. How may I help you? **B:** Pedro, this is Melissa Green. My husband and I had an accident! **A:** Oh, no! Are you OK? **B:** Yes, we're fine. No one was hurt. **A:** Thank goodness. Was there much damage to the car? **B:** Well, we'll have to replace the headlights. And fix the hood and the bumper.

Option: (+15 minutes) Have students look at the third and fourth pictures and make notes about the accident and its causes. Encourage students to look at the list of words on the board from the Group Story and to read the car parts Vocabulary on page 40. After students have finished writing, have pairs read each other's writing and compare details they included.

Option: Oral Progress Assessment

• Use the illustrations on page 49. Encourage students to use the language practiced in this unit.

• Point to the different items in the illustrations and have students identify them.

• Ask information questions; for example, *Where are they? What are they doing? Where do they want to go? What's this? What is he doing? Who is she talking to? What happened? How did the accident happen?*

• Invite a student to role-play a telephone conversation with you. Play the role of the woman and ask the student to play the receptionist at Multi Car Rentals.

• Evaluate the student on intelligibility, fluency, correct use of grammar, and appropriate use of vocabulary.

 Oral Progress Assessment Charts

Option: *Top Notch* Project

Have students research a news article about a car accident and prepare a presentation to the class.

Idea: Have students bring articles about car accidents to the class. The articles do not have to be in English.

Tell students to work in pairs and choose one article to present. Have pairs make notes about the article they choose, using the questions as a guide.

Students can refer to their notes when they present the accident to the class.

EXTRAS

On the Internet:
• Online Teacher Resources: pearsonelt.com/topnotch3e/

Additional printable resources on the ActiveTeach:
• Assessment
• Just for Fun
• *Top Notch Pop* Song Activities
• *Top Notch TV* Video Program and Activity Worksheets
• Supplementary Pronunciation Lessons
• Conversation Activator Video Scripts
• Audioscripts and Answer Keys
• Unit Study Guides

ORAL REVIEW

GROUP STORY Together, create a story about the pictures. Each person adds one sentence to the story. Begin with January 16. Use the past continuous and the simple past tense in your story. Start like this:

They picked up their rental car in Temuco on January 16 . . .

PAIR WORK

1 Create conversations for the people in the first three pictures. For example:

   A: *We'd like to rent a car.*
   B: *Certainly. What kind of a car do you need?*

2 Create a phone conversation for the fourth picture. The woman reports the accident to Multi Car Rentals. The agent responds. Say as much as you can. For example:

   We had an accident. My husband was . . .

January 16

January 17

January 18

Later

✓ NOW I CAN

☐ Discuss a car accident.
☐ Describe a car problem.
☐ Rent a car.
☐ Discuss good and bad driving.

COMMUNICATION GOALS

1 Ask for something in a store.
2 Make an appointment at a salon or spa.
3 Discuss ways to improve appearance.
4 Define the meaning of beauty.

UNIT 5 Personal Care and Appearance

PREVIEW

THE APEX SPA and FITNESS CENTER
For a better-looking—and better—you!

WORLD CLASS TOP NOTCH SALON SERVICES ▾

haircuts

facials

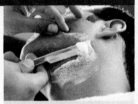

shaves

FULLY EQUIPPED SPA ▾

manicures

pedicures

massage:
Swedish, therapeutic, or shiatsu

GROUP EXERCISE CLASSES ▾

yoga ...

kickboxing ...

Pilates ...

spinning ... and more

STATE OF THE ART GYM ▾

The latest in exercise equipment

Make an appointment
with our personal
trainers.

A ▶ 3:02 **VOCABULARY • *Salon services*** Read and listen. Then listen again and repeat.

| a haircut | a facial | a shave | a manicure | a pedicure |

B **PAIR WORK** With a partner, discuss the Apex Club services. What are the advantages of combining exercise and fitness with spa and massage services in one club?

UNIT 5 Personal Care and Appearance

PREVIEW

Before Exercise A, give students a few minutes of silent time to examine the spa brochure.

Suggested teaching time:	12–17 minutes	Your actual teaching time:

- Introduce the topic by writing *spa* on the board. Ask *What kinds of services does a spa offer? Have you or has anyone you know ever been to a spa?*
- Check comprehension by asking:
  What is this brochure for? (A spa and fitness center.)
  What can you do at this place? (Take exercise classes, work out at a gym, make an appointment with a personal trainer, use salon services, get a massage.)
- Tell students to discuss these questions in pairs: *In your opinion, which of these services are the most essential at a spa? Which are the least essential?*

> **Language and culture**
> - *Swedish massage* includes five basic massage strokes and focuses on the muscles and connective tissues in the body.
> - *Shiatsu* is a Japanese form of massage that focuses on pressure points and energy paths in the body. Some people believe shiatsu massage can relieve muscle and joint pain by correcting energy imbalances in the body.

A Vocabulary

Suggested teaching time:	3 minutes	Your actual teaching time:

V Vocabulary Flash Card Player

- After students read and listen once, have them look at the photos that illustrate the services in the brochure. Ask questions to test comprehension of the vocabulary. For example: *Which salon service are you getting when someone is cutting your toenails?* (A pedicure.)
- Explain that we use the verbs *give* or *get* with the salon services. A customer <u>gets</u> the service and the salon worker <u>gives</u> the service.

 Learning Strategies

B Pair work

Suggested teaching time:	3 minutes	Your actual teaching time:

- Draw a chart on the board with two headings: *Advantages* and *Disadvantages*. Tell pairs to copy the chart and to fill it in with the advantages and disadvantages they discuss.
- Call on pairs to share their ideas with the class.

C ▶ 3:03 Photo story

Suggested teaching time:	12–15 minutes	Your actual teaching time:

- To prepare students, tell them to look at the photos and answer these questions:

  Why do you think the man is in the salon? (To get a haircut.)

  What does the woman give the man? (A towel. Maybe he's there to get a massage and a haircut.)

- Have students read and listen to the conversation. Make sure students understand the meaning of *while I'm at it* (while I am doing something else).

- Have students listen and read a second time. To check comprehension, ask:

  What services is the client interested in? (A massage and a haircut.)

  What time will he get his massage? (11:00, since someone canceled his or her appointment.)

  What time can he get a haircut? (12:00.)

  Is this salon in Europe? How do you know? (Yes, it's in Europe. The price is quoted in euros.)

  What does the client ask the receptionist at the end of the conversation? (If he should tip the staff.)

Language and culture

- At places where appointments are necessary, such as salons, businesses, or doctors' offices, it is common to refer to people by the time of their appointment; for example, *Your one o'clock is here.* OR *Your nine o'clock canceled.*

- *Would it be possible to . . .* is a way to make a request when the speaker wants a special favor.

Option: (+8 minutes) For an alternative approach before reading the Photo Story, ask students to cover the conversation. Tell them to use the photos to predict what the people are saying.

D Focus on language

Suggested teaching time:	5 minutes	Your actual teaching time:

- Model the activity by doing the first item with the class. Then tell students to work individually and underline the phrases in the conversation. Move around the room and explain unfamiliar vocabulary as needed.

- Review the answers as a class and have pairs practice the conversation.

Option: (+5 minutes) Assign pairs one of the expressions they underlined and have them create a two-line conversation using it. For example:

A: *I really need a haircut.*

B: *You're in luck. There's a hair salon in this hotel.*

Answers to Exercise D

1. Would it be possible to get a massage?
2. You're in luck. Our eleven o'clock just called to cancel his appointment.
3. How much will the massage and haircut come to?
4. It will be 110 euros in all.
5. Not a problem.
6. Well, that's up to you.

SPEAKING

A Personalize

Suggested teaching time:	5–10 minutes	Your actual teaching time:

- Give students a moment to skim the different services. If necessary, refer them to the previous page to review vocabulary. Then ask students to read the words and phrases and to indicate how often they get the services. Explain as needed: *once in a while* means sometimes. Point out that the words and phrases are listed from least often to most often. Explain that *I do this for myself!* means that the person never goes to the salon to get these services; instead they do the services for themselves.

- Before pairs compare answers, write on the board *How often do you get a ___?* Remind students that customers use the verb *get* to talk about services they receive and that these are countable nouns.

B Pair work

Suggested teaching time:	5–7 minutes	Your actual teaching time:

- Ask students to rank the salon services in Exercise A from 1 (most useful) to 6 (least useful). Have students explain their ranking in groups using the samples in quotes as models. Then have students compare opinions with a partner.

- When the groups have finished, survey the class responses to find which salon services are considered the most and least useful.

Workbook

C ▶3:03 **PHOTO STORY** Read and listen to a conversation in a spa salon.

ENGLISH FOR TODAY'S WORLD
Understand English speakers from
different language backgrounds.
Receptionist = French speaker

Receptionist: Can I help you, sir?

Client: Would it be possible to get a massage? I don't have an appointment.

Receptionist: Well, actually, you're in luck. Our eleven o'clock just called to cancel his appointment.

Client: Terrific.

Receptionist: Let me show you to the dressing area.

Client: Thanks. Oh, while I'm at it, do you think I could get a haircut, too?

Receptionist: Yes. But you might have to wait a bit. We don't have anything until 12:00.

Client: Not a problem. By the way, how much will the massage and haircut come to?

Receptionist: Let's see . . . it will be 110 euros in all.

Client: Great. One more question. Is it customary to tip the staff?

Receptionist: Well, that's up to you. But most clients give the stylist and the masseuse a euro or two each.

D **FOCUS ON LANGUAGE** Answer the questions, using language from the Photo Story.   See page T51 for answers.

1 How does the client ask for a massage?

2 How does the receptionist indicate that the client can have a massage without an appointment?

3 How does the client ask about the price of a massage and a haircut?

4 What phrase does the receptionist use to tell the client the total cost of the salon services?

5 How does the client say "That's OK"?

6 What expression does the receptionist use to tell the client that the amount to tip is <u>his</u> decision?

SPEAKING

A **PERSONALIZE** Check the word or phrase that best describes how often you get these salon services. Then compare charts with a partner.

	weekly	monthly	once in a while	never	I do this for myself!
haircut	☐	☐	☐	☐	☐
facial	☐	☐	☐	☐	☐
shave	☐	☐	☐	☐	☐
manicure	☐	☐	☐	☐	☐
pedicure	☐	☐	☐	☐	☐
massage	☐	☐	☐	☐	☐

B **PAIR WORK** In your opinion, what is the value of each service? Compare opinions with a partner.

❝ I think massages are great for backaches. A massage helps me feel better. ❞

❝ A shave? Are you kidding? I do that myself. I don't go to salons! ❞

GOAL Ask for something in a store

DIGITAL FLASH CARDS

VOCABULARY *Personal care products*

A ▶ 3:04 Read and listen. Then listen again and repeat.

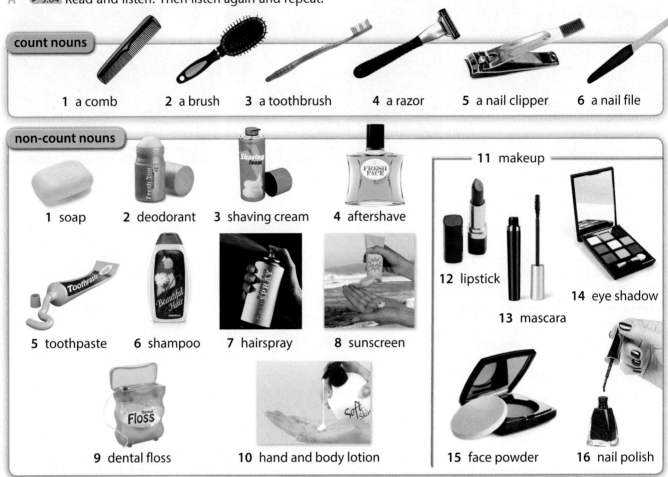

count nouns

1 a comb   2 a brush   3 a toothbrush   4 a razor   5 a nail clipper   6 a nail file

non-count nouns

1 soap   2 deodorant   3 shaving cream   4 aftershave

5 toothpaste   6 shampoo   7 hairspray   8 sunscreen

11 makeup

12 lipstick   13 mascara   14 eye shadow

9 dental floss   10 hand and body lotion

15 face powder   16 nail polish

B ▶ 3:05 **LISTEN TO INFER** Listen and circle the kind of product each ad describes.

1 Spring Rain (shampoo / deodorant)
2 Rose (soap / nail polish)
3 Pro-Tect (sunscreen / hand and body lotion)

4 All Over (face powder / hand and body lotion)
5 Scrubbie (toothpaste / shaving cream)
6 Maximum Hold (hairspray / shampoo)

GRAMMAR *Quantifiers for indefinite quantities and amounts*

Use some and any with both plural count nouns and non-count nouns.

some: affirmative statements
We bought some combs. Now we have some.
They need some soap. We have some.

any: negative statements
I don't have any razors. I don't want any.
We don't want any makeup. We don't need any.

some or any: questions
Do you want any aftershave?   OR   Do you want some aftershave?
Does she have any nail files?   OR   Does she have some nail files?

VOCABULARY

A ▶3:04 Read and listen . . .

Suggested teaching time:	10–15 minutes	Your actual teaching time:

Ⓥ Vocabulary Flash Card Player

- Ask a student to read the caption from the first item in each group of products. (A comb, soap.) Ask *Which word has an article?* (Comb.) *Why? Which group does* comb *belong to?* (Count nouns.) Remind students that non-count nouns do not have articles.

- Have students listen and repeat. Make sure they repeat the indefinite articles with the count nouns.

- Check comprehension by having students close their books. Write these products on the board: *toothbrush, toothpaste, razor, shaving cream.* Ask *Which do we use to clean our teeth? To shave our faces or legs?* Write on the board *a toothbrush and toothpaste, a razor and shaving cream.* Emphasize the use of the indefinite article with the two count nouns.

> #### Language and culture
> - *Soap, toothpaste,* and *shampoo* are non-count nouns, but they often appear in these countable phrases: *a bar of soap, a tube of toothpaste,* and *a bottle of shampoo.*
> - The term *makeup* is a category and includes all the items in the picture: lipstick, mascara, eye shadow, face powder, and nail polish.

Option: *(+5–7 minutes)* For additional practice, play a game. Tell students to look at all the vocabulary items for two minutes and then close their books. Ask them how many of the items they can remember. Have students work in pairs from memory to complete a list of all twenty-two items from the vocabulary. The pair who remembers the most items or completes the list first is the winner.

B ▶3:05 Listen to infer

Suggested teaching time:	5–8 minutes	Your actual teaching time:

- Before students listen, read the product names. Based on the name, ask students to predict the type of product each one is. Explain that the brand names are listed first and the type of product appears in parentheses. Tell them to underline their predictions and then listen once or twice to check if their predictions were correct. Have students compare their answers in pairs.

- Tell students to listen again and write key words from each ad that suggest what the product is. (Possible responses: 1. hair. 2. hands clean, washing your hands, clean hands; 3. protect your skin from the sun; 4. skin dry and rough, skin feels dry. 5. brighter, whiter teeth; dental cream. 6. keep your hair in place.)

- Invite students to share their words with the class.

> #### AUDIOSCRIPT
> **1 M:** Do you want softer, cleaner-smelling hair every time you wash? Ask for Spring Rain at your local drugstore or cosmetics store. Or order online at www.springrain.com.
> **2 F:** Can't get your hands clean after a day in the garden? Try washing your hands with Rose. You'll get clean hands fast!
> **3 M:** Doctors say it's important to protect your skin from the sun. So, even on a cloudy day, don't go out without ProTect and keep your skin healthy and young.
> **4 F:** Does soap make your skin dry and rough? Well, All Over is the answer. All Over Liquid Smoother. Use All Over after bath or shower. Use All Over whenever your skin feels dry.
> **5 M:** For brighter, whiter teeth, use Scrubbie Dental Cream twice a day, morning and night, and see results in less than a week. And have sweeter-smelling breath from day one!
> **6 F:** Windy day? Hate to wear a hat? Maximum Hold will keep your hair in place even in the worst weather. Just shampoo, dry, and style your hair as usual. Then apply twice before going out. Your hair will look as good at the end of the day as it does when you step out. Get Maximum Hold for your hair.

GRAMMAR

Suggested teaching time:	10–12 minutes	Your actual teaching time:

- To introduce *some* and *any*, write on the board: *1. some—affirmative statements, 2. any—negative statements, 3. some or any—questions.* Read the example sentences in the Grammar box and ask *Which category does each one belong in?*

- Review the first point in the Grammar box. Emphasize that the noun is not repeated in the shortened second sentence. Explain that it is possible to use *some* and *any* with and without nouns. Here it is also possible to say *Now we have some combs. We have some soap. I don't want any razors. We don't need any makeup.*

- Review the second point in the Grammar box. Explain that *some* and *any* have the same meaning in questions, and they can be used interchangeably.

GRAMMAR (Continued)

* Go over the rule and example sentences for *a lot of* and *lots of*. Tell students that these two quantifiers are interchangeable. Then ask *What about you? Do you have a lot of razors? Do you use a lot of sunscreen? Do you buy a lot of makeup?* (I have / don't have <u>a lot of</u> razors. I use / don't use <u>a lot of</u> sunscreen. I buy / don't buy <u>a lot of</u> makeup.)

* Have students read the rule and example sentences for *many* and *much*. On the board, write *hairspray, toothbrush, comb, soap.* Tell students to add *many* or *much* to each item and create a negative sentence.

Option: GRAMMAR BOOSTER *(Teaching notes p. T132)*

 Inductive Grammar Charts

Grammar practice

Suggested teaching time:	3 minutes	Your actual teaching time:	

* Have students complete the conversation. Encourage them to refer to the Grammar box, if necessary.

* Review answers with the class.

 Extra Grammar Exercises

CONVERSATION MODEL

A ▶3:06 Read and listen . . .

Suggested teaching time:	2–3 minutes	Your actual teaching time:	

> These conversation strategies are implicit in the model:
> * Use "Excuse me" to initiate a conversation with a salesperson.
> * Confirm information by repeating it with rising intonation.
> * Use "No problem" to show you don't mind an inconvenience.

* Use the photo to predict the conversation. Ask:
  Where are the two men? (In a store / a drugstore.)
  Who are they? (A customer and a store clerk.)
  What do you think the clerk is doing? (Showing the customer where something is.)

* Have students read and listen. Then ask:
  What does the customer want to buy? (Sunscreen and razors.)
  How does he ask for the sunscreen? (Where would I find sunscreen?)

B ▶3:07 Rhythm and intonation

Suggested teaching time:	3 minutes	Your actual teaching time:	

* Have students repeat chorally. Make sure they:
  ○ use falling intonation for *Where would I find sunscreen?*
  ○ use rising intonation for *Sunscreen?* and *Anything else?*
  ○ pause slightly after *Actually.*

C Find the grammar

Suggested teaching time:	2 minutes	Your actual teaching time:	

* After students find and underline the quantifiers, ask *Which sentences are affirmative?* (Those with *some*.) *Negative?* (Those with *any*.)

* Then ask *What noun do the first two sentences refer to?* (Sunscreen.) *The second two sentences?* (Razors.) *Which is a count noun?* (Razor.) *Non-count?* (Sunscreen.)

NOW YOU CAN Ask for something in a store

A Conversation activator

Suggested teaching time:	8–13 minutes	Your actual teaching time:	

 Conversation Activator Video

* *Note:* You can print the script or you can show a running transcript on the video player on the ActiveTeach. The script also appears on page 184 of this Teacher's Edition.

* Encourage students to use the directory and the language in the Recycle box in their conversations, along with the Vocabulary on page 52. Model the conversation with a more confident student, using this language.

> DON'T STOP! Encourage students to keep their conversations going by asking more questions. For example: *Where would I find the toothpaste?*

* For more support, play the Conversation Activator Video before students do this activity themselves. In Scene 1, the actors use different words in the gaps from the ones in the Conversation Model. In Scene 2, the actors extend the conversation. After each scene, ask students how the model has been changed by the actors.

Conversation Activator Video Script; Conversation Activator Pair Work Cards; Learning Strategies

B Change partners

Suggested teaching time:	5 minutes	Your actual teaching time:	

* Encourage students to practice the conversation in other types of stores. Ask *What kind of store can you buy clothes / food / electronics in?* (Possible responses: Department stores; grocery stores / convenience stores; electronics stores / appliance stores /office supply stores.) Review specific products that might be found in each type of store.

* Remind students to change partners when finished.

* Invite pairs to role-play their conversations for the class. Check comprehension by asking *What items was the person looking for?*

EXTRAS

Workbook or MyEnglishLab

 Speaking Activities: Unit 5, Activity 1

Use <u>a lot of</u> or <u>lots of</u> with both plural count nouns and non-count nouns in statements and questions. They have the same meaning.

That store has **a lot of** (or **lots of**) razors. They don't have **a lot of** (or **lots of**) sunscreen. Do they have **a lot of** (or **lots of**) makeup?

Use <u>many</u> and <u>much</u> in negative statements.

many: with plural count nouns	**much:** with non-count nouns
They don't have **many** brands of makeup.	The store doesn't have **much** toothpaste.

GRAMMAR BOOSTER p. 132

- <u>Some</u> and <u>any</u>: indefiniteness
- <u>Too many</u>, <u>too much</u>, and <u>enough</u>
- Comparative quantifiers <u>fewer</u> and <u>less</u>

GRAMMAR PRACTICE Complete the conversation between a husband and wife packing for a trip.

Dana: Do we have (1 <u>any</u>/ many) shampoo?

Neil: Yes. We have (2 many / <u>lots of</u>) shampoo.

Dana: And Maggie uses (3 much / <u>a lot of</u>) sunscreen. Is there (4 many / <u>any</u>)?

Neil: No, there isn't (5 some / <u>any</u>). And we don't have (6 <u>much</u> / many) toothpaste, either. I can pick (7 <u>some</u> / any) up on my way back from work.

Dana: Hey, Adam's shaving now. Does he need (8 <u>any</u> / many) shaving cream?

Neil: He doesn't shave every day. He can use mine!

CONVERSATION MODEL

A ▶3:06 Read and listen to someone looking for personal care products in a store.

A: Excuse me. Where would I find sunscreen?

B: Sunscreen? Have a look in the cosmetics section, in aisle 2.

A: Actually, I did, and there wasn't <u>any</u>.

B: I'm sorry. Let me get you <u>some</u> from the back. Anything else?

A: Yes. I couldn't find <u>any</u> razors either.

B: No problem. There are <u>some</u> over there. I'll show you.

B ▶3:07 **RHYTHM AND INTONATION** Listen again and repeat. Then practice the Conversation Model with a partner.

C **FIND THE GRAMMAR** Find and underline the four quantifiers in the Conversation Model.

NOW YOU CAN Ask for something in a store

A **CONVERSATION ACTIVATOR** With a partner, use the store directory to change the Conversation Model. Use the Vocabulary and quantifiers. Then change roles.

A: Excuse me. Where would I find .... ?
B: .... ? Have a look in ....
A: Actually, I did, and there .... any.
B: I'm sorry. Let me get you .... from the back. Anything else?
A: ....

DON'T STOP!

- Ask about other personal care products.

🔁 **RECYCLE THIS LANGUAGE.**

How much [is that aftershave / are those nail clippers]?
Can I get this [shampoo] in a larger / smaller size?
Can I get this lipstick in [black]?
Do you have any cheaper [razors]?

Cosmetics Plus

DIRECTORY

	Aisle
Hair Care	3
Tooth Care	4
Skin Care	2
Nail Care	2
Makeup	2
Shaving Supplies	1

B **CHANGE PARTNERS** Practice the conversation again, asking for other products.

GOAL Make an appointment at a salon or spa

CONVERSATION MODEL

A ▶3:08 Read and listen to someone make an appointment for a haircut.

A: Hello. Classic Spa and Salon.

B: Hello. This is Monica Morgan. I'd like to make an appointment for a haircut.

A: When would you like to come in, Ms. Morgan?

B: Today, if possible.

A: Let me check. . . . Sean has an opening at 2:00.

B: Actually, that's a little early for me. Is someone available after 4:00?

A: Yes. Yelena can see you then.

B ▶3:09 **RHYTHM AND INTONATION** Listen again and repeat. Then practice the Conversation Model with a partner.

GRAMMAR *Indefinite pronouns: someone / no one / anyone*

Someone, no one, and anyone are indefinite pronouns. Each refers to an unnamed person. Use indefinite pronouns when the identity of the person is unknown or unimportant.

Affirmative statements

| Someone / No one | is available. |

| Someone / No one | is waiting for the manicurist. |

I saw **someone** at the front desk.

Questions

| Can | anyone / someone | wash my hair? |

| Is there | anyone / someone | at the front desk? |

| Did you see | anyone / someone | waiting for a shave? |

Negative statements

There isn't **anyone** waiting.
I didn't see **anyone** at the salon.

Be careful!
Use anyone, not no one, with the negative form of a verb.
 I didn't speak to **anyone**.
 NOT I didn't speak to no one.

GRAMMAR BOOSTER p. 133
• Indefinite pronouns: something, anything, everything, and nothing

A ▶3:10 **LISTEN TO ACTIVATE VOCABULARY AND GRAMMAR** Listen to the conversations. Complete each statement with someone or anyone and the salon service(s).

1 They can't find ....anyone.... to give her a ....manicure.... this afternoon.

2 ...Someone... can give him a ....shampoo.... and a ..haircut / cut.. at 4:00.

3 There is ....someone.... who can give her a ....manicure.... and a ....pedicure.... at 6:30.

4 There isn't ....anyone.... who can give him a ....shave.... today.

CONVERSATION MODEL

A ▶3:08 **Read and listen . . .**

Suggested teaching time:	3 minutes	Your actual teaching time:

This conversation strategy is implicit in the model:
• Use "Let me check" to ask someone to wait while you check information.

• Have students read and listen to the conversation. Explain any unknown vocabulary.

• To check comprehension, ask:
  What does the woman want to make an appointment for? (A haircut.)
  When does Sean have an opening? (At 2:00.)
  When does the woman want to come in? (After 4:00.)

• Have students read and listen a second time.

Language and culture
• The verbs used frequently with *appointment* are *make* and *have*. A person *makes an appointment with someone* and *has* (or *makes*) *an appointment* to do something.

Option: *(+3 minutes)* To expand the activity, write the phrases below on the board after students have listened again. Tell them to find other ways of saying them in the Conversation Model.
  is available (= has an opening)
  can give you a haircut (= can see you)

B ▶3:09 **Rhythm and intonation**

Suggested teaching time:	2 minutes	Your actual teaching time:

• Have students repeat each line chorally. Make sure they use rising intonation for *When would you like to come in* and *Is someone available after 4:00?*

GRAMMAR

Suggested teaching time:	8–13 minutes	Your actual teaching time:

• While a student reads the explanations in the Grammar box, write examples on the board: *I asked someone at the desk for an appointment. I didn't ask anyone for a manicure. Did you ask anyone for a massage?*

• Have pairs study the sentences and notice the difference in usage between *someone* and *anyone*. Ask *Do we use someone or anyone in affirmative statements?* (Someone.) *In negative statements?* (Anyone.) *In questions?* (Someone or anyone.) *When do we use* no one? (In affirmative statements.)

• Call on students to read the example sentences under each category in the Grammar box.

• Read the Be careful! note. To check understanding, write on the board: *I didn't call no one. / I didn't call anyone.* Ask *Which sentence is correct?* (The second one.)

Option: **GRAMMAR BOOSTER** *(Teaching notes p. T133)*

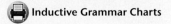 **Inductive Grammar Charts**

A ▶3:10 **Listen to activate vocabulary and grammar**

Suggested teaching time:	7–9 minutes	Your actual teaching time:

• Have students listen to the conversations about the salon services and complete the statements. If students need help, write on the board *shave, manicure, haircut, shampoo, pedicure* or refer students to page 50. Play the audio and allow students to listen again.

• Tell students to identify affirmative statements by writing *A* and negative statements by writing *N*. (1. N; 2. A; 3. A; 4. N)

• Have students listen again and decide which indefinite pronoun to use. Encourage them to refer to the Grammar box, if necessary.

• Have students compare answers with a partner.

AUDIOSCRIPT

CONVERSATION 1
F1: I don't have an appointment. But I've been working in the garden and my hands are a mess. Is there any possibility for this afternoon?
F2: Let me check the book. I'm sorry. Dora and the others are all booked up today. Could you make it in tomorrow?

CONVERSATION 2
F: Demirjian Hair Salon. How can I help you?
M: This is Mr. Banks. Is Eva available for a shampoo and a cut sometime today?
F: Let me check . . . Yes, she has a cancellation at 4:00. She could see you then.
M: Great. See you at 4:00.

CONVERSATION 3 [F = Australian English]
M: Pretty Hands and Feet.
F: Hello. This is Helen Jones. I have a seven o'clock appointment for a manicure. Would it be possible to get a pedicure, too? Sorry for the last-minute request.
M: Actually, umm . . . if you could come in a little earlier, we could do that.
F: How much earlier?
M: Six-thirty?
F: Great. See you then.

CONVERSATION 4 [M1 = Russian]
M1: Good morning, Mr. Lane. Hmm . . . we don't have you down for an appointment today.
M2: Actually, I don't have one. But I can't stand this beard another day. Is one of the barbers available? I don't mind waiting.
M1: I'm so sorry to disappoint you, but Vinnie's out sick and there's just no one else available.

B Grammar practice

Suggested teaching time:	5–8 minutes	Your actual teaching time:	

- To prepare students for the activity, have them skim the exercise and label each sentence by its type: affirmative (A), negative (N), or question (Q). (1. A; 2. N; 3. Q; 4. N; 5. A; 6. A; 7. N; 8. A; 9. N; 10. N; 11. A; 12. N.)
- Tell students to fill in the blanks individually. Refer them to the Grammar box, if necessary.
- Have students review answers in pairs.

 Extra Grammar Exercise

PRONUNCIATION

A ▶3:11 The vowel in an unstressed syllable . . .

Suggested teaching time:	2 minutes	Your actual teaching time:	

 Pronunciation Coach Video

- After students read the directions and the words, tell them to pay attention to the vowel reduction in the unstressed syllable as they listen. Explain that this reduced vowel sound is called a *schwa* and is one of the most common vowel sounds in English.
- Have students listen again and repeat in the pauses.

B Now practice saying the words . . .

Suggested teaching time:	2 minutes	Your actual teaching time:	

- After students practice individually, tell them to practice reading the words to each other in pairs. Move around the room and listen for correct stress.
- Ask students to read individual words to the class.

 Pronunciation Activities

NOW YOU CAN Make an appointment at a salon or spa

A Conversation activator

Suggested teaching time:	8–11 minutes	Your actual teaching time:	

 Conversation Activator Video

- *Note:* You can print the script or you can show a running transcript on the video player on the ActiveTeach. The script also appears on page 184 of this Teacher's Edition.
- To prepare students, give them a moment to skim the list of salon services. Refer students to the Conversation Model on page 54 to review requesting a salon service.

DON'T STOP! Extend the conversation. Encourage students to use the language in the Recycle box to continue the conversation. Tell them to number the language in the Recycle box in the order they use it.

- For more support, play the Conversation Activator Video before students do this activity themselves. In Scene 1, the actors use different words in the gaps from the ones in the Conversation Model. In Scene 2, the actors extend the conversation. After each scene, ask students how the model has been changed by the actors.
- Be sure to reinforce the use of the conversation strategy.
- Role-play the conversation with a more confident student.
- Have pairs role-play conversations, referring to the list of services and names of staff. Review meaning as needed. Encourage students to be creative as they continue the conversation.
- Move around the room and listen for the use of recycled language as pairs continue their conversations. Remind students to change roles to get more practice.

 Conversation Activator Video Script; Conversation Activator Pair Work Cards

B Change partners

Suggested teaching time:	8–10 minutes	Your actual teaching time:	

- To form new pairs, tell students to count off alternating A and B. Then tell them to find a new partner with the same letter. Tell pairs to create new conversations for different services.
- Encourage students to continue the conversation using the list of services and the language in the Recycle box.
- If time permits, invite partners to share their role plays. Then survey the class about which service they would choose to get.

EXTRAS

Workbook or MyEnglishLab

 Speaking Activities: Unit 5, Activity 2

B **GRAMMAR PRACTICE** Complete each statement or question with <u>someone</u>, <u>no one</u>, or <u>anyone</u>. In some cases, more than one answer is correct.

1 There's _someone (or no one)_ at the front desk.

2 They didn't tell _anyone_ it would be a long wait.

3 Did you see _someone/anyone_ giving a manicure?

4 I didn't ask _anyone_ about the price.

5 There will be _someone_ here to give you a pedicure in a few minutes.

6 _Someone_ can cut your hair at 12:30 if you can wait.

7 Please don't tell _anyone_ the price. It was very expensive!

8 _Someone_ called and left you this message while you were getting your shampoo.

9 There wasn't _anyone_ there when she called for an appointment.

10 I didn't speak to _anyone_ about the bad haircut.

11 _Someone / No one_ told me the salon offers shiatsu massage now.

12 I don't have the nail file. I gave it to _someone_ .

PRONUNCIATION *Pronunciation of unstressed vowels*

A ▶3:11 The vowel in an unstressed syllable is often pronounced /ə/. Read and listen, paying attention to the syllable or syllables marked with /ə/. Then listen again and repeat.

1 ma ssage
  /ə/

2 fa cial
    /ə/

3 ma ni cure
     /ə/

4 pe di cure
    /ə/

5 de o do rant
    /ə/ /ə/

B Now practice saying the words on your own.

NOW YOU CAN Make an appointment at a salon or spa

A **CONVERSATION ACTIVATOR** With a partner, change the Conversation Model, using services and staff from the list. Then change roles.

A: Hello. ....
B: Hello. This is .... I'd like to make an appointment for ....
A: When would you like to come in, ... ?
B: .... if possible.
A: Let me check. . . . . has an opening at ....
B: Actually, that's a little .... for me. Is someone available .... ?
A: Yes. .... can see you then.

DON'T STOP!
• Ask about other services.
• Ask about prices and payment.

🔄 **RECYCLE THIS LANGUAGE.**

Is someone available on / at __?
How much is [a pedicure]?
How long is [a massage]?
Can someone [wash my hair]?
I need [a shave].
Is the tip included?
Do you accept credit cards?

THE **APEX**
SPA and FITNESS CENTER

SERVICES	STAFF
haircut	Christopher/Diana
pedicure	Karin/Carlota
shave	Nick/Giorgio
manicure	Sonia/Marie
massage	Vladimir/Edouard
personal training	Igor/Betty

B **CHANGE PARTNERS** Practice the conversation again, making an appointment for other services.

GOAL Discuss ways to improve appearance

BEFORE YOU READ

PREDICT Look at the photos and title of the article. What questions do you think the people will ask Dr. Weiss?

READING ▶ 3:12

Cosmetic surgery
. . . for everyone?

Contact Doctor Weiss at Personal Health Magazine: weiss@personalhealth.rx

BEFORE surgery

AFTER surgery

Some people consider cosmetic surgery no more serious than visiting a spa or a salon. But others say, "I think I'll pass." They're aware that cosmetic surgery is, in fact, surgery, and surgery should never be taken lightly. Fitness editor Dr. Gail Weiss answers readers' questions about cosmetic surgery.

Dear Dr. Weiss:

I'm at my wits' end with my face. I have wrinkles and sun damage. I'm only 30, but I look 50. Do you think a face-lift is an option for me?

Josephine

Dear Josephine:

This popular and effective surgery lifts the face and the neck in one operation. But a face-lift is surgery, and afterwards you will have to stay home for a number of days. It takes time to recover. Before you decide to have a face-lift, ask your dermatologist or a cosmetic surgeon about a chemical peel. A chemical peel removes the top layer of skin and can improve the appearance of the skin without surgery. Compared to surgery, a half-hour visit to your dermatologist would be a piece of cake! Good luck!

Gail Weiss, M.D

Dear Dr. Weiss:

I'm a 24-year-old man who is already losing his hair. Dr. Weiss, I'm looking for a wife, and I'm afraid no woman will want to marry a 25-year-old bald guy. I need some advice.

Calvin

Dear Calvin:

There are several surgical procedures which a cosmetic surgeon can perform to help treat hair loss and restore hair for both men and women. But if that's not practical, remember that some of the world's most attractive men are bald!

Gail Weiss, M.D.

Dear Dr. Weiss:

When I was young, I was a chocoholic. I ate a lot of chocolate, but I never gained any weight. Now that I'm older, I can't eat anything without gaining weight! I've heard that liposuction is the answer to an overweight person's dreams. Is that true?

Dawson

Dear Dawson:

It's true that liposuction can remove fat deposits that don't respond to dieting and exercise, but it's expensive and can be dangerous. It would be a good idea to ask your doctor for some help in dieting first. Then, if you are unsuccessful, be sure to find a surgeon with a lot of experience before deciding on liposuction.

Gail Weiss, M.D.

A PARAPHRASE Find and circle each underlined expression in the article. Then circle the correct word or phrase to complete each statement.

1 If you say <u>I think I'll pass</u>, you mean (*"No, thanks"*)/ "That's a great idea").

2 If you are <u>at your wits' end</u> about something, you are (happy /(unhappy)) about it.

3 <u>It takes time to recover</u> means that you (will /(won't)) feel better immediately.

4 Something that is <u>a piece of cake</u> is ((easy)/ difficult).

B UNDERSTAND FROM CONTEXT With a partner, find these procedures in the Reading and write a definition for each one. Answers will vary.

1 liposuction surgical procedure that can remove fat

2 hair restoration a way of treating hair loss

3 a face-lift surgical procedure that "lifts" the face and neck to get rid of wrinkles and sun damage

4 a chemical peel a procedure that removes the top layer of skin without surgery

BEFORE YOU READ

Suggested teaching time:	5 minutes	Your actual teaching time:

Predict

- Give students two minutes to look at the photos and title of the article. Then ask *How is this article organized?* (It's a series of letters from people asking questions and the doctor's answers.)

- Write on the board students' predictions about what the letters will ask. (Possible responses: Getting cosmetic surgery or facials, etc.) Leave the predictions on the board to refer to after reading the article.

▶3:12 READING

Suggested teaching time:	12–17 minutes	Your actual teaching time:

- To introduce the topic, ask *What do you think of when you see the words "cosmetic surgery"?* Write students' ideas on the board. (Possible responses: Improving your appearance, changing your nose or lips.)

- Call on a student to read the article title. Ask *What do the Q and A next to the title mean?* (Questions and answers.) Write on the board *Cosmetic surgery—for everyone?* Ask *What does the title ask?* (Is cosmetic surgery for everyone?) Ask students for their opinions.

- Have students look at the "before" and "after" woman's photos. Ask *How is the "after" photo different?* (The woman's nose is straighter.)

- After students have read the article, ask them to list the kinds of cosmetic surgery and procedures the article mentions. (Liposuction, surgery to treat hair loss, face-lifts, chemical peels.)

- To check comprehension of the introductory paragraph, ask:

  What do many people think about cosmetic surgery? (That it isn't serious.)

  What does Dr. Weiss think about cosmetic surgery? (It is serious, and it should never be taken lightly.)

- Review the main idea with the class. Ask *What do you think Dr. Weiss's views are about cosmetic surgery? Does she generally think it's a good idea or a bad idea?* (That depends. She suggests that patients be careful and try other procedures first. She also says that patients need to choose a good surgeon.)

Option: (+5–10 minutes) For additional practice, have the class brainstorm natural ways to improve appearance. (Possible responses: Diet, exercise, plenty of sleep, eight glasses of water per day, using sunscreen, not smoking.) Discuss how each tip can contribute to a better appearance and, as a result, avoid the need for cosmetic surgery. For example, *Exercise keeps you in good shape. Then you don't need liposuction.*

A Paraphrase

Suggested teaching time:	5 minutes	Your actual teaching time:

- Tell students that after they find the expressions in the article and underline them, they should read the sentences near each expression (the context) to figure out what the expressions mean.

- Have students compare answers in pairs. Then go over the answers with the class.

B Understand from context

Suggested teaching time:	10 minutes	Your actual teaching time:

- Model the activity by doing the first item as a class. Ask students to find *liposuction* in the article. (In the last Q & A.) Say *Look at the sentence after the second liposuction. What does it say?* (Can remove fatty deposits.) Ask *What is the definition of liposuction?* (Cosmetic surgery that removes fat deposits.) Point out that words are often defined by the sentences before and after them in writing.

- Tell partners to try to write the definitions without using a dictionary.

- To provide more support, write definitions for the procedures on the board (in a different order) and have students choose from the list.

- Have students check their definitions in a dictionary.

 **Learning Strategies**

C Confirm content and apply information

Suggested teaching time:	10 minutes	Your actual teaching time:

- While students are scanning the article, copy the chart on the board. As a class, fill in the information about Josephine. Say *In the article, Josephine says that she has wrinkles. What are wrinkles?* (Lines in the skin, usually around the eyes and mouth.) Ask *Now what is Josephine's problem? What is the doctor's advice? What is your advice?* Write the answers in the chart.

- Have pairs scan the article for the remaining names in the chart and find the information requested.

- Review Dr. Weiss's advice with the class. Ask *Did you usually agree with Dr. Weiss's advice?*

 Extra Reading Comprehension Exercises

NOW YOU CAN Discuss ways to improve appearance

A Frame your ideas

Suggested teaching time:	5–7 minutes	Your actual teaching time:

- Tell students to skim the ways to improve appearance in the first column of the survey. Make sure they remember what each one means. Refer students to the article or the unit vocabulary as necessary.

- Ask a student to read the words across the top of the chart. Point out that *definitely* and *absolutely not* suggest strong opinions, and that *maybe* and *probably not* suggest less certainty.

- Have students complete the survey individually and then compare answers in groups and discuss differing opinions.

- Review answers with the class. Ask individuals which ways to improve appearance they marked *definitely* or *absolutely not.* Encourage students to explain their feelings about these procedures.

B Notepadding

Suggested teaching time:	3–6 minutes	Your actual teaching time:

- Model the activity by reviewing the example on the notepad. Tell students to suggest other advantages and disadvantages of dieting.

- Refer students to any answers they marked *definitely* or *maybe* on the survey above. If they don't have any of these answers, tell them to imagine a popular celebrity and write the celebrity's answers.

- Have students write the advantages and disadvantages of two other methods, and compare notes in pairs.

C Discussion

Suggested teaching time:	10–15 minutes	Your actual teaching time:

- Ask students to suggest additional ways to improve appearance that have not already been listed and discussed.

Text-mining: Focus students' attention on the box. Tell students to skim the article on page 56 and underline useful language. Then write students' findings on the board for them to refer to during the discussion.

- Have students work in groups to discuss what they think is the best way and the worst way to improve appearance. Tell students to mention the advantages and disadvantages of the methods to explain their choices. Encourage them to use their notes and any useful language they discovered from text-mining.

- Review answers with the class. Vote on the most popular and least popular way(s) to improve appearance.

Option: (+10 minutes) To challenge your students, have them write a letter to Dr. Weiss, using the letters on page 56 as models. Encourage students to make up a problem if they don't feel comfortable discussing personal problems. Then have pairs exchange letters and write responses to each other's letters. Encourage students to include non-surgical remedies (such as diet, exercise, plenty of sleep, eight glasses of water per day, sunscreen, not smoking, etc.) in their responses.

EXTRAS

Workbook or MyEnglishLab

 Speaking Activities: Unit 5, Activity 3

C **CONFIRM CONTENT AND APPLY INFORMATION** Complete the chart with information from the article. Then, with a partner, give your own advice for each person.

	Problem	Dr. Weiss's advice	Your advice
Josephine	wrinkles and sun damage	chemical peel	
Calvin	hair loss	surgical procedure	
Dawson	overweight	try dieting before considering surgery	

A **FRAME YOUR IDEAS** Take the opinion survey about ways to improve appearance.

How far would you go to improve your appearance?

Would you try ...

	definitely	maybe	probably not	absolutely not!
diet?	○	○	○	○
exercise?	○	○	○	○
massage?	○	○	○	○
hair restoration?	○	○	○	○
cosmetics and makeup?	○	○	○	○
facials?	○	○	○	○
face-lifts?	○	○	○	○
liposuction?	○	○	○	○
chemical peels?	○	○	○	○

B **NOTEPADDING** Choose one method you would try and one method you would not try. On the notepad, write advantages and disadvantages.

Method	Advantage(s)	Disadvantage(s)
I would try diet.	free, safe	It's hard to do!

Method	Advantage(s)	Disadvantage(s)

C **DISCUSSION** What's the best way to improve your appearance? What ways would you NOT try? Explain. Use your notepad for support.

Text-mining (optional)
Find and underline three words or phrases in the Reading that were new to you. Use them in your Discussion.
For example: "surgical procedures."

GOAL Define the meaning of beauty

BEFORE YOU LISTEN

DIGITAL FLASH CARDS

A ▶3:13 **VOCABULARY** • *Discussing beauty* Read and listen. Then listen again and repeat.

physical features skin, hair, body shape and size, eyes, nose, mouth, etc.

beauty the physical features most people of a particular culture consider good-looking

attractive having a beautiful or pleasing physical or facial appearance

unattractive the opposite of *attractive*

youth appearing young; the opposite of looking old

health the general condition of one's body and how healthy one is

B **EXPLORE YOUR IDEAS** Write a statement or two describing, in your opinion, the characteristics of an attractive man or woman.

> *An attractive woman has long hair and dark eyes.*

C **PAIR WORK** Use your statements to talk about the physical features you consider attractive for men and women. Use the Vocabulary.

> 66 In my opinion, attractive people have . . . 99

LISTENING COMPREHENSION

A ▶3:14 **LISTEN TO RECOGNIZE SOMEONE'S POINT OF VIEW** Listen to the interview. Check all of the statements that summarize Maya Prasad's and Ricardo Figueroa's ideas about beauty.

Maya Prasad

☐ I'm very lucky to be so beautiful.

☑ All the contestants were beautiful. I was just lucky.

☑ Physical beauty only lasts a short time.

☐ Love makes people beautiful.

Ricardo Figueroa

☐ Physical beauty is not important at all.

☑ Both physical beauty and inner beauty are important.

☐ Only inner beauty is important.

☑ Prasad represents an almost perfect combination of inner and outer beauty.

B ▶3:15 **LISTEN TO TAKE NOTES** Listen and take notes about what Figueroa says about each of the qualities below. Then compare your notes with the class.

warmth:	She expresses her love for others easily.
patience:	She's a wonderful listener and lets others speak. She doesn't rush them.
goodness and kindness:	She spends time helping other people who have difficulties. Last year she taught art to children in a public hospital.

BEFORE YOU LISTEN

A ▶3:13 Vocabulary

Suggested teaching time:	2–4 minutes	Your actual teaching time:

V Vocabulary Flash Card Player

- To introduce the topic, write on the board *beauty*. Ask *What does beauty mean to most people?* (Possible responses: A certain height or weight; the shape and color of eyes; hair length and color.) Encourage students to share their personal ideas as well.

- Have students read and listen and then listen again and repeat.

B Explore your ideas

Suggested teaching time:	3–6 minutes	Your actual teaching time:

- Review physical features with the class. To support weaker students, list characteristics on the board.
  hair (long, medium, short)
  skin (dark, light, medium)
  shape (thin, medium build, heavy-set)
  eyes (blue, brown, hazel, light, dark)
  nose (short, long, curved, straight)
  lips (full, thin)
  height (tall, medium or average, short)

- Encourage students to describe characteristics both for a man and woman. Help with vocabulary as needed.

C Pair work

Suggested teaching time:	5 minutes	Your actual teaching time:

- Tell students to form pairs to discuss their ideas of attractive physical features.

- Invite volunteers to share their answers with the class. Ask *Did any answers surprise you? Why?*

LISTENING COMPREHENSION

A ▶3:14 Listen to recognize someone's point of view

Suggested teaching time:	5 minutes	Your actual teaching time:

- To prepare students before they listen, tell them to skim the statements next to the pictures and predict which ones the people in the pictures will make.

- Have students listen to the interview once and then listen again to check the correct statements.

- Review answers with the class.

FYI: Maya does not explicitly say that she believes love makes people beautiful. Based on her comment about the song, one could infer that she believes this statement. Have students listen again and discuss whether Maya believes this or not.

AUDIOSCRIPT

[F1 = British English, F2 = Indian, M = Spanish]

F1: This is Nigella Compton with the DBC radio network and Eye on the Globe. We're talking to the new Miss Universal Beauty, Maya Prasad, who has just won her title at the tenth annual Miss Universal Beauty pageant in Kuala Lumpur. And we're also talking to Ricardo Figueroa, the chief judge of the contest this year. Welcome, Ms. Prasad—or, should I say, Welcome Miss Universal Beauty?

F2: Hello, Nigella. Please call me Maya. Thank you for inviting me.

F1: And welcome, Mr. Figueroa.

M: Thank you.

F1: My pleasure. Maya, please tell our listeners what it's like to have been chosen Miss Universal Beauty. Do you feel like the most beautiful woman in the world?

F2: Uh . . . actually, no. To tell you the truth, the idea is very flattering, but I don't actually feel that beautiful. All the contestants were beautiful. Many, I think, were much more attractive than I am. I think I was very lucky.

F1: One of the things that's special about the Miss Universal Beauty contest is that it emphasizes both inner and outer beauty. Mr. Figueroa, could you say a few words about that for us?

M: Certainly. The Miss Universal Beauty contest tries to choose contestants who exhibit all the features of traditional physical beauty: youth, health, beautiful skin and hair, a lovely body—those things everyone understands to represent beauty. But, true beauty goes beyond that. Helen Keller, who was both blind and deaf, said something very profound and true about beauty: "The best and most beautiful things in the world cannot be seen, nor touched . . . but are felt in the heart." We at the Miss Universal Beauty contest have tried to make that our motto. We try to find that beauty that touches our hearts.

AUDIOSCRIPT continues on page T59.

 Learning Strategies

B ▶3:15 Listen to take notes

Suggested teaching time:	6–9 minutes	Your actual teaching time:

- Read the qualities on the notebook paper. Explain vocabulary as needed.

- To focus students' attention, ask pairs to fill in the note with what they remember before they listen again. Then play the interview again.

- Tell pairs to compare answers. Play the interview again as needed. Then ask *In addition to the qualities on the notepad, what's one other quality that Maya has?* (She's modest. OR Modesty.)

- Review the answers with the class. Ask *Do any of these qualities describe you or someone you know? Are these qualities important to you?*

Option: (+5–10 minutes) Have students choose one of the five qualities that they think is the most important in inner beauty. Have them discuss it with a partner. Then bring the class together and survey student opinions.

C Discussion

Suggested teaching time:	8–10 minutes	Your actual teaching time:

- Divide the class into four groups and assign each group one of the discussion topics to talk about in detail. Have each group choose one student to record ideas to then present to the class. Move around the room and assist as needed.

- Ask each representative to present the ideas discussed in his or her group. Invite other students to contribute ideas.

Option: (*+15 minutes*) To challenge students, have them write about one of the topics for homework. Encourage students to develop their points of view by providing examples. Tell students they can include ideas from the group discussions.

 Graphic Organizers

NOW YOU CAN Define the meaning of beauty

A Notepadding

Suggested teaching time:	3–5 minutes	Your actual teaching time:

- Write on the board *inner beauty*. Review the qualities of inner beauty and write these on the board: *warm, patient, good, kind, modest*. Ask students to suggest other qualities; for example, friendly, funny, fun, pleasant, sweet, thoughtful.

- Call on a volunteer to read the sample sentences. On the board write *He / She looks . . .* Tell students that this means that the people *seem* to have these qualities, since we have no way of knowing about inner beauty from appearance only.

- Have students complete their lists individually.

B Pair work

Suggested teaching time:	3 minutes	Your actual teaching time:

- Have pairs discuss the qualities they wrote down. Move around the room as students discuss.

- Review answers with the class. Ask *Which of the four people seems most beautiful to you? Why?* Have students specify qualities of inner and outer beauty.

C Discussion

Suggested teaching time:	10–13 minutes	Your actual teaching time:

- To wrap up the lesson, tell students to think back to their definition of beauty at the beginning of the lesson. Ask *Do you have a different idea of beauty at the end of this lesson?*

- Call on a volunteer to read the sample quote. Invite students to think of a person they consider beautiful and then share their views using this person as an example. Encourage students to go beyond physical beauty.

Option: (*+15 minutes*) Have students expand on their definitions of beauty and write a short essay. Tell them to use the sample quote at the bottom of a page as a model.

EXTRAS

Workbook or MyEnglishLab

 Speaking Activities: Unit 5, Activity 4; "Find Someone Who . . ." Activity

---

Continued, for page T58 (Listening Comprehension)

F1: Very interesting. And all the more so since Helen Keller was blind and couldn't see what people looked like. She still had a concept of beauty. "The most beautiful things are felt in the heart." What, in your opinion, are those things—those beautiful things—that we feel in the heart?

M: Well, I think Helen Keller was describing inner beauty—those qualities that last longer than youth and can exist even when health has gone. Qualities such as goodness, kindness to other people, truthfulness—qualities that everyone appreciates—no matter where in the world they live.

F2: I've always felt that physical beauty can't last forever. People think it's beauty that brings you love, but I'm not so sure. I've always loved the Oscar Hammerstein song that says: "Do you love me because I'm beautiful, or am I beautiful because you love me?"

F1: Hmm. Very interesting food for thought. I would imagine that that attitude will help you lead a happy life.

M: I'd like to say that the judges thought that Maya presented an almost perfect balance between outer and inner beauty. Her happiness with life is one of the strongest features of her inner beauty. But before we finish, let me just read a little from their written comments: Maya has warmth: She expresses her love for others easily. Patience: She is a wonderful listener and lets other speak. She doesn't rush them.

F2: Oh, Mr. Figueroa. I can't believe anyone said all this about me. I'm just a regular person!

M: Maya, that comment shows us that you are also very modest—modesty is actually another of the features of your inner beauty. But let me continue . . . Maya's also a woman of great goodness and kindness: She spends time helping other people who have difficulties. Last year she taught art to children in the public hospital. So her happiness, her warmth, her patience, and her kindness shine through and make her physical beauty all the more radiant.

F1: Thank you to you both.

C **DISCUSSION** Talk about one or more of the questions.

1 In what ways do you agree or disagree with Prasad's and Figueroa's ideas about beauty?

2 Do you think the Miss Universal Beauty contest sounds better than the usual beauty contest? Why or why not?

3 Do you think there should be beauty contests for men as well as for women? Why or why not? What in your opinion is the difference between a woman's beauty and a man's beauty?

4 How do you explain these words in the song Prasad talks about: "Do you love me because I'm beautiful, or am I beautiful because you love me"?

NOW YOU CAN Define the meaning of beauty

A **NOTEPADDING** Look at the four photos. What qualities of beauty do you find in each person? Write notes.

1	Outer beauty	Inner beauty
	She has beautiful skin.	She looks warm and friendly.

1) Outer beauty

Inner beauty

2) Outer beauty

Inner beauty

3) Outer beauty

Inner beauty

4) Outer beauty

Inner beauty

B **PAIR WORK** Discuss the qualities of beauty you found in the people in the pictures. Compare your opinions. Use your notepads for support.

C **DISCUSSION** Define the meaning of beauty.

> " I think beauty is hard to describe. It's a combination of things. I consider my grandmother really beautiful because . . . "

A ▶ 3:16 Listen to the conversations. Infer what kind of product the people are discussing. Complete each statement.

1 Hawaii Bronzer is a brand of ....sunscreen.......................... .

2 Swan is a brand of ....soap.......................... .

3 Truly You is a brand of ....makeup.......................... .

4 Mountain Fresh is a brand of ....toothpaste.......................... .

5 Silk 'n Satin is a brand of ....body lotion.......................... .

6 Fresh as a Flower is a brand of ....deodorant.......................... .

B Complete each statement or question.

1 There aren't (many / much) customers in the store right now.

2 Do they sell (any / many) sunscreen at the hotel gift shop? I forgot to pack some.

3 Your sister doesn't want (some / any) body lotion.

4 She doesn't wear (much / some) makeup. She doesn't need to—she has beautiful skin.

5 My son uses (any / a lot of) shaving cream.

6 There's (anyone / someone) on the phone for you. Do you want me to take a message?

7 There are (any / a lot of) salons in this neighborhood.

C Complete each statement about services at a salon or spa.

1 There's nothing like a professional ....shave.......... when you're sick and tired of your beard.

2 If your hair is too long, get a ....haircut.......... .

3 In the summer, before you wear sandals for the first time, your feet will look great if you get a ....pedicure.......... .

4 When your hands are a mess, you can get a ....manicure.......... .

5 When your muscles are sore from too much work or exercise, a ....massage.......... can help.

D Complete each conversation with the correct procedure.

1 A: I look so old! Look at my neck and my eyes.
   B: Why don't you get (a massage / a facelift)?

2 A: My back and shoulders are sore from too much exercise.
   B: They say (a chemical peel / a massage) can really help.

3 A: Look at this! I'm getting bald!
   B: Have you thought about (liposuction / hair restoration)?

WRITING

Re-read the letters on page 56. Choose one letter and write a response, using your own opinion and making your own suggestions. Explain what you think is OK or appropriate for men and women.

WRITING BOOSTER p. 147
- Writing a formal letter
- Guidance for this writing exercise

For additional language practice . . .

♫ **TOP NOTCH POP** • Lyrics p. 153
"Piece of Cake"

DIGITAL SONG   DIGITAL KARAOKE

REVIEW

A ▶ 3:16 **Listen to the conversations . . .**

Suggested teaching time:	6 minutes	Your actual teaching time:

• Before students listen, tell them to read through the sentences with blanks for each conversation.

• Refer students to the Vocabulary on page 52. Then have students listen to determine the products.

• Tell students to listen again and write down any key words that suggest what each product is. (1. Beach, burned; 2. washed her hands, bar; 3. lipstick, eye shadow; 4. teeth, brush; 5. skin, dry, itchy; 6. fresh as a flower, not perfume, not soap, not shampoo.)

AUDIOSCRIPT

CONVERSATION 1 [F = U.S. regional]
F: Let's stop by the drugstore and get some of that Hawaii Bronzer before we go to the beach. I don't want to get burned.
M: OK.

CONVERSATION 2
M: Honey, I think we're out of Swan. There's none in our bathroom and no more in the closet.
F: Have you had a look in the kids' bathroom? Laura wanted to wash her hands and she was out of it, so maybe she took the bar from ours. I'll pick some up this afternoon when I go shopping.

CONVERSATION 3
F1: Excuse me. What aisle are the Truly You products in?
F2: It depends. What are you looking for?
F1: I'm looking for lipstick and eye shadow.
F2: I don't think we carry the eye shadow, but the lipstick is in aisle three.
F1: Thanks.

CONVERSATION 4
M1: I need something better than Sparkledent. My teeth are sensitive, and it hurts every time I brush.
M2: Well, I use Mountain Fresh. It tastes great, and it's good for sensitive teeth.

CONVERSATION 5
M: My skin is so dry and itchy. What should I do?
F: Well I use Silk 'n Satin after my shower, and my skin is great.

CONVERSATION 6
F1: Wow! Is that a new perfume?
F2: Actually, no. Can you guess what it is?
F1: Is it soap?
F2: Nope.
F1: Shampoo?
F2: No. Want a clue?
F1: OK.
F2: Well, their ad is "Fresh as a Flower—Hour after Hour."
F1: You're kidding! I would have never guessed. I want some of that, too.

B **Complete each statement . . .**

Suggested teaching time:	3 minutes	Your actual teaching time:

• To prepare students, tell them to mark the sentences *Q* for questions (2); *N* for negative statements (1, 3, 4); and *A* for affirmative statements (5, 6, 7). Then have them note if the nouns following the choices are count (1, 7) or

non-count nouns (2–5). (There is no noun following the choices in item 6.) Tell students to use these clues to help them choose the correct answers.

• Review answers with the class.

C **Complete each statement . . .**

Suggested teaching time:	3 minutes	Your actual teaching time:

• Have students skim the sentences and underline clues about the salon service in question. (1. Sick and tired of your beard; 2. hair is too long; 3. before you wear sandals; 4. hands are a mess; 5. muscles are sore.)

• Review answers with the class.

D **Complete each conversation . . .**

Suggested teaching time:	3 minutes	Your actual teaching time:

• Have pairs look at the context. (1. look so old, neck and eyes; 2. sore from exercise; 3. bald.)

• After students complete the activity, have them compare responses in pairs.

WRITING

Suggested teaching time:	10–15 minutes	Your actual teaching time:

• To introduce the activity, write on the board *I think cosmetic surgery is a good way to improve appearance. / I think people should seek natural ways to improve their appearance.* Tell students to choose which statement they agree with more and write their reasons.

• Then ask *What is appropriate for men? Women?* Encourage students to write down more notes to answer the questions.

• Invite students to exchange letters with a partner. Have them ask each other questions if something is not clear.

Option: *Option: (+10–15 minutes)* For additional speaking practice, divide the class into two groups, matching student views from the writing exercise above if possible. Tell each group to prepare arguments to support one of the statements on the board from the exercise above. Allow students to refer to the letters they wrote to Dr. Weiss and to the article on page 56 for ideas. Invite groups to share their arguments, allowing each side to respond. Write the arguments on the board. Then have students read the arguments to determine which group made a stronger case.

Option: **WRITING BOOSTER** *(Teaching notes p. T147)*

 Writing Process Worksheets

 Top Notch Pop **Song Video and Karaoke Video**

UNIT 5, REVIEW   **T60**

 Digital Games

ORAL REVIEW

Before the first activity, give students a few minutes of silent time to become familiar with the picture.

Contest

Suggested teaching time:	8–13 minutes	Your actual teaching time:

- Give pairs a minute to study the picture. Then have them close their books and write down as many products and services as they can remember.

- As a class, have students check their lists against the picture. Tell them to cross out any items on their lists that are not in the picture. Then have them count. The pair with the most words wins.

Possible responses . . .

manicure, pedicure, shampoo, haircut, massage, facial, shave, conditioner, hair spray, nail polish, shaving cream, lotion

Pair work 1

Suggested teaching time:	5 minutes	Your actual teaching time:

- Model the activity by asking a more confident student to role-play a conversation with you.

Possible responses . . .

A: Hi. I have a 2:30 appointment for a facial. **B:** Yes, Annette will be right with you. **A:** Do you think I could get a massage, too? **B:** Yes, but you might have to wait a bit. Markus doesn't have anything open until 4:00. **A:** Not a problem. One more question. How much will the services cost? **B:** A facial and massage will be 100 euros. You can charge it to your room if you like. **A:** Great. Thank you.

Pair work 2

Suggested teaching time:	7–12 minutes	Your actual teaching time:

- Tell students to look at the two people sitting on the bench waiting. Ask *What services do you think the man is here for?* (Possible responses: A shave and a haircut.) *The woman?* (Any of the services.)

- Have pairs write conversations for the two people. Encourage students to use details from the picture (the man looking at his watch). Move around the room and assist as needed.

Possible responses . . .

A: What are you here for? **B:** A haircut. Do you know if it is customary to tip the staff? **A:** Yes, about 3 euros for a haircut. **B:** Thank you. What about you? What are you here for? **A:** I'm here for a shave. But Andy is with someone else, and I am in a hurry. **B:** Look, Andy's finished and his client is leaving. **A:** Oh, good. This beard may take a while!

 Oral Progress Assessment Charts

Option: *Top Notch* Project

Groups evaluate the effectiveness of different ads and present their results to the class.

Idea: Have groups choose an ad from a newspaper, magazine, or the Internet. Write the following questions on the board and ask students to discuss them.

What does the product do?
What part of the body is it for?
Who should use it?
Do you believe it's a good product? Why? Why not?
Would you buy it?

Have students put their ads on a bulletin board. Tell students to look at the ads, decide which are the most convincing, and explain why.

EXTRAS

On the Internet:
- Online Teacher Resources: pearsonelt.com/topnotch3e/

Additional printable resources on the ActiveTeach:
- Assessment
- Just for Fun
- *Top Notch Pop* Song Activities
- *Top Notch TV* Video Program and Activity Worksheets
- Supplementary Pronunciation Lessons
- Conversation Activator Video Scripts
- Audioscripts and Answer Keys
- Unit Study Guides

ORAL REVIEW

CONTEST Look at the picture for a minute, and then close your books. With a partner, try to remember all the products and services in the picture. The pair who remembers the most products and services wins.

PAIR WORK

1 Create a conversation between the client and the clerk at the front desk of the salon. Start like this:

Hi. I have a 2:30 appointment for . . .

2 Create a conversation for the man and woman waiting for salon services. For example:

What are you here for?

NOW I CAN

☐ Ask for something in a store.
☐ Make an appointment at a salon or spa.
☐ Discuss ways to improve appearance.
☐ Define the meaning of beauty.

UNIT 6 Eating Well

COMMUNICATION GOALS
1 Talk about food passions.
2 Make an excuse to decline food.
3 Discuss lifestyle changes.
4 Describe local dishes.

PREVIEW

A HEALTHY DIET

The right balance of foods will keep you healthy.

FATS, OILS, SWEETS — eat rarely

DAIRY — 2-3 servings per day for calcium

FRUIT — 2-4 servings per day for vitamins and fiber

VEGETABLES — 3-5 servings per day for vitamins and fiber

BREAD, GRAINS, PASTA — 6-11 servings per day for carbohydrates

MEAT, FISH, BEANS — 2-3 servings per day for protein and vitamins

▶ 3:19 **VOCABULARY**

Calcium:
Dairy products and leafy green vegetables provide calcium for healthy bones and teeth.

Carbohydrates:
Grains, pasta, and bread are sources of healthy carbohydrates.

Protein:
Meat, fish, poultry, eggs, legumes, and nuts are rich sources of protein.

Vitamins:
Vitamins A, B, C, and D come from a variety of foods, and they are important for good health.

A Look at the suggestions above for eating a healthy diet. Do you think this diet is healthy? Why or why not?

B Complete the chart about the foods you eat each day. Compare charts with a partner.

C **DISCUSSION** How are the Healthy Diet suggestions different from your chart? Which do you think is a healthier diet? Explain.

2–3 servings a day
3–5 servings a day
More than 5 servings a day

UNIT 6 Eating Well

PREVIEW

Before beginning Exercise A, give students a few minutes of silent time to examine the food guide.

Suggested teaching time:	10–15 minutes	Your actual teaching time:

- For a warm-up and review, ask the class general information questions about food. For example: *Is your diet healthy? Do you eat a lot of healthy foods? How many fruits and vegetables do you eat in a day?*

- Tell students to look at the food items in the food guide while volunteers read the labels. Make sure that students know that *rarely* means not often.

- ▶ 3:19 **Vocabulary** After students listen to the audio, have them find the words in the food guide. Ask volunteers to read the definitions aloud.

- Tell pairs to name the individual items pictured in the different categories. (Fats, oils, sweets: chocolate, candy, doughnuts, oil; Dairy: milk, cheese, yogurt; Fruit: apples, oranges, grapes, kiwis, pomegranates, pears, lemons, melons; Bread, grains, pasta: bread, pasta; Vegetables: carrots, cauliflower, broccoli, squash, garlic, tomatoes, cucumbers; Meat, fish, beans: fish, meat, chicken, peanuts, kidney beans, eggs.)

- Explain that the foods and the number of recommended servings in food guides can vary depending on national dietary habits and current research. Ask *Have you seen any other food guides?* If the answer is *yes*, ask *In these other food guides, were the categories the same? Were the sample foods different? What was different?* If the answer is *no*, ask *What are some other food categories that could appear on this food guide? What are other foods that could be examples?*

- After students answer the questions, have them work in pairs to discuss foods they never eat. Then have pairs share the foods they never eat with the class.

Language and culture
- *Fruit* can be both a count and a non-count noun. For example, *I eat a lot of fruit* (non-count) and *I bought many different fruits at the supermarket* (types of fruit—count).
- A serving can be measured by volume, by weight, or by the piece (for example, one banana, one slice of bread). Serving size depends on the culture. For example, in North America, serving sizes are often larger than they are in Asia.

A Look at the suggestions . . .

Suggested teaching time:	2 minutes	Your actual teaching time:

- Tell students to discuss the question in pairs.
- Then have pairs share their ideas with the class.

B Complete the chart . . .

Suggested teaching time:	6–10 minutes	Your actual teaching time:

- For a warm-up, have students list the foods they ate for breakfast, lunch, dinner, and snacks for the past two or three days.

- Refer students to the empty chart on the right and tell them to use their list to fill it in. (If students need more space, tell them to copy the chart on a separate sheet of paper.) After they have finished, have pairs compare their charts.

- Ask the class *What category of foods do you eat most— for example, fruits, meat, dairy? Are you surprised by the numbers of different foods you eat?*

Option: (+5 minutes) For an alternative approach, have students fill in the chart with the foods they would *ideally* like to eat. Have students compare charts in pairs and then share their answers with the class. To review describing preferences, refer students to the Conversation Model on page 19.

C Discussion

Suggested teaching time:	5 minutes	Your actual teaching time:

- To prepare students for the activity, tell them to work individually and compare their chart to the one in the Student's Book. Circle any differences they find.

- Divide students into groups. Refer them to their charts, and tell them to discuss the questions.

Option: (+5 minutes) To expand the activity, draw the chart below on the board and give students copies of it. Tell groups to create a week's ideal menu, basing their choices on the chart in the Student's Book. Then have pairs discuss whether or not they would enjoy following this menu for a month.

	Mon	Tues	Wed	Thur	Fri	Sat	Sun
Breakfast							
Lunch							
Dinner							
Snacks							

 **Graphic Organizers**

D ▶3:20 Photo story

Suggested teaching time:	10–12 minutes	Your actual teaching time:

- Preview the photos by asking *Where are the two women?* (In a cafeteria / lunchroom / self-service restaurant.) *In the second picture, what is the woman in the blue shirt doing?* (Offering some cake to the woman in the red shirt.) *Does the woman in the red shirt want any cake?* (No.)

- Tell students to close their books and listen to the conversation. Then ask *What are the two women talking about?* (Dieting, eating chocolate cake.)

- Have students read and listen to the conversation. Highlight the fact that rising intonation is used with *Want to try some?* Point out the word with the asterisk below the conversation. If students need a definition, refer them to the glossary on page 62.

- Check comprehension by asking *Has Joy been trying to eat fewer sweets?* (Yes.) *What is she eating in the picture?* (Chocolate cake.) *What does Rita ask about the cake?* (How many calories does it have?) *Does Rita eat some cake?* (Yes.) *How much does she eat?* (A bite.)

- Make sure students understand that *You only live once* means take advantage of opportunities and enjoy the pleasures of life now because it's your only opportunity to live.

Language and culture

- In informal spoken English, questions are often reduced. For example, *Want to try some?* is a reduced form of the question *Do you want to try some cake?* In reduced questions, the auxiliary verb and the subject are omitted and the question is formed by intonation.

Option: (+3–5 minutes) To personalize the activity, write these questions on the board for group discussion: *Have you ever been on a diet? What foods did and didn't you eat? How long did you stay on the diet? Was it successful?*

E Focus on language

Suggested teaching time:	5 minutes	Your actual teaching time:

- To prepare students, draw their attention to the eight underlined phrases in the Photo Story. Read them or ask a student to read them aloud.

- Move around the room as students work in pairs to match phrases from the story with the phrases and sentences in the exercise.

- Review answers with the class.

SPEAKING

Suggested teaching time:	7–10 minutes	Your actual teaching time:

- Give pairs a few minutes to read the diet descriptions. Refer students to the glossary on page 62 if needed. Then have them answer the questions.

- Bring the class together and ask the students their opinions. Then ask *Which of these diets does not list disease prevention?* (Mushroom diet and Atkins diet.) *Do you think disease prevention is important for a diet?*

Option: (+10 minutes) To extend the activity, have pairs choose a diet and create a menu for a couple of days. Then have pairs work with another pair to discuss if they would enjoy following this menu.

Option: (+5–10 minutes) To challenge students, ask *In addition to changing eating habits, what else can a person do to lose weight? To gain weight?* Divide the class in half and assign each half either weight loss or weight gain. Have the groups discuss ways to lose or gain weight and then present them to the class. (Lose weight: exercise, drink a lot of water, count calories, use more calories than you consume; Gain weight: exercise less, drink a lot of water, count calories, use fewer calories than you consume.)

Workbook

Rita: Didn't you tell me you were avoiding sweets?

Joy: I couldn't resist! I had a craving for chocolate.

Rita: Well, I have to admit it looks pretty good. How many calories are in that thing anyway?

Joy: I have no idea. Want to try some?

Rita: Thanks. But I think I'd better pass. I'm avoiding carbs.*

Joy: You? I don't believe it. You never used to turn down chocolate!

Rita: I know. But I'm watching my weight now.

Joy: Come on! It's really good.

Rita: OK. Maybe just a bite.

Joy: Hey, you only live once!

*carbs (informal) = carbohydrates

E **FOCUS ON LANGUAGE** Find an underlined sentence or phrase in the Photo Story with the same meaning as each of the following.

1 I don't know. .... I have no idea. ....

2 I should say no. .... I'd better pass. ....

3 I couldn't stop myself. .... I couldn't resist. ....

4 I'm trying not to get heavier. I'm watching my weight.

5 I really wanted . . . . I had a craving for ....

6 I agree . . . . I have to admit ....

7 say no to .... turn down ....

8 I'll try a little. .... just a bite ....

SPEAKING

Read the descriptions of diets. Would you ever try any of them? Why or why not?

> " I don't believe in the Atkins Diet. A lot of meat, eggs, and cheese doesn't sound like the right balance of foods for good health. "

The Mushroom Diet

For weight loss.
Replace lunch or dinner every day—for two weeks—with a mushroom dish.

The Vegan Diet

For better health and prevention of disease.
Avoid all animal products, including dairy and eggs. Eat lots of grains, beans, vegetables, and fruits.

The Atkins Diet

For weight loss.
Eat high-protein foods such as meat, eggs, and cheese. Avoid foods that are high in carbohydrates, such as potatoes, bread, grains, and sugar.

The Juice Fast

For better health and prevention of disease.
Instead of food, drink four to six glasses of fresh vegetable and fruit juices for anywhere from three days to three weeks. Get plenty of rest and avoid exercise during the fast.

GOAL Talk about food passions

VOCABULARY *Food passions*

A ▶3:21 Read and listen. Then listen again and repeat.

I'm **crazy about** seafood.
I'm **a big** meat **eater**.
I'm **a big** coffee **drinker**.
I'm **a chocolate addict**.
I'm **a pizza lover**.

I **can't stand** fish.
I'm **not crazy about** chocolate.
I **don't care for** steak.
I'm **not much of a pizza eater**.
I'm **not much of a coffee drinker**.

B ▶3:22 **LISTEN TO ACTIVATE VOCABULARY** Circle the correct words to complete each statement about the speakers' food passions.

1 She (is crazy about / doesn't care for) sushi.
2 He (loves / can't stand) asparagus.
3 She (is a mango lover / doesn't care for mangoes).
4 He (is a big pasta eater / isn't crazy about pasta).
5 She (is an ice cream addict / can't stand ice cream).

sushi

mangoes

pasta

ice cream

asparagus

C **PAIR WORK** Tell your partner about some of your food passions.

❝ I'm really a seafood lover, but I'm not crazy about clams. ❞

GRAMMAR *Use to / used to*

Use use to and used to + the base form of a verb to describe things that were true in the past but are no longer true in the present.

I **used to be** crazy about candy, but now I don't care for it.
She **didn't use to eat** cheese, but now she has it all the time.

Did you **use to eat** a lot of fatty foods? | Yes, I did. / No, I didn't. OR Yes, I used to. / No, I didn't use to.

What **did** you **use to have** for breakfast? (Eggs and sausage. But not anymore.)
Why **did** you **use to eat** so much? (Because I didn't use to worry about my health.)

Be careful!

They **used** to . . . BUT | They didn't **use** to . . .
Did they **use** to . . . ?

GRAMMAR BOOSTER p. 134
• Use to / used to: use and form, common errors
• Be used to vs. get used to
• Repeated actions in the past: would + base form, common errors

VOCABULARY

A ▶3:21 Read and listen . . .

Suggested teaching time:	2 minutes	Your actual teaching time:

V Vocabulary Flash Card Player

- For a warm-up, read the lesson goal and ask *What is a passion?* (A strong emotional feeling, positive or negative.) *Do you have any food passions?* Model the answer by expressing one of your own food passions, such as *I'm really crazy about chocolate. I love it!*

- After students listen to the audio and repeat, ask *Which person likes a lot of different foods?* (The man.) *Which person doesn't like a lot of foods?* (The woman.)

- Point out that the positive ways of expressing food passions are on the left. Those on the right are negative, in varying degrees. *I can't stand* is stronger than the three other negative statements.

Language and culture

- An *addict* usually means someone who is dependent on drugs or alcohol. In this context, it means having an extremely strong passion for something.
- **From the Longman Corpus:** English speakers only use the negative in expressions such as *I can't stand . . . , I don't care for . . . ,* or *I'm not much of a . . . .* They never say *I stand . . . . , I care for . . . ,* or *I'm much of a . . .* when referring to food or things they like.

 Learning Strategies

B ▶3:22 Listen to activate vocabulary

Suggested teaching time:	5–7 minutes	Your actual teaching time:

- Before students listen, have them look at the pictures and read the names of the foods. Ask individuals *How do you feel about these foods?* Encourage students to use the Vocabulary in Exercise A in their answers.

- While students listen to the audio, tell them to write down key words that suggest whether each speaker likes or doesn't like the food. Make sure students listen for each speaker's opinion. (1. biggest passion, sushi addict; 2. I really don't care for it, doesn't agree with me, can't look at it; 3. big mango eater, mmm; 4. I don't touch it, not much of a pasta lover; 5. I like it too much, think about it all the time.)

- Have students complete the exercise. If necessary, let them listen again before checking answers in pairs.

AUDIOSCRIPT

1 [F = Portuguese]
F: My biggest passion is sushi. I'm definitely a sushi addict. I have it, oh, probably twice a week. There's a terrific restaurant around the corner from where I live in Rio. And they make amazing sushi.

2
M: My wife is crazy about asparagus, but I really don't care for it. I don't know why. It just doesn't agree with me. I can't even look at it.

3
F: When I was a kid, I didn't use to like them. I thought they tasted funny. But now, I've turned into a big mango eater. There's really nothing quite like slices of fresh mango. Mmm.

4 [M = Spanish]
M: My family loves pasta. We have it several times a week, but I don't touch it. The truth is, we just have it TOO much—with tomato sauce, pesto sauce, garlic and oil—you name it. I'll eat anything, but I'm really not much of a pasta lover.

5 [F = Chinese]
F: The problem with ice cream is I like it too much. When I'm on a diet, I can't eat it. But that doesn't mean I don't think about it all the time. I do.

C Pair work

Suggested teaching time:	3–5 minutes	Your actual teaching time:

- As students discuss their food passions in pairs, encourage them to use the expressions from Exercise A.

- Once they have finished, ask pairs to share with the class their partner's food passions.

GRAMMAR

Suggested teaching time:	8–10 minutes	Your actual teaching time:

- To introduce the grammar point, write on the board *I used to eat a lot of sweets. But now I try to watch my weight.* Ask *Did I eat a lot of sweets in the past, or do I eat a lot of sweets now?* (In the past.)

- Review the usage information and the example statements in the Grammar box. Explain that in the first two examples, the second half contradicts the information in the first part of the statement.

- Ask *How does the form of* used to *differ in the first two example sentences?* Point out that *used to* becomes *didn't use to* in the negative; the *d* disappears because *didn't* is in the simple past.

- Shift attention to the example questions in the Grammar box. Read the exchanges, then ask *How does the form of* used to *change in a question?* (*Used to* becomes *use to.*) Point out that the auxiliary *did* is always followed by a base form in questions and negatives. *Use to* is the base form.

- Model the pronunciation of *used to* /ustə/ and *use to* /ustə/. Point out that the *d* is elided, and so the pronunciation of both forms is the same.

- Review the information in the Be careful! box.

Language and culture

- **From the Longman Corpus:** Both learners of English and native speakers of English make the mistake of writing *didn't use**d** to* instead of *didn't use to.*

Option: GRAMMAR BOOSTER *(Teaching notes p. T134)*

 Inductive Grammar Charts

Grammar practice

Suggested teaching time:	8 minutes	Your actual teaching time:

- Tell students to skim the sentences and underline *now* in the second part of each item. Point out that the second part talks about present behavior that is different from past behavior.
- Then have students complete each sentence. Remind students to write *didn't use to* in the negative sentences. If necessary, model an example for the last item.
- Have students compare answers with a partner.

 Extra Grammar Exercise

PRONUNCIATION

▶ 3:23 **Notice how the pronunciation . . .**

Suggested teaching time:	2 minutes	Your actual teaching time:

 Pronunciation Coach Video

- Have students read and listen to the sentences, paying attention to how /tu/ in the phrases *used to* and *use to* is reduced to /tə/.
- After students listen again and repeat, have them practice reading the sentences to a partner.
- Move around the room and listen for correct reduction.

 Pronunciation Activities

CONVERSATION MODEL

A ▶ 3:24 **Read and listen . . .**

Suggested teaching time:	2 minutes	Your actual teaching time:

This conversation strategy is implicit in the model:
- Provide an emphatic affirmative response with "Definitely."

- After students read and listen, write the phrases below on the board and have students find them in the conversation. Ask students to suggest other ways of saying them.
  Are you a big coffee drinker? (= Do you drink a lot of coffee?)
  I'm crazy about coffee. (= I love coffee.)
  I've cut back. (= I used to drink a lot, but now I drink less.)
- Have students read and listen again. To check comprehension, ask *Does the man like coffee?* (Yes. He's crazy about it.) *Who used to drink a lot of coffee?* (The woman.) *Would the man really die without coffee?* (No, not really, but he can't imagine his life without coffee.)

B ▶ 3:25 **Rhythm and intonation**

Suggested teaching time:	3–5 minutes	Your actual teaching time:

- Have students repeat each line chorally. Make sure they:
  ○ use rising intonation for *Are you a big coffee drinker?*
  ○ stress the word *coffee*.

NOW YOU CAN Talk about food passions

A **Notepadding**

Suggested teaching time:	3–6 minutes	Your actual teaching time:

- Ask students to list the foods. Make sure they remember that *crazy about* means they like the food and *can't stand* means they don't like it. Move around the room and help students as needed.
- Have students compare lists with a partner.

B **Conversation activator**

Suggested teaching time:	4–6 minutes	Your actual teaching time:

 Conversation Activator Video

- *Note:* You can print the script or you can show a running transcript on the video player on the ActiveTeach. The script also appears on page 185 of this Teacher's Edition.
- To review talking about food passions, refer students to the Conversation Model above.
- Reinforce the use of the conversation strategies.
- Model the activity by role-playing the conversation with a more confident student. Play the role of Student B.

DON'T STOP! Encourage students to keep their conversations going by asking more questions. For example: *Are you a big ice cream fan? Did you use to eat a lot of meat?*

- For more support, play the Conversation Activator Video before students do this activity themselves. In Scene 1, the actors use different words in the gaps from the ones in the Conversation Model. In Scene 2, the actors extend the conversation. After each scene, ask students how the model has been changed by the actors.
- Move around the room while students role-play their conversations and help students as needed. Encourage students to change roles.

Conversation Activator Video Script; Conversation Activator Pair Work Cards

C **Change partners**

Suggested teaching time:	5–7 minutes	Your actual teaching time:

- When pairs have finished, invite them to role-play their conversations for the class. After each conversation, ask *What are this person's food passions? Are they negative or positive?*

EXTRAS

Workbook or MyEnglishLab

 Speaking Activities: Unit 6, Activity 1

GRAMMAR PRACTICE Use the context to help you complete each sentence with <u>used to</u> or <u>didn't use to</u>. Then write two sentences about yourself.

1 Gary ....<u>used to</u>........ go out to eat a lot, but now he eats at home more often.

2 Nina ....<u>didn't use to</u>........ eat a lot of pasta, but now she does.

3 Vinnie ....<u>didn't use to</u>........ drink a lot of coffee, but now he's a coffee addict.

4 Anton ....<u>used to</u>........ eat a lot of vegetables, but now he doesn't.

5 Cate ....<u>used to</u>........ hate seafood, but now she's crazy about fish.

6 Ted ....<u>used to</u>........ eat a lot of fatty foods, but now he avoids them.

7 Burt ....<u>didn't use to</u>........ drink a lot of water, but now he has several glasses a day.

8 May ....<u>didn't use to</u>........ like salad, but now she has salads several times a week.

9 (used to) I ......(Answers will vary)...................................
....

10 (didn't use to) I ......(Answers will vary)..............................
....

PRONUNCIATION *Sound reduction: <u>used to</u>*

▶3:23 Notice how the pronunciation of <u>to</u> in <u>used to</u> changes to /tə/ in natural speech. Read and listen. Then listen again and repeat. Practice the sentences on your own.

1 I used to be a big meat eater.

2 Jack used to like sweets.

3 Sally used to be crazy about fries.

4 They didn't use to like seafood.

CONVERSATION MODEL

A ▶3:24 Read and listen to two people talking about their food passions.

A: Are you a big coffee drinker?

B: Definitely. I'm crazy about coffee. What about you?

A: I used to drink it a lot. But recently I've cut back.

B: Well, I couldn't live without it.

B ▶3:25 **RHYTHM AND INTONATION** Listen again and repeat. Then practice the Conversation Model with a partner.

NOW YOU CAN Talk about food passions

A **NOTEPADDING** Complete the notepad with foods you like and dislike.

My food passions	
Foods I'm crazy about	Foods I can't stand

B **CONVERSATION ACTIVATOR** With a partner, change the Conversation Model, exchanging information about your food passions. Talk about what you used to and didn't use to eat or drink. Use your notepad and the Vocabulary from page 64.

A: Are you a big .... ?

B: .... What about you?

A: ....

DON'T STOP!
• Ask about more foods and drinks.

C **CHANGE PARTNERS** Talk about other food passions.

LESSON **2** **GOAL** Make an excuse to decline food

CONVERSATION MODEL

A ▶3:26 Read and listen to a dinner guest make an excuse to decline food.

A: Please help yourself.

B: Everything looks great! But I'll pass on the chicken.

A: Don't you eat chicken?

B: Actually, no. I'm a vegetarian.

A: I'm sorry. I didn't know that.

B: It's not a problem. I'll have something else.

B ▶3:27 **RHYTHM AND INTONATION** Listen again and repeat. Then practice the Conversation Model with a partner.

▶3:28 **Variations**
It's not a problem.
Don't worry.
I'm fine.

VOCABULARY *Excuses for not eating something*

DIGITAL FLASH CARDS

A ▶3:29 Read and listen. Then listen again and repeat.

Coffee **doesn't agree with me**.

I'm **on a diet**. / I'm **trying to lose weight**.

I don't eat beef. It's **against my religion**.

I'm **allergic to** chocolate.

I'm **avoiding** sugar.

I **don't care for** broccoli.

B ▶3:30 **LISTEN TO ACTIVATE VOCABULARY** Listen to each conversation. Write the letter to complete each statement. Then listen again to check your work.

...c... **1** Cindy . . .   **a** is a vegetarian.

...d... **2** Frankie . . .   **b** is avoiding fatty, salty foods.

...e... **3** Marie . . .   **c** is trying to lose weight.

...a... **4** Susan . . .   **d** is allergic to something.

...b... **5** George . . .   **e** doesn't care for seafood.

C **PAIR WORK** Talk about foods or drinks you avoid. Explain why.

> ❝ I usually don't eat fried foods. I'm trying to lose weight. ❞

CONVERSATION MODEL

A ▶3:26 Read and listen . . .

Suggested teaching time:	2 minutes	Your actual teaching time:

These conversation strategies are implicit in the model:
• Offer food with "Please help yourself."
• Acknowledge someone's efforts by saying something positive.
• Soften the rejection of an offer with "I'll pass on the ___."
• Use a negative question to express surprise.
• Use "It's not a problem" to downplay inconvenience.

• Tell students to look at the photo to predict the conversation and ask:
   What are they doing? (Having dinner.)
   What is the woman trying to do? (She's trying to give / offer the man some food.)
   Does the man want the food? (No.)

• Have students read and listen to the conversation. To check comprehension, ask:
   What does the man say about the food? (Everything looks great.)
   Does the man eat chicken? (No.) *Why not?* (He's a vegetarian.)
   Why do you think the woman apologizes? (She's sorry she didn't cook something else.)

Language and culture
• The informal expression *Help yourself* means don't wait to be served; take the food that you want. For example, *All the desserts are in the kitchen. Help yourself.*
• The expression *I'll pass on ___* or *I'll pass* is an indirect way to decline an offer. It is more polite than being direct and saying *I don't want any ___.*

B ▶3:27 Rhythm and intonation

Suggested teaching time:	3 minutes	Your actual teaching time:

• Have students repeat chorally. Make sure they:
   ◦ put stress on *Everything* and *great*.
   ◦ use rising intonation for *Don't you eat chicken?*

▶3:28 Variations

• Have students listen and repeat the expressions in the box. Have them substitute *Don't worry* and *I'm fine* for *It's not a problem* as they practice the Conversation Model.

VOCABULARY

A ▶3:29 Read and listen . . .

Suggested teaching time:	3–5 minutes	Your actual teaching time:

V Vocabulary Flash Card Player

• After students listen and repeat, ask them to give the excuses in other words.

Language and culture
• The verb *care* has different meanings, depending on the attached preposition. For example, *To not care for* means not to like something or someone (*I don't care for him*). *To care about* means to have concern for something or someone (*I care about the environment*).

Option: (+5 minutes) To extend the activity, ask pairs to provide acceptable excuses for declining food in their culture. As pairs call out their excuses, write these excuses on the board. Then review each one and ask *How many of you agree this excuse is OK? Raise your hands.*

B ▶3:30 Listen to activate vocabulary

Suggested teaching time:	6–11 minutes	Your actual teaching time:

• Before students listen, ask them to read the phrases in the second column and the names in the first column. Tell them to listen for the names in the conversations.

• Have students listen and complete the activity. Let them listen again before checking answers in pairs.

> **AUDIOSCRIPT**
>
> CONVERSATION 1
> **M:** Cindy, don't you like pasta?
> **F:** I love it. That's the problem. I'm on a diet.
> **M:** Well, then have some vegetables. They're good for you.
> **F:** Thanks.
>
> CONVERSATION 2
> **F:** Doesn't Frankie eat fruit salad?
> **M:** Actually, he can't. It has strawberries, and he can't eat them. He's allergic. His skin gets red all over when he does.
> **F:** Oh, I'm sorry. I didn't know that.
> **M:** Oh, that's OK. He'll be fine.
>
> CONVERSATION 3 [F = French]
> **M:** Aren't you going to try the grilled fish, Marie?
> **F:** Actually, I'm not too crazy about fish.
> **M:** How about the clams?
> **F:** I'll pass. They really don't agree with me.
> **M:** Well, how about some grilled chicken then?
> **F:** That sounds great.
>
> **AUDIOSCRIPT** continues on page T68.

🖨 **Learning Strategies**

C Pair work

Suggested teaching time:	6–8 minutes	Your actual teaching time:

• Model the activity by reading the sample in the quotes and then writing on the board some foods and drinks that you avoid. Allow individuals a minute or two to brainstorm foods they avoid. Then have pairs use the Vocabulary to talk about foods on their lists.

• Have pairs share their partner's information along with the excuse used to decline the food.

GRAMMAR

Suggested teaching time:	8 minutes	Your actual teaching time:

- To introduce negative questions, write on the board 1. *Is Tanya allergic to nuts? 2. Isn't Tanya allergic to nuts?* Point out the difference between the two sentences. (1. Asks a *yes / no* question; 2. Asks a negative *yes / no* question to check information that the speaker thinks is true. The speaker thinks Tanya is allergic to nuts.)

- Read the first bullet point and examples in the Grammar box. Point out that a negative *yes / no* question can be answered affirmatively or negatively. Give alternative answers; for example, *No, she isn't. No, he didn't.*

- Write additional negative *yes / no* questions on the board that check information the class thinks is true about you. For example, *Aren't you a teacher? Don't you have children?* Tell pairs to ask each other negative *yes / no* questions to check information they think is true.

- After reading the second and third bullet points and their examples, have students suggest additional questions. For example, *Wasn't the homework difficult? Don't you love that new TV show? Aren't you going to give us homework? Isn't there a quiz today?* Have students respond with short answers.

Option: (+2 minutes) For additional practice, ask students to find an example of a negative *yes / no* question in the Conversation Model (Don't you eat chicken?) Ask *How is this negative question used?* (To express surprise.)

Option: GRAMMAR BOOSTER (*Teaching notes p. T135*)

 Inductive Grammar Charts

Grammar practice

Suggested teaching time:	4 minutes	Your actual teaching time:

- Before students complete the exercise, tell them to skim the conversations to get the context. (1. Aren't; 2. Wasn't; 3. Didn't; 4. Hasn't; 5. Isn't; 6. Didn't.)

- After students complete the exercise, review the answers as a class. Then have students identify how each negative question is used. (1. To confirm information / express surprise; 2. To get someone to agree; 3. To confirm information; 4. To confirm information; 5. When you want someone to agree with you; 6. To express surprise.)

⭐🖨 Extra Grammar Exercises

 **NOW YOU CAN** Make an excuse to decline food

A Notepadding

Suggested teaching time:	3 minutes	Your actual teaching time:

- To prepare students, have them look at the pictures and read the names of the different foods.

- Ask *Why might someone "pass" on [shellfish]?* Have students volunteer possible excuses for not eating each food pictured. (Possible responses: I am allergic to . . . ; I don't care for shellfish; shellfish doesn't agree with me.)

- If necessary, refer students to the Vocabulary on page 66.

- Allow students to complete the activity individually, then form pairs to compare excuses.

B Conversation Activator

Suggested teaching time:	5–7 minutes	Your actual teaching time:

 Conversation Activator Video

- *Note:* You can print the script or you can show a running transcript on the video player on the ActiveTeach. The script also appears on page 185 of this Teacher's Edition.

- To review making excuses to decline food, refer students to the Conversation Model on page 66.

DON'T STOP! Extend the conversation. Encourage students to use all the language in the Recycle box to continue the conversation. Tell them to cross out each phrase as they use it and not reuse the same phrase.

- For more support, play the Conversation Activator Video before students do this activity themselves. In Scene 1, the actors use different words in the gaps from the ones in the Conversation Model. In Scene 2, the actors extend the conversation. After each scene, ask students how the model has been changed by the actors.

- Be sure to reinforce the conversation. Model the conversation by role-playing it with a more confident student. Play the role of Student B to stress rising intonation after *Don't you . . . ?*

- Have pairs role-play conversations referring to the foods pictured and their notes. Remind them to change roles.

 Conversation Activator Video Script; Conversation Activator Pair Work Cards

C Change partners

Suggested teaching time:	5–8 minutes	Your actual teaching time:

- After students find a new partner, have them repeat the conversation using foods from their notes. Move around the room and help as needed.

- Invite pairs to role-play their conversations for the class. After each conversation, check comprehension by asking *What food did the person pass on? Why?*

EXTRAS

Workbook or MyEnglishLab

🖨 Speaking Activities: Unit 6, Activity 2

GRAMMAR *Negative yes / no questions*

Use negative yes / no questions . . .
- **to confirm information you think is true.**
  Isn't Jane a vegetarian? (Yes, she is.)
  Didn't he go on a diet last week? (Yes. He's trying the Atkins Diet.)
- **when you want someone to agree with you.**
  Don't you love Italian food? (Yes, it's delicious!)
  Wasn't that a terrible dinner? (Actually, no. I thought it was good.)
- **to express surprise.**
  Aren't you going to have cake? (I'm sorry, but I'm on a diet.)
  Hasn't he tried the chicken? (No. He's a vegetarian.)

GRAMMAR BOOSTER p. 135
- Negative yes / no questions: short answers

GRAMMAR PRACTICE Complete each negative yes / no question.

1 A: ....Aren't........ you allergic to tomatoes?
   B: Me? No. You're thinking of my brother.
2 A: ....Wasn't........ that lunch yesterday delicious?
   B: It was fantastic!
3 A: ....Didn't........ we already have steak this week?
   B: Yes, we did.

4 A: ....Hasn't........ your husband been on a diet?
   B: Yes. But it's driving him crazy.
5 A: ....Isn't........ asparagus disgusting?
   B: Actually, I like it.
6 A: ....Didn't........ you like your pasta?
   B: Actually, it was a little too spicy for me.

NOW YOU CAN Make an excuse to decline food

A **NOTEPADDING** Look at the photos. On a separate sheet of paper, use the Vocabulary to write an excuse to decline each food.

B **CONVERSATION ACTIVATOR** With a partner, change the Conversation Model to role-play a dinner conversation. Use the photos to offer foods. Use your notepad to make excuses to decline that food. Then change roles. OPTION: Role-play a dinner conversation with more than one classmate.

A: Please help yourself.
B: Everything looks .... ! But I'll pass on the ....
A: Don't you eat .... ?
B: Actually, ...
A: I'm sorry. I didn't know that.
B: .... I'll have ....

DON'T STOP!
- Offer drinks and other foods.
- Talk about food passions.

RECYCLE THIS LANGUAGE.

be crazy about __	can't stand __
be a big __ eater / drinker	be not crazy about __
be a(n) __ addict / lover	not care for __

C **CHANGE PARTNERS** Practice the conversation again.

octopus   shellfish

tofu   steak

broccoli   beets

chocolate

BEFORE YOU READ

EXPLORE YOUR IDEAS Do you think people's eating habits are better or worse than they used to be? Explain with examples.

READING ▶ 3:31

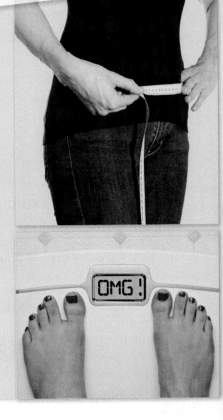

How Can It Be?
Americans gain weight . . . while the French stay thin

Have you ever wondered why Americans struggle with watching their weight, while the French, who consume all that rich food—the bread, the cheese, the wine, and the heavy sauces—continue to stay thin? Now a report from Cornell University suggests a possible answer. A study of almost 300 participants from France and the U.S. provides clues about how lifestyle and decisions about eating may affect weight. Researchers concluded that the French tend to stop eating when they feel full. However, Americans tend to stop when their plate is completely empty, or they have reached the end of their favorite TV show.

According to Dr. Joseph Mercola, who writes extensively about health issues, the French see eating as an important part of their lifestyle. They enjoy food and, therefore, spend a fairly long time at the table. In contrast, Americans see eating as something to do quickly as they squeeze meals between the other activities of the day. Mercola believes Americans have lost the ability to sense when they are actually full. So they keep eating long after the French would have stopped. In addition, he argues that, by tradition, the French tend to shop daily, walking to small shops and farmers' markets where they have a choice of fresh fruits, vegetables, and eggs as well as high-quality meats and cheeses for each meal. In contrast, Americans tend to drive their cars to huge supermarkets to buy canned and frozen foods for the whole week.

Despite all these differences, new reports show that recent lifestyle changes may be affecting French eating habits. Today, the rate of obesity—or extreme overweight—among adults is only 6%. However, as American fast-food restaurants gain acceptance, and the young turn their backs on older traditions, the obesity rate among French children has reached 17%—and is growing.

A UNDERSTAND FROM CONTEXT Use the context of the article to help you choose the same meaning as each underlined word or phrase.

1 Have you ever wondered why Americans <u>struggle with</u> watching their weight . . .
   a have an easy time   **b** have a difficult time   **c** don't care about

2 . . . while the French, who consume all that <u>rich food</u>, ...
   a fatty, high-calorie food   **b** low-fat, low-calorie food   **c** expensive food

3 . . . continue to <u>stay thin</u>?
   a worry about their weight   **b** not become overweight   **c** gain weight

4 Researchers concluded that the French tend to stop eating when they feel <u>full</u>.
   a like they can't eat any more   **b** worried about their weight   **c** hungry

5 . . . the French see eating as an important part of their <u>lifestyle</u>.
   a personal care and appearance   **b** culture or daily routine   **c** meals

BEFORE YOU READ

Explore your ideas

Suggested teaching time:	2 minutes	Your actual teaching time:	

- Introduce the topic by having students discuss the question in pairs. Then ask the class *How many think people's eating habits are better? Worse?* Call on individual students to give a reason to support their answer.

- Then ask the class *Are your eating habits better or worse than they used to be? Why?*

READING ▶3:31

Suggested teaching time:	13 minutes	Your actual teaching time:	

- Read the title of the article. Make sure students understand that *How can it be?* means *How can it be true?* Based on the title, ask students to predict the content of the article. Ask *Do you think it is true that Americans gain weight while the French stay thin? What differences between American and French cultures do you think the article will discuss?* (Possible responses: Americans eat a lot of fast food and drink a lot of soda. French people eat more fruits and vegetables and healthy breads.) Write the responses on the board.

- To check comprehension, ask:
  Do the French eat mostly low-fat foods? (No, they eat rich [high-calorie] foods.)
  What is the secret of the French? (They stop eating when they feel full.)
  What are some problems with American eating habits? (People eat quickly in between other activities or while watching TV.)
  What is the bad news for the French? (Recent lifestyle changes are affecting their eating habits and more children are obese than in the past.)

- Then write on the board I spend a lot of time eating at the table with my family or friends. I eat quickly while watching TV. Ask *Which sentence applies to you? Who do you relate to more in the article, the French or Americans? Why?*

Option: (+10 minutes) Ask *Are you surprised by the information in this article?* Have groups discuss the question and give reasons for their answer.

A Understand from context

Suggested teaching time:	5 minutes	Your actual teaching time:	

- Tell pairs to scan the article for the underlined words and circle them. Then have pairs study the context of the words (the sentences before and after them) and determine their meanings.

- Move around the room and help students as needed.

- Review answers with the class.

Option: (+10 minutes) To challenge students, have them write new sentences on a separate sheet of paper using the underlined words. Tell them the sentences don't have to be connected to the content of the article. For example: *My sister struggles with learning English grammar.* Then have pairs exchange papers and read and comment on each other's papers.

🖨 Learning Strategies

AUDIOSCRIPT Continued, for page T66 (**B** Listen to Activate Vocabulary)

CONVERSATION 4
F: Isn't Susan going to have some steak?
M: Actually, she doesn't eat meat.
F: Never?
M: Never.

CONVERSATION 5
M: I think I'll pass on the french fries.
F: Why's that, George? Don't you like french fries?
M: Yes. But my doctor thinks I should eat less salt and oil.
F: Oh, I see.

B Summarize

Suggested teaching time:	4–6 minutes	Your actual teaching time:

- To prepare students for the activity, draw on the board the two-column chart below. Tell students to copy the chart and then work in pairs to fill in the columns with reasons from the article why the French stay thin and Americans gain weight.

The French	The Americans

- Tell individuals to use the chart to write their summaries. Move around the room and help students form comparative sentences.
- Invite volunteers to write their summaries on the board and review the summaries with the class. (Possible responses: The French stop eating when they feel full, and Americans continue to eat until they finish all the food on their plate. The French spend a lot of time at the table, but Americans eat quickly between other daily activities. Americans usually shop for food weekly in huge supermarkets; in contrast, the French tend to shop daily in small shops and markets.)

C Compare and contrast

Suggested teaching time:	3–6 minutes	Your actual teaching time:

- Model the activity by reading the questions to the class and having a student read the sample quote. Have students form groups to discuss the questions.
- Move around the room and help students as needed. Encourage students to respond to the various points made in the article; for example, stopping eating when full, spending a lot of time at the table, shopping daily for food.
- Have pairs report their discussion results with the class. If students say that lifestyles in their country are closer to French lifestyles, ask *Are recent lifestyle changes affecting eating habits in your country? Do you know if the obesity rate in your country has increased in recent years?*

 Extra Reading Comprehension Exercises

 **Discuss lifestyle changes**

A Frame your ideas

Suggested teaching time:	5 minutes	Your actual teaching time:

- To introduce the questionnaire, tell students to look at the photo. Ask *Does he have a healthy diet?* Ask students to read the numbered questions in the survey. Make sure students understand that *cut back* means *eat less.*
- While individuals fill in the survey, walk around the room and make sure students complete the explanations.
- Have pairs compare surveys. Encourage them to explain any items they check as "other."

Option: (+10 minutes) As an alternative approach, instead of comparing answers in pairs, tell students to mingle and compare answers with their classmates. Students should keep track of answers and total them when they are finished.

B Class survey

Suggested teaching time:	3–8 minutes	Your actual teaching time:

- To review the survey results, write the survey questions on the board. Read each question and ask for a show of hands. Write the totals on the board.
- Read the first two questions in the "How many students . . ." box below the survey and ask for a show of hands for each. Discuss answers with the class. Then write on the board *most, some, few.* Model how to use the words in statements about the class; for example, *Most students have gone on a diet. Few students have been successful with a diet.*
- Then have pairs use the totals on the board to answer the remaining questions in the box about the survey.

Option: (+5 minutes) For classes who used the alternative option in Exercise A, ask students the questions in the green box. Have students call out the totals they have from their class survey.

C Discussion

Suggested teaching time:	10–15 minutes	Your actual teaching time:

Text-mining: Review the instructions with the class, then have students skim the article and underline useful language. Write students' findings on the board for them to refer to during the discussion.

- Read the sample quote at the bottom of the page. Then have students form groups to discuss the questions in the book. Encourage students to come to an agreement on their conclusion. Assign one student the role of taking notes.
- On the board write *Healthy Lifestyle.* Write students' ideas for having a healthy lifestyle on the board. (Possible responses: To have a healthy lifestyle, people need to balance their time well. They should make time to sit down and have a meal. They should exercise.)

EXTRAS

Workbook or MyEnglishLab

 Speaking Activities: Unit 6, Activity 3

B SUMMARIZE According to the article, why do the French stay thin while Americans gain weight? Write a four-sentence summary of the Reading. Then share your summary with the class.

> Compared to Americans, the French stay thin because . . .

C COMPARE AND CONTRAST In your country, do people generally stay thin or do they struggle with watching their weight? Are lifestyles in your country closer to those of France or the U.S., as described in the article?

> 44 I think people here are more like people in France. They like to eat, but they don't gain weight easily. 77

NOW YOU CAN Discuss lifestyle changes

A FRAME YOUR IDEAS Complete the lifestyle self-assessment.

1 Have you ever changed the way you eat in order to lose weight? ● yes ● no

If so, what have you done?
○ ate less food
○ cut back on desserts
○ avoided fatty foods
○ other (explain) _____

Were you successful? ○ yes ○ no
Why or why not? Explain. _____
_____

2 Have you ever changed the way you eat in order to avoid illness? ● yes ● no

If so, what changes have you made?
○ stopped eating fast foods
○ started eating whole grains
○ started eating more vegetables
○ other (explain) _____

Were you successful? ○ yes ○ no
Why or why not? Explain. _____
_____

3 Have you ever tried to lead a more active lifestyle? ● yes ● no

If so, what have you done?
○ started working out in a gym
○ started running or walking
○ started playing sports
○ other (explain) _____

Were you successful? ○ yes ○ no
Why or why not? Explain. _____
_____

B CLASS SURVEY On the board, summarize your class's lifestyles.

How many students . . .
• want to make some lifestyle changes?
• have gone on a diet to lose weight?
• have changed their diet to improve their health?
• have been successful with a diet?
• lead an active lifestyle?

C DISCUSSION How do you think your classmates compare to most people in your country? Are they generally healthier or less healthy? What do you think people need to do to have a healthy lifestyle?

> 44 I think my classmates are healthier than most people in this country. Too many people eat fast foods. They need to eat healthier food and exercise more. 77

Text-mining (optional)
Find and underline three words or phrases in the Reading that were new to you. Use them in your Discussion.
For example: "gain weight."

BEFORE YOU LISTEN

A ▶ 3:32 **VOCABULARY • *Food descriptions*** Read and listen. Then listen again and repeat.

It **looks** terrific.

It **smells** terrible.

It tastes { sweet. / spicy. / salty. / sour. }

It **smells like** }
It **tastes like** } chicken.
It **looks like** }

It's { soft. / hard. }

It's { chewy. / crunchy. }

B **PAIR WORK** Use the Vocabulary to describe foods you know.

❝ Apples are crunchy. ❞

LISTENING COMPREHENSION

A ▶ 3:33 **LISTEN FOR DETAILS** First, listen to the descriptions of foods from around the world and write the letter of each food. Then listen again and choose the Vocabulary that completes each description.

...c.... **1** It's (crunchy / chewy / hard), and it tastes (salty / sweet / sour).

...d.... **2** It tastes (salty / sweet / spicy), and it's (soft / hard / crunchy).

...f.... **3** It's (soft / chewy / crunchy), and it tastes (salty / sweet / spicy).

...e.... **4** It tastes (salty / sweet / spicy). Some think it (tastes / smells / looks) awful.

...b.... **5** It (smells / tastes / looks) great, and it (smells / tastes / looks) awful.

...a.... **6** They're (crunchy / chewy / hard), and they taste (salty / sweet / spicy).

kim chee / Korea cabbage

caviar / Russia

chapulines / Mexico grasshopper

cho dofu / China

mochi / Japan

Jell-O ® **/ United States**

BEFORE YOU LISTEN

A ▶3:32 Vocabulary

Suggested teaching time	5–7 minutes	Your actual teaching time:

 Vocabulary Flash Card Player

- Before students listen, tell them to look at the pictures and read the food descriptions. Make sure students can identify the foods pictured for sweet (candy), spicy (pepper), salty (salt), sour (lemon), soft (tofu or cheese), hard (tofu or cheese).

- After students listen and repeat, ask:
  What other food is sweet? Spicy? Salty? Sour?
  What other food is soft? Hard?
  What other food is chewy? Crunchy?
  Permit students to answer with foods that are familiar to them.

- Then have students listen and repeat again.

 Learning Strategies

B Pair work

Suggested teaching time	5–8 minutes	Your actual teaching time:

- Tell pairs to brainstorm a list of different foods. Then have them use the words in the Vocabulary to describe them.

- Move around the room and listen for correct pronunciation and use. Provide help as needed.

- Have pairs share their descriptions with the class.

LISTENING COMPREHENSION

A ▶3:33 Listen for details

Suggested teaching time	12–17 minutes	Your actual teaching time:

- For a warm-up, look at the pictures and ask *Have you ever tried any of these foods? If so, which one(s)? How did it (they) taste?*

- Focus on picture b. Ask *How do you think this food tastes?* Have students predict what the other foods taste like, and write their predictions on the board.

- Have students listen to the descriptions once or twice and write the letter of each food. If necessary, have students listen again.

- Then ask students to listen again and complete each description.

- Review answers with the class. Then have students compare the descriptions to their predictions earlier.

Option: *(+10 minutes)* Have pairs choose a popular local food and write a description of it without mentioning the name of the food. Tell students to say how the food tastes and smells, if it's hard or soft, chewy or crunchy. Then have pairs read their descriptions to the class and ask students to guess the food.

AUDIOSCRIPT

1 [F = Japanese]
F: Mochi is made from a sweet rice and it's really delicious. We always eat mochi to celebrate the new year. It tastes sweet, and it's very, very chewy. As a matter of fact, some old people have to be very careful if they eat it. But it tastes great.

2 [M = U.S. regional]
M: When I was growing up, my mother used to make Jell-O all the time. It comes in beautiful colors and it comes in at least twenty-six different flavors. Grape, lemon, orange, mixed fruit, cherry, mango. It's soft and cool, and it's sweet and kids just love it. Where I come from, we make it into all kinds of salads with fruit.

3 [F = Korean]
F: In Korea we eat kim chee a lot. It's a kind of salad that we eat with most meals. There are actually about 180 different kinds of kim chee. But most are made with cabbage. It's very hot and spicy. And it's nice and crunchy.

4 [M = Russian]
M: When I have guests in my home in Moscow, I always serve them caviar. It's a real Russian specialty. You know caviar? It's fish eggs—and you can buy it red or black. In other countries, it's very expensive, but in Russia it's not too bad. Some people think it looks awful, but I think it's beautiful. It's wonderful and salty, and you should always eat it cold—and in small bites.

5 [F = Chinese]
F: Have you ever tried cho dofu? Well, if you haven't, you'll be very surprised because it smells very bad! That's what the name means—bad-smelling tofu. But the flavor is quite delicious—a little salty. I didn't use to like it myself. But now I'm crazy about it.

6 [M = Spanish]
M: I'm from Oaxaca, and we have a special food called chapulines. Chapulines means grasshoppers, actually. But they're really good and they're really good for you. They're pretty salty, and . . . uh . . . crunchy. They really do taste great, though.

B ▶3:34 Listen to personalize

Suggested teaching time:	5 minutes	Your actual teaching time:

- Have students listen again. Stop the audio after each description and allow pairs to discuss if they would like to try that food.
- While students discuss, write a list of all the foods on the board. After listening to all the descriptions, ask the class *Who would like to try ___?* Ask for a show of hands and write the numbers on the board.
- Invite students to study the survey on the board and determine the most and least popular food.

 **Learning Strategies**

NOW YOU CAN Describe local dishes

A Frame your ideas

Suggested teaching time:	8–10 minutes	Your actual teaching time:

- Have pairs brainstorm popular foods in their country and then write these on the board. Leave the list on the board for use in Exercise B.
- Tell pairs to complete their notes by choosing three foods they would serve a visitor to their country. Tell them to refer to the list on the board or suggest other foods.
- After students complete the activity, have pairs present their choices to the class. If more than one pair chooses the same food, have the class compare descriptions and ingredients.
- Ask *Is there any local food you would not serve a visitor? Why not?*

Option: (+10 minutes) To challenge students, have pairs write a recipe for one of the foods they chose. Ask different pairs to share their recipes with the class.

B Pair work

Suggested teaching time:	10–13 minutes	Your actual teaching time:

- For review, refer students to the Vocabulary on page 70.
- Give students a few minutes to skim the language in the Recycle box. Review meaning as necessary. Encourage students to keep the conversation going by using the language in the box. Tell them to cross out each sentence that they use.
- Model the activity by role-playing a conversation with a more confident student. Use the sample quotes.
- Then have pairs role-play conversations referring to the foods they described in their notes in Exercise A.
- Have pairs role-play their conversations for the class. After the role plays are finished, ask *What food did the first / second / third pair describe? What is it like? What's in it?*

Option: (+10 minutes) To challenge students, have pairs pretend they are at a local restaurant looking at a menu (the items they outlined in Exercise A). Have them discuss the foods and then decide what they would like to order.

EXTRAS

Workbook or MyEnglishLab

Speaking Activities: Unit 6, Activity 4; "Find Someone Who . . ." Activity

B ▶ 3:34 **LISTEN TO PERSONALIZE** Listen again. After each food, discuss with a partner whether you would like to try that food. Explain why or why not.

NOW YOU CAN Describe local dishes

A **FRAME YOUR IDEAS** Choose three local dishes that you would recommend to a visitor to your country. Write notes about each.

Name of dish:
Rain doughnuts

Description:
soft and sweet

What's in it?
flour, eggs, milk

Name of dish:

Description:

What's in it?

1

Name of dish:

Description:

What's in it?

3

Name of dish:

Description:

What's in it?

2

B **PAIR WORK** Role-play a conversation in which one of you is a visitor to your country. Introduce and describe your dishes to the "visitor." Use the Vocabulary. For example:

❝ Have you tried rain doughnuts? ❞

❝ No, I haven't. What are they like? ❞

❝ Well, they're soft. And they taste sweet . . . ❞

"rain doughnuts" / Brazil

🔄 **RECYCLE THIS LANGUAGE.**

Ask about the dish	Comment on the dish	
What's in [it / them]?	It sounds / they sound [great].	I'm allergic to __.
Is it / Are they [spicy / sweet]?	I'm crazy about __.	I'm avoiding __.
How do you make [it / them]?	I'm a big __ eater.	__ [don't / doesn't] agree with me.
Is it / Are they [popular]?	I'm a(n) __ [addict / lover].	__ [is / are] against my religion.
Does it / Do they taste [salty]?	I [used to / didn't use to] eat __.	I'm not much of a __ [eater].
	I don't care for __.	I'm [on a diet / trying to lose weight].

REVIEW

A ▶3:35 Listen to the conversation in a restaurant. Cross out the foods that the speakers don't mention.

~~beef and broccoli~~	chicken	clams	~~noodles~~	pasta
pizza	salmon	scallops	shrimp	steak

B ▶3:36 Now listen again and complete the statements.

The man doesn't care for ....seafood.......... .

He would rather eat ....steak............... .

C Complete the negative yes / no question for each situation.

1 The weather today is sunny and beautiful. You turn to your friend and say: "......Isn't...... the weather fantastic?"

2 You've just finished dinner. It was a terrible meal. As you leave, you say to your friend: "......Wasn't...... that meal awful?"

3 You're sightseeing in China. From your tour bus window you see a long wall in the distance. You say to the person sitting next to you: "..........Isn't.......... that the Great Wall?"

4 You're surprised to see your friend eating breakfast at 11:30. You say: "......Haven't...... you ...had / eaten... breakfast yet?"

5 You see a woman on the street. You're pretty sure it's Norah Jones, the singer. You go up to her and ask: "..........Aren't.......... you Norah Jones?"

D Write five sentences about things you used to or didn't use to do or think when you were younger. For example:

> I didn't use to like coffee when I was younger.

E Write short descriptions of the following foods.

apples	bananas	carrots	grapefruit
ice cream	onions	squid	steak

> Carrots are orange, and they're sweet and crunchy.

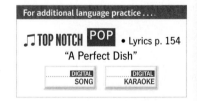

For additional language practice . . .

♫ TOP NOTCH **POP** • Lyrics p. 154
"A Perfect Dish"

| DIGITAL SONG | DIGITAL KARAOKE |

WRITING

Write a paragraph on the following topic: Do you think people are eating healthier or less healthy foods than they used to? Give examples to support your opinion.

> I think people are eating a lot of unhealthy foods today.
>
> People used to eat a lot of fresh foods. However, lately . . .

WRITING BOOSTER p. 148

• Connecting ideas:
  subordinating conjunctions
• Guidance for this writing exercise

REVIEW

A ▶3:35 Listen to the conversation . . .

Suggested teaching time:	3 minutes	Your actual teaching time:

- Tell students to close their books. Play the conversation. To check comprehension ask *Where does the conversation take place?* (In a restaurant.)
- Have students open their books and read the food choices in the box. Ask *Which of these are seafood?* (Clams, salmon, scallops, shrimp.) Then have them listen again as needed to complete the exercise.
- Tell students to compare answers with a partner.

Option: (+5–10 minutes) Have pairs or small groups discuss their food passions. Ask *Which of these foods are you crazy about? Which ones do you not care for?*

AUDIOSCRIPT

M: Nice restaurant.
F: Yeah. You're going to love the menu. The fish is really fresh.
M: Hmm, do they have pizza?
F: Not here. How about some pasta? They have it with shrimp, clams, scallops . . .
M: That's OK. I'll pass.
F: Do you like salmon?
M: Uh . . . Chicken would be good.
F: I don't think they have chicken. Sorry.
M: OK, the truth is I'm not crazy about seafood. I just don't like it. Actually, I'm really a meat eater at heart.
F: Well, why didn't you say something! We didn't have to come to a seafood restaurant.
M: Don't worry about it. I'll be fine.
F: Hey, look. They have steak.
M: OK, now you're talking.

B ▶3:36 Now listen again . . .

Suggested teaching time:	3 minutes	Your actual teaching time:

- Ask a volunteer to read the list of food in Exercise A again. Then have students listen again and complete the statements. Clarify that *would rather* means *prefer.*
- Review the answers with the class. Then ask *Does anyone dislike seafood as much as the man in the audio? Has anyone ever ordered steak in a seafood restaurant?*

C Complete the negative <u>yes</u> / <u>no</u> question . . .

Suggested teaching time:	3 minutes	Your actual teaching time:

- Before students open their books, read aloud the situation in item 1. On the board, write ___ *the weather fantastic?* Explain this is a negative question and ask a student to complete it.
- Tell students to think about the context and verb tense of each situation before completing the questions.
- When students have finished, review answers with the class. Check comprehension by asking *Which negative questions check information the speaker thinks is true?* (3, 5.) *Which negative question expresses surprise?* (4.) *Which negative questions show that the speaker wants the listener to agree?* (1, 2.)

D Write five sentences . . .

Suggested teaching time:	4–6 minutes	Your actual teaching time:

- To review *used to* in affirmative and negative statements, write on the board *When I was younger, I used to watch TV a lot. I didn't use to go to the movies.* Ask *Did you use to watch TV a lot when you were younger? Did you use to go to the movies?*
- After students complete the activity, have them share their sentences in pairs. Make sure they reduce the vowel in *to.*

E Write short descriptions . . .

Suggested teaching time:	4–7 minutes	Your actual teaching time:

- After students read the different foods, ask *Which of these foods have you eaten? What are they like?* Ask students to share their opinions.
- After students complete the activity, have them work in pairs and tell them to read their descriptions to their partners out of order. Their partners will try to guess which food is being described.

WRITING

Suggested teaching time:	10–15 minutes	Your actual teaching time:

- Write the question on the board. Have students take notes to support their opinion. Then tell them to start their paragraph with *I think people are eating healthier / less healthy . . .*
- Have students form pairs. While they work, write *Do you agree with your partner? Why? Why not?* Have pairs exchange paragraphs. Then have them discuss the question on the board.

Option: **WRITING BOOSTER** *(Teaching notes p. T148)*

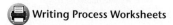 **Writing Process Worksheets**

 *Top Notch Pop* **Song Video and Karaoke Video**

 **Digital Games**

ORAL REVIEW

Before the first activity, give students a few minutes of silent time to become familiar with the descriptions.

Challenge

Suggested teaching time:	5–7 minutes	Your actual teaching time:

- Have students look at the pictures of the selections and skim the ingredients. Ask *Has anyone ever had any of these dishes?*
- Then have students choose the dish that interests them most. Tell students to study the ingredients for a minute and then close their books.
- Call on students to describe the dishes they chose. If students chose the same dish, invite students to help each other describe the ingredients.
- Then ask individual students *Why did you choose the dish?* (Possible response: It seemed very tasty. / It seemed strange. / I like spicy foods.)

Pair work 1

Suggested teaching time:	5–7 minutes	Your actual teaching time:

- Refer students to the Vocabulary on page 64 to review talking about food passions.
- Then have pairs role-play conversations.

Possible responses . . .
A: Have you tried pad thai? It's terrific. **B:** Is it spicy? I don't care for spicy foods. I like salty foods, though. **A:** Then you should try some pot stickers. You'll love them.

Pair work 2

Suggested teaching time:	5 minutes	Your actual teaching time:

- Refer students to the Vocabulary on page 66 to review how to make excuses.
- Then have pairs role-play conversations.

Possible responses . . .
A: Would you like some pot stickers? **B:** Actually, I don't eat pork. **A:** Oh, I didn't know you are a vegetarian. **B:** I'm not. I don't eat pork because it's against my religion.

Pair work 3

Suggested teaching time:	5–8 minutes	Your actual teaching time:

- Refer students to the Vocabulary on page 70 to review talking about dishes.
- Then have pairs role-play conversations.

Possible responses . . .
A: Have you ever tried chicken mole? **B:** No, but it looks delicious. What's in it? **A:** Chicken, hot peppers, tomatoes, and chocolate. **B:** It smells terrific. I'd like to try some.

FYI: Chocolate is a common ingredient of many mole sauces, but not all.

Language and culture
These foods are typically pronounced as follows in English:
Pad thai = /pɑd'taɪ/; *Bi bim bop* = /bi'bim·bap/; *Mole* = /'mo·leɪ/; *Tabouleh* = /ta·'bu·li/; *Rocoto* = /ro·'ko·to/

Option: *(+10 minutes)* To challenge students, have them role-play a conversation between a server (waiter or waitress) and a customer at a restaurant.

Option: Oral Progress Assessment
- Use the photographs on page 73. Encourage students to use the vocabulary, grammar, rhythm, and intonation practiced in this unit.
- Ask information questions:
  Are you allergic to any of these foods?
  Which foods have ingredients you can't stand?
  Which dish would you like best? Why?
  Which foods seem especially healthy? Why?
- Invite a student to role-play a conversation with you.
- Evaluate the student on intelligibility, fluency, correct use of grammar, appropriate use of vocabulary.

 Oral Progress Assessment Charts

Option: *Top Notch* Project
Idea: Have students do some research on the Internet or in a library about a dish from another country for a presentation about the dish to the class.

- Write these questions on the board for pairs to discuss:
  What does the dish look like?
  What does it taste like?
  How is it served?
  Is it served on any special occasions?
- Tell students to bring photos and a recipe for their presentations. Then combine them into a class cookbook for distribution in a later class session.

EXTRAS

On the Internet:
- Online Teacher Resources: pearsonelt.com/topnotch3e/

Additional printable resources on the ActiveTeach:
- Assessment
- Just for Fun
- *Top Notch Pop* Song Activities
- *Top Notch TV* Video Program and Activity Worksheets
- Supplementary Pronunciation Lessons
- Conversation Activator Video Scripts
- Audioscripts and Answer Keys
- Unit Study Guides

International Buffet
Today's Selections

Pad Thai • Thailand

Ingredients: rice noodles, tofu, peanuts, fish sauce, sugar, lime juice, vegetable oil, garlic, shrimp, eggs, hot peppers

Bi Bim Bop • Korea

Ingredients: rice, beef, soy sauce, sesame oil, garlic, black pepper, salt, eggs, lettuce, rice wine, hot peppers

Chicken Mole • Mexico

Ingredients: chicken, salt, vegetable oil, onions, garlic, tomatoes, chocolate, hot peppers

Potato Soup • Colombia

Ingredients: chicken, three kinds of potatoes, corn, avocados

Tabouleh Salad • Lebanon

Ingredients: parsley, mint, onions, tomatoes, salt, black pepper, cracked wheat, lemon juice, olive oil

Pot Stickers • China

Ingredients: flour, cabbage, pork, green onions, sesame oil, salt

Stuffed Rocoto Peppers • Peru

Ingredients: onions, garlic, ground beef, hard-boiled eggs, raisins, cheese, rocoto peppers, vegetable oil

ORAL REVIEW

CHALLENGE Choose a dish and study the photo and the ingredients for one minute. Then close your book. Describe the dish.

PAIR WORK

1 Create a conversation for the man and woman in which they look at the foods and talk about their food passions. For example:

Have you tried Pad Thai? It's terrific!

2 Create a conversation in which the man or the woman suggests and offers foods. The other makes excuses. Start like this:

A: *Would you like some __?*
B: *Actually, __.*

3 Choose a dish and create a conversation between someone from that country and a visitor. For example:

Have you ever tried __?

✓ NOW I CAN

☐ Talk about food passions.
☐ Make an excuse to decline food.
☐ Discuss lifestyle changes.
☐ Describe local dishes.

COMMUNICATION GOALS
1 Get to know a new friend.
2 Cheer someone up.
3 Discuss personality and its origin.
4 Examine the impact of birth order.

PREVIEW

The **Psychology** of Color

According to research, colors have a powerful effect on us. Take the test and then see if your answers are confirmed by the research. You may be surprised! (Check your answers below.)

Color test

1) What color is the most attention-getting?

● black   ○ yellow   ● red   ○ other

2) What color is most likely to make people feel angry?

● black   ○ yellow   ● pink   ○ other

3) What color is best for a hospital room?

○ pink   ○ white   ● green   ○ other

4) What color often makes people feel tired?

● green   ● blue   ● pink   ○ other

5) What is the least appealing color for food?

● black   ○ yellow   ● blue   ○ other

Answers

1) Experts say red attracts the most attention. Using red for traffic lights and warning lights makes them more noticeable.

2) Studies have shown that being in a yellow room makes it more likely for adults to lose their tempers and for babies to cry.

3) Green is the easiest color on the eye, and it causes people to relax. Painting a hospital room green helps patients get the rest they need.

4) Research has shown that looking at pink can cause people to feel tired. Some sports teams have painted the dressing room of the opposing team pink to reduce the players' energy.

5) Researchers in marketing have found that using blue in processed foods is unappealing. They believe that this is because blue is rare in nature. Painting a restaurant red, on the other hand, increases the appetite. Many restaurants are painted red.

Questionnaire

What are your color preferences?
Look at the colors below.

YELLOW-GREEN   EMERALD GREEN   BRIGHT ORANGE   DARK GRAY   LIGHT BLUE   TOMATO RED   LILAC

Which color do you find the most appealing? _____

Which color do you most associate with happiness? _____

Which color do you most associate with being sad? _____

A **CLASS SURVEY** How many classmates answered the questions on the test correctly? Which color on the questionnaire was the most appealing to your classmates?

B **DISCUSSION** In your opinion, what makes people like some colors and dislike others?

❝ I think people like colors that remind them of things they like. ❞

❝ I agree. I love blue. It reminds me of the sky. I love being outdoors. ❞

UNIT 7 About Personality

PREVIEW

Suggested teaching time:	8–13 minutes	Your actual teaching time:	

- To introduce the topic, write on the board *Colors*. With books closed, have students name as many different colors as they can. Write these on the board.
- Tell students to open their books, and give them a few minutes of silent time to examine the color test and the questionnaire.
- Ask *Do you think colors have effects on us?*
- Then focus students' attention on the test. After students complete the test, have them compare answers in pairs. Then look at the upside-down answer key for numbers 1–5.
- Ask individual students *Were you surprised by any of the answers? Do you disagree with any of them? If yes, why?*

> ### Language and culture
> - In American English, *color* is spelled without a *u*; in other varieties of English, the same word is spelled with a *u*: *colour*.

A Class survey

Suggested teaching time:	4 minutes	Your actual teaching time:	

- Ask students if they guessed the correct colors to the questions in the test.
- Focus attention on the questionnaire section. Have students compare the colors on the board with the colors in the book. Ask *How are these colors different?* Point out that the colors in the book are varieties of colors. Ask students to give examples of other varieties of colors and then fill in the blanks. Make sure students understand *appealing* means *interesting* and *attractive*.
- Ask for a show of hands to determine the most and least popular color. Write numbers on the board. Ask *Why do you think ___ is the most / the least popular color?*
- Draw the chart below on the board. Have students share which colors they associate with each emotion.

Happiness	Sadness

B Discussion

Suggested teaching time:	5 minutes	Your actual teaching time:	

- Read the question to the class and ask two students to read the sample quotes. Model a statement showing disagreement; say *I don't really agree. I like red a lot, but it doesn't remind me of anything. I just like the color.*
- Divide the class into small groups to discuss the question. As students work, write on the board *Do color preferences come from your culture or from personal taste?* Tell groups to include this question in their discussion.
- Review answers with the class. Invite volunteers to share their points of view.

> ### Language and culture
> - Colors appear in many English idioms. Here are a few of them: *To see red* means to feel very angry; a successful business is *in the black*, and a failing business is *in the red*; someone who is feeling very envious is *green with envy*.

C ▶ 4:02 **Photo story**

Suggested teaching time:	10–15 minutes	Your actual teaching time:

- To prepare students, tell them to look at the photos. Ask:
  Do these two people know each other? (Yes.) *Where are they?* (At home / in a living room.)
  What do you think they are talking about?

- Have students read and listen to the conversation.

- To check comprehension, ask:
  What are Chelsea and Chad talking about?
    (Replacing the wallpaper.)
  Do they like the wallpaper? (No.)
  What color did Chelsea want to paint the walls?
    (Pink; soft rose.)
  Why didn't Chad like that color? (He thought it was too feminine.)
  What colors do they discuss? (Blue and white.)
  What color do they choose? (White.)

- Have students close their books and listen again. In small groups, ask them to summarize the conversation as a chain story. Have them begin their summaries *Chelsea and Chad are discussing . . . .* When groups finish, have them form new groups to compare their summaries.

Language and culture

- In informal spoken English, *way* is used to express a high degree. When Chelsea says *Way too masculine* it means *Much too masculine*.

D **Paraphrase**

Suggested teaching time:	5 minutes	Your actual teaching time:

- Tell students to work in pairs and find and underline the quoted phrases in the conversation. Tell them to use the context to figure out the meaning. If necessary, model the activity by doing the first item with the class.

- Have pairs share answers with the class. Then ask:
  Why do Chelsea and Chad decide blue is not a good color? (They're not sure their furniture would look good with it.)
  Why do Chelsea and Chad choose white as their color?
    (Because everything looks good with white.)

E **Think and explain**

Suggested teaching time:	5–7 minutes	Your actual teaching time:

- Model the activity by reading the first item and example. Have students work individually. Tell them to find the place in the Photo Story that proves a statement is false. Move around the room as students work, and help as needed.

- Review answers with the class.

Answers to Exercise E
2. Chad says, "You wanted pink . . ."
3. Chelsea says, "I'm pulling your leg, silly! Blue would be great."
4. Chelsea says, "I'm not sure the furniture would go with it."
5. Chad says, "I'd hate to have to get all new stuff . . ."
6. Chad says, "All of a sudden, I'm thinking white."
7. Chelsea says, "It goes with everything!"

SPEAKING

Suggested teaching time:	8–11 minutes	Your actual teaching time:

- Refer students to the color test on page 74. Make sure they review the information in the answer key. Ask *What do studies say about using yellow as a room color?* (It makes adults lose their tempers and babies cry more.) *Pink?* (It makes people feel tired.) *Green?* (It relaxes people.)

- Tell students to choose their colors and write their reasons. Refer them also to the Photo Story for ideas. Move around the room as students work.

- After pairs compare charts, invite volunteers to share colors and reasons. Ask *Did anyone suggest yellow or pink? Why?*

EXTRAS

Workbook

GRAMMAR

Suggested teaching time:	8–13 minutes	Your actual teaching time:

- To introduce the grammar point, write on the board I'd like <u>to repaint</u> the kitchen. I don't mind <u>repainting</u> it. Be sure to underline the infinitive and the gerund.

- Ask a student to read the sentences on the board. Then ask another student to give the subject and verb in each sentence. (I, would like; I, don't mind.) Explain that infinitives and gerunds are used after certain verbs such as *like* and *don't mind*.

- Review the first point in the Grammar box. Then ask a student to read the example sentence using a gerund in the Grammar box. Have another student read the example sentence using an infinitive.

- Ask *What's the subject and verb in each example sentence?* (She, enjoys; He, wants.) *What are the verb tenses in the example sentences?* (Simple present tense.) Repeat that the verb in *She enjoys painting* is *enjoys*, and that *painting* functions as a direct object noun. Make sure students don't confuse the *-ing* gerund form with a continuous form. Point out that gerunds and infinitives can be used with verbs in different tenses.

- Make sure that students read and understand the Remember note about other *-ing* forms. If necessary, refer students to the participial adjectives on page 10.

- Ask volunteers to read the lists of verbs that are followed by gerunds, infinitives, or both.

- Note that for this initial presentation in Lesson 1, students should understand that gerunds and infinitives function as nouns and that they follow certain verbs. Lesson 2 covers the use of gerunds as objects of prepositions.

Option: (+5–8 minutes) To extend the activity, have students review the lists of verbs in the Grammar box and then close their books. Divide the class in half. Call out a verb and have alternating teams decide if the verb is followed by a gerund or an infinitive. For each correct answer, the team gets a point. The team with the most points wins.

> ### Language and culture
> - **From the Longman Corpus:** Confusion over whether to follow a verb with a gerund or infinitive is very common among English learners of all language backgrounds. Incorrect sentences such as *I enjoy to go camping* and *I'd like going to the seaside* are commonplace.

Option: GRAMMAR BOOSTER *(Teaching notes p. T136)*

 **Inductive Grammar Charts**

A Grammar practice

Suggested teaching time:	5–7 minutes	Your actual teaching time:

- To prepare students, read the title of the paragraph. Ask *What are some ways to make new friends?*

- Tell students to scan the first verb in each pair of verbs and decide if it should be followed by a gerund or an infinitive. Then have students complete the exercise.

- Review answers with the class. Read the first sentence and then ask students to read the completed sentences aloud.

B Find the grammar

Suggested teaching time:	4–5 minutes	Your actual teaching time:

- Before students begin the exercise, remind them that not all verbs ending in *–ing* are gerunds. Refer them to the note in the Grammar box at the top of the page.

- Review answers with the class. (Gerunds: 1. using; 2. being; 3. painting; 4. looking; 5. marketing, using, painting. Infinitives: 2. to lose, to cry; 3. to relax; 4. to feel, to reduce.)

FYI: These participial adjectives also appear in the answers to the questionnaire on page 74: *warning, dressing, opposing,* and *unappealing.*

 Extra Grammar Exercises

Answers to Exercise B

1. Experts say red attracts the most attention. <u>Using</u> red for traffic lights and warning lights makes them more noticeable.
2. Studies have shown that <u>being</u> in a yellow room makes it more likely for adults <u>to lose</u> their tempers and for babies <u>to cry</u>.
3. Green is the easiest color on the eye, and it causes people <u>to relax</u>. <u>Painting</u> a hospital room green helps patients get the rest they need.
4. Research has shown that <u>looking</u> at pink can cause people <u>to feel</u> tired. Some sports teams have painted the dressing room of the opposing team pink <u>to reduce</u> the players' energy.
5. Researchers in marketing have found that <u>using</u> blue in processed foods is unappealing. They believe that this is because blue is rare in nature. <u>Painting</u> a restaurant red, on the other hand, increases the appetite. Many restaurants are painted red.

PRONUNCIATION

▶4:03 **Notice how an unstressed <u>to</u> . . .**

Suggested teaching time:	2 minutes	Your actual teaching time:

 Pronunciation Coach Video

- Before students read and listen to the sentences, tell them to pay attention to how unstressed *to* becomes /tə/ in infinitive phrases.

- Then have students listen again and repeat.

- Tell students to practice reading the sentences to a partner. Move around the room and listen for correct reduction of *to*.

 Pronunciation Activities

CONVERSATION MODEL

A ▶4:04 Read and listen . . .

Suggested teaching time:	2 minutes	Your actual teaching time:

> These conversation strategies are implicit in the model:
> • Clarify an earlier question with "Well, for example. . . ."
> • Buy time to think with "Let's see."
> • Use auxiliary "do" to emphasize a verb.

- For a warm-up, write on the board *What are your likes and dislikes?* Ask *What does this question mean?* (What things do you like and what things do you not like?) Explain that students will listen to a conversation about likes and dislikes.

- Then tell students to look at the picture and ask *Where are the people?* (At a café / restaurant.) *Do you think they know each other?*

- Play the audio while students read and listen to the conversation. Explain that *So do I* is another way of saying *I do, too.*

- Ask:
  What does the woman like to do in her free time? (Play tennis, go to the movies.)
  Why does she like to play tennis? (She finds it relaxing.)
  Does the man think tennis is relaxing? (No, he finds it boring.)
  What does the man like to do? (Go to the movies.)

B ▶4:05 Rhythm and intonation

Suggested teaching time:	3 minutes	Your actual teaching time:

- Have students repeat each line chorally. Make sure they:
  ○ use falling intonation for *What would you like to know?* and *What do you like doing in your free time?* and *What about you?*
  ○ put stress on *relaxing* and *boring.*
  ○ use emphatic stress with *do.*

Option: (+3 minutes) For additional fluency practice, ask students to try to repeat the conversation from memory while looking at their partner. Allow them to keep their books open the first time but have them close their books the second. Find out how much they can remember.

NOW YOU CAN Get to know a new friend

A Notepadding

Suggested teaching time:	6–8 minutes	Your actual teaching time:

- Ask a volunteer to read the sample likes and dislikes. Ask individual students *Is cooking something you like to do?*

- Tell students to write their likes and dislikes in gerund form on the notepad. Encourage them to describe their likes and dislikes with the lists of adjectives or their own ideas.

- Move around the room to make sure students have written gerunds on their notepads.

B Conversation activator

Suggested teaching time:	7–10 minutes	Your actual teaching time:

 Conversation Activator Video

- *Note:* You can print the script or you can show a running transcript on the video player on the ActiveTeach. The script also appears on page 186 of this Teacher's Edition.

- Model the activity by role-playing the conversation with a more confident student.

- As pairs practice their conversations, move around the room and monitor their use of gerunds and infinitives as well as rhythm and intonation. Encourage them to refer to their notepads for ideas to continue the conversation. Remind them to change roles once their conversation has finished.

- Be sure to reinforce the use of conversation strategies; for example, using emphatic stress with *I <u>do</u> like*, and pausing slightly after *Well, for example . . .*

DON'T STOP! Extend the conversation. Encourage students to use all the times and occasions in the "Other times and occasions" box and all the adjectives in the Recycle box.

- For more support, play the Conversation Activator Video before students do this activity themselves. In Scene 1, the actors use different words in the gaps from the ones in the Conversation Model. In Scene 2, the actors extend the conversation. After each scene, ask students how the model has been changed by the actors.

 Conversation Activator Video Script; Conversation Activator Pair Work Cards

C Change partners

Suggested teaching time:	7–10 minutes	Your actual teaching time:

- After students have found a new partner, tell them to create new conversations. Encourage them to change roles when they have finished.

- Invite pairs to share their role plays with the class. After each conversation, ask *What are this person's likes and dislikes?*

EXTRAS

Workbook or MyEnglishLab

Speaking Activities: Unit 7, Activity 1

CONVERSATION MODEL

A ▶4:06 Read and listen . . .

| Suggested teaching time: | 2 minutes | Your actual teaching time: | |

These conversation strategies are implicit in the model:
• Thank someone for showing interest.
• Offer empathy with "I know what you mean."

• To introduce the conversation, have pairs look at the picture and take turns saying as much as they can about it to each other. (Possible responses: There are two men. They are at work / school / in a hall. The man on the right looks sad / depressed.)

• Have students predict what the conversation will be about, based on the picture. Ask *What do you think they're talking about?*

• While students read and listen to the conversation, write on the board *the same old grind* (pronounced /graɪnd/). Ask students to find the context clue that explains the meaning of this phrase. (I'm tired of working, too.)

• Tell students to read and listen to the conversation again. Check comprehension by asking:
  Why is Speaker B down? (He's tired of the same old grind.)
  How does Speaker A feel? (He's tired of working, too.)
  What do the two men decide to do to cheer up? (Go to a movie.)

Language and culture
• The expressions *to be down* and *to be down in the dumps* both mean *to be depressed. The same old grind* is an informal expression that refers to depressing, boring, routine work.
• The expression *I know what you mean* is frequently used in spoken English to show empathy.

B ▶4:07 Rhythm and intonation

| Suggested teaching time: | 3 minutes | Your actual teaching time: | |

• Have students repeat each line chorally. Make sure they use falling intonation for *What's up?* and *How about a movie?* and stress *go* in *Let's go!*

• ▶4:08 **More adjectives** Have students listen and repeat the expressions in the box. Explain that these adjectives all mean the same thing. Tell students they can substitute the other adjectives for *down* as they practice the Conversation Model.

GRAMMAR

| Suggested teaching time: | 10–15 minutes | Your actual teaching time: | |

• To introduce the grammar point, write on the board *She wrote a poem about roses.* If necessary, briefly review the function of prepositions. (They are words that specify place, direction, and time.)

• Ask:
  What is the preposition in the sentence? (About.)
  What is the object of the preposition? (Roses.)
  What are some other prepositions? (On, in, of, with.)

• Write on the board *She's excited about writing poems.* Then ask *What is the preposition in the sentence?* (About.) *What is the object of the preposition?* (Writing [poems].)

• Explain that because a gerund such as *writing* functions as a noun, it can be the object of a preposition.

• Read the first point and the example sentences in the Grammar box. Ask:
  What are the prepositions in the sentences? (Of, with, to.)
  What are the objects of the prepositions? (Of: flying; with: cooking; to: discussing.)

• Ask a student to read the Be careful! note in the Grammar box.

• Go over the expressions followed by gerunds in the box, and make sure students understand them. Point out that the best way to learn these combinations is to memorize them.

FYI: Make sure students understand that *to* in the expression *object to* is a preposition, and it is followed by a gerund. The *to* is not part of an infinitive. For example, saying *I object to go* is incorrect. The correct form is *I object to going.*

Option: GRAMMAR BOOSTER *(Teaching notes p. T136)*

 Inductive Grammar Charts

A Grammar practice

| Suggested teaching time: | 4–6 minutes | Your actual teaching time: | |

• To prepare students for the activity, tell them to circle the word or words before each blank in the exercise and identify them as verbs or adjectives. (Ted: 1. believes, verb; 2. complains, verb; 3. worry, verb; 4. afraid, adj.) (Nicole: 5. object, verb; 6. bored, adj; 7, 8. sick and tired, adj; 9. angry, adj; 10. afraid, adj; 11. excited, adj.) Then have them complete the exercise.

• After students complete the exercise, have them compare answers with a partner. Point out that items 7 and 8 complement the same adjectives, *sick and tired.*

FYI: In item 8, it is grammatically correct to omit or include *of* in the answer; for example, *. . . she's sick and tired of writing so many long reports and (of) taking exams.*

• Review answers with the class by asking volunteers to read complete sentences aloud.

• An *extrovert* is a person who is outgoing and confident and likes to be around other people.
• An *introvert* is a person who prefers to spend time alone and focus on his or her own interests.
• The expression *sick and tired of* means exhausted and bored with something. It can be followed by a noun (*Nicole is sick and tired of exams.*) or a gerund (*Nicole is sick and tired of studying for exams.*).

B Pair work

Suggested teaching time:	5–8 minutes	Your actual teaching time:

• Invite a student to read the sample quotes. Ask *What form comes after* happy about*?* (A gerund, *getting.*) Then have a student read the adjectives in the chart. (*Happy, excited, bored, sick and tired.*)
• After students complete the forms and share information in pairs, ask individual students to share their answers with the class.

  Extra Grammar Exercise

NOW YOU CAN Cheer someone up

A Notepadding

Suggested teaching time:	7 minutes	Your actual teaching time:

• Ask students to read the sample. Then ask them for their own suggestions. Be sure they express their suggestions as gerunds.
• Have students share what they're tired of. See if students have similar answers.

B Conversation activator

Suggested teaching time:	7–10 minutes	Your actual teaching time:

 Conversation Activator Video

• *Note:* You can print the script or you can show a running transcript on the video player on the ActiveTeach. The script also appears on page 186 of this Teacher's Edition.
• Refer students to the Conversation Model on page 78 to review cheering someone up.
• Model the activity by role-playing the conversation with a more confident student. Play the role of Student A.
• Be sure to reinforce the use of the conversation strategies. For example, make sure students use appropriate facial expressions when expressing thanks or empathy with *I know what you mean.*

DON'T STOP! Extend the conversation. Encourage students to use the ideas and the language in the Recycle box to continue the conversation. Tell them to number the language in the Recycle box in the order in which they use it.

• For more support, play the Conversation Activator Video before students do this activity themselves. In Scene 1, the actors use different words in the gaps from the ones in the Conversation Model. In Scene 2, the actors extend the conversation. After each scene, ask students how the model has been changed by the actors.

 Conversation Activator Video Script; Conversation Activator Pair Work Cards

C Change partners

Suggested teaching time:	7–9 minutes	Your actual teaching time:

• Assign students new partners and have them create new conversations. Encourage them to change the situation from a restaurant to work, school, or their own idea.
• Invite partners to share their role plays with the class.

EXTRAS

Workbook or MyEnglishLab

 Speaking Activities: Unit 7, Activity 2

AUDIOSCRIPT Continued, for page T82 (Listening Comprehension)

PART 2
F1: So what about Annie?
F2: Annie's a whole 'nother story.
F1: How so?
F2: Well, you know what they say about middle children—it's hard for them to feel special. They have no special status—they're not the first and not the "baby"—they're just "in between." Most middle children at least have a little time to be "the baby" and feel special. But in Annie's case, she never did. Her sister Lucy was born when Annie was really still a baby.
F1: I didn't realize that. How old was Annie when her sister was born?
F2: Thirteen months—just over a year. Annie wasn't even walking or talking yet.
F1: Hmm. How did Lucy's arrival affect her?
F2: Well, Annie's not an unhappy kid. But she struggles with the things people say middle children usually have a hard time with. Maybe a little more than the typical middle child.
F1: What kinds of things?
F2: Well, Annie's sort of jealous of both her siblings. She's jealous of Brian because we're always saying how great he is. And she's jealous of Lucy because she thinks Lucy gets more attention. Remember, Annie never had a chance to be the "baby." We think that's why she's a little bit of a rebel.
F1: Annie's a rebel? She's only seven. How can she be such a rebel?
F2: Well, nothing terrible, but . . . We know that if we're going out, there's going to be an argument with Annie about clothes. I ask her to wear shoes, and she wants to wear sandals. We get dressed up to go to a nice restaurant and she wants to wear jeans. Sometimes we just give in and let her wear what she wants. We hate to keep fighting with her all the time. This would never happen with Brian.
F1: You know, it sounds like she may be trying to get the attention she thinks the other two are getting.
F2: You may be right. But, on the other hand, we don't really worry about her. She's very popular. No one has more friends than Annie. People just love her. She's always been very popular.
F1: You know that's what they say about middle children. They're usually very popular.

AUDIOSCRIPT continues on page T80.

BEFORE YOU READ

Suggested teaching time:	5 minutes	Your actual teaching time:	

- For a warm-up, have students look at the picture and describe what they see. (Possible response: A family taking a walk.) Ask students to read the title of the article. Then ask *Why do you think this picture goes with the Reading?* (Because it has symbols of nature [genes/chromosomes] and nurture [parents].)

- Tell students to discuss the question in the book in pairs. Then have pairs share their ideas with the class.

READING ▶4:09

Suggested teaching time:	10–15 minutes	Your actual teaching time:	

- Ask a student to read the title. Focus on the word *Personality*. Ask students to work in pairs to answer these questions:
  What is your definition of personality?
  What kind of personality do you have?

- Have students read the first paragraph of the article to themselves. Then ask:
  How many of you have an easygoing personality?
  How many of you have a more emotional personality?
  Do you sometimes wish you had a different personality?
  Do you think you can change your personality?

- Have students read the last two paragraphs of the article. Ask:
  Which school of thought believes that a baby is born without a personality? (The nurture school.)
  Which school of thought believes that personality is inherited? (The nature school.)
  Why is it impossible to settle the nature vs. nurture controversy? (Because you can't put people in a laboratory and watch them develop.)
  Do you think nature and nurture both influence a person's personality? In what ways?

Option: (+10 minutes) To challenge students, have them do this activity as a timed reading. Give students a time limit to read each paragraph. When the time is up, tell them to close their books and to answer your questions as a class or in small groups without looking at the article.

Option: (+10 minutes) Have students listen to the audio of the first paragraph. Ask them to summarize what they heard about personality.

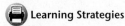 Learning Strategies

A Understand vocabulary from context

Suggested teaching time:	5–7 minutes	Your actual teaching time:	

- Have students skim the two columns and try to match the words with their definitions. If students need help, tell them to find the words in the article and use the context to help them with the meaning.

- Have pairs compare answers. Move around the room and help as needed.

B Make personal comparisons

Suggested teaching time:	5 minutes	Your actual teaching time:	

- To prepare students for the activity, tell them to skim the first paragraph of the article about personalities and underline the personality type and traits that best describe their parents' personalities and their own.

- Tell students to discuss the questions in pairs. Then ask *Did you find many similarities between you and your parents? Were you surprised by the similarities or differences between you and your parents?*

⭐ 🖨 **Extra Reading Comprehension Exercises**

AUDIOSCRIPT Continued, for page T82 (Listening Comprehension)

PART 3

F1: And what about the "baby"? I guess if Annie's seven, Lucy must be six?

F2: Right.

F1: Well, you said that Brian and Annie are typical first and middle children. What about Lucy? Is she a typical youngest child?

F2: I guess she is. She's pretty independent. Maybe that's because we didn't have as much time for her as the others. Annie was only thirteen months old when Lucy was born, so we were still pretty busy taking care of Annie. We kind of just let Lucy develop on her own. But that definitely had an effect on her personality. Like any kid, she wanted our attention.

F1: What did she do to get it?

F2: Well, she learned how to make us laugh. There's nothing Lucy likes more than clowning around and making people laugh. She's the family clown. Everyone loves her.

F1: Lucy is a lovable kid. Very charming. I smile every time I think of her.

F2: Sometimes I worry, though, that she's a little bit of a show-off, but they say that many youngest children like to show off. How better to get attention, right?

F1: Right.

F2: But I have to tell you—that that doesn't stop her from being a bit of a pain, too. Last week she decided to paint the dining room walls. Thank goodness she only had washable paint!

F1: Sorry! I shouldn't laugh. Well, they do say the baby is usually the most creative!

F2: Well, that's our Lucy! But seriously, though, she is creative: piano; children's theater; ballet lessons; all that stuff. She just can't get enough. We just wish she'd grow up a little. It seems like she'll always be "the baby." She drives her older brother and sister crazy with all the attention she gets.

F1: Well, they say the youngest child has the longest childhood. It looks like all three of your kids are a textbook case on birth order.

F2: You can say that again. Well, I've got to be going. This was really fun. Next time, you'll have to have lunch at my place.

F1: I'll take you up on that. I'll give you a call sometime next week, OK?

NOW YOU CAN Discuss personality and its origin

A Frame your ideas

Suggested teaching time:	5 minutes	Your actual teaching time:	

- Ask a student to read the title of the survey. Survey the class. Ask *How many of you think you're an introvert? How many of you think you're an extrovert?*
- Ask a volunteer to read the instructions and then have students read each pair of personality traits. Make sure students understand that *interact* means *to talk to or work with other people.*
- Find out how many extroverts, introverts, and mixtures of both there are in the class. Ask *Did you identify your personality type correctly before completing the survey? Was anyone surprised by the results of the survey?*

Option: (+5 minutes) For additional grammar practice, have students read the survey again and circle each gerund. (1. Being; 2. interacting; 5. thinking, talking.) Have students identify the reason for each gerund.
(1. After the verb *enjoy*; 2. after the verb *avoid*; 5. after the preposition *without*.)

B Pair work

Suggested teaching time:	7–10 minutes	Your actual teaching time:	

- Invite two students to read the examples in the speech bubbles. Ask *Which person is an introvert?* (The woman.) *An extrovert?* (The man.)
- After pairs discuss their personality traits, bring the class together and have students share some of the examples that explain their traits.

Option: (+10 minutes) To extend the activity, write on the board *introvert, extrovert, mixture of both.* Have students number a piece of paper from 1 to 6. Then read the six statements below, and tell students to write down whether each person's personality type is extrovert, introvert, or a mixture of both.
1. *I like to go out with friends, but I also enjoy spending time at home.* (A mixture of both.)
2. *I always think carefully about what I'm going to say.* (Introvert.)
3. *I can't stand being alone.* (Extrovert.)
4. *I have a lot of friends, but I don't know them very well.* (Extrovert.)
5. *I talk a lot, but I'm also a good listener.* (A mixture of both.)
6. *It takes time for other people to get to know me.* (Introvert.)

Option: (+10–15 minutes) To challenge students, have them write a paragraph describing the personality traits of a friend or family member who has the opposite personality from theirs. Have students explain how they get along, considering these differences in personality. Invite students to read their paragraphs to the class.

C Discussion

Suggested teaching time:	8–13 minutes	Your actual teaching time:	

Text-mining: Review the instructions with the class, then have students skim the article and underline useful language. Write students' findings on the board for them to refer to during the discussion.

- Read the questions. Review that *nurture* is another word for *genetics,* and *nature* is another word for *environment.*
- Divide the class into groups of four or five. Point out the language in the Recycle box and encourage students to use all of it in their discussion.
- While groups discuss the question, move around the room. Encourage students to provide examples; for example: "I have a pretty easygoing personality, but my mom is really emotional. When I'm around her, I get stressed. I'm not sure if I learned this stress from her or if I inherited it."
- Have groups share their ideas with the class. To help students get started, ask:
   Who believes nurture formed their personality?
   Who believes it was nature?
   Who believes it was both?

Option: (+15 minutes) To challenge students, let them debate the following question. Write on the board *Is personality formed by nature or nurture?* Divide the class into two teams and assign each team one answer. Tell each group to prepare arguments to support their assigned answer for homework. Have students refer to the article for ideas. In the next class, have groups share their arguments, allowing each side to respond. Write the arguments on the board. Then have students read the arguments to determine which group made a stronger case.

EXTRAS

Workbook or MyEnglishLab

 Speaking Activities: Unit 7, Activity 3

T81   UNIT 7, LESSON 3

BEFORE YOU LISTEN

Explore your ideas

Suggested teaching time:	3–5 minutes	Your actual teaching time:

- Have a student read the lesson goal. Ask *What is birth order?* (The order in which children in a family are born.) Explain to students that they will be examining how the order children are born affects their personalities.

- Ask several students *Do you have any brothers or sisters? If yes, are you the youngest, the oldest, or a middle child?*

- Make sure students understand that *siblings* means brothers and sisters. Tell pairs to discuss the question.

- After the discussion is finished, invite students to share their opinions with the class. Encourage them to be specific. If necessary, refer students to the ideas on page 77.

LISTENING COMPREHENSION

A ▶4:10 Listen for main ideas

Suggested teaching time:	6 minutes	Your actual teaching time:

- Read the three choices to the class.

- Before playing the audio, explain to students that the listening is a long one and that they should not expect to understand all the details. They only have to listen for the main idea.

- After students listen and complete the task, review answers with the class.

FYI: The complete audio is quite long. Students will have the opportunity to hear it again. Play the complete audio once in Exercise A.

> **Language and culture**
> - *A show-off* is an informal term for a person who likes to exhibit his or her abilities so other people will admire them.
> - The term *the baby* refers to the youngest child in a family. Even an adult can say *I am the baby of the family* to mean that he or she is the youngest family member.

AUDIOSCRIPT

PART 1

F1: Would you like some more dessert?

F2: No, thanks, Linda. Everything was delicious, but I couldn't eat another bite! Thanks so much.

F1: So, Jeanne, how are your kids doing?

F2: Well, that depends on which one . . .

F1: Well, how about the oldest? That's Brian, right? How old is he now?

F2: He's fifteen. Brian's fine. Brian's always fine. He's doing great at school. I'm sure he'll get into a great university in a couple of years. He's a great kid—works hard, he plays by the rules, and he's successful at almost everything he does. The only thing that sometimes worries me about Brian is that he can be a little too self-critical.

F1: Self-critical? How so?

F2: Well, Brian can be pretty hard on himself: no matter how well he does at something, he's not satisfied. He always feels he could do better.

F1: That's so interesting. Our first, Eric, is like that, too.

F2: Really?

F1: You know, I once read this article in one of those popular psychology magazines. It said that first children are often self-critical because parents push them to succeed more than they do with their other children. I don't mean to suggest you did that, and I don't think we did that with Eric, but it's interesting because it's so common. I just wonder why.

F2: Well, I do think there's some truth to that in our case. Harvey and I were involved in everything Brian did—music lessons, karate lessons, Chinese class on Saturday—we drove him to all his classes. We picked him up after they were over. We always asked him a lot of questions about how he was doing. He probably thought our message to him was that he had to be good at everything. But we were just interested. We didn't actually push him to be good at everything, but he may have thought we expected a lot of him. Kids internalize those messages.

F1: I imagine that's pretty typical. It's no one's fault.

F2: And one more thing—if you buy into that—you know—"nurture theory."

F1: Yeah?

F2: Brian's sister Annie wasn't born 'til Brian was eight. He really had more contact with us and other adults than he did with someone closer to his age. I'm sure all that contact with us probably had a huge impact. And, interestingly, Brian has always been comfortable with adults.

F1: From what you're saying, it sounds like Brian is the classic first child. They say that first children often feel more comfortable with people older than themselves. They seem to have a short childhood and grow up fast.

AUDIOSCRIPT continues on page T79.

 Learning Strategies

B ▶4:11 Listen for specific information

Suggested teaching time:	9–12 minutes	Your actual teaching time:

- To help students with the detailed listening, draw the chart below on the board and hand out copies to students. Ask volunteers to write the names of the children in the appropriate columns (Oldest—Brian, Middle—Annie, Youngest—Lucy). Tell students they can refer to this chart as they listen.

Oldest	Middle	Youngest

- Play the audio for Parts 1, 2, and 3 separately while students complete the exercises for each part respectively. Then play each part again as students listen and check their answers.

- Have pairs review the answers to each part. If necessary, let students listen again to whichever part they need.

 Graphic Organizers

C Classify information

Suggested teaching time:	8 minutes	Your actual teaching time:

- To prepare students, tell them to skim the personality traits and underline any unknown vocabulary. Review the vocabulary with the class. Then ask students to circle the traits that describe themselves. Tell them they will refer to this information later.
- Have students do the exercise in pairs. If necessary, allow students to listen again.
- Review answers with the class.
- Refer students to the traits they circled during the warm-up. Ask individual students *Are the traits you circled typical of people with young birth order position?*

Language and culture

- When there is just one child in a family, that child is referred to as an *only child*. Because an only child is the oldest, youngest, and the middle child, only children often show personality traits of all three birth-order categories.

Option: (+5 minutes) To extend the activity, ask the following question, and have students discuss it in groups: *Which child do you think has the most difficult place in the birth order? Why?*

Option: (+10 minutes) To challenge students, divide the class into three groups. Assign each group one of the children from the listening and have them write a summary describing his or her personality. Encourage students to use the information in the chart to help them. If necessary, let students listen again.

NOW YOU CAN Examine the impact of birth order

A Frame your ideas

Suggested teaching time:	3–5 minutes	Your actual teaching time:

- Before students fill out the checklist, make sure they understand all the descriptions.

Language and culture

- The article *the* is used for the oldest and youngest child, but the article *a* is used for a middle child. There is only one oldest and youngest child, but in families with three or more children, there can be one or more middle children.

B Group work

Suggested teaching time:	6–9 minutes	Your actual teaching time:

- Divide the students into three groups according to their birth order. If a group has only one member, combine it with another group.
- Ask each group *What generalizations can you make about your group?* Read the sample answer in quotes.
- Tell students to make notes about the personality traits of their group members as they compare checklists. For example, *Everyone has a lot of friends. A lot of us are rebels.*
- Have groups share their findings with the class, referring to their notes.

C Discussion

Suggested teaching time:	10–15 minutes	Your actual teaching time:

- For a warm-up, ask *What traits did the first / only children have? Did they have similar personalities?*
- Have groups discuss how birth order can affect a person's personality. Refer them to the Ideas box. Then have students share ideas with the class.

Option: (+10 minutes) To extend the activity, write on the board *Do you agree with the statement that first children are often the most successful?* Have students work in pairs. Then have pairs share ideas with the class. Ask follow-up questions such as *What does a person have to do to achieve success in life? Do you know any very successful middle or youngest children? If yes, what do you think influenced their success?*

EXTRAS

Workbook or MyEnglishLab

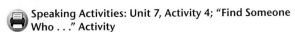 **Speaking Activities: Unit 7, Activity 4; "Find Someone Who . . ." Activity**

A ▶4:12 Listen to the conversations . . .

Suggested teaching time:	4–8 minutes	Your actual teaching time:

- Tell students to listen to the conversations with their books closed. Then have them open their books and complete as many statements as they can.
- Allow students to listen again as needed to complete the activity. Then have students compare answers in pairs.
- Review answers with the class and discuss any difficulties that students may have had.

AUDIOSCRIPT

CONVERSATION 1
F: You look a little blue, Andy. What's up?
M: I don't know. Nothing in particular. I'm just feeling bored with my job. Every day it's the same old thing.
F: I'm sorry to hear that.
M: Thanks.

CONVERSATION 2
F1: Let's have a party. I'm in the mood to have a lot of people for dinner.
F2: Mollie! You never stop! You've got to be the most active person I know.
F1: I just hate sitting around and thinking. I like a lot of action.

CONVERSATION 3 [M = U.S. regional]
M: Let's just stay home tonight. I need some peace and quiet.
F: Greg! I'm getting sick and tired of staying home. Don't you want to get out and see our friends?
M: Sometimes. But most nights I'd rather just be with you and read or listen to music.

CONVERSATION 4
M: So, Millie, where do you stand on the nature-nurture controversy?
F: Me? I guess I think the family is the most important factor. A happy early childhood makes a person cheerful for life.

CONVERSATION 5
M: So, Vera, what do you think is the best way to make your children have cheerful personalities?
F: Are you kidding? People are born either happy or sad. The parents have nothing to do with it. Once you're born, it's too late.

B Complete the paragraph . . .

Suggested teaching time:	2–4 minutes	Your actual teaching time:

- Ask students to circle the verb or adjective in front of each blank. To help students, tell them to ask themselves which preposition follows each verb or adjective. If students have difficulty, write these words on the board: *about, in, to, with.*
- After students complete the activity, have them compare answers with a partner. Refer students to the Grammar box on page 78 if necessary.

C Complete each personal statement . . .

Suggested teaching time:	6–9 minutes	Your actual teaching time:

- To prepare students for the activity, have them begin by underlining the verb in each sentence and then deciding if a gerund or infinitive should follow. If necessary, refer students to the Grammar boxes on pages 76 and 78 for help.
- After students complete the statements, have them compare answers in pairs. As pairs work together, move around the room and help as needed.
- Have pairs share their answers with the class. Ask *Did any partners have similar personal statements?*

D Complete each statement . . .

Suggested teaching time:	2 minutes	Your actual teaching time:

- After students complete each statement, have them compare answers with a partner. If necessary, refer students to pages 80–83 for help.

WRITING

Suggested teaching time:	10–15 minutes	Your actual teaching time:

- On the board, write *Personality traits.* Have students brainstorm different traits; for example, *self-critical, creative, conservative, introvert / extrovert, a clown, a rebel.*
- Have students decide who they will write about. Students may feel more comfortable sharing descriptions of someone they know well rather than descriptions of themselves.
- Invite students to read their descriptions to the class.

Option: **WRITING BOOSTER** *(Teaching notes p. T149)*

 **Writing Process Worksheets**

 *Top Notch Pop* **Song Video and Karaoke Video**

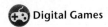 Digital Games

ORAL REVIEW

Before the first activity, give students a few minutes of silent time to become familiar with the pictures.

Pair work 1

Suggested teaching time:	5 minutes	Your actual teaching time:

- Before students create conversations, encourage them to look through the unit for vocabulary and ideas. Refer them to the Conversation Model on page 78.
- Invite pairs to act out their conversations for the class.

> **Possible responses . . .**
> **A:** You look down. What's up? **B:** Oh, nothing serious. I'm just tired of the same old grind. But thanks for asking. **A:** I know what you mean. I'm tired of studying, too. How about going for a bike ride? That always helps me. **A:** Great idea. Let's go right now!

Pair work 2

Suggested teaching time:	5 minutes	Your actual teaching time:

- Before students create conversations, encourage them to look through pages 80–83 for ideas.

> **Possible responses . . .**
> **A:** So, who is the youngest in your family? **B:** My sister Kate. I have two sisters. I'm in the middle. **A:** Really? I'm the oldest. I have a younger brother. **B:** You're lucky. I hate being in the middle. My parents pay more attention to my sisters. **A:** Are you an introvert or an extrovert? **B:** I'm more of an introvert by nature.

Group work

Suggested teaching time:	12 minutes	Your actual teaching time:

- Write on the board *What is personality, and how does it develop?*
- Divide the class into groups of four. Have students choose one person to be the recorder and take notes as the group discusses the question on the board. Encourage students to use themselves as examples.
- Have each group choose a person to role-play the professor and present the notes to the rest of the class.
- Invite groups to share their notes with the class. After each professor speaks, encourage students to ask questions.

> **Possible responses . . .**
> Some people say a person is born with a personality, and there is no way to change it. But life is not that simple. Environment affects how a person grows and develops, and it can influence his or her personality. For example, Myra here is the youngest of five children. She says birth order definitely influenced who she is. As the baby of the family, she never had many responsibilities. There was always someone older to do things for her. Now as an adult, she says it took her a long time to learn to take care of her responsibilities . . .

Option: Oral Progress Assessment

- Use the pictures on page 85. Encourage students to use the vocabulary, grammar, rhythm, and intonation practiced in this unit.
- Ask:
  In Picture 1, what are the people doing?
  In Picture 2, what are the women talking about?
  In Picture 3, what is the professor talking about?
- Invite a student to role-play a conversation about the second picture with you. Play the role of the man, and have the student play the woman.
- Evaluate the student on intelligibility, fluency, correct use of grammar, and appropriate use of vocabulary.

 Oral Progress Assessment Charts

Option: *Top Notch* Project

Have students research the birth order of a famous person and prepare a presentation for the class.

Idea: In pairs, have students brainstorm a list of well-known successful people they admire and then choose one person to focus on.

- Tell students to use the Internet or the library to find out about the person's family background, including the number of siblings he or she has and the person's place in the birth order. Include pictures if possible.
- When students make their presentations, have them draw a family tree on the board.

EXTRAS

On the Internet:
- Online Teacher Resources: pearsonelt.com/topnotch3e/

Additional printable resources on the ActiveTeach:
- Assessment
- Just for Fun
- *Top Notch Pop* Song Activities
- *Top Notch TV* Video Program and Activity Worksheets
- Supplementary Pronunciation Lessons
- Conversation Activator Video Scripts
- Audioscripts and Answer Keys
- Unit Study Guides

ORAL REVIEW

PAIR WORK

1 Create a conversation for photo 1 in which the girl on the left cheers up her friend. Use gerunds and infinities.

2 Role-play a discussion between the two people in photo 2. They discuss the birth order of their siblings and their personalities.

GROUP WORK Choose one person to be the professor in photo 3. Help that person create a lecture about personality development. Then the other classmates listen to the lecture and ask questions.

You look down . . .

1

So, who is the youngest in your family?

2

Today we're discussing the nature-nurture controversy . . .

3

✓ NOW I CAN

☐ Get to know a new friend.
☐ Cheer someone up.
☐ Discuss personality and its origin.
☐ Examine the impact of birth order.

PREVIEW

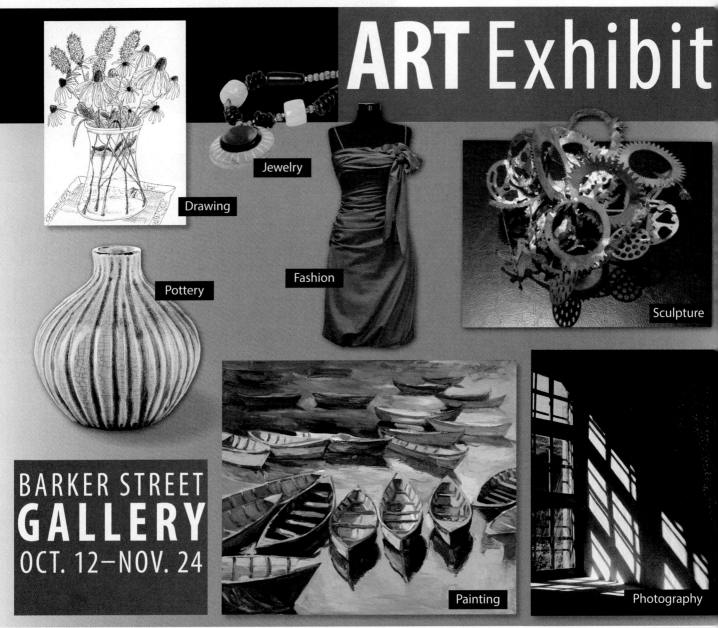

ART Exhibit

Drawing

Jewelry

Fashion

Pottery

Sculpture

BARKER STREET
GALLERY
OCT. 12–NOV. 24

Painting

Photography

DIGITAL
FLASH
CARDS

A ▶4:15 **VOCABULARY • *Kinds of art*** Read and listen. Then listen again and repeat.

B **DISCUSSION** What kinds of art do you like? Which pieces of art in the Preview do you like? Why? Use some of the adjectives.

❝ I'm not really into paintings, but I think this one's beautiful. ❞

❝ I like jewelry, but I don't think the necklace is very interesting. ❞

Adjectives to describe art

beautiful	awful	feminine
exciting	boring	masculine
fascinating	weird	unusual
relaxing	silly	practical
thought-provoking	depressing	interesting

UNIT 8 The Arts

PREVIEW

Suggested teaching time:	10–12 minutes	Your actual teaching time:	

- For a warm-up, tell students to close their books. Write on the board *Art.* Have students work in pairs and brainstorm as many words as they can connected to this topic. (Possible responses: Museum, paintings, sculptures.)

- Have students open their books and spend a few minutes reading and examining the poster silently. Ask *Do you see any words from your brainstorm on this poster? Have you ever been to an art exhibit? If yes, where?*

- Check comprehension by asking:
  Where can you go to see these art pieces? (To the Barker Street Gallery.)
  When is the exhibit? (October 12 to November 24.)
  Would you go see this exhibit? Why? Why not?

- Have students complete a survey about their favorite pieces of art. Draw the chart below on the board or print out a copy for each student. Have students walk around the room and mingle to complete the chart.

Name	What's your favorite . . .?			
	Painting	Sculpture	Photo	Drawing
_____	_____	_____	_____	_____
_____	_____	_____	_____	_____
_____	_____	_____	_____	_____
_____	_____	_____	_____	_____
_____	_____	_____	_____	_____

 **Graphic Organizers**

A ▶4:15 Vocabulary

Suggested teaching time:	5 minutes	Your actual teaching time:	

V Vocabulary Flash Card Player

- Before students read and listen to the vocabulary, have them skim the labels on each kind of art.

- After students read and listen once, check comprehension. Ask:
  For which kind of art do you use a camera? (Photography.)
  For which kind of art do you use a pencil? (Drawing.)
  For which kind of art do you use paints and a paintbrush? (Painting.)
  Which kinds of art can you wear on your body? (Fashion and jewelry.)

- Have students listen again and repeat.

B Discussion

Suggested teaching time:	5–8 minutes	Your actual teaching time:	

- Begin by focusing students' attention on the "Adjectives to describe art" box. Model correct pronunciation by reading the adjectives aloud. Explain words as needed. Invite students to suggest additional words; for example, *pretty, ugly, colorful, boring.* Write students' words on the board for them to refer to later.

- Divide the class into small groups to discuss the questions. Move around the room and monitor pronunciation and stress, providing help as needed.

- Invite students to share their preferences with the class. Encourage students to explain their art preferences.

C ▶ 4:16 Photo story

Suggested teaching time:	10–15 minutes	Your actual teaching time:

- To prepare students for the activity, tell them to cover the conversation and look at the photos. Ask:
  Where are the two people? (At an art exhibit.)
  What are they doing? (Looking at pieces of art.)
  What kind of art are they looking at in Photo 1? (Painting.)
  In Photo 2? (Photography.) *In Photo 3?* (Sculpture.)

- Tell students to study the people's body language, then ask *What do you think they are saying about the painting in Photo 1?* Refer students to the list of adjectives to describe art on page 86 if they have difficulty answering the questions. (Possible responses: It's beautiful / relaxing.)
  In Photo 2? (Possible responses: It's fascinating / unusual.)
  In Photo 3? (Possible responses: It's weird / unusual / awful / interesting.)

- With the conversation uncovered, play the audio.

- Check comprehension by asking:
  Who is an artist: the man or the woman? (The man.)
  Which piece of art did he create? (The painting.)
  Which pieces of art did Teo's boss create? (The photos.)

- Play the audio again while students read and listen to the conversation.

Language and culture

- The expression *to each his own* means that everyone has his or her own opinion or preference.
- The word *just* is commonly used to call someone's attention to something. *Just* is also used in this way with verbs such as *think, imagine,* and *listen.*
- **From the Longman Corpus:** The expression *not really into [something]* is commonly used in informal spoken English.

D Activate vocabulary

Suggested teaching time:	5 minutes	Your actual teaching time:

- Go over the types of art in the box before students do the exercise.

- Have students complete the exercise individually and then compare their answers in pairs.

- Ask students to explain what the different words mean. Ask *What is realistic art?* (Art that looks like real things or people.) *What is abstract art?* (Art that has shapes and patterns that do not look like real things or people.) *What is traditional art?* (Art that is based on ideas or methods that have existed for a long time.) *What is modern art?* (Art that rejects traditional forms and shows new or different ideas and methods.)

E Focus on language

Suggested teaching time:	5–8 minutes	Your actual teaching time:

- To prepare students for the activity, ask volunteers to read the underlined phrases in the Photo Story.

- Move around the room while pairs match phrases from the story with the definitions in the exercise.

- If students have difficulty, suggest that they look at each phrase in the exercise one by one and then scan all the underlined phrases in the Photo Story until they find one with the same meaning. Then tell them to make a check mark next to it to indicate that it has been used.

- Review answers with the class.

Language and culture

- The expression *you can't judge a book by its cover* can be used to talk about people or things. It means that you can't form an opinion about the quality of something or someone's character just by looking at the outside.

Option: (+10 minutes) To challenge students, have pairs create short dialogues using expressions from the Photo Story. Model a conversation with a more confident student; for example:
  A: *Believe it or not, I made this sculpture.*
  B: *Really? How do you like that. I had no idea you had so much talent.*

SPEAKING

Suggested teaching time:	10–12 minutes	Your actual teaching time:

- Tell students to look at the pieces of art in the Photo Story and in Exercise D. Ask, *Which pieces are realistic? Which pieces are abstract? Which pieces are traditional? Which pieces are modern?* Students' answers may vary. Ask them to explain their answers. For example: *The first painting in the Photo Story is realistic because you can see that it's a painting of buildings.*

- Ask students to read the sample quotes. Then have pairs discuss their preferences.

- Tell pairs to continue their discussion preferences and to refer to the list of types of art in Exercise D and the sample answers in the book for ideas.

Option: (+5–10 minutes) For an alternative approach, have students look at the pieces of art individually and write words that the pieces of art make them think of. Then have students work in pairs to compare their words. Invite pairs to share their interpretations of what the pieces of art represent.

 EXTRAS

Workbook

C ▶4:16 **PHOTO STORY** Read and listen to a conversation at an art show.

Lynn: Teo, this is just great. I had no idea you had so much talent!

Teo: Thank you!

Lynn: I mean it. Your work is very impressive.

Teo: It's so nice of you to say that. I don't think I'm particularly talented. I just love to paint.

Teo: Believe it or not, these were taken by Paul Johns.

Lynn: Your boss? How do you like that! They're really quite good.

Teo: I know. He doesn't look like the artistic type, does he?

Lynn: No. I had no idea he took photos. I guess you can't always judge a book by its cover.

Teo: Hey, this is an interesting piece. I kind of like it.

Lynn: You do? I find it a little weird, actually.

Teo: But that's what makes it so fascinating.

Lynn: Well, to each his own. I guess I'm just not really into abstract art.

D **ACTIVATE VOCABULARY** Circle the three kinds of art Lynn and Teo discuss:

(painting)   fashion   (sculpture)   (photography)   drawing   jewelry

E **FOCUS ON LANGUAGE** With a partner, discuss and find an underlined expression in the Photo Story to match each of the phrases.

1 I didn't know . . .   I had no idea

2 I don't really like . . .   I'm just not really into

3 Everyone has a different opinion.   to each his own

4 I have some information that may surprise you.
   Believe it or not

5 I'm really surprised!   How do you like that!

6 You can't really know someone just by looking at him or her.   You can't always judge a book by its cover.

7 In my opinion, it's . . .   I find it

SPEAKING

" I prefer more realistic art. I'm just not into abstract paintings. "

What kinds of art do you prefer? Explain why.

" I'm into fashion. I like clothes that are really modern. "

Art can be **realistic** . . .

or **abstract**.

It can be **traditional** . . .

or **modern**.

GRAMMAR *The passive voice*

Most sentences are in the active voice: the subject of a sentence performs the action of the verb. In the passive voice, the receiver of the action is the subject of the sentence.

Active voice: Architect Frank Gehry designed the Guggenheim Museum in Bilbao, Spain.

Passive voice: The Guggenheim Museum in Bilbao, Spain, was designed by architect Frank Gehry.

Form the passive voice with a form of <u>be</u> and the past participle of a verb.

These vases are made in Korea.
The museum was built in the 1990's.
The *Mona Lisa* has been shown at the Louvre Museum since 1797.

It is common to use the passive voice when the performer of the action is not known or not important. Use a <u>by</u> phrase in a passive voice sentence when it is important to identify the performer of an action.

Pottery is made ~~by people~~ in many parts of the world. (not important)
This bowl was found ~~by someone~~ in Costa Rica. (not important)
This dress was designed **by Donatella Versace**. (important)

GRAMMAR BOOSTER p. 137
• Transitive and intransitive verbs
• The passive voice: other tenses

A UNDERSTAND THE GRAMMAR Read each passive voice sentence and decide if the <u>by</u> phrase is necessary. If it isn't necessary, cross it out.

1 The glass pyramids were added to the Louvre Museum in Paris ~~by workers~~ in 1989.

2 The sculpture *The Thinker* was created by French artist Auguste Rodin.

3 Antoni Gaudí designed and built some of the most famous buildings in Spain. His plans for the Casa Milà in Barcelona were completed ~~by him~~ in 1912.

4 The melody of "Ode to Joy" is known by people all over the world. It was written by German composer Ludwig van Beethoven.

5 China's famous Terracotta Army figures in Xi'an were discovered by farmers in 1974.

B GRAMMAR PRACTICE Change each sentence from the active to the passive voice. Use a <u>by</u> phrase.

1 Leonardo da Vinci painted the *Mona Lisa* in the sixteenth century.
   The *Mona Lisa* was painted by Leonardo da Vinci in the sixteenth century.

2 Brazilian photographer Sebastião Salgado took that photograph in 2007.
   That photograph was taken by Brazilian photographer Sebastião Salgado in 2007.

3 Mexican filmmaker Alfonso Cuarón directed the 2013 3D film *Gravity*.
   The 2013 3D film *Gravity* was directed by Mexican filmmaker Alfonso Cuarón.

4 Japanese master printmaker Katsushika Hokusai made that print over a century ago.
   That print was made over a century ago by Japanese master printmaker Katsushika Hokusai.

5 Korean fashion designer Sang A Im-Propp created these beautiful handbags.
   These beautiful handbags were created by Korean fashion designer Sang A Im-Propp.

6 Weavers have produced beautiful Persian rugs for several thousand years.
   Beautiful Persian rugs have been produced by weavers for several thousand years.

GRAMMAR

Suggested teaching time:	10–15 minutes	Your actual teaching time:

- To introduce the passive voice, write on the board the first two example sentences from the Grammar box, circling *Architect Frank Gehry* and the *Guggenheim Museum*.

- Explain that the first sentence is in the active voice. The active voice focuses attention on the performer of the action (what the subject *does*). The performer in this case is Frank Gehry. The second sentence is in the passive voice. We use the passive voice to focus on the receiver of an action (what *happens to* the subject), which in this case is the Guggenheim Museum.

- Review the second point and the examples with the class. Point out that the passive voice can be used in different tenses. Ask *What tenses do you see in the example sentences?* (Simple present, simple past, present perfect.)

- Review the last point and examples. Ask *Do we know who makes the pottery?* (No.) Explain that if students are unsure whether or not to use the *by* phrase, they should put the sentence into the active voice. Demonstrate by writing on the board *Donatella Versace designed this dress.*

- Tell students to use their own ideas to write four sentences in the passive voice. When they have finished, have them read their sentences to a partner.

> **Language and culture**
> - **From the Longman Corpus:** The following expressions almost always occur in the passive: *be born, be based on,* and *be located (at / in).*

Option: GRAMMAR BOOSTER *(Teaching notes p. T137)*

 Inductive Grammar Charts

A Understand the grammar

Suggested teaching time:	4–7 minutes	Your actual teaching time:

- To prepare students for the activity, have them circle the *by* phrase in each sentence. Then, in pairs, have students study the sentences to decide if the *by* phrase is necessary.

- Tell students to change the sentence into the active voice to see if the performer of the action is important for understanding the sentence. Model this with the first item. (Workers added the glass pyramids . . .)

- Move around the room and help students as needed.

- Review answers with the class.

B Grammar practice

Suggested teaching time:	5–8 minutes	Your actual teaching time:

- Before students complete the activity, tell them to scan the sentences and identify the tenses of the verbs. (1–5: simple past; 6: present perfect.) Ask *How do you form the past tense of the passive?* (Use *was / were* + past participle.) *The present perfect?* (Use *have been / has been* + past participle.)

- Remind students to use a *by* phrase to identify who performed the action.

- When students have completed the activity, have them compare answers in pairs.

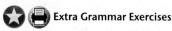 **Extra Grammar Exercises**

CONVERSATION MODEL

A ▶4:17 Read and listen . . .

Suggested teaching time:	2 minutes	Your actual teaching time:

> These conversation strategies are implicit in the model:
> • Say "Be sure not to miss ___" to emphasize the importance of an action.
> • Introduce support for an opinion with "For one thing."
> • Express enthusiasm for what someone has said with "No kidding!"

• Tell students to work in pairs and discuss what they think is happening in the painting. Then have pairs share their interpretations with the class.

• Have students read and listen. Then ask:
  Where is the Louvre Museum? (Paris.)
  What famous painting is kept there? (The *Mona Lisa.*)
  Has the woman seen the Mona Lisa? (No.)

Language and culture

• Leonardo da Vinci was an Italian painter, sculptor, architect, musician, mathematician, engineer, inventor, geologist, and writer, among other things. In the early 1500s, he painted the *Mona Lisa*, the most popular painting in the Louvre Museum. It is thought to be a portrait of Lisa Gherardini, a wealthy Italian woman. The painting's unique background and Mona Lisa's mysterious smile has made it one of the most famous works of art in the world.

• **From the Longman Corpus:** A frequent expression in spoken English, *for one thing* is used when the speaker is about to give a reason for something he or she has just said. Sometimes the speaker will just say *Well, for one.*

B ▶4:18 Rhythm and intonation

Suggested teaching time:	3 minutes	Your actual teaching time:

• Have students repeat each line chorally. Make sure they:
  ○ use rising intonation for *Really?* and falling intonation for *Why's that?*
  ○ stress *kid* in *kidding.*
  ○ stress *love* in *You'll love it.*

PRONUNCIATION

A ▶4:19 Notice how stress . . .

Suggested teaching time:	2 minutes	Your actual teaching time:

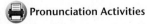 **Pronunciation Coach Video**

• Have students read and listen to the sentences, paying attention to the stress.

• Allow students to listen again and repeat in the pauses.

• Ask students to practice saying the sentences to a partner.

FYI: Some people pronounce *interesting* with four syllables.

🖨 **Pronunciation Activities**

B Now practice saying . . .

Suggested teaching time:	2 minutes	Your actual teaching time:

• To prepare students for the activity, write on the board *That's terrific!* Read the sentence with emphatic stress and circle *-ri-.* Have students repeat. Model the remaining sentences and tell students to circle the parts of the sentences that need emphatic stress.

• Review answers with the class by asking volunteers to read the sentences with emphatic stress. Correct as needed.

• Tell students to practice reading the sentences in pairs. Move around the room and listen for correct emphatic stress.

NOW YOU CAN Recommend a museum

Conversation activator

Suggested teaching time:	17–22 minutes	Your actual teaching time:

 Conversation Activator Video

• *Note:* You can print the script or you can show a running transcript on the video player on the ActiveTeach. The script also appears on page 187 of this Teacher's Edition.

• Ask volunteers to read the descriptions of the three museums and the names of the pieces of art (*El Dorado's Raft, The Chinese Cabbage, Starry Night*).

• Ask:
  Have you ever been to any of these museums?
  If yes, did you see these pieces of art?
  If not, which museum would you like to visit? Why?

• Ask what other museums students know of.

• Model the activity by role-playing the conversation with a more confident student.

• Remind students to change roles after they have finished their conversations.

DON'T STOP! Extend the conversation. Encourage students to use the information on the page to continue their conversations. Point out the language in the Recycle box.

• For more support, play the Conversation Activator Video before students do this activity themselves. In Scene 1, the actors use different words in the gaps from the ones in the Conversation Model. In Scene 2, the actors extend the conversation. After each scene, ask students how the model has been changed by the actors.

• After pairs have completed the activity, ask them to present their role plays to the class. After each conversation, check comprehension. Ask *What museum was recommended? Why was it recommended?*

 Conversation Activator Video Script; Conversation Activator Pair Work Cards

EXTRAS

Workbook or MyEnglishLab

🖨 **Speaking Activities: Unit 8, Activity 1**

CONVERSATION MODEL

A ▶4:17 Read and listen to someone recommend a museum.

A: Be sure not to miss the Louvre while you're in Paris.

B: Really? Why's that?

A: Well, for one thing, that famous painting, the *Mona Lisa*, is kept there.

B: No kidding! I've always wanted to see the *Mona Lisa*!

A: Well, they have a great collection of paintings. You'll love it.

B: Thanks for the suggestion!

B ▶4:18 **RHYTHM AND INTONATION** Listen again and repeat. Then practice the Conversation Model with a partner.

The *Mona Lisa* by Leonardo Da Vinci

PRONUNCIATION *Emphatic stress*

A ▶4:19 Notice how stress is emphasized to show enthusiasm. Read and listen. Then listen again and repeat.

1 No KIDDing! 2 That's fanTAstic! 3 That's PERfect! 4 How INteresting!

B Now practice saying the following statements with emphatic stress.

1 That's terRIfic! 2 That's WONderful! 3 How exCIting! 4 How NICE!

NOW YOU CAN Recommend a museum

CONVERSATION ACTIVATOR With a partner, change the Conversation Model to recommend a museum. Use the information in the pictures or museums you know. Use the passive voice and emphatic stress. Then change roles.

A: Be sure not to miss .... while you're in ....
B: Really? Why's that?
A: Well, for one thing, ... is kept there.
B: .... ! I've always wanted to see ....
A: Well, they have a .... collection of .... You'll love it.
B: Thanks for the suggestion!

DON'T STOP!
- Recommend other things to see or do.

RECYCLE THIS LANGUAGE.

Have you ever . . .
- tried __?
- climbed __?
- gone to the top of __?
- gone sightseeing in __?
- taken a tour of __?

THE GOLD MUSEUM - BOGOTÁ

Famous for its large collection of jewelry and sculpture

El Dorado's Raft (gold and emeralds)

THE MUSEUM OF MODERN ART
NEW YORK CITY

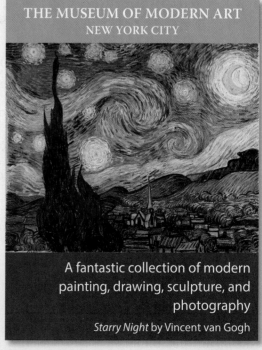

A fantastic collection of modern painting, drawing, sculpture, and photography

Starry Night by Vincent van Gogh

THE NATIONAL PALACE MUSEUM
TAIPEI

Known for its huge collection of traditional Chinese painting, pottery, and sculpture

The Chinese Cabbage sculpture (jade)

CONVERSATION MODEL

A ▶4:20 Read and listen to someone asking about an object.

A: Excuse me. What's this figure made of?

B: Wood. It's handmade.

A: Really? Where was it made?

B: Mexico. What do you think of it?

A: It's fantastic!

B ▶4:21 **RHYTHM AND INTONATION** Listen again and repeat. Then practice the Conversation Model with a partner.

DIGITAL
FLASH
CARDS

VOCABULARY *Objects, handicrafts, and materials*

A ▶4:22 Read and listen. Then listen again and repeat.

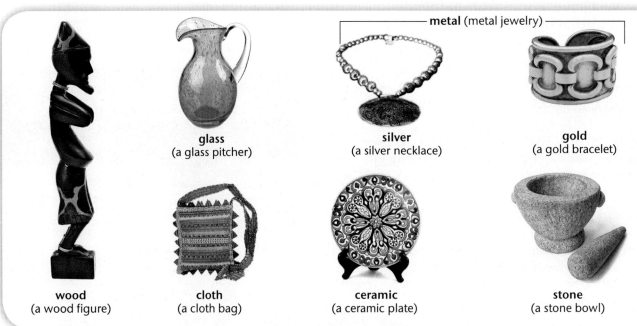

metal (metal jewelry)

glass
(a glass pitcher)

silver
(a silver necklace)

gold
(a gold bracelet)

wood
(a wood figure)

cloth
(a cloth bag)

ceramic
(a ceramic plate)

stone
(a stone bowl)

B **PAIR WORK** Tell your partner about some of your favorite objects in your home.

> On my vacation last year, I bought a large stone bowl. It's in my kitchen, and I use it for serving.

GRAMMAR *The passive voice: questions*

Was this stone figure **carved** by hand?	Yes, it was. / No, it wasn't.
Were these wood bracelets **made** in Thailand?	Yes, they were. / No, they weren't.
What **is** this **made** of?	It's made of wood.
What **is** this ceramic bowl **used** for?	It's used for preparing food.
When **was** this picture **painted**?	It was painted in the 1980s.
Where **were** these cloth figures **made**?	In Brazil.
How **were** those handbags **manufactured**?	By machine.

GRAMMAR BOOSTER p. 138
• Yes / no questions in the passive voice: other tenses

CONVERSATION MODEL

A ▶4:20 **Read and listen . . .**

Suggested teaching time:	2 minutes	Your actual teaching time:

> This conversation strategy is implicit in the model:
> • Invite someone's opinion with "What do you think of ___?"

- Tell students to look at the picture and say as much as they can about it to a partner.
- Ask students to read and listen to the conversation.
- Invite volunteers to read aloud the last sentence in the Conversation Model. Ask *What other positive adjectives do you know?* (Possible responses: Beautiful, great, amazing, awesome.)
- Check comprehension by asking *Does the woman like the figure?* (Yes, she thinks it's fantastic.) *In what country was the figure made?* (Mexico.)
- Have students read and listen again. Then write these questions from the Conversation Model on the board, underlining the verbs:
  1. What's this figure <u>made</u> of?
  2. Where <u>was</u> it <u>made</u>?
  Ask students which tense the underlined verbs are in. (1. Present simple; 2. Simple past.) Then ask them *Are these questions in the active or passive voice?* (Passive.)

> **Language and culture**
> • **From the Longman Corpus:** It is common to ask someone what he or she thinks *of* or *about* something. *Think of* is more commonly used to talk about objects. *Think about* is more commonly used to talk about ideas or actions.

B ▶4:21 **Rhythm and intonation**

Suggested teaching time:	3 minutes	Your actual teaching time:

- Have students repeat each line chorally. Make sure students:
  ○ use falling intonation for *What's this figure made of?, Where was it made?* and *What do you think of it?*
  ○ use rising intonation for *Really?*
  ○ stress *tas* in *fantastic.*

VOCABULARY

A ▶4:22 **Read and listen . . .**

Suggested teaching time:	3 minutes	Your actual teaching time:

Ⓥ Vocabulary Flash Card Player

- Explain that *handicrafts* are pieces of art made by hand.
- Review the names of the materials, handicrafts, and objects with the class. Have students listen and repeat.
- Ask *Which materials are considered more valuable than the others?* (Gold and silver.)

> **Language and culture**
> • **From the Longman Corpus:** *Wooden* is also used to describe objects that are made from wood such as *wooden furniture, wooden bowls,* and *wooden boxes.* However, one exception is *floors: We have wood floors.*

🖨 Learning Strategies

B **Pair work**

Suggested teaching time:	3–5 minutes	Your actual teaching time:

- Tell students to look at the materials in the Vocabulary and write a list of objects they have in their home that are made from these materials. (Possible responses: Wood spoon; glass vase; silver medal; gold earrings; cloth toy; clay pot; stone fireplace.)
- Ask a student to read the sample quote. Then have pairs talk about the items they wrote in their lists.

GRAMMAR

Suggested teaching time:	6–11 minutes	Your actual teaching time:

- Write on the board:
  This stone figure was carved by hand.
  Was this stone figure carved by hand?
  Yes, it was.
- Point out that in the question, a form of *be* (*was*) and the past participle (*carved*) are separated by the subject (*this stone figure*). Explain that short answers in the passive don't include the past participle. They simply use a form of *be.*
- Review the questions and answers in the Grammar box with the class. Explain that the first two questions are *yes / no* questions, and the others are information questions.
- Write on the board *These cloth figures were made in Brazil. Where were these cloth figures made?*
- Point out that *were* (a form of *be*) and *made* (the past participle) are separated by the subject (*these cloth figures*), and *where* is added. Other information words that can be used are *when, what, how,* and *why.*
- Help students to focus on the information words in the last five questions in the Grammar box by circling them (*what, what, when, where, how*).

Option: **GRAMMAR BOOSTER** *(Teaching notes p. T138)*

🖨 Inductive Grammar Charts

A Grammar practice

Suggested teaching time:	3–6 minutes	Your actual teaching time:

- To prepare students for the activity, have them circle the passive voice verb in each answer (A). (1. Are made; 2. are made; 3. 's dyed; 4. are sewn; 5. are used.) As students work, write on the board: *What? When? Where? Why? How?*

- Tell students to underline the information following the verb and decide which question word best asks for that information. (1. In Vietnam = where; 2. of cloth = what; 3. in different colors = how; 4. by hand = how; 5. to tell stories = for what.) Read the first answer as a model. Explain that *in Vietnam* hints that *Where* would be the best question word.

- Move around the room and help students as needed. Then have pairs compare answers.

- Review any outstanding questions with the class.

B Complete the conversations . . .

Suggested teaching time:	5–7 minutes	Your actual teaching time:

- Begin by having students follow the procedure from Exercise A: circle the passive voice verb in each statement. Look at the information following the verb and decide which question word best asks for that information. (1. By hand = how; 2. for serving sugar = what; 3. of gold = what; 4. in Venezuela = where; 5. by machine = how; 6. of ceramic = what.)

- Tell students to use this information to write the questions.

- After they have completed the exercise, have students compare questions in pairs. Move around the room and help students as needed.

 Extra Grammar Exercises

 NOW YOU CAN Ask about and describe objects

A Conversation activator

Suggested teaching time:	5–7 minutes	Your actual teaching time:

Conversation Activator Video

- *Note:* You can print the script or you can show a running transcript on the video player on the ActiveTeach. The script also appears on page 187 of this Teacher's Edition.

- After students have looked at the pictures of the art objects, ask them to work in pairs and write down the material each is made of. (Possible answers: wood, glass, silver, ceramic, stone.)

- If necessary, refer students to the Conversation Model on page 90 to review discussing an art object.

- Model the activity by role-playing the conversation with a more confident student. Play the role of Student B and use indication gestures such as pointing at or facing the object when asking *What do you think of ___?*

- As students role-play the conversation, move around the room and monitor the correct use of passive voice and rhythm and intonation. If necessary, refer students to the list of adjectives to describe art on page 86.

DON'T STOP! Extend the conversation. Encourage students to continue the conversation by using other passive voice questions. Write on the board the information question words *What? When? Where? Why? How? Who?* and review some possible questions in the passive. (Possible questions: Why are they considered valuable? When was it created?)

- For more support, play the Conversation Activator Video before students do this activity themselves. In Scene 1, the actors use different words in the gaps from the ones in the Conversation Model. In Scene 2, the actors extend the conversation. After each scene, ask students how the model has been changed by the actors.

- Be sure to reinforce the use of conversation strategies; for example, make sure students show interest when asking *What do you think of ___?*

 Conversation Activator Video Script; Conversation Activator Pair Work Cards

B Change partners

Suggested teaching time:	5–7 minutes	Your actual teaching time:

- Once students choose new partners, have them role-play conversations about other objects. Encourage them to use the language in the Recycle box and ask a variety of passive voice questions.

- Move around the room and help students as needed.

- To review the role play, have pairs report their partner's reactions to the different kinds of art.

C Discussion

Suggested teaching time:	10 minutes	Your actual teaching time:

- Tell students to work in pairs, and then write down the object that they have chosen and brainstorm words to describe it. Remind them they can recycle the colors they studied in the previous unit.

- Have pairs work with another pair and describe their partner's object. Tell them to ask one another questions about the objects they described. Refer students to the list of information words on the board to help them. (Possible questions: What is the vase made of? Where was it made? How was it made? When was it made? What color is it?)

EXTRAS

Workbook or MyEnglishLab

 Speaking Activities: Unit 8, Activity 2

A GRAMMAR PRACTICE   Complete the questions in the interview. Use a question word and the passive voice.

> We interviewed Brian Tardiff at the Sanford Gallery about the exhibit of modern Hmong cloth quilts.
>
> **Q** ....*Where are*.... these quilts .....*made*.... ?
>   1 make
> **A** These beautiful quilts are made in Vietnam by women from the Hmong tribe.
>
> **Q** ....*What are*.... they ....*made*.... of?
>   2 make
> **A** They're made of cloth. The pieces of cloth are cut by hand and sewn together.
>
> **Q** ....*Is*.... the cloth ....*dyed*.... ?
>   3 dye
> **A** It's dyed in different colors, using plants and beeswax. It takes a lot of time.
>
> **Q** ....*How are*.... they ....*sewed*.... ?
>   4 sew
> **A** They are sewn by hand. Each is unique.
>
> **Q** ....*What are*.... they ....*used*.... for?
>   5 use
> **A** Many people just use them for decoration. However, Hmong culture doesn't have a written tradition, so some are used to tell stories about the women's lives.

B   Complete the conversations. Write information questions, using the passive voice.

1 A: ....How were the [glass] cups made?.... ?
 B: The glass cups? They were made by hand.

2 A: ....What is that [silver] bowl used for?.... ?
 B: That silver bowl? It's used for serving sugar.

3 A: ....What is this [beautiful] figurine made of?.... ?
 B: This beautiful figure? It's made of gold.

4 A: ....Where were these [wood] chairs made?.... ?
 B: These wood chairs? They were made in Venezuela.

5 A: ....How was that [Chinese] bag made?.... ?
 B: That Chinese bag? It was made by machine.

6 A: ....What is this cup made of?.... ?
 B: This cup? It's made of ceramic.

NOW YOU CAN   Ask about and describe objects

A CONVERSATION ACTIVATOR   With a partner, change the Conversation Model to ask about and describe one of the objects. Use the Vocabulary. Then change roles.

A: Excuse me. What .... made of?
B: ....
A: .... Where .... made?
B: .... What do you think of .... ?
A: ....

DON'T STOP!
- Ask about other objects.
- Ask other passive voice questions.

a figure / Greece

a plate / Italy

a vase / China

dolls / Russia

cups / Thailand

B CHANGE PARTNERS   Practice the conversation again about other objects.

C DISCUSSION   Describe an object in your own home. Ask your classmates questions about the objects they describe.

> 66 In my living room, I have a small figure. It's made of wood. It's a piece of traditional art. I bought it on my vacation last year. 99

RECYCLE THIS LANGUAGE.

fantastic	cool
awesome	interesting
terrific	beautiful

BEFORE YOU READ

WARM-UP Do you do anything artistic? Do you paint, draw, or do handicrafts? Why or why not?

> " I paint sometimes. I find it relaxing. "

> " Actually, I'm not interested in art. I don't really think I have any ability. "

READING ▶ 4:23

Is it talent or hard work?

When children are asked to draw or paint a picture, they are happy to oblige. And they are willing to talk about and show their creation to anyone they meet. But when adults are asked to do the same thing, they typically get nervous and refuse to even try, claiming that they have no talent.

Most adults see themselves as lacking the "artistic gene." However, when you look at drawings made by artists when they were children, their work doesn't differ much from the scribbles and stick figures all children draw when they are young. When Don Lipski, who makes a successful living as a professional artist, looks back at drawings that he made as a child, he doesn't find any early evidence of his own artistic talent. "I was always making things . . . doodling and putting things together. I didn't think of myself as a creative person. I was just doing what all kids do."

The general belief is that artistic talent is something one is born with: a person either has talent or does not. Clearly, great artists like Michelangelo or Picasso had natural talent and possessed more artistic ability than the average person. However, one factor that isn't often considered is the role that years of training, practice, and

All young children scribble, doodle, and draw stick figures.

hard work have played in the creation of great pieces of art. In addition, most artists are successful because they are passionate about their art—they love what they do. Their passion motivates them to continue to create— and improve their ability—day after day. While natural talent may be an advantage, hard work appears to be a necessary part of the creative process.

In *Drawing on the Right Side of the Brain*, author Betty Edwards argues that while few people are born with natural artistic talent, all of us have the potential to improve our artistic ability. We just have to be willing to keep working at it. She claims that anyone can learn to use the right side of the brain, the side that governs visual skills like drawing and painting. In other words, artistic ability can be learned.

A **RECOGNIZE THE MAIN IDEA** Choose the main idea of the article.

a Artistic skill can be taught.

b Children are better artists than adults.

c To draw well, you have to be born with artistic talent.

d Few people are born with artistic talent.

BEFORE YOU READ

Warm-up

Suggested teaching time:	5–8 minutes	Your actual teaching time:

- To introduce the topic, write on the board *artistic talent*. Ask *Who here is an artist?* Ask for a show of hands and write the number on the board.

- Read the questions and ask volunteers to read the sample quotes. Now that they have thought about different kinds of artistic abilities, ask *Have you changed your mind? Are you an artist?*

- Ask students to talk about their artistic abilities with the class.

Option: (+10 minutes) To challenge students, write on the board *What is art?* Divide students into small groups and tell them to write a definition of *art*. Emphasize that there is no right or wrong answer. If groups cannot agree on a single definition, tell them to discuss and write two definitions. Have groups share their definitions with the class. (Possible response: Art is something you make, such as a painting, sculpture, or photograph, because you think it's beautiful or to express your feelings.) Then have a student look up *art* in a dictionary and read the definition. Ask *Do you agree with the definition?*

READING 4:23

Suggested teaching time:	15–17 minutes	Your actual teaching time:

- To prepare students for the activity, tell them to look at the picture. Ask *What is the picture of? What age do you think the artist was?* (Possible responses: 1. A house, trees, flowers, the sun, a person; 2. Probably a child who is about three or four years old.) Then ask *Do you think this is art?*

- Ask a volunteer to read the caption. Explain that *scribble* and *doodle* have similar meanings: children *scribble*, which means to make meaningless marks on a paper; *doodle* means to draw without thinking. Adults often *doodle* while talking on the phone. Ask *Do you agree that this picture is scribbling and doodling?*

- Read the title of the article. As students read the article, move around the room and explain vocabulary as needed.

- Once students have read the article, return to the title. Ask *According to the article, does art require talent or hard work?* (Hard work. Talent can give an advantage, but hard work is a necessary part of the creative process.) Ask individual students if they agree with the article.

Option: [+5 minutes] To challenge students, have them close their books and listen to the audio of the Reading after they have discussed the title. Once they have listened to the article, return to the title and have them discuss the main idea.

Language and culture

- Michelangelo Buonarroti (1475–1564), commonly known as Michelangelo, was an Italian Renaissance painter, sculptor, architect, poet, and engineer. He is best known for his paintings in the Sistine Chapel and his sculpture of *David* in Florence, Italy. (There is a picture of *David* on page 97.)
- Pablo Ruiz Picasso (1881–1973) was a Spanish artist famous for his paintings, drawings, pottery, and sculpture.

 Learning Strategies

A Recognize the main idea

Suggested teaching time:	3 minutes	Your actual teaching time:

- Tell students to read the choices for the main idea. Tell them to make a checkmark next to each statement that is supported by the article (a, d). Then instruct them to choose the statement that summarizes the main idea of the article (a).

- Have pairs compare answers and discuss.

B Identify supporting details

Suggested teaching time:	5 minutes	Your actual teaching time:

- Have students check the answers *True* or *False* first without referring to the article. Then, if needed, let them look back at the article.
- Instruct pairs to compare answers. Tell them to return to the article to look up any questions they don't agree on.
- Review answers with the class. Then tell pairs to rewrite the false statements so that they are true. Encourage students to first find the true information in the article to help them. (3. paragraph 2: However, when you look at drawings . . . ; 4. paragraph 3: Clearly . . . ; 5. paragraph 3: However, one factor . . .) Move around the room as students work. Help students as needed. (Possible responses: 3. It is difficult to tell which children are going to be artists because most children draw stick figures and scribbles. 4. Famous artists clearly possess more natural talent and artistic ability than the average person. 5. Years of training, practice, and hard work play an important role in the creation of great pieces of art.)

C Paraphrase

Suggested teaching time:	7 minutes	Your actual teaching time:

- Have students scan the Reading for the title of the book *Drawing on the Right Side of the Brain* (the last paragraph). Then invite a volunteer to read the paragraph.
- Tell students to paraphrase Edwards's theory. Stress that *to paraphrase* means to say something in your own words, so students should not copy anything from the article word for word. (Possible response: Betty Edwards argues that with hard work anyone can improve his or her artistic ability.)
- Have pairs share their paraphrases. Tell them to make sure the other person did not copy anything word for word from the article. Move around the room and check students' work.
- Ask individual students *Do you agree with Betty Edwards's theory? Why? Why not?*

 Extra Reading Comprehension Exercises

 NOW YOU CAN Talk about artistic talent

A Frame your ideas

Suggested teaching time:	5–10 minutes	Your actual teaching time:

- Have students skim the survey. Focus on question 5. Make sure students understand that all the listed items are considered art. Clarify that *handicrafts* are art pieces created by hand. Then instruct students to answer the questions.

- Invite pairs to compare surveys. Encourage them to discuss their talents in more detail.
- Have students share details from their surveys with the class. Invite them to share what they listed in the *other* category. (Possible responses: Digital art, filmmaking, collages.)
- Poll the class by asking *Do you think you have artistic ability?*

Option: (+10 minutes) If appropriate, have students bring something to the next class that they have created which demonstrates their artistic ability. These items could include such things as drawings, some photos, a song or dance, a video clip, a cake, etc. In the next class, have students form groups to present and discuss their creations.

B Discussion

Suggested teaching time:	5–10 minutes	Your actual teaching time:

Text-mining: Focus students' attention on the box. Tell students to skim the article on page 92 and underline useful language; for example, *when you look at drawings . . . ; I didn't think of myself as . . . ; The general belief is . . . ; Clearly . . . ; one factor that isn't always considered . . .* Then write students' language on the board for them to refer to during the discussion.

- Divide the class into small groups to discuss the questions. Encourage students to use examples from the article, history, and their own lives. Tell them they can refer to real-life artists such as those mentioned in the unit.

EXTRAS

Workbook or MyEnglishLab

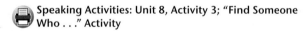 **Speaking Activities: Unit 8, Activity 3; "Find Someone Who . . ." Activity**

B **IDENTIFY SUPPORTING DETAILS** Read each statement. Check <u>True</u> or <u>False</u>, according to the article. Support your choice with details from the article.

		True	False
1	Young children generally don't worry if they are talented or not.	☑	☐
2	Most adults think they are not talented.	☑	☐
3	It's easy to see which children are going to be artists when you look at their drawings.	☐	☑
4	There isn't much difference between famous artists and other people.	☐	☑
5	Talent is all one needs to create great artistic work.	☐	☑
6	People who don't have natural talent can improve their artistic skill.	☑	☐

C **PARAPHRASE** Read the paragraph in the article about *Drawing on the Right Side of the Brain* again. In your own words, restate Betty Edwards's theory about artistic ability.

| According to Betty Edwards, . . . |
| |

NOW YOU CAN Talk about artistic talent

A **FRAME YOUR IDEAS** Complete the survey. Then compare responses with a partner.

Who's Got Talent?

1. Do any of your family members or friends have artistic talent? ○ yes ○ no

   Relationship to you: _____

   In which of the arts? _____

   Where do you think this talent comes from?

   _____

2. Do you think you have natural artistic talent?
   ○ yes ○ no ○ not sure

3. Do other people think you're talented?
   ○ yes ○ no ○ not sure

4. How would you rate your own artistic talent on a scale of 1 to 5?

1	2	3	4	5
POOR		AVERAGE		EXCELLENT

5. In which of the arts do you think you may have talent? Explain.

   example
   ☑ music <u>I sing and play several musical instruments.</u>

   ○ music _____

   ○ drawing / painting _____

   ○ handicrafts _____

   ○ acting _____

   ○ dancing _____

   ○ photography _____

   ○ other _____

B **DISCUSSION** Do you think people are born with artistic talent? Or is it developed through years of training, practice, and hard work?

Text-mining (optional)
Find and underline three words or phrases in the Reading that were new to you. Use them in your Discussion.
For example: "have talent."

GOAL Discuss your favorite artists

BEFORE YOU LISTEN

A ▶4:24 **VOCABULARY** • *Passive participial phrases* Read and listen. Then listen again and repeat.

be inspired by He is inspired by nature. He tries to capture nature's beauty in his photographs.

be influenced by She was influenced by Stella McCartney's work. You can see similarities between McCartney's fashion designs and her own.

be fascinated by He has always been fascinated by the life of Vincent van Gogh. He thinks the artist was extremely fascinating.

be moved by You will be moved by Charlie Chaplin's films. Even though they are funny, their themes of life and love really touch your heart.

Stella McCartney
fashion designer

Vincent van Gogh
painter

Charles Chaplin
actor, filmmaker

B **PAIR WORK** Tell your partner what inspires, influences, interests, fascinates, and moves you. Use passive participial phrases.

> " I'm inspired by my parents. They work really hard. "

LISTENING COMPREHENSION

A ▶4:25 **UNDERSTAND FROM CONTEXT** Listen to the interviews. Complete each statement with the name of the artist.

1 Burt Hildegard is fascinated by the work of ....Ang Lee............ .

2 Susan Wallach is influenced by the work of ......Henri Cartier-Bresson...... .

3 Katherine Wolf is inspired by the work of ....Valentino............ .

4 Nick Jenkins is moved by the work of ....Frida Kahlo............ .

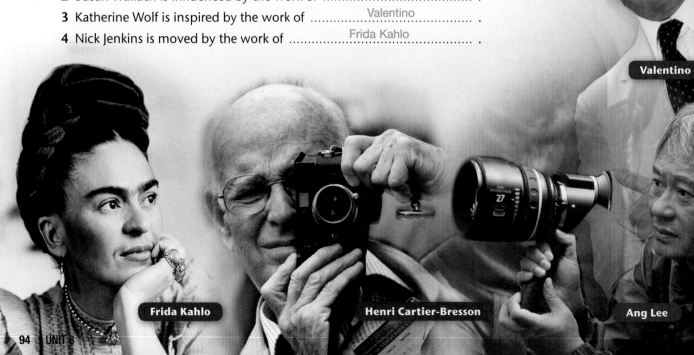

Frida Kahlo   Henri Cartier-Bresson   Ang Lee

Valentino

BEFORE YOU LISTEN

A ▶4:24 Vocabulary

Suggested teaching time:	3–7 minutes	Your actual teaching time:

 Vocabulary Flash Card Player

- After students listen and read, point out that the second sentence in each pair expands on the meaning of the expression. Have pairs create additional sentences to explain the meanings; for example, for *be fascinated by*: He has visited cities where van Gogh used to live.

- Ask *Are these expressions in the active or the passive voice?* (Passive.) Have students say what tenses they are. (1. Simple present tense; 2. simple past tense; 3. present perfect; 4. future with *will*.)

- Have students listen and repeat again.

> ### Language and culture
> - Stella McCartney, the daughter of former Beatle Paul McCartney, is a successful fashion designer.
> - Charlie Chaplin (1889–1977) is one of the most important figures in film history. He was an English actor, comedian, and director who made many silent films in the early 20th century. He often played a beloved character called "The Tramp" who always dressed in a black suit and a bowler hat.
> - Vincent van Gogh (1853–1890) was a Dutch post-impressionist painter. He had little success during his lifetime. After his death, his fame grew quickly, and today he is one of the most popular artists in the world.
> - **From the Longman Corpus:** Each of these verbs (*inspire, influence, fascinate, move*) is more commonly used in the passive voice than in the active voice.

Learning Strategies

B Pair work

Suggested teaching time:	4–8 minutes	Your actual teaching time:

- Have students answer the questions individually. Tell them that their answers don't have to relate to art; for example, *I'm interested in old cars.*

- Have students work in pairs to compare answers.

LISTENING COMPREHENSION

A ▶4:25 Understand from context

Suggested teaching time:	10–15 minutes	Your actual teaching time:

- For a warm-up, ask students to skim the pictures and captions. Ask *What kinds of artists are these people?* (Ang Lee: film director; Frida Kahlo: painter; Valentino: fashion designer; Henri Cartier-Bresson: photographer.) *Which of these artists do you know about?*

- Before students listen, tell them to skim the exercise items with the names of the four people being interviewed. Tell students that each interview will focus on one of the artists.

- Have students listen once. If necessary, have them listen a second time. Review answers with the class.

AUDIOSCRIPT

INTERVIEW 1

M1: Welcome to *Focus on the Arts*. I'm Paul Green, and we're broadcasting today from beautiful downtown San Francisco, where we're asking people about their favorite artists. Excuse me, sir! Sir? Excuse me.

M2: Yes?

M1: I'm Paul Green from *Focus on the Arts*. I wonder if I could ask for one minute of your time to tell us if you have a favorite movie director.

M2: My favorite director? Sure. That would be Ang Lee, from Taiwan. I find his work really fascinating.

M1: In what way?

M2: Well, for one thing, all his films are really different from each other.

M1: How so?

M2: Some of his best movies are in Chinese, like *Eat Drink Man Woman* . . . *Crouching Tiger / Hidden Dragon* . . . And he also makes great movies in English that are set in England . . . or the U.S. . . . and they really explore the culture in those countries.

M1: Mm-hmm.

M2: Some of his movies are really artistic and others are very commercial. I think he's not afraid to try new things. I like that.

M1: Great. Thank you so much. And your name is?

M2: Burt. Burt Hildegard.

M1: Well, thank you so much for your time.

INTERVIEW 2

M1: Let's find someone else . . . Oh, there's a woman over here taking pictures. Ma'am? Excuse me, ma'am? Would you be willing to talk with us?

F1: Me? I'm in a little bit of a hurry, but . . . Well, OK. I guess.

M1: Great. Well, first of all, can I get your name?

F1: Susan. Susan Wallach.

M1: Hi Susan. I couldn't help but notice that you're a photographer.

F1: Well, not professionally.

M1: I'm wondering if you have a favorite photographer.

F1: A favorite photographer? That would definitely be Henri Cartier-Bresson, the French photographer. He was a real twentieth-century artist. I think he died a few years ago.

M1: What do you like about his work?

F1: Well for one thing his photographs are just beautiful to look at.

M1: Mmm.

F1: He traveled all over the world to take photos and he captured some of the most important historical images of the twentieth century.

M1: I see.

F1: You know, his work is all in black and white, but the images are unforgettable. He had this ability to photograph people at just the right moment. I read somewhere that often he would wait for hours for the right time to take a photo.

M1: I believe I've heard that, too.

F1: Believe it or not, his work has really influenced my own. As a matter of fact, when you came over to speak to me, I was waiting for the right moment to take a shot.

M1: I'm sorry I interrupted you!

F1: Oh, that's OK. It was fun talking with you.

AUDIOSCRIPT continues on page T95.

B ▶4:26 Listen to take notes

Suggested teaching time:	5 minutes	Your actual teaching time:

- Ask students to skim the chart in the book. Invite students to interpret the notes.
- Have students listen again to each interview and write down additional notes in the chart.
- Have students compare notes in pairs.

C Discussion

Suggested teaching time:	5 minutes	Your actual teaching time:

- Divide the class into groups of three to discuss the artists. Remind students to refer to their notes in Exercise B to explain why they find the artist fascinating.
- To wrap up, invite students to offer names for these categories: favorite movie director, favorite photographer, favorite fashion designer, favorite painter or sculptor.

NOW YOU CAN Discuss your favorite artists

A Frame your ideas

Suggested teaching time:	5 minutes	Your actual teaching time:

- Invite a volunteer to read the questionnaire. Explain vocabulary as needed.
- After students complete the questionnaire, have them compare answers in pairs.

B Notepadding

Suggested teaching time:	7 minutes	Your actual teaching time:

- To prepare students for the activity, focus on the types of artists and art listed in the two boxes. Write some types on the board.
- To help students come up with artists, tell them to work in pairs and brainstorm examples of each type of artist. Give them a few minutes.
- When students have finished, ask for their examples and write them on the board. Have students discuss what types of art the artists created, providing examples when possible.
- If students still have difficulty naming artists, have students help each other think of the names. If necessary, have students use the Internet to find a favorite artist.
- Tell students to work individually to complete the information on the notepad.

C Group work

Suggested teaching time:	5–7 minutes	Your actual teaching time:

- Call on students to read the speech bubbles above the photos.
- Have students work in groups to discuss their favorite artists. Ask students to give examples of the artists' work and describe their style. Encourage students to follow the format of the comments in the speech bubbles.

- Review the comments with the class and ask if any students in the groups named the same artists.

EXTRAS

Workbook or MyEnglishLab

 Speaking Activities: Unit 8, Activity 4

AUDIOSCRIPT Continued, for page T94 (Listening Comprehension)

INTERVIEW 3
M1: There's a very nicely dressed young woman over here . . . Excuse me. Would you mind talking to our listeners today? I'm with *Focus on the Arts*.
F2: Oh, I love that show! Are you Paul Green?
M1: I am. Nice to meet you, uh . . .
F2: Katherine. Katherine Wolf. Thank you!
M1: Hi, Katherine. Katherine, I wonder if you have a favorite fashion designer.
F2: A favorite fashion designer . . . Well, I really like the Italian designer Valentino. He doesn't design dresses anymore, but he's a classic.
M1: Wasn't there a film about him?
F2: Actually, I saw it. *Valentino, the Last Emperor*. I really loved the passion he has for his art.
M1: So what do you especially like about his work?
F2: Well, I find his dresses really elegant and very original. In the movie, he says his greatest desire was to make women look beautiful. I think he was very successful at doing that. His designs are very flattering to women.
M1: I see.
F2: You know, seeing him in that movie made me want to have a creative job. He inspired me to take fashion design classes myself.
M1: Really? That's terrific! Thank you, Katherine.
F2: You're welcome.

INTERVIEW 4
M1: We have time for one more. Let's see . . . Excuse me! Sir! Could I take just a minute of your time?
M3: Sure. What's going on?
M1: Hi, I'm Paul Green from *Focus on the Arts,* and I'm asking people today about their favorite artists. What about you? Do you have a favorite painter or sculptor?
M3: Cool! Well, actually I'm very fond of the paintings of Frida Kahlo.
M1: Oh, the Mexican painter. I love her work, too. By the way, can you tell me your name please?
M3: Oh, sure. Nick Jenkins.
M1: So, Nick, what is it that you like so much about Kahlo's work?
M3: You know, Kahlo had a very hard life. She was very sick as a child, and as a young woman she was in a terrible accident. So she was always in pain, and she couldn't have any children.
M1: Really? I didn't know that.
M3: Yeah. Her work reflects her life experiences. And of course she was married to Diego Rivera, the great Mexican muralist. It wasn't always a happy marriage, so she had a lot of material for creating her art.
M1: What a life she had!
M3: You know, her self-portraits really touch my heart. They move me much more than Diego Rivera's work, actually. And he's great.
M1: Well, they were both great artists with natural talent. Thanks, Nick. It was nice talking with you.
M3: Hey, my pleasure.
M1: Well, that's all the time we have for today. And remember, keep focused on the arts!

B ▶4:26 **LISTEN TO TAKE NOTES** Listen again to each interview and write some of the details you hear about each artist. Compare notes with a partner.

1 Ang Lee	2 Henri Cartier-Bresson	3 Valentino	4 Frida Kahlo
explores culture Films different from each other Not afraid to try new things From Taiwan	*took black-and-white photos* Images of 20th century Take at the right time French	*is Italian* Passion for his art Dresses; elegant and original Designs flattering to women Italian	*was sick as a child* Hard life, sick as a child, accident Her life influenced her work Difficult marriage

C **DISCUSSION** Which of the artists described in the Listening do you find the most fascinating? Use your notes to explain why.

NOW YOU CAN Discuss your favorite artists

A **FRAME YOUR IDEAS** Complete the questionnaire. Then compare answers with a partner.

WHICH QUALITIES ATTRACT YOU TO AN ARTIST?
Check all that apply.

HIS OR HER WORK . . .

- ○ is realistic / traditional.
- ○ is abstract / modern.
- ○ is easy to understand.
- ○ makes you think.
- ○ touches your heart.
- ○ makes you laugh.
- ○ other: _____

HE OR SHE . . .

- ○ is a rebel.
- ○ is creative.
- ○ tries new things.
- ○ has his or her own style.
- ○ inspires people.
- ○ other: _____

Types of artists
a painter
a writer
a sculptor
a filmmaker / director
a fashion designer
an architect
a photographer
an actor
a singer
a dancer

Types of art
drawing
painting
sculpture
photography
jewelry
pottery
fashion
handicrafts

B **NOTEPADDING** On your notepad, write about some of your favorite artists.

	Artist's name	Type of artist	Why I like this artist
1			
2			
3			

C **GROUP WORK** Discuss your favorite artists. Tell your class why you like them. Ask your classmates questions about the artists they describe.

I'm a real fan of the Mexican painters Frida Kahlo and Diego Rivera. I'm fascinated by their lives.

Donatella Versace is my favorite designer. Her fashions are so creative!

One of my favorite Japanese artists is Naoki Urasawa. His drawings in the comic book *Yawara!* are really exciting.

A ▶4:27 Listen and write the letter of the piece of art each person is talking about. Then listen again and circle the best way to complete each statement.

a 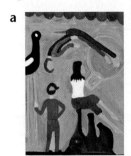 b  c  d  e

............e............ **1** She thinks it's ((beautiful) / ugly / abstract).

............c............ **2** He thinks it's (traditional / ugly / (fascinating)). She thinks it's (fantastic / (OK) / abstract).

............d............ **3** She thinks it's (OK / awful / (great)). He thinks it's too (abstract / (dark) / traditional).

B On a separate sheet of paper, change each sentence from active to passive voice.

1 César Pelli designed the Petronas Twin Towers in Kuala Lumpur.
    The Petronas Twin Towers in Kuala Lumpur were designed by César Pelli.
2 The great Iranian filmmaker Majid Majidi directed *Children of Heaven* in 1998.
    Children of Heaven was directed by the great Iranian filmmaker Majid Majidi in 1998.
3 Henri Matisse made the print *Icarus* in 1947.
    The print *Icarus* was made by Henri Matisse in 1947.
4 Annie Leibovitz took that photograph of John Lennon in 1980.
    That photograph of John Lennon was taken by Annie Leibovitz in 1980.
5 The Japanese artist Hokusai produced *The Great Wave of Kanagawa* in the early 1830s.
    The *Great Wave of Kanagawa* was produced by Hokusai in the early 1830s.

C List materials under each category. Answers may vary.
Answers may vary

Materials that are expensive	Materials that weigh a lot	Materials that break easily
gold Silver	Stone, wood	Glass, ceramic

D Complete the statements.

1 The art of designing clothes is called ....fashion.......... .

2 One type of ....sculpture.......... is a figure carved from wood or stone.

3 Two types of metal often used to make jewelry are ....gold..........
and ....silver.......... .

4 Art in a conservative style from the past is called ....traditional.......... art.

5 A piece of art made with a pen or pencil is called a ....drawing.......... .

For additional language practice . . .

🎵 TOP NOTCH **POP** • Lyrics p. 154
"To Each His Own"

| .... DIGITAL SONG | .... DIGITAL KARAOKE |

WRITING

Choose a favorite object that decorates your home. Describe it in a paragraph.

WRITING BOOSTER p. 150
• Providing supporting details
• Guidance for this writing exercise

Ideas
• a painting or drawing
• a photo or poster
• a piece of furniture
• a figure or sculpture
• a plate, bowl, or vase
• (your own idea) ___

REVIEW

A ▶4:27 Listen and write . . .

Suggested teaching time:	3 minutes	Your actual teaching time:

- Review vocabulary by asking students to identify the kind of art each illustration represents. (a. Painting; b. sculpture / figure; c. sculpture; d. painting; e. figure.) Then have them listen to the conversations.
- Have students listen again and complete the exercise. Review answers with the class.

AUDIOSCRIPT

CONVERSATION 1 [M = Arabic]
M: So what do you think of this one?
F: It's gorgeous. I really love it.
M: So you like gold figures?
F: I sure do. What do you think?
M: It's not bad.

CONVERSATION 2
M: Wow! That's an interesting piece.
F: You like stone sculpture?
M: Yeah, I do. It's a very handsome piece.
F: It's not too bad.

CONVERSATION 3
F: I really love this one!
M: Don't you find it a little dark?
F: That's the artist's style. I find his work very interesting.
M: Well, dark is not my style. I'd prefer a little more color.

Option: (+10 minutes) For a challenge, assign pairs the remaining items not included in the audio track (the colorful painting and the sculpture / figure labeled "b") and have them role-play conversations about them. Tell them to use the conversations they heard as models. If necessary, have students listen to the audio again. Then invite pairs to present their role plays to the class.

B On a separate sheet of paper, . . .

Suggested teaching time:	3 minutes	Your actual teaching time:

- Have students underline the verb in each sentence. (1. designed; 2. directed; 3. made; 4. took; 5. produced.) Review the formation of the passive voice in the simple past (a form of *be* + past participle) and have students make a note of the past participle of each verb.
- Remind students to use a *by* phrase to identify the artist who performed each action.
- Have students change the sentences to the passive voice and compare answers in pairs.

C List materials . . .

Suggested teaching time:	3–8 minutes	Your actual teaching time:

- If students have difficulty thinking of materials, refer them to the Vocabulary on page 90 for help. Encourage students to think of additional materials. (Possible responses: Bronze, copper, crystal, silk.)
- Have students compare lists in pairs.
- Review answers with the class by compiling all the materials in a chart on the board.

D Complete the statements . . .

Suggested teaching time:	3 minutes	Your actual teaching time:

- Tell students to complete the statements individually. If students have difficulty completing the statements, refer them to the Vocabulary on pages 86 and 90.
- Have students compare answers in small groups.

Option: (+10 minutes) To challenge students, turn the task into a competition. Give each group a time limit, for example, two minutes, to come up with as many items as they can for each category. Have teams share their answers with the class. The team that has the most items is the winner.

WRITING

Suggested teaching time:	15 minutes	Your actual teaching time:

- To prepare students for the activity, tell them to skim the Ideas in the box. For review, also remind them of discussions they had earlier in the unit (Vocabulary Exercise B on page 90, and Now You Can Exercise C on page 91 where they described objects that they like.)
- Tell students to identify the kind of art their favorite object is. If possible, students should also name the piece of art and the artist and then describe what the object looks like. Then they should explain how it makes them feel and why it's important to them.
- After students complete the writing assignment, tell them to check their papers. Ask *Is the passive voice used correctly? Have you included by phrases when important?*
- Then have students exchange papers with a partner. Have them ask questions if something is not clear.

Option: **WRITING BOOSTER** *(Teaching notes p. T150)*

 Writing Process Worksheets

 Top Notch Pop **Song Video and Karaoke Video**

 **Digital Games**

ORAL REVIEW

Before the first activity, give students a few minutes of silent time to become familiar with the pictures.

Contest

Suggested teaching time:	3 minutes	Your actual teaching time:

- With books closed, have students write sentences in the passive to describe the details on the page. Move around the room and determine which student has the most correct sentences.
- Write on the board *The horse is made of ___. The Statue of David is kept in the ___.* Call on volunteers to fill in the blanks of the model sentences. (Wood, the Accademia Gallery.) Then ask students to write their sentences on the board.

> *Possible responses . . .*
> The statue of *David* was made by Michelangelo. *Apples and Oranges* was painted by Paul Cézanne. It is kept in the Musée d'Orsay in Paris. The doll is made of cloth. It was made in Peru. The bracelet is made of silver. It was made in India. The cup was made in China. The horse is made of wood. It was made in Sweden.

Pair work 1

Suggested teaching time:	5–7 minutes	Your actual teaching time:

- Have pairs skim the information on the European museum pamphlet.
- To review language for making museum recommendations, refer students to the Conversation Model on page 89.

> *Possible responses . . .*
> **A:** Be sure not to miss the Musée d'Orsay while you're in Paris.
> **B:** Actually, I don't care for his work. I find it a little boring. **A:** Really? I'm fascinated by his work. **B:** Well, to each his own. I prefer classic paintings like the *Mona Lisa*.

Pair work 2

Suggested teaching time:	5–8 minutes	Your actual teaching time:

- Have students change partners and create a conversation for the two men at the bottom of the page. Encourage students to discuss what all the objects are made of and where they were made. Invite them to also guess when they were made.

> *Possible responses . . .*
> **A:** Excuse me. What's this bowl made of? **B:** Wood. It's handmade.
> **A:** Really? Where was it made? **B:** In Colombia. What do you think of it? **A:** It's interesting. I like it.

Discussion

Suggested teaching time:	5–10 minutes	Your actual teaching time:

- Have pairs talk about the pieces they prefer and explain why. Refer students to the Now You Can on page 95 for ideas. Then have them share ideas with the class.

> *Possible responses . . .*
> I like *Apples and Oranges.* The colors in this piece are fantastic. I'm fascinated by the work of Paul Cézanne.

Option: Oral Progress Assessment

- Use the photographs and information on page 97. Encourage students to use the vocabulary, grammar, rhythm, and intonation practiced in this unit.
- Point to the different items on the page and ask students what they are.
- Say *Ask me three questions in the passive voice for one of the objects; for example, "Where was the cloth doll made?"*
- Invite a student to role-play a conversation with you between the man and the woman. Play the role of the woman and have the student play the man.
- Evaluate the student on intelligibility, fluency, correct use of grammar, and appropriate use of vocabulary.

 Oral Progress Assessment Charts

Option: *Top Notch* Project

Have students research an artist and prepare a presentation and / or a class book about the artist.

Idea: Have students use the Internet or visit the library to research the life of an artist. Encourage students to include examples of the artist's work and include their sources (names and authors of books and / or websites) at the end of the biography.

EXTRAS

On the Internet:
- Online Teacher Resources: pearsonelt.com/topnotch3e/

Additional printable resources on the ActiveTeach:
- Assessment
- Just for Fun
- *Top Notch Pop* Song Activities
- *Top Notch TV* Video Program and Activity Worksheets
- Supplementary Pronunciation Lessons
- Conversation Activator Video Scripts
- Audioscripts and Answer Keys
- Unit Study Guides

ORAL REVIEW

CONTEST Look at the page for one minute and close your books. Using the passive voice, who can describe the most objects and art?

The horse figure is made of __. The statue of David is kept in the __.

PAIR WORK

1. Create a conversation for the man and woman. Recommend a museum. Start like this:

Be sure not to miss the __ while you're in __.

2. Create a conversation for the customer and the store clerk. Ask about the objects. Start like this:

Excuse me. What's this __ made of?

DISCUSSION Talk about the pieces of art in the photos. Say what you like or don't like about each one.

1

2

THE GREAT MUSEUMS OF EUROPE

The Accademia Gallery
FLORENCE, ITALY

The world's largest collection of statues by Michelangelo!

David by Michelangelo

Musée d'Orsay
PARIS, FRANCE

Home of the best collection of 19th-century French art, including famous painters such as Monet, Degas, and Renoir

Apples and Oranges by Paul Cézanne

China

India

NOW I CAN

☐ Recommend a museum.
☐ Ask about and describe objects.
☐ Talk about artistic talent.
☐ Discuss my favorite artists.

Peru

Sweden

Living in Cyberspace

COMMUNICATION GOALS

1 Troubleshoot a problem.
2 Compare product features.
3 Describe how you use the Internet.
4 Discuss the impact of the Internet.

PREVIEW

x

Our Community

Friends   Search   Home

FRANK CARUSO

✏ Edit

🔍 Search

✉ Messages

📷 My photo albums

🎥 Videos

👥 Groups

⬆ Upload

 Frank Caruso Hey, I'm in Rome now! How do you like my new profile pic? That's the Colosseum behind me. This place is awesome!

 Kathy Chu Wow! You take good selfies, Frank! You look like you're having fun! Hey, didn't you just post a message from Tokyo two days ago?

 Frank Caruso I did. But I've always wanted to see Italy, so someone suggested visiting my airline's web page to look for specials. I got a great deal on a return ticket with a stop here. I'm heading back home to Boston on Friday. Did you all catch the Japan photos I posted?

 Nardo Madureira No. What album are they in?

 Frank Caruso Actually, they're not here. They're on that new photo-sharing site, GlobalPhoto. Log on and add me to your friends. Or I can send you a link. Click on it to go right to the pics.

 Kathy Chu Well, I just looked and they're very cool. Can't wait to see the ones from Italy. I hope they're as nice as the ones from Japan! Nice chatting with you guys! Ciao!

A   PAIR WORK   Read the posts on the social network website. Are you on any similar sites? Do you post regularly? Why or why not?

B   DISCUSSION   Discuss these questions.

1   What photo-sharing services do you know about online? Do you store your photos on any of these sites? What are the advantages and disadvantages of photo-sharing services?

2   Have you ever posted photos while you were traveling? Do you know anyone who has?

UNIT 9 Living in Cyberspace

PREVIEW

Before Exercise A, give students a few minutes of silent time to examine the website.

Suggested teaching time:	10 minutes	Your actual teaching time:

- After students have looked at the website for a few minutes, ask *What kind of website is this?* (A social networking or photo sharing site.) *What do people do on this site?* (They connect with friends and share their photos.)
- Ask a few questions to test comprehension. For example: *Where is Frank right now?* (Rome.) *Where was he two days ago?* (Tokyo.) *Where does he live?* (In Boston.)
- Explain any vocabulary students do not understand.

A Pair work

Suggested teaching time:	4–7 minutes	Your actual teaching time:

- Model the task by writing the questions on the board. Then answer with your own information. For example: *I am on Facebook and Twitter, but I don't post very often because I don't have time.*
- After pairs discuss the questions, call on a few pairs to share their answers with the class.

B Discussion

Suggested teaching time:	5–8 minutes	Your actual teaching time:

- Divide students into small groups to discuss the questions. To introduce the topic, ask *What are some photo-sharing services you know about?* Write the answers on the board.
- Draw the chart below on the board. Do not include the possible responses.

Advantages	Disadvantages
1. You can show your photos to other people very easily.	1. Some people you don't know may be able to see your photos.
2. You can get positive feedback from people on your photos.	2. You can get negative feedback from people on your photos.
3. You don't need to print out your photos.	3. It sometimes takes a long time to upload your photos onto the site.
4. You can see other people's photos very easily.	

Tell students to copy the table into their notebooks and to write down the advantages and disadvantages they discuss. As you review answers to item 1 with the class, complete the chart with students' responses.

- Have groups discuss the questions in item 2. Then take a poll. Ask *How many people have posted photos while they were traveling?* Have students raise their hands. Then call on students to tell the class about the photos they posted.

C ▶5:02 Photo story

Suggested teaching time:	10–15 minutes	Your actual teaching time:

- To prepare students, tell them to look at the pictures for one minute and say as much as they can about them to a partner.
- After students listen and read, check comprehension by asking:
  What is Dee doing? (Possible responses: She's using her computer; She's instant messaging.)
  What kind of problem does Amy have? (Her computer froze after she clicked on an attachment.)
  What does Dee recommend to Amy? (She recommends that Amy shut down the computer and restart it.)

D Focus on language

Suggested teaching time:	5 minutes	Your actual teaching time:

- Tell students to read the five underlined phrases in the Photo Story and think about what they mean before they do the matching. Then tell them to write the expressions next to the meanings.
- To support weaker students, suggest that they look at each phrase in the exercise one by one and then scan all the underlined phrases in the Photo Story until they find one with the same meaning. Then tell them to write a check mark next to it to indicate that it has been used.
- Have students compare answers in pairs.
- Review answers with the class. Point out that two of the items have the same meaning: *takes care of it, does the trick.* Ask volunteers to read each sentence using the expression from the other sentence. Explain that both these items can be used interchangeably.

Option: (*+10 minutes*) To challenge students, have them create and role-play their own conversations using the underlined expressions.

SPEAKING

Suggested teaching time:	9–13 minutes	Your actual teaching time:

- Before students complete the chart, explain any new vocabulary as needed.
- After students check their answers, tell them to read the list of possible computer solutions. Invite them to write their own idea.
- Ask students to think of the last real computer problem they had and to discuss possible solutions in pairs.
- Move around the room and help as needed.
- Invite pairs to share their experiences with the class.

Language and culture

- Certain verbs always appear together with computer terms; for example, we *log on to the Internet, go online, run software, browse the Web,* and *visit a website.*

Option: (*+5 minutes*) To extend the activity, write students' solutions on the board and have the class vote on the best solution for each problem.

Option: (*+8 minutes*) To expand the activity, have students work in pairs and role-play a conversation or live chat between a person with a computer problem and a support technician.

Workbook

C ▶5:02 **PHOTO STORY** Read and listen to a conversation in an office.

Amy: What are you doing here at this hour? I wasn't sure I'd find you.

Dee: Oh hi, Amy. I'm just fooling around online. I guess I forgot about the time!

Amy: Am I interrupting you?

Dee: Not at all. Paul and I are just instant messaging.

Amy: Sorry to bother you. But I'm a little worried about something.

Dee: What's wrong?

Amy: I just got this e-mail from someone I don't know, and I clicked on the attachment to see what it was. My computer totally crashed. Everything froze, and no matter what I do, nothing happens.

Dee: Actually, you should never open an attachment if you don't know the sender. It could be malware or carry a virus.

Amy: I know. I don't know what I was thinking! It just happened so fast.

Dee: Look. First, try shutting down and restarting, OK? Sometimes that takes care of it.

Amy: You think that would work?

Dee: It couldn't hurt. Listen, Paul's still there. Let me send a quick response, OK? I'll just be a second.

Amy: No problem. I'll go and try restarting to see if that does the trick.

D **FOCUS ON LANGUAGE** Look at the five expressions from the Photo Story. Write the letter of the meaning of each expression. (Two expressions have the same meaning.)

...b... **1** just fooling around   **a** won't take a long time

...d... **2** takes care of it   **b** not doing anything serious

...c... **3** couldn't hurt   **c** is worth trying

...a... **4** I'll just be a second   **d** fixes the problem

...d... **5** does the trick

SPEAKING

Do you know how to solve computer problems? Complete the chart. Then compare answers with a partner and discuss some possible solutions.

Do you know what to do if . . .	Yes	No	Not sure
1 you think you have a virus?	☐	☐	☐
2 your printer won't print?	☐	☐	☐
3 you click on a link and nothing happens?	☐	☐	☐
4 your computer is really slow?	☐	☐	☐
5 your computer crashes?	☐	☐	☐
6 you forget your password?	☐	☐	☐

Some computer solutions
- try restarting
- check if it's turned on
- buy a new computer
- [your own idea]

GOAL Troubleshoot a problem

CONVERSATION MODEL

A ▶5:03 Read and listen to people troubleshooting a computer problem.

A: Eugene, could you take a look at this?

B: Sure. What's the problem?

A: Well, I clicked on the toolbar to save a file, and the computer crashed.

B: Why don't you try restarting? That sometimes works.

A: OK. I'll give that a try.

B ▶5:04 **RHYTHM AND INTONATION** Listen again and repeat. Then practice the Conversation Model with a partner.

▶5:05 **Ways to reassure someone**
That sometimes works.
That sometimes helps.
That sometimes does the trick.

DIGITAL FLASH CARDS

VOCABULARY *The computer screen, components, and commands*

A ▶5:06 Read and listen. Then listen again and repeat.

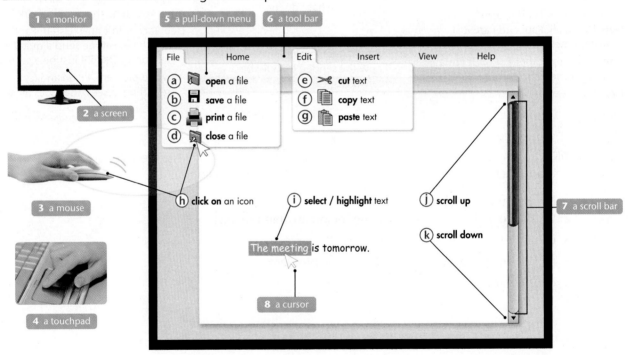

B ▶5:07 **LISTEN TO ACTIVATE VOCABULARY** Listen. Check the computer command each person needs.

	📁	💾	🖨	✂	📄	📋	▲	▼
1 He needs to click on . . .	☐	☐	☐	☐	☑	☐	☐	☐
2 She needs to click on . . .	☐	☐	☐	☐	☐	☐	☐	☑
3 He needs to click on . . .	☐	☑	☐	☐	☐	☐	☐	☐
4 She needs to click on . . .	☑	☐	☐	☐	☐	☐	☐	☐
5 He needs to click on . . .	☐	☐	☐	☐	☐	☑	☐	☐
6 She needs to click on . . .	☐	☐	☑	☐	☐	☐	☐	☐

CONVERSATION MODEL

A ▶5:03 Read and listen . . .

Suggested teaching time:	2 minutes	Your actual teaching time:

These conversation strategies are implicit in the model:
• Ask for assistance with "Could you take a look at ___?"
• Introduce an explanation with "Well, ..."
• Make a suggestion with "Why don't you try ___ing?"

• Play the audio as students read. Then ask *What's the woman's problem?* (Her computer crashed.) Point out that the word *crash* has the connotation of something catastrophic happening. *What's the man's suggestion?* (Try restarting the computer.)

• Write the phrases below on the board and encourage students to suggest other ways of saying them:
  the computer crashed (The computer stopped working.)
  try restarting (Try turning the computer off and then turning it on again.)
  I'll give that a try. (I'll try that.)

• Ask *What is another way of saying* restart? (Reboot.) If necessary, refer students to the Photo Story on page 99 to find the term.

• Have students read and listen again.

Language and culture
• *Give [something] a try* means basically the same as *try [something]* and is very commonly used in spoken English.

B ▶5:04 Rhythm and intonation

Suggested teaching time:	3 minutes	Your actual teaching time:

• Have students repeat each line chorally. Make sure they:
  ○ use rising intonation for *Could you take a look at this?*
  ○ use falling intonation for *What's the problem?*
  ○ pause slightly after *Well.*

• ▶5:05 **Ways to reassure someone** Have students listen and repeat the expressions in the box. Have them substitute *That sometimes helps* and *That sometimes does the trick* for *That sometimes works* as they practice the Conversation Model.

VOCABULARY

A ▶5:06 Read and listen . . .

Suggested teaching time:	4–6 minutes	Your actual teaching time:

 Vocabulary Flash Card Player

• Ask students to look at the toolbar and read the computer commands.

• Point out the arrow pictured next to the picture of the hand with a mouse. Explain that the arrow is called a *cursor*. Write on the board *Cursor.*

FYI: Note that a cursor can change forms when it is moved outside of the document to another part of the screen.

• Play the audio and have students listen and read. Ask:
  How do you save a file? (Click on the pull-down menu and click on *save a file.*)
  How can you open a file? (Click on the pull-down menu and click on *open a file.*)
  How do you move up and down on a page? (Click on the arrows on the scroll bar on the right.)

• Have students listen and repeat.

B ▶5:07 Listen to activate vocabulary

Suggested teaching time:	8–10 minutes	Your actual teaching time:

• Play the audio once. Tell the students that they may hear more than one command mentioned, but they should check only the commands the person needs to use. Play the audio again as students complete the exercise.

AUDIOSCRIPT

CONVERSATION 1
M: Fran, can you give me a hand?
F: Sure. What's up?
M: Well, I just want to copy this text.
F: Oh, that's easy. Just select the text and click on this icon here.
M: Ah. Thanks.

CONVERSATION 2 [F = Portuguese]
F: Dave, I'm going to need some help here.
M: No problem. What do you need?
F: I just want to see what's on the next page.
M: Oh, that's easy. Put your cursor on the scroll bar and scroll down.
F: Thanks a lot.

CONVERSATION 3
M: OK, Beth. I'm finished.
F: Great! Did you remember to save?
M: Yikes! I always forget! Thanks.
F: No problem.

CONVERSATION 4 [M = Eastern European]
F: Rick, can you help me out here?
M: Of course. What are you trying to do?
F: Well, I just want to open a new file.
M: OK. Just click on this icon here.
F: Oh, that's right.

CONVERSATION 5 [F = Japanese]
M: Uh-oh.
F: What's the matter?
M: I just selected some text and clicked on this icon. It's gone.
F: No problem. That was the *cut* command. You just need to click on the *paste* icon.
M: Ah, there it is. Thanks!

CONVERSATION 6
F: OK, I'm done.
M: So you're ready to print?
F: Uh-huh. What do I click on?
M: Right here.
F: Got it. Thanks.

GRAMMAR

Suggested teaching time:	5–8 minutes	Your actual teaching time:	

- Ask a student to read the first point and the example sentences in the Grammar box.
- Write on the board two additional examples:
  1. I clicked on the tool bar to save a file.
  2. Press this key to print the document.
- Ask *How else can you say each sentence?* (1. I clicked on the toolbar <u>because</u> I <u>wanted</u> to save a file. 2. Press this key <u>if</u> you <u>want</u> to print the document.) Make sure students understand the contrast: The clause which follows *because* and *if* must contain a subject and verb; the infinitive is followed by a noun.
- Have a student read the second point and the example sentences. Then ask individual students *Why are you taking this class?* Tell them to use a short answer with an infinitive. (Possible responses: To improve my English, to get a better job, to meet new people.)

Option: **GRAMMAR BOOSTER** *(Teaching notes p. T139)*

 Inductive Grammar Charts

A Find the grammar

Suggested teaching time:	2 minutes	Your actual teaching time:	

- When students have identified the sentence, write it on the board. (I clicked on the tool bar to save a file.)
- After students rewrite the sentence with *because*, ask pairs to write another sentence with an infinitive of purpose and then rewrite it with *because*.

B Pair work

Suggested teaching time:	5–7 minutes	Your actual teaching time:	

- For a warm-up, ask *Do you make to-do lists? Do you have a smart phone? If you don't, how do you remember to do things?*
- To model the activity, ask two volunteers to read the sample quotes. Then ask a volunteer to read the list of tasks on the smart phone. Have students work in pairs to ask and answer questions about the to-do list.

C Grammar practice

Suggested teaching time:	4–6 minutes	Your actual teaching time:	

- Tell students to work individually to complete each statement. After students complete the exercise, have them compare answers in pairs.
- Ask several students the questions below. Have students answer with short answers and infinitives of purpose.
  Why did you buy a new scanner?
  Why did you e-mail your friend?
  Why did you connect to the Internet?

⭐ **Extra Grammar Exercises**

NOW YOU CAN Troubleshoot a problem

A Conversation activator

Suggested teaching time:	6–8 minutes	Your actual teaching time:	

 Conversation Activator Video

- *Note:* You can print the script or you can show a running transcript on the video player on the ActiveTeach. The script also appears on page 187 of this Teacher's Edition.
- Begin by asking students to read the computer problems in the Recycle box and write a check mark next to the ones they've experienced. Ask *Which computer problems have you had?* Invite students to complete the last item with a different problem and share that problem with the class.
- Model the activity by role-playing the conversation with a more confident student. Play the role of Student A.
- Have pairs choose one or two computer problems for their role play. Refer them to the Conversation Model and Vocabulary on page 100 as necessary. Remind students to change roles when they have finished.
- Move around the room and help students as needed.

DON'T STOP! Extend the conversation. Encourage students to use the ideas in the box to continue their conversations.

- For more support, play the Conversation Activator Video before students do this activity themselves. In Scene 1, the actors use different words in the gaps from the ones in the Conversation Model. In Scene 2, the actors extend the conversation. After each scene, ask students how the model has been changed by the actors.

 Conversation Activator Video Script; Conversation Activator Pair Work Cards; Learning Strategies

B Change partners

Suggested teaching time:	6–8 minutes	Your actual teaching time:	

- Assign new partners and have pairs role-play conversations using the other problems on the list.
- Move around the room and listen for correct intonation. Help students as needed.
- Have selected pairs role-play their conversations for the class. After each conversation, check comprehension. Ask *What is Student A's computer problem? What suggestion does Student B make?*

EXTRAS

Workbook or MyEnglishLab

 Speaking Activities: Unit 9, Activity 1

GRAMMAR *The infinitive of purpose*

GRAMMAR BOOSTER p. 139
- Expressing purpose with <u>in order to</u> and <u>for</u>

An infinitive can be used to express a purpose.

I scrolled down **to read** the text. (= because I wanted to read the text)
Put the cursor on the toolbar **to choose** a file. (= if you want to choose a file)

Answering a <u>Why</u> question with an infinitive of purpose is similar to answering with <u>Because</u>.

Why did you click on that icon?   **To save** the file before I close it. (= Because I want to save it.)
Why did you highlight that word?   **To select** it so I can copy it. (= Because I want to copy it.)

A **FIND THE GRAMMAR** Look at the Conversation Model on page 100. Find an infinitive of purpose. Restate the sentence, using <u>because</u>.

B **PAIR WORK** Look at Cathy's to-do list. Ask and answer questions, using infinitives of purpose.

    ❝ Why is Cathy going shopping? ❞

    ❝ To get something for dinner. ❞

TO DO TODAY

- go shopping – get something for dinner
- call Dad – wish him Happy Birthday!
- meet Brandy – talk about next weekend
- talk to Mark – ask for help with scanner
- e-mail Hillary – send her my new photos
- drop off car at service station – fix windshield wipers
- visit Katonah Museum – see new art exhibit
- call salon – make appointment for manicure

C **GRAMMAR PRACTICE** Complete each sentence in your own way. Use infinitives of purpose. *Answers will vary.*

1 Don't forget to click on the save icon ...*to save your document*........ .
2 You can click on the print icon ....
3 Put the cursor on the pull-down menu ....
4 I bought a new scanner ....
5 I e-mailed my friend ....
6 I connected to the Internet ....

NOW YOU CAN Troubleshoot a problem

A **CONVERSATION ACTIVATOR** With a partner, change the Conversation Model. Create a conversation in which one of you asks for help with a computer problem. Use the computer vocabulary from page 100 and an infinitive of purpose. Then change roles.

A: .... , could you take a look at this?
B: Sure. .... ?
A: Well, I clicked on .... to .... , and ....
B: Why don't you try .... ? That ....
A: .... I'll give that a try.

DON'T STOP!
- Discuss other problems.
- Offer other suggestions.

RECYCLE THIS LANGUAGE.
- The computer crashes.
- The screen freezes.
- The printer won't print.
- The file won't [open / close / print].
- The [mouse] doesn't work.
- Nothing happens.
- (your own idea) __

B **CHANGE PARTNERS** Practice the conversation again with other problems.

GOAL Compare product features

GRAMMAR *Comparisons with as . . . as*

To express similarity

Use <u>as</u> . . . <u>as</u> with an adjective to indicate how two things are equal or the same. Use the adverb <u>just</u> for emphasis.

> The new speakers are as good as the old ones.
> The iFriend tablet is just as nice as the F40.

Use the adverb <u>almost</u> in affirmative statements to indicate that two things are very similar but not exactly the same.

> The Zeta B is almost as fast as the Panasox.

To express difference

Use <u>not as</u> . . . <u>as</u> to indicate how two things are different. Use <u>not quite</u> when the difference is very small. Use <u>not nearly</u> to indicate that there's a big difference.

> Our new printer isn't as noisy as the old one.
> The G4 isn't quite as expensive as the Z90.
> The Panasox isn't nearly as affordable as the Zeta B.

You can use shortened statements with <u>as</u> when the meaning is clear.

> The old monitor was great. But the new one is just as good. (= just as good as the old one)
> Have you seen Carl's new laptop? My laptop isn't as nice. (= as nice as his laptop)

GRAMMAR BOOSTER p. 139
- As . . . as to compare adverbs
- Comparatives and superlatives: review
- Comparison with adverbs

A **GRAMMAR PRACTICE** Read each statement about a product. Write a sentence with <u>as</u> . . . <u>as</u> and the cue to compare the products.

1 The new Shine keyboard is popular. The one from Digitek is popular, too.
   (just) The new Shine keyboard is just as popular as the one from Digitek.

2 The XCue joystick is easy to use. The JRock joystick is also easy to use.
   (just) The XCue joystick is just as easy to use as the JRock joystick.

3 The C50 monitor is large. The C30 monitor is a little larger than the C50.
   (almost) The C50 monitor is almost as large as the C30 monitor.

4 Comtec's new mini-tablet is very small. Sango's new mini-tablet is also very small.
   (just) Comtec's new mini-tablet is just as small as Sango's new mini-tablet.

5 The CCV speakers are very powerful. The Soundtec speakers are much more powerful.
   (not / nearly) The CCV speakers are not nearly as powerful as the Soundtec speakers.

6 The Icon monitors are very inexpensive. The Sentinel monitors are a little more expensive.
   (not / quite) The Sentinel monitors are not quite as inexpensive as the Icon monitors.

a joystick

B On a separate sheet of paper, write five statements comparing things you are familiar with. Use <u>as</u> . . . <u>as</u>.

> In my opinion, the Mardino sports car isn't nearly as good as the Strega.

Ideas for comparisons
- cars
- electronic products
- stores
- restaurants
- (your own idea) ___

DIGITAL
MORE
EXERCISES

GRAMMAR

Suggested teaching time:	12–18 minutes	Your actual teaching time:

- Write on the board *My smart phone is as good as your laptop*. Ask *Is my smart phone better than your laptop?* (No, they're the same quality.)

- Review the first two points and their examples in the Grammar box. Ask:
  Which speakers are better—the new ones or the old ones? (They are equally good.)
  Which has more new features—the iFriend or the F40? (They have the same number of new features.)
  Emphasize that *as . . . as* is used to say that two things are equal or the same.

- Ask *What is the difference between the Zeta B and the Panasox?* (The Zeta B is a little slower than the Panasox.)

- Tell the class to think of pairs of sentences using *as . . . as* and *almost as . . . as*, comparing students' hair length, height, age, and other characteristics. For example, *My hair is as long as yours. I am almost as tall as you. But you're a little taller.*

- Review the third point and examples in the Grammar box. Ask:
  Which printer is noisier: the old one or the new one? (The old one.) *Which is more expensive: the G4 or the Z90?* (The Z90.) *Is the Z90 a lot more expensive?* (No.) *Is the Zeta B cheaper than the Panasox?* (Yes.)
  Emphasize that *not as . . . as* is used to say that two things are different.

- To further illustrate the difference between *not quite* and *not nearly*, write these sentences on the board:
  1. *My computer isn't quite as fast as your computer.*
  2. *My computer isn't nearly as fast as your computer.*
  Ask:
  Which sentence says that your computer is only a little bit faster than mine? (1.) *Which sentence says that your computer is much faster than mine?* (2.)
  Which words mean that the difference between the computers is very small? (Not quite as . . . as.)
  Which words mean that there's a big difference between the computers? (Not nearly as . . . as.)

- Ask a volunteer to read the last point in the Grammar box. Ask the class to think of additional examples.

Language and culture

- *Just* and *quite* add emphasis to a comparison. *Just as . . . as* emphasizes the similarity in a comparison. *Not quite as . . . as* emphasizes that the difference is very small.
- Comparisons with *as . . . as* can focus on an adjective (*as good as*), an adverb (*not cost quite as much as*), or a noun (*as many new features as . . .*).
- In British English, *quite* can have two meanings. It can mean *a little bit but not very* when the stress is on *quite*. For example, the sentence *He was quite intelligent* means *He was a little bit intelligent, but not very intelligent*. When the stress is on the adjective, then *quite* means *very*. For example, *The meal was quite good* means *The meal was very good*. In American English, *quite* always means *very*.

FYI: Although adverbs often end in *-ly*, here are four adverbs that are the same as their adjective forms: *hard, fast, early,* and *late*. *Hardly* and *lately* are adverbs, but they have very different meanings from *hard* and *late*.

Option: **GRAMMAR BOOSTER** *(Teaching notes p. T139)*

 Inductive Grammar Charts

A Grammar practice

Suggested teaching time:	7–12 minutes	Your actual teaching time:

- Have pairs underline the point of comparison. (1. Is popular; 2. is easy to use; 3. is large; 4. is small; 5. are powerful; 6. are inexpensive.)

- Have students write the sentences individually.

- Review answers by asking students to write the sentences on the board. Discuss any difficulties.

Option: (+5–10 minutes) For a challenge, have partners create pairs of sentences about themselves. For example, *My phone has many games. Daniela's phone also has many games.* Then have students exchange sentences with another pair to determine if the sentences show similarity or difference. Write a new sentence using *as . . . as*; for example, *My phone has just as many games as Daniela's phone.*

B On a separate sheet of paper . . .

Suggested teaching time:	0 minutes	Your actual teaching time:

- Read the "Ideas for comparisons." Write the list on the board. Ask *What can you compare in each category?* (Cars: speed, safety; electronic products: cost; stores: popularity, selection; restaurants: good food, atmosphere, prices.)

- Tell students to suggest ideas for other things to compare. Write these on the board. Have students suggest examples of points of comparison.

- Encourage students to use various forms introduced in the Grammar box when writing their comparisons. For example, *Mel Air isn't quite as safe as Tempo. And the food on Mel Air isn't nearly as good as on Tempo. The service, however, is just as good.*

 Extra Grammar Exercises

PRONUNCIATION

A ▶5:08 Read and listen . . .

Suggested teaching time:	2 minutes	Your actual teaching time:

 **Pronunciation Coach Video**

- Ask students to read and listen to the sentences, paying attention to the stress in *as . . . as* phrases.
- Have students listen again and repeat in the pauses.
- Tell students to practice reading the sentences to a partner. Move around the room and listen for correct stress.

🖶 **Pronunciation Activity**

B Read the statements you wrote . . .

Suggested teaching time:	2 minutes	Your actual teaching time:

- Have students practice stress with *as . . . as* by reading four of the sentences they wrote in Exercise B on page 102. Help them distribute stress appropriately.

CONVERSATION MODEL

A ▶5:09 Listen to someone . . .

Suggested teaching time:	2 minutes	Your actual teaching time:

These conversation strategies are implicit in the model:
- Express interest informally with "Oh, yeah?"
- Use "Everyone says . . ." to introduce a popular opinion.
- Say "Well, I've heard ___" to support a point of view.

- To prepare students, tell them to look at the picture. Ask *Do these two people know each other?* (Yes.) *What is the man thinking about?* (A game controller.)
- Play the audio while students read and listen. Check comprehension by asking:
  What are the people talking about? (Buying a new game controller.)
  What kind of game controller is the man thinking about getting? (A Macro.)
  According to the woman, which is better—a Panatel or a Macro? (Both are equally good.)
  According to the woman, which is more expensive—a Panatel or a Macro? (A Macro.)
- Allow students to read and listen again. Then ask:
  Which game controller does the woman recommend? (A Panatel.)
  Why does she recommend this brand? (It's as good as a Macro and it's cheaper.)
  Will the man buy a Panatel? (Maybe. He'll check it out first.)

B ▶5:10 Rhythm and intonation

Suggested teaching time:	3 minutes	Your actual teaching time:

- Have students repeat each line chorally. Make sure they:
  ○ use rising intonation for *Oh, yeah?* and *Really?*

○ use falling intonation for *What kind?*
○ stress *good* in *as good as.*

NOW YOU CAN Recommend a better deal

A Conversation activator

Suggested teaching time:	5 minutes	Your actual teaching time:

 Conversation Activator Video

- *Note:* You can print the script or you can show a running transcript on the video player on the ActiveTeach. The script also appears on page 188 of this Teacher's Edition.
- Ask students to skim the two lists of electronic products from the magazines.
- Refer students to the Conversation Model to review recommending a better deal. Point out the instruction to use *as . . . as.*
- Model the activity by role-playing the conversation with a more confident student.
- As pairs practice their conversations, move around the room and help students as needed. Encourage them to use their own ideas to keep the conversation going. Be sure to reinforce the use of the conversation strategies. For example, make sure students show interest by using rising intonation and appropriate facial expressions with *Oh, yeah?* and *Really?*
- Remind students to change roles once they have finished.

DON'T STOP! Extend the conversation. Encourage students to use all of the language in the Recycle box. Tell them to ask about other features of the products to continue the conversation. Have them place a check mark next to the language in the Recycle box as they use it.

- For more support, play the Conversation Activator Video before students do this activity themselves. In Scene 1, the actors use different words in the gaps from the ones in the Conversation Model. In Scene 2, the actors extend the conversation. After each scene, ask students how the model has been changed by the actors.

🖶 **Conversation Activator Video Script; Conversation Activator Pair Work Cards; Learning Strategies**

B Change partners

Suggested teaching time:	5 minutes	Your actual teaching time:

- Have students find new partners and role-play conversations about other products and features.
- After pairs practice their role plays, invite pairs to present their conversations to the class. After each conversation, check comprehension. Ask *What does Student A want to buy? What does Student B recommend? Why?*

EXTRAS

Workbook or MyEnglishLab

 Speaking Activities: Unit 9, Activity 2

PRONUNCIATION *Stress in <u>as</u> . . . <u>as</u> phrases*

A ▶5:08 Read and listen. Then listen again and repeat.

1 The new printer is as slow as the old one.

3 The X12 mouse isn't nearly as nice as the X30.

2 My old smart phone is just as small as the new one.

4 The M200 keyboard isn't quite as cheap as the Z6.

B Read the statements you wrote in Exercise B on page 102 aloud, paying attention to stress.

CONVERSATION MODEL

A ▶5:09 Listen to someone compare product features.

A: I'm thinking about getting a new game controller.

B: Oh, yeah? What kind?

A: Everyone says I should get a Macro.

B: Well, I've heard that the Panatel is as good as the Macro, but it costs a lot less.

A: Really? I'll check it out.

B ▶5:10 **RHYTHM AND INTONATION** Listen again and repeat. Then practice the Conversation Model with a partner.

NOW YOU CAN Compare product features

A **CONVERSATION ACTIVATOR** With a partner, change the Conversation Model, using the magazine ratings to compare features of different products. Use <u>as</u> . . . <u>as</u>. Then change roles.

A: I'm thinking about getting a new ....
B: .... ? What kind?
A: Everyone says I should get ....
B: Well, I've heard that ....
A: Really? ....

DON'T STOP!

• Ask about other features.

RECYCLE THIS LANGUAGE.

Which . . .
is more popular?	is newer?
is easier / harder to use?	is quieter / noisier?
is lighter / heavier?	is slower / faster?
is larger / smaller?	has more features?
is less / more expensive?	looks nicer?
costs less / more?	gets better reviews?

B **CHANGE PARTNERS** Now practice the conversation again, using other products and features.

Buyer's Friend *Magazine*

Our recommendations!

■ eMax Wireless Mouse	very good	US $25
■ eMax X15 Wireless Keyboard	very comfortable	US $30
■ eMax Y80 Webcam	easy to use	US $52
■ eMax Z40 Monitor	15 inches / 38 centimeters	US $250

THE ELECTRONICS GUIDE

YOUR BEST BUYS!

Klick Wireless Mouse	very good	US $12
Klick P40 Wireless Keyboard	very comfortable	US $25
Klick Ultra Webcam	easy to use	US $52
Klick P20 Monitor	19 inches / 48.3 centimeters	US $99

GOAL Describe how you use the Internet

BEFORE YOU LISTEN

DIGITAL FLASH CARDS

▶ 5:11 **VOCABULARY** • *Internet activities* Read and listen. Then listen again and repeat.

visit a website go to a specific address on the Internet and read its content

surf the Internet visit a lot of different websites for information that interests you

join (an online group) become a member of an Internet group to meet friends and share information about your hobbies and interests

post (a message) add your comments to an online discussion on a message board, a blog, or a social networking site

attach (a file) place a document or photo into an e-mail

upload (a file) move a document, music file, or picture from a personal computer, phone, or MP3 player onto the Internet

share (a link) send an e-mail or post a message with the address of an interesting website you want someone to visit

download an application download a useful program that you can use to play games, get information, or perform tasks

send an instant message "chat" with someone online in real time by typing messages

look up information go to a website to learn about something

> **Remember also:**
> • download (a file)
> • stream a video
> • check e-mail

LISTENING COMPREHENSION

A ▶ 5:12 **LISTEN FOR THE MAIN IDEA** Listen to people describe how they use the Internet. Write a checkmark next to the person who seems to enjoy the Internet the least. Explain your answer.

☐ **1** George Thomas ☐ **2** Sonia Castro ☑ **3** Robert Kuan ☐ **4** Nadia Montasser

B ▶ 5:13 **LISTEN FOR DETAILS** Listen again and check the activities each person does.

	George Thomas	Sonia Castro	Robert Kuan	Nadia Montasser
buys products	☐	☐	☐	☑
downloads music	☐	☐	☐	☑
checks the latest news	☑	☐	☐	☐
participates in online groups	☑	☑	☐	☐
plays online games	☐	☐	☐	☐
sends instant messages	☑	☐	☐	☐
surfs the Internet	☑	☐	☐	☐
uploads photos	☐	☑	☐	☐
uses a computer at work	☑	☐	☑	☐

BEFORE YOU LISTEN

▶ 5:11 **Vocabulary**

Suggested teaching time:	3 minutes	Your actual teaching time:	

V Vocabulary Flash Card Player

- Before students read and listen, tell them to skim the Internet activities in boldface type (including the phrases in the "Remember also" box).

- Have students listen and repeat. Then ask *Which of these things do you do once a month? Once a week? Every day?*

- Have students listen and practice again with their books closed.

Option: (+3–7 minutes) For additional practice with the Vocabulary, have students form teams and play a game. Read the definitions but not the words. Teams compete to be the first to raise their hands and give the correct matching words. Each student can answer only once until all of the team members have answered. The team with the most correct answers is the winner. To challenge students, replay the game in reverse. Read the words and ask students to supply the correct definitions.

 Learning Strategies

LISTENING COMPREHENSION

A ▶ 5:12 **Listen for the main idea**

Suggested teaching time:	4–6 minutes	Your actual teaching time:	

- For a warm-up, ask the class *Who enjoys spending time on the Internet? Who does not?* Have students make a statement comparing the numbers of students who answered *Yes* and *No.*

- Tell students they will listen to four people describe how they use the Internet.

- Play the audio once and review the answer with the class.

- Ask *Is anyone here like Robert Kuan?*

AUDIOSCRIPT

1 George Thomas
M: I think I probably spend at least ten hours a day online. I know that's hard to believe, but . . . I'm pretty much what you'd call a computer addict . . . no doubt about it. I'm always surfing the Internet to see what's new. I'm a news junkie, so I visit CNN.com several times a day to see what's in the news. And I belong to a bunch of online groups. There are usually new messages posted every day, but I'm not that interested in responding. I just like to read. My friend Nick usually sends me instant messages throughout the day, so of course I have to respond to those . . . I end up fooling around most of the day . . . a lot more than I'm working, I'm afraid. It's a good thing no one knows . . . well, OK, <u>you</u> know.

---

2 Sonia Castro [F = Spanish]
F: I joined Facebook a few months ago, and I'm, like, totally into it now. People are constantly inviting me to be their friend, so I've got more than a hundred friends on my Facebook page now. I check it a lot each day to see what's new . . . and there always is something new. And I love that you can upload into the photo section. I've been wasting a lot of time scanning tons of photos . . . photos of my family, photos of my friends, photos of my cat . . . I used to spend a lot of time surfing the Net, but now I spend most of my time on Facebook.

3 Robert Kuan [M = Chinese]
M: I really don't have a lot of time for fooling around on the Internet. I'm the kind of guy who sends a few e-mails to his friends and family once in a while . . . and when I need to use the Internet, I'm in and I'm out. I don't like surfing around . . . to me it's just a total waste of time. Mainly, I just use my computer for work. There are a few programs I have to use . . . you know, Word, Excel . . . And of course people in the office communicate a lot more by e-mail than they do in person . . . or even by phone.

4 Nadia Montasser [F = Arabic]
F: I find the Internet really convenient. When you want to buy something, you can do some quick research and find out which product is the most popular or if there are any problems with it. There are a lot of things I used to do by mail or in person, but now I just do them online. I generally buy most of my music online now—it's easy to pay online and download the files onto my MP3 player. And there are a lot of things you can buy at a lower price if you do a little research. You can compare prices really easily.

B ▶ 5:13 **Listen for details**

Suggested teaching time:	8–11 minutes	Your actual teaching time:	

- Before students listen for details, ask them to read the computer activities on the chart and circle the ones they do. Invite students to share what they circled with the class.

- Tell students to listen once without checking the activities. Then have them listen again and complete the exercise.

- Have students compare answers in pairs. Then have pairs compare the activities they circled with the activities of the four people from the listening. Ask *Which person do you share the most computer activities with? What do you spend the most time doing on the computer?*

Option: (+5 minutes) Write on the board Do you think social sites like Facebook are safe places to keep in touch with friends? Why? Have groups discuss the questions and give examples to support their opinions. Bring the class together and have groups share their opinions.

NOW YOU CAN | Describe how you use the Internet

A Frame your ideas

Suggested teaching time:	12–17 minutes	Your actual teaching time:

- Have students complete the survey individually while you move around the room and help as needed.
- To review, refer students to the Vocabulary on page 104.
- After students complete the survey, have them compare answers in pairs.
- Review responses with the class. Ask several students *What other things do you use a computer for? Can you imagine your life without a computer? Can you imagine your life without the Internet?*

B Group work

Suggested teaching time:	10–13 minutes	Your actual teaching time:

- Review the information in the chart and the Ideas box with the class. Remind students that *avoid* means *keep away from.*
- Ask pairs to form questions from the information and select students to write the questions on the board. (1. Are you an Internet expert? 2. Are you an Internet addict? 3. Are you uncomfortable using the Internet? 4. Do you use the Internet to meet people? 5. Do you use the Internet to avoid people?)
- Then have students move around the room to complete the exercise by asking their classmates the questions. Encourage them to ask follow-up questions to get more information.

C Discussion

Suggested teaching time:	8–10 minutes	Your actual teaching time:

- Draw a chart on the board like the one below or print and distribute copies to students.

Internet experts	Internet addicts	Isn't comfortable using the Internet	Uses Internet to meet people	Uses Internet to avoid people

- To model the activity, ask a volunteer to read the sample answer in quotes. Ask individual students to tell the class about someone they spoke to. Write students' names in the chart. Invite the person being talked about to tell the class more by answering the question that applies to him or her. For example, ask:
  1. *Why do you call yourself an Internet expert? How much do you know about the Internet?* (Possible response: I know a lot about the Internet.)
  2. *Why do you call yourself an Internet addict? How many hours a day do you spend on the Internet?* (Possible response: I spend twelve hours a day on the Internet.)
  3. *Why are you uncomfortable using the Internet? What happened?* (Possible response: I don't know how to use the Internet.)
  4. *How do you use the Internet to meet people? Where do you go to meet people face to face?* (Possible response: I use social sites. I meet people through friends.)
  5. *How do you use the Internet to avoid people?* (Possible response: I never go anywhere. I do all my shopping online.)

Option: *(+10 minutes)* To extend the activity, write this situation on the board: *Imagine that your computer or device has broken down, and you have no Internet access for a week. How does this affect your life?* Have groups discuss their week without the Internet. Bring the class together and ask students to share. As a challenge, follow up the discussion by having students write two to three paragraphs describing the week without the Internet. For more advanced groups, have students write without discussing.

 Graphic Organizers

EXTRAS

Workbook or MyEnglishLab

 Speaking Activities: Unit 9, Activity 3

A FRAME YOUR IDEAS Complete the survey about your own Internet use.

New Tab ×

Internet User Survey

1. I usually spend ___ hours a week online.
- ○ 0 – 10
- ○ 11 – 20
- ○ 21 – 30
- ○ 31 – 40
- ○ 41 – 50
- ○ over 50

2. I use . . .
- ○ a desktop
- ○ a laptop
- ○ a smart phone
- ○ a tablet
- ○ (none of these)

3. I use the Internet . . .
- ○ for work
- ○ for study
- ○ for fun
- ○ I never use the Internet.

4. I use the Internet . . .

○ to search for new websites	○ to send instant messages	○ to download music
○ to upload photos	○ to keep in touch with friends	○ to upload videos
○ to download photos	○ to keep in touch with family	○ to download videos
○ to design websites	○ to meet new people	○ to send and receive e-mail
○ to look up information	○ to watch movies	○ to play games
○ to create art	○ to look at my bank accounts	○ to pay bills
○ to shop for things	○ to sell things	○ to read or watch the news
○ to take classes	○ to practice English	○ to just fool around
		○ other: ....

5. Check the statements that are true about you.
- ○ People consider me to be a technology expert. They come to me for help.
- ○ You could say I'm an Internet addict. I'm always online.
- ○ Compared to most people, I spend a lot of time on the Internet.
- ○ I spend just as much time on the Internet as most people.
- ○ I don't spend nearly as much time on the Internet as most people.
- ○ I'm really not comfortable using the Internet.

B GROUP WORK Walk around your classroom and ask your classmates about their Internet use. Ask questions to get more information and take notes.

Ideas for questions
Why . . . ?   When . . . ?
Where . . . ?   How . . . ?

Find someone who. . .	Name	Notes
is an Internet expert.		
is an Internet addict.		
isn't comfortable using the Internet.		
uses the Internet to meet people.		
uses the Internet to avoid people.		

C DISCUSSION Tell your class what you found out about your classmates and how they use the Internet.

❝ May spends a lot of time online. She uses her tablet to meet new people and keep in touch with friends. Gary spends a lot of time online with his smart phone. He uploads photos and . . . ❞

BEFORE YOU READ

1 What kinds of problems have you had on the Internet?

2 What kinds of Internet problems have you heard about on the news?

READING ▶5:14

Identity Thieves Steal 40 Million Credit Card Numbers

Eleven hackers around the world were accused of stealing more than 40 million credit card numbers on the Internet. They included three people from the U.S. who are accused of hacking into the wireless networks of popular online stores.

Once inside these networks, they searched for customers' credit card numbers, passwords, and personal information so they could pretend to be those customers. When the identity theft was completed, credit card numbers and other details were then sold on the Internet, allowing criminals to withdraw thousands of dollars at a time from ATMs.

Cyberbullying Leads to Teenager's Death

Megan Taylor Meier, age 13, joined an online social networking group where she became online friends with a 16-year-old boy named Josh. Megan and Josh never communicated by phone or in person, but she enjoyed exchanging messages with him in the group.

Over time, Josh changed. He began to bully her daily—criticizing her personality and telling her what a bad person she was. Some of their communications were posted so everyone could see them. Josh's last message to her said, "The world would be a better place without you." A short time later, Megan committed suicide.

After her death, it was discovered that there was no "Josh." The messages came from the mother of one of Megan's classmates. The mother had been angry with Megan because she believed Megan had said some untrue things about her daughter.

Computer Viruses Are Getting Harder to Prevent

"We're losing the battle against computer viruses," says David Farber, professor of computer science at Carnegie Mellon University. These viruses, which can enter computer systems through junk e-mail from hackers, have reached epidemic proportions, slowing down computers—and sometimes causing whole office computer systems to crash—in both large and small companies. In one year alone, they were reported to have caused $13 billion USD in damage.

Companies have been trying for years to protect themselves with anti-virus programs, but criminals are creating newer, improved viruses faster than these programs can keep up with.

A **UNDERSTAND FROM CONTEXT** Use the context of the articles to help you to complete each definition.

..c.. **1** A hacker is . . .

..a.. **2** A computer virus is . . .

..f.. **3** A criminal is . . .

..e.. **4** Junk e-mail is . . .

..b.. **5** An anti-virus program is . . .

..g.. **6** A cyberbully is . . .

..d.. **7** An identity thief is . . .

a a software program that causes problems in computers.

b a software program that tries to stop the spread of viruses.

c a person who enters computer systems without permission.

d a person who steals other people's personal information.

e an advertisement you didn't request.

f a person who breaks the law; for example, by stealing money.

g a person who sends cruel and negative messages to another person online.

B **RELATE TO PERSONAL EXPERIENCE** What news stories have you heard about the Internet? Do you ever worry about using the Internet? Why or why not?

BEFORE YOU READ

Suggested teaching time:	5 minutes	Your actual teaching time:

- After pairs discuss the questions, ask students to share their answers with the class. Write student responses on the board in two columns:

Problems students have had	Problems students have heard about

- Discuss ways to resolve these problems with the class.

 **Learning Strategies**

READING ► 5:14

Suggested teaching time:	10–15 minutes	Your actual teaching time:

- Before students read, have volunteers read the titles of the articles. Ask *What problems will these articles talk about?* (Identity thieves, computer viruses, and cyberbullying.) If necessary, explain *cyberbullying* by dividing the word into its parts: *cyber* refers to messages and information on the Internet; *to bully* means to scare someone by showing power or threatening violence. Write the problems on the board.

- Tell students to keep their books closed and work in pairs to discuss what they know about these problems. Then have students open their books and read the articles.

- Check comprehension by asking *What do hackers do?* (They use computers to get into websites or computer systems without permission.) *How can viruses enter computer systems?* (Through junk e-mail.) *Where did Megan meet Josh?* (On an online social network.)

- As a class, discuss which problem students think is the most serious. Have students keep their books open so they can refer to specific information in the articles.

Option: (+5 minutes) To challenge students, have them close their books and listen to the audio of each article before reading. After each article, ask students what they remember about it. When students have finished, have them open their books and check their ideas in the Reading.

Option: (+5–10 minutes) To extend the activity, have students discuss the following questions in groups: *Has your computer ever had a virus? If yes, what happened?*

Option: (+10 minutes) As an alternative approach, do a jigsaw reading. Divide the class into three groups. Assign each group one article and have them summarize the problem and discuss ways to prevent it. When they've finished, have each group give a short presentation to the class, including a summary of the article and suggestions for handling the problem.

Option: (+15 minutes) For a challenge, have students write a "letter to the editor" to respond to one of the three articles. Tell students to give advice on what people can do to avoid the problems discussed. Have students exchange letters and give each other feedback.

A Understand from context

Suggested teaching time:	4–6 minutes	Your actual teaching time:

- Begin by having students match each of the terms in the exercise to the article in which it appeared. (First article: hacker, criminal, identity thief; second article: computer virus, junk e-mail, anti-virus program; third article: cyberbully.)

- Encourage students to try to complete the exercise without looking back at the articles. If necessary, tell them to look up any words they didn't know.

- Have students compare answers in pairs.

B Relate to personal experience

Suggested teaching time:	8–10 minutes	Your actual teaching time:

- Divide the class into small groups to discuss the questions. Assign one student in each group the role of recorder.

- After groups discuss the questions, have each recorder share the group's conclusions with the class.

- To follow up, ask:
  Do you post pictures or videos on the Internet?
  Do you belong to any social networks?
  Why do you think some people might be uncomfortable on the Internet?

 Extra Reading Comprehension Exercises

NOW YOU CAN Discuss the impact of the Internet

A Notepadding

Suggested teaching time:	8–11 minutes	Your actual teaching time:

- Have students close their books. Write on the board *The Internet has changed the way people . . .* Invite students to share some ideas to complete the sentence. (Possible responses: Communicate, find information, pay bills, relax, shop.)

- Have students open their books and read aloud the four statements about how the Internet has impacted people's lives. Ask students to suggest examples for the first statement. (Possible responses: Good changes: You can find information about almost anything very quickly simply by typing a few words into a search engine online. Bad changes: The information people find isn't always reliable or true.)

- As students work in pairs to discuss and list ideas, encourage them to think of more than one example of a good and bad impact for each statement.

- If necessary, refer students to the articles on page 106 for additional problems.

B Discussion

Suggested teaching time:	10–13 minutes	Your actual teaching time:

Text-mining: Focus students' attention on the box. Tell students to scan the articles on page 106 and underline useful language. Then write students' examples on the board for them to refer to during the discussion.

- Divide the class into groups, making sure that the pairs from the previous activity are not in the same group.

- As students compare notes, encourage them to write on their notepads any additional items that they hear about or think of.

- Bring the class together and draw the chart below on the board or print out a copy for each student. Do not include the possible responses. As you review answers with the class, complete the chart with students' responses. Then add up the answers in each column.

Benefits	Problems
Banking online saves trips to the bank.	Your private information can be stolen.
Social networks allow you to reconnect with old friends.	You have to be careful what you write because other people can read things you post.

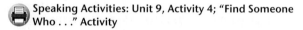 **Graphic Organizers**

EXTRAS

Workbook or MyEnglishLab

Speaking Activities: Unit 9, Activity 4; "Find Someone Who . . ." Activity

A **NOTEPADDING** With a partner, discuss each statement. Write at least one good change and one bad change for each.

1	The Internet has changed the way people find information.
Good changes:	
Bad changes:	

2	The Internet has changed the way people work in offices.
Good changes:	
Bad changes:	

3	The Internet has changed the way people shop.
Good changes:	
Bad changes:	

4	The Internet has changed the way people communicate.
Good changes:	
Bad changes:	

B **DISCUSSION** Do you think that computers and the Internet have brought more benefits or more problems? Support your opinions with examples.

Text-mining (optional)
Find and underline three words or phrases in the Reading that were new to you. Use them in your Discussion.
For example: "exchanging messages."

In my opinion, there are more benefits than problems. For example, it's easy to look up information, and it's really fast.

I think the Internet is OK, but there are really too many problems. First of all, you have to be very careful if you shop online with a credit card.

A ▶ 5:15 Listen to the conversations. Circle T for true and F for false. Then listen again and infer how to complete each statement.

1 She recommends the C40.	T	(F)
2 She recommends the Hip web camera.	(T)	F
3 He recommends the new Sender tablet.	T	(F)
4 He recommends the Play Zone 3.	T	(F)

1 The C40's monitor is .... the X8's.
(a) the same size as   **b** larger than   **c** smaller than

2 The Hip web camera is .... the Pentac web camera.
a the same price as   (b) cheaper than   **c** more expensive than

3 Sender's new model is .... Sender's old model.
a the same as   **b** nicer than   (c) worse than

4 Play Zone 3 is .... Play Zone 2.
a as cool as   (b) less cool than   **c** more cool than

B Answer each question in your own words, using infinitives of purpose.

1 Why do people join social networking sites? ....

2 Why do people send instant messages? ....

3 Why do people surf the Internet? ....

4 Why do people shop online? ....

5 Why are you studying English? ....

C Complete each statement.

1 ...... Click ...... on an icon on the screen to select it.

2 If you want to print a document, click on the print icon on the ...... tool bar ....

3 To read more text on your monitor's ...... screen ...... , use the scroll ...... bar ...... to scroll down.

4 Click on <u>File</u> on the toolbar so you can choose an icon from the ...... pull-down ...... menu.

5 When you're finished working on a document, don't forget to ...... save ...... it before you close the file.

D Unscramble the letters of the words in the box to complete each sentence.

chatated	clorls	doalwond	esmou	rekcha	rusvi

1 Last year, a ...... hacker ...... got into the company's computer systems and stole important information.

2 Use the ...... mouse ...... to click on a file and open it.

3 It isn't difficult to ...... download ...... songs from the Internet.

4 Use the ...... scroll ...... bar to see more text on the screen.

5 Her computer isn't working now because she downloaded a ...... virus ...... from a piece of junk e-mail.

6 I ...... attached ...... the photos to the e-mail I sent this morning.

WRITING

Write two paragraphs about the benefits and the problems of the Internet. Use your notepads from page 107 for support.

For additional language practice . . .

♫ TOP NOTCH **POP**   • Lyrics p. 154
"Life in Cyberspace"

| DIGITAL SONG | DIGITAL KARAOKE |

WRITING BOOSTER p. 151
• Organizing ideas
• Guidance for this writing exercise

REVIEW

A ▶5:15 Listen to the conversations . . .

Suggested teaching time:	6–10 minutes	Your actual teaching time:

- Tell students to listen to the conversations with their books closed. After each conversation, ask *What are the people talking about?* (1. Monitors; 2. web cameras; 3. tablets; 4. computer games.)

- Have students listen to the conversations again with their books open and complete the exercise. Tell them to listen carefully to the *as . . . as* comparisons. Remind students that the adverb *just* emphasizes similarity. The adverb *almost* indicates that two things are similar but not exactly the same. Negatives with *not as . . . as* suggest difference.

- Allow students to listen again to check their answers.

- Review answers with the class. If necessary, write on the board any lines from the conversations that students had trouble with.

AUDIOSCRIPT

CONVERSATION 1 [F = Spanish]
F: You know, I was planning to buy a new C40 computer, but I changed my mind.
M: Why? the C40 is a good model.
F: I know, but I've heard that the X8 computer comes with a better monitor.
M: Really? The C40 monitor is just as large as the one that comes with the X8. They're both 21 inches.
F: True. But the X8 monitor has a brighter screen.

CONVERSATION 2 [M = Japanese]
M: I'm thinking of getting the Hip Web Camera. What do you think?
F: Well, I've heard the Hip isn't quite as expensive as the Pentac Web Camera, but it's just as good.
M: Really? Are you sure?
F: That's what I've heard. Check it out for yourself.

CONVERSATION 3 [M = Jamaican]
F: Didn't you get a new Sender tablet?
M: Yeah. I replaced my old model.
F: Are you satisfied with the new one?
M: Well, to tell the truth, Sender's new model isn't as nice as the old one.
F: Really! That's too bad.

CONVERSATION 4
F: I'm thinking of getting the new Play Zone 3 computer game for my kids. Is it any good?
M: Well my son has the Play Zone 2. He really likes it.
F: Really? But what about the Play Zone 3?
M: Well, he says it's almost as cool as the Play Zone 2.
F: Almost as cool? That doesn't sound so good.
M: That's why we still have the Play Zone 2.

B Answer each question in your own words . . .

Suggested teaching time:	4–7 minutes	Your actual teaching time:

- After students answer the questions, have them compare answers in pairs.

- Ask several students the last question and compare their responses.

C Complete each statement.

Suggested teaching time:	2 minutes	Your actual teaching time:

- If students have difficulty completing the sentences, refer them to the Vocabulary on page 100. To support weaker students, write on the board *click, tool bar, screen, bar, pull-down, save* in a different order. Tell students to choose answers from these words as they complete the exercise.

- After students complete each statement, have them compare answers in pairs.

D Unscramble the letters of the words . . .

Suggested teaching time:	5–8 minutes	Your actual teaching time:

- Give pairs a few minutes to unscramble any words that they can. Then have them look at the sentences for context and unscramble any remaining words. Move around the room and help students as needed.

- Review answers with the class.

WRITING

Suggested teaching time:	10–15 minutes	Your actual teaching time:

- Ask students to look at their notes on page 107 and organize their ideas. Tell students that they can organize their ideas as they wish. For example, they can focus on one topic like communication on the Internet and discuss benefits and problems. Or they can just focus on benefits or just problems of the Internet.

- Move around the room and help students organize their ideas. Encourage them to use the infinitive of purpose and comparisons with *as . . . as* in their writing.

- After students complete the writing assignment, tell them to check their papers. Ask *Are your comparisons clear? Are the spelling and punctuation correct?*

- Then have students exchange papers with a partner. Tell them to ask questions if something is not clear.

Option: **WRITING BOOSTER** *(Teaching notes p. T151)*

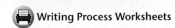 **Writing Process Worksheets**

 *Top Notch Pop* **Song Video and Karaoke Video**

 **Digital Games**

ORAL REVIEW

Before the first activity, give students a few minutes of silent time to become familiar with the pictures.

Contest

Suggested teaching time:	3 minutes	Your actual teaching time:

- Ask students to write down all the computer parts and activities they can remember. The student with the most words wins the contest.

Possible responses . . .

Uploading, downloading, troubleshooting, scanning, printing, computer, monitor, keyboard, mouse, touchpad, printer, laptop, scanner.

Pair work 1

Suggested teaching time:	5 minutes	Your actual teaching time:

- Tell students to look at the photo of the man and the woman and suggest possible conversations. Encourage students to use details from the picture. Have them look at the Vocabulary on pages 98 and 100 for ideas.

Possible responses . . .

A: Could you take a look at this? **B:** Sure. What's the problem? **A:** Well, my computer is frozen. **B:** Why don't you try saving the document, shutting down your computer, and then restarting it? That sometimes works. **A:** OK. I'll give that a try.

Pair work 2

Suggested teaching time:	5 minutes	Your actual teaching time:

- Have students look at the photo of the two men. Ask *What's the man on the left holding? What's on the computer screen?* Suggest possible conversations. To review, refer students to the Conversation Model on page 103.

Possible responses . . .

A: I'm thinking about getting a new printer. **F:** Oh, yeah? What kind? **A:** Everyone says I should get an Amplex. I'm looking at their website right now. **F:** Well, I've heard that the Amplex isn't as good as the Zimtel, and it costs a lot more. Look at this ad in the newspaper for the Zimtel. **M:** Really? I'll check it out.

Pair work 3

Suggested teaching time:	5 minutes	Your actual teaching time:

- Have students look at the photos of the two women on the phone and suggest possible conversations. Refer students to the Conversation Model on page 100 for ideas.

Possible responses . . .

A: Hi, Mona, am I interrupting you? **B:** No, Sue. I'm just downloading music and scanning some photos. **A:** That's cool. How are the photos? **B:** They're great. They look just as good as a professional print. I'll send you one. **A:** Yes, please do. You know I'm thinking about buying a digital camera. **B:** Oh, yeah? What kind? **A:** Well, the thing is, I don't know much about them, so I'm not sure what kind to get. **B:** Why don't you go online and visit some camera store websites to get some ideas? **A:** Great idea. I'll give that a try.

Option: Oral Progress Assessment

- Use the photos on page 109. Encourage students to use the vocabulary, grammar, rhythm, and intonation practiced in this unit.

- Point to the different items in the photos and ask students what they are. (Possible responses: Computer, keyboard, mouse, monitor, laptop, printer, phone.)

- Ask information questions:
  Why do you think the man in the first picture looks worried?
  What is the woman in the first picture doing?
  What are the people in the middle picture doing?
  Why are the women in the bottom pictures talking on the phone?

- Ask a student to role-play a conversation about the first picture with you. Play the role of the woman, and have the student play the role of the man.

- Evaluate the student on intelligibility, fluency, correct use of grammar, and appropriate use of vocabulary.

 Oral Progress Assessment Charts

Option: *Top Notch* Project

Have students prepare summaries of articles about computer benefits or problems.

Idea: Bring articles about computers to class or help students look up articles on the Internet.

- Ask students to read and summarize the articles. Tell them to make sure the summary clearly describes the benefit or problem.

EXTRAS

On the Internet:
- Online Teacher Resources: pearsonelt.com/topnotch3e/

Additional printable resources on the ActiveTeach:
- Assessment
- Just for Fun
- *Top Notch Pop* Song Activities
- *Top Notch TV* Video Program and Activity Worksheets
- Supplementary Pronunciation Lessons
- Conversation Activator Video Scripts
- Audioscripts and Answer Keys
- Unit Study Guides

ORAL REVIEW

CONTEST   Look at the photos for one minute. Then close your books. Who can name all the computer parts and activities in the photos? For example:

There's a printer and . . . OR
He's trying to print photos . . .

PAIR WORK

1 Create a conversation for the man and the woman. They are troubleshooting a problem. Start like this:
Could you take a look at this?

2 Create a conversation for the two men. One is asking for a product recommendation. Start like this:
I'm thinking about getting a new . . .

3 Create a conversation for the two women on the phone. One is asking the other about what she is doing on the computer. Start like this:
Am I interrupting you?

NOW I CAN

☐ Troubleshoot a problem.
☐ Compare product features.
☐ Describe how I use the Internet.
☐ Discuss the impact of the Internet.

UNIT **10** Ethics and Values

COMMUNICATION GOALS

1 Discuss ethical choices.
2 Return someone else's property.
3 Express personal values.
4 Discuss acts of kindness and honesty.

PREVIEW

A **GROUP WORK** Have you ever been faced with a moral dilemma similar to the ones in the pictures? Tell your classmates what happened.

UNIT **10** Ethics and Values

PREVIEW

Before Exercise A, give students a few minutes of silent time to examine the dilemmas.

Suggested teaching time:	7 minutes	Your actual teaching time:

- Write on the board *moral dilemma*. Explain that a *dilemma* is a problem. When we must make a difficult choice, we say that we are *faced with* a problem or dilemma. Ask students to infer the meaning of moral dilemma from the context. Ask *What moral dilemma is each person facing?* (Whether to take the box with the cheaper price; what to do with the watch someone forgot; whether to say something about the wrong total; whether to keep two windbreakers even though only one was ordered.)
- Model the activity by asking the class about the first photo. Ask *What do you think he should do?*
- Have students work in pairs and discuss what the people should do in the three other situations.
- If necessary, explain these items on the guest check: *Shrimp cocktail* is a small dish of cold, cooked shrimp and a sauce eaten at the beginning of the meal; *tomato bisque* is a thick, creamy tomato soup; *sirloin* is a steak; *sparkling water* is a carbonated spring or mineral water.
- Ask the class:
  What's the correct total on the guest check? ($45.20.)
  Who do you think will have to pay the balance if the customer doesn't correct the mistake? (Possibly the waiter / server.)
  What do you think will happen to the windbreaker company if the man keeps two windbreakers? (Probably nothing.)
  Will the man have to pay to mail the second windbreaker back?
  Do you think that makes it OK to keep two windbreakers?
- Ask individual students for their opinion on what the people should do.

Language and culture
- *Uh-oh* is an informal exclamation that indicates that someone has made a mistake. It has a rising then falling intonation.
- In British English, the list you are given in a restaurant that shows what you must pay is called the *bill*. In American English it is called the *check*.

A Group work

Suggested teaching time:	10–12 minutes	Your actual teaching time:

- Divide the class into small groups to discuss the question. If any students don't feel comfortable discussing their own moral dilemmas, ask them to talk about those of people they know or moral dilemmas from TV shows.
- Review responses with the class. Then ask the class *Were you surprised by some of your classmates' moral dilemmas? Were you surprised by their actions?*

Option: (+10 minutes) To extend the activity, dictate the questions below to students or write them on the board. Then have students ask and answer the questions in pairs. Encourage them to elaborate on their answers with details.

How honest are you?
  1. *Have you ever driven faster than the speed limit?*
  2. *Have you ever traveled on a bus or train without paying the fare?*
  3. *Have you ever charged your phone or other device at work or school?*
  4. *Have you ever copied someone's answers on a test?*

B ▶5:18 Photo story

Suggested teaching time:	12–16 minutes	Your actual teaching time:

- To prepare students for the activity, have them look at the photos. Ask:
  Where are the two people? (In a department store.)
  What is the man holding in the first photo? (A broken plate.)
  What do you think the man with the plate is saying in the second photo?
  What do you think his friend is saying in the last photo?

- Tell students to close their books and listen to the conversation.

- To check comprehension, ask:
  How did the plate break? (It broke when he picked it up.)
  Is the dish expensive? (Yes.)
  What does Noah want to do? (Put the plate back on the shelf and leave.)

- Have students open their books. Play the audio again as students read and listen to the conversation.

- Ask pairs to study the pictures and then read the conversation again. As students work, write on the board *Are you more like Matt or Noah?* Call on students to answer the question.

- Ask students *What do you think will happen next?*

C Focus on language

Suggested teaching time:	4–7 minutes	Your actual teaching time:

- Tell students to read the five underlined phrases in the Photo Story and think about their meanings.

- Ask volunteers to read aloud the idioms in Exercise C. Then tell students to complete the exercise.

- To support weaker students, suggest that they scan all the underlined phrases in the Photo Story until they find one with the same meaning. Then tell them to cross it out to indicate that it has been used.

- Have students compare answers in pairs. Move around the room and help students as needed.

- Review answers with the class.

D Think and explain

Suggested teaching time:	5–7 minutes	Your actual teaching time:

- Tell students to scan the Photo Story and underline parts of the conversation that answer the questions. Have them write the number of the question next to the text that supports it.

- Ask volunteers to answer the questions. Make sure students support their answers with quotations from the story.

SPEAKING

A Survey

Suggested teaching time:	7 minutes	Your actual teaching time:

- Before students complete the survey, ask volunteers to read the statements aloud.

- Have students think of what else a person could do in each situation; for example, for item 5 (Matt), offer to pay the damage or offer to replace the plate.

Option: *(+10 minutes)* As an alternative approach, conduct the survey as a class activity. For each statement, first ask students who agree to raise their hands, then ask students who disagree to raise their hands. Write the numbers for agree and disagree on the board for each statement. Discuss reasons with the class.

B Group work

Suggested teaching time:	4–7 minutes	Your actual teaching time:

- Divide the class into groups of three or four. After the groups compare their answers and explain their reasons, ask, *Did everyone in your group have the same answers on the survey? If you had different answers, what were your reasons?* Have groups share the results of their discussion with the class.

Workbook

B ▶ 5:18 **PHOTO STORY** Read and listen to a conversation about a moral dilemma.

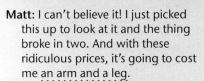

Matt: I can't believe it! I just picked this up to look at it and the thing broke in two. And with these ridiculous prices, it's going to cost me an arm and a leg.

Noah: Oh, forget it. I'll bet it was already broken.

Matt: You're probably right.

Noah: Just put it back on the shelf. The place is empty. No one saw. Let's just split.

Matt: I couldn't do that.

Noah: Why not? You said it yourself. The prices are ridiculous.

Matt: Well, put yourself in the owner's shoes. Suppose the plate were yours? How would you feel if someone broke it and didn't tell you?

Noah: Well I'm *not* the owner. And, anyway, for him it would be just a drop in the bucket. To *you* it's a lot of money.

Matt: Maybe so. But if I ran out without telling him, I couldn't face myself.

C **FOCUS ON LANGUAGE** Match each idiom from the Photo Story with its meaning.

1 an arm and a leg   c
2 split   e
3 put yourself in someone's shoes   d
4 a drop in the bucket   a
5 I couldn't face myself.   b

a a small amount of money
b I would feel bad about it.
c a lot of money
d imagine another person's point of view
e leave

D **THINK AND EXPLAIN** Answer the following questions. Support your answers with quotations from the Photo Story.
Answers may vary.
1 Does Noah think Matt broke the plate?
No, he doesn't think Matt broke it because he says, "I'll bet it was already broken."
2 Why does Noah think it would be easy to leave without saying anything? Noah thinks it would be easy
to leave without saying anything because "The place is empty. No one saw (what happened)."
3 What does Matt want to do about the plate?
He wants to tell the owner to make himself feel better about what happened. ". . . if I ran out without telling
him, I couldn't face myself."

SPEAKING

A **SURVEY** Look at "Moral Dilemmas" and the Photo Story again. Do you agree with the statements below? Circle <u>yes</u> or <u>no</u>, and then give a reason for your answers.

1 Andrew should buy the chocolate with the lower price.	yes / no	
2 Victoria should keep the watch.	yes / no	
3 Amber should tell the waiter there's a mistake.	yes / no	
4 Daniel should send the second jacket back.	yes / no	
5 Matt should tell the store owner what happened.	yes / no	

B **GROUP WORK** Form small groups. Compare your answers and explain your reasons.

GOAL Discuss ethical choices

GRAMMAR *The unreal conditional*

> **Remember:** Conditional sentences express the results of actions or conditions. The real conditional expresses the results of real conditions—conditions that exist.
> If I don't use English in class, I won't learn to speak it.

Meaning

Unreal conditional sentences describe the results of unreal conditions—conditions that don't exist.

unreal action or condition	result (if it were true)
If I **found** a wallet in the street,	I'**d try** to return it. (unreal: I haven't found one.)

> **Contraction**
> would → 'd

Formation

In the if clause, use the simple past tense. For the verb be, always use were.
In the result clause, use would + a base form.

unreal action or condition	result (if it were true)
If I **had** to make a hard decision,	I **would try** to do the right thing
If she **knew** how to speak French,	she'**d help** them.
If you **broke** something in a store,	**would** you **pay** for it?
If you **were** Matt,	what **would** you **do**?
If I **were** you,	I **wouldn't do** that.
If you **weren't** my friend,	I **wouldn't tell** you what happened.

Note: In real and unreal conditional sentences, the clauses can occur in either order. Use a comma if the if clause comes first.

If I knew, I would tell you. OR I would tell you if I knew.

> **Be careful!**
> Don't use **would** in the **if** clause.
> If I knew his name, I would tell you.
> NOT If I ~~would know~~ his name . . .

> **GRAMMAR BOOSTER** p. 140
> Expressing ethics and obligation: expansion
> • should, ought to, had better
> • have to, must, be supposed to

A UNDERSTAND THE GRAMMAR Check the conditional sentences that describe an unreal condition.

- ☑ **1** If we ate in a restaurant, I would pay the bill.
- ☐ **2** I'll pay the bill if we eat in a restaurant.
- ☐ **3** If you get a haircut, you'll look younger.
- ☑ **4** His wife would worry if he came home really late.

- ☑ **5** If I were you, I'd tell him the truth.
- ☐ **6** If I have problem with my office computer, I always ask my co-worker Jim to help.
- ☑ **7** If they sent me the wrong pants, I would return them.

B GRAMMAR PRACTICE Complete each unreal conditional sentence with the correct forms of the verbs.

1 If they ......**put**...... the wrong price on the coat, ...**would**...... you ......**buy**...... it without telling
the clerk?
<small>put</small> <small>buy</small>

2 I'm sure you ......**would say**...... something if the restaurant check ......**were**...... wrong.
<small>say</small> <small>be</small>

3 If I ......**found**...... an expensive piece of jewelry in a public bathroom and ......**couldn't**...... find the owner,
I ......**wouldn't keep**...... it.
<small>find</small> <small>can not</small>
<small>not keep</small>

4 If you ......**were**...... friends with someone who did something wrong, ...**would**...... you ......**say**......
something to him or her?
<small>be</small> <small>say</small>

5 If you ......**had**...... two tickets, ...**would**...... you ......**give**...... one to a friend?
<small>have</small> <small>give</small>

6 What ...**would happen**... if it ......**snowed**...... here tomorrow?
<small>happen</small> <small>snow</small>

7 They ......**would go**...... to India if they ......**had**...... the money.
<small>go</small> <small>have</small>

8 If you ......**received**...... two jackets instead of the one you ordered, ...**would**...... you ......**send**...... one
of them back?
<small>receive</small> <small>send</small>

9 If they ......**were**...... here, I ......**would tell**...... them what happened.
<small>be</small> <small>tell</small>

GRAMMAR

Suggested teaching time:	12–17 minutes	Your actual teaching time:	

- On the board, write *conditional sentences*. Direct students' attention to the Remember box and example sentence. Be sure students understand that a conditional sentence has an *if* clause, which introduces the condition, and a result clause. Explain that the real conditional expresses the results of real conditions that actually exist.

- Ask students to suggest other results for the condition *If I don't use English in class*. (Possible response: My teacher will give me a bad grade.)

- On the board, write *The unreal conditional*. Explain that, unlike the real conditional, the unreal conditional describes an imaginary situation and its result. Write on the board *If I were you, I would study harder.* Ask *Is it possible for me to be you?* (No.)

- Ask a student to read the explanation under *Meaning* and the example sentence. Write it on the board. Have students circle the verbs in each clause. (Found; 'd try.) Make sure students understand that *'d* is the contraction for *would*.

- Read the *Formation* grammar point. Call on students to read the example sentences. After each one, ask if the person actually has to do what is proposed in the *if* clause:

  Do I have to make a hard decision? (No.)
  Does she know how to speak French? (No.)
  Did you break something in a store? (No.)
  Are you Matt? (No.)
  Am I you? (No.)
  Are you my friend? (Yes.)

- Read the Note and then ask students to change the order of the clauses in the example sentences. Tell students that in information questions, it's more common to begin with the question: *What would you do if . . .* although it's correct to say questions with the clauses in either order.

- Direct students' attention to the Be careful! box. Make sure they understand not to use *would* in the *if* clause.

Option: GRAMMAR BOOSTER *(Teaching notes p. T140)*

 Inductive Grammar Charts

A Understand the grammar

Suggested teaching time:	5–8 minutes	Your actual teaching time:	

- To review, ask *What's an unreal condition?* (A condition that doesn't exist.)

- Have a volunteer read item 5. Then ask *Am I you?* (No, therefore the condition is unreal.) Point out that the form provides another hint that the condition is unreal. Ask *What is the verb form in the* if *clause?* (Simple past tense: *were.*) *What is the form in the result clause?* (Would + base form, *tell.*)

- Have students complete the rest of the exercise in pairs. Then review answers with the class.

Option: *(+5 minutes)* To expand the exercise, have pairs write two questions for each sentence. For example,
1. Would you pay the bill if we ate in the restaurant? Who would pay if we ate in a restaurant? Move around the room and help as needed. Then ask pairs to read their questions to the class. Call on volunteers to answer the questions.

B Grammar practice

Suggested teaching time:	6–9 minutes	Your actual teaching time:	

- Write on the board If I found money on the street, I would probably keep it. Ask *What is the verb in the* if *clause of this unreal conditional sentence?* (Found.) *What is the verb in the result clause?* (Would keep.)

- Reverse the order of clauses and write on the board I would probably keep the money if I found it on the street. Ask *Does this sentence have the same meaning?* (Yes.) Then ask students to change the sentence into a question. (Would you keep the money if you found it on the street?)

- Tell students to complete the exercise and watch the order of clauses. Remind them that the simple past is in the *if* clause and *would* + base form appears in the result clause.

- Review answers with the class.

 **Extra Grammar Exercises**

CONVERSATION MODEL

A ▶5:19 Read and listen . . .

Suggested teaching time:	2 minutes	Your actual teaching time:

These conversation strategies are implicit in the model:
• Say "You think so?" to reconfirm someone's opinion.
• Provide an emphatic response with "Absolutely."

• Tell students to look at the photo. Ask *Where are they?* (In a restaurant / café.)
• After students read and listen to the conversation, read aloud the woman's first line and have students suggest another way of saying *They didn't charge us for the desserts.* (The restaurant didn't include the cost of the desserts in the check.)
• Have students read and listen again. Ask a student to read the confirming responses that can replace *Absolutely*, and then play the accompanying audio.
• Have students work in pairs to practice the last two lines of the Conversation Model, trying out the different confirming responses. Move around the room as students work.

B ▶5:20 Rhythm and intonation

Suggested teaching time:	3 minutes	Your actual teaching time:

• Have students repeat each line chorally. Make sure they:
  ◦ use rising intonation for *Really?* and *You think so?*
  ◦ put extra stress on the third syllable in *Absolutely*.
• Point out that the second syllable of *didn't* is greatly reduced in spoken English.
• ▶5:21 **Express an ethical obligation** Have students listen and repeat the expressions in the box. Have them substitute *We should tell the waiter* and *We ought to tell the waiter* for *We'd better tell the waiter* as they practice the Conversation Model.

PRONUNCIATION

A ▶5:22 Notice how the /d/ . . .

Suggested teaching time:	2 minutes	Your actual teaching time:

 Pronunciation Coach Video

• As students read and listen to the questions, tell them to notice how /d/ + /y/ becomes /dʒ/. Point out that these are information questions and use falling intonation.
• Have students listen again and repeat in the pauses.
• Ask students to practice reading the sentences in pairs. Move around the room and listen for correct assimilation of sounds and correct intonation.

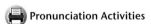 Pronunciation Activities

B Pair work

Suggested teaching time:	4 minutes	Your actual teaching time:

• Give students a few minutes to fill in the questions. Move around the room and help as needed. Make sure students use the correct verb forms.
• Then have pairs ask each other the questions and answer them. Listen for the assimilation of *would you*.

NOW YOU CAN Discuss ethical choices

A Conversation activator

Suggested teaching time:	6–8 minutes	Your actual teaching time:

 Conversation Activator Video

• *Note:* You can print the script or you can show a running transcript on the video player on the ActiveTeach. The script also appears on page 188 of this Teacher's Edition.
• ▶5:23 **Situations that require an ethical choice** Have students look at the pictures in the box as they listen and repeat the expressions. Make sure they understand the different moral dilemmas. Explain as needed. Ask *Have you ever had experiences like these?* Have students explain.
• Model the activity by role-playing the conversation with a more confident student, and demonstrate ways of continuing the conversation. Play the role of Student A.

DON'T STOP! Encourage students to keep their conversations going by saying more. Tell them to use the language in the Recycle box.

• For more support, play the Conversation Activator Video before students do this activity themselves. In Scene 1, the actors use different words in the gaps from the ones in the Conversation Model. In Scene 2, the actors extend the conversation. After each scene, ask students how the model has been changed by the actors.

 Conversation Activator Video Script; Conversation Activator Pair Work Cards; Learning Strategies

B Discussion

Suggested teaching time:	5–7 minutes	Your actual teaching time:

• Ask students to work with a new partner to discuss ethical choices. If students are reluctant to talk about their own choices, tell them to talk about someone they know. Remind students to use the simple past.
• Make a list on the board of ethical situations. Ask students to share how they would act in the different situations. Listen for the correct use of the unreal conditional: *If there were extra money in my paycheck, I wouldn't say anything.*

EXTRAS

Workbook or MyEnglishLab

 Speaking Activities: Unit 10, Activity 1

CONVERSATION MODEL

A ▶5:19 Read and listen to people discussing an
ethical choice.

A: Look at this. They didn't charge us for the desserts.

B: Really? I think we'd better tell the waiter.

A: You think so?

B: Absolutely. If we didn't tell him, it would be wrong.

B ▶5:20 **RHYTHM AND INTONATION** Listen again
and repeat. Then practice the Conversation
Model with a partner.

▶5:21 **Express an ethical obligation**

We'd better tell	
We should tell	the waiter.
We ought to tell	

PRONUNCIATION *Blending of d + y in would you*

A ▶5:22 Notice how the /d/ and /y/ sounds blend to /dʒ/ in questions
with "would you." Read and listen. Then listen again and repeat.

1 What would you do if the waiter didn't charge you for the dessert?

2 What would you do if you found a wallet on the street?

3 Who would you call if you were sick?

4 Where would you go if you wanted a great meal?

B **PAIR WORK** Complete the following questions. Ask a partner the questions, using blending
with <u>would you</u>. Then answer your partner's questions.

1 What would you do if .... ?

2 Where would you go if .... ?

3 When would you eat if .... ?

NOW YOU CAN Discuss ethical choices

A **CONVERSATION ACTIVATOR** With a partner,
change the Conversation Model. Discuss
ethical choices, using the situations in the
pictures. Then change roles.

A: Look .... They ....

B: .... ? I think .... 'd better ....

A: You think so?

B: Absolutely. If .... , ...

DON'T STOP!
• Say more.

 RECYCLE THIS LANGUAGE.
I couldn't face myself.
Put yourself in [his / her / their] shoes.
If you don't tell the [clerk], [she'll have to pay for it].
If [he didn't charge us], [we would tell him].

▶5:23 **Situations that require an ethical choice**

They didn't charge us for the cake.

They undercharged me.

They gave me too much change.

They gave me more than I ordered.

B **DISCUSSION** Tell your classmates about an
ethical choice <u>you</u> had to make in the past.

GOAL Return someone else's property

CONVERSATION MODEL

A ▶5:24 Read and listen to a conversation about returning property.

A: Excuse me. I think you forgot something.

B: I did?

A: Isn't this jacket hers?

B: Oh, you're right. It is. That's nice of you.

A: Don't mention it.

▶5:26 **Acknowledging thanks**
Don't mention it.
My pleasure.
You're welcome.
Not at all.

B ▶5:25 **RHYTHM AND INTONATION** Listen again and repeat. Then practice the Conversation Model with a partner.

GRAMMAR *Possessive pronouns / Whose*

Possessive pronouns can replace nouns and noun phrases. They answer questions with Whose and clarify answers to questions with Which.

A: **Whose** coat is that? **B:** It's **mine**. (= It's my coat.)
A: **Which** is <u>her cup</u>? **B:** This one is **hers**.

subject pronouns	possessive adjectives	possessive pronouns	
I	my	mine	That's <u>my jacket</u>. / It's **mine**.
you	your	yours	<u>Your dinner</u> was great. / **Yours** was great.
he	his	his	Are these <u>his keys</u>? / Are these **his**?
she	her	hers	She drives <u>her car</u> to work. / She drives **hers** to work.
we	our	ours	These are <u>our shoes</u>. / These are **ours**.
they	their	theirs	They finished <u>their assignment</u>. / They finished **theirs**.

Be careful!
• Don't use a possessive adjective in place of a possessive pronoun.
  Is this **yours**? NOT Is this ~~your~~?
• Don't use a noun after a possessive pronoun.
  These shoes are **mine**. NOT These are ~~mine shoes~~.

GRAMMAR BOOSTER p. 141
• Possessive nouns: review and expansion
• Pronouns: summary

A **GRAMMAR PRACTICE** Replace the noun phrases with possessive pronouns.

1 Those gloves are ~~my gloves~~. *(mine)*

2 That is ~~her coat~~. *(hers)*

3 The books on that table are ~~Mr. Davison's~~. *(his)*

4 Their car and ~~our car~~ are parked on the same street. *(ours)*

5 Are those my tickets or ~~her tickets~~? *(hers)*

6 The white house is ~~my mother's house~~. *(hers)*

7 Is this painting ~~your painting~~ or ~~her brother's painting~~? *(yours) (his)*

8 The newspaper under the chair is ~~his daughter's paper~~. *(hers)*

9 Is this DVD ~~your DVD~~ or ~~your friends'~~? *(yours) (theirs)*

10 Are these ~~your son's shoes~~? *(his)*

CONVERSATION MODEL

A ▶5:24 **Read and listen . . .**

Suggested teaching time:	2 minutes	Your actual teaching time:

> This conversation strategy is implicit in the model:
> • Acknowledge thanks with "Don't mention it."

- Before students read and listen to the conversation, give them a minute to study the picture. Then tell them to close their books. Ask *Where are the people in the picture?* (In a restaurant / café.) *What do you think the woman is saying to the man?* (Here's your daughter's jacket.)
- Have students read and listen to the conversation.
- Check comprehension by asking:
  Whose jacket is the woman holding? (The girl's.)
  How do you know? (She says, "Isn't this jacket hers?")
  Why does the man say "I did?"? (Because he doesn't realize he forgot something.)
  What do you think the woman means when she says "Don't mention it."? (You're welcome.)

Option: (+5 minutes) For a challenge, have pairs thank each other and respond with the different expressions for acknowledging thanks. For example:
A: *Thank you for helping me with the computer.*
B: *No problem.*

A: *Thanks for going with me to the art museum.*
B: *Sure.*

B ▶5:25 **Rhythm and intonation**

Suggested teaching time:	3 minutes	Your actual teaching time:

- Have students repeat each line. Make sure they:
  ◦ use rising intonation for *I did?* and *Isn't this jacket hers?*
  ◦ pause after *Oh.*
  ◦ stress *right* in *You're right.*
  ◦ use equal stress on all words in *Don't mention it.*

- ▶5:26 **Acknowledging thanks** Point out the phrases for acknowledging thanks and play the accompanying audio. Ask pairs of students to read the last two lines in the conversation, replacing *Don't mention it* with the different expressions.

> **Language and culture**
> • The most common way of acknowledging thanks is *You're welcome.* The expressions *My pleasure, Don't mention it,* and *Not at all* are considered more formal. *No problem* is less formal, and *Sure* is very informal.

GRAMMAR

Suggested teaching time:	6–11 minutes	Your actual teaching time:

- Have students read the first three lines in the Grammar box and the examples. Ask *What words does* mine *replace?* (My coat.) *What words does* hers *replace?* (Her cup.)

- Hold up a book and say *This is my book. This book is mine.* Give the book to Student A and say *This is John's book. This book is his.* Have Student A give the book to Student B and answer the question *Whose book is this?* Have students continue passing the book and answering the question.

- To practice clarifying answers to questions with *which,* show students your pen and then borrow a pen from a student. Ask *Which pen is his / hers? Which pen is mine?*

- Go over the chart comparing subject pronouns, possessive adjectives, and possessive pronouns and the examples.

- Ask volunteers to read the sentence pairs.

- Read the Be careful! note to differentiate possessive adjectives and possessive pronouns. Write on the board *That's my jacket. It's my.* Ask *Why is that incorrect?* (My is a possessive adjective.) Then write *It's mine jacket.* Ask *Why is that incorrect?* (We don't use a noun after a possessive pronoun.)

> **Language and culture**
> • **From the Longman Corpus:** A common error of English learners is confusing possessive pronouns and possessive adjectives, such as using *yours, hers, ours,* and *theirs* to modify plural nouns. Possessive pronouns are never used as possessive adjectives.

Option: (+5–10 minutes) To extend the activity, read the first sentence in each of the following pairs and have students complete the second sentence. *1. These aren't your keys. These keys are ___.* (Possible responses: mine, his, hers, ours, theirs. [Any logical possessive pronoun is correct.]) *2. The green house is Mary's. This house is ___. 3. My phone number is 555-3430. What's ___? 4. Here's Edwin's car. Where's ___? 5. Do you have your book? I have ___. 6. I showed you my license. Now show me ___.*

Option: GRAMMAR BOOSTER (*Teaching notes p. T141*)

 **Inductive Grammar Charts**

A **Grammar practice**

Suggested teaching time:	3–5 minutes	Your actual teaching time:

- To model the task, focus on item 6. Draw students' attention to the words that are crossed out. Ask *What possessive pronoun will replace* my mother's house? (Hers, NOT mine.) Tell students to pay particular attention to numbers 6–10 and not be deceived by the possessive adjectives that precede the nouns.

- Have students complete the task in pairs. Move around the room and help students as needed.

- Review answers with the class by asking students to read the corrected sentences aloud.

B Grammar practice

Suggested teaching time:	3–4 minutes	Your actual teaching time:

- Begin by reminding students that a possessive *adjective* is followed by a noun, and a possessive *pronoun* is not followed by a noun. Have students find the items that require a possessive adjective. (2B parents; 3A suitcase; 3B suitcase; 4B necklace; 5A car; 6A house; 6B office.)
- After students complete the statements and questions, tell them to compare answers with a partner.
- Review answers by calling on pairs to read the conversations.

C ▶5:27 Listen to activate grammar

Suggested teaching time:	4–6 minutes	Your actual teaching time:

- Before students listen, have them skim the statements. Ask *Which item can you answer before the listening?* (Second blank in 2.) *Why?* (Because we know we need a possessive pronoun to replace "Brad's wife," a woman, hers.)
- As students prepare to listen, tell them to pay attention if a male or female is speaking and if the person speaking refers to one or two people.
- Play the audio. Have students compare answers in pairs, and then discuss any questions with the class.

AUDIOSCRIPT

CONVERSATION 1
F: Hey! Look what I found under the table!
M: What?
F: A shopping bag from the Emporium. It's full of clothes.
M: No kidding. I wonder whose it is?
F: Maybe it belongs to that woman paying at the cashier.
M: You're right . . . Excuse me! Is this bag yours? It was under our table.
F2: Yes, it is. Thanks so much. That's so kind of you!
M: No problem.

AUDIOSCRIPT continues on page T117

 **Extra Grammar Exercises**

NOW YOU CAN Return someone else's property

A Conversation activator

Suggested teaching time:	8 minutes	Your actual teaching time:

 **Conversation Activator Video**

- *Note:* You can print the script or you can show a running transcript on the video player on the ActiveTeach. The script also appears on page 188 of this Teacher's Edition.
- Ask students to name the personal items on the page. (Wallet, glove, jacket, cell phone, handbag, pen, books, glasses.) Explain that these are items people often lose or forget.

- Refer students to the Conversation Model on page 114 to review returning someone else's property. Have students also review the ways of acknowledging thanks.
- Be sure to reinforce the use of the conversation strategy. For example, for "Don't mention it" and "Not at all," do a quick wave of your hand to demonstrate that a *Thank you* is not necessary.
- Model the activity by role-playing the conversation with a more confident student and demonstrate ways of continuing the conversation.
- Remind students to change roles after they have finished their conversations.
- After pairs have completed the activity, have students role-play their conversations for the class.
- For more support, play the Conversation Activator Video before students do this activity themselves. In Scene 1, the actors use different words in the gaps from the ones in the Conversation Model. In Scene 2, the actors extend the conversation. After each scene, ask students how the model has been changed by the actors.

 Conversation Activator Video Script; Conversation Activator Pair Work Cards

B Group work

Suggested teaching time:	8–10 minutes	Your actual teaching time:

- To prepare students, explain that they will now role-play returning someone else's property.
- Have all students contribute one or two items to make a lost property pile on a desk or table. Tell students to pick up one item (not their own) from the table and then mingle, asking questions to find the owner. Once they find the owner, they role-play a conversation.
- Model the activity. Approach a student with a pencil in your hand and say *Excuse me. I think you forgot something. Is this yours?* Write on the board *No, it's not mine.*
- Encourage students to follow the model in the book. Explain that the activity is not finished until they find the chosen object's owner and their own object has been returned to them.

C Extension

Suggested teaching time:	8–10 minutes	Your actual teaching time:

- Divide the class into two groups and have each student in each group place two completely different items on a table or desk. Read the instructions and the sample quotes. Encourage students to use *whose* and *which* in their questions.
- Move around the room and monitor language. Correct students as needed.

EXTRAS

Workbook or MyEnglishLab

 Speaking Activities: Unit 10, Activity 2

B **GRAMMAR PRACTICE** Complete the conversations. Circle the correct adjectives and pronouns.

1 A: Whose umbrella is this, (he / **his**) or (her / **hers**)?
   B: I'm not sure. Ask them if it's (their / **theirs**).

2 A: Who is more conservative about clothes? Your parents or your husband's parents?
   B: (He / **His**), I think. (**My** / Mine) parents are pretty liberal.

3 A: Is this (ours / **our**) suitcase?
   B: No, I already got (**our** / ours) suitcase, so this one can't be (our / **ours**).

4 A: I found this necklace near Carrie's desk. Is it (her / **hers**)?
   B: No, it's (**my** / mine) necklace. I'm so happy someone found it!

5 A: Is that (**their** / theirs) car?
   B: No, (their / **theirs**) is the black one over there.

6 A: Where should we meet? At (**your** / yours) house or (my / **mine**)?
   B: Neither. Let's meet at (**my** / mine) office.

C ▶5:27 **LISTEN TO ACTIVATE GRAMMAR** Listen to the conversations and complete each statement with a possessive pronoun.

1 The bag is ......**hers**...... .
2 The phone is ......**his**...... , but the keys belong to Brad's wife. They're ......**hers**...... .
3 The coat isn't ......**his**...... .
4 The concert tickets aren't ......**theirs**...... .

NOW YOU CAN **Return someone else's property**

A **CONVERSATION ACTIVATOR** With a partner, change the Conversation Model to role-play returning the items in the pictures. Then change roles.

A: Excuse me. I think you forgot something.
B: I did?
A: .... yours?
B: Oh, you're right. .... That's nice of you.
A: ....

B **GROUP WORK** First, collect personal items from your classmates. Then role-play returning someone else's property. Walk around the room to find the owners. Use possessive pronouns.

C **EXTENSION** Place all your classmates' personal items on a table. Ask about each item. Identify the owner, using possessive pronouns.

❝ Whose phone is this? ❞

❝ It's his. ❞

BEFORE YOU LISTEN

EXPLORE YOUR IDEAS Which actions would be OK, and which wouldn't be OK for the following people: you? your parents? your grandparents? your own teenaged child?

> " It wouldn't be OK if my grandmother pierced her nose. Face piercing is for young people. She's too old. "

get a tattoo

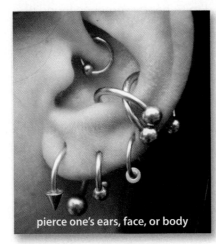
pierce one's ears, face, or body

dye one's hair a wild color

LISTENING COMPREHENSION

A ▶5:28 **LISTEN FOR MAIN IDEAS** Listen to each conversation. Then circle the correct word or phrase to complete each statement.

1 a Beth thinks it's (OK / not OK) to wear an earring to the office.

  b Beth (convinces / doesn't convince) Luke.

2 a Celia's husband thinks it's (OK / wrong) for a woman to have a tattoo.

  b Celia's husband thinks it's (OK / wrong) for a man to have a tattoo.

3 a The first man is (happy / not happy) that his daughter is going to law school.

  b He wants his daughter to (stay home / work).

4 a Kate's dad is (worried / not worried) about what people think of Kate.

  b Kate is (worried / not worried) about what people think of her.

B **UNDERSTAND VOCABULARY FROM CONTEXT** Read the following quotations from the conversations. Then choose the meaning of each underlined word or phrase. Listen again if necessary.

1 "But lots of people are old-fashioned, and they don't think men should wear earrings."

  a preferring the way things were in the past

  b preferring the way things are now

2 "What a double standard!"

  a having the same rules for everyone

  b having different rules for different people

3 "That's a little sexist, if you ask me!"

  a not treating men and women in the same way

  b treating men and women in the same way

4 "But modesty is very important for girls."

  a wearing clothes that cover one's body

  b wearing clothes that show one's body

BEFORE YOU LISTEN

Explore your ideas

Suggested teaching time:	5–8 minutes	Your actual teaching time:

- Begin by reviewing the pictures and their captions with the class. Provide vocabulary as needed.

- Ask a volunteer to read the questions. Then draw the chart below on the board.

	You	Your parents	Your grandparents	Your teenaged child
Get a tattoo				
Pierce one's ears, face, or body				
Dye one's hair a wild color				

- To model the activity, ask volunteers to share their opinions while you write them in the chart. Invite students to give examples of themselves or people they know who have tattoos, body piercings, or wild-colored hair.

Option: (+5–10 minutes) You could print and distribute copies of the chart. Have students work in pairs or small groups to discuss their answers and fill in their charts.

 Graphic Organizers

LISTENING COMPREHENSION

A ▶5:28 Listen for main ideas

Suggested teaching time:	6–8 minutes	Your actual teaching time:

- After students listen with their books closed, ask them to summarize each conversation. (1. Should a man wear an earring to the office on his first day at a new job? 2. A man has a tattoo but doesn't like his wife having a tattoo. 3. A father wants his daughter to stay home and have children rather than be a lawyer. 4. A father wants his daughter to dress modestly.)

- Before listening again, ask students to open their books and try to complete as many statements as they can.

- If necessary, have students listen again to complete the exercise. Have them compare answers in pairs.

- Review answers with the class and explain any unknown terms; for example, *That's crazy* is a very informal but strong way to disagree. Tell students to use it carefully as it could be interpreted as insulting in more formal situations. The phrase *You got it* is an informal way of saying *Yes, that's right* or *Yes, you understood. You got it*

can also be used as an informal affirmative response to a request. For example:
   A: *Could you finish the report by 2:00?*
   B: *You got it.*

- Tell pairs to correct all of the false statements. If necessary, allow students to listen once more to check their answers.

AUDIOSCRIPT

CONVERSATION 1
  F: Luke! Tomorrow's your first day in your new job. You're not going to wear that earring, are you?
  M: I was going to. Why not?
  F: Well, if I were you, I wouldn't wear it. It may not be appropriate in the office.
  M: That's crazy. What's wrong with an earring, Beth?
  F: Nothing. But lots of people are old-fashioned, and they don't think men should wear earrings . . . at least at the office.
  M: You're only twenty-eight and you sound like my grandmother. This is the twenty-first century. In any case, I need to be who I am. I'm an individualist.

CONVERSATION 2
  F1: Celia, what a great tattoo! When did you get it?
  F2: Just last week. But my husband thinks it's awful.
  F1: Doesn't he have one, too?
  F2: Yes. But he says it's not the same thing.
  F1: You mean he thinks it's OK for a man but not for a woman?
  F2: You got it.
  F1: What a double standard!

CONVERSATION 3
  M1: Mark, I'm really unhappy. My daughter wants to go to law school.
  M2: That's great! What's the problem?
  M1: Well, I was hoping she'd marry a lawyer, not be one!
  M2: Why's that?
  M1: Well, it's just that I think men should be lawyers and women should stay home and have children.
  M2: That's a little sexist, if you ask me!

CONVERSATION 4
  M: Kate! You can't go out in those clothes. I can see your tummy!
  F: So? That's the style. Don't you watch TV? Read magazines?
  M: I don't care. Girls should be modest. People will think you're a bad girl.
  F: But, Dad. You know I'm a good person. I follow all the rules. Everyone knows that!
  M: That's true. But modesty is very important for girls. If you're modest, people will know you're a good girl.

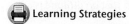 Learning Strategies

B Understand vocabulary from context

Suggested teaching time:	5 minutes	Your actual teaching time:

- After reading the directions, have students work in pairs to choose the correct definitions, and then review answers with the class.

- To check comprehension, ask *What's the double standard referred to in the conversation between Celia and her friend?* (Celia's husband has a tattoo but doesn't think it's OK for a woman to have one.) *What sexist ideas does the man in the third conversation have?* (His daughter should not go to law school and become a lawyer but should get married, stay home, and have children.)

C Apply new vocabulary

Suggested teaching time:	4 minutes	Your actual teaching time:

- Ask students to complete the task individually. Move around the room as students work. If they have difficulty with the vocabulary, refer them to Exercise B.
- After students write their examples, tell them to compare examples in pairs.
- Invite students to share their examples with the class without mentioning the word or phrase it illustrates. Have the class guess if the example illustrates *old-fashioned, a double standard, sexist,* or *modesty.*
- After each example, ask the class *Do you agree that this is a [double standard]? Why? Why not?*

D Pair work

Suggested teaching time:	4–7 minutes	Your actual teaching time:

- Ask the class to look at the photo. Have a student read the caption. Ask *Would you see something like this today?* (Not in most places in the U.S.)
- Have pairs look at the sample answer in quotes and discuss the picture in more detail using the words as indicated.
- Move around the room and help as needed.

Option: (+5–10 minutes) To challenge students, tell them to imagine they are one of the people in the photograph. Have them write a paragraph describing what they were thinking and feeling when the photograph was taken. Then group students together who imagined they were the same person and have them compare reactions. Finally have groups share their reactions with the class.

NOW YOU CAN Express personal values

A Idea framing

Suggested teaching time:	5–8 minutes	Your actual teaching time:

- Ask a student to read the title of the self-test. Ask *What are values?* (They are a person's beliefs about what is right and what is wrong.)
- Have volunteers read the sentences in the test. Make sure students understand them. Explain that *an attitude* is an opinion or point of view.
- Tell students to work individually to complete the self-test and then compare responses in pairs.
- Ask students to share their answers and examples with the class.

B Notepadding

Suggested teaching time:	6–8 minutes	Your actual teaching time:

- Read the questions aloud. Make sure students understand the questions and the task.
- Move around the room as students work individually. Help with examples as needed.

C Group work

Suggested teaching time:	10–13 minutes	Your actual teaching time:

- Direct students' attention to the language in the Recycle box. Ask volunteers to read the ways to express agreement and disagreement, likes and dislikes, and adjectives.
- Divide the class into small groups to discuss their opinions on the various topics. Encourage students to use all the language in the Recycle box. Ask them to number the language in the order they use it. Remind students that they should give examples for their reasons.

EXTRAS

Workbook

 Speaking Activities: Unit 10, Activity 3

AUDIOSCRIPT continued for page T115 (**C** Listen to Activate Grammar)

CONVERSATION 2 [F = Korean]
F: Brad! I think you might have dropped your keys and cell phone.
M: What? I don't think so. My phone's right here in my pocket . . . Hey! No, it isn't. Let me have a look at that phone.
F: Here you go.
M: Wow. You're right! That is mine. Where did you find it?
F: Here. Right next to these keys. I suppose these are yours, too.
M: Well, actually, the keys are my wife's. She's going to be so happy I didn't lose them.

CONVERSATION 3 [M = U.S. regional]
M: I don't believe it! This coat isn't mine.
F: What do you mean it isn't yours?
M: It isn't mine. Remember when we got to the restaurant? I hung up my coat with all the others. You know how it is. All these raincoats look the same.
F: What are you going to do?
M: I'll drive back to the restaurant and see if my coat's still there.
F: And what if it isn't?
M: I don't know. Maybe the person who took my coat will call. I have my name and address in the vest pocket. Anyway, I'll cross that bridge when I come to it.

CONVERSATION 4
F: What is going on here? These aren't the right tickets!
M: What are you talking about?
F: They're for tomorrow, not tonight.
M: How could that have happened?
F: Uh-oh.
M: What?
F: Did you get these from the kitchen counter or the dining room table?
M: The dining room.
F: Oh, no. Those were the tickets I got for Julie and Glenn! I told you to take the ones from the kitchen.
M: Oops.

C **APPLY NEW VOCABULARY**   Write an example for each word or phrase from your own experience. Compare examples with a partner.

> 66 I think an example of old-fashioned is not letting teenagers go out on dates. 99

old-fashioned	
a double standard	
sexist	
modesty	

D **PAIR WORK**   Discuss the picture. Use the following words and phrases in your discussion: old-fashioned, sexist, double standard, modesty.

> 66 He's measuring the woman's swimsuit. If she were a man, he wouldn't measure it. That's a double standard. 99

Man measuring the length of a woman's swimsuit (U.S., 1920s)

NOW YOU CAN Express personal values

A **IDEA FRAMING**   Complete the Values Self-Test. Then compare answers with a partner. Do you have the same values?

Values Self-Test

Check the boxes that best describe your values. Include a specific example.

1. ❏ I'm modern in my attitudes about modesty.
   ❏ I'm old-fashioned in my attitudes about modesty.
   Explain. _____
   _____
   _____

2. ❏ I think tattoos and body piercing are OK for men.
   ❏ I think tattoos and body piercing are OK for women.
   Explain. _____
   _____
   _____

3. ❏ I think it's OK to have a double standard for different people.
   ❏ I think the rules should be the same for everyone.
   Explain. _____
   _____
   _____

4. ❏ Some people might say I'm sexist.
   ❏ Nobody would say I'm sexist.
   Explain. _____
   _____
   _____

B **NOTEPADDING**   Answer each question and explain your opinion, using examples.

Is it sometimes OK to have a double standard for men and women?
_____
_____
_____

Can people be sexist when they talk about men, or only about women?
_____
_____
_____

Are old-fashioned ideas usually better or worse than modern ideas?
_____
_____
_____

C **GROUP WORK**   Now discuss each question, expressing your personal values. Expect people to disagree with you!

RECYCLE THIS LANGUAGE.

Agreement and disagreement	Likes and dislikes	Adjectives
I agree.	I like __.	liberal
I disagree.	I dislike __.	conservative
It depends.	I hate __.	strict
	I can't stand __.	modest
	I don't mind __.	
	__ drives me crazy!	

BEFORE YOU READ

PREDICT   Look at the headlines of the three news stories. In what way do you think the stories will be similar?

READING   ▶ 5:29

Homeless Man Returns Wallet with $900
Posted on: Monday, 17 April

SANTA ANA, Calif. - A homeless man searching through trash bins for recyclable cans found a missing wallet and returned it to its owner. Kim Bogue, who works in the city, realized that her wallet was missing last week and doubted she'd ever get back the $900 and credit cards inside. "I prayed that night and asked God to help me," said Bogue, who was saving the money for a trip to her native Thailand.

Days later, a homeless man found the wallet wrapped in a plastic bag in the trash, where Bogue had accidentally thrown it away with her lunch. He gave it to Sherry Wesley, who works in a nearby building. "He came to me with the wad of money and said, 'This probably belongs to someone that you work with. Can you return it?'" Wesley said.

"He has a very good heart," said Bogue, who gave the man a $100 reward. "If someone else had found it, the money would have been gone."

Man Risks Life to Save Another

Many people who ride a busy urban subway wonder, "What would happen if I fell off the platform and onto the tracks? What would I do?" Others wonder, "What would I do if someone else fell?"

That question was answered in a split-second decision made by "subway hero" Wesley Autrey, a fifty-year-old New York City construction worker on his way to work. Autrey jumped onto the tracks to save a fellow passenger from an oncoming New York City subway train.

The passenger, Cameron Hollopeter, 20, a film student at the New York Film Academy, had fallen between the tracks after suffering a seizure. Autrey rolled Hollopeter into a gap between the rails and covered him with his own body just as the train entered the station. Both men survived.

"I don't feel like I did something spectacular; I just saw someone who needed help," Mr. Autrey said. "I did what I felt was right."

An act of honesty by airport screener

NEW DELHI: In a display of honesty, a security agent at the Indira Gandhi International Airport handed over a small plastic bag with US $3,000 in cash to a passenger who had completely forgotten the bag after it passed through the airport screening machine.

Noticing that the bag had been left behind, Dalbir Singh made an announcement asking passengers to come forward to claim it. However, when no one claimed it, Singh inspected the baggage tag and guessed it probably belonged to a passenger en route to Mumbai. An announcement was made on the next flight to Mumbai, and the owner of the bag came forward to collect it.

Singh was given a cash reward for his honesty.

A   **SUMMARIZE**   Summarize one of the articles. Close your book and tell the story in your own words.

B   **INTERPRET INFORMATION**   Discuss each person's motives for his or her actions.

    1 Why did Kim Bogue give the homeless man a reward?   Because he had a good heart.

    2 Why did Wesley Autrey risk his life to save a stranger?   Because he saw someone who needed help.

    3 Why do you think Dalbir Singh returned the money to the passenger?   (Answers will vary)

C   **RELATE TO PERSONAL EXPERIENCE**   Think of a story you have heard about someone who helped a stranger in need. Tell it to the class.

DIGITAL
MORE
EXERCISES

BEFORE YOU READ

Predict

Suggested teaching time:	2 minutes	Your actual teaching time:

- To introduce the topic, ask a student to read the headlines of the articles. Then read the question aloud. Write on the board *kindness and honesty*. Ask students to give examples of kindness and then of honesty. Write them on the board under the appropriate heading. (Possible responses: Helping an older person carry something heavy; reporting finding a lost credit card.)

READING ▶ 5:29

Suggested teaching time:	12–15 minutes	Your actual teaching time:

- As students read the articles, write on the board:
  Which two articles are about money? ("Homeless man . . ." and "An act of honesty . . .")
  In which article could a person have died? ("Man risks life . . .")
  Which act of kindness / honesty could you imagine performing?
- Check comprehension by having students answer the questions in pairs and then reviewing answers with the class.

FYI: If students are having problems with the names in the reading, have them read along a second time while playing the audio. Hearing the names will help students sound them out the next time they read the articles.

 **Learning Strategies**

A Summarize

Suggested teaching time:	3–5 minutes	Your actual teaching time:

- To help students with their summaries, ask *What are five information questions words?* Write on the board *What? When? Where? Why? How?* Explain that students will need to use these words to help them choose important facts about the article.

- Tell students to work individually. Give them a few minutes to choose an article and take notes.

- With their books closed, have students work in pairs and summarize their articles for each other. Encourage students, while they are listening to their partner, to ask questions about anything they don't understand.

- Have students open their books and make sure their summaries are correct.

- Invite volunteers to share their summaries with the class. If appropriate, prompt students by asking questions such as *What happened? Where did it happen? How . . .*

Option: (+8 minutes) As an alternative approach, do this exercise as a jigsaw. Have students form groups of three and count off *1, 2, 3*. Assign each number a different article and tell them to read it individually. Once students have had time to read the article and make notes, tell them to work in their groups and listen to one another's summaries and take notes.

Option: (+8 minutes) Alternatively, have students listen to the audio of the articles and take notes of the main points. Have students prepare their summaries based on their notes.

B Interpret information

Suggested teaching time:	3 minutes	Your actual teaching time:

- Model pronunciation of the names by reading the questions about the articles aloud (Bogue = /boʊg/; Autrey = /'a tri/). Tell students to discuss the questions in pairs.

- After pairs discuss the questions, have students share answers with the class.

C Relate to personal experience

Suggested teaching time:	5 minutes	Your actual teaching time:

- Model the activity by focusing on one article and telling the students a similar story that you have heard. Then ask students to think of stories they've heard or experienced themselves.

- Give students a few minutes to think and make notes. Then ask volunteers to share stories. Encourage students to ask more questions about the stories. After each one, ask *If you were that person, would you act the same way?*

 Extra Reading Comprehension Exercises

NOW YOU CAN Discuss acts of kindness and honesty

A Notepadding

Suggested teaching time:	12–20 minutes	Your actual teaching time:

- Ask students to skim the pictures and situations. Ask *Have any of these situations happened to you?*

- Call on a student to read the first situation and the four questions. Review the meaning of *could*, *should*, and *would*: *Could* + base form expresses possibility; *should* + base form expresses obligation; *would* indicates an unreal condition. To remind students what an unreal conditional is, ask *Did you find my cell phone? What would you do if you found my cell phone?*

- Give the students a few minutes to write their answers. After students answer the questions for each situation, have them compare answers with a partner.

> **Language and culture**
> - An ATM is called a *cashpoint* in British English and a *bank machine* in Canadian English.

B Group work

Suggested teaching time:	8–10 minutes	Your actual teaching time:

Text-mining: Encourage students to find and underline words or phrases that were new to them, and that could be useful in the Group Work discussion. (Possible answers: *wad of money, split-second decision, display of honesty, come forward, cash reward.*) Tell them to try to use the language as they complete the task.

- Ask a student to read the sample quote.

- Divide the class into groups of three or four students. Remind students to: use the unreal conditional, pronounce the /d/ of *would* and the /y/ of *you* as /dʒ/, and use correct rhythm and intonation.

- While students are discussing their responses, move around the room and listen for the correct use of *could* + base form, *should* + base form, and *would* + base form in the result clause of the unreal conditional sentences.

- To review the answers, draw the graphic organizer below on the board or print it out and distribute to students. Do not include the possible responses. Tell students to fill in the first two columns, then discuss. Write students' answers in the last two columns.

Could do	Should do	Would do (you)	Would do (most people)
• accept the coffee • refuse the coffee and order a new one • say Thank you	• refuse it	• accept it from a friend • refuse it from a stranger ✓✓✓	• accept it

- For each situation, ask each student *What would you do [if you found a wallet full of cash]?* Write the responses in the third column. For every repeated answer, add a check mark next to the response.

- Count the responses to see what most people in the class would do. Ask *Do you think this class is an honest group of people?*

 **Graphic Organizers**

EXTRAS

Workbook or MyEnglishLab

 Speaking Activities: Unit 10, Activity 4; "Find Someone Who . . ." Activity

A **NOTEPADDING** Answer the questions about each situation.

Situation: Someone ahead of you at a coffee bar has paid for your coffee.

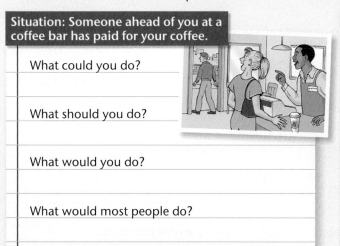

What could you do?

What should you do?

What would you do?

What would most people do?

Situation: A blind man is crossing a street in front of you and a car is coming.

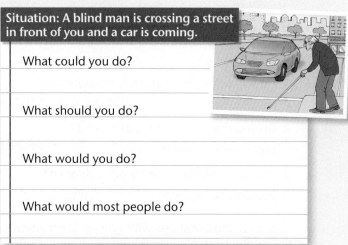

What could you do?

What should you do?

What would you do?

What would most people do?

Situation: You find a wallet full of cash in a restaurant.

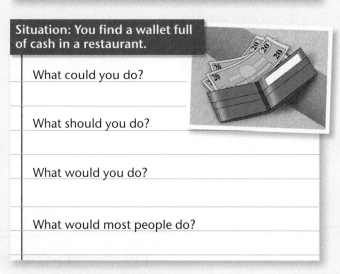

What could you do?

What should you do?

What would you do?

What would most people do?

Situation: You find cash at an ATM.

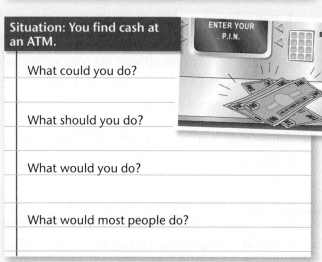

What could you do?

What should you do?

What would you do?

What would most people do?

Situation: The cashier undercharges you.

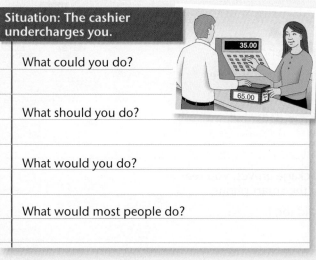

What could you do?

What should you do?

What would you do?

What would most people do?

Situation: You find a gold watch in a department store dressing room.

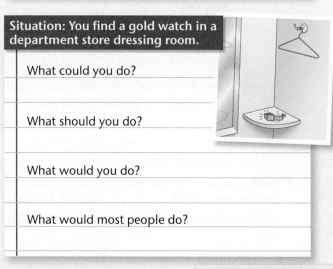

What could you do?

What should you do?

What would you do?

What would most people do?

B **GROUP WORK** Compare your notes. Would you all do the same things in these situations? Use the unreal conditional and expressions from the Photo Story on page 111.

> 66 If I found cash near an ATM, I would keep it. There would be no way to find the owner. 99

Text-mining (optional)
Find and underline three words or phrases in the Reading that were new to you. Use them in your Group Work
For example: "a split-second decision."

REVIEW

A ▶5:30 Listen to the conversations. Check <u>Yes</u> or <u>No</u> to answer each question and explain your answers. (Explanations will vary)

	Yes	No
1 Do you think John has a double standard?	☑	☐

Explain your answer: *He thinks it's OK for young people to get tattoos, but not old people.*

2 Do you think Jessica's mom is sexist?   ☑   ☐

Explain your answer: *She has different rules for her son's curfew than her daughter's.*

3 Do you think Alex's dad is old-fashioned?   ☑   ☐

Explain your answer: *He wants his son to open the car door for his date.*

B Complete the questions with <u>Whose</u>. Then answer each question, using possessive pronouns. Follow the example.

1 Those shoes belong to my daughter. *Whose are* they? *They're hers.*
2 That sweater belongs to my son. *Whose is* it? *It's his.*
3 The house across the street is my parents' house. *Whose is* it? *It's theirs.*
4 These tickets are my husband's and mine. *Whose are* they? *They're ours.*
5 The table over there is your table. *Whose is* it? *It's mine.*

C Complete each conditional sentence in your own words.

1 If the weather were good, ...
2 If .... , I'd go out to eat tonight.
3 If I found your wallet, ...
4 If .... , I'd call home.
5 I'd be angry with my children if ....
6 If I had a new car, ...
7 I would choose a new career if ....

> **For additional language practice...**
> ♫ **TOP NOTCH** POP • Lyrics p. 154
> "What Would You Do?"
> DIGITAL SONG | DIGITAL KARAOKE

D What would you do? Complete each unreal conditional sentence.

1 You order two sandwiches for lunch, but they only charge you for one.
YOU "If the restaurant undercharged me, I ...."

2 You pay for a newspaper that costs one dollar with a five-dollar bill. The merchant gives you nine dollars change.
YOU "If the merchant gave me too much change, I ...."

3 You buy a smart phone from a website. When the package arrives, you see that the company has sent you two MP3 players and the smart phone.
YOU "If the company sent me more items than I paid for, I ...."

WRITING

Write three paragraphs about Matt's dilemma in the Photo Story on page 111. In the first paragraph, summarize the situation. In the second paragraph, write about what Matt could or should do. In the third paragraph, write what you would do if you were Matt. Explain your reasons, using the unreal conditional.

> **WRITING BOOSTER** p. 152
> • Introducing conflicting ideas
> • Guidance for this writing exercise

REVIEW

A ▶5:30 **Listen to the conversations . . .**

Suggested teaching time:	5 minutes	Your actual teaching time:

- Have students listen to the conversations with their books closed. After each conversation, ask *What are the people talking about?* (1. A grandmother getting a tattoo; 2. A girl having to be home earlier than a boy; 3. A boy opening the door for a girl.)

- Have students open their books and answer the questions *Yes* or *No*.

- Have students listen to the conversations again and then write explanations for their answers.

- Have students compare answers with a partner. Call on volunteers to share their explanations with the class.

Language and culture
- The expression *You've got to be kidding* is common in spoken English. It indicates that a speaker thinks that what someone is saying is silly or ridiculous.

AUDIOSCRIPT

CONVERSATION 1
M: Grandma! You're going to get a tattoo? You've got to be kidding!
F: Why? What's wrong with a tattoo?
M: You're too old. Tattoos are for young people.
F: So, John, you think there should be different rules for young people and old people?

CONVERSATION 2
F1: Jessica, please be home by ten.
F2: Ten? Mom, that's ridiculous.
F1: I don't think so.
F2: But Mark doesn't have to be home until midnight.
F1: Mark is a boy.
F2: Mom! Why should boys and girls have different rules?

CONVERSATION 3
M1: Alex, let me give you some fatherly advice.
M2: Sure, Dad. What is it?
M1: When you take Allison out tomorrow, be sure to open the car door for her when she gets into your car.
M2: You're not serious.
M1: I am. That kind of thing really impresses a young woman.
M2: No offense, Dad. But that's pretty old-fashioned. Allison is my age. Save that stuff for Mom, OK?

B **Complete the questions . . .**

Suggested teaching time:	3 minutes	Your actual teaching time:

- Have students fill in the first blanks with *Whose are* or *Whose is*, replacing the singular or plural subjects. Then have them answer the questions.

- Go over the answers with the class.

C **Complete each conditional sentence . . .**

Suggested teaching time:	3–5 minutes	Your actual teaching time:

- Before students complete the sentences, have them look at the verbs in the clauses and identify what type of conditional is used in the sentences. (All are unreal conditionals.) Review the formation of the unreal conditional. (*If* clause: simple past tense; result clause: *would* + base form.)

- Then have students compare sentences with a partner. Tell pairs to check for correct formation of the conditional sentences. Refer them to the Grammar box on page 112 if necessary.

- Ask students to share their sentences with the class.

D **What would you do?**

Suggested teaching time:	5–10 minutes	Your actual teaching time:

- Have students look at the illustrations on page 113 and identify the situation that applies to each sentence. (1. They undercharged me. 2. The merchant gave me too much change. 3. They gave me more than I ordered.)

- As a class, brainstorm possibilities for the first situation. Ask *What would you do if they undercharged you?* (Possible response: I would tell the waiter.)

- After students decide what they would do in each situation, have them complete the result clauses.

- After students compare completed sentences with a partner, call on students to read their sentences to the class.

WRITING

Suggested teaching time:	10–15 minutes	Your actual teaching time:

- Write on the board the outline below :
  1. Summary of Matt's dilemma 2. What could / should Matt do? 3. If I were Matt, I would . . .

- Tell students they will write three paragraphs in response to the points on the board. For the first paragraph, remind students that a summary should consist of a few sentences describing the dilemma Matt finds himself in. For the second paragraph, have students think of different things Matt could or should do in the situation. For the final paragraph, tell students to imagine they were Matt (unreal conditional) and explain what they would do in the situation.

- Have pairs exchange papers. Ask them to discuss their responses in the last paragraphs.

- Ask the class *Did you and your partner agree on what you would do if you were Matt?*

- Collect student work and give feedback.

Option: **WRITING BOOSTER** *(Teaching notes p. T152)*

 **Writing Process Worksheets**

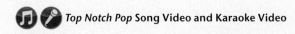 *Top Notch Pop* **Song Video and Karaoke Video**

 **Digital Games**

ORAL REVIEW

Before the first activity, give students a few minutes of silent time to become familiar with the pictures.

Contest

Suggested teaching time:	5 minutes	Your actual teaching time:	

- Divide the class into teams of three or four students. Have teams study the pictures and then tell them to close their books and make notes about as many details as they can. Encourage students to cooperate with one another.

- Have students put their pencils down. Ask teams to present the details they wrote down. Make sure students don't write down more details as another team works. The team with the most details is the winner.

> **Possible responses . . .**
> Details in the pictures include people, a phone, an airplane, an airport, a gate, a terminal, a clock. The plane has just landed. People are leaving the plane. A woman notices that someone forgot a phone on the seat. She picks up the phone and runs after a man and a woman to see if it's theirs.

Pair work 1

Suggested teaching time:	7 minutes	Your actual teaching time:	

- Have pairs look at the two pictures together and suggest different situations to talk about. Encourage students to look at the unit for vocabulary and ideas.

- Ask students to write down what they would do in this situation. Tell them to use the unreal conditional. For example, *If I found a phone, I would . . .*

> **Possible responses . . .**
> If I found a phone on the plane, I would try to find the owner. If I couldn't find the owner, I would give the phone to a flight attendant. If I lost my phone, I would be very upset. If someone returned my phone, I would be very happy.

Pair work 2

Suggested teaching time:	7 minutes	Your actual teaching time:	

- Divide the class into groups of three and focus on the second picture. Have them create a conversation for the three people. Encourage students to use possessive pronouns.

> **Possible responses . . .**
> **A:** Excuse me. Is this your phone? **B:** Oh, that phone isn't mine. It's hers. **C:** Oh! Where did you find it? **A:** You left it on your seat. **C:** Thanks so much. **A:** Don't mention it. I'm glad I found you.

Option: Oral Progress Assessment

- Use the illustrations on page 121. Encourage students to use the vocabulary, grammar, rhythm, and intonation practiced in this unit.

- Point to the different items in the illustrations and ask students what they are. (Possible responses: Man, woman, phone, airplane, airport, gate, terminal, clock.)

- Ask:
  In the first picture, what does the woman on the plane see?
  Whose phone is it?
  What does she do with the phone?
  Does she keep the phone?
  Does the woman find the owner of the phone?
  What does the man say?
  What does the woman say?

- Ask a student to role-play a conversation about the second picture with you. Play the role of the woman in the yellow jacket and have the student play the man.

- Evaluate the student on intelligibility, fluency, correct use of grammar, and appropriate use of vocabulary.

Option: *Top Notch* Project

Have students research magazines to create an appearance *Do's and Don'ts* list to present to classmates.

Idea: Have pairs find examples of clothing and accessories. Tell students to create a *Do's* page and a *Don'ts* page and paste the examples on it.

- Have pairs exchange pages with another pair. Tell them to comment on the clothing choices.

EXTRAS

On the Internet:
- Online Teacher Resources: pearsonelt.com/topnotch3e/

Additional printable resources on the ActiveTeach:
- Assessment
- Just for Fun
- *Top Notch Pop* Song Activities
- *Top Notch TV* Video Program and Activity Worksheets
- Supplementary Pronunciation Lessons
- Conversation Activator Video Scripts
- Audioscripts and Answer Keys
- Unit Study Guides

ORAL REVIEW

CONTEST Form teams. With your team, look at the two pictures for one minute. Then close your books and tell the story you saw in the pictures. The team that remembers more details wins.

PAIR WORK

1 Tell your partner what you would do if you were the woman who found the lost object. Use the unreal conditional. Start like this:

If I found . . . , I would . . .

2 Create a conversation for the people in the second picture. Use possessive pronouns. Start like this:

Excuse me. Is this your . . .

A few minutes later

GATE 22 B

departures

NOW I CAN

- [ ] Discuss ethical choices.
- [ ] Return someone else's property.
- [ ] Express personal values.
- [ ] Discuss acts of kindness and honesty.

121

Reference Charts

PRONUNCIATION TABLE

Vowels

Symbol	Key Words
i	beat, feed
ɪ	bit, did
eɪ	date, paid
ɛ	bet, bed
æ	bat, bad
ɑ	box, odd, father
ɔ	bought, dog
oʊ	boat, road
ʊ	book, good
u	boot, food, flu
ʌ	but, mud, mother
ə	banana, among
ɚ	shirt, murder
aɪ	bite, cry, buy, eye
aʊ	about, how
ɔɪ	voice, boy
ɪr	deer
ɛr	bare
ɑr	bar
ɔr	door
ʊr	tour

Consonants

Symbol	Key Words	Symbol	Key Words
p	pack, happy	z	zip, please, goes
b	back, rubber	ʃ	ship, machine, station, special, discussion
t	tie		
d	die	ʒ	measure, vision
k	came, key, quick	h	hot, who
g	game, guest	m	men
tʃ	church, nature, watch	n	sun, know, pneumonia
dʒ	judge, general, major	ŋ	sung, ringing
f	fan, photograph	w	wet, white
v	van	l	light, long
θ	thing, breath	r	right, wrong
ð	then, breathe	y	yes
s	sip, city, psychology		
ţ	butter, bottle		
tˀ	button		

IRREGULAR VERBS

base form	simple past	past participle
be	was / were	been
become	became	become
begin	began	begun
break	broke	broken
bring	brought	brought
build	built	built
buy	bought	bought
catch	caught	caught
choose	chose	chosen
come	came	come
cost	cost	cost
cut	cut	cut
do	did	done
draw	drew	drawn
dream	dreamed / dreamt	dreamed / dreamt
drink	drank	drunk
drive	drove	driven
eat	ate	eaten
fall	fell	fallen
feed	fed	fed
feel	felt	felt
fight	fought	fought
find	found	found
fit	fit	fit
fly	flew	flown
forget	forgot	forgotten
get	got	gotten
give	gave	given
go	went	gone
grow	grew	grown
have	had	had
hear	heard	heard
hit	hit	hit
hold	held	held
hurt	hurt	hurt
keep	kept	kept
know	knew	known

base form	simple past	past participle
leave	left	left
let	let	let
lose	lost	lost
make	made	made
mean	meant	meant
meet	met	met
pay	paid	paid
put	put	put
quit	quit	quit
read /rid/	read /rɛd/	read /rɛd/
ride	rode	ridden
ring	rang	rung
rise	rose	risen
run	ran	run
say	said	said
see	saw	seen
sell	sold	sold
send	sent	sent
shake	shook	shaken
sing	sang	sung
sit	sat	sat
sleep	slept	slept
speak	spoke	spoken
spend	spent	spent
stand	stood	stood
steal	stole	stolen
swim	swam	swum
take	took	taken
teach	taught	taught
tell	told	told
think	thought	thought
throw	threw	thrown
understand	understood	understood
wake up	woke up	woken up
wear	wore	worn
win	won	won
write	wrote	written

1   THE PRESENT OF BE

Statements

I	am	
You We They	are	late.
He She It	is	

2   THE SIMPLE PRESENT TENSE

Statements

I You We They	speak English.
He She	speaks English.

Yes / no questions

Do	I you we they	know them?
Does	he she	eat meat?

Short answers

Yes,	I you we they	do.
	he she it	does.

No,	I you we they	don't.
	he she it	doesn't.

Information questions

What do	you we they	need?
When does	he she it	start?
Who	wants needs likes	this book?

3   THE PRESENT CONTINUOUS

Statements

I	am	watching TV.
You We They	are	studying English.
He She It	is	arriving now.

Yes / no questions

Am	I	
Are	you we they	going too fast?
Is	he she it	

Short answers

Yes,	I	am.
	you	are.
	he she it	is.
	we they	are.

No,	I'm not.
	you aren't / you're not.
	he isn't / he's not.
	she isn't / she's not.
	it isn't / it's not.
	we aren't / we're not.
	they aren't / they're not.

Information questions

What	are	you we they	doing?
When	is	he she it	leaving?
Where	am	I	staying tonight?
Who	is		driving?

4   THE PAST OF BE

Statements

I He She It	was late.
We You They	were early.

(The past of be–continued)

Yes / no questions

Was	I he she it	on time?
Were	we you they	in the same class?

Short answers

Yes,	I he she it	was.
	we you they	were.

No,	I he she it	wasn't.
	we you they	weren't.

Information questions

Where	were	we? you? they?	
When	was	he she it	here?
Who	were	they?	
Who	was	he? she? it?	

5 THE SIMPLE PAST TENSE

Many verbs are irregular in the simple past tense.
See the list of irregular verbs on page 123.

Statements

I You He She It We They	stopped working.

I You He She It We They	didn't start again.

Yes / no questions

Did	I you he she it we they	make a good dinner?

Short answers

Yes,	I you he she it we they	did.

No,	I you he she it we they	didn't.

Information questions

When did	I you he she it we they	read that?
Who		called?

6 THE FUTURE WITH BE GOING TO

Statements

I'm You're He's She's It's We're They're	going to	be here soon.

I'm You're He's She's It's We're They're	not going to	be here soon.

Yes / no questions

Are	you we they	going to want coffee?
Am	I	going to be late?
Is	he she it	going to arrive on time?

Short answers

Yes,	I	am.
	you	are.
	he she it	is.
	we they	are.

No,	I'm not.
	you aren't / you're not.
	he isn't / he's not.
	she isn't / she's not.
	it isn't / it's not.
	we aren't / we're not.
	they aren't / they're not.

Information questions

What	are	you we they	going to see?
When	is	he she it	going to shop?
Where	am	I	going to stay tomorrow?
Who	is		going to call?

Grammar Booster

The Grammar Booster is optional. It offers a variety of information and extra practice. Sometimes it further explains or expands the unit grammar and points out common errors. In other cases, it reviews and practices previously learned grammar that would be helpful when learning new grammar concepts. If you use the Grammar Booster, you will find extra exercises in the Workbook in a separate section labeled Grammar Booster. The Grammar Booster content is not tested on any *Top Notch* tests.

UNIT 1 Lesson 1

The present perfect: information questions

Form information questions by inverting <u>have</u> and the subject of the sentence.
What have you seen in Paris?
What (OR Which) countries have you visited?
Where has she gone scuba diving?
How have your parents been?
How many cities have you visited this week?
Who have you traveled with?

Note: When <u>Who</u> is the subject of the sentence, there is no inversion.
Who has traveled to Miami in the last two months?

On a separate sheet of paper, write information questions. Use the present perfect.   See page T126 for answers.

1 what dishes / she / try / in Mérida
2 who / you / invite / to the party
3 where / he / work / before
4 which movies / they / see
5 how / your children / be
6 who / climb / Grouse Mountain
7 what / they / hear / about the new school
8 how many times / she / take / that class

UNIT 1 Lesson 2

The present perfect: use and placement of <u>yet</u> and <u>already</u>

Remember: Use <u>yet</u> or <u>already</u> in questions.
Have you read the book yet? OR Have you already read the book?

Use <u>already</u> in affirmative statements. Place <u>already</u> before the main verb or at the end of the statement.
I've already read the book. OR I've read the book already.

Use <u>yet</u> in negative statements. Place <u>yet</u> at the end of the statement or between <u>have</u> and the base form.
I haven't read the book yet. OR I haven't yet read the book.

Be careful!
Don't use <u>yet</u> in affirmative statements. Don't use <u>already</u> in negative statements.
DON'T SAY Yes, I've read the book yet. / No, I haven't already read the book.

Don't use <u>ever</u> with <u>yet</u> or <u>already</u>.
DON'T SAY Have you ever read the book yet? / Have you ever read the book already?

A On a separate sheet of paper, rewrite each statement or question, using <u>already</u> or <u>yet</u>.   See page T126 for answers.

1 (yet) Has she finished the homework?
2 (yet) They haven't seen the movie.
3 (already) We've tried fried clams several times.
4 (already) Has your father left?

B On a separate sheet of paper, rewrite each sentence, using <u>already</u> or <u>yet</u>.   See page T126 for answers.

1 I haven't had dinner.
2 She's been to London, Berlin, and Rome.
3 They haven't called home.
4 We've finished our class.

Grammar Booster

Note about the Grammar Booster

Many will elect to do the Grammar Booster as self-study. However, if you choose to use the Grammar Booster with the classroom activity instead, teaching notes are included here.

UNIT 1 Lesson 1

The present perfect: information questions

Suggested teaching time:	5 minutes	Your actual teaching time:

- Read the first rule in the Grammar box aloud. Make sure students know that *invert* means to *change the order of*. To check understanding, write on the board *You have seen the Eiffel Tower in Paris.* Ask which *Wh-* word could replace the information *Eiffel Tower*? (What.) Write *What* under the sentence on the board. Then ask *What is the subject of the sentence?* (You.) Ask a volunteer to invert *have* and *you* and write out the rest of the sentence.

- Call on volunteers to read the remainder of the information questions. Point out the inversion in each one.

- Read the note aloud. Write the example sentence on the board. Underline *Who* and restate that it is the subject of the sentence. Explain that with *who,* there is no inversion.

On a separate sheet of paper . . .

Suggested teaching time:	6 minutes	Your actual teaching time:

- Move around the room as students write sentences. Refer them to the example sentences to help them. Remind them that the *Wh-* words begin the sentence.

- Review the answers with the class. Write out on the board any sentences that give students difficulty.

Answers to Unit 1, Lesson 1
1. What dishes has she tried in Mérida?
2. Who have you invited to the party?
3. Where has he worked before?
4. Which movies have they seen?
5. How have your children been?
6. Who has climbed Grouse Mountain?
7. What have they heard about the new school?
8. How many times has she taken that class?

UNIT 1 Lesson 2

The present perfect: use and placement . . .

Suggested teaching time:	8 minutes	Your actual teaching time:

- Ask volunteers to read the rules and the example sentences. Focus on the placement of the words in blue. Write on the board
  1 *I've eaten dinner.*
  2 *I haven't eaten dinner.*
  3 *Have you eaten dinner?*

- Have a volunteer place *already* or *yet* into the sentence. (1. I've already eaten dinner. I've eaten dinner already. 2. I haven't eaten dinner yet. I haven't yet eaten dinner. 3. Have you eaten dinner yet? Have you already eaten dinner? Have you eaten dinner already?)

- Read the Be careful! notes to the class, and write the following sentences on the board for students to correct: 1 *I haven't eaten dinner already.* (Replace *already* with *yet.*) 2 *Yes, I've eaten dinner yet.* (Replace *yet* with *already.*) 3 *Have you ever eaten sushi yet?* (Cross out *yet.*)

A On a separate sheet of paper . . .

Suggested teaching time:	2 minutes	Your actual teaching time:

- Review answers with the class.

Answers to Unit 1, Lesson 2—Exercise A
1. Has she finished the homework yet?
2. They haven't seen the movie yet. / They haven't yet seen the movie.
3. We've tried fried clams several times already. / We've already tried fried clams several times.
4. Has your father already left? / Has your father left already?

B On a separate sheet of paper . . .

Suggested teaching time:	2 minutes	Your actual teaching time:

- Ask *Which sentences are affirmative?* (2 and 4.) *Negative?* (1 and 3.) Say, *Use already or yet correctly in each sentence.*

- Move around the room and help students. Ask *Can you use yet in the affirmative statements?* (No.) *Can you use already in the negative statements?* (No.)

- Review answers with the class.

Answers to Unit 1, Lesson 2—Exercise B
1. I haven't had dinner yet. / I haven't yet had dinner.
2. She's already been to London, Berlin, and Rome. / She's been to London, Berlin, and Rome already.
3. They haven't called home yet. / They haven't yet called home.
4. We've already finished our class. / We've finished our class already.

The present perfect: _ever_, _never_, and _before_

Suggested teaching time:	4 minutes	Your actual teaching time:	

- Call on volunteers to read the first rule and the example question and answers. Write additional questions for students to answer; for example, _Have you ever traveled on a ship? Have you ever gone sky diving? Have you ever driven a tractor?_
- Have a student read the second rule. Invite students to share things they have never done before. Then ask students if anyone in class has done any of these things.
- Tell students to read the last rule silently. Then call on volunteers to tell the class about something they have _never ever_ done.

C On a separate sheet of paper . . .

Suggested teaching time:	4 minutes	Your actual teaching time:	

- For a warm-up, poll the class with several questions from the exercise.
- Have students write the answers. Remind them to use _ever, never,_ and _before_ in their answers.
- Move around the room and help students as they write. For the second part of the exercise, remind students to use the simple past tense to describe when something happened.
- Have pairs compare their answers and experiences.

UNIT 2 Lesson 1

The present perfect and the present . . .

Suggested teaching time:	5 minutes	Your actual teaching time:	

- Read the introductory information to the class.
- Then ask a volunteer to read the first way to talk about unfinished actions. Write the example on the board and underline _2001_. Ask _What other start time could we use in this sentence?_ (Possible answers: January, Monday, Last week, I was born.)
- Ask students to suggest additional present perfect statements using _since_; for example, say _We have been in class since [2:00]. Are we still in class?_ (Yes.)
- Ask a student to read the second way to talk about unfinished actions. Write the example on the board, and underline _five years_. Ask _What other start time could we use in this sentence?_ (Possible answers: Six months, three weeks, a long time.)
- Have a student read the third way to talk about unfinished actions.

- Read the final note to the class aloud. Write on the board _I have been reading since this morning. I have been reading for three hours._ Ask:
  Did the action begin in the past?
  When did the action begin?
  Am I still reading?
  May I continue to read into the future?
- Ask students to suggest additional present perfect continuous statements to describe unfinished actions. Have them create statements using both _since_ and _for_.

A Read the sentences . . .

Suggested teaching time:	4 minutes	Your actual teaching time:	

- To review, ask _What words indicate unfinished action in sentences in the present perfect (continuous)?_ (For / since.)
- Have students complete the exercise. If they need help, hint to them to look for sentences that use _for_ or _since_.
- Review answers with the class. Point out that items 3, 6, and 8 are all finished actions.

B Complete each statement . . .

Suggested teaching time:	3 minutes	Your actual teaching time:	

- After students complete the exercise, invite volunteers to read each sentence aloud. Focus students' attention on the verb in each sentence and how it emphasizes continuity of the action.

Option: (+3 minutes) Have students underline the _for_ and _since_ phrases in the exercise. Then have them replace the _for_ phrases with _since_ phrases.

The present perfect: _ever_, _never_, and _before_

Use _ever_ in questions. Use _never_ in negative statements and short answers. Do not use _ever_ in affirmative statements.

Have you **ever** made sushi?

Yes, I have. OR Yes, I've made sushi. NOT Yes, I've ~~ever~~ made sushi.

No, I **never** have. OR No, I've **never** made sushi.

You can also use _before_ in negative statements with _never_.

I've **never** been to Thailand **before**.

In very informal speech, _ever_ is sometimes used with _never_ for strong emphasis. This meaning of _ever_ is similar to "in my whole life."

I've **never ever** seen a Charlie Chaplin movie.

C On a separate sheet of paper, answer each question, using real information. If the answer is _yes_, write when this happened.   Answers will vary.

1 Have you ever gone on a cruise?

2 Have you ever tried Indian food?

3 Have you ever been to Hawaii?

4 Have you ever met a famous person?

5 Have you ever fallen in love?

6 Have you ever played golf?

UNIT 2 _Lesson 1_

The present perfect and the present perfect continuous: unfinished (or continuing) actions

Unfinished (or continuing) actions are those that began in the past, continue in the present, and may possibly continue into the future. Here are three ways to talk about unfinished actions:

1 **the present perfect with _since_**: Use _since_ with a stated start time in the past.

I've lived here **since** 2001. (2001 is the stated start time. I still live here, so the action "continues.")

2 **the present perfect with _for_**: Use _for_ to describe the period of time from its start until the present.

I've lived here **for** five years. (Emphasis is on the five-year period. I still live here, so the action "continues.")

3 **the present perfect continuous with _for_ or _since_**: Form the present perfect continuous with the present perfect of _be_ and a present participle.

I've **been living** here since 2001. OR I've **been living** here for five years. (In both cases, the action "continues.")

When describing unfinished or continuing actions with _for_ and _since_, the present perfect and the present perfect continuous are both correct. Some people feel the present perfect continuous emphasizes the continuing time a bit more.

A Read the sentences with the present perfect. Check each sentence that describes an unfinished or continuing action.

☑ 1 The Pitts have lived in China since the late nineties.

☑ 2 Carmen has been living in Buenos Aires since last year.

☐ 3 I've visited Paris three times.

☑ 4 Ted has been visiting Paris since 2005.

☑ 5 We have eaten in that great Indian restaurant for years.

☐ 6 They've eaten in that Indian restaurant before.

☑ 7 My brother has been playing tennis for many years.

☐ 8 Min-ji has played tennis twice.

B Complete each statement with the present perfect continuous.

1 _Rio_ ...._has been playing_............ (play) at the Children's Classics Cinema every Saturday since 2010.

2 Robert ...._has been waiting_............ (wait) in the ticket holders' line for a pretty long time.

3 People ...._have been worrying about_....... (worry about) violence in movies since the sixties.

4 I'_ve been talking about_.................... (talk about) that movie for weeks.

5 We'_ve been coming_......................... (come) to this classics movie theater for two years.

Spelling rules for the present participle: review

Add -ing to the base form of the verb

speak ➔ speaking

If the base form ends in a silent -e, drop the -e and add -ing.

have ➔ having

In verbs of one syllable, if the last three letters are a consonant-vowel-consonant (C-V-C) series, double the last consonant and then add -ing.

C V C

s i t ➔ sitting

Be careful! Don't double the last consonant in words that end in -w, -x, or -y.

flow ➔ flowing

fix ➔ fixing

pay ➔ paying

In verbs of more than one syllable that end in a consonant-vowel-consonant series, double the last consonant only if the stress is on the last syllable.

con • tról ➔ controlling   BUT   ór • der ➔ ordering

C   Write the present participle for these base forms.

1 find _finding_	8 go _going_	15 come _coming_	22 forget _forgetting_	29 begin _beginning_
2 be _being_	9 make _making_	16 leave _leaving_	23 eat _eating_	30 tell _telling_
3 lose _losing_	10 fix _fixing_	17 drive _driving_	24 pay _paying_	31 bring _bringing_
4 put _putting_	11 know _knowing_	18 meet _meeting_	25 stand _standing_	32 take _taking_
5 get _getting_	12 speak _speaking_	19 blow _blowing_	26 think _thinking_	
6 say _saying_	13 hear _hearing_	20 give _giving_	27 buy _buying_	
7 write _writing_	14 let _letting_	21 run _running_	28 see _seeing_	

UNIT 2   Lesson 2

Like, want, would like, would rather: review and expansion; common errors

Use like and want + a direct object to express likes, dislikes, and desires.

They **like** documentaries. We **don't like** science fiction.

She **wants** a ticket to the late show.

Use would like + a direct object to make a polite offer or a request.

A: **Would** you **like** tickets for *Casablanca*?

B: Yes, please. We**'d like** two tickets for the 8:00 show.

Use would like + an infinitive (to + base form) to make a polite offer or to express wants.

Would you **like to stream** a movie on your tablet?

Where **would** you **like to go**?

I**'d like to download** a movie onto my tablet.

She**'d like to see** a comedy.

Use would rather + a base form to express a preference for an activity.

A: Would you like to see the movie downtown or at the theater in the mall?

B: I**'d rather see** it at the mall.

Use than with would rather to contrast preferences.

I**'d rather** stream a movie **than** go to the theater.

They**'d rather** go to a Woody Allen film **than** a Martin Scorsese film.

Be careful!

Don't use a base form after would like.

My friends **would like to meet** in front of the theater.   NOT   My friends ~~would like meet~~ in front of the theater.

Don't use an infinitive after would rather.

We**'d rather get** tickets for the early show.   NOT   We~~'d rather to get~~ tickets for the early show.

Spelling rules for the present participle: review

Suggested teaching time:	3 minutes	Your actual teaching time:	

- To review, write the words *vowel* and *consonant* on the board. Ask students to provide examples of each (Vowels = *a, e, i, o, u,* and sometimes *y;* consonants are all the other letters of the alphabet.)
- Give students a few minutes to read the spelling rules. As students read, write the following words on the board *think, make, run, mix, wonder.* Ask *Which of these words are examples of C-V-C?* (*Run* and *mix.*) For which word do you double the consonant? (run = running) Then elicit the present participle for the other words. (thinking, making, mixing, wondering)

C Write the present participle . . .

Suggested teaching time:	8 minutes	Your actual teaching time:	

- Have students work in pairs to complete the exercise.
- To review the answers, have students write the words on the board for easy correction.
- If time permits, divide the class into two teams and hold a spelling bee to practice spelling of the present participle form.

UNIT 2 Lesson 2

Like, want, would like, would rather . . .

Suggested teaching time:	5 minutes	Your actual teaching time:	

- Have a student read aloud the first rule and examples. If necessary, review the definition of a *direct object* (The person or thing directly affected by the verb; the receiver of the action in a sentence.)
- Go over the *would like* rules and examples. Make sure students understand that they can use *would like* with either nouns or infinitives to make polite offers. Remind students that the contraction for *would* is *'d.*
- Go over the *would rather* rules and examples. Make sure the students understand the difference between the *base form* and the *infinitive* form of verbs (for example: *play* versus *to play*). Remind students that *than* must be added when two preferences are contrasted.
- Review the Be Careful! Note. Explain that *would like* is followed by the infinitive form, but *would rather* is followed by the base form.
- To test understanding, write a few incorrect sentences on the board and ask students to correct them. For example:

  I would like buy a DVD. (I would like to buy a DVD.)

  I would rather to go to a movie. (I would rather go to a movie.)

  I would rather eat pizza eat Chinese food. (I would rather eat pizza than eat Chinese food.)

A On a separate sheet of paper . . .

Suggested teaching time:	6 minutes	Your actual teaching time:

- Move around the room as students work, providing help as necessary. Tell students to refer to the Grammar box for help as well. Make sure that students invert *would* + the pronoun in the question form in 2 and 4.
- Review the answers with the class.

Answers to Unit 2, Lesson 2—Exercise A
1. They would like to see the Woody Allen film.
2. What time would you rather meet?
3. Who would like to order eggs for breakfast?
4. Would they rather watch TV or go out?
5. Jason would like to have a large container of popcorn.
6. I'd rather rent a sci-fi film tonight.
7. Her parents would rather not watch anything too violent.
8. Who'd rather not see that silly animated film?

B Correct the errors . . .

Suggested teaching time:	5 minutes	Your actual teaching time:

- If necessary, quickly review the rules in the grammar chart, especially the information in the Be Careful! box.
- Do the first item with the class as an example. Write *I'd rather to stay home than to go out.* on the board. Ask, *What are the mistakes in this sentence?* Cross out *to* in both places in the sentence (I'd rather stay home than go out.)
- Have students correct the errors individually. Then have them compare answers with a partner.

C On a separate sheet of paper . . .

Suggested teaching time:	3 minutes	Your actual teaching time:

- After students answer the questions, have them interview a partner and share their answers.
- If time permits, compare preferences among students in the entire class.

UNIT 3 Lesson 1

Will: expansion

Suggested teaching time:	4 minutes	Your actual teaching time:

- Ask several students *Do you know the weather for tomorrow?* Write students' predictions on the board. Make sure that you have examples with *will* and *be going to.*
- Call on a student to read the first rule. Ask students to make additional predictions about the future, such as *Our team will win the football game. The pool is going to reopen in July.*

FYI: *Be going to* is used to make predictions more often when there is obvious evidence; for example, *It's going to rain.* (There are black clouds in the sky, which give us obvious evidence.) *Will* is used slightly more often when

making a prediction based on opinion. However, these distinctions are not always observed and the forms are used interchangeably in informal spoken English.

- Read the second rule aloud. Then write *Weekend plans: I'm going to . . .* Ask students to share what they are going to do this weekend.
- Focus on the third rule and read the example sentence. Say *I don't have any plans after school today. Maybe I'll go grocery shopping. Or maybe I'll go to the park and read a book.* Clarify that these are ideas you came up with right now for the immediate future.
- Read the fourth rule and the example sentence aloud. Invite students to share things they are and are not willing to eat.
- Go over the rules for can, should, and have to with future meaning. Make sure that students understand that they should never use can and should with will, but they can use will + have to together to express future obligation.
- Ask students to give you more examples of sentences that include can, should, and have to with future meaning. Write their sentences on the board. Possible responses:

  We can go to the beach tomorrow. It's going to be hot.

  You should visit Disney World during your trip to Florida next month.

  I'll have to go to the airport at 8 o'clock tomorrow morning.

A On a separate sheet of paper . . .

Suggested teaching time:	4 minutes	Your actual teaching time:

- Move around the room as students work and make sure they use *be going to* to write about their weekend plans.
- Have students exchange their papers with a classmate and read about their plans.
- If time permits, have each student report his or her partner's plans to the class.

A On a separate sheet of paper, write sentences and questions using these words and phrases. See page T129 for answers.

1 They / would like / see / the Woody Allen film.
2 What time / you / would rather / meet?
3 Who / would like / order / eggs for breakfast?
4 they / rather / Would / watch TV or go out?
5 Jason / would like / have / a large container of popcorn.
6 I'd rather / rent / a sci-fi film tonight.
7 Her parents / rather / not / watch / anything too violent.
8 Who'd rather / not / see / that silly animated film?

B Correct the errors in these sentences.

1 I would rather ~~to~~ stay home than ~~to~~ go out.
2 She would like ^{to} buy a ticket to tonight's show.
3 My friends would ~~like~~ ^{rather} download movies from the Internet.
4 Would they rather ~~to~~ see an animated film than an action film?
5 ^{Would} ~~Do~~ they rather see movies at home?
6 Who would like ^{to} go to the late show tonight?
7 My husband ~~likes~~ $^{would like}$ two tickets to the concert.

C On a separate sheet of paper, answer each question in a complete sentence, expressing your own preference. Answers will vary.

1 What genre of movie do you usually like?
2 What movie do you want to see this weekend?
3 What would you like to have for dinner tonight?
4 Would you rather see a comedy or a horror film?
5 Would you like to rent a DVD or go to the movies?

UNIT 3 · Lesson 1

Will: expansion

Will and be going to
Use **will** or **be going to** for predictions about the future. The meaning is the same.
It'll rain tomorrow. = It's going to rain tomorrow.

Use **be going to**, NOT **will**, when you already have a plan for the future.
A: Are you going to come to class tomorrow?
B: No. I'm going to go to the beach instead. NOT No. I'll go to the beach instead.

Other uses of will
Use **will**, NOT **be going to**, to talk about the immediate future when you do not already have a plan.
Maybe I'll go to the beach this weekend. NOT Maybe I'm going to go to the beach this weekend.

Use **will**, NOT **be going to**, to express willingness.
I'll pay for Internet service, but I won't pay for the airport shuttle. (= I'm willing to pay for Internet service, but I'm not willing to pay for the airport shuttle.)

Can, should, and have to: future meaning
Can and **should** are modals and should never be used with **will**.

You can use **can** alone to express future possibility.
Tomorrow morning you can ask the hotel for a rollaway bed.
They can't go to the museum tomorrow. It's closed on Mondays.

You can use **should** alone to express future advice.
You should visit the Empire State Building next week. It's great.

However, you can use **will** with **have to** + a base form to express future obligation.
I'll have to leave the 2:00 meeting early.
We won't have to make a reservation at a restaurant tonight.

A On a separate sheet of paper, write five sentences about your plans for the weekend, using **be going to**. Then write the sentences again, using **will**. Answers will vary.

B   On a separate sheet of paper, write five sentences with <u>will</u> or <u>won't</u> for willingness
    on one of the following topics.
    Answers will vary.

> **Topics**
> • kinds of exercise you're willing (or not willing) to do
> • kinds of food you're willing (or not willing) to eat for breakfast
> • kinds of clothes you're willing (or not willing) to wear

C   Complete the sentences, using <u>will</u> or <u>won't</u> with <u>have to</u>.

    1 She will have to call .... (she / have to / call) the office before 6:00.
    2 They will have to reserve . (they / have to / reserve) their tickets by Monday.
    3 We will not have to cancel (we / not have to / cancel) the meeting if Mr. Carson's flight is on time.
    4 I have to leave .... (I / have to / leave) a message for my boss.
    5 You will not have to order (you / not have to / order) room service if you arrive before 10:00 P.M.
    6 We have to take .... (we / have to / take) a taxi to the airport.

UNIT 3 *Lesson 2*

The real conditional: present

Use the present real conditional to express general and scientific facts. Use the simple present tense
or the present tense of <u>be</u> in both clauses.
   If it **rains**, flights **are** late. [fact]
   If you **heat** water to 100 degrees, it **boils**. [scientific fact]

In present real conditional sentences, <u>when</u> (or <u>whenever</u>) is often used instead of <u>if</u>.
   When (or **Whenever**) it rains, flights are late.
   When (or **Whenever**) you heat water to 100 degrees, it boils.

A   On a separate sheet of paper, write present real conditional sentences.   See page T130 for answers.

    1 Water (freeze) when you (lower) its temperature below zero degrees.
    2 Whenever my daughter (take) her umbrella to school, she (forget) to bring it home.
    3 She (go) on vacation every August if she (not have) too much work.
    4 He (run) in the park if the weather (be) dry.
    5 In my company, if cashiers (make) a mistake, they (repay) the money.

The real conditional: future

Use the future real conditional to express what you believe will happen in the future under certain
conditions or as a result of certain actions. Use the simple present tense or the present of <u>be</u> in the <u>if</u>
clause. Use a future form (<u>will</u> or <u>be going to</u>) in the result clause.
   If I **go** to sleep too late tonight, I **won't be able to** get up on time. (future condition, future result)
   If she **comes** home after 8:00, I'**m not going to make** dinner. (future condition, future result)

Remember: Use a comma when the <u>if</u> clause comes first. Don't use a comma when the <u>if</u> clause comes
at the end of the sentence.
   If I see him, I'll tell her.   I'll tell her if I see him.

Be careful! **Don't use a future form in the <u>if</u> clause.**
   If I see him, I'll tell her. NOT If I ~~will see~~ him, I'll tell her. NOT If I'~~m going to see~~ him, I'll tell her.

B   Circle the correct form to complete each future real conditional sentence.

    1 If they (like)/ will like) the movie, they (see /(will see) it again.
    2 I ('m going to talk)/ talk) to her if she (does)/ 's going to do) that again.
    3 If you (buy)/ are going to buy) some eggs, I (make /'ll make) you an omelet tonight.
    4 If they (see)/ will see) her tomorrow, they (drive /'ll drive) her home.
    5 (Are you going to study)/ Do you study) Italian if they (offer)/ will offer) it next year?

B On a separate sheet of paper . . .

Suggested teaching time:	4 minutes	Your actual teaching time:

- Direct students' attention to the list of topics in the box.

- For a warm-up, write on the board *exercise, breakfast food, clothes.* Say *I'll ride my bike, but I won't run. I'll have yogurt, but I won't eat oatmeal. I'll wear a skirt, but I won't wear shorts.* Invite students to share additional examples.

- After students write their sentences on the topic of their choice, call on each student to read his or her sentences and have the class identify the topic: exercise, breakfast food, or clothes. Students will be able to see how they compare with their classmates.

Option: (+4 minutes) Tell students to imagine that the class is going to have a party. Have students use *will* in an offer to bring in different things; for example, *I'll bring soda. I'll bring chips and salsa.* If necessary, to get them started, ask *Who is willing to bring things? Who'll bring paper plates? Who'll bring cookies?*

C Complete the sentences . . .

Suggested teaching time:	4 minutes	Your actual teaching time:

- Do the first item with the class as an example. Have a student write the correct answer on the board (*She will have to call the office before 6:00.*) Remind students that when they see *not have to* in parentheses, they should use *won't* in their answers.

- Have students compare answers in pairs.

UNIT 3 Lesson 2

The real conditional: present

Suggested teaching time:	5 minutes	Your actual teaching time:

- Write on the board *If you heat ice, it melts.* Explain that this sentence states a scientific fact. Ask students *What tense are the verbs in the two clauses?* (Present.)

- Read the first present real conditional rule and examples. Make sure that students understand that the present tense is used in both clauses to express general and scientific facts.

- Go over the second rule and example. Go back to the example sentence on the board. Ask, *Can we use when instead of if in this sentence?* (Yes: *When you heat ice, it melts.*)

A On a separate sheet of paper . . .

Suggested teaching time:	5 minutes	Your actual teaching time:

- Remind students that they must use the simple present tense in both clauses.

- After students complete the exercise, have them compare answers in pairs.

Answers to Unit 3, Lesson 2—Exercise A
1. Water <u>freezes</u> when you <u>lower</u> its temperature below zero degrees.
2. Whenever my daughter <u>takes</u> her umbrella to school, she <u>forgets</u> to bring it home.
3. She <u>goes</u> on vacation every August if she <u>doesn't have</u> too much work.
4. He <u>runs</u> in the park if the weather is dry.
5. In my company, if cashiers <u>make</u> a mistake, they have to <u>repay</u> the money.

The real conditional: future

Suggested teaching time:	5 minutes	Your actual teaching time:

- Read the first future real conditional rule and examples, and direct students' attention to the Be Careful! note. Make sure that students understand that in future real conditional sentences, the present tense is used in the if clause even though it describes a future event. The future tense is used in the result clause.

- Direct students' attention to the Remember! Note. Write these sentences on the board: *If we go we'll have fun. We'll have fun if we go.* Ask, Where do I put a comma? (After *if we go* in the first sentence.)

B Circle the correct form . . .

Suggested teaching time:	5 minutes	Your actual teaching time:

- To provide more support, have students circle *if* in all the sentences in the exercise. Remind them that they must use the simple present tense in the verb that follows *if* clause, and the future tense in the other (result) clause.

- After students complete the exercise, have them compare answers in pairs.

C On a separate piece of paper . . .

Suggested teaching time:	5 minutes	Your actual teaching time:

- Remind students that they must insert a comma after the *if* clause when the *if* clause comes first in the sentence.
- Move around the room, helping students as needed.
- To review answers, call on a few students to share their sentences with the class.

UNIT 4 Lesson 1

The past continuous: expansion

Suggested teaching time:	5 minutes	Your actual teaching time:

- Have a volunteer read the first rule and example sentences.
- Write the following additional example on the board: I was downloading a picture when my computer crashed. Ask:
  Which activity happened first? (Downloading a picture.)
  What interrupted the activity? (The computer crashing.)
  Which was the continuous action? (Downloading a picture.)
  Which was the completed action? (The computer crashed.)
  Point out the relative placement of *while* and *when: while* appears before the continuous clause; *when* follows the continuous clause.
- Read the second rule and examples. Then write the following on the board: While I was watching TV, my brother was sleeping. Ask *Which activity happened first?* (Neither one. Both were happening at the same time in the past.)

On a separate sheet of paper . . .

Suggested teaching time:	5 minutes	Your actual teaching time:

- Model the activity by completing item one with the class. Write on the board take a test / hear the fire alarm. Ask *Which of these activities do you think happened first?* Place a **1** next to *take a test* and write the complete sentence on the board.
- Tell students to complete the remaining items in the same way: Number the activity according to which they think happened first and then write complete sentences.
- Move around the room, helping students as needed. If students have numbered any actions incorrectly, help them see why a particular action happened first.
- Review answers by having students write their sentences on the board and correcting them with the class.

Answers to Unit 4, Lesson 1

1. She was taking a test at school when she heard the fire alarm.
2. While I was talking to my mother on the phone, the TV show started.
3. Mr. Park was cooking dinner when Mrs. Park finished the laundry.
4. Mr. Kemp was working in the garden when the rain began.
5. While Claudia was picking up their rental car, Alex called their hotel.
6. While Nancy was shopping at the grocery store, she saw an old friend.

UNIT 4 Lesson 2

Nouns and pronouns: review

Suggested teaching time:	5 minutes	Your actual teaching time:

- Have students read the definition of a noun. Ask them to give additional examples of common nouns and proper nouns.
- Read the second rule aloud. Then write on the board Jack Hendrickson sells computers. Ask *What is the proper noun in this sentence?* (Jack Hendrickson.) *The common noun?* (Computers.) *Which noun performs the action?* (Jack.) *Which receives the action?* (Computers.) Stress that the noun that performs the action is the *subject,* and the noun that receives the action is the *object.* Leave the sentence on the board to refer to later.
- Ask students to read the last rule and example sentences. Check understanding by asking students to change the nouns in the sentence on the board into pronouns. (He sells them.) Ask *Which is the subject pronoun?* (He.) *The object pronoun?* (Them.)

C On a separate sheet of paper, complete each future real conditional sentence with true information. Use a comma when the if clause comes first. Answers will vary.

1 If I live to be 100 . . .
2 My family will be angry if . . .
3 If I don't practice English every day . . .
4 If I go to my favorite restaurant next week . . .
5 I'll buy a new smart phone if . . .
6 If I need new shoes . . .

UNIT 4 Lesson 1

The past continuous: expansion

The past continuous describes an action that was continuous until (and possibly after) the moment at which another action took place. The words <u>when</u> or <u>while</u> are often used in sentences that contrast continuing and completed actions.

He was talking on the phone when the storm began. (continuous action, then completed action)
While I was living in Chile, I got married. (continuous action, then completed action)

The past continuous also describes two continuing actions occurring in the same period of time.

While she was driving, her husband was reading the newspaper.
They were eating, and the music was playing.

On a separate sheet of paper, use the prompts to write logical sentences. Use the past continuous and the simple past tense in each sentence. See page T131 for answers.

1 She / take a test at school / when / she / hear the fire alarm
2 While I / talk to my mother on the phone / the TV show / start
3 Mr. Park / cook dinner / when / Mrs. Park / finish the laundry
4 Mr. Kemp / work in the garden / when / the rain / begin
5 While / Claudia / pick up / their rental car / Alex / call / their hotel
6 While / Nancy / shop at the grocery store / she / see / an old friend

UNIT 4 Lesson 2

Nouns and pronouns: review

A <u>noun</u> is a word that names a person, a place, or a thing. Nouns are either common or proper. A proper noun is capitalized.

common nouns: car, windshield, doctor, woman, father
proper nouns: Martin, Caracas, Carla's Restaurant

Two functions of nouns in sentences are subjects and direct objects. The subject performs the action of the verb. The object receives the action.

    subject   direct object
Carla's Restaurant serves breakfast all day long.

A <u>pronoun</u> is a word that represents or replaces a noun. Pronouns also function as subjects and direct objects.

subject pronouns: I, you, he, she, it, we, they
object pronouns: me, you, him, her, it, us, them

subject		direct object	
My parents	drove	the car	to the airport.
They		it	

First, underline the subjects and circle the objects in these sentences. Then label each noun as either "common" or "proper." Finally, put a check (✓) above each pronoun. (Note: Not every sentence contains a pronoun.)

proper   *common*
Italians drive fast (cars.)

1 We love big (vans.)

2 The children broke the side-view (mirror.)

3 Ms. Workman picked up the (car) this morning.

4 Rand loves (sports cars,) and his wife loves (them,) too.

5 A man driving a sports car hit our (minivan.)

6 I returned the rental (car) at the airport.

7 A-1 Rental Agency called (me) about the reservation.

UNIT 5   Lesson 1

Some and any: review

Some and any are indefinite quantifiers. They indicate an indefinite number or amount.

There are some toothbrushes in aisle 2. (We don't know how many.)

They are buying some shaving cream. (We don't know how much.)

Could I get some nail files? (We're not asking for a specific number of nail files.)

Do they have any makeup in this store? (We're not asking specifically how much.)

Be careful to use some and any correctly with count and non-count nouns:

Some: with non-count nouns and plural count nouns in affirmative statements

        non-count noun   plural count noun

We need some sunscreen and some combs. They have some here.

Any: with non-count nouns and plural count nouns in negative statements

            non-count noun   plural count noun

A: She doesn't want any shampoo, and he doesn't need any nail clippers.

B: Good! We don't have to buy any, then. I'm out of cash.

Any or some: with count and non-count nouns in questions

Do they need any toothpaste or sunscreen for the trip?

Do we need any razors or toothbrushes?

> **Remember:** Count nouns name things you can count individually. They have singular and plural forms (1 nail file, 3 combs). Non-count nouns name things you cannot count individually. They don't have plural forms. Use containers, quantifiers, and other modifiers to make non-count nouns countable.
>
> a bottle of shampoo / aftershave
> a tube of toothpaste / lipstick
> a bar of soap
> a can of hairspray / deodorant / shaving cream
> 250 milliliters of sunscreen

A On a separate sheet of paper, change these sentences from affirmative to negative. Follow the example. *See page T132 for answers.*

    There is some shampoo in the shower. *There isn't any shampoo in the shower.*

1 There are some razors next to the sink.

2 We have some nail clippers.

3 They need some brushes for the children.

4 She's buying some mascara.

5 The manicurists need some new nail polish.

6 I want some sunscreen on my back.

7 There is some dental floss in aisle 4.

8 They need some deodorant for the trip.

B Complete each sentence with some or any.

1 I don't need ...*any*... more hand lotion.

2 There isn't ...*any*... makeup in the bag.

3 We don't see ...*any*... scissors in the whole store.

4 They need ...*some*... soap to wash their hands.

5 It's too bad that there isn't ...*any*... toothpaste.

6 I don't see ...*any*... combs or brushes on those shelves.

7 I know I had ...*some*... nail files in my bag. Now I can't find them.

First, underline the subjects . . .

Suggested teaching time:	5 minutes	Your actual teaching time:

- Before students complete the exercise, ask *How do you know a noun is proper?* (It begins with a capital letter.) Remind students to underline only nouns. Refer them to the definition in the Grammar box.

- Have students place check marks next to the pronouns in the sentences. Move around the room as students complete the exercise, providing help as necessary.

- Review answers with the class. Have students call out the subjects and objects of each sentence and identify them as proper nouns, common nouns, or pronouns.

UNIT 5 Lesson 1

Some and any: review

Suggested teaching time:	10 minutes	Your actual teaching time:

- Give students a few minutes to study the information in this section.

- To review the information, ask *What are count nouns?* (Things you can count individually.) *What are non-count nouns?* (Things you cannot count individually.) Write some examples of each on the board: *Count: apples, pickles, chocolate bars; Non-count: ice cream, rice, juice.* Call on volunteers to create affirmative and negative sentences for the words on the board. (Possible responses: I bought some apples at the store. The store didn't have any vanilla ice cream.)

- Read the information from the Remember note aloud and review the containers. To give students additional information on containers and quantifiers, draw the chart below on the board.

Containers	Quantifiers
a bag	a cup
a bottle	a gallon
a box	a gram
a can	a kilo
a carton	a liter
a container	170 milliliters
a jar	an ounce
a package	a piece
a tube	a pound
	a quart
	a slice
	a spoonful

A On a separate sheet of paper . . .

Suggested teaching time:	7 minutes	Your actual teaching time:

- Have students look at the example sentence as a class. Then have them rewrite the sentences.

- Move around the room, helping students as needed. Then review answers with the class.

- Have students identify if each noun is countable (1. razors; 2. nail clippers; 3. brushes) or non-countable (4. mascara; 5. nail polish; 6. sunscreen; 7. dental floss; 8. deodorant). Then ask *How can we make the uncountable nouns countable?* (Add a container, quantifier, or other modifier; for example, tube of mascara, bottle of nail polish, bottle of sunscreen, box of dental floss, stick of deodorant.)

Answers to Unit 5, Lesson 1—Exercise A

1. There aren't any razors next to the sink.
2. We don't have any nail clippers.
3. They don't need any brushes for the children.
4. She isn't buying any mascara.
5. The manicurists don't need any new nail polish.
6. I don't want any sunscreen on my back.
7. There isn't any dental floss in aisle 4.
8. They don't need any deodorant for the trip.

B Complete each sentence . . .

Suggested teaching time:	3 minutes	Your actual teaching time:

- For a warm-up and review, ask *What kind of sentences use any?* (Questions and negatives.) Have students find the questions and negative statements and circle them. (1, 2, 3, 5, 6.) Have students fill in the blanks with *any.* Then have students fill in the remaining affirmative statements with *some.*

- For further practice, call on volunteers to identify the count and non-count nouns, as in Exercise A.

Too many, too much, and enough

Suggested teaching time:	4 minutes	Your actual teaching time:

- Write on the board *Sheila has too much homework.* Ask *Does Sheila need more homework?* (No.) *Would she like less homework?* (Probably.) Call on volunteers to create example sentences using *too much*.
- Read the rules with students. Ask volunteers to rewrite the first two example sentences on the board. (There aren't too many customers waiting in line. There isn't too much toothpaste on the toothbrush.)
- You may wish to point out that *not too much* can mean literally that the quantity or amount is not more than necessary. *Not too much* can also mean that there's almost not enough, for example: *There's not too much cheese in the fridge. We should buy some more.*

C Complete each sentence . . .

Suggested teaching time:	6 minutes	Your actual teaching time:

- Have students circle the count nouns (4. choices; 6. brands; 7. people) and underline the non-count nouns (1. nail polish; 2. perfume; 3. fruit; 5. soap; 8. money). Then have students fill in the blanks. Remind them to think about the sentence logically when choosing which word to write.
- After students complete the exercise, have them compare their answers in pairs.

Comparative quantifiers fewer and less

Suggested teaching time:	4 minutes	Your actual teaching time:

- Have students read the information.
- Write *hours / time; dollars / money* on the board. Ask *Which word in each pair is countable? Non-countable?* Have students suggest example sentences for each pair, using *fewer* and *less*. For example, I work fewer hours this year than last year. This project is taking less time.

D Complete each sentence . . .

Suggested teaching time:	3 minutes	Your actual teaching time:

- Have students scan the noun after each blank and decide if it is countable or noncountable. (1. students—countable; 2. cheese—noncountable; 3. ingredients—countable; 4. kinds of cars—countable; 5. movies—countable; 6. body lotion—noncountable)
- Ask *Which quantifier goes with count nouns?* (Fewer.) *Non-count nouns?* (Less.)
- After students complete the exercise, have them compare their answers in pairs.

UNIT 5 Lesson 2

Indefinite pronouns: something, anything . . .

Suggested teaching time:	4 minutes	Your actual teaching time:

- Write on the board *I don't have anything to tell you. I have nothing to tell you.* Ask *What's the difference in meaning between these two sentences?* (There isn't any difference.) Then ask students to suggest a sentence with the opposite meaning. (I have something to tell you.)
- Give students a few minutes to read the rules and example sentences.
- Write these sentences on the board and have students correct them:
  1 *I don't have nothing to do today.* (I don't have anything to do today.)
  2 *Dora hasn't said something about her problem.* (Dora hasn't said anything about her problem.)
  3 *He didn't read nothing about the news.* (He didn't read anything about the news.)
- Write these sentences on the board: 1 *We didn't find _____ at the mall.* 2 *I have _____ to give you.* Tell students to fill in the blanks. Point out that one item has two possible answers. (**1** anything; **2** something / nothing)

Too many, too much, and enough

The word <u>too</u> indicates a quantity that is excessive—more than someone wants or needs. Use <u>enough</u> to indicate that a quantity or amount is satisfactory.

Use <u>too many</u> and <u>not too many</u> for count nouns.
There are too many customers waiting in line.

Use <u>too much</u> and <u>not too much</u> for non-count nouns.
There's too much toothpaste on the toothbrush.

Use <u>enough</u> and <u>not enough</u> for both count and non-count nouns.
There's enough shampoo, but there aren't enough razors.

C Complete each sentence with <u>too many</u>, <u>too much</u>, or <u>enough</u>.

1 Let's do our nails. Do we have ....enough........ nail polish for both of us?
2 This shampoo has ......too much..... perfume. It smells awful!
3 It's not a good idea to buy ......too much......... fruit. We're not going to be home for a few days.
4 This menu has ......too many...... choices. I can't make up my mind.
5 Check the bathroom shelf to see if we have ....enough........ soap. Mom and Dad are coming to visit.
6 I don't like when there are ......too many...... brands. I can't decide which one to buy.
7 There's no way to get a haircut today. ......Too many...... people had the same idea!
8 They don't want to spend ......too much....... money on makeup. They're trying to save money.

Comparative quantifiers <u>fewer</u> and <u>less</u>

Use <u>fewer</u> for count nouns. Use <u>less</u> for non-count nouns.
The Cosmetique store has fewer brands of makeup than the Emporium.
There's less shampoo in this bottle than in that tube.

D Complete each sentence with <u>fewer</u> or <u>less</u>.

1 Which class has ....fewer......... students—the early class or the late one?
2 The recipe calls for ....less.......... cheese than I thought.
3 It has ....fewer........ ingredients, too.
4 Don't rent from Cars Plus. They have ....fewer......... kinds of cars than International.
5 The Cineplus has ....fewer......... movies this weekend than usual.
6 Is there ....less.......... body lotion in the small size or the economy size?

UNIT 5 Lesson 2

Indefinite pronouns: <u>something</u>, <u>anything</u>, <u>everything</u>, and <u>nothing</u>

Use <u>something</u>, <u>nothing</u>, or <u>everything</u> in affirmative statements.
There's something in this box.
Nothing can convince me to get a pedicure.
Everything is ready.

Use <u>anything</u> in negative statements.
There isn't anything in the fridge.

Use <u>something</u>, <u>anything</u>, or <u>everything</u> in <u>yes</u> / <u>no</u> questions.
Is there something we should talk about? Is anything wrong?
Do you have everything you need?

<u>Nothing</u> has the same meaning as <u>not anything</u>. Don't use <u>nothing</u> in negative statements.
There isn't anything in the fridge. = There's nothing in the fridge. NOT There ~~isn't nothing~~ in the fridge.

Choose the correct indefinite pronoun to complete each sentence.

1 I need to go to the store to buy (something)/ anything).
2 There is (something)/ anything) I can do to help.
3 There isn't (everything /(anything) you can do to make yourself taller.
4 I went on the Internet to find (something)/ anything) about how to use sunscreen.
5 They have (something)/ anything) that helps you lose weight.
6 There's (anything /(nothing) that can make you look young again.
7 They can't get (anything)/ nothing) to eat there after ten o'clock.

UNIT 6 Lesson 1

Use to / used to: use and form

Use to and **used to** express a past habitual action, but one that is no longer true today.
  When I was a kid, I **didn't use to eat** vegetables. But now I do.

Remember: In yes / no questions and negative statements, use use to NOT used to.
  I **used to** stay up late. Now I don't.
  I **didn't use to** (NOT used to) get up early. Now I do.
  Did you **use to** (NOT used to) go dancing more often?

> **Note:** The simple past tense can express a past habitual action if there is a reference to a period of time in the past.
>   When I was a kid, I **didn't eat** peppers. I still don't today.

A On a separate sheet of paper, change each statement into a yes / no question.   See page T134 for answers.

  I used to go running every day. *Did you use to go running every day?*

1 There used to be a large tree in front of your house.   3 Their grandmother used to put sugar in their orange juice.
2 Mr. and Mrs. Palmer used to go dancing every weekend.   4 Luke used to be very overweight.

B On a separate sheet of paper, use the prompts to write logical sentences with negative or affirmative forms of use to / used to.   See page T134 for answers.

1 Jason and Trish / get lots of exercise, but now they go swimming every day.
2 There / be a movie theater on Smith Street, but now there isn't.
3 No one / worry about fatty foods, but now most people do.
4 English / be an international language, but now everyone uses English to communicate around the world.
5 Women in North America / wear pants, but now it's very common for them to wear them.

Be used to / get used to

Be used to + a noun phrase means to be accustomed to something. Compare use to / used to with be used to.
  I **didn't use to** like spicy food. But now I do. (used to + base form)
  I'm **used to** the noise now. But at first, it really bothered me. (be used to + a noun phrase)

Get used to + a noun phrase means to become accustomed to something.
  You'll **get used to** the new menu after a few days.

Be careful! With be used to, don't change used in negative statements or questions.
  He **wasn't used to** the weather there. NOT He wasn't use to . . .
  Are you **used to** life here? NOT Are you use to . . .

Choose the correct . . .

Suggested teaching time:	3 minutes	Your actual teaching time:

- Have students circle the negative sentences. (3 and 7) Ask *Which indefinite pronoun do you use with negative statements?* (Anything.) Make sure students remember that *nothing* cannot be used in negative statements. Then have them complete the exercise.
- Review answers with the class.

UNIT 6 *Lesson 1*

Use to / *used to*: use and form

Suggested teaching time:	4 minutes	Your actual teaching time:

- Tell the class *When I was little, I used to carry my blanket everywhere.* Ask *Do I still carry my blanket everywhere?* (No.) Point out that we use *used to* in order to talk about a past habitual action that is no longer true.
- Invite students to share something they used to do when they were little.
- Then call on volunteers to read the rules. Focus on the last point—in negative statements and in *yes / no* questions, *used to* changes to *use to*.

A On a separate sheet of paper . . .

Suggested teaching time:	3 minutes	Your actual teaching time:

- Review that a *yes / no* question is one that elicits the answer "yes" or "no." Ask a student to read the sample question in blue. Based on the sentence before it, ask *Is the answer to the question yes or no?* (Yes.) Point out the form change from *used to* to *use to* in the question format.
- Have students complete the exercise. Then review answers with the class.

Answers to Unit 6, Lesson 1—Exercise A
1. Did there use to be a large tree in front of your house?
2. Did Mr. and Mrs. Palmer use to go dancing every weekend?
3. Did their grandmother use to put sugar in their orange juice?
4. Did Luke use to be very overweight?

B On a separate sheet of paper . . .

Suggested teaching time:	3 minutes	Your actual teaching time:

- Have students work in pairs. Encourage them to think carefully about the meaning of the sentence before deciding to use *used to* or *use to*. Model the first sentence. Say *Now Jason and Trish go swimming every day. What makes more sense: that in the past they didn't use to get a lot of exercise, or that they used to get a lot of exercise?* (That they didn't use to get a lot of exercise.)
- Move around the room as pairs discuss and write the sentences. Then review answers with the class. If necessary, break down the explanations as modeled above.

Answers to Unit 6, Lesson 1—Exercise B
1. Jason and Trish didn't use to get lots of exercise, but now they go swimming every day.
2. There used to be a movie theater on Smith Street, but now there isn't.
3. No one used to worry about fatty foods, but now most people do.
4. English didn't use to be an international language, but now everyone uses English to communicate around the world.
5. Women in North America didn't use to wear pants, but now it's very common for them to wear them.

Be used to / *get used to*

Suggested teaching time:	4 minutes	Your actual teaching time:

- Write on the board *I didn't like our new house when we moved into it, but I am used to it now.* Ask *What does* used to *mean in this sentence?* (That I am accustomed to our house.)
- Call on volunteers to read the rules. Clarify the explanations and example sentences as needed.
- Direct students' attention to the Be careful! information. To test understanding, write these two sentences on the board:

    1. I didn't _____ to like cheese, but I do now.

    2. Is she _____ to working in an office now?

Ask, *For the first sentence, should I write* use *or* used? (use) *For the second sentence, should I write* use *or* used? (used)

C Check the sentences . . .

Suggested teaching time:	3 minutes	Your actual teaching time:	

- Have students work in pairs to read the sentences and discuss the meaning. Write cues on the board to help students: *Does the sentence describe a past habitual action? Does the sentence describe getting accustomed to something?*
- When students finish, focus on the unchecked items that describe past habitual action. (2, 3, 6.) For each item, ask if the situation is true now. (No.)

D Write . . .

Suggested teaching time:	5 minutes	Your actual teaching time:	

- After students complete the exercise, have them compare their answers in pairs.
- Review answers with the class. Focus on the incorrect items. For example, ask *Why is number 1 incorrect?* (*Used to* in this sentence means *accustomed to* and does not change form in the negative and question forms.)

E On a separate sheet of paper . . .

Suggested teaching time:	4 minutes	Your actual teaching time:	

- Write on the board *I'm used to . . . I'm not used to . . .* Orally complete each sentence. For example, *I'm used to getting up early. I'm not used to the traffic in this city.*
- Have students write four of their own sentences. Make sure they understand that they are writing sentences with *used to* meaning *accustomed to*—not describing past habitual actions.
- To review answers, call on students to share their sentences with the class.

Repeated actions in the past: *would* + base form

Suggested teaching time:	4 minutes	Your actual teaching time:	

- Write on the board *When I was little, I used to carry my blanket everywhere.* Say *Another way to say this sentence is "When I was little, I would carry my blanket everywhere."* Call on a student to read the first rule.
- Read the Be careful! note. Provide a few more incorrect sentences for students to correct on the board; for example, *When I was young . . . I ~~would~~ (used to) have a lot of free time. I ~~would~~ (used to) live in Canada. I ~~would~~ (used to) like cotton candy.*

F If it is possible . . .

Suggested teaching time:	4 minutes	Your actual teaching time:	

- Review that *would* can only be used to describe habitual past action. It cannot be used to describe possession, likes and dislikes, situations, or locations in the past.
- Make sure that students understand that each sentence could be completed with *used to*. The task is to see which sentences can also be completed with *would*. (1, 4, 5)
- After students have completed the exercise, have them compare their answers in pairs.

UNIT 6 Lesson 2

Negative *yes* / *no* questions: short answers

Suggested teaching time:	3 minutes	Your actual teaching time:	

- Have students read the rules in the box to themselves.
- Then bring the class together. Ask individual students questions such as *Isn't your name Mark? Don't you have an older sister?* Encourage students to use short answers to answer your questions.

C Check the sentences in which <u>used to</u> means "accustomed to something."

☑ 1 When the school term ended, I was finally used to the new teacher.
☐ 2 In our other class, the teacher used to be very strict.
☐ 3 They used to like red meat, but now they don't.
☑ 4 Because we lived in the mountains, we weren't used to fresh seafood.
☑ 5 I'm sure she'll get used to her new apartment soon.
☐ 6 These shoes used to be comfortable, but now they're too loose.
☑ 7 I'm sure she'll get used to wearing high-heeled shoes.

D Write ✓ if the sentence is correct. Write ✗ if it is incorrect and make corrections.

              used
☒ 1 I'll never get ~~use~~ to the traffic here.
☑ 2 We didn't use to take vacations very often.
         used
☒ 3 Is he ~~use~~ to his new roommate yet?
             used
☒ 4 Will she ever get ~~use~~ to life in the city?
☑ 5 What did you used to do on weekdays when you weren't working?

E On a separate sheet of paper, write two sentences about something you're used to and two sentences about something you're not used to. Answers will vary.

Repeated actions in the past: <u>would</u> + base form

You can also use <u>would</u> + the base form of a verb to describe repeated past actions. In this use, <u>would</u> has the same meaning as <u>used to</u>.

  When we were young, our parents would go camping with us. (= used to go camping with us.)

Be careful! With non-action verbs that don't describe repeated actions, use <u>used to</u>, not <u>would</u>.

  I used to have a lot of clothes. NOT I ~~would have~~ a lot of clothes.
  My hometown used to be Dakar. NOT My hometown ~~would be~~ Dakar.
  I used to be a terrible English student. NOT I ~~would be~~ a terrible English student.
  My friends and I used to hate baseball. NOT My friends and I ~~would hate~~ baseball.

F If it is possible, complete the sentence with <u>would</u>. If not, use a form of <u>used to</u>.

1 They ....would.... go to the beach every Saturday in the summer.
2 I ....used to.... have a really large kitchen in my old house.
3 My husband never ....used to.... like coffee, but now he can't get enough of it.
4 Almost every evening of our vacation we ....would.... eat at a terrific outdoor restaurant.
5 Before the microwave, people ....would.... heat up soup on the top of the stove.
6 Sigrid ....used to.... be a tour guide, but now she's a professional chef.
7 There ....used to.... be three or four Italian restaurants in town, but now there aren't any.

UNIT **6** *Lesson 2*

Negative <u>yes</u> / <u>no</u> questions: short answers

Answer negative <u>yes</u> / <u>no</u> questions the same way as you would answer affirmative <u>yes</u> / <u>no</u> questions.

Is Jane a vegetarian?	Yes, she is. / No, she isn't.
Isn't Jane a vegetarian?	
Do they have two sons?	Yes, they do. / No, they don't.
Don't they have two sons?	

Answer each negative question with a short answer. (Use the information for your answer.)

1 A: Isn't Jeremy a lawyer?
   B: .....No, he isn't..... He's not a lawyer.

2 A: Doesn't Bob have two brothers?
   B: .....Yes, he does..... He has two younger brothers.

3 A: Haven't you been to Siberia before?
   B: .....No, I haven't..... I've never been here before.

4 A: Aren't you learning English right now?
   B: .....Yes, I am..... I'm studying English at the institute.

5 A: Wasn't Nancy at the movies last night?
   B: .....No, she wasn't... She didn't go to the movies.

6 A: Don't Sachiko and Tomofumi have a car?
   B: .....Yes, they do.... They own a minivan.

UNIT 7 Lesson 1

Gerunds and infinitives: usage within sentences

Gerunds (-ing form of a verb) and infinitives (to + base form) function as nouns within sentences.

Gerunds

Like nouns, gerunds can be subjects, subject complements, direct objects, and objects of prepositions.
   Painting is my favorite leisure-time activity. (subject)
   My favorite activity is **painting**. (subject complement; usually follows be)
   I enjoy **painting**. (direct object)
   I read a book about the history of **painting**. (object of the preposition of)

Infinitives

Infinitives can be subjects, subject complements, and direct objects.
   To paint well is a talent. (subject)
   The only thing he needs is **to paint**. (subject complement; usually follows be)
   I want **to paint**. (direct object)

Underline the gerunds and circle the infinitives in these sentences. How is each used in the sentence? On the line next to each sentence, write *S* for subject, *C* for subject complement, *DO* for direct object, or *OP* for object of a preposition.

...do... 1 I enjoy watching old movies every night on TV.

...do... 2 Her greatest dream was (to see) all of her children attend college.

...op... 3 What's the point of creating a nice environment at home if genetics is the only thing that counts?

...s... 4 Avoiding too much pressure helps children become less critical.

...do... 5 My niece plans (to study) personality development next semester.

UNIT 7 Lesson 2

Negative gerunds

A gerund can be made negative by using a negative word before it.
   I like **not going** to bed too late.
   They complained about **never having** enough time.

Answer each negative question . . .

Suggested teaching time:	4 minutes	Your actual teaching time:

- Have students work individually to complete the exercise. Tell them to use the information in the exchange to answer the question correctly. Model item 1 for students. Ask *How do we know whether Jeremy is a lawyer?* (The last sentence in 1B says *He's not a lawyer.*)

- Review answers with the class. Have students point out the information that helped them answer the questions.

Option: (+5 minutes) Have pairs choose one of the conversations and continue it for one or more exchanges. Tell them to use negative yes / no questions; for example, A: *Isn't Jeremy a lawyer?* B: *No, he isn't.* A: *Really? Didn't he go to law school?* B: *Yes, he did, but then he became a policeman.*

UNIT 7 Lesson 1

Gerunds and infinitives: usage . . .

Suggested teaching time:	10 minutes	Your actual teaching time:

- On the board, write 1. I love *dancing*. 2. I love *to dance*. Ask *Do these sentences have the same meaning?* (Yes.) *What's the difference between them?* (Sentence 1 uses a gerund. Sentence 2 uses an infinitive.)

- Call on a student to read the first rule and example sentences in the box. Point to the underlined words in the sentences and ask *How do these words function—as nouns or verbs?* (They all function as nouns.)

- Ask students to suggest additional sentences that use a gerund as a subject, subject complement, object of a preposition, and direct object. Explain these terms as necessary. (For example: a *subject complement* describes or renames the subject of the sentence.) Possible responses:
   subject (Dancing is a healthy exercise.)
   subject complement (My favorite kind of exercise is dancing.)
   object of a preposition (I wrote an essay about dancing.)
   direct object (I enjoy dancing at clubs.)

- Call on a student to read the second rule and example sentences. Ask students to suggest additional sentences that use an infinitive in the following ways:
   subject (To sing opera is difficult.)
   subject complement (What I really want is to sing.)
   direct object (I love to sing jazz.)

- Move around the room and help students as needed. Provide additional examples such as:
   subject: Skating is a popular Olympic sport.
   subject complement: A popular Olympic sport is skating.
   direct object: I like skating.
   object of a preposition: I am interested in skating.

Underline the gerunds . . .

Suggested teaching time:	3 minutes	Your actual teaching time:

- For a warm-up, ask *What form is a gerund?* (Base form of verb + *-ing*.) Before completing the exercise, instruct students to scan the sentences for all the gerunds and underline them. Repeat this process for infinitives, and have students circle them in the sentences.

- In pairs, have students identify the parts of speech and label them. Encourage students to discuss any statements they are not sure about. Move around the room and help students as needed.

- Review any outstanding questions.

UNIT 7 Lesson 2

Negative gerunds

Suggested teaching time:	4 minutes	Your actual teaching time:

- Ask a volunteer to read the rule and example sentences in the box. Write on the board I *really don't like . . .* Complete the sentence with a negative gerund; for example, *not seeing my friends during the summer.* Then call on several students to finish the sentence with their own ideas.

- Write on the board I'm *worried about never having enough money to pay rent.* Ask *Can we replace* never *with* not? (Yes.) *Is the meaning the same?* (Not exactly.) Explain that in the sentence above, *never* suggests that not having money is an ongoing, continuous situation, whereas *not having enough money* refers to the situation right now.

Complete the paragraph . . .

Suggested teaching time:	3 minutes	Your actual teaching time:

- Tell students to read the paragraph carefully. Have them complete the exercise individually, thinking carefully about the context.
- When students have completed the exercise, have them compare their answers in pairs. Move around the room and help students with any problem areas.

Option: (+8 minutes) On the board, write *I really want to do something to improve* . . . Have students write a paragraph describing what they would like to improve about themselves or their surroundings. Tell them to use both affirmative and negative gerunds in their paragraphs.

UNIT 8 Lesson 1

The passive voice: transitive verbs . . .

Suggested teaching time:	7 minutes	Your actual teaching time:

- Ask a volunteer to read the first rule and example sentences in the box aloud. Read the Remember note to students and ask *What is the subject in the first example sentence?* (Picasso.) *What is the verb?* (Painted.) *What is the direct object?* (Guernica.)
- Call on a volunteer to read the second rule. Focus students' attention to the example sentences. Ask *What is the direct object in each of the sentences?* (There is none. The verbs are intransitive, so there is no receiver of the action.)
- Tell students to scan the list of common intransitive verbs on the right. Tell them to try to attach direct objects to the verbs, such as *I arrived on time. I walk to school. Don't fall down.*
- Invite students to suggest additional sentences that use transitive verbs; for example, *They sold their house last week.* For each sentence, ask *What is the receiver of the action?*

A Check each sentence . . .

Suggested teaching time:	4 minutes	Your actual teaching time:

- For a warm-up, have students scan the sentences and underline the verbs. (1. arrives; 2. has bought; 3. stole; 4. lived; 5. sent; 6. is coming; 7. opened.) Before students complete the exercise, make sure they remember that intransitive means there is no direct object. Then as students work, move around the room and help them as needed.
- Review answers with the class.

Option: (+2 minutes) For a challenge, have students locate the direct objects in the sentences with transitive verbs. (2. two drawings; 3. painting; 5. *Sunflowers*; 7. a new gallery.)

The passive voice: form

Suggested teaching time:	7 minutes	Your actual teaching time:

- Remind students that unlike intransitive verbs, transitive verbs can be used in the active or passive voice.
- Have students look at the first set of example sentences. Walk them through the transformation. Ask:
  What is the verb in the first sentence? (Buy.)
  What is the receiver of the action? (Famous paintings.)
  Who is the performer of the action? (Art collectors.)
  How does the passive sentence differ from the active one? (In the passive sentence, the focus is more on the receiver of the action.)
- Point out the *by* phrase (also known as the *agent*) in the passive sentences and tell students to underline it. Ask *Did any sentence not have a* by *phrase?* (The second sentence and the last one.) *Why do you think there is no* by *phrase?* (Because it isn't important to name who is showing the films and the drawings. The important information is the films / drawings and the locations—the Film Center and the Tate Modern.)

Complete the paragraph with affirmative and negative gerunds.

I really want to do something to improve my appearance and lose weight. I'm sick of .....**not being**..... able to fit into my
                                                                                        1 be
clothes. I know it's not enough to complain about ......**gaining**...... weight—I need to do something about it! I plan to spend
                                                         2 gain
every afternoon ....**riding**........ my bike. Also, I want to go on a diet, but I'm afraid of ......**feeling**...... hungry all the time.
                    3 ride   4 feel
I worry about .....**not having**.... enough energy to exercise if I'm .....**not getting**... enough to eat.
                 5 have   6 get

UNIT 8 *Lesson 1*

The passive voice: transitive verbs and intransitive verbs

A transitive verb can have a direct object. Transitive verbs can be used in the active voice or passive voice.

active voice	passive voice

Picasso **painted** *Guernica* in 1937. → *Guernica* **was painted** in 1937.

An intransitive verb cannot have a direct object. With an intransitive verb, there is no "receiver" of an action.

The painting **arrives** tomorrow.
The *Mona Lisa* **will stay** at the Louvre.
That new sculpture **looks** like a Botero.

> **Remember:** The subject of a sentence performs the action of the verb. A direct object receives the action of the verb.

Common intransitive verbs

arrive	happen	sit
come	laugh	sleep
die	live	stand
fall	rain	stay
go	seem	walk

A Check each sentence that has an intransitive verb.

☑ 1 Pedro Almodóvar's new film arrives in theaters this fall.
☐ 2 A Canadian art collector has bought two of Michelangelo's drawings.
☐ 3 Someone stole Edvard Munch's painting *The Scream* in 2004.
☑ 4 The painter Georgia O'Keeffe lived in the southwestern part of the United States.
☐ 5 The Van Gogh Museum in Amsterdam sent *Sunflowers* on a world tour.
☑ 6 The traveling collection of ancient Roman sculpture is coming to San Diego this week.
☐ 7 The Metropolitan Museum of Art opened a new gallery last year.

The passive voice: form

Form the passive voice with a form of <u>be</u> and the past participle of a verb.

	Active voice	Passive voice
Simple present tense	Art collectors **buy** famous paintings all over the world.	Famous paintings **are bought** by art collectors all over the world.
Present continuous	The Film Center **is showing** Kurosawa's films.	Kurosawa's films **are being shown** at the Film Center.
Present perfect	Some world leaders **have bought** Yu Hung's paintings.	Yu Hung's paintings **have been bought** by some world leaders.
Simple past tense	I. M. Pei **designed** the Grand Pyramid at the Louvre.	The Grand Pyramid at the Louvre **was designed** by I. M. Pei.
Past continuous	In 2010, the museum **was selling** copies of Monet's paintings.	In 2010, copies of Monet's paintings **were being sold** by the museum.
Future with <u>will</u>	Ang Lee **will direct** a new film next year.	A new film **will be directed** by Ang Lee next year.
Future with <u>be going to</u>	The Tate Modern **is going to show** Van Gogh's drawings next month.	Van Gogh's drawings **are going to be shown** at the Tate Modern next month.

B　On a separate sheet of paper, rewrite each sentence in the passive voice. Use a <u>by</u> phrase only if it is important to know who is performing the action.　See page T138 for answers.

1　Someone actually stole the *Mona Lisa* in 1911.
2　Paloma Picasso designed these pieces of silver jewelry.
3　Someone will repair the sculpture when it gets old.
4　People have paid millions of U.S. dollars for some of Van Gogh's paintings.
5　They are showing some new paintings at the Smith Gallery this week.
6　The Malcolm Museum is going to exhibit ten sculptures by Asian artists.
7　Frida Kahlo was painting these pieces while she was sick in bed.
8　People built great pyramids throughout Central America during the height of the Mayan civilization.

C　On a separate sheet of paper, rewrite the sentences in Exercise A that have a transitive verb, changing the active voice to the passive voice.　See page T138 for answers.

UNIT 8 Lesson 2

The passive voice: <u>yes</u> / <u>no</u> questions

To form <u>yes</u> / <u>no</u> questions in the passive voice, move the first auxiliary verb before the subject.

Simple present tense	Are famous paintings ~~are~~ bought by art collectors?
Present continuous	Are Kurosawa's films ~~are~~ being shown at the Film Center?
Present perfect	Have Yu Hung's paintings ~~have~~ been bought by some world leaders?
Simple past tense	Was the Grand Pyramid at the Louvre ~~was~~ designed by I. M. Pei?
Past continuous	Were copies of Monet's paintings ~~were~~ being sold by the museum?
Future with <u>will</u>	Will a new film ~~will~~ be directed by Ang Lee next year?
Future with <u>be going to</u>	Is a collection of Van Gogh's drawings ~~is~~ going to be shown next month?

On a separate sheet of paper, rewrite the sentences as <u>yes</u> / <u>no</u> questions in the passive voice.
See page T138 for answers.

1　That new film about families is being directed by Gillian Armstrong.
2　One of da Vinci's most famous drawings has been sold by a German art collector.
3　A rare ceramic figure from the National Palace Museum in Taipei will be sent to the Metropolitan Museum of Art in New York.
4　A new exhibit is going to be opened at the Photography Gallery this week.
5　Some new paintings have been bought by the Prado Museum for their permanent collection.
6　*Las Meninas* can be seen at the Prado Museum in Madrid.
7　The *Jupiter* Symphony was written by Mozart.
8　Some of Michelangelo's work was being shown around the world in the 1960s.

B On a separate sheet of paper . . .

Suggested teaching time:	4 minutes	Your actual teaching time:

• To help students complete the exercise, have them underline the verb and circle the direct object in each sentence. Then instruct them to scan the subject of each sentence. Ask *Which subject seems like it can be omitted?* (Subjects such as *Someone, People, They* in items 1, 3, 4, 5, 8.) Explain to students that these sentences will not have a *by* phrase when they are converted into the passive voice; for example, in item 1: *The Mona Lisa was stolen in 1911.* It is understood that someone stole the painting. That information is not important.

Answers to Unit 8, Lesson 1—Exercise B

1. The *Mona Lisa* was actually stolen in 1911.
2. These pieces of silver jewelry were designed by Paloma Picasso.
3. When the sculpture gets old, it will be repaired.
4. Millions of U.S. dollars have been paid for some of Van Gogh's paintings.
5. Some new paintings are being shown at the Smith Gallery this week.
6. Ten sculptures by Asian artists are going to be exhibited at the Malcolm Museum.
7. These pieces were being painted by Frida Kahlo while she was sick in bed.
8. Great pyramids were built throughout Central America during the height of the Mayan civilization.

C On a separate sheet of paper . . .

Suggested teaching time:	3 minutes	Your actual teaching time:

• As students focus on sentences 2, 3, 5, and 7, remind them to look for the performer of the action and decide if the performer is important to the meaning of the sentence (items 2 and 5) or not important (item 3). This will help them decide whether to use the *by* phrase or not.

Answers to Unit 8, Lesson 1—Exercise C

2. Two of Michelangelo's drawings were bought by a Canadian art collector.
3. Edvard Munch's painting *The Scream* was stolen in 2004.
5. *Sunflowers* was sent on a world tour by the Van Gogh Museum in Amsterdam.
7. A new gallery was opened by the Metropolitan Museum of Art last year.

FYI: The answer to item 7 implies that the museum management funded the gallery, but the new gallery is not located inside the museum. To indicate that the gallery is located in the museum, change the preposition to *at*.

UNIT 8 Lesson 2

The passive voice: yes / no questions

Suggested teaching time:	5 minutes	Your actual teaching time:

• Give students a few minutes to study the sentences in the chart. As students work, write on the board *This class is being offered again next semester.* When students finish reading, ask a volunteer to apply the rule they observed in the example sentences to the sentence on the board. (They should move *is* to the beginning of the sentence.)

On a separate sheet of paper . . .

Suggested teaching time:	6 minutes	Your actual teaching time:

• To help form the *yes / no* questions, first instruct students to underline the full verb in each sentence and circle the first auxiliary. Then tell them to follow the models in the chart if they need help.

• After students rewrite the sentences, review answers with the class. Call on volunteers to read the sentences. Help students and offer explanations as needed.

Answers to Unit 8, Lesson 2

1. Is that new film about families being directed by Gillian Armstrong?
2. Has one of da Vinci's most famous drawings been sold by a German art collector?
3. Will a rare ceramic figure from the National Palace Museum in Taipei be sent to the Metropolitan Museum of Art in New York?
4. Is a new exhibit going to be opened at the Photography Gallery this week?
5. Have some new paintings been bought by the Prado Museum for their permanent collection?
6. Can *Las Meninas* be seen at the Prado Museum in Madrid?
7. Was the *Jupiter* Symphony written by Mozart?
8. Was some of Michelangelo's work being shown around the world in the 1960s?

 **UNIT 9** *Lesson 1*

Other ways to express a purpose

Suggested teaching time:	5 minutes	Your actual teaching time:

- Write on the board *I e-mailed the company. I wanted to complain about the product.* Ask students to combine these sentences. (Possible responses: I e-mailed the company because I wanted to complain about the product. I e-mailed the company to complain about the product. I wanted to complain about the product, so I e-mailed the company.) Write *I e-mailed the company in order to complain about the product.*

- Call on a student to read the first rule and example sentences in the box. Write on the board *I am taking this English class . . .* Call on volunteers to complete the sentence; for example, *. . . in order to speak English better; . . . because I want to travel to England; . . . to meet new people.*

- Read the second rule in the box. Have students read the example sentences to themselves. Tell them to underline the noun phrases and gerund phrases. Point out in the Be careful! note that it is not possible to use *for* before an infinitive.

A On a separate sheet of paper . . .

Suggested teaching time:	4 minutes	Your actual teaching time:

- For a warm-up, have students underline the infinitive of purpose in each sentence. Then have them rewrite the sentences using *in order to*.

- Review the answers with the class. For a challenge, have students suggest other ways to say each sentence; for example, *She joined Facebook because she wanted to meet new people.*

Answers to Unit 9, Lesson 1—Exercise A
1. She joined Facebook in order to meet new people.
2. Jason surfs the Internet in order to see what's new.
3. Alison uses online banking in order to pay all her bills.
4. They always print their documents first in order to read them carefully.
5. I never use the pull-down menu in order to open files.
6. He used an online telephone service in order to call his family.

B Complete each sentence . . .

Suggested teaching time:	3 minutes	Your actual teaching time:

- Give students a few minutes to scan the sentences and mark those that have noun or gerund phrases following the blank. Ask *Which word would best complete these sentences?* (For.) Then ask *What form of the verb follows to?* (The base form of the verb.) Have students fill in the blanks with the correct word.

- After students have completed the exercise, have them check their answers in pairs. Move around the room to answer any questions.

UNIT 9 *Lesson 2*

Comparison with adjectives: review

Suggested teaching time:	5 minutes	Your actual teaching time:

- Give students a few minutes to review comparative and superlative forms. Then have students work in pairs to compare themselves to each other. Ask them to make statements in the comparative and superlative about different students in the entire class; for example, *I am taller than Michel. I am not as talkative as Michel. Damian is the smartest student in the class.*

UNIT 9   *Lesson 1*

Other ways to express a purpose

In order to

You can use <u>in order to</u> with a base form of a verb to express a purpose. The following three sentences have the same meaning.

    I scrolled down in order to read the text.

    I scrolled down because I wanted to read the text.

    I scrolled down to read the text.

For

You can use <u>for</u> to express a purpose before a noun phrase or gerund phrase.

    She e-mailed me for some advice.

    They shop online for electronic products.

    I use my smart phone for e-mailing clients.

Be careful! Don't use <u>for</u> before an infinitive of purpose.

    DON'T SAY She e-mailed me ~~for~~ to ask a question.

A   On a separate sheet of paper, rewrite the sentences with <u>in order to</u>.   See page T139 for answers.

  1   She joined Facebook to meet new people.

  2   Jason surfs the Internet to see what's new.

  3   Alison uses online banking to pay all her bills.

  4   They always print their documents first to read them carefully.

  5   I never use the pull-down menu to open files.

  6   He used an online telephone service to call his family.

B   Complete each sentence with <u>for</u> or <u>to</u>.

  1   My friend e-mailed me …to… say he's getting married.

  2   Jane shops online …for… clothing.

  3   I went online …to… find a new keyboard.

  4   Matt created a web page …for… keeping in touch with his family and friends.

  5   Sometimes I use my computer …to… download movies.

  6   We both log on to the Internet …for… information.

  7   Just click the icon …to… open the file.

  8   When Gina's computer crashed, her brother came over …to… help her.

UNIT 9   *Lesson 2*

Comparison with adjectives: review

As . . . as

Use <u>as</u> . . . <u>as</u> to indicate how two things are equal or the same. Use <u>not as</u> . . . <u>as</u> to indicate how two things are different.

    The new Jax 10 monitor is just as good as the Jax 20.

    The Jax 10 monitor is not as big as the Jax 20.

Comparatives

Use comparatives to show how two things are not equal. Use <u>than</u> if the second item is mentioned.

    My laptop is heavier than John's (is).   OR My laptop is heavier.

    Regular mail is less convenient than e-mail. OR Regular mail is less convenient.

Superlatives

Use superlatives to show how one thing is different from two or more other things. Remember to use <u>the</u> with the superlative.

    The M2, LX, and Bell printers are all good. But the Bell is the best.

    The Gatt 40 monitor is the least expensive one you can buy.

A Correct the error in each sentence.

1 The Orca speakers aren't as ~~heavier~~ *heavy* as the Yaltas.

2 My old laptop didn't have as many problems ~~than~~ *as* my new laptop.

3 I checked out the three top brands, and the Piston was definitely the ~~better.~~ *best*

4 Maxwell's web camera is much more expensive ~~as~~ *than* their digital camera.

5 Of all the monitors I looked at, the X60 is definitely ~~larger.~~ *the largest*

6 The Jaguar is *the* most powerful computer in the world.

Comparison with adverbs

Comparatives

My new computer **runs faster than** my old one.
The X20 **operates more quietly than** the X30.

As . . . as

My new phone **works as well as** my old one.
The Macro laptop **doesn't run as slowly as** the Pell does.

Superlatives

Of these three laptops, the MPro **starts up the most slowly.**

> **Remember:** Adverbs often give information about verbs.
> My phone works **well**.   My printer prints **fast**.
>
> **Many adjectives can be changed to adverbs by adding -ly.**
> | | | | | | |
> |---|---|---|---|---|---|
> | loud | → **loudly** | quick | → **quickly** | quiet | → **quietly** |
> | poor | → **poorly** | bad | → **badly** | slow | → **slowly** |

B On a separate sheet of paper, rewrite each pair of sentences into a single sentence using comparatives. Then write single sentences using <u>as . . . as</u>.   See page T140 for answers.

1 My brother's smart phone downloads music quickly. My MP3 player doesn't download quickly.

2 My new computer doesn't log on slowly. My old computer logs on slowly.

3 Your old monitor works well. My new monitor doesn't work well.

4 The Rico printer prints quickly. The Grant printer doesn't print quickly.

5 The Pace scanner doesn't run quietly. The Rico scanner runs quietly.

UNIT 10 Lesson 1

Should and ought to; had better

Use <u>should</u> or <u>ought to</u> + a base form to state an opinion or give advice, especially about an ethical choice. <u>Ought to</u> has the same meaning as <u>should</u>, but <u>should</u> is slightly less formal.
  You **should** (or **ought to**) **return** the wallet. You **shouldn't keep** it.

Use <u>had better</u> + a base form to state an opinion or give stronger advice. The meaning is similar to <u>should</u> and <u>ought to</u>, but <u>had better</u> expresses the idea that there is a consequence for not doing something.
  You'd **better tell** the waiter that the check is wrong. If you don't, he will have to pay.
  You'd **better not eat** at the Fairway Café. I got sick there the last time I did.

Remember: <u>Should</u>, <u>ought to</u>, and <u>had better</u> precede other verbs and give them a special meaning. They never change form.

> **Note:** In American English it's very uncommon to use <u>ought to</u> in negative statements or questions. Use <u>should</u> or <u>shouldn't</u> instead.

A On a separate sheet of paper, complete the statements about an ethical choice, expressing your own ideas.
Answers will vary.

1 Colleagues in an office should always ....

2 Parents of young children should not ....

3 We ought to tell the store owner when ....

4 You forgot to pay your check? You had better ....

5 We had better not .... It's too expensive.

B On a separate sheet of paper, write five suggestions to a visitor to your country, using <u>had better</u> or <u>had better not</u>.
Answers will vary.

> ❝ You'd better not take the local train to Bradbury. It's too slow. ❞

A Correct the error . . .

Suggested teaching time:	4 minutes	Your actual teaching time:

- Tell students to correct the errors in the sentences. Encourage them to refer to the rules in the box if they need help.

- Have students compare their answers with a partner. Move around the room and help students as needed.

- Review answers with the class. Ask *Which sentences are in the superlative?* (3, 5, and 6.) Then for a challenge, ask students for a different way to state item 1. (*The Yaltas are heavier than the Orca.*)

Comparison with adverbs

Suggested teaching time:	3 minutes	Your actual teaching time:

- To review what an adverb is, have students look at the Remember note. Call on volunteers to suggest sentences that use the adverbs in the list; for example, *She hurt herself badly. Please talk quietly—everyone is asleep.*

- Tell students to read the rules about making comparisons with adverbs and study the example sentences.

- Write on the board *She didn't do as poorly as I did on the exam.* Tell students to suggest another way to say the same sentence. (*I performed more poorly on the exam than she did. She performed better on the exam than I did.*)

FYI: Although many adverbs end in -*ly*, there are four adverbs that are the same as their adjective forms: *hard, fast, early,* and *late*. Their comparative forms are *harder, faster, earlier,* and *later*.

B On a separate sheet of paper . . .

Suggested teaching time:	4 minutes	Your actual teaching time:

- For a warm-up, have students underline the common verb in each pair of sentences. Then have them combine the sentences into one, using the comparative form. Move around the room and help students as needed.

- Have students work in pairs to write single sentences using *as*. Remind students to use negatives where needed in order to maintain the same meaning.

Answers to Unit 9, Lesson 2—Exercise B

1. My brother's MP3 player downloads music more quickly than my MP3 player. / My MP3 player doesn't download music as quickly as my brother's MP3 player.
2. My old computer logs on more slowly than my new computer. / My new computer doesn't log on as slowly as my old computer.
3. Your old monitor works better than my new monitor. / My new monitor doesn't work as well as your old monitor.
4. The Rico printer prints more quickly than the Grant printer. / The Grant printer doesn't print as quickly as the Rico printer.
5. The Rico scanner runs more quietly than the Pace scanner. / The Pace scanner doesn't run as quietly as the Rico scanner.

UNIT 10 *Lesson 1*

Should and ought to; had better

Suggested teaching time:	5 minutes	Your actual teaching time:

- Call on students to read the first rule and example sentence. Point out that *should* and *ought* to have the same meaning, and both can be used to state an opinion or give advice.

- Direct students' attention to the Note about *ought to* in negative statements and questions.

- Read the second rule and examples. Make sure that students understand that *had better* is stronger than *should* and *ought to*.

- Go over the Remember note. Stress that *should, ought to,* and *had better* never change form.

A On a separate sheet of paper . . .

Suggested teaching time:	5 minutes	Your actual teaching time:

- If necessary, review the rules in the grammar chart before students start the exercise.

- Move around the room, helping students as needed.

- To review answers, call on a few students to share their sentences with the class.

B On a separate sheet of paper . . .

Suggested teaching time:	5 minutes	Your actual teaching time:

- Direct students' attention to the sample answer in the box. Remind them that they should use *had better* to give stronger advice, when there will be consequences if the advice is not followed.

- To review answers, have students compare answers in pairs. Then ask pairs to share their sentences with the class.

Have to, must, and be supposed to

Suggested teaching time:	6–8 minutes	Your actual teaching time:

- Call on students to read the *have to / must* rule and example sentences. Point out that these two forms are used when there is no other choice of action available.
- Direct students' attention to the Note. Write three examples on the board:

    I must finish this report.

    I have to finish this report.

    I have got to finish this report.

Ask *Is there a difference in meaning between these three sentences?* (No.) *Which sentence sounds the most formal?* (The one with *must*.) *Which sentence sounds the least formal?* (The one with *have got to*.)

- Read the rules and examples for *don't have to* and *must not*. Make sure that students understand that *don't have to* is used when there are different choices of action available, and *must not* is used when someone is not allowed to do something.
- Call on volunteers to read aloud the rule and examples for *be supposed to*. Explain that *be supposed to* is not as strong as *have to* and *must*. We use *be supposed to* when someone expects us to do something, but it is not necessary or required.

C On a separate sheet of paper . . .

Suggested teaching time:	5 minutes	Your actual teaching time:

- Do the first item with the class as an example. Have a volunteer write the two answers on the board (*Drivers must obey the speed limit. Drivers have to obey the speed limit.*)
- Review the answers as a class. Ask, *Who might say these things?* (Possible answers: 1. A policeman; 2. A teacher; 3. A restaurant worker; 4. A restaurant worker.)

D On a separate sheet of paper . . .

Suggested teaching time:	6–8 minutes	Your actual teaching time:

- Have students do this activity in pairs.
- Call on pairs to share their answers with the class. Ask *Does everyone agree about what students are supposed to do?* Write a list of "rules" for your school on the board.

E Choose the sentence . . .

Suggested teaching time:	5 minutes	Your actual teaching time:

- To provide support, briefly review the differences between the verbs used in this exercise before students start: *should, ought to,* and *had better* are close in meaning and are used for advice. *Have to* and *must* are close in meaning and are used to express obligation. *Be supposed to* is used when you are expected to do something, but it is not necessary. *Don't have to* is used when it is not necessary to do something, and *must not* is used when you are not allowed to do something.
- Have students do the exercise individually and then compare their answers in pairs.

UNIT 10 Lesson 2

Possessive nouns: review and expansion

Suggested teaching time:	3 minutes	Your actual teaching time:

- Give students a few minutes to read the rules in the box.
- Write the following words on the board: *lawyer / fees; Hendersons / lake house; kids / toys; Mike and Linda / anniversary.* Call on volunteers to write the possessive form for each pair or group of words. (*Lawyer's fees; Hendersons' lake house; kids' toys; Mike and Linda's anniversary.*)

Have to, must, and be supposed to

Have to and must

Use <u>have to</u> or the modal <u>must</u> + a base form to express obligation when there is no other choice of action available.

> Students **must take** this exam.
> You **have to take** the 6:00 train if you want to arrive on time.

Use <u>don't have to</u> (NOT <u>must</u>) to express a lack of obligation.

> You **don't have to pay** for the shoes if you don't like them. You can return them.

Use <u>must not</u> (NOT <u>don't have to</u>) for a strong or legal prohibition.

> Passengers **must not leave** their baggage unattended in the waiting area.

Be supposed to

Use <u>be supposed to</u> (or <u>not be supposed to</u>) + a base form to express an expected, but not a required, action. The degree of obligation is weaker than with <u>have to</u> or <u>must</u>.

> We're **supposed to pay** our check at the front of the coffee shop, not at the table. (The restaurant expects diners to pay at the front.)
> Hotel guests **are not supposed to use** the towels from their rooms at the pool.

> **Note:** <u>Must</u> is very formal and not very common in speaking. It is generally used by a person in authority (e.g., a teacher or boss) to state policy or law. <u>Have to</u> is much more common in both speaking and writing. The more informal <u>have got to</u> is also common in spoken English.
>
> > Sorry. I**'ve got to hurry**. I'm going to be late.
>
> Don't use <u>must not</u> for a lack of obligation. Use <u>don't have to</u> or <u>doesn't have to</u>.

C On a separate sheet of paper, write each sentence two ways: with <u>must</u> and with <u>have to</u>.

1. Drivers / obey the speed limit.
2. Students / arrive on time for class.
3. In this beach restaurant / diners / wear shoes. If you are barefoot, don't come in.
4. You / have a reservation to eat at the Palace Restaurant.

1. Drivers must obey the speed limit. / Drivers have to obey the speed limit.
2. Students must arrive on time to class. / Students have to arrive on time to class.
3. In this beach restaurant diners must wear shoes. / In this beach restaurant diners have to wear shoes.
4. You must have a reservation to eat at the Palace Restaurant. / You have to have a reservation to eat at the Palace Restaurant.

D On a separate sheet of paper, write five sentences that describe actions your school expects from its students. Use <u>be supposed to</u>. Answers will vary.

> Students are supposed to come on time to class. They're not supposed to be late.

E Choose the sentence closer in meaning to each numbered statement or question.

1. Do you think the Milton Restaurant is a good place to eat?
   - **a** Do you think I should eat at the Milton Restaurant?
   - b Do you think I have to eat at the Milton Restaurant?

2. If you don't have a reservation, the restaurant won't give you a table.
   - a The restaurant is supposed to give you a table.
   - **b** You had better have a reservation.

3. They don't accept credit cards in this store. They only accept cash.
   - **a** You have to pay with cash.
   - b You ought to pay with cash.

4. Don't wear shorts in the restaurant.
   - **a** You must not wear shorts in the restaurant.
   - b You don't have to wear shorts in the restaurant.

UNIT 10 Lesson 2

Possessive nouns: review and expansion

Add <u>'s</u> (an apostrophe + <u>s</u>) to a name or a singular noun.

> Where is Glenn's car?   What's your daughter's married name?
> This is Ms. Baker's class.   I love Dickens's novels.

Add an apostrophe to plural nouns that end in <u>s</u>. For irregular plurals, such as <u>women</u> or <u>children</u>, add <u>'s</u>.

> the women's room   the boys' clothes   the Jacksons' car

Add <u>'s</u> to the name or noun that comes last in a list of two or more.

> Jean and Ralph's house

A   Correct the following sentences, adding an apostrophe or an apostrophe + s to the possessive nouns.

Carmen's jacket is under the table.

1 The two girls' keys are lost.
2 Mr. Stiller's English is really fluent.
3 The doctor's office is downstairs.
4 Sarah and Tom's children are at the Taylor School.

5 That man's car is parked in a no-parking zone.
6 Julia's friend's brother is going to get married tonight.
7 The Smiths' garden is beautiful.

Pronouns: summary

Subject pronouns

Subject pronouns represent subject nouns and noun phrases. The subject pronouns are I, you, he, she, it, we, and they.

Matt didn't break the plate = **He** didn't break the plate.

Object pronouns

Object pronouns represent nouns (and noun phrases) that function as direct objects, indirect objects, and objects of prepositions. The object pronouns are me, you, him, her, it, us, and them.

They gave Susan the toy car for the children.

They gave it to her for them.

B   On a separate sheet of paper, rewrite the sentences, replacing the underlined nouns and noun phrases with pronouns.   See page T142 for answers.

Matt didn't break the plate. *He didn't break it.*

1 Our children love TV.
2 Janet and I never buy food at that store.
3 Do you and I have the car this afternoon?
4 Sylvia's family laughs at her jokes.
5 My friends are speaking with Ms. Rowe today.

6 Mr. Harris is teaching the students with Mr. Cooper.
7 All the students are speaking English very well this year.
8 Does Carl need to give the paper to his teachers?
9 Martin and Larry returned the money to the woman.

A Correct the following . . .

Suggested teaching time:	4 minutes	Your actual teaching time:

- Have students underline the possessive nouns in the sentences. Call their attention to item 6, which has two possessive nouns. Then have students complete the exercise.
- Review answers with the class. Answer any outstanding questions.

Pronouns: summary

Suggested teaching time:	3 minutes	Your actual teaching time:

- To review subject and object pronouns, have students read the rules in the box. Review the definitions of *subject, direct object, indirect object,* and *object of a preposition* as needed.
- Students may be least familiar with the indirect object, which comes before the direct object and indicates *to whom* or *for whom* the action of the verb is being performed. Indirect objects usually appear with verbs such as *take, tell, bring, give, show, offer, send, sell.* An indirect object only appears in a sentence that has a direct object.
- Focus on the last example sentence in the box to make sure students see how the direct and indirect object pronouns switch position.

B On a separate sheet of paper . . .

Suggested teaching time:	4 minutes	Your actual teaching time:

- Hint to students that the words at the beginning of each sentence are the subject pronouns.
- Review answers with the class.

Answers to Unit 10, Lesson 2—Exercise B
1. They love it.
2. We never buy it at that store.
3. Do we have it this afternoon?
4. They laugh at them.
5. They are speaking with her today.
6. He is teaching with them or him.
7. They are speaking English very well this year.
8. Does he need to give it to them?
9. They returned it to her.

Writing Booster

Note about the Writing Booster

These teaching notes and suggested teaching times are provided if you choose to use the Writing Booster in class.

UNIT 1

Avoiding run-on sentences

Suggested teaching time:	15–20 minutes	Your actual teaching time:

- Ask a volunteer to read the first rule in the box. Call on students to say what the subject and verb is in each sentence.

- Read the Remember note aloud. Make sure students understand what *capital letter* means. If necessary, write uppercase and lowercase examples on the board, such as *H h, P p, L l*. Review that a *period* is a form of punctuation. Ask *What are other forms of punctuation?* (Comma, question mark, exclamation point, etc.)

FYI: An exclamation point should only be used at the end of a command or to indicate very strong emotion.

- Write on the board *He is walking to school.* Ask *Is this an independent clause?* (Yes. It has a subject and a verb.) Call on a student to circle the verb in the sentence on the board. (Is walking.) Review that the verb shows action in a sentence. Ask *What is the subject?* (He.) Point out that the sentence expresses a complete idea.

- Write on the board *He is walking to school usually he takes the bus.* Ask *What is wrong with this sentence?* (Possible answers: It has more than one complete idea; it has two independent clauses.) Invite a volunteer to read the second and third rules. Ask a volunteer to correct the sentence on the board using the model for ideas. (Separate into two sentences or connect using a comma and *but*.)

- Finally, have students read the Be careful! note to themselves.

A Write X . . .

- Have students underline the independent clauses in each item. If necessary, refer students to the first rule in the box if they need to review independent clauses.

- Then tell students to analyze whether the independent clauses are connected correctly or if there is a run-on sentence.

- Have students review their answers in pairs. Move around the room and help students as needed.

- Bring the class together and ask *Which sentences are correct?* (4 and 7) *Why?* (4. The two independent clauses are treated as separate sentences. 7. The two independent clauses are connected with a comma and the coordinating conjunction *but*.)

B On a separate sheet of paper . . .

- Ask students to work individually to correct the run-on sentences. Tell them that more than one answer may be possible. Move around the room and help students as needed.

- Have students compare their answers with a partner.

- Then bring the class together. Ask *Did you and your partner have different answers?* If yes, invite students to share both possible answers. Make sure students understand that the coordinating conjunction *but* isn't used simply to connect two ideas like *and* is. *But* is used to express unexpected contrast; for example, item 1: *Ann is Canadian, but she doesn't speak French.* The implication is that someone who is Canadian would likely know some French.

Answers to Unit 1, Exercise B

1. Ann is Canadian. She doesn't speak French. / Ann is Canadian, but she doesn't speak French.
2. They're good students. They work very hard. / They're good students, and they work very hard.
3. My brother is a lawyer. He lives in Hong Kong. / My brother is a lawyer, and he lives in Hong Kong.
5. Some people think cities are beautiful. I don't agree. / Some people think cities are beautiful, but I don't agree.
6. I have been to three foreign countries. I have never been to the United States. / I have been to three foreign countries, but I have never been to the United States.
8. I have never been to the top of the Empire State Building in New York. I have been to the top of Taipei 101 in Taipei. / I have never been to the top of the Empire State Building in New York, but I have been to the top of Taipei 101 in Taipei.

C Guidance for the Writing Exercise (on page 12)

- Tell students to read their paragraphs from page 12 and underline all the independent clauses. Move around the room and help students as needed. Ask students if they see any run-on sentences. Have students make necessary corrections.

- Then have students read a partner's paragraph and see whether their partner missed any run-on sentences. Encourage pairs to offer suggestions. Move around the room and help students as needed.

- Collect students' work and give feedback.

Writing Booster

The Writing Booster is optional. It is intended to teach students the conventions of written English. Each unit's Writing Booster is focused both on a skill and its application to the Writing exercise from the Unit Review page.

UNIT 1   Avoiding run-on sentences

An independent clause is a sentence with a subject and a verb.

subject	verb
I	saw a photo of the mountain.
It	looked very high.

> **Remember:** A sentence begins with a capital letter and ends with a period.

In writing, don't combine independent clauses without using a coordinating conjunction, such as <u>and</u> or <u>but</u>.

Run-on sentence   ✗ ~~I saw a photo of the mountain it looked very high.~~

Correct a run-on sentence by (a) using a period to separate it into two sentences, or (b) using a coordinating conjunction to combine the two independent clauses. A comma before the conjunction is optional.

✓ I saw a photo of the mountain. It looked very high.
✓ I saw a photo of the mountain, **and** it looked very high.

Be careful! Do not use a comma to combine independent clauses. Use a period to separate them.

Run-on sentence   ✗ ~~A new student arrived yesterday, he is from Santos.~~
                   ✓ A new student arrived yesterday. He is from Santos.

A   Write ✗ if the item contains a run-on sentence. Write ✓ if the item is written correctly.

- [✗] **1** Ann is Canadian she doesn't speak French.
- [✗] **2** They're good students they work very hard.
- [✗] **3** My brother is a lawyer, he lives in Hong Kong.
- [✓] **4** Victor and Lisa came home late last night. They stayed up until 4:00 A.M.
- [✗] **5** Some people think cities are beautiful I don't agree.
- [✗] **6** I have been to three foreign countries, I have never been to the United States.
- [✓] **7** We haven't tried Polish food, but we have tried Hungarian food.
- [✗] **8** I have never been to the top of the Empire State Building in New York, I have been to the top of Taipei 101 in Taipei.
- [✗] **9** I visited Jeju in Korea, and it was really beautiful.

B   On a separate sheet of paper, write each of the run-on sentences in Exercise A correctly.
See page T143 for answers.

C   Guidance for the Writing Exercise (on page 12) After you write about your interesting experience, check carefully to see if you have written any run-on sentences. Use a period to separate the independent clauses, or use the coordinating conjunctions <u>and</u> or <u>but</u> to combine them.
Answers will vary.

A paragraph is a group of sentences that relate to a topic or a theme. When your writing contains sections about a variety of topics, it is a good idea to divide it into separate paragraphs.

When there is more than one paragraph, it is customary, though not required, to include **a topic sentence** in each paragraph that summarizes or announces the main idea of the paragraph. The other sentences in the paragraph traditionally include details or facts that support the main idea. Using topic sentences makes paragraphs clearer and easier to understand.

In the writing model to the right, there are two paragraphs, each beginning with a topic sentence (highlighted in yellow).

In the first paragraph, the topic sentence informs us that the paragraph will contain details about violence in movies "before the 1960s."

In the second paragraph, the topic sentence informs us that the paragraph will shift focus. The word "Today" lets the reader know what the focus of the paragraph will be.

Without the topic sentences, the ideas would run together and be difficult to follow.

Remember: Indent the first word of each new paragraph so readers know that a new section of the writing is beginning.

indent ──────► [   ]Before the 1960s, most movies did not show much graphic violence. When fighting or shooting occurred on the screen, it was clean: Bang! You're dead! The victim fell to the ground and died, perhaps after speaking a few final words. The viewer never saw blood or suffering. But in the late 1960s, filmmakers such as Arthur Penn and Sam Peckinpah began making movies with more graphic violence, such as *Bonnie and Clyde* and *The Wild Bunch*. They believed that if audiences could see how truly horrible real violence was, people would be less violent in their own lives.

Today, special-effects technology has made it possible to create very realistic images of bloodshed and violence. Steven Prince, author of *Savage Cinema: Sam Peckinpah and the Rise of Ultraviolent Movies*, describes the difference between early movies and the movies of today: ". . . filmmakers can create any image that they can dream up." So, Prince believes, because of technology, movies today are more and more violent and bloody.

A   Choose a topic sentence for each paragraph.

1

_____ . Some people are worried that viewing a lot of violence in movies and video games can be dangerous. They feel that it can make violence seem normal and can cause people to imitate the violent behavior, doing the same thing themselves. Other people disagree. They believe that showing violence is honest and can even be helpful.

   a Many people say violence in movies can be harmful.
   (b) People have different opinions about how violence can affect viewers.
   c People imitate violent behavior they see in movies.

2

_____ . This 1967 Arthur Penn movie is about a real gang of violent bank robbers who terrorized the U.S. Southwest in the 1930s. Bonnie (Faye Dunaway) and Clyde (Warren Beatty), and their gang were believed to be responsible for thirteen deaths and many robberies before they were finally killed.

   (a) *Bonnie and Clyde* is based on a true story.
   b Arthur Penn is one of the most famous directors of the 1960s.
   c There were a lot of bank robberies in the 1930s.

3

_____ . The U.S. documentary *Spellbound* visits the homes of eight finalists for the National Spelling Bee and then follows them to the finals in Washington, D.C. We get to know the kids and their families.

   a Spelling bees are popular in the U.S., and there have been a number of them in Washington.
   b The finals of the National Spelling Bee take place in Washington, D.C.
   (c) Some documentaries give us an intimate view of people and their lives.

UNIT 2

The paragraph

Suggested teaching time:	15–20 minutes	Your actual teaching time:

- Have students read the description of a paragraph. To check comprehension, ask:
  - *What is a paragraph?* (It's a group of sentences about one topic or theme.)
  - *What is a topic sentence?* (It's a sentence that announces the main idea of a paragraph.)
  - *Where in a paragraph is the topic sentence?* (It's usually the first sentence.)

- Call on volunteers to read the topic sentences in the two sample paragraphs. Ask *What information does each topic sentence give you?* (The first paragraph will be about violence in movies before the 1960s; the second paragraph will be about violence in movies today.)

- Tell students to read the model paragraphs to themselves. Then ask *Do the supporting sentences in each paragraph support the topic sentences?* (Yes.)

- Have a volunteer read the Remember note. If necessary, explain what *indent* means by pointing out the space at the beginning of the sample paragraphs. Tell students that instead of indenting, some people create paragraphs simply by leaving spaces between blocks of text.

FYI: In a paragraph, the first line is usually indented about five spaces from the left margin.

A Choose a topic sentence . . .

- Before students complete the exercise, remind them that the topic sentence announces the main idea of the paragraph. Tell them to read the choices carefully to pick the one that best depicts the main idea.

- Have pairs compare their answers. If they have different topic sentences, encourage students to analyze which one best depicts the main idea. Move around the room and help students as necessary.

- Bring the class together to discuss any outstanding issues.

B On a separate sheet of paper . . .

- Read the directions and the situations that students will describe in each paragraph. Give students a few minutes to work individually and brainstorm ideas. Then have students work in pairs and share ideas of what they will write about.

- Have students write their paragraphs. Tell them to refer to their brainstormed lists for supporting details. Write on the board *Does your paragraph have a topic sentence? Does it summarize or announce the main idea of your paragraph?*

- Ask students to read the questions on the board and then reread their paragraphs.

- Then have pairs exchange paragraphs and comment on their topic sentences and supporting sentences.

C Guidance for the Writing Exercise (on page 24)

- Before students complete the exercise, write on the board *Do you think watching violence is harmful? Why? Do you think watching violence is OK? Why?* Call on a few volunteers to share their ideas with the class.

- Tell students to take notes and organize their ideas on the notepad. Move around the room and help students as needed.

- Have pairs share their paragraphs. Encourage students to read their topic sentences carefully and suggest ways to improve them.

- Collect students' work and give feedback.

UNIT 3

Avoiding sentence fragments . . .

Suggested teaching time:	15–20 minutes	Your actual teaching time:

- Give students a few minutes to read through the rules in the box. Then write on the board *I prefer the Hotel Casablanca because it looks interesting.* Explain that *I prefer the Hotel Casablanca* is an independent clause because it can stand by itself as a sentence. Then ask *What is the dependent clause?* (Because it looks interesting.) Ask *Can the dependent clause stand by itself?* (No.) *Why?* (Because it doesn't express a complete idea.) Point out that a *dependent* clause *depends* on another clause.

FYI: Note that *since* can be used to express time or to give a reason for something. If there is any possibility of confusion between the two uses of *since*, such as in *Since I was young*, use *because* to give reasons.

- Call on a volunteer to read the first rule and example sentence in the box.

- Have students look at the example sentence on the board again. Erase the dependent clause and put it at the beginning of the sentence. Ask *Can a dependent clause appear at the beginning of the sentence?* (Yes.) Invite a student to read the next rule.

- Read the third rule, which is about sentence fragments. Then write a couple of examples on the board: *Because we like to stay at fancy hotels. Since we made a reservation online, we saved 20%.* Ask *Which is a complete sentence?* (The second one.) *Which is a sentence fragment?* (The first one.) Erase the second sentence, but keep the sentence fragment on the board.

- Have a student read the last rule and example sentences. Then return to the sentence fragment on the board. Ask *How can you make the fragment into a complete sentence?* (By adding an independent clause such as *We decided on the Royal Plaza*.) Point out that the independent clause can be placed before or after the dependent clause.

A In the following paragraph . . .

- Tell students to scan the paragraph for *because* and *since* and circle each occurrence they find. Then have students study each use of *because* and *since* and underline the sentence fragments.

- Ask *Which uses of* because *or* since *in the paragraph are correct?* (Only the first. The dependent clause is attached to an independent clause.)

- Call on volunteers to read the four sentence fragments.

B On a separate sheet of paper . . .

- Tell students that the sentence fragments can be corrected in different ways. Move around the room and help students as needed.

- Remind students that a dependent clause has to be connected to an independent clause or rewritten to become an independent clause. Explain that two dependent clauses *cannot* be connected to make an independent clause.

- Have pairs compare their paragraphs for any outstanding sentence fragments. Suggest solutions.

- Invite students to compare paragraphs and see if they solved the sentence fragments differently.

Answers to Unit 3, Exercise B
When I was a child, I had three very important dreams. Because I was young, I thought they would all come true. The first one was that I wanted to be an architect because I loved modern buildings. Since I wanted to help people, the second dream was to be a doctor. The last one was to be a flight attendant since I liked to travel. Only one of my dreams became a reality. I am an architect today. Because I really love my job, I think it was really the right choice for me.

C Guidance for the Writing Exercise (on page 36)

- Tell students to read the paragraphs they wrote about hotels they want to stay at and underline all the uses of *because* and/or *since*. Ask *Are there any sentence fragments?* Have students make necessary corrections.

- Then have students read a partner's paragraph and see if their partner missed any sentence fragments. Encourage pairs to offer suggestions. Move around the room and help students as needed.

- Collect students' work and give feedback.

B   On a separate sheet of paper, write two paragraphs of three to five sentences each with details about the following topics. Make sure you have included a topic sentence for each paragraph that summarizes or announces the main idea of the paragraph.   Answers will vary.

Paragraph 1	Paragraph 2
The story of a time you (or others) were late to meet someone for an event	The story of what you (or the others) did after the event

C   Guidance for the Writing Exercise (on page 24) On the notepad, write notes about why some people think watching violence is harmful and why others think it isn't. Use your notes as a guide for your paragraphs about violence. Include a topic sentence for each paragraph to summarize the main ideas.   Answers will vary.

Harmful:

Not harmful:

UNIT 3   Avoiding sentence fragments with <u>because</u> or <u>since</u>

Remember: You can use the subordinating conjunctions <u>because</u> or <u>since</u> to give a reason. <u>Because</u> and <u>since</u> answer a <u>Why</u> question. A clause that begins with <u>because</u> or <u>since</u> is called a dependent clause. A dependent clause gives information about an independent clause.

—— independent clause ——   —————— dependent clause ——————
I prefer the Hotel Casablanca   because (or since) it looks very interesting.

A dependent clause with <u>because</u> or <u>since</u> can also come at the beginning of a sentence. If it comes first, use a comma.

Because it looks very interesting, I prefer the Hotel Casablanca.

In writing, a dependent clause alone is an error called a "sentence fragment." It is not a sentence because it does not express a complete idea.

Sentence fragment   ✗ I prefer the Hotel Casablanca. ~~Because it looks very interesting.~~

To correct a sentence fragment with <u>because</u> or <u>since</u>, make sure it is combined with an independent clause. Or rewrite the sentence without <u>because</u> or <u>since</u> to create an independent clause.

✓ I prefer the Hotel Casablanca because it looks very interesting.
✓ I prefer the Hotel Casablanca. It looks very interesting.

A   In the following paragraph, underline four sentence fragments with <u>because</u> or <u>since</u>.

When I was a child, I had three very important dreams. Because I was young, I thought they would all come true. The first one was that I wanted to be an architect. <u>Because I loved modern buildings. Since I wanted to help people.</u> The second dream was to be a doctor. The last one was to be a flight attendant. <u>Since I liked to travel.</u> Only one of my dreams became a reality. I am an architect today. <u>Because I really love my job.</u> I think it was really the right choice for me.

B   On a separate sheet of paper, write the paragraph again. Correct all the sentence fragments. Combine the dependent clauses with independent clauses to make complete sentences. See page T145 for answers.

C   Guidance for the Writing Exercise (on page 36) In your paragraph about a hotel, include at least three reasons using <u>because</u> or <u>since</u>. Then check carefully to make sure that there are no sentence fragments.   Answers will vary.

<u>And</u>

<u>And</u> connects two or more words in a series. Use commas to separate words when there are more than two in the series. (The last comma is optional.)

I'm concerned about aggressive and inattentive driving. (no comma: <u>and</u> connects two adjectives.)

Inattentive drivers sometimes eat and talk on their cell phones while they are driving. (no comma: <u>and</u> connects two verbs with the same subject.)

Gesturing, staring, and multitasking are three things aggressive drivers often do. (A comma is necessary: <u>and</u> connects more than two words in a series. The comma after <u>staring</u> is optional.)

<u>And</u> can also combine two separate complete sentences into one sentence. In the new sentence, the two original sentences are called "independent clauses." The comma is common but optional.

———————— complete sentence ———————— —— complete sentence ——
Aggressive drivers do many dangerous things. They cause a lot of crashes.

———————— independent clause ———————— —— independent clause ——
Aggressive drivers do many dangerous things, **and** they cause a lot of crashes.

A   Insert commas where necessary or optional in the sentences.

1 She enjoys swimming, hiking, and fishing.
2 I don't like SUVs and other large cars.
3 We're traveling to France, Italy, and Spain.
4 Marianne and Sally are coming with us.
5 I'm renting a car, and I'm driving it to Chicago.
6 This agency has nice convertibles, vans, and sports cars.

B   On a separate sheet of paper, combine each pair of sentences into one sentence consisting of two independent clauses. Use <u>and</u>. See page T146 for answers.

1 They made a call to a car rental company. They reserved a minivan for the weekend.
2 The left front headlight is broken. It won't turn on.
3 We rented a full-size sedan with a sunroof. We opened it because the weather was beautiful.
4 I hit the car in front of me. A passenger in the back seat was hurt.
5 You can drop the car off at nine o'clock. You can pick it up in the late afternoon.

<u>In addition</u>, <u>Furthermore</u>, and <u>Therefore</u>

Use <u>In addition</u> and <u>Furthermore</u> to add to the ideas in a previous sentence. <u>In addition</u> and <u>Furthermore</u> are approximately equal in meaning, but <u>Furthermore</u> is a little more formal. You can use both in the same writing to avoid repetition.

People should pay attention to their own driving. **In addition**, they should be aware of the driving of others.

I think defensive driving makes sense. **Furthermore**, it has been proven to reduce the number of accidents.

Use <u>therefore</u> to introduce a result.

——————————————————— result ———————————————————
Ron has had a lot of accidents. **Therefore**, the rental company said he couldn't rent one of their cars.

Note: It's customary to use a comma after <u>In addition</u>, <u>Furthermore</u>, and <u>Therefore</u>.

C   Complete the statements with <u>In addition</u> or <u>Therefore</u>.

1 The other driver was speeding. <u>In addition</u>, she wasn't paying attention.
2 No one was hurt. <u>Therefore</u>, we didn't have to go to the hospital after the crash.
3 I was taking a business trip with a lot of equipment. <u>Therefore</u>, I rented a car with a lot of trunk space.
4 They need to rent a minivan for their trip to Montreal. <u>In addition</u>, they have to stay in a pet-friendly hotel because they plan to bring their pet dog.

D   Guidance for the Writing Exercise (on page 48) In your paragraph about good and bad drivers, use <u>And</u>, <u>In addition</u>, <u>Furthermore</u>, and <u>Therefore</u>. Then check your paragraph carefully to see if you have used commas correctly. Answers will vary.

UNIT 4

And, In addition, Furthermore, . . .

Suggested teaching time:	15–20 minutes	Your actual teaching time:	

And

- Call on a student to read the first rule and example sentence in the box. Write the first example sentence on the board and have a student circle the adjectives connected by *and*. (Aggressive, inattentive.) Stress that when *and* connects two words, a comma is not needed.

- Write the next example sentence on the board. Ask *What is the subject?* (Inattentive drivers.) *What is the verb?* (There are two: *eat, talk*.)

- Read the third example sentence aloud. Ask *What does and connect in this sentence?* (Three words: *gesturing, staring, multitasking*.) Ask *Why are there commas?* (Because there are more than two words in the series.) Stress that the comma after the second word is optional. Explain that it is a style preference.

FYI: When *and* joins the last two items in a series and a comma appears before *and,* this is called a *serial comma.*

- Finally, have students read the last rule to review that *and* can be used to connect two independent clauses.

A Insert commas where necessary . . .

- Tell students to circle *and* in each sentence and underline the words it connects. Then have them complete the exercise.

- Bring the class together and ask *Which sentences need commas?* (Sentences 1, 3, and 6 need two or three commas, depending on your style preference; sentence 5 needs a comma because *and* connects two independent clauses.) Ask *Why don't the other sentences need commas?* (Because *and* only connects two words.)

Option: (+5 minutes) Have students identify the words being connected in each sentence. (1: gerunds; 2, 3, 4 and 6: nouns; 5: verbs.)

B On a separate sheet of paper . . .

- After students have completed the exercise, have them check that each independent clause has a subject and verb.

- Then have students compare their answers with a partner.

- Bring the class together and ask *Did you put a comma before and?* Reiterate that the comma is optional.

- Have students suggest additional ways to combine the pairs of sentences. Tell them that they don't need to have two independent clauses in the combined sentence. More than one answer will be possible.

Answers to Unit 4, Exercise B

Answers may vary but might include the following:
1. They made a call to a car rental company, and they reserved a minivan for the weekend.
2. The left front headlight is broken, and it won't turn on.
3. We rented a full-sized sedan with a sun roof, and we opened it because the weather was beautiful.
4. I hit the car in front of me, and a passenger in the back seat was hurt.
5. You can drop the car off at nine o'clock, and you can pick it up in the late afternoon.

In addition, Furthermore, and *Therefore*

- Have students read the first rule in the box to themselves. Then call on volunteers to read the example sentences aloud. Ask *Can we use furthermore in the first sample sentence?* (Yes.) *Can we use in addition in the second sample sentence?* (Yes.) *How do the sentences change?* (Using *furthermore* in a sentence makes it a little more formal.)

- Read the second rule and example sentence. Ask *Can we replace therefore with in addition or furthermore?* (No.) *Why not?* (*Therefore* has a different meaning; it introduces a result.)

- Read the note regarding punctuation.

C Complete the statements . . .

- On the board write *Does the sentence introduce a result? Does the sentence add ideas?* Tell students to refer to these questions when choosing the correct answer.

- Ask *Is more than one answer possible for any item?* (No.)

D Guidance for the Writing Exercise (on page 48)

- On the board write *and, in addition, furthermore,* and *therefore.* Review that *and* connects two or more words in a series, *in addition* and *furthermore* add ideas, and *therefore* introduces a result. Encourage students to use these words in their paragraphs about good and bad drivers.

- When they are finished, tell students to read their paragraphs and underline all the uses of *and.*

- Ask *Did you use commas to separate more than two words in a series?* Have students make necessary corrections.

- Then have students work in pairs to read their partner's paragraph and see if he or she missed any commas. Remind students that the comma before *and* is optional. Encourage pairs to offer suggestions. Move around the room and help students as needed.

- Collect students' work and give feedback.

UNIT 5

Conventions of formal letter writing

Suggested teaching time:	20–30 minutes	Your actual teaching time:

- Ask students to close their books. Write on the board *Formal letters*. Ask *How are formal letters different from e-mails or handwritten social notes?* (Possible responses: They are more formal in tone. You don't use abbreviations or emoticons in formal letters. You are more careful with grammar and spelling.) Ask *In what situations might you write a formal letter?* (Possible responses: To apply for a job, to request a service, to file a complaint.)

- Have students open their books and call on a volunteer to read the rules in the box. Make sure students understand that the *recipient* is the person receiving the letter.

- Give students a few minutes to study and read the sample letter. Have them look at the labels carefully.

- Bring the class together. Ask *What is the* complimentary close *in the letter?* (Sincerely.) Have students read the note with the other common complimentary closes.

- Ask *Does the writer of the letter know the recipient's name?* (No, she just addresses the letter to the manager of the spa.) *How does she write the salutation?* (Dear Sir or Madam.) Then ask a student to read the note in the box. Have pairs write formal salutations to each other.

A Think of a business . . .

- Have students work in small groups. Give them a few minutes to discuss their ideas and make notes.

B On a separate sheet of paper . . .

- Using their notes, have students write their letters. Point out that their letters should be more formal in nature than the response letters on page 56. Tell them to refer to the letter in this section for a model.

- After students write their letters, have them use the bulleted list in the box as a checklist. Tell students to make any necessary corrections needed.

- Students can handwrite their first drafts. If possible, encourage students to type their second drafts.

- Collect students' work and give feedback.

FYI: *Unless* and *if . . . not* can both be used to say that what you will do depends on something else happening: Unless *Brad comes soon, I'm going without him.* / If *Brad does not come soon, I'm going without him.*

C Guidance for the Writing Exercise (on page 60)

- Give students a few minutes to read the directions silently. Make sure that they understand that the original letters on page 56 don't all list three advantages and disadvantages. Students will have to supply the missing information.

- Allow students a few minutes to take notes on the notepad, listing methods, advantages, and disadvantages about improving one's appearance. (Possible responses for losing weight: A *method* could be exercise; the *advantage* could be that it's inexpensive; the *disadvantage* could be that it's difficult to stay on track with any exercise routine.)

- When students have finished writing, have them work in pairs and read their partner's letter. Have them check for name, address, the date, a salutation, and a complimentary close as well as correct use of commas.

There aren't many rules for informal social communication such as e-mails, text messages, and handwritten social notes. There are, however, important rules and conventions for formal written communication, such as business letters, memos, and e-mails. For these, be sure to include the following elements:

- your address
- the recipient's name, position, and address
- the date
- a salutation
- a complimentary close
- your typewritten name and, in a letter or memo, your handwritten signature

Note: When business correspondence is an e-mail, it's not necessary to include addresses.

If you know the recipient's name, the salutation should use the following format: Dear [title + last name]. It's common in a formal letter to use a colon (:) after the name. In less formal letters, a comma is appropriate.

Dear Mr. Smith: Dear Marie,

If you don't know the recipient's name or gender, use this format:

Dear Sir or Madam: OR   To whom it may concern:

Follow the layout and punctuation in the writing model to the right.

your address ⎰ 657 Boulevard East
              ⎱ New Compton, Fortunia
              ⎱ e-mail: fclasson@vmail.gr

date ⎰ December 14, 2016

Manager
The Tipton Spa
Tipton Hotel   ⎰ recipient's address
2200 Byway Street
Sylvania, Sorrento

Dear Sir or Madam: ⎰ salutation

I'm writing to tell you that I was very happy with the service provided by the staff of the Tipton Spa when I was in Sylvania last week. The hair stylist gave me a wonderful haircut, and the masseur was really top notch. I particularly enjoyed the relaxing music that played over the public address system. Finally, the prices were fair, and I left the spa feeling great.

I want you to know that I am recommending the Tipton Spa to all my friends and have told them that they should visit you even if they are staying in another hotel or if they are in Sylvania for the day. In fact, I have told them that it's worth traveling to Sylvania just to visit the spa. Congratulations on such a wonderful spa.

Sincerely, ⎰ complimentary close
Francine Classon ⎰ signature
Francine Classon ⎰ typewritten name

Other common complimentary closes
Cordially,
Sincerely yours,
Best regards,

A Think of a business, such as a hotel, a store, a salon, a gym, or a restaurant where you have received good service. On the notepad, write notes about the business. *Answers will vary.*

Name of business:
Address:
Why you are happy with the service:

B On a separate sheet of paper, write a letter of thanks to the manager of the business in Exercise A. Explain what you like about the service. Use your notes and the writing model above as a guide. *Answers will vary.*

C Guidance for the Writing Exercise (on page 60) Look at the letter that you chose from page 56. On the notepad below, list three methods that the writer could use to improve his or her appearance. Make notes of the advantages and disadvantages of each method. Then use your notes as a guide to help you write your response letter. Be sure to include your name and address, the date, a salutation, and a complimentary close in your letter. *Answers will vary.*

Method	Advantages	Disadvantages
1.		
2.		
3.		

A subordinating conjunction connects a dependent clause to an independent clause.

Subordinating conjunctions	
because	unless
since	although
if	(even) though

——— independent clause ——— ——— dependent clause ———
People are eating more fast foods today **because** they want to save time.
      I generally avoid carbohydrates **even though** it isn't easy.

A dependent clause can also come at the beginning of a sentence. Use a comma after the dependent clause when it comes first.

——— dependent clause ——— ——— independent clause ———
Because people want to save time, they are eating more fast foods today.
      Even though it isn't easy, I generally avoid carbohydrates.

Use the subordinating conjunction <u>if</u> to express a condition. Use <u>unless</u> to express a negative condition.
      You will be healthy **if** you eat right and exercise regularly.
      You will gain weight **unless** you eat right and exercise regularly. (= if you don't)

Use the subordinating conjunctions <u>although</u>, <u>even though</u>, or <u>though</u> to express a contradiction.
Although
Even though   they knew fatty foods were unhealthy, people ate them anyway.
Though

Remember: Use <u>because</u> or <u>since</u> to give a reason.

A   Choose the best subordinating conjunction to complete each sentence.

1 (Though / **If** / Unless) I learn to speak English well, I will be very happy.

2 (**Even though** / Because / If) she is an artist, she is interested in science.

3 Studying English is important (although / **because** / unless) it can help you do more.

4 (Unless / **Although** / Since) English grammar isn't easy, I like studying it.

5 They have to go on a diet (**because** / unless / though) they're overweight.

6 He cut back on desserts and sodas (**even though** / if / because) he didn't want to.

7 (**Even though** / Because / Unless) my grandmother is 80 years old, she is in very good health.

8 (Unless / Because / **Though**) I think I'm going to get sick, I don't want to change my eating habits.

9 She won't eat red meat (because / **unless** / although) she has to.

10 (Unless / **Even though** / Since) she's a vegetarian, she sometimes eats fish.

B   Read each sentence. Then, on a separate sheet of paper, write and connect a clause to the sentence, using the subordinating conjunction.   Answers will vary.

1 Most people don't want to change their eating habits. (even though)

2 Children become overweight. (if)

3 Obesity will continue to be a global problem. (unless)

4 Eating too much fast food is bad for you. (because)

5 Most people continue to eat unhealthy foods. (although)

> *1 Most people don't want to change their eating habits even though they have health problems.*

C   Guidance for the Writing Exercise (on page 72) Using four different subordinating conjunctions, write four sentences: two about eating habits in the past and two about eating habits in the present. Use your sentences in your paragraph about eating habits.   Answers will vary.

UNIT 6

Connecting ideas: subordinating . . .

Suggested teaching time:	20–30 minutes	Your actual teaching time:

- Write *subordinating conjunctions* on the board. Ask students for examples and refer them to the list at the top right of the page. Review that subordinating conjunctions connect an independent clause to a dependent clause. Have students read the first two rules and example sentences to themselves.

- Have volunteers read the rule about *if* and *unless* aloud. Explain that an *if-* or *unless-* clause is paired with a result clause that describes what will happen under that condition. Ask *Which clause is dependent?* (The *if-* clause— it can't stand alone.) *Which clause is independent?* (The result clause—it can stand alone.) Have students read the example sentences.

- Read the next rule to the class. Invite volunteers to read the sentences using the words *Although, Even though,* and *Though.* Ask students to state the sentence in a different way to express contradiction. (Possible answer: People know that fatty foods are unhealthy, but they eat them anyway.)

A Choose the best . . .

- Write the following on the board:
  Does the sentence
  -give a reason? (because, since)
  -express a contradiction? (although, even though)
  -express a condition? (if, unless)

- Tell students to refer to the questions to help them decide which subordinating conjunction to use.

- Have students compare their answers with a partner. Then bring the class together and answer any questions.

B Read each sentence . . .

- Have students skim the exercise. Ask *Are these dependent or independent clauses?* (They're independent—they express complete thoughts.) Tell students to look at the context and create dependent clauses. Remind students that *if* and *unless* express a condition, *because* gives a reason, and *although* expresses a contradiction.

- As students complete the exercise, move around the room and provide help as needed.

- Review students' answers with the class.

C Guidance for the Writing Exercise (on page 72)

- On the board, write *Do you think people are eating healthier or less healthy foods than they used to?*

- Tell students to take notes and write sentences about eating habits: two about the past and two about the present. Write *because, since, if, unless, although* on the board for students to refer to.

- After students write their paragraphs, have them check their papers for the correct use and punctuation of subordinating conjunctions.

- Collect students' work and give feedback.

UNIT 7

Parallel structure

Suggested teaching time:	15–20 minutes	Your actual teaching time:	

- Read the introduction to parallel structure. Have students read the example sentences. Point out that all items in the list are gerunds. Read the Be careful! note. Ask *How would you correct that sentence?* (Change the infinitive *to play* to a gerund or change the gerunds *painting* and *dancing* to infinitives.)

- On the board, write *He spends a lot of time listening to music, texting his friends, and surfing the web.* Ask *Does the sentence have parallel structure?* (Yes.) Have students underline the parallel structures. (Listening, texting, surfing.)

- Ask a student to read the second rule and example sentences. Then read the Remember note. On the board, write *This summer I would like to . . .* Invite volunteers to come to the board and write three things they would like to do this summer. Remind students to repeat *to* with each verb or only to mention it the first time. After volunteers complete their sentences, have students comment as to whether the parallel structure is correct.

- Read the Remember note and example sentence to the students to review punctuation of items in a series. Refer to students' sentences on the board to illustrate comma use when listing three items.

A Correct the errors . . .

- Have students circle the verb in each sentence and underline the items in the series. Then have them identify the mistakes in the sentences.

- Have students compare their answers in pairs. Move around the room and help students as needed.

- Review answers with the class.

Answers to Unit 7, Exercise A
Answers will vary, but might include the following:
1. I have begun studying psychology and <u>learning</u> about personality development.
2. They avoid arguing about the nature nurture controversy and <u>disagreeing</u> about which is more important.
3. The Bersons love to run, <u>swim</u>, and lift weights.
   OR
   The Bersons love to run, to swim, and <u>to</u> lift weights.
4. She's both responsible and social. She prefers to study early in the evening and <u>to go</u> out afterwards.
   OR
   She's both responsible and social. She prefers to study early in the evening and go out afterwards.

5. Introverts hate <u>talking</u> about their feelings and being with a lot of people.
   OR
   Introverts hate to talk about their feelings and <u>be</u> with a lot of people.
   OR
   Introverts hate to talk about their feelings and <u>to be</u> with a lot of people.
6. Marjorie is a classic extrovert. She likes to be very active, <u>know</u> a lot of people, and <u>seek</u> excitement.
   OR
   Marjorie is a classic extrovert. She likes <u>being</u> very active, knowing a lot of people, and <u>seeking</u> excitement.
   OR
   Marjorie is a classic extrovert. She likes to be very active, <u>to know</u> a lot of people, and to seek excitement.
7. To be quiet, to be hard to know, and to seek peace are traits typical of the introvert's personality.
8. Psychologists of the nineteenth century continued <u>to believe</u> in the importance of genetics and <u>to write</u> about it in books and articles.

B Guidance for the Writing Exercise (on page 84)

- Have students write their answers to each question. Direct their attention to the words to describe likes/dislikes in the box. Encourage students to use these words in their answers, and to check off the words as they use them. Remind students to be careful of parallel structure when listing items.

- When students have finished, tell them to return to their answers and underline any series of items. Refer them to the Be careful! note to check for correct structure, and then ask them to make any necessary corrections.

- Finally, have students use the information in their answers to write their paragraphs.

UNIT 7   Parallel structure

When writing a series of words or phrases in a sentence, be sure that all items in the series are in the same grammatical form. This feature of good writing is called "parallel structure."

Lucy is creative. She likes painting, playing the piano, and dancing. (all items in the series are gerunds)

Be careful! Don't combine gerunds and infinitives in the same series.
Don't write: Lucy is creative. She likes painting, ~~to play~~ the piano, and dancing.

In a series of infinitives, it is correct to use <u>to</u> before each item in the series or to use <u>to</u> only before the first item.

✗ I decided to study medicine, get married, and ~~to~~ have children before my thirtieth birthday.

✓ I decided to study medicine, to get married, and to have children before my thirtieth birthday.

✓ I decided to study medicine, get married, and have children before my thirtieth birthday.

Remember: When a sentence includes a series of more than two words or phrases, separate them with commas. Use <u>and</u> before the last item in the series. The comma before <u>and</u> is optional.

no comma (two items)   commas (three items)
Jake and May have three favorite activities: painting, singing, and dancing.

A   Correct the errors in parallel structure in the sentences.   See page T149 for answers.

1 I have begun studying psychology and to learn about personality development.

2 They avoid arguing about the nature-nurture controversy and to disagree about which is more important.

3 The Bersons love to run, to swim, and lift weights.

4 She's both responsible and social. She prefers to study early in the evening and going out afterwards.

5 Introverts hate to talk about their feelings and being with a lot of people.

6 Marjorie is a classic extrovert. She likes to be very active, knowing a lot of people, and to seek excitement.

7 To be quiet, be hard to know, and to seek peace are traits typical of the introvert's personality.

8 Psychologists of the nineteenth century continued believing in the importance of genetics and to write about it in books and articles.

B   Guidance for the Writing Exercise (on page 84)   On a separate sheet of paper, write sentences to answer some or all the following questions about the person you chose. If appropriate, use verbs and phrases from the box on the right. Be careful to use parallel structure. Use the sentences in your paragraphs about the person.

Answers will vary.

- Who is the person?
- What is his or her relation to you?
- Who are the people in his or her family?
- How many siblings does he or she have?
- What kind of personality does he or she have?
- What are his or her likes and dislikes?
- Are there some things he or she is excited about, bored with, angry about, or worried about right now?
- Are there some things he or she is excited about, bored with, angry about, or worried about right now?

Words to describe likes / dislikes	
avoids	hopes
hates	would like
can't stand	is happy about
doesn't mind	is excited about
enjoys	is bored with
expects	is sick and tired of

Remember: A good paragraph has a topic sentence that clearly states what the main idea of the paragraph is.

In addition, a paragraph should have **supporting details**—that is, information that provides support for, and is clearly tied to, the topic sentence.

Be careful! If a detail doesn't support the topic sentence or isn't tied to it clearly, then it may not belong in the paragraph.

In the writing model to the right, the topic sentence of the paragraph is highlighted in yellow. The sentences that follow are details. Two of the sentences are crossed out because they do not support the topic sentence and should not be included in the paragraph. These two sentences do not provide information about the chair and do not indicate why the writer likes the chair. The remaining sentences are supporting details—they all support the topic sentence and are clearly tied to it. They provide more information about the chair and they explain why the writer likes the chair.

> In my living room, my favorite possession is an old wooden chair. My parents gave it to me when I left home. ~~A wooden chair can be very expensive if it is an antique.~~ It has lots of memories for me because it was in my parents' bedroom when I was growing up. ~~It's important to take very good care of wooden furniture.~~ The chair is very comfortable, and I used to sit in it a lot as a child.

A Read each topic sentence. Circle the detail that does not support the topic sentence.

1 Many French artists in the nineteenth century were influenced by Japanese art and printmaking.
   a Today, the work of Hokusai, Japan's most famous printmaker, is popular in Western countries. *(circled)*
   b Looking at the work of the French impressionists, it is clear that they chose to imitate the Japanese artistic styles of the time.
   c A number of French artists had collections of Japanese art.

2 I love my poster of Álvaro Saborío, the Costa Rican soccer player, but my wife hates it.
   a I think Saborío is a great player.
   b My wife doesn't think I should keep it in our bedroom.
   c The number on Saborío's uniform is 15. *(circled)*

3 Rodin's statue, *The Thinker*, is probably one of the most famous sculptures in the world.
   a This metal sculpture of a man deep in thought is recognized all over the world.
   b Rodin was born on November 12, 1840. *(circled)*
   c The image of *The Thinker* can be seen in popular art and advertisements.

4 On a side table in my dining room, I have two small ceramic figures of lions from my trip to Taipei.
   a They have beautiful colors including red, green, blue, and yellow.
   b You should visit the National Palace Museum when you are in Taipei. *(circled)*
   c I bought them together from a small shop at a temple I was visiting.

5 My sister has always shown a lot of talent in the performing arts.
   a We've had our differences, and we haven't always agreed on everything. *(circled)*
   b She has acted in school plays since she was about ten years old.
   c I think she's going to follow a career as an actor or dancer.

6 I think artistic talent is something you're born with.
   a I've tried many times to improve my ability at drawing, but it hasn't worked.
   b I have friends who are very talented in art, but they've never taken any special classes.
   c My aunt studied art at the Art Institute of Chicago for four years. *(circled)*

Supporting details

Suggested teaching time:	15–20 minutes	Your actual teaching time:

- Give students a few minutes to read the information and the sample paragraph. Then read the Remember and Be careful! notes aloud to the class. Refer students to the highlighted and crossed out portions of the paragraph as you read about them.
- Give students a few minutes to read the paragraph again. Review by asking *Why are the two sentences crossed out?* (They do not support the topic sentence or show why the writer likes the chair.)

A Read each topic sentence . . .

- Have students complete the exercise in pairs. Encourage them to discuss which details best support the topic sentence. Move around the room and help students as needed.
- Bring the class together and review answers. Have students explain why one of the details does *not* support the topic sentence; for example, 1. *Option a* talks about Japan's most famous printmaker today—there is no mention of Japanese artists' influence on French artists in the nineteenth century.

B Guidance for the Writing Exercise (on page 96)

- Call on volunteers to say what they will write about. Then invite students to reread the paragraph on page 146 about the chair and pay attention to the topic sentence and supporting details.

- Then have students work on filling out the outline on the notepad. Move around the room and help them as needed. Make sure all students have a clear topic sentence.

- Give students a few minutes to reread their supporting details. Tell them to cross out any sentences that do not support the topic sentence. Then tell them to replace any crossed-out sentences with ones that do support the topic sentence. Students will use this information in their paragraphs.

- If appropriate for your class, have pairs exchange outlines and offer each other feedback.

UNIT 9

Organizing ideas

Suggested teaching time:	20–30 minutes	Your actual teaching time:

- Write *Organizing ideas* on the board. Tell students that the most important thing to remember when writing something is to organize ideas clearly. There are different ways of doing this, usually depending on how long a piece of writing is.

- Focus on Approach 1. Have students read the information. Explain that the handwritten notes are just ideas that a writer would then organize into a paragraph. This writer would list the advantages first and then the disadvantages.

- Read the information after Approach 1 to the class and have students read Approach 2. Explain that the sentences in capital letters are examples of topic sentences. They introduce what each paragraph will be about.

- Finally, read Approach 3 to the class. Point out that this approach produces the longest piece of writing of the three, developing the topic in great detail. If time permits, invite students to suggest additional ideas for their individual paragraphs.

B   **Guidance for the Writing Exercise (on page 96)** On the notepad, write the favorite object you chose. Create a topic sentence that states the most important thing you want to say about that object. Then write five supporting details to use in your paragraph.   Answers will vary.

Favorite object:
Topic sentence:
Details to support my topic sentence:
1.
2.
3.
4.
5.

UNIT 9   Organizing ideas

When you want to describe the benefits and problems of an issue, there are different ways you can organize your ideas. Here are some approaches.

Approach 1: In one paragraph
One way is to describe all the advantages and disadvantages in one paragraph. Following are notes of the details that will be included in the paragraph.

THE ADVANTAGES AND DISADVANTAGES OF SMART PHONES
Advantages: are easy to carry, don't miss calls, keep you connected with family and friends
Disadvantages: bother other people, make people dependent, are easy to lose

This approach is good for a short piece of writing consisting of only a few sentences. However, if you want to develop those ideas in more than just a few sentences, it is easier for the reader to follow if you can organize the details in one of the following ways:

Approach 2: In two paragraphs
In this approach, you can use a first paragraph to describe all the advantages. Then you can use a second paragraph to describe all the disadvantages. Following are notes of the details that will be included in each paragraph.

Paragraph 1: SMART PHONES HAVE ADVANTAGES
are easy to carry, don't miss calls, keep you connected with family and friends
Paragraph 2: BUT THEY ALSO HAVE DISADVANTAGES
bother other people, make people dependent, are easy to lose

Approach 3: In more than two paragraphs
In this approach, you can use a separate paragraph to focus on each different topic. In each paragraph, you can describe both advantages and disadvantages. Following are notes of the details that will be included in each paragraph.

Paragraph 1: (THEY'RE SMALL.) smart phones easy to carry, but also easy to lose
Paragraph 2: (THEY'RE CONVENIENT.) won't miss calls, but you can also bother other people
Paragraph 3: (THEY'VE CHANGED OUR LIVES.) keep people connected with family and friends, but also
can make people dependent

A   Using Approach 2, organize the ideas into two paragraphs: paragraph 1 is about the benefits of renting a car; paragraph 2 is about the problems. Write 1 or 2 next to each idea.

__1__ It gives you the freedom to go wherever you want to go whenever you want.

__1__ You might see places you can't see by bus or train.

__2__ You could have an accident during your trip.

__1__ You have more control over whether or not you will have an accident during your trip.

__1__ You can carry more luggage and other things you might need.

__2__ To drive safely, you have to become familiar with the local driving rules.

__1__ If you're traveling with a group of people, it could cost less than paying for bus and train tickets.

__2__ You may have to understand road signs that are in a different language.

__2__ If you have to do all the driving, it can be very stressful and tiring.

__2__ If you're traveling alone or with one other person, it could cost a lot of money in rental fees and gas.

B   Now, on a separate sheet of paper, practice using Approach 3. Organize the sentences from Exercise A by topic into three or more separate paragraphs. Don't forget to include a topic sentence.   Students' own answer

C   Guidance for the Writing Exercise (on page 108) Use your notes on page 107 to write your paragraphs about the benefits and problems of the Internet. Choose Approach 2 or Approach 3 to organize your writing.   Answers will vary.

UNIT 10   Introducing conflicting ideas: <u>On the one hand</u>; <u>On the other hand</u>

Use <u>On the one hand</u> and <u>On the other hand</u> to present conflicting ideas or two sides of an issue. The following two sentences present the two sides together, one right after the other.

On the one hand, I would want to tell the truth. **On the other hand**, I wouldn't want to get in trouble.

Remember: You can also present conflicting or contradictory information with <u>Even though</u>, <u>Although</u>, and <u>However</u>.

Even though I'm basically an honest person, I don't always tell the truth.
Although Matt didn't think he broke the dish, it's possible that he did.
Matt wanted to tell the owner of the store what happened. **However**, Noah didn't agree.

When one paragraph presents one side of an issue and the next one presents the other, writers don't usually use <u>On the one hand</u> in the first paragraph. Instead, they just begin the next paragraph with <u>On the other hand</u> to let the reader know that the conflicting idea will follow. Look at the writing model to the right.

> Being honest has many advantages. If you always tell the truth, you don't have to remember an untruth you said before. People who tell the truth don't have trouble sleeping. They can look at themselves in the mirror and feel good.
>
> On the other hand, there are times when telling a lie makes sense. For example, your friend Andrew might ask you if you like his new jacket, and you think it's ugly. If you told him that, it would hurt his feelings. It's possible that not being absolutely truthful might make more sense.

A   Reread the Photo Story on page 111. Write a summary of the story in three to five sentences. Answer the questions below.   Student's own answers

- Where was Matt?
- Who was he with?
- What happened?
- What did the two friends discuss?

B   Answer the questions below. Write three to five sentences about Matt's choices. Then write the consequences of each choice. Use <u>If</u> and the unreal conditional in at least one sentence.

- What should he do?
- What could he do?
- What would most people do?   Student's own answers

C   Write three to five sentences about what you would do if you were Matt. Answer the questions below.

                                           Answers will vary.

- What would you do?
- What would happen if you did that?
- What would happen if you didn't?

D   Guidance for the Writing Exercise (on page 120) In your paragraphs about Matt's dilemma, use <u>On the one hand</u>, <u>On the other hand</u>, <u>Even though</u>, <u>Although</u>, and <u>However</u> to connect conflicting ideas.   Answers will vary.

A Below are ideas . . .

- To help students visualize the expected organization of their writing, write the following on the board:
  Renting a car during a vacation overseas
  Paragraph 1: Benefits
  Paragraph 2: Disadvantages
- Tell students to organize the list of ideas in the book into the two categories. Model the activity by choosing the topic sentence with the class. (There are advantages and disadvantages to renting a car while you're on vacation overseas.) They will write **1** for sentences that describe the benefits of renting a car, and **2** for sentences that describe the disadvantages of renting a car.
- Review answers with the class.

B Now, on a separate sheet of paper . . .

- Have students work in pairs to organize the ideas about renting a car during a vacation overseas into two or more paragraphs. Encourage them to think of mini-topics for the separate paragraphs, such as cost, safety, and stress. Tell pairs to look at the model (Approach 3) on page 147.
- Tell pairs they don't have to write out the paragraphs but just have to organize their notes like the sample presented. Move around the room and help students as needed.

C Guidance for the Writing Exercise (on page 108)

- On the board write Benefits and Problems of the Internet. Tell students they will organize their notes on page 107 into two or more paragraphs. Tell students to look through their notes and study Approaches 2 and 3 to decide which one will work best to organize their ideas.
- Tell students to organize their notes like the sample given. Move around the room and help students as needed. Check in with each student to offer input.
- Have students write out the paragraphs for homework. Focus individual feedback on organization of ideas.

UNIT 10

Introducing conflicting ideas . . .

Suggested teaching time:	20–30 minutes	Your actual teaching time:

- Begin by explaining the idiom *on the one hand . . . on the other hand.* Use actual hand gestures to explain that this is an expression you say when presenting two different ways of thinking about a situation. Give an example, such as *On the one hand* [hold out your left hand], *my new job will give me new opportunities to grow; on the other hand* [hold out your right hand], *I'll spend a lot more hours working.*
- Invite a student to read the first rule and example sentences. Write on the board On the one hand, . . . / On the other hand, . . . Invite volunteers to share some contrasting opinions on the topic of telling the truth.

- Read the Remember note. Ask a volunteer to restate the first example sentence using *Even though, Although,* or *However.* (Possible response: I want to tell the truth; however, I don't want to get into trouble.)
- Read the last rule. Then ask volunteers to read the two paragraphs on the right aloud.

A Reread the Photo Story . . .

- Have students answer the questions in pairs. Then have them write the summaries individually.
- Tell pairs to swap summaries and respond. Move around the room and help students as needed.

B Answer the questions . . .

- To help students take notes, write the following questions on the board:
  What could Matt do? (Possible response: Put the broken plate on the shelf.)
  What should Matt do? (Possible response: Tell the owner.)
  What would most people do? (Possible response: Put the plate on the shelf.)
  If Matt puts the plate back on the shelf . . .
  If Matt doesn't tell the owner about the plate . . .
- Move around the room and help students as needed. Then bring the class together and call on students to share their points of view.

C Write three to five sentences . . .

- On the board, write If I were Matt, I would . . . Call on volunteers to share their ideas. Correct any mistakes in the usage of the unreal conditional.
- Tell students to write a few sentences describing what they would do if they were Matt and to describe the consequences of these unreal actions.

D Guidance for the Writing Exercise (on page 120)

- Tell students to refer to their notes from the previous exercises and write two paragraphs about Matt's dilemma. Tell students to use the language they learned to introduce conflicting ideas. Remind students that if they choose to present one side of the story in one paragraph and the other side in the second paragraph, they should follow the model paragraphs in the book and begin the second paragraph with *On the other hand.*
- Have pairs exchange their paragraphs and compare their ideas.
- Give individual feedback, focusing on introducing conflicting ideas.

Top Notch Pop Lyrics

▶ 1:16–1:17 **Greetings and Small Talk**
[Unit 1]
You look so familiar. Have we met before?
I don't think you're from around here.
It might have been two weeks ago, but I'm not sure.
Has it been a month or a year?
I have a funny feeling that I've met you twice.
That's what they call déjà vu.
You were saying something friendly, trying to be nice—and now you're being friendly, too.
One look, one word.
It's the friendliest sound that I've ever heard.
Thanks for your greetings.
I'm glad this meeting occurred.

(CHORUS)
Greetings and small talk
make the world go round.
On every winding road I've walked,
this is what I've found.

Have you written any letters to your friends back home?
Have you had a chance to do that?
Have you spoken to your family on the telephone?
Have you taken time for a chat?
Bow down, shake hands.
Do whatever you do in your native land.
I'll be happy to greet you
in any way that you understand.

(CHORUS)

Have you seen the latest movie out of Hollywood?
Have you read about it yet?
If you haven't eaten dinner, are you in the mood for a meal you won't forget?
Bow down, shake hands.
Do whatever you do in your native land.
I'll be happy to greet you
in any way that you understand.

(CHORUS)

▶ 1:35–1:36 **Better Late Than Never**
[Unit 2]
Where have you been? I've waited for you.
I'd rather not say how long.
The movie began one hour ago.
How did you get the time all wrong?
Well, I got stuck in traffic, and when I arrived
I couldn't find a parking place.
Did you buy the tickets? You're kidding—
for real?
Let me pay you back, in that case.

(CHORUS)
Sorry I'm late.
I know you've waited here forever.
How long has it been?
It's always better late than never.

When that kind of movie comes to the big screen,
it always attracts a crowd,
and I've always wanted to see it with you—
but it looks like we've missed it now.
I know what you're saying, but actually,
I would rather watch a video.

So why don't we rent it and bring it back home?
Let's get in the car and go.

(CHORUS)

Didn't you mention, when we made our plans, that you've seen this movie recently?
It sounds so dramatic, and I'm so upset,
I'd rather see a comedy!
Well, which comedy do you recommend?
It really doesn't matter to me.
I still haven't seen 'The World and a Day'.
I've heard that one is pretty funny.

(CHORUS)

▶ 2:17–2:18 **Checking Out** **[Unit 3]**
Ms. Jones travels all alone.
She doesn't need much space—
a single room with a nice twin bed
and a place for her suitcase.
Her stay is always satisfactory,
but in the morning she's going to be checking out.
Mr. Moon will be leaving soon,
and when he does I'll say,
"Thank you, sir, for staying with us.
How do you want to pay?"
And in the end it isn't hard.
He'll put it on his credit card. He's checking out.
Would you like to leave a message?
Could you call back later?
Do you need some extra towels
or today's newspaper?
Can I get you anything?
Would you like room service?
I'm so sorry.
Am I making you nervous?
Good evening.
I'll ring that room for you.
Is that all?
I'll be glad to put you through.
I'm sorry, but he's not answering.
The phone just rings and rings.
The couple in room 586
have made a king-size mess.
Pick up the laundry. Turn down the beds.
We have another guest
coming with his family.
You'd better hurry or they will be checking out. . .

▶ 2:36–2:37 **Wheels around the World** **[Unit 4]**
Was I going too fast
or a little too slow?
I was looking out the window,
and I just don't know.
I must have turned the steering wheel
a little too far
when I drove into the bumper
of that luxury car.
Oh no!
How awful!
What a terrible day!
I'm sorry to hear that.
Are you OK?

(CHORUS)
Wheels around the World
are waiting here with your car.
Pick it up.
Turn it on.
Play the radio.
Wheels around the World—
"helping you to go far."
You can drive anywhere.
Buckle up and go.

Did I hit the red sedan,
or did it hit me?
I was talking on the cell phone
in my SUV.
Nothing was broken,
and no one was hurt,
but I did spill some coffee
on my favorite shirt.
Oh no!
Thank goodness you're still alive!
I'm so happy that
you survived.

(CHORUS)

What were you doing when you hit that tree?
I was racing down the mountain, and the brakes failed me.
How did it happen? Was the road still wet?
Well, there might have been a danger sign,
But I forget.
The hood popped open and the door fell off.
The headlights blinked and the engine coughed.
The side-view mirror had a terrible crack.
The gearshift broke. Can I bring the car back?
Oh no!
Thank goodness
you're still alive!
I'm so happy that
you survived.

(CHORUS)

▶ 3:17–3:18 **Piece of Cake** **[Unit 5]**
I need to pick up a few things
on the way back to school.
Feel like stopping at a store with me?
I'd like to, but I think I'll pass.
I don't have time today.
It's already nearly a quarter to three.

(CHORUS)
Don't worry. We'll be fine.
How long can it take?
It's easy. It'll be a piece of cake.

I need a tube of toothpaste and
a bar of Luvly soap,
some sunscreen, and a bottle of shampoo.
Where would I find makeup?
How about a comb?
Have a look in aisle one or two.

(CHORUS)

I have an appointment
for a haircut at The Spa.
On second thought, they're always
running late.
My class starts in an hour.
I'll never make it now.
How long do you think we'll have to wait?

(CHORUS)

They say there's someone waiting
for a trim ahead of me.
Can I get you some coffee or some tea?
OK. In the meantime,
I'll be getting something strong
for this headache at the pharmacy!

(CHORUS)

▶ 3:37–3:38 **A Perfect Dish**   [Unit 6]

I used to eat a lot of fatty foods,
but now I just avoid them.
I used to like chocolate and lots of sweets,
but now those days are gone.
To tell you the truth,
it was too much trouble.
They say you only live once,
but I'm not crazy about feeling sick.
What was going wrong?
Now I know I couldn't live without this.
Everything's ready.
Why don't you sit down?

(CHORUS)
It looks terrific,
but it smells pretty awful.
What in the world can it be?
It smells like chicken,
and it tastes like fish—
a terrific dish
for you and me—
a perfect dish for you
and me.

I used to be a big meat eater,
now I'm vegetarian,
and I'm not much of a coffee drinker.
I can't stand it anymore.
I'm avoiding desserts with sugar.
I'm trying to lose some weight.
Some things just don't agree with me.
They're bad for me, I'm sure.
Would you like some?
Help yourself.
Isn't it so good for you health?

(CHORUS)

Aren't you going to have some?
Don't you like it?
Wasn't it delicious?
Don't you want some more?

(CHORUS)

▶ 4:13–4:14 **The Colors of Love**   [Unit 7]

Are you sick and tired of working hard day
and night?
Do you like to look at the world in shades of
black and white?
Your life can still be everything that you were
dreaming of.
Just take a look around you and see all the
colors of love.
You wake up every morning and go through
the same old grind.
You don't know how the light at the window
could be so unkind. If blue is the color that
you choose when the road is rough, you know
you really need to believe in the colors of love.

(CHORUS)
The colors of love
are as beautiful as a rainbow.

The colors of love
shine on everyone in the world.

Are negative thoughts and emotions painful
to express?
They're just tiny drops in the ocean of
happiness.
And these are the feelings you must learn to
rise above.
Your whole life is a picture you paint with the
colors of love.

(CHORUS)

▶ 4:28–4:29 **To Each His Own**   [Unit 8]

He doesn't care for Dali.
The colors are too bright.
He says that Picasso
got everything just right.
She can't stand the movies
that are filmed in Hollywood.
She likes Almodóvar.
She thinks he's really good.
He's inspired by everything
she thinks is second-rate.
She's moved and fascinated
by the things he loves to hate.
He's crazy about art that only
turns her heart to stone.
I guess that's why they say
to each his own.
He likes pencil drawings.
She prefers photographs.
He takes her to the the art museum,
but she just laughs and laughs.
He loves the Da Vinci
that's hanging by the door.
She prefers the modern art
that's lying on the floor.
"No kidding! You'll love it. Just wait and see.
It's perfect in every way."
She shakes her head. "It's not for me.
It's much too old and gray."
She thinks he has the worst taste
that the world has ever known.
I guess that's why they say
to each his own.
But when it's time to say goodbye,
they both feel so alone.
I guess that's why they say
to each his own.

▶ 5:16–5:17 **Life in Cyberspace**   [Unit 9]

I'm just fooling around.
Am I interrupting you?
Well, I wanted to know—
what are you up to?
I tried to send some photos,
but it's been so long
that I almost don't remember
how to log on.
So I'm thinking about getting a
new computer.
I don't know what kind. I should have done
it sooner.
But I heard the Panatel is as good as
the rest.
Check it out. Check it out.
You should really check it out.

(CHORUS)
Let's face it—that's life.
That's life in cyberspace.

When you download the pictures,
then you open the files.
If your computer's slow,
then it can take a little while.
From the pull-down menu,
you can print them, too.
But don't forget to save
everything you do.
Scroll it up. Scroll it down.
Put your cursor on the bar.
Then click on the icon,
and you'll see my new car!
The car goes as fast
as the one I had before.
Check it out. Check it out.
You should really check it out.

(CHORUS)

Am I talking to myself, or are you still there?
This instant message conversation's
going nowhere.
I could talk to Liz.
She isn't nearly as nice.
It isn't quite as much fun.
I've done it once or twice.
What's the problem?
Come on. Give it a try.
If you don't want to be friends,
at least tell me why.
Did you leave to make a call
or go out to get some cash?
Did the photos I sent make your
computer crash?

(CHORUS)

▶ 5:31–5:32 **What Would You Do?**
[Unit 10]

What would you do
if I got a tattoo with your name?
What would you say
if I dyed my hair for you?
What would you do
if I sang outside your window?
What would you think
if I told you I loved you?

(CHORUS)
I hate to say this,
but I think you're making a big mistake.
By tomorrow,
I'm sure you'll be sorry.

What would you do
if I sent you a love letter?
Would you say it was wrong
and send it back to me?
What would you think
if I pierced my ears? Would you care?
Would you think
that I had lost all my modesty?

(CHORUS)

Well, give it some thought.
I know I could make you happy.
Are you kidding?
You'd have to be nuts to ask me.
It's no mistake. I'm sure
that my heart is yours.
I have to find a way
to make you mine.

(CHORUS)

Top Notch TV Teaching Notes

For some general guidelines on using the *Top Notch TV* sitcom and interviews, see the Teaching Ideas document in the *Top Notch TV* folder on the ActiveTeach. **Note:** The Answer Keys included in these Teaching Notes provide answers to the Activity Worksheet exercises on the ActiveTeach.

UNIT 1

Sitcom: *Have we met before?*

Social language
- Get reacquainted with someone
- Discuss tourist activities

Grammar
- The present perfect

SCENE 1

PREVIEW

- Have students brainstorm activities and places and write them on the board—for example, *visit / Paris*. Then have students create questions using the present perfect; for example, *Have you ever visited Paris?* In pairs, students take turns asking and answering the questions.

REVIEW

- Ask comprehension questions. Play the video episode again if necessary.
    Does Marie look familiar to Ms. Novak? (yes)
    Does Ms. Novak look familiar to Marie? (no)
    Where does Ms. Novak think she has seen Marie before? (Chicago, Egypt, China, Australia, Peru)
    Has Marie ever been to any of these places? (no)
    Why does Marie look familiar to Ms. Novak? (Marie was roommates with Ms. Novak's sister when she lived in Paris, and Ms. Novak remembers seeing Marie in pictures.)

EXTENSION

Oral work

- Pair work: role play. Have students work in pairs to role-play Marie and Ms. Novak and reenact what happened in the video episode.
- Pair work: role play. Have students work in pairs to role-play a conversation between Ms. Novak and her sister about Ms. Novak's meeting with Marie.

Written work

- Pair work. Have students work in pairs to summarize the story in the video episode. Write these sentences on the board to help them begin:
    A woman named Ms. Novak came into Top Notch Travel with Mr. Evans. He introduced her to the receptionist Marie . . .
- Pair work. Have students work in pairs to continue the dialogue between Marie and Ms. Novak for a few more exchanges. Write these lines on the board to help them begin:
    Marie: So how is Katerina?
    Ms. Novak: . . .

LANGUAGE NOTE: When Ms. Novak says, "I never forget a face," she means that she always remembers the face of someone she has met before.

VIDEO SCRIPT

Mr. Evans introduces Marie to Ms. Novak, a new client.

Mr. Evans: Marie, this is Ms. Novak. She's from Chicago. Marie is our receptionist.
Marie: It's nice to meet you.
Ms. Novak: It's nice to meet you, too.
Mr. Evans: I'll get your tickets.
Ms. Novak: You look very familiar to me, Marie. **Have** we **met** before?
Marie: I don't think so. No.
Ms. Novak: Well, I never forget a face. I'm sure I know you from somewhere. I don't look familiar to you?
Marie: I'm sorry. No.
Ms. Novak: I know! We met in Chicago. You were a waitress in a restaurant near the Art Institute.
Marie: I**'ve** never **been** to Chicago.
Ms. Novak: **Have** you ever **driven** a taxi in Egypt?
Marie: No.
Ms. Novak: Oh, you were the pilot on a small airplane in China. You flew me over the Great Wall.
Marie: No.
Ms. Novak: **Have** you ever **gone** snorkeling in Australia?
Marie: No.
Ms. Novak: **Driven** a bus in Peru?
Marie: No. Ms. Novak, I'm quite sure we**'ve** never **met** before. I came here only a year ago from Paris.
Ms. Novak: Paris? My sister, Katerina, lived there for a year.
Marie: Katerina? Katerina Novak?! She lived with me!

Ms. Novak: Of course! You were in all the
pictures she sent home.
Marie: What a coincidence!
Ms. Novak: You see, I never forget a face.

SCENE 2

PREVIEW

- Think of different sites in your city. They can be
historical sites, nature sites, popular stores, and so on.
Ask individual students *Have you ever been to . . . ?
Have you ever visited . . . ? Have you ever seen . . . ?*
If students keep saying *yes*, ask *Have you done
everything in this city? What haven't you done yet?*

REVIEW

- Ask comprehension questions. Play the video
episode again if necessary.
    *Is Ms. Novak going sightseeing? (No. She is
    going back to her hotel room to read.)*
    *How many times has she been in this city before?
    (many times—she has been coming there once
    a month for eight years)*
    Does she believe there is a Museum of Cheese? (no)
    *What is the Museum of Cheese really? (a cheese
    shop)*
    *Why does Mr. Evans call it the Museum of
    Cheese? (because they have every kind of
    cheese, and some of it is very old)*
    *Where is the cheese shop? (at the corner of
    Seventh and Oak)*
    *What time is Mr. Evans meeting Ms. Novak? (at
    4:00)*

EXTENSION

Oral work

- Discussion. Remind students that Ms. Novak has
been coming to this city once a month for eight
years. Ask *Why do you think Ms. Novak comes to
this city so often?* Write students' guesses on the
board—for example, *business, family, friends.* Then
ask students whether there is a city they visit often.
If the answer is yes, ask *What things have you done
there?* If the answer is no, ask *What city would you
like to visit often? Why?*

- Tell students to make up a place in their city, like
Mr. Evans's Museum of Cheese. Have them tell the
class where it is and why they should go there.

Written work

- Have students write a summary of the story in
the video episode. To help students begin, write
on the board: *Mr. Evans asked Ms. Novak if she is
going sightseeing. She said . . .*

- Pair work. Ask students *What happens when Ms.
Novak meets Mr. Evans at the Museum of Cheese?*
Have students work in pairs to write a story. Then
bring the class together, and call on pairs to read
their stories to the class.

VIDEO SCRIPT

*Mr. Evans tries to come up with something Ms.
Novak hasn't seen or done in the city.*

Mr. Evans: I have your tickets.
Ms. Novak: Thank you. Did you know that Marie
knows my sister, Katerina?
Mr. Evans: Really? It's a small world, isn't it? So
are you going sightseeing before you leave?
Ms. Novak: No. I'm going back to the hotel to read.
Mr. Evans: What?! You're visiting our great city
and you're not even going to see it?
Ms. Novak: **I've come** here once a month for
eight years. **I've seen** it all before.
Mr. Evans: I'm sure I can think of something you
haven't seen.
Ms. Novak: I think you're wrong.
Mr. Evans: **Have** you **visited** the Riley Museum
of Art?
Ms. Novak: Twenty times.
Mr. Evans: **Have** you ever **been** to the top of the
Olson Building?
Ms. Novak: Just last month.
Mr. Evans: **Have** you **eaten** at Andre's Café?
Ms. Novak: Twice.
Mr. Evans: Ever **been** to Cold Beach?
Ms. Novak: Yes.
Mr. Evans: **Seen** the City Opera?
Ms. Novak: Yes.
Mr. Evans: **Toured** the Japanese Gardens?
Ms. Novak: Yes.
Mr. Evans: You can't **have done** everything in
this city.
Ms. Novak: I'm afraid it's true.
Mr. Evans: **Have** you ever **visited** the Museum
of Cheese?
Ms. Novak: There's no Museum of Cheese.
Mr. Evans: Aha! It is really amazing. Everyone
goes there. I can't believe you **haven't been**
there yet! Marie, could you call the Museum
of Cheese and reserve a ticket for Ms. Novak
and me?

Ms. Novak: You're not serious.

Mr. Evans: I am. It's at the corner of Seventh and Oak. I'll see you there at 4:00.

Ms. Novak: OK. I'll see you there. Thank you. Good-bye, Marie.

Marie: Say hello to Katerina for me.

(Ms. Novak leaves.)

Marie: Mr. Evans, is there really a Museum of Cheese at Seventh and Oak?

Mr. Evans: It's a wonderful little cheese shop. They have every kind of cheese. Some of it's very old, so, yes, I'd say it's a museum of cheese. Ms. Novak will love it.

ANSWER KEY

A. 1. c 2. b 3. c 4. a 5. a

B. 1. False 2. True 3. False 4. False 5. False

C. 1. Have you visited 2. Have you ever been to the top of 3. Have you eaten 4. Ever been to 5. Have you ever visited

 Top Notch Pop and Karaoke: *Greetings and Small Talk*

UNIT 2

Sitcom: *Have you chosen a movie yet?*

Social language
- Apologize for lateness
- Disagree politely

Grammar
- The present perfect
- *Would rather*

SCENE 1

PREVIEW
- On the board, write *horror film, drama, action film.* Ask students *Do you like any of these genres?* Give examples of movies you know for each of these genres, and describe what the movies are about.

REVIEW
- Ask comprehension questions. Play the video episode again if necessary.

  Do Paul and Bob go to the movies often? (yes)
  Have they chosen a movie yet? (no) Why not? (Paul and Bob have seen almost everything.)
  Is The Last Train to Hong Kong *an action film? (yes)*

Have Paul and Bob seen it? (yes)
Is On the Bridge *a romantic film or a violent film? (a romantic film)*
Has Cheryl seen it? (no)
What kind of film is The Hand? *(a horror film)*
Why does Cheryl say the movie tickets are her treat? (because she wants Paul and Bob to stop acting out the movies and attracting attention in the restaurant)

EXTENSION

Oral work
- Group work: role play. Divide the class into groups of four. Have students role-play the characters and reenact what happened in the video episode.
- Discussion. Ask *Which of the movies would you rather see? Why?* Have students discuss the three movies from the video episode.

Written work
- Pair work. Have pairs of students continue the conversation among the four friends for a few more exchanges. Tell students to have these people choose a movie to see in the end. Call on pairs to read their conversations to the class.
- Pair work. Have pairs of students choose one of the movies from the video episode and create an imaginary summary and movie review.

LANGUAGE NOTES: *To run out of time* means no longer to have any time left.

My treat means *I am paying.*

VIDEO SCRIPT

In the café, Bob, Marie, Paul, and Cheryl try to pick a movie to go to.

Paul: Give us another one, Marie.

Marie: We're running out of time. Oh, there she is.

Cheryl: I'm sorry I'm late. I couldn't find a parking space. **Have** you **been** here long?

Bob: Since yesterday. But it's no problem. The waiter brought us food and we slept on the floor.

Cheryl: **Have** you **chosen** a movie yet?

Marie: We've been trying. Unfortunately, these guys **have seen** almost everything.

Paul: We like the movies.

Marie: What about the action film *The Last Train to Hong Kong?*

Bob: "Where is this train going?"

Paul: "Believe me, you**'d rather not know**."

Bob: "We're going to Hong Kong, aren't we?"

Paul: "**Would** you **rather** stay here and fight the 100 men?"

Bob: "No. And I've always **wanted** to see Hong Kong."

Paul: "Look out!"

Marie: *(to Cheryl)* They've been doing this for a half hour.

Cheryl: That looks a little too violent for me. What about *On the Bridge?* I hear it's great.

Bob: "You're late, Frederick."

Paul: "I'm sorry."

Bob: "And I've **waited** for you for so long."

Paul: "I . . . got stuck in traffic."

Bob: "For two years?!"

Marie: Very romantic.

Cheryl: How about the horror movie *The Hand?*

Paul: "I've just **returned** from the train station. **Have** you **seen** anything lately?"

Bob: "No. We should go inside."

Paul: "Good idea. I don't want to see that terrible hand."

Bob: "Do you really think there's a hand out there that . . . ARRRGGGGHHH!"

Cheryl: Stop doing that right now, and the movie tickets are my treat.

Paul and Bob: Deal!

Cheryl: I'm not buying you popcorn.

ANSWER KEY

A. 1. b 2. b 3. c 4. c 5. c 6. b

B. 1. Have you, a movie yet 2. Have you seen anything lately

C. 1. you'd rather not know 2. Would you rather stay 3. I've always wanted

SCENE 2

PREVIEW

- Ask individual students *Have you ever seen a movie star or a singer on the street or in a restaurant? Did you talk to him or her? If yes, what did you say?*

REVIEW

- Ask comprehension questions. Play the video episode again if necessary.

  Who notices David Doolittle in the café—Paul or Marie? (Marie)

  Who is David Doolittle? (a famous British actor)

  Does Cheryl go to meet David Doolittle? (no)

  Are Paul and Bob fans of David Doolittle? (yes)

  What do Paul and Bob tell David Doolittle? (They say that they like his movies and that he is great.)

  What was the name of the movie where David Doolittle was a dancer? (The Dancer)

  What did he play in Doctor Fork? (a chef)

  When did Paul see Songs of Love again? (last week)

  What did David Doolittle play in Pie in the Sky? (a pilot)

  Why did David Doolittle invite Bob and Paul to join him? (because he could see that they would not leave)

EXTENSION

Oral work

- Pair work. Call on students to recall the names of the four movies and write them on the board: *The Dancer, Doctor Fork, Songs of Love, Pie in the Sky.* Have students work in pairs to guess the genres of the movies. Then have them discuss which of these movies they would rather see.

- Discussion. Tell students to think of questions to ask a famous actor or actress. Point out that Cheryl and Marie did not go to see David Doolittle because they were embarrassed. Ask *Are you more like Cheryl and Marie or Paul and Bob?*

Written work

- Pair work. Have students work in pairs to write two or three sentences about each Doolittle movie, describing what each one is about.

- Ask students to pretend that they see a famous movie star in a restaurant. Have them write a conversation between themselves and the star they meet.

LANGUAGE NOTES: *To take it easy* means to relax. The expression *Take it easy,* however, can also mean *good-bye.*

Doolittle says, "Would you guys care to join me?" This is another way of saying *Would you guys like to join me?*

VIDEO SCRIPT

Paul and Bob strike up a conversation with David Doolittle, a famous British actor.

Marie: So, what do you want to do? Hey, isn't that David Doolittle, the famous British actor?

Cheryl: You're right! It is!

Bob: Let's go say hi.

Cheryl: No, don't! What are you doing?!

Paul: Aren't you David Doolittle?

Doolittle: Yes, I am.

Bob: Wow! We really like your movies.

Doolittle: Thank you.

Paul: You're great!

Doolittle: Thank you very much.

Paul: Remember that movie where you're that dancer? What was that called?

Doolittle: *The Dancer.*

Paul: That's it! That was unforgettable!

Bob: I love that one where you're the chef. What's that one called?

Doolittle: *Doctor Fork?*

Bob: That's it. That was so funny! Unforgettable, man.

Doolittle: Thank you.

Paul: My favorite is the one where you're that robot musician named . . .

Doolittle: DD-42.

Paul: Yeah! Yeah! I just saw that movie again last week. That's a great movie. What's that called?

Doolittle: *Songs of Love.*

Paul: Yeah. Man, that's unforgettable.

Doolittle: Thanks. You know what? I have to go soon, and I should finish my lunch . . .

Bob: Oh, right. Yeah, sorry. It was nice to meet you.

Doolittle: You, too. Take it easy.

Bob: Take it easy. Isn't that what you say at the end of that movie where you're the pilot?

Doolittle: *Pie in the Sky.*

Paul: Yeah! That was unforgettable, man.

Bob: Unforgettable.

Doolittle: Would you guys care to join me?

Paul: What's your favorite movie?

ANSWER KEY

A. 1. dancer 2. chef 3. robot musician 4. pilot
B. 1. b 2. c 3. b 4. a 5. c
C. 1. a 2. b 3. b

Interview: *Do you think there's too much violence in movies?*

PREVIEW

• Ask students the following questions:
  What are some different genres of movies? (for example, comedy, action, drama)
  How many of you watch violent movies?
  What are the titles of some violent movies you have seen?
  Do you think it's OK for children to watch violent movies?

REVIEW

• Ask comprehension questions. Play the video segment again if necessary.
  Is comedy Emma's favorite genre? (no)
  Does San think violence in movies is harmful to children? (yes)
  Which person thinks that violence in movies is OK sometimes? (Stephan)
  When does Stephan think that violence in movies is OK? (when the violence helps the plot along and when there's a point to the violence)
  How does Stephan decide what movies to see? (He chooses films that get good reviews and films by filmmakers he likes.)
  Does Joe think violent movies are dangerous? Why? (No, he thinks people are dangerous, not movies.)

EXTENSION

Oral work

• Pair work. Have students work in pairs to discuss which interviewees they agree or disagree with. Have them explain why. Then bring the class together and ask students' opinions. Encourage students to refer to movies they have seen to support their points of view.

• Discussion. Ask students *How do you decide what movies to see?* Have individual students share their answers with the class.

Written work

• Pair work. Have students work in pairs to write summaries of what each interviewee said.

• Have each student choose one interviewee and write a paragraph explaining why he/she agrees or disagrees with the interviewee's point of view.

LANGUAGE NOTES: *To portray violence "graphically"* means to show a lot of blood, killing, and so on.

To help the plot along means to keep the story moving.

"A point to" the violence means that there is "a purpose for" showing the violence.

Turns me off means *I don't like it.*

To tend to do something means to usually do something.

To sway means to influence.

Movies "of that nature" means "those kinds of" movies.

To have good judgment skills means to be able to tell right from wrong.

OOPS! San says that children should not see violent movies because "they're a little more *influential* and don't have the judgment skills that adults do." She misuses the word *influential*, which means having an influence on others. What she means to say is that children are "more easily influenced" by violent movies than adults.

VIDEO SCRIPT

Interviewer: Do you have a favorite genre of movie?

Emma: I love drama. I love comedy, but my favorite is drama.

Interviewer: Do you think there's too much violence in movies?

Stephan: I think sometimes some films portray violence a little too graphically, but I feel that if it helps the plot along, and there's sort of a point to the violence, then it's OK, but unnecessary violence really turns me off.

Interviewer: So do you choose to go see movies if you know they're going to be violent?

Stephan: I usually tend to see films that get good reviews or are by filmmakers whom I admire. I don't think violence would really, you know, sway me one way or the other.

Interviewer: Do you ever go to see violent movies yourself?

Joe: Yes, I've seen violent movies—thrillers and movies of that nature.

Interviewer: Can violent movies be dangerous?

Joe: I think people are dangerous. I don't know that movies are dangerous.

Interviewer: Should children be allowed to see violent movies?

Emma: No. I don't think children need to be watching violent movies.

Interviewer: What's your feeling about violence? Is it harmful, particularly to children?

San: It is. I think violence is harmful, especially in movies. Movies . . . children of certain ages should not see violent movies because they're a little more influential and don't have the judgment skills that adults do.

ANSWER KEY

A. 1. c 2. b 3. a 4. d

B. films by filmmakers he likes, films that get good reviews

C. 1. False 2. True 3. False 4. False 5. True
6. False 7. False 8. False

 Top Notch Pop and Karaoke:
Better Late Than Never

UNIT 3

Sitcom: *Can I take a message?*

Social language
- Take messages
- Discuss hotel amenities

Grammar
- The future with *will*
- *Had better*

SCENE 1

PREVIEW

- Ask the following questions:
  What information do you usually give when you leave a phone message?
  Do you leave or take messages often on your job?
  Have you ever taken a message incorrectly? What happened?

REVIEW

- Ask comprehension questions. Play the video episode again if necessary.
  Does Mr. Evans write down every message? (yes)
  Who do the callers want to speak to? (Cheryl)
  Is Mrs. Beatty calling from her hotel? (yes)
  What is the problem? (She is not happy with the hotel; there is no bellman.)
  Is Mr. Rashid calling from a hotel? (no)
  What is his message? (He wants a cheaper hotel in Budapest.)
  Is Ms. Novak calling from a hotel? (no)
  What is her message? (She wants to know if her cat can stay at her hotel in Rio, and she asks for a king-size bed.)
  Does Cheryl understand Mr. Evans's messages? (no)

EXTENSION

Oral work

- Role play. Ask *What does Mr. Evans say to each person who calls? (He says that Cheryl's not there and that she will call back.)* Play the three phone calls again, and have students listen to the different ways Mr. Evans says the same thing. Stop after each phone call and write Mr. Evans's words on the board.
  I'm afraid Cheryl's not here . . . Cheryl will call you back.
  Cheryl's not here. Can I take a message? . . . I'll give Cheryl your message.
  She'll be right back. Is there a message? . . . I'll ask her to check and call you.

  Have students role-play Mr. Evans taking down the messages, using the prompts on the board.

- Pair work: role play. Have students work in pairs to role-play a conversation between a client and Mr. Evans. Tell students to make up their own requests or complaints.

Written work

- Pair work: role play. Replay Mr. Evans's conversation with Mrs. Beatty. Write Mr. Evans's part of the conversation on the board. Leave blanks for Mrs. Beatty's part, which we can't hear. Have students work in pairs to complete the conversation by making up Mrs. Beatty's part.

Hello.

Hi, Mrs. Beatty.

Cheryl? I'm afraid Cheryl's not here.

You're not satisfied with your hotel?

No bellman? I'm sorry.

Cheryl will call you back.

OK. Good-bye.

- Have students write a short summary of each caller's phone message.

LANGUAGE NOTE: *To be satisfied* means to be happy with something.

VIDEO SCRIPT

Mr. Evans takes phone messages for Cheryl.

Mr. Evans: Hello, Top Notch Travel. One moment please.
Hello, Top Notch. Just a moment please.
Top Notch. Hold please.

Hello. Hi, Mrs. Beatty. Cheryl? I'm afraid Cheryl's not here. You're not satisfied with your hotel? No bellman? I'm sorry. Cheryl **will call** you back. OK. Good-bye.

Hello? Yes, hello, Mr. Rashid. Cheryl's not here. Can I take a message? You want a cheaper hotel in Budapest—a hotel without breakfast is OK. Very good. I**'ll give** Cheryl your message. Good-bye.

Hello? Oh, hi, Ms. Novak. She**'ll be** right back. Is there a message? Can your cat stay with you at your hotel in Rio? And you'd like to reserve a king-size bed. I**'ll ask** her to check and call you. Bye-bye.

(Cheryl enters.)
Oh! You're back. I have three messages for you. Let's see. Mrs. Beatty wants a cheaper cat. Mr. Rashid isn't satisfied with his breakfast. And Ms. Novak thinks the bellman needs a king-size bed. They**'ll explain** it all to you.
Cheryl: What?

ANSWER KEY

A. 1. False 2. False 3. True 4. True 5. False
6. False 7. False 8. True
B. 1. Mrs. Beatty is not happy about her hotel. There is no bellman. 2. Mr. Rashid wants a cheaper hotel in Budapest. A hotel without

breakfast is OK. 3. Ms. Novak wants to bring her cat with her to the hotel in Rio. She also wants a king-size bed in her hotel room.
C. 1. cat 2. breakfast 3. bellman 4. bed

SCENE 2
PREVIEW

- Ask individual students the following questions:
  Have you ever had problems at a hotel?
  What happened?
  What did you do about the problems?

REVIEW

- Ask comprehension questions. Play the video episode again if necessary.
  Is Mrs. Beatty in Los Angeles? (yes)
  What's the problem? (The hotel isn't very nice.)
  What floor is her room on? (the fifth floor)
  Is there a bellman? (no) Or an elevator? (no)
  Does she have a smoking or a non-smoking room? (a smoking room)
  Did she want a smoking room? (no)
  What kind of bed did she request? (king-size bed)
  What kind of bed did she get? (twin bed)
  Is Mrs. Beatty at the right hotel? (no)
  How will she get her bags to the front desk? (She will ask a student to help her.)

EXTENSION
Oral work

- Pair work: role play. Have students work in pairs to role-play Cheryl and Mrs. Beatty and reenact the phone conversation from the video episode.
- Discussion. Have students discuss the problems Mrs. Beatty has at the hotel and decide which would be problems for them and which would not.

Written work

- Pair work. Have students work in pairs to write a summary of the problems Mrs. Beatty has at the hotel. Then bring the class together, and have pairs read their summaries.
- Pair work. Have students work in pairs to write a phone conversation between Cheryl and Mrs. Beatty after Mrs. Beatty has checked into the new hotel. Invite students to read their conversations to the class.

VIDEO SCRIPT

On the phone, Mrs. Beatty complains to Cheryl about the hotel she's staying at.

Cheryl: Hello. I'd like to speak to a guest—Mrs. Beatty in Room 514. Thank you.

Mrs. Beatty: Hello?

Cheryl: Hello, Mrs. Beatty? This is Cheryl from Top Notch. How's Los Angeles?

Mrs. Beatty: Well, the hotel isn't very nice, dear.

Cheryl: I'm sorry to hear that. Are you OK? You sound tired.

Mrs. Beatty: My room is on the fifth floor. I had to walk up—with my luggage.

Cheryl: There's no bellman? No elevator?

Mrs. Beatty: No. And I wanted a non-smoking room with a king-size bed.

Cheryl: And I requested that for you.

Mrs. Beatty: Well, they gave me a smoking room with a twin-size bed. It's all they have.

Cheryl: I**'d better check** your reservation. What hotel are you at?

Mrs. Beatty: The Candle Inn, I think. And another thing. They didn't make up the room. The towels are dirty.

Cheryl: Did you call housekeeping?

Mrs. Beatty: They're not answering. And there are all these students everywhere. I thought you said that movie stars stay at this hotel.

Cheryl: Mrs. Beatty, your reservation is for the Chandler Inn. You're in the wrong hotel. The Chandler Inn is a much nicer hotel.

Mrs. Beatty: Oh! Well! I**'d better call** a taxi.

Cheryl: How **will** you **get** your bags to the front desk?

Mrs. Beatty: I'm sure I can find a student to help. I**'ll say** I'm a movie star. I**'ll be** fine.

Cheryl: OK. Good luck.

Mrs. Beatty: Good-bye.

ANSWER KEY

A. There is no elevator. There is no bellman. She has a smoking room. She doesn't have a king-size bed. They didn't make up the room. The towels are dirty. There are students everywhere.

B. 1. Los Angeles 2. 514 3. fifth 4. nice 5. students 6. wrong

C. 1. I'd better call 2. will 3. get 4. I'll say 5. I'll be

Interview: *What's important to you in a hotel?*

PREVIEW

• Ask students to brainstorm different hotel facilities, services, amenities, and other factors that are important in choosing a hotel. Write them on the board—for example, *a fitness center, a pool, a business center, a gift shop, room service, atmosphere, location, price.* Then ask individual students *What things are important to you in choosing a hotel?*

REVIEW

• Ask comprehension questions. Play the video segment again if necessary.

Is a fitness center important to James when choosing a hotel? (no)
Is a pool important to him? (no)
What is important to him? (location)
Is Blanche a big fan of hotels? (no)
What is important to her? (The hotels have to be comfortable.)
Does Chris use room service in a hotel? (no) Why not? (He likes to go out and see the city where he is staying.)
According to Christiane, what makes a hotel special? (the people who work there)
Who once brought flowers to Christiane's hotel room? (a bellman)
Did the flowers make Christiane's stay at the hotel even more pleasant? (yes)
Did Chris talk about a good or bad hotel experience? (bad)
Why did Chris say noisy hotel neighbors are unpleasant? (It is a distraction, and this is bad especially when you have to get up early in the morning.)

EXTENSION

Oral work

• Pair work: role play. Have students work in pairs to role-play separate conversations between the interviewer and Christiane and between the interviewer and Chris. Tell students to try to include all the information they talked about.

• Discussion. Have students discuss their best and worst hotel experiences. Ask *Where was the hotel? How long were you there? Do you recommend the hotel?* Then ask *What do you do when you have a bad experience like Chris did? (complain, never return, don't recommend the hotel to other people) Do you do anything when you have a good experience like Christiane did? (tell the management, write a letter, leave a tip)*

Written work

• On the board, write *What is important to James in a hotel?* Have students write a short summary of his answer.

• Have students choose either Chris's bad experience or Christiane's good experience and write a letter to the hotel either to complain or to express thanks for a wonderful stay. Remind students to make the tone of the letter formal. Then have students exchange letters with a partner and read them.

OOPS! When Herb says, "She doesn't like twin beds" he means to say "She doesn't like two separate beds."

VIDEO SCRIPT

Interviewer: Could you tell me some of the things that are important to you in a hotel, such as a fitness center or a pool or gift shop or restaurant, a business center?

James: I look more for location in a hotel than anything else. I want to be close and convenient to whatever I'm doing in town. If I'm there to enjoy myself, for example, then I want to be near the beach. So location's more important to me than anything else.

Blanche: I don't pay too much attention to the hotel.

Herb: She likes one bed. She doesn't like twin beds.

Blanche: I'm not a big fan of hotels. If they have . . . if they're comfortable, I'm happy with it.

Interviewer: When you stay in a hotel, do you use room service?

Chris: No. I try not to use room service because I like to go out and see a little bit of the town or the city I'm staying in.

Interviewer: Thinking about a really good hotel experience, could you tell me about that?

Christiane: Really what makes the hotel special is the people who work there. If people there are very nice and friendly, and people say "Good morning" and know you by name and they . . . when you come back to the hotel . . . they greet you and they ask you how your day was, and they just make the difference. If . . . when I stayed in a hotel I had . . . I had a bellman bring me flowers that were left over and put them in my room, and those are those little touches that I think make your experience or your stay in a hotel much more pleasant than when you just stay anywhere else.

Interviewer: How about a worst hotel experience?

Chris: Well, I have had experiences, on more than one occasion, where I've been in a room next to people that are rather noisy and so that can be . . . that can be a distraction, especially when you've got to be up early in the morning.

ANSWER KEY

A. 1. b 2. c 3. a 4. d

B. They ask about your day. They say "Good morning." They know your name. They are nice and friendly.

C. *Following are expected answers. Students may produce variations that are also correct.*

1. There were extra flowers left over at the hotel, and the bellman put them in her room.
2. The people in the next room were noisy.

 Top Notch Pop and Karaoke: *Checking Out*

UNIT 4

Sitcom: *What happened to you?!*

Social language
- Describe a car accident
- Express concern and sympathy
- Rent a car

Grammar
- The past continuous
- Phrasal verbs: direct object placement

SCENE 1

PREVIEW

- Ask students *What can cause a car accident?* Have students brainstorm the answers and write them on the board—for example, *speeding, tailgating, talking on a cell phone, not paying attention, problems with the car, another driver, something on the road.* Then ask *What can a person do to not have a car accident?*

REVIEW

- Ask comprehension questions. Play the video episode again if necessary.
  What happened to Paul? (He had a car accident.)
  Was he driving a van? (yes)
  Was he wearing a seat belt? (yes)
  Where was he driving? (on Sixth Street)
  Why was the road slippery? (There were fish on the road.)
  What happened to the steering wheel? (It came off.)
  Does he have the steering wheel with him? (yes)
  Did Paul hit a stop sign? (No, another driver did, and it fell on Paul's van.)
  What were the causes of the accident? (the fish, the problem with the steering wheel, the car that was tailgating, the car that hit the stop sign, the piano)
  Was Paul hurt? (no)
  What part of the van is still OK? (the steering wheel)

EXTENSION

Oral work

- Discussion. Have students discuss the following questions:

  Where do you think the fish came from?
  Where do you think the piano came from?
  What can Paul do to not have an accident in the future?

- Group work: role play. Have students work in groups of four to role-play the characters and reenact what happened in the video episode.

Written work

- Pair work. Have students work in pairs to write a summary of what happened to Paul.

- Group work. Ask students *What do you think Paul will do now?* Have students work in groups of four to continue the conversation among Paul, Marie, Bob, and Cheryl for a few more exchanges. Invite groups to read their scenarios to the class.

VIDEO SCRIPT

In the café, Paul describes a car accident he just had to Bob, Cheryl, and Marie.

Paul: Hello.
Marie: Paul, what happened to you?
Paul: I had an accident with the van.
Cheryl: Oh, no! Are you OK?
Paul: I'm fine. I **was wearing** my seat belt. No one was hurt, but I think we're going to need a new van.
Bob: What happened?
Paul: I **was driving** on Sixth Street and there were a lot of fish on the road.
Marie: A lot of what?
Paul: Fish.
Marie: Why were there fish in the road?
Paul: I don't know. Anyway, I tried to turn but I had a problem with the steering wheel.
Bob: The steering wheel broke?
Paul: No, it came off. So I drove over the fish. The fish made the road slippery, so when I tried to stop, I hit a parked car.
Bob: Oh, no!
Paul: I'm not finished. The car behind me **was tailgating**, so he hit me. A car on the opposite side of the road hit a stop sign. The stop sign fell and smashed my hood.
Cheryl: Oh, no!
Paul: Then, worst of all, when I got out to look at the damage, a piano fell on the van.
Marie: What? Where did it come from?
Paul: I don't know. But the van does not look good. The bumpers are damaged. So is the

hood. The doors won't open. The windows won't close. The engine's not working. The headlights are smashed. The horn won't honk. And it smells like fish.
Bob: Are there any parts that are OK?
Paul: The steering wheel still looks good.
Bob: Great. All we need is a van to go with it.

ANSWER KEY

A. 6, 4, 2, 1, 5, 3, 7, 8
B. 1. b 2. a 3. b 4. c 5. c
C. 1. bumpers 2. hood 3. doors 4. windows
   5. engine 6. headlights 7. horn

SCENE 2

PREVIEW

- Remind students that Paul cannot drive the van after the accident. Ask *What do you think he should do?* Write students' suggestions on the board.

REVIEW

- Ask comprehension questions. Play the video episode again if necessary.

  When do they need the van? (this afternoon)
  What is Paul doing this afternoon? (taking tourists from Chile to the museum)
  Why does Paul not want a fish sandwich? (He just had a bad experience with fish.)
  When will they pick up the van? (right away)
  How long will they need it for? (two weeks)
  When will they return it? (on the fifteenth of the month)
  Why does Paul want a four-wheel drive van? (to take a group from France to the mountains)
  Does AutoRent have luxury vans with DVD and stereo? (They only have vans with stereo, but no DVD.)
  Does AutoRent have convertible vans? (no)
  What color van will Paul get? (white)
  Why does Cheryl ask for lots and lots of insurance? (because Paul just had an accident)

EXTENSION

Oral work

- Discussion. Ask students the following questions:
  What happens when Cheryl asks for a convertible van? (The person on the phone laughs.)
  Why do you think the person laughs? Do you think they even make convertible vans?
  Do you think they make four-wheel drive vans?

- Pair work: role play. Have students work in pairs to role-play Cheryl and Paul and reenact what happened in the video episode.

Written work

- Pair work. Have students work in pairs to write additional questions Cheryl can ask AutoRent during her phone call. For example, *Does the van have air- conditioning? Is it automatic or manual transmission? How many people can ride in this van? How much does the van cost per day?* Then combine pairs into groups of four and have them exchange and answer each other's questions.

- Pair work. Tell students they will create True and False quizzes. Have students work in pairs to write true and false statements about the video episode. Then combine pairs into groups of four and have them exchange and answer each other's quizzes. Finally, have the writers of the quizzes check the answers.

VIDEO SCRIPT

Cheryl calls a car rental agency to rent a van for Paul.

Cheryl: We're going to need a van this afternoon. You're taking the tourists from Chile to the museum. I'll call the rental company.

Bob: Are you hungry? Want some of my fish sandwich? Oh, sorry. Guess not.

Cheryl: Hi. Is this AutoRent? I need a rental car.

Paul: A van.

Cheryl: Do you rent vans? That's great. We'll need to **pick it up** right away. We'll probably need it for two weeks. Could we return it on the fifteenth of the month? Great.

Paul: Four-wheel drive. We could take the group from France to the mountains.

Cheryl: Do you have any four-wheel drive vans? *(to Paul)* They don't have four-wheel drive vans.

Paul: How about a luxury van with DVD player and stereo?

Cheryl: Do you have any luxury vans with DVD and stereo? *(to Paul)* Stereo, yes. DVD, no.

Paul: How about a convertible van? Ask them!

Cheryl: Do you have any convertible vans? *(to Paul)* No. What color do you want?

Paul: Blue. No, red. No, green.

Cheryl: White will be fine. Insurance? Yes, we'd like insurance. Lots and lots of insurance, please.

ANSWER KEY

A. 1. False 2. False 3. True 4. False 5. True
   6. False
B. 1. a 2. b 3. a 4. b
C. 1. They don't have four-wheel drive vans.
   2. Stereo, yes. DVD, no. 3. No.

 Top Notch Pop and Karaoke: *Wheels around the World*

UNIT 5

Sitcom: *How about a manicure?*

Social language

- Discuss personal care
- Suggest ways to improve appearance

Grammar

- Count and non-count nouns
- Indefinite quantities and amounts

SCENE 1

PREVIEW

- Ask individual students *Do you care about how you look? What do you do to take care of your appearance every day?*

REVIEW

- Ask comprehension questions. Play the video episode again if necessary.

    Is Cheryl using a new shampoo? (yes)
    Where did she buy it? (at her salon)
    Does Bob want to try this new shampoo? (no)
    What does this new shampoo do to hair? (makes it softer and cleaner-smelling)
    What does Bob do to take care of his appearance? (He shampoos, showers, and shaves every day.)
    What else do Cheryl and Marie think he should do? (use skin care products, use conditioner, get manicures)
    What does Bob say about conditioner? (He says that it's for women.)
    Does Bob get manicures? (No. He doesn't know men get manicures.)
    Will he let Cheryl and Marie give him a manicure? (yes)
    Why is Bob so worried at the end of the video episode? (Cheryl says they can talk about a face-lift.)

EXTENSION

Oral work

- Discussion. Ask students the following questions:
  *What does Bob say when Marie says, "Do you
  use any conditioner?" (That's for women.)*
  *Do you agree that some personal care products
  are for women only? Which ones?*
  *Do you agree with Marie that women like men
  who take care of their appearance?*
  *Do you think it is also true that men like women
  who take care of their appearance?*

- Pair work. Have students work in pairs to continue
  the conversation between Cheryl and Bob for a
  few more exchanges. Invite students to perform
  their scenarios for the class.

Written work

- Have students write what they do every day to
  take care of their appearance.

- Pair work. Have students work in pairs to write
  a summary of the story in the video episode. To
  help students begin, write these sentences on the
  board:
  *Cheryl and Marie are discussing Cheryl's new
  shampoo. Cheryl asks Bob if he would like to
  try it too. Bob says . . .*

LANGUAGE NOTE: Cheryl says Bob's nails are *a
mess.* This means they don't look good.

VIDEO SCRIPT

*In Cheryl's apartment, Cheryl, Marie, and Bob
discuss personal appearance.*

Marie: Cheryl, your hair looks gorgeous.
Cheryl: Thank you! I have a new **shampoo**—
Bright 'n Clean.
Marie: I'd like to try it. Did you find it at the
drugstore?
Cheryl: No, I bought it at my salon on Friday. I'll
pick **some** up for you next time I'm there.
Marie: Great, thanks!
Cheryl: Would you like **some** too, Bob?
Bob: I have **shampoo**, thanks.
Cheryl: But mine will make your hair softer and
cleaner-smelling.
Bob: Uh, thanks, but no thanks.
Marie: Come on, Bob, don't you care about how
you look?
Bob: Of course I do. I shampoo, shower, and
shave every day.
Marie: That's all?
Bob: Is there more to do?
Marie: Don't you use **any** skin care products—
body lotion or **skin cream**?
Bob: No. Should I?

Marie: If you want your skin to stay young and
healthy. Do you use **any conditioner**?
Bob: That's for women.
Cheryl: Lots of men use it, too.
Bob: Really?
Marie: Sure. Women like men who take care of
their appearance.
Bob: Really? OK. Well, what else should I do?
You don't want me to wear **makeup**, do you?
Lipstick, **mascara**, **eye shadow** . . .
Cheryl: No. But how about a manicure? I'm
serious. Look at your nails. They're a mess.
Bob: Men get manicures?
Marie: Many do, yes.
Cheryl: We can give you one right here.
Bob: Really?
Cheryl: Piece of cake.
Bob: Well . . . OK.
Cheryl: Great. Then we can talk about your
haircut, facial, and face-lift.
Bob: What?

ANSWER KEY

A. 1. Marie 2. softer 3. healthy 4. shampoo
5. conditioner 6. nails 7. manicure 8. face-lift
B. 1. b 2. b 3. a 4. b
C. 1. hair 2. shampoo 3. drugstore 4. salon

SCENE 2

PREVIEW

- Ask individual students *How often do you get a
  haircut? Do you spend a lot of time doing your hair
  every day? Do you use any personal care products in
  your hair?*

REVIEW

- Ask comprehension questions. Play the video
  episode again if necessary.
  How does Bob's facial mask taste? (terrible)
  *What did Cheryl do to Bob's hair? (She cut it and
  put some hair spray in it.)*
  *What does Bob say about his nails? (He says they
  look great.)*
  What does he ask Marie for? (a pedicure)
  Does she say yes? (no)
  *What does Bob say about his hair? (He says it
  looks great, too.)*
  Do Cheryl and Marie think Bob looks good? (yes)
  Does Bob give Cheryl a tip? (no)
  *What does Bob do to thank Cheryl and Marie?
  (He treats them to pizza.)*
  *What does he ask at the end of the video episode?
  (to make an appointment for another manicure)*

Oral work

- Discussion. Ask students the following questions:
  What does Bob say to Marie and Cheryl about the facial at the end of the video episode? (that they can never tell anyone about it)
  Why does he say this?
  Do you think men are usually embarrassed by personal care services?

- Group work: discussion. On the board, write the following questions and have groups discuss them:
  Do you ever use any of the personal care services mentioned in the episode?
  If yes, which ones? How often? Where do you go?
  If not, why not?

Written work

- Pair work. Have students work in pairs to write a summary of the story in the video episode. To help students begin, write this sentence on the board:
  Cheryl and Marie gave Bob a facial . . .

- Pair work. Have students work in pairs to write a conversation between Paul and Bob later that day when Paul notices that Bob looks different. Then have pairs read their conversations to the class.

VIDEO SCRIPT

Cheryl and Marie give Bob a facial, a haircut, and a manicure.

Bob: What is this stuff on my face?
Cheryl: It makes your skin soft and smooth.
Bob: It tastes terrible.
Cheryl: Oh! Sorry.
Bob: I can't believe you cut my hair. And what did you put in it?
Cheryl: **Some hair spray**.
Bob: **Hair spray**!
Cheryl: **Not much**. You'll like it. There.
Bob: Wow. My nails look great! Could I get a pedicure, too?
Marie: Uh, no.
Bob: My hair looks great, too!
Cheryl: See what a little personal care can do?
Bob: Wow. Thank you so much.
Marie: You know, it's customary to tip the person who gives you a haircut.
Bob: How do I look?
Marie: Good.
Cheryl: You look really, really good! You look amazing!
Bob: Then let's get pizza—my treat.
Marie: Great!
Bob: You can never tell anyone about this. Especially the facial.

Cheryl: Deal.
Bob: Now when can I get an appointment for another manicure?

ANSWER KEY

A. 1. facial 2. haircut 3. manicure 4. pedicure
B. 1. True 2. True 3. False 4. False 5. False
   6. False
C. 1. Some 2. Not much 3. anyone

 Top Notch Pop and Karaoke:
Piece of Cake

UNIT 6

Sitcom: *Help yourself, everyone!*

Social language

- Offer and decline food
- Talk about food passions
- Discuss habits and lifestyles

Grammar

- *Used to*
- Suggestions with *Why don't . . . ?*
- Negative *yes / no* questions

SCENE 1

PREVIEW

- Ask individual students *Are there any foods you don't eat? If yes, what foods? Why don't you eat them?*

REVIEW

- Ask comprehension questions. Play the video episode again if necessary.
  Who cooked dinner? (Cheryl)
  Does Mr. Evans eat most of the food Cheryl cooked? (no)
  Why doesn't he eat much chicken? (He's not a big chicken eater.)
  Why doesn't he eat potatoes? (He's avoiding potatoes—maybe he's on a diet.)
  Why doesn't he eat broccoli? (It doesn't agree with him.)
  What food is he allergic to? (cabbage)
  What food is he crazy about? (rice)
  Why is Bob not eating much? (He is on a diet.)
  What kind of diet is Paul on? (He is trying to gain weight.)

EXTENSION

Oral work

- Discussion. Ask students the following questions:
  How does Cheryl feel when she sees that Mr. Evans doesn't eat most of the food she cooked? When you are at a dinner party, do you ever eat food that you normally don't like very much?

- Pair work: role play. Have students work in pairs to role-play Mr. Evans and Cheryl. Tell the students role-playing Mr. Evans to use their own food preferences to accept or decline food. Tell students to give reasons for the foods they decline.

Written work

- Have students write a summary of Mr. Evans's food preferences. Then have them write which foods on Cheryl's menu they can eat. If there's anything they don't like or can't eat, have them explain why.

- Pair work. On the board, write *Bob's diet* and *Paul's diet*. Ask *Who is trying to lose weight? Who is trying to gain weight?* Have students work in pairs to write sentences describing which foods on Cheryl's menu are good for Bob's diet and which foods are good for Paul's diet. Then have students suggest additional foods that will help each person's diet.

LANGUAGE NOTES: *I'll pass* means *I won't have any.*

Pass the [food] means *Hand the [food] to me.*

VIDEO SCRIPT

Cheryl hosts a dinner for the entire Top Notch Travel staff.

Cheryl: I think everything's ready. **Why don't** we sit down?

Marie: This smells so wonderful! What are we having to eat?

Cheryl: There's roast chicken, baked potatoes, salad, broccoli with garlic, red cabbage, and rice. Help yourself, everyone.

Paul: Wow! That's a lot of vegetables.

Cheryl: Vegetables are very healthy for you. Mr. Evans, would you like some chicken?

Mr. Evans: Just a little, thank you. I'm not a big chicken eater.

Cheryl: How about some potatoes?

Mr. Evans: I'm sorry. I'm avoiding potatoes.

Cheryl: Some broccoli?

Mr. Evans: I'll pass. I'm afraid it doesn't agree with me.

Cheryl: Cabbage?

Mr. Evans: Sorry. I'm allergic.

Cheryl: Mr. Evans, I'm so sorry. There's very little here for you to eat.

Mr. Evans: I'm crazy about rice.

Cheryl: Well, then pass the rice please.

Marie: Cheryl, this tastes so delicious. Bob, you're not eating very much tonight. **Don't** you like the food?

Cheryl: Bob's on a diet.

Bob: I'm trying to lose weight.

Mr. Evans: Good for you, Bob.

Paul: I'm on a diet, too.

Marie: Why are *you* on a diet? You're so skinny.

Paul: I'm trying to *gain* weight.

Bob: I can't stand it.

All: Bob!

SCENE 2

PREVIEW

- Have students name different desserts and write them on the board. Then ask individual students *Which is your favorite dessert? Do you eat it often? Do you usually eat dessert after a meal?*

REVIEW

- Ask comprehension questions. Play the video episode again if necessary.
  What dessert does Cheryl bring out first? (cookies)
  How many cookies does Marie take? (one) Paul? (four)
  Does Mr. Evans eat sweets? (no) Did he use to? (yes)
  Will Bob have dessert? (no)
  What did Marie see Bob eating at work today? (cookies and candy)
  What did she see him eating yesterday? (ice cream)
  What does Bob say? (He says that he was eating carrots, an apple, and fruit salad.)
  What else does Cheryl have for dessert? (strawberries and chocolate cake)
  Does Mr. Evans like strawberries? (Yes. They are his passion.)

EXTENSION

Oral work

- Discussion. Replay the part of the video where Marie talks about sweets she saw Bob eating at work. Ask students the following questions:
  Do you think Bob was really eating sweets?

Why is Bob so nervous? (He doesn't want Cheryl to think that he's eating sweets at work.)
Do you think Bob's diet is successful?

• Pair work: role play. Have students work in pairs to role-play Marie and Bob and reenact their conversation in the video episode.

Written work

• Ask *Do you think Bob needs Cheryl's help with his diet?* Have students write a paragraph about Bob's diet and comment if he seems serious about it.

• Pair work. Tell students they will create True and False quizzes. Have students work in pairs to write true and false statements about the video episode. Then combine pairs into groups of four and have them exchange quizzes and answer them. Finally, have the writers of each quiz check the answers.

LANGUAGE NOTE: The expression *You only live once* suggests that a person should take advantage of opportunities, enjoy the pleasures of life, and live life to the fullest.

VIDEO SCRIPT

After dinner, Cheryl serves desserts.

Paul: Cheryl, that was fantastic.
Mr. Evans: The rice was terrific.
Cheryl: Cookies, anyone?
Marie: Yes, one please!
Paul: I'll take two, thanks. Or three. Or four.
Cheryl: Do you eat sweets, Mr. Evans?
Mr. Evans: I **used to**. But I can't anymore.
Marie: No dessert for you, Bob?
Cheryl: Not on his diet.
Marie: But **weren't** you eating cookies today at work?
Bob: I was eating carrots.
Marie: **Didn't** I see you snacking on candy this afternoon?
Bob: That was an apple.
Marie: What about that ice cream you ate yesterday?
Bob: Fruit salad.
Marie: My mistake.
Paul: These cookies are terrific.
Cheryl: If you like the cookies, you'll love this cake. Would you eat some strawberries, Mr. Evans?
Mr. Evans: Strawberries are my passion!
Cheryl: Really?
Mr. Evans: I'd eat strawberries on anything—cereal, pasta, even rice.
Paul: I'm crazy about chocolate cake! I can gain weight with every bite!
Cheryl: I think I'll have a cookie. Bob, could you pass the . . . oh, where'd they go?

Marie: I have one.
Paul: I have four.
Mr. Evans: I have none.
Bob: Hey . . . you only live once.

ANSWER KEY

A. 1. b 2. c 3. b 4. a 5. c 6. b
B. 1. I have one. 2. I have four. 3. I have none.
C. 1. weren't you eating cookies 2. carrots
    3. Didn't I see you 4. candy 5. apple
    6. ice cream 7. Fruit salad

 Top Notch Pop and Karaoke:
A Perfect Dish

UNIT 7

Sitcom: *What do you think of this color?*

Social language
• State color preferences
• Talk about mood
• Cheer someone up

Grammar
• Gerunds and infinitives

SCENE 1

PREVIEW

• Have students name different colors and write them on the board. Ask individual students *What is your favorite color? Which colors make you feel happy? Which colors make you feel sad?* Have students answer using the colors on the board.

REVIEW

• Ask comprehension questions. Play the video episode again if necessary.
    Does Bob like the colors Cheryl is showing him? (no)
    How do all the colors make Paul feel? (happy)
    How do all the colors make Marie feel? (sad)
    What does Bob want Cheryl to do? (He wants her to leave the walls the way they are.)
    What does Cheryl ask Bob to do? (She asks Bob to find a color everyone likes.)
    Does Bob find a color? (yes) What color is it? (green)

Does Cheryl want to paint her apartment green?
(no) Why not? (because her sofa is green)
What does Bob tell Cheryl to do? (He tells her
to change the color of the sofa to yellow—the
current color of the walls.)

EXTENSION

Oral work

• Pair work. Play the video episode again. Then have students work in pairs to choose a color for Cheryl's walls. Have pairs share their color with the class and explain their choice.

• Group work: role play. Divide the class into groups of four. Have students role-play the characters and reenact what happened in the video episode. Tell students role-playing Cheryl and Bob to be friendly to each other.

Written work

• Pair work. Have students work in pairs to continue the dialogue between Cheryl and her friends for a few more exchanges. Write these lines on the board to help them begin:

Cheryl: Do you really think green would look nice?
Bob: Yes, I do.

• Ask *Why do you think Paul always says the colors make him feel happy, and Marie says they make her feel sad?* Have students write a few sentences answering this question.

VIDEO SCRIPT

Cheryl tries to pick a color to repaint her apartment.

Cheryl: What do you think about this color?
Paul: What is that color?
Cheryl: It's tomato red. How does this color make you feel?
Paul: Happy.
Marie: Sad.
Bob: Tired. I don't feel like **looking** at any more colors.
Cheryl: Quit **complaining**. How about this one?
Paul: Happy.
Marie: Sad.
Bob: Awful. I can't stand **looking** at it. Do you plan **to do** this all night?
Cheryl: This one? Be sure **to look** carefully.
Marie: Sad.
Paul: Happy.
Bob: Very, very nervous.
Cheryl: Nervous about what?
Bob: I'm nervous you're going to paint the whole wall that color.
Cheryl: It's my apartment, Bob.
Bob: Yeah, but we come here a lot. Can we discuss **leaving** the walls just like this?

Cheryl: I'm tired of **looking** at yellow walls.
Bob: Fine. Can you at least choose a color we'll all be excited about?
Cheryl: There is no color you all like. Paul's feeling happy about everything, Marie's feeling sad about everything, and you just seem to hate color, don't you Bob?
Bob: I love color. Just not those colors.
Cheryl: OK. Then why don't you find a color that everybody likes?
Bob: What do you think of this color?
Paul: I like it.
Marie: I like it too, actually.
Bob: I love it.
Cheryl: I'm not painting the walls the same color as my sofa. The whole room would be green.
Bob: You could change the color of the sofa.
Cheryl: To what?
Bob: The color of the walls would be a nice color.

ANSWER KEY

A. 1. a 2. b 3. c 4. b 5. c 6. b
B. 1. looking, complaining 2. looking, to do, to look
C. 1. tired of, excited about 2. happy about, sad about

SCENE 2

PREVIEW

• Take a poll. Ask students *Are you generally a happy person or a sad person?* Then ask *Do you like to laugh? Do you ever laugh for no reason?*

REVIEW

• Ask comprehension questions. Play the video episode again if necessary.

What's wrong with Marie? (She's feeling down in the dumps.)
Why does she feel this way? (She doesn't know.)
Who wants to help her? (Paul)
What did people call him in school? (Dr. Cheer)
Why did they call him that? (because he is always happy and enjoys cheering people up)
How does Paul stay happy all the time? (He practices laughing every day.)
What does he laugh at? (nothing)
Does Marie think this is a good idea? (No. She says this is not in her nature.)
Does she try? (yes) Does it work? (no)
What works in the end? (chocolate)
Does chocolate work for you?

Oral work

- Discussion. Have students try Paul's trick and laugh for no reason. On the board, write *That's not in my nature.* Point out that Marie says this when Paul tells her to laugh. Ask individual students *Do you think it is in your nature to laugh for no reason? Do you think you would feel better?*

- Pair work: role play. Have students work in pairs to role-play Paul and Marie and reenact what happened in the video episode. Encourage students to have fun acting the laughing part.

Written work

- Have students write a summary of the story in the video episode. To help students begin, write these sentences on the board: *Marie is feeling blue, and Paul wants to cheer her up. He says that at school people called him Dr. Cheer . . .*

- Pair work. Have students work in pairs to make a list of at least six things Marie can do to cheer up when she is feeling blue. Then bring the class together and have students read their ideas to the class.

VIDEO SCRIPT

Marie is feeling blue, and Paul tries to cheer her up.

Cheryl: Marie, you've been so quiet. Are you OK?

Marie: I'm just a little down in the dumps.

Cheryl: Oh, I'm sorry. We've been arguing about colors and you're feeling blue. Hmm. Blue . . .

Paul: What's wrong, Marie?

Marie: Don't know. I can't put my finger on it. I've just been feeling . . . out of sorts.

Paul: Don't worry. I can help. Dr. Cheer is here.

Marie: Doctor who?

Paul: At school, people called me Dr. Cheer because I'm always happy and I enjoy **cheering** people up.

Bob: You know, that's true. You're always cheering me up.

Marie: How do you do that?

Paul: I practice **laughing** every day.

Marie: Laughing at what?

Paul: Nothing. I just choose **to laugh**.

Marie: You just decide **to laugh**? I can't do that. It's not in my nature.

Paul: How do you know? Just try it. Let me hear you laugh.

Marie: Ha-ha.

Paul: Louder.

Marie: HA-HA.

Paul: Come on, keep **laughing**. You're right. It's not your personality.

Marie: What now, Dr. Cheer?

Paul: Chocolate?

Marie: Yes!

Paul: Works every time.

ANSWER KEY

A. 1. at school 2. cheering people up 3. nothing
    4. choose to laugh 5. a chocolate bar
B. 1. down in the dumps 2. feeling blue 3. put
    my finger on it 4. feeling out of sorts
C. 1. b 2. a 3. b

Interview: *How would you describe your personality?*

PREVIEW

- Ask students *Are you the youngest, middle, or oldest child in your family? Do you think birth order has an effect on personality?*

REVIEW

- Ask comprehension questions. Play the video segment again if necessary.

    Who is Alvino most like in his family? (his mother) Why? (because she smiles a lot)
    How many brothers and sisters does Cortyan have? (four—one brother and three sisters)
    What kind of personality does Cortyan have? (She is quiet and calm.)
    Do Cortyan and her sisters have the same personalities? (no)
    Who was the oldest child in Lorayn's family? (her brother)
    Did he have the same rules as Lorayn and her sister did? (no)
    How did their parents treat him differently? (He was able to go to concerts at an earlier age than Lorayn and her sister; Lorayn and her sister helped around the house more than he did.)

EXTENSION

Oral work

- Discussion. Ask students the following questions:
    Has anyone had a similar experience to Lorayn's? (having an older brother or sister who got special treatment from parents)
    What does Alvino say is a benefit of being the youngest child in a family? (You get clothes.) Do you agree this is a benefit?
    What are other benefits of being the youngest child in a family?

- Pair work: interviews. Pair students. One student role-plays the interviewer, and the other student role-plays someone who is the only girl or boy in a family. Write these interview questions on the board to help students:

How many brothers / sisters do you have?
Do you like being the only girl / boy in your family?
Do your parents treat you differently? How?

Encourage students to make up additional questions.

Written work

- Pair work. Tell students they will create True and False quizzes. Have students work in pairs to write true and false statements about the video segment. Then combine pairs into groups of four and have them exchange quizzes and answer them. Finally, have the writers of each quiz check the answers.

- On the board, write _____ *and I have the same personality.* Tell students to write the name of the family member they are most like. Then ask them to write a paragraph describing how they are alike. For example, *My Dad and I have the same personality. We are both introverts . . .* Then have students read their description to the class.

LANGUAGE NOTES: *To get away with something* means to not get in trouble for doing something.

To "get out of" household duties means to "not have to do" household duties.

VIDEO SCRIPT

Interviewer: Who are you most like in terms of personality?
Alvino: My mother.
Interviewer: And why do you say that?
Alvino: Outgoing—she smiles a lot.
Interviewer: Do you have any brothers or sisters?
Cortyan: One brother, two . . . three sisters.
Interviewer: And how are you different? Is, say, one more extroverted than the other, or more introverted?
Cortyan: Well, I'm quiet, calm. I don't really get excited over things and just take it easy. I don't let things bother me a lot, while my sisters, they will get excited and get upset, so I'm not like that.
Interviewer: OK. How about first children? Do you think that they have certain traits that they share?
Lorayn: Well, I think my brother, being the oldest and the only boy, was allowed to get away with things a lot more than my sister and I. And what I mean by that is as the oldest and as a boy, he was able to go to concerts at an earlier age than my sister or I. He kind of got out of household duties that my sister and I had because he was babysitting us.

Interviewer: And how about if you're the last in a big family? Do you think that you get special benefits from that?
Alvino: Yeah, you get clothes.
Interviewer: What about birth order? Do you think that makes a difference, who's the oldest and who's the youngest?
Maiko: I don't think so.
Interviewer: Not important?
Maiko: I don't think it's important. It's just the personality.

ANSWER KEY

A. 1. Alvino 2. Cortyan 3. Lorayn 4. Maiko
B. 1. True 2. False 3. True 4. True 5. False
C. 1. an outgoing 2. a calm 3. concerts 4. clothes

 Top Notch Pop and Karaoke:
The Colors of Love

UNIT 8

Sitcom: *What do you think?*

Social language
- Describe art
- Describe how art affects people

Grammar
- The passive voice

SCENE 1

PREVIEW

- On the board, write *art.* Have students name different kinds of art (for example, *painting, drawing, photography, sculpture, fashion, film, pottery*). Ask students *Which types of art do you prefer? Do you understand art? Is there any kind of art you don't like?*

REVIEW

- Ask comprehension questions. Play the video episode again if necessary.
    What art pieces has Ms. Novak brought to the office? (a painting, a sculpture, and a photograph)
    What is the painting of? (an orange circle on blue)
    What is the sculpture of? (a gold square)
    What is the photograph of? (snow in a park)

Does anyone like the art pieces? (Mr. Evans and Ms. Novak)
Do the others say what they really think? (no)
Which piece does Marie prefer—the painting or the sculpture? (the painting)
Which pieces does Mr. Evans decide to buy? (all of them)

EXTENSION

Oral work

- Discussion. On the board, write *I think I can do that.* Ask the following questions:
  Who said this? (Paul)
  About what? (about the painting)
  Do you think you could paint that painting?
  Do you ever feel that way about art?
  In your opinion, what is real art?

- Group work: role play. Divide the class into groups of six. Have students role-play the characters and reenact what happened in the video episode.

Written work

- Have students write a review of the three art pieces from Ms. Novak's gallery. Tell students to describe what each piece looks like, write information they know about it from the video episode, and then say what they think about each piece.

- Pair work. Point out that Bob tells Mr. Evans the sculpture would look good in his office. Ask *Why do you think he said this?* Then have students work in pairs to continue the dialogue for several more exchanges. Write these lines on the board to help students start:
  Mr. Evans: Where should we put these wonderful art pieces?
  Bob: There is no room on my desk.

VIDEO SCRIPT

Ms. Novak brings three pieces of art to show the staff of Top Notch Travel.

Mr. Evans: Hello, everyone. You remember Ms. Novak.
Ms. Novak: Hello.
Mr. Evans: Ms. Novak has just opened an art gallery here. I've asked her to find some pieces to decorate our office. She's brought some things for us to look at today.
Ms. Novak: I have a painting, a sculpture, and a photograph that I think you'll like. Here's the painting. This **was painted** by a Russian artist that I really like. It**'s called** *Sun on the Water*. The artist **was inspired** by looking at the sea. What do you think?
Paul: I think I can do that.
Cheryl: It's . . . fantastic.
Marie: How . . . interesting!

Bob: It's very . . . blue.
Ms. Novak: Yes.
Mr. Evans: It's gorgeous!
Ms. Novak: Oh, good. Here's the sculpture. It **was made** by a British sculptor. It**'s called** *City of Gold*.
Paul: Is it really gold?
Ms. Novak: No. It**'s made** of wood. It **was painted** gold. What do you think?
Cheryl: It's . . . cool.
Bob: Mr. Evans, I think it would look good in your office.
Marie: I think I prefer the painting.
Mr. Evans: I**'m fascinated** by it!
Ms. Novak: Good. And here's the photograph. It**'s called** *Winter*. It **was photographed** in Paris.
Paul: There's nothing there.
Ms. Novak: It's a photograph of snow in a park.
Mr. Evans: Maybe I should buy them all. What do you think?
All: Great!
Ms. Novak: Excellent.

ANSWER KEY

A. 1. b 2. e 3. c 4. a 5. d
B. 1. True 2. False 3. False 4. True 5. False 6. True
C. 1. was painted 2. was inspired 3. was made 4. 's made 5. was painted 6. was photographed
D. 1. *Sun on the Water* 2. *City of Gold* 3. *Winter*

SCENE 2

PREVIEW

- Ask individual students *Do you take pictures often? Do you enjoy taking pictures? Have you ever sold any of your pictures? What do you think makes a good photographer?*

REVIEW

- Ask comprehension questions. Play the video episode again if necessary.
  Is Paul serious when he says, "I'm an artist"? (no)
  What is the name of his latest work? (Office Walls)
  Does Ms. Novak think Paul has talent? (yes)
  Is Paul surprised? (yes)
  What does she want to do with his photos? (sell them)
  When is he bringing more pieces to Ms. Novak? (Friday)
  Where does Paul tell Cheryl to hang the painting Mr. Evans bought? (by Paul's desk) Why? (because he feels he is an artist now)

Oral work

- Discussion. Replay the beginning of the video episode where Paul talks about his "latest work." Ask these questions:

    Do you think everyone can be an artist?
    Are there qualifications you think people need to be artists?
    If yes, what are they?
    If not, why not?
    Do you learn art skills, or are you born with them?

- Pair work: role play. Have students work in pairs to create a new scenario where Ms. Novak does *not* like Paul's photographs. Have pairs decide what she will do—either say her honest opinion or pretend to like them the way everyone pretended to like the pieces she sold Mr. Evans. Invite pairs to perform their scenarios to the class.

Written work

- Have students write a summary of the story in the video episode. To help students begin, write these sentences on the board: *Paul says he is an artist. He takes a picture of a wall and calls it* Office Walls.

- Pair work. Have students predict what Paul's meeting with Ms. Novak will be like on Friday. What photographs will he show her? Will she be impressed by his work? Have students work in pairs to write the conversation they'll have. Then invite pairs to read their conversation to the class.

VIDEO SCRIPT

Ms. Novak discusses Paul's photography with Paul.

Paul: Hey, look. I'm an artist. Here's my latest work. It**'s called** Office Walls. I **was inspired** by looking at the walls of the office.

Ms. Novak: Are you a photographer?

Paul: Yes, well, no, I . . . I take a lot of pictures.

Ms. Novak: Hmmm. I'm not so crazy about that one, but I do like what you've done here. I**'m** very **moved** by it, actually. It's a fascinating mixture of Eastern and Western traditions. You have talent.

Paul: I do?

Ms. Novak: I think I could sell this.

Paul: Really?

Ms. Novak: It's very good.

Paul: I'm crazy about photography.

Ms. Novak: Do you have any more of your work here?

Paul: Uh, no.

Ms. Novak: Here's my card. Why don't you bring me some pieces on Friday?

Paul: OK.

Ms. Novak: Bye-bye.

Paul: Bye-bye.

Cheryl: So . . . where are we going to put *this* thing?

Paul: Hang it by my desk.

Marie: Really?

Paul: Yeah. As an artist, I'm really starting to like it. As a matter of fact, I think it's . . . one of the most interesting works I've ever seen.

ANSWER KEY

A. 1. a 2. b 3. c 4. b

B. 1. was inspired by 2. not so crazy about 3. moved by

C. "I think I could sell this." "It's very good." "Why don't you bring me some pieces on Friday?"

D. *Individual responses may include variations like the following:*
Paul tells Marie to hang the picture by his desk. He says now that he is an artist, he's really starting to like it. He thinks this is one of the most interesting works he has ever seen.

 Top Notch Pop and Karaoke: *To Each His Own*

UNIT 9

Sitcom: *Can you help me with something?*

Social language
- Ask for and offer help
- Suggest a solution

Grammar
- The infinitive of purpose
- Comparisons with *as . . . as*

SCENE 1

PREVIEW

- Ask students *Is it OK to play computer games at work? Send instant messages? E-mail friends? Surf the Internet for fun?* Then take a poll: *Do you think it is OK not to work 100 percent of the time you are at work?*

REVIEW

- Ask comprehension questions. Play the video episode again if necessary.

    Does everyone ask Bob computer questions? (yes)
    Does Bob seem to be very busy? (yes)

What is Marie's computer problem? (The printer won't work.)

What is Paul's computer problem? (His computer crashed.)

What is Cheryl's computer problem? (She thinks someone sent her an e-mail with a virus in it.)

Does Bob solve everyone's problem? (yes)

Is he happy about helping people? (no)

What happens on his computer? (It says "Game over.")

EXTENSION

Oral work

- Group work: role play. Divide students into groups of four. Have students role-play Bob and each person who comes to him for help. Ask students to come up with their own computer problems. When they get advice, they should ask why they need to do that. Tell students role-playing Bob to use an infinitive of purpose when answering why.

- Discussion. Ask these questions:
    What was Bob doing on his computer? (playing a computer game)
    Should he play games at work?
    Do you think he does this a lot?
    What do you think Bob's coworkers think when he plays games at work?
    Do you think his boss knows he plays games at work?

Written work

- Pair work. Have students work in pairs to create a list of computer problems and write suggestions Bob would make.

- Pair work. Tell students to imagine that Mr. Evans was in the room when Bob's computer said "Game over." Have students work in pairs to write a conversation between Mr. Evans and Bob. Then invite pairs to read their conversation to the class.

LANGUAGE NOTE: *To need a hand with something means to need help with something.*

VIDEO SCRIPT

In the office, Bob troubleshoots computer problems for Marie, Paul, and Cheryl.

Marie: Bob, can you help me with something?
Bob: Sure.
Marie: I'm trying to print a file, but the printer won't work.
Bob: Push the green button on the printer.
Marie: Why?
Bob: **To turn** it on. It won't print unless it's on.
Marie: Oh, right. Silly me. Thank you.

Paul: Hey, Bob. My laptop crashed, and I can't get it to do anything. I type on the keyboard and nothing happens.
Bob: Stick this here.
Paul: Why?
Bob: **To restart** the computer.
Paul: You sure? OK. Thanks.
Cheryl: Bob, I could use a hand with something.
Bob: What is it?
Cheryl: Somebody sent me an e-mail, but I think it has a virus in it.
Bob: Don't open the attachment. Click on the No-Virus icon on the toolbar.
Cheryl: Why?
Bob: **To clean** the computer and stop the virus.
Cheryl: Thanks!
Marie: Bob, can I ask you another question?
Bob: I'm sorry, but I can't get any work done with all these questions! Please. I have some very important stuff I need to finish right now.
Marie: Very important stuff?
Bob: How can I help you?

ANSWER KEY

A. 1. True 2. False 3. False 4. False 5. True
   6. False
B. 1. print a file, printer 2. crashed, keyboard
   3. e-mail, virus
   a. 3 b. 1 c. 2
C. 1. turn the printer on (turn on the printer)
   2. restart the computer 3. clean the computer and stop the virus

SCENE 2

PREVIEW

- Ask students *Have you ever built a website? What technology do you need to build a website? (a computer, digital camera, scanner, and so on)*

REVIEW

- Ask comprehension questions. Play the video episode again if necessary.
    What did Mr. Evans ask Bob to do? (to build a website for the company)
    What new technology does Bob say he needs? (a new scanner, a digital camera, a new laptop, a new DVD drive, and a new joystick)
    What is a joystick for? (computer games)
    Does Bob really need it? (no)
    Is Mr. Evans happy about the cost for all the new items? (no)
    What will Bob get in the end? (nothing) Why? (Mr. Evans fools him and makes him take back what he has asked for.)

EXTENSION

Oral work

- Pair work: role play. Have students work in pairs to role-play Mr. Evans and Bob and reenact what happened in the video episode.

- Pair work: role play. Have students work in pairs to role-play Bob and Cheryl. Have Bob complain to Cheryl about how Mr. Evans refused to buy any new technology.

Written work

- Have students role-play Bob and write an e-mail to Mr. Evans, asking for the two items he originally said OK to—the scanner and digital camera. Tell students to make a good argument why he needs them. Then have students exchange letters with a partner and write a reply from Mr. Evans.

- Pair work. Tell students they will create True and False quizzes. Have students work in pairs to write true and false statements about the video episode. Then combine pairs into groups of four and have them exchange quizzes and answer them. Finally, have the writers of each quiz check the answers.

VIDEO SCRIPT

Bob asks Mr. Evans for some new technology in order to build a website.

Bob: Hey, Mr. Evans?

Mr. Evans: Yes?

Bob: You asked me to build a website for the company.

Mr. Evans: Oh, yes. How's it coming along?

Bob: Well, sir, I think I need some new technology.

Mr. Evans: What do you need?

Bob: A new scanner.

Mr. Evans: What's that?

Bob: It's a scanner, sir, but it's **not nearly as good as** this one. This one will give us much better photos.

Mr. Evans: OK.

Bob: And a digital camera would be good.

Mr. Evans: What's that?

Bob: It's not a digital camera, sir. It won't take pictures **as easily as** this one.

Mr. Evans: OK.

Bob: And also a new laptop. It's **not as fast as** this one.

Mr. Evans: I see. Anything else?

Bob: A new DVD drive. And I could also use a new joystick.

Mr. Evans: A joystick? Isn't that for computer games?

Bob: Well, I don't really need the joystick.

Mr. Evans: What's all this going to cost me? What?!

Bob: Well, actually, we can do without the DVD drive . . . and the laptop . . . and the camera . . . and the scanner.

Mr. Evans: Great!

ANSWER KEY

A. scanner, digital camera, laptop, DVD drive, joystick

B. 1. True 2. True 3. False 4. True 5. False

C. 1. scanner, nearly as good as 2. digital camera, as easily as 3. laptop, as fast as

D. 1. Mr. Evans says OK to the new scanner and the digital camera. 2. DVD drive, laptop, camera, and scanner 3. *Individual responses may include variations like the following:* Mr. Evans is happy because he doesn't have to spend money.

Interview: *Are you a computer addict?*

PREVIEW

- Ask individual students *How many hours do you spend on the computer? Do you think you are a computer addict?*

REVIEW

- Ask comprehension questions. Play the video segment again if necessary.

  Does Lisa use a computer at work? (yes)

  What does she use the computer for? (to make schedules and to e-mail friends and coworkers)

  Is Deepti a computer addict? (yes)

  What does Angelique think about playing games, surfing, and chatting? (too much is not a good idea)

  What does she think about researching projects on the Internet? (You can spend as much time as you want.)

  Does Deepti think children should use the Internet? (yes, but with guidance)

  What does James say are the advantages of the Internet? (communication and the knowledge you can get)

  Why does Lisa think there are dangers on the Internet for children? (because they are curious and cannot always decide what is right or wrong)

EXTENSION

Oral work

- Discussion. Ask students these questions:

  Have you ever found information online that was not true?

How can you be sure the information you have found is true or correct?
What are some good websites you use?

- Discussion. Ask students these questions:
  Angelique says it's OK to spend as much time as you like on the computer researching projects. Do you agree?
  Do you agree with Angelique that playing games, surfing, and chatting on the computer a lot is similar to watching a lot of TV? How much do you think is too much?

Written work

- Have students summarize James's comments about the advantages of the Internet. Have students write whether they agree and add their own ideas.
- On the board, write *Do you think children should be allowed to use the Internet?* Have students write a paragraph responding to this question. Tell them to write whether they agree with Deepti's and Lisa's comments about the topic.

VIDEO SCRIPT

Interviewer: Could you tell me some of the things you use a computer for?

Lisa: I use my computer every day at work to make schedules. I do a lot of that at my job. Also to e-mail friends and coworkers about things that need to get done for the day.

Interviewer: Would you say you're a computer addict?

Deepti: Yes. I am a computer addict.

Interviewer: How about just overall time spent on the computer?

Angelique: I think it kind of depends on what you use the time for. 'Cause if you're doing, you know, researching projects and things like that, spend as much time as you like on the computer, you know, 'cause it's easy and it's fast.

Interviewer: But how about games and surfing and chat?

Angelique: I don't know. I mean, it's probably about the same as television. Too much of it isn't a good idea, I mean, when you can get outside and enjoy the city.

Interviewer: Do you think children should be allowed to use the Internet?

Deepti: With guidance, I think they should be allowed to use the Internet.

Interviewer: What do you see as the advantages of the Internet?

James: Well, communication is certainly an advantage. With, like I said, with e-mail you keep in touch with friends all over the country, practically free of charge. Also, the wealth of

knowledge that you can pick up. You can ask the computer with your search engines any question at all and come up with thousands of answers. You have to choose the one you like.

Interviewer: Do you see some particular dangers, for you even, but particularly for children?

Lisa: I mean, at this point I feel as though I'm, you know, like an adult, so I can kind of censor what I want to look at and things like that, but kids don't necessarily have that and are a little bit more curious, so I think that they definitely need that supervision.

ANSWER KEY

A. e-mail coworkers, play games, make schedules, chat, do research projects, surf the Internet
B. 1. True 2. False 3. True 4. False 5. True 6. True
C. 1. b 2. a 3. c 4. a 5. c 6. b

 Top Notch Pop and Karaoke: *Life in Cyberspace*

UNIT 10

Sitcom: *That's David Doolittle!*

Social language
- Return lost property
- Identify ownership
- Express ethical beliefs

Grammar
- Possessive pronouns
- Conditionals: factual and unreal

SCENE 1

PREVIEW

- Ask students *What would you do if you saw a person forget something in a restaurant? What if the person were a famous actor?*

REVIEW

- Ask comprehension questions. Play the video episode again if necessary.
  Where are Marie and Cheryl? (in a restaurant)
  Who do they see? (David Doolittle—an actor)
  What has he forgotten? (his hat, gloves, cell phone, and keys)
  What does Marie give back to him first? (his hat)

Where did Marie say she found it? (under the table)
What does Cheryl tell Marie to do? (to return the rest of his things)
What does Marie do? (She returns the gloves.)
Does she introduce herself to David Doolittle? (yes)
What is the last thing she returns? (his keys)
Does she return his cell phone? (no)
Why does David Doolittle give Marie his phone number? (so Marie can call him at his office if she finds his cell phone)

EXTENSION

Oral work

- Discussion. Ask students these questions:
  Why does Marie decide to keep Mr. Doolittle's cell phone?
  Do you think Marie will call David Doolittle to return his cell phone? Why or why not?
  Do you think what Marie does is OK?
  Have you ever done something similar?

- Pair work: role play. Have students work in pairs to predict what will happen next and role-play a scene. Tell students to decide whether the scene will be with Cheryl and Marie or with Marie and David Doolittle. Invite students to perform their role plays to the class.

Written work

- On the board, write *If I were Marie, I would . . .* Have students finish this sentence and write a paragraph describing what they would do.

- Ask *Do you think David Doolittle knows Marie has his cell phone? Does he want her to call him?* Tell students to write a story from Mr. Doolittle's point of view.

LANGUAGE NOTE: *Mobile* is another word for *cell phone*. It is more common in British English.

VIDEO SCRIPT

Cheryl and Marie are having desserts in the café when Marie finds things left behind by the actor David Doolittle.

Cheryl: I can't believe I'm eating this.
Marie: I can't believe you are eating it either.
Cheryl: You know, that man looks like someone I know. That man just left something at his table.
Marie: That's David Doolittle . . . the actor! He left his hat. And his gloves. And his cell phone. And his keys. Hold these.
Cheryl: What are you doing?
Marie: I'm giving him back his hat.
Cheryl: What about these?
Marie: Sir! Excuse me, sir! Is this hat **yours**?
Doolittle: That's **mine**, yes, thank you. Did I leave it here?
Marie: I saw it under your table.

Doolittle: Thanks again.
Marie: You're welcome.
Cheryl: **If** you **don't give** him back the rest of his things, I **will**.
Marie: Just wait. Sir! Excuse me, sir!
Doolittle: Yes?
Marie: Are these gloves **yours**?
Doolittle: Yes, they're **mine**. I'm forgetting everything, aren't I?
Marie: Aren't you David Doolittle?
Doolittle: Well, I am, yes.
Marie: I'm Marie LePage. I'm a big fan.
Doolittle: Thank you. And thanks for these.
Marie: My pleasure. Mr. Doolittle?
Doolittle: What would I do without you? You know, I'm missing my mobile. Have you seen it?
Marie: I don't see it under your table.
Doolittle: Well, I'm in a hurry. **If** you do **find** it, **would** you be so kind as to call me at my office?
Marie: I'd be happy to.
Doolittle: Thank you. Bye.
Marie: I have David Doolittle's phone number. And his cell phone.

ANSWER KEY

A. 1. True 2. False 3. True 4. False 5. False
B. 1. b 2. b 3. c 4. c
C. 1. yours, That's mine 2. yours, Yes, they're mine

SCENE 2

PREVIEW

- Take a poll. Ask *Do you think when Marie didn't return David Doolittle's cell phone, it was stealing? Do you think it was the wrong thing to do?*

REVIEW

- Ask comprehension questions. Play the video episode again if necessary.
  What are Cheryl and Marie talking about? (David Doolittle's cell phone)
  Does Cheryl think what Marie did is OK? (no)
  Does Marie think it was OK? (yes) Why? (She says she didn't steal the cell phone and that she is returning it tonight.)
  Does Cheryl think it's OK for a woman to invite a man to dinner? (no) Does Marie? (yes)
  How did Bob and Cheryl meet? (They met in a park, where Cheryl lost her bag and Bob helped her find it.)
  What did Bob do that is similar to what Marie is doing now? (He waited two hours to tell Cheryl that he found her bag.)

Why does Bob tell Cheryl this story now? (to show her that what Marie is doing is not so wrong)

EXTENSION

Oral work

- Discussion. On the board, write *Women don't ask men to dinner.* Ask *Who said this? (Cheryl) Does Marie agree? (no) Do you agree? Why or why not?*

- Group work: role play. Divide the class into groups of four. Have students role-play the characters and reenact what happened in the video episode.

Written work

- Point out that Cheryl keeps saying that she thinks what Marie did is wrong. Ask students *Do you think it's wrong?* Have students write a paragraph explaining their opinion.

- Have students write a summary of Cheryl's version of how she and Bob met.

VIDEO SCRIPT

Cheryl and Marie argue about the fact that Marie didn't return David Doolittle's cell phone.

Cheryl: Well, I still think it's wrong.

Marie: Cheryl . . .

Bob: What's going on?

Cheryl: Marie just stole David Doolittle's cell phone.

Paul: David Doolittle was here?

Marie: I didn't steal it. He left it, and I'm waiting to return it until tonight.

Cheryl: He asked if it was under the table. You said it wasn't.

Marie: It wasn't under the table because it was in my pocket.

Cheryl: Well, I think that's wrong.

Marie: It's not wrong. He'll get his phone back.

Cheryl: What do you two think?

Bob: Well . . .

Paul: Um . . .

Cheryl: What are you going to do now?

Marie: I'm going to call him tonight, tell him I found his phone, and ask him to meet me for dinner.

Cheryl: You're going to ask him to dinner?

Marie: Sure. Why not?

Cheryl: Women don't ask men to dinner. Do they?

Marie: Oh, don't be so old-fashioned, Cheryl. This is the twenty-first century. Women ask men out to dinner all the time. Don't they?

Cheryl: Well, I still think it's wrong. You should have given him the phone.

Bob: Cheryl, I have to tell you something.

Cheryl: What?

Bob: Do you remember when we met?

Cheryl: Of course. I was at the park. I'd lost my bag and you helped me find it. It took us two

hours. We talked and talked and I became more interested in Bob than in finding the bag.

Bob: Well, actually, I found your bag in two minutes, but I waited two hours to tell you. I thought you were the most amazing woman I had ever met. If you had found your bag right away, you would have left and we wouldn't be here right now.

Cheryl: That is so romantic! That's why I love this man!

Marie: See? **If** it **worked** for Bob, it **might work** for me.

Cheryl: You and David Doolittle! That would be fantastic! Call! Call him!

Interview: *What would you do?*

PREVIEW

- Tell students to imagine that they are walking down the street and see some cash on the ground. There is no one around. Ask individual students *What would you do?*

REVIEW

- Ask comprehension questions. Play the video segment again if necessary.
    What three ethical decisions do the people talk about? (incorrect bill at a restaurant, mistake on a price tag in a store, and money found on the street)
    What would Jessica do if there were a mistake on a restaurant bill? What would Martin do? (Both of them would tell the waiter or waitress.)
    What would Catherine do if there were a mistake on a price tag in a store? What would Jessica do? (Both of them would ask the cashier.)
    What would Catherine do if she found cash on the street? (She would take it.) What would Christiane do? (She would leave it if she saw a poor person around.)

EXTENSION
Oral work

- Pair work: role play. Have students work in pairs to choose one of the characters from the video segment and role-play the short conversation between the interviewer and the interviewee.

- Group work: discussion. Have students work in groups to discuss the three situations. Ask *Would you do the same things as any of the people interviewed? What would you do differently?*

Written work

- On the board, write *You make judgments all the time and not everything is equal.* Then tell students to write a paragraph and say whether they agree or disagree with Martin and explain why.

- Pair work. Have students work in pairs to think of another ethical situation and write it down as a question. Combine pairs into groups of four and have them exchange questions and answer them. Then have each group discuss the situations.

VIDEO SCRIPT

Interviewer: If you got a bill in a restaurant that was obviously wrong, what would you do?

Jessica: I would tell the waitress and ask her if everything's OK.

Martin: I think they should tell the waiter.

Interviewer: And what should they tell them?

Martin: That they're given too much change or they're undercharged.

Interviewer: How about if a person's shopping in a department store and an expensive piece of clothing has a tag on it that's obviously wrong—it's priced too low—should that person tell the cashier or just pay for it?

Catherine: I usually ask. That's me, though.

Jessica: Well, I would go to the cashier, or I think everybody should go to the cashier, at least ask if that's right. And if he says it's right, then at least you tried it.

Interviewer: And then suppose you found some cash on the street, not in a wallet, just some cash lying on the street. What would you do with it?

Catherine: I'd pick it up and put it in my pocket.

Christiane: I usually do not pick up money if a very poor person is around because I think a poor person needs it more than I do, so I'd leave it lying there.

Interviewer: So are the three situations—the restaurant, the department store, and the cash on the street—the same or different?

Martin: I think each one is different.

Interviewer: Why?

Martin: You make judgments all the time and not everything is equal.

ANSWER KEY

A. 1. c 2. b 3. b 4. a 5. a

B. *Following are expected answers. Students may produce variations that are also correct.*
   1. tell the waiter there is a mistake 2. ask the cashier 3. pick it up and put it in her pocket

---

 Top Notch Pop and Karaoke: *What Would You Do?*

Conversation Activator Video Script

Unit 1, Lesson 1

Scene 1
M1: Peter, have you met Emma?

M2: No, I haven't.

M1: Emma, I'd like you to meet Peter.

F: Hi, Peter. You look familiar. Have we met before?

M1: I don't think so.

F: I know! Last week. We were at my friend Carrie's house.

M1: Oh, that's right! How have you been?

Scene 2
M1: Zoe, have you met Mark?

F1: No, I haven't.

M1: Mark, I'd like you to meet Zoe.

M2: Hi, Zoe. You look familiar. Have we met before?

F1: I don't think so.

M2: I know! Last week. You were at the meeting at the Science Museum.

F1: Oh, that's right! How have you been?

M2: Great. How about you?

F1: Fine, thanks. So have you been to one of those meetings before?

M2: No. It was my first time. How about you?

F1: It was my first time too. It was really interesting.

M2: Yeah, it was.

F2: Hi, Mark. Hi, Peter.

M2: Hey, Emma. Have you met Zoe?

F2: No I haven't. Hi!

M2: Zoe, this is our friend Emma.

F1: Hi, Emma. Nice to meet you. Actually you look familiar.

F2: Really? Have we met before?

F1: I think so. I know! Three days ago. We didn't meet, but I saw you at the pharmacy.

Unit 1, Lesson 2

Scene 1
F: Welcome to Chicago. Have you ever been here before?

M: No, it's my first time. But yesterday I went to the top of Willis Tower. It was amazing!

F: That's great. Have you been to the Art Institute yet?

M: The Art Institute? No, I haven't. What's that?

F: It's a famous Chicago art museum. I think you'll like it.

Scene 2
M: Welcome to New York. Have you ever been here before?

F: No, it's my first time. But yesterday I went sightseeing. It was great!

M: Cool. Have you gone to the top of the Empire State Building yet?

F: The Empire State Building? No, I haven't.

M: It's really nice. I think you'll like it. Hey, do you like museums?

F: Yes, I do.

M: Then you should go to the Metropolitan Museum of Art. It's fantastic.

F: Sounds great. Could you recommend any good restaurants?

M: Sure. What kind of food do you like?

F: I love Italian.

M: Then you should try Mario's on West 51st Street. It's the best.

F: Thanks!

Unit 2, Lesson 1

Scene 1

F: Have you been here long?

M: For about a half hour.

F: Sorry I'm late. I missed the bus. Did you get the tickets?

M: Yes. But *Cancun Holiday* started fifteen minutes ago. I got tickets for *Fifth Avenue*. I hope that's OK.

F: That's fine. I've heard it's great. How much do I owe?

Scene 2

M: Have you been here long?

F: For about five minutes.

M: Sorry I'm late. I couldn't get a taxi. Did you get tickets?

F: Yes. But the 7:45 show for *Monster Dance* is sold out. But I got tickets for the 9:00 show. I hope that's OK.

M: That's fine. I've always wanted to see *Monster Dance*. I love horror movies. So how much do I owe?

F: Nothing. It's my treat.

M: Well, thanks! Next time it's on me. Would you like to have dinner after the show? It gets out at 11:15.

F: Hmm. 11:15? That's past my bedtime. Let's get something now, OK?

Unit 2, Lesson 2

Scene 1

F: What would you rather do: stay home and stream a movie or go to the theater?

M: I'd rather stay home. Is that OK?

F: OK. Would you rather see *The Boats of Tanzania* or *Captain Silly*?

M: Are you kidding? I can't stand documentaries and to tell you the truth, I'm not that big on animated films.

F: Well, how about *City Nights?*

M: It's a deal!

Scene 2

M: What would you rather do: stay home and stream a movie or go to the theater?

F: I'd rather go out. Is that OK?

M: Sure! Would you rather see *Love Under the Stars* or *Gangster Holiday*?

F: Are you kidding? I can't stand love stories, and to tell you the truth, I'm not that big on violent films.

M: Well, how about an animated film? *Mrs. Kangaroo and Her Babies* is playing. I've heard that's great.

F: Well, I hate animated films.

M: *Titanic* in 3D?

F: Actually, I'd really like to see that. I've never seen that one.

M: OK! That works for me.

Unit 3, Lesson 1

Scene 1

F: Hello? I'd like to speak to Martin Vacarro. He's a guest.

M: I'll ring that room for you. . . . I'm sorry. He's not answering. Would you like to leave a message?

F: Yes. Please tell him Lorna Nader called. I'll call him back tonight at six.

M: Is that all?

F: Yes, it is. Thank you.

Scene 2

M: Good morning. I'd like to speak to Tina James. She's a guest.

F: Is that J-A-M-E-S?

M: That's right.

F: I'll ring that room for you. . . . I'm sorry. She's not answering. Would you like to leave a message?

M: Yes, thank you. Please tell her Tom Byrne called.

F: Excuse me. How do you spell your last name?

M: Sure. It's B as in Brazil, Y as in yes, R as in Russia, N as in New York, E as in English.

F: Thank you. Is that all?

M: Actually, no. Please tell her I'll meet her at the Lenox Restaurant at five o'clock.

F: The Lenox Restaurant, five o'clock. Do you have the address?

M: Oh, of course. It's at 25 King Street.

F: Twenty five King.

M: Oh, and please tell her I'll bring the report. She'll understand.

F: You'll bring the report.

M: Thank you very much.

F: My pleasure. Have a good day.

M: Thanks. Bye.

Unit 3, Lesson 2

Scene 1

M1: Hi. I'm checking in. The name's Franklin.

M2: Let's see. That's a single for three nights. Smoking?

M1: Actually, no. Non-smoking.

M2: No problem. May I have your credit card?

M1: Here you go. By the way, is the business center still open?

M2: It closes at five. But if you hurry, you'll still make it.

M1: Thanks.

Scene 2

F: Hi. I'm checking in. The name's Greeley.

M: Let's see. That's a suite for four nights? Non-smoking?

F: That's right.

M: Welcome to the Parker Hotel, Ms. Greeley. May I have your credit card?

F: Here you go. By the way, is the gift shop still open?

M: Yes it is. It closes at nine. But if you hurry, you'll make it.

F: Thanks. What about the pool? Does it close at nine too?

M: Actually, it's open till ten o'clock.

F: Perfect. By the way, what floor is my room on?

M: You're in 206, on the second floor.

F: Is there a soda machine on that floor?

M: Yes. There's a machine on every floor. And if you'd like to order room service, it's open 24 hours.

F: Great. Oh, I need wake up service for tomorrow morning.

M: No problem. What time would you like to get up?

F: 6:30, please.

M: Very good. You'll get a phone call at 6:30 tomorrow morning. Do you need anything else?

F: Oh, do you have free Internet service?

M: Yes, we do. Here's the information about our Internet service.

F: Thank you. Are the elevators over there?

M: That's right.

Unit 4, Lesson 1

Scene 1

M1: I had an accident.

M2: How awful. Are you OK?

M1: I'm fine. No one was hurt.

M2: What a relief! How did it happen?

M1: Well, the other driver was turning, and I hit her car.

M2: That's terrible. Was there much damage?

M1: Yes. I'll have to replace my headlights.

Scene 2

F: I had an accident.

M: I'm so sorry. Are you OK?

F: Yes, I am.

M: That's good. How did it happen?

F: Well, the other driver was talking on the phone, and he hit my car.

M: Oh, no! Was there much damage?

F: Yes. I'll have to replace a door.

M: That's terrible. Where were you?

F: I was at Smith Street and Main. Thank goodness the other driver wasn't speeding!

M: What about his car?

F: Oh, he'll have to replace his hood and his headlights.

M: Well, you're OK. What a relief!

Unit 4, Lesson 2

Scene 1

M: I'm dropping off my car.

F: Was everything OK?

M: Well, actually, the brakes are making a funny sound.

F: Really? Any other problems?

M: No. That's it.

Scene 2

F: I'm dropping off my car.

M: Was everything OK?

F: Well, actually, the turn signals aren't working.

M: Oh no. Any other problems?

F: Yes. The sunroof won't open.

M: You're kidding!

F: And the clutch is making a funny sound.

M: Oh no.

F: And the trunk won't close.

M: That's awful! Anything else?

F: No, that's it!

M: Thank goodness!

Unit 5, Lesson 1

Scene 1

F: Excuse me. Where would I find brushes?

M: Brushes? Have a look in the hair care section, in aisle 1.

F: Actually, I did, and there weren't any.

M: I'm sorry. Let me get you some from the back. Anything else?

F: Yes. I couldn't find any dental floss either.

M: No problem. There's some over there. I'll show you.

Scene 2

M: Excuse me. Where would I find hand lotion?

F: Hand lotion? Have a look in the skin care section, in aisle 5.

M: Actually, I did, and there wasn't any.

F: I'm sorry. Let me get you some from the back. Anything else?

M: Yes, please. I need shaving cream and aftershave.

F: Sure. We have those right over here. I'll show you.

M: Thanks. How much is that aftershave?

F: Let me check. . . . It's six dollars and 95 cents.

M: Can I get it in a smaller size?

F: I'm not sure. . . . Oh, yes. We have it in a small travel size. It's only two dollars.

M: Great! Thanks.

Unit 5, Lesson 2

Scene 1

M1: Hello. Super Gym and Fitness Center.

M2: Hello. This is Art Blake. I'd like to make an appointment for personal training.

M1: When would you like to come in, Mr. Blake?

M2: Today, if possible.

M1: Let me check. . . . Mike has an opening at three.

M2: Actually, that's a little late for me. Is someone available this morning?

M1: Yes. Hobson can see you at ten.

Scene 2

F1: Hello. Seabourn Spa.

F2: Hello. This is Elaine Townsend. I'd like to make an appointment for a massage.

F1: When would you like to come in, Ms. Townsend?

F2: On Friday morning, if possible.

F1: Let me check. . . . Svetlana has an opening at 11:15.

F2: Actually, that's a little late for me. Is someone available earlier?

F1: Yes. Natasha can see you at ten.

F2: That's great. Oh. And I'd like to make an appointment for a facial too.

F1: On Friday morning?

F2: Yes, if possible.

F1: Actually, Natasha can give you a facial too, after your massage.

F2: That's great. How much will the massage and the facial be?

F1: That'll be 75 dollars.

F2: Is the tip included?

F1: Yes, Ms. Townsend. It is.

Unit 6, Lesson 1

Scene 1

M: Are you a big tea drinker?

F: Not really. I'm not crazy about tea. What about you?

M: I didn't use to drink tea. But now I drink it all the time.

F: Well, I usually drink coffee. I couldn't live without it.

Scene 2

F: Are you a big meat eater?

M: Definitely. I'm crazy about steak. What about you?

F: I used to eat a lot of meat. But I've been cutting back.

M: Really?

F: Yeah. I eat a lot more seafood and beans. They have a lot of protein.

M: Well, I eat meat with every meal. I couldn't live without it.

F: What about fish? Do you eat that too?

M: Actually, I'm not a big fish eater.

F: Well, I'm a seafood addict now. I love it.

M: So what do you usually drink with your meals?

F: Me? Usually water. What about you?

M: I'm a big soda drinker. I love soda.

Unit 6, Lesson 2

Scene 1

M: Please help yourself.

F: Everything looks fantastic! But I'll pass on the fried squid.

M: Don't you eat fried squid?

F: Actually, no. I don't care for squid.

M: I'm sorry. I didn't know that.

F: Don't worry. I'll have something else.

Scene 2

F1: Please help yourself.

F2: Everything looks wonderful! But I'll pass on the pasta.

F1: Don't you eat pasta?

F2: Actually, I'm crazy about pasta. But I'm trying to lose weight.

F1: I'm sorry. I didn't know that.

F2: I'm fine. I'll have some broccoli.

F1: Would you like some pasta?

(continued)

M: Sure! I'm a pasta addict.

F1: And how about some broccoli?

M: I'm sorry. Broccoli doesn't agree with me.

F1: Really? How about some beets?

M: Actually, I'm not a big vegetable eater. Sorry. But the pasta looks great!

F2: Well, I'm crazy about beets. They're low calorie, and they have lots of vitamins.

F1: Great. Please help yourself.

F2: Thanks!

F1: Soda?

F2: Not for me, thanks. I'll just have water.

M: I'll have some. Thank you! Everything looks excellent.

F2: Wonderful!

F1: Thank you!

Unit 7, Lesson 1

Scene 1

F: So tell me something about yourself.

M: What would you like to know?

F: Well, for example, what do you like doing on weekends?

M: Let's see. Most of all, I enjoy watching old classic movies. I think they're fascinating. What about you?

F: Well, I find watching old movies a little boring. But I do love to go walking in the park.

M: So do I. We should go walking in the park together sometime, then.

Scene 2

M1: So tell me something about yourself.

M2: What would you like to know?

M1: Well, for example, what activities do you like doing outside of the office?

M2: Let's see. Most of all, I enjoy going bungee jumping. I think it's thrilling.

M1: Really? I find extreme sports scary. But I do like being outside, and I like camping in the mountains.

M2: So do I. So do you plan to do that on your vacation?

M1: Actually, my wife can't stand camping. She doesn't like to sleep outside. So on my next vacation, I'd like to take my family to Ocean World.

Unit 7, Lesson 2

Scene 1

M1: You look depressed. What's up?

M2: Oh, nothing serious. I'm just tired of getting up so early every day. But thanks for asking.

M1: I know what you mean. I hate getting up early too. How about going to bed earlier? That always helps me.

M2: Good idea.

Scene 2

F1: You look upset. What's up?

F2: Oh, nothing serious. I'm just a little depressed about having way too much work. I don't get home until 11 at night.

F1: I know what you mean. How about having a talk with your boss?

F2: I don't know. I'm worried about saying anything. She gets angry sometimes.

F1: Well, be sure to say that you're not complaining about working hard. Just say that you need to get home a little earlier at night. I'm sure she'll understand. I believe in telling the truth.

F2: That's actually a great idea.

Unit 8, Lesson 1

Scene 1

F: Be sure not to miss the Bright Museum while you're in Greenville.

M: Really? Why's that?

F: Well, for one thing, that famous drawing *Sleeping Dogs* is kept there.

M: No kidding! I've always wanted to see *Sleeping Dogs*!

F: Well, they have a great collection of drawings. You'll love it.

M: Thanks for the suggestion!

Scene 2

M: Be sure not to miss the Kent Museum while you're in Lancaster.

F: Really? Why's that?

M: Well, for one thing, that famous sculpture by Henry Owen is kept there.

F: *The Hat*? No kidding! I've always wanted to see that!

M: Well, they have a great collection of Owen's sculptures. You'll love it.

F: Thanks for the suggestion!

M: By the way, have you ever taken a tour of the Mason House in Lancaster?

F: No, I haven't. Is it interesting?

M: Definitely. You should do that, too.

F: I will.

M: And have you tried grilled ice cream?

F: Grilled ice cream? No, I haven't. Is it good?

M: Lancaster is famous for its grilled ice cream.

F: Thanks! Great suggestions.

Unit 8, Lesson 2

Scene 1

M: Excuse me. What's this bowl made of?

F: Glass, actually. It's handmade.

M: Really? Where was it made?

F: China. What do you think of it?

M: It's very cool!

Scene 2

F: Excuse me. What are those bracelets made of?

M: They're silver. They're handmade.

F: Really? Where were they made?

M: Let me check. They were made in Poland. What do you think of them?

F: They're wonderful! And what about these necklaces?

M: The gold ones? Those were made in Spain. Aren't they nice?

F: Yes, they are. That clay pot is great, too. What is it used for?

M: The small one? It's for serving salt.

F: Salt? Really?

M: That's right.

Unit 9, Lesson 1

Scene 1

M: Zoe, could you take a look at this?

F: Sure. What's up?

M: Well, I clicked on this icon to open up the document and nothing happened.

F: Why don't you try clicking on the toolbar? That might do the trick.

M: Thanks. I'll give that a try.

Scene 2

F: Mark, could you take a look at this?

M: Sure. Is there a problem?

F: Well, I clicked on this word to highlight it and nothing happened.

M: Really? Why don't you try cutting and pasting the word again? That sometimes works.

F: Oh. I'll give that a try.

M: If that doesn't work, try restarting your computer. That might help.

F: OK. . . Actually, I have a question. My screen sometimes freezes. What should I do?

(continued)

M: It's always a good idea to restart when that happens. Also, if you open too many files, that may be the problem. You should always close any files you aren't using.

F: Thanks. I'll do that.

Unit 9, Lesson 2

Scene 1

F: I'm thinking about getting a new monitor.

M: No kidding! What kind?

F: Everyone says I should get a MegaMax Z40.

M: Well, I've heard that the Klik P20 isn't nearly as expensive as the MegaMax.

F: Really? I'll think about that.

Scene 2

M: I'm thinking about getting a new keyboard.

F: Cool! What kind?

M: I'm thinking about the MegaMax Wireless Keyboard. But everyone says I should get a Klik Wireless.

F: Well, I've heard that the Klik is very comfortable. The MegaMax is good, too, but it isn't quite as cheap as the Klik.

M: Really? I didn't know that.

F: Also, the Klik comes in different colors. The MegaMax only comes in black.

M: Well, I like black. But I guess the Klik is more affordable.

F: Actually, they're both very affordable. You should get the one you like.

Unit 10, Lesson 1

Scene 1

M1: Look at this. They gave us too much change.

M2: Really? I think we should tell the waitress.

M1: You think so?

M2: Absolutely. If we didn't tell her, I would feel bad.

Scene 2

M: Look at this. They undercharged us.

F: Really? I think we ought to go back to the store.

M: You think so?

F: Absolutely. If we didn't tell the clerk, I couldn't face myself.

M: Oh! And look at this.

F: Wow. What a nice sweater!

M: It is really nice, but I didn't buy it.

F: You're kidding. Did they charge us for the sweater?

M: No, they didn't. Let's just keep it.

F: No way. It's a nice store. If you don't take the sweater back, the clerk will have to pay for it. Put yourself in his shoes.

M: You're right. Let's go.

Unit 10, Lesson 2

Scene 1

M1: Excuse me. I think you forgot something.

M2: I did?

M1: Aren't these glasses yours?

M2: Oh, you're right. They are. That's nice of you.

M1: My pleasure.

Scene 2

F1: Excuse me. I think you forgot something.

F2: I did?

F1: Isn't this purse yours?

F2: Oh! You're right. It is! That's so nice of you.

F1: And what about this earring? It was under the table. Is it yours too?

F2: No. It's beautiful, but it isn't mine. Thanks, anyway.

F1: Not at all.